CRAVING FOR
ECSTASY
AND NATURAL HIGHS

A Positive Approach to Mood Alteration

Praise for the first edition

Psychologist Harvey Milkman and chemist Stanley Sunderwirth explore why our relentless search for pleasure sometimes leads to dangerous addictions and show us healthy ways to achieve happiness." - *Scientific American Mind*

"This book is extremely useful for a broad range of readers. This book reflects the extensive scientific and clinical expertise of the authors and is compelling reading for anyone interested in addictive behaviors. It is one of the rare books that from page one immediately engrosses, educates and broadens your perspective." - Alex Blaszczynski, The University of Sydney, *International Journal of Mental Health Addiction*

"Written clearly and in a free flowing manner, and handsomely illustrated by Kenneth Axen, a biomedical research scientist, the book is a welcome addition to the arsenal of all the players in the 'War on Addiction,' a war that is slowly beginning to appear winnable, more and more."- Vijay Nagaswami, Book Review, *The Hindu*

"A beautifully written and organized book... a thrill ride through the most innovative and insightful perspectives that science and clinical experience have to offer... hip and artistic, reflecting a deep understanding of addiction... a major contribution to the field; it is must reading." - Howard J. Shaffer, PhD, Associate Professor, *Harvard Medical School* and Director of the Division on Addictions

"Reading this book is in itself an ecstatic experience!"... "A fascinating journey that explores the benefits and risks of pleasure and the universal desire to feel good... It's quite a trip." - G. Alan Marlatt, PhD., Director, *Addictive Behaviors Research Center*, University of Washington

If there is but one book that you read about pleasure, addiction, and recovery this is by far THE book. *Craving for Ecstasy* is the most comprehensive, informative, and ground breaking book that I have read on these broad subjects. Fascinating as it is fun to read, it is a gold mine of cutting edge science and a go-to book for insights on drug and natural highs.

John B. Arden, PhD, author of *Mind-Brain-Gene*

There is not a society on earth that does not regularly employ intoxicants. The human desire to transport our minds to states of awe, wonder, and ecstasy is ubiquitous. It is akin to a basic instinct, like hunger, sex and attachment.

We learned this crucial lesson, now essential to beat back the opioid and other drugs epidemic and a world encased in ennui, from Dr. Milkman in the groundbreaking first edition of *Craving for Ecstasy*. Now we can learn so much more as Dr. Milkman updates us—in his always engaging style—on what is new and revelatory in the science and culture of hedonic practices, including drug use and abuse.

The 2nd Edition of Craving is remarkably timely and exceptionally relevant. You will want to read it, and you will enjoy the read.

Lloyd I. Sederer, MD
Adjunct Professor, Columbia University School of Public Health
Chief Medical Officer, New York State Office of Mental Health

Bassim Hamadeh, CEO and Publisher
Kassie Graves, Director of Acquisitions
Jamie Giganti, Senior Managing Editor
Sean Adams, Production Editor
Alexa Lucido, Licensing Coordinator

Cover image copyright © Depositphotos/Furian; Depositphotos/Leonardi; Depositphotos/Surovtseva; Depositphotos/ktsdesign; Copyright © 2011 by iStockphoto LP/Sashkinw; Source: https://commons.wikimedia.org/wiki/File:Henri_Rousseau_005.jpg.

Printed in the United States of America

ISBN: 978-1-5165-0819-8 (pbk) / 978-1-5165-0820-4 (br)

CRAVING FOR ECSTASY
AND NATURAL HIGHS

A Positive Approach to Mood Alteration

Second Edition

Harvey B. Milkman,
Stanley G. Sunderwirth,
and Katherine G. Hill

Illustrations by Kenneth Axen

cognella® | ACADEMIC PUBLISHING

CONTENTS

CHAPTER 6 The Great Psychiatric Tavern   109

CHAPTER 7 Nicotine: The World's Antidepressant   125

PROLOGUE

Look to this day!
For it is life, the very life of life.
For yesterday is but a dream
And tomorrow is only a vision
But today well lived makes
every yesterday a dream of happiness
And tomorrow a vision of hope.
Look well, therefore, to this day!
Such is the salutation of the dawn.

—Kalidasa, 3rd century A.D. Sanskrit poem

PREFACE

T he explosions of Internet technology, international terrorism, political and economic instability, have altered the landscape of human experience. How are people coping with such dramatic change? Some rely on drugs and alcohol—old standbys when times get rough. Others take refuge in a gamut of tension-relieving pursuits, including unhealthy eating, online pornography, promiscuity, gambling, or joining fundamentalist cults. Some simply live out their days in quiet desperation.

This book is designed to provide insight into how ordinary people, from all walks of life, somehow fall off track and lose themselves in a web of counterfeit pleasures. Almost everyone has experienced cravings or urges that he or she couldn't or wouldn't control. If we are not personally affected, someone that we deeply care about is entrenched in a cycle of unhealthy mood control. Many of us have watched the lives of loved ones unravel to the point of utter despair, or even death. Our aim is to provide readers with the understandings, skills, and attitudes to take a positive approach to mood alteration and the pursuit of pleasure. By knowing the fundamental principles of mood alteration, readers not only improve their capacity to manage stress and live more fully, but they can also serve as strong allies to those who would benefit from an educated perspective.

Craving for Ecstasy and Natural Highs: A Positive Approach to Mood Alteration is aimed at all those who seek science-based answers to two basic questions: (1) How is the mind so easily corrupted by unhealthy pleasures? and (2) How can we take charge to increase the likelihood of lasting happiness and fulfillment? Our approach brings together state-of-the-art theory and research from brain science, human development, and the new and exciting field of positive psychology. We present a cogent picture of how to orchestrate positive feeling states, conducive to improved physical and mental well-being.

After exploring biological, psychological, and social pathways to pleasure, need gratification, and dependence—on food, sex, drugs, the Internet, gambling ... or whatever—readers discover healthy means for feeling good (i.e., natural highs), favorable to achieving happiness throughout the life span. The following discussion outlines our systematic examination of these topics.

In the eight years since publication of *Craving for Ecstasy and Natural Highs: A Positive Approach to Mood Alteration*, much has changed in the domains of compulsive pleasure seeking and healthy means for achieving happiness. Consequently, we have updated each chapter with current perspectives on the array of behaviors that could be considered addictive. On counterpoint, we have advanced our presentation of positive means to enhance neural functioning, resulting in heightened pleasure and meaningful life experiences. As in our earlier edition, we aspire to provide "... a thrill ride through the most innovative and insightful perspectives that science and clinical experience have to offer" (Shaffer, 2009, 1st edition cover).

During the past decade, the most striking occurrence in the study of pleasure has been the broad social movement toward medicalization and legalization of marijuana. As of March 2018, in the United States, medical marijuana is legal in 30 states and the District of Columbia, plus the territories of Guam and Puerto Rico. Recreational pot, which may be smoked or otherwise ingested in a variety of ways, is legal in eight states and the District of Columbia. Because the opportunity for chemically-induced pleasure has expanded so dramatically, we have devoted a new chapter, "Cannabis: Reefer Madness Revisited," to examining the widespread availability of tetrahydrocannabinol (THC).

Another shift in the tide of compulsive drug use is the epidemic of opioid addiction and an unprecedented rise in opioid related fatalities. Drug overdose is the leading cause of accidental death in the U.S., with opioid addiction driving this epidemic. Although much of the problem is related to the misuse of prescription narcotics, the "dark web," where buyers can use special browsers (and make anonymous purchases) allows powerful synthetic opioids such as fentanyl to penetrate nearly every region of the country. To deal with the complex problem of prescription and black-market opioid and heroin abuse, we address both the negative and positive aspects of compounds that have profound efficacy in healing and reducing human suffering. We have devoted a new chapter, "Feeling No Pain: The Opioid Era," to shedding light on this topic.

With the attention surrounding legal marijuana and the opioid epidemic, nicotine, arguably the world's most dangerous drug, often gets short shrift. Annual deaths from smoking are nearly 7x greater than opioid-related deaths. Nicotine is the most widely used drug of abuse and smoking tobacco is responsible for more deaths and more financial expenditures due to health problems and lost productivity than all other legal and illegal drugs combined. The chapter entitled "Nicotine: The World's Antidepressant" includes research on nicotine's effects on the brain, health effects of smoking, trends in teenage use of e-cigarettes, and the increasing popularity of hookah bars. Questions around how far society should enforce smoking bans and the establishment of a nationwide legal age of 21 for the purchase of any nicotine-containing products are examined.

Aside from drugs, common vehicles for compulsive pleasure include behaviors such as eating, gambling, and the Internet; also wish-fulfilling fantasies, often driven by longings for sex, power, or immortality. In Western society, heterosexual men have had mostly free reign, not only in discussing their sexual fantasies, but also in accessing pornographic materials and commercial sex venues, e.g., prostitution, strip clubs. The last decade has marked a dramatic change in society's attitudes. There is a shift from the relatively heteronormative culture of bars, sex clubs, and pornographic images, to a more diverse band of patronage. In consideration of the trend toward increased inclusiveness, we describe how current venues for the expression of sexual fantasies may play a role in the onset and progression of sexually-oriented dependencies.

Wish-fulfilling fantasies are by no means relegated to the sexual realm. The world struggles to comprehend how killing can be justified by seemingly unalterable assumptions about supernatural phenomena. Apocalyptic dreams are fueled by ancient prophesies of "the end days" and "heaven on earth." Fantasies of a "new beginning" are among the most compelling of all, as they suggest a complete surcease from suffering. Apocalyptic fantasies are subject to the same principles of reinforcement as other need-satisfying activities, hence potentially addictive. Current waves of faith-justified violence are examined in terms of the psycho/bio/social processes that facilitate widespread proliferation.

Regarding prevention and treatment, there has been major progress in the past decade. In terms of the latter, we explain well-documented success in our ability to inject natural highs into the everyday lives of children, successfully immunizing them against dangerous means to achieve pleasure and reduce stress. Regarding treatment, we not only describe current and effective models for evoking prosocial change, but discuss strategies for integrating formerly separate treatments into unified strategies that operate synergistically to provide optimal results.

We explore critical segues into natural highs including: mindfulness meditation, healthy eating, exercise, positive relationships, and meaningful engagement in one's areas of interest or talent. Imaging data show that meditation has the capacity to enhance brain function, with corresponding improvements in mental and physical health. Neurotransmitter levels can also be improved by intake of micronutrients from the diet and by engaging in exercise. Healthy intimate relationships and engaging in satisfying hands-on activities also enhance feel-good brain chemistry. These activities can be powerful reinforcers in the lives of any person. For someone struggling to recover from addiction or to remain sober, they allow reconnection with natural and healthy pleasures, thereby facilitating the attainment of a comfortable and responsible lifestyle.

Finally, in the Digital Age, the Internet is an enormous resource for accessing information on *Craving for Ecstasy and Natural Highs*. Exclusive reliance on the printed word is an inadequate representation of the available knowledge in most fields of scientific inquiry. To meet this challenge, we have dubbed a unique feature of this volume: "See for Yourself." Each chapter is punctuated by carefully selected links to video presentations or other media portrayals of relevant topics, developed by some of the most respected news and scientific entities of our time, e.g., *TED Talks, The New York Times, Scientific American, National Geographic*, etc. Because of the vast array of web-based resources, those presented in the "See for Yourself" section for each chapter are not intended as an exhaustive collection. Some sources, such as National Geographic *Drugs, Inc.* have been included in several chapters in clip form, though the full series provides a wealth of relevant video content. The full episode guide for *Drugs, Inc.* can be found through the National Geographic Channel website, and via this link: **https://www.nationalgeographic.com/tv/drugs-inc-the-fix/.**

On behalf of all those who have made this book possible, we wish you a most pleasant and meaningful journey!

ABOUT THE AUTHORS

Harvey B. Milkman, PhD, is Professor Emeritus, Department of Psychology, Metropolitan State University of Denver, where he teaches classes on cravings and addiction, and abnormal psychology. He is Visiting Professor (2015-present) and Fulbright Scholar (2019) at Reykjavik University, Iceland. He was a Fulbright Scholar at the National University of Malaysia (1985–1986) and represented the United States Information Agency as a consultant and featured speaker in Australia, Brazil, Iceland, The Netherlands, Peru, Turkey, and Yugoslavia. He is Founder and Director of Project Self-Discovery, a National Demonstration grant for adolescent substance abuse prevention (1992–2002). Dr. Milkman delivered master classes on "Adolescent Problem Behaviors" for the *US/Russia Peer-to-Peer* program on "Working with At-Risk Youth," July 2016, Moscow State University, Moscow, Russia. Dr. Milkman was a featured guest on *NPR's* "Here and Now" on March 10, 2017. Dr. Milkman is author of numerous scholarly articles and books on the causes, consequences, and treatment choices for the broad spectrum of addictive behaviors.

Stanley G. Sunderwirth, PhD, was Professor Emeritus at Indiana University–Purdue University Columbus. Dr. Sunderwirth received his doctorate in organic chemistry from The Ohio State University in 1955 and held teaching positions at Colorado State University and at Pittsburg State University in Kansas. He had been the chairman of the Chemistry Department of Pittsburg State University, Dean and Vice President at Metropolitan State College of Denver, and Vice President at Community College of Philadelphia. Dr. Sunderwirth received five Fulbright Awards, four to Uruguay and one to India. Dr. Sunderwirth authored many scientific publications on brain chemistry and its effect on mind, mood, and behavior.

Katherine G. Hill, PhD, pursued graduate work in behavioral neuroscience at Kansas State University. After earning her PhD, Dr. Hill did postdoctoral training at Oregon Health & Science University, where she continued her studies with rodent models of drug and alcohol reward. She spent several years teaching psychology at a small liberal arts college in the East before returning to her home state of Colorado. She is currently an Associate Professor of Psychology at Metropolitan State University of Denver where she teaches courses in cravings & addictions, psychopharmacology, behavioral neuroscience, and statistics & research methods in psychology.

ABOUT THE ILLUSTRATOR

Kenneth Axen, PhD, designed and rendered more than 50 illustrations in this book. Dr. Axen is a research scientist who has written and illustrated books on physiology, exercise physiology, and pulmonary disease. He is an adjunct full professor at Brooklyn College, CUNY, where he teaches undergraduate and graduate classes in physiology, exercise physiology and pathophysiology.

SECTION I

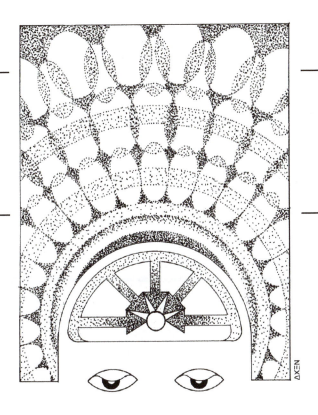

The Universal Desire To Feel Good

INTRODUCTION

Our discussion begins with a fundamental source of human unrest: the relentless urge to feel wonderful. Consider a conversation between the legendary comic strip characters Calvin and Hobbes:

Bill Waterson. Copyright © 1990 by Andrews McMeel Universal. Reprinted with permission.

The desire to have *more* of everything, to "experience only peaks," is basic to the human psyche. *Craving for ecstasy*—the root cause of compulsive pleasure seeking—springs from one's early encounters with pleasurable activities. For most, sugar (in a myriad of presentations) provides entry into pleasure from an ingestible substance. Just as a toddler discovers that spinning oneself into a dizzy heap can ramp up feelings of intoxication and bliss, the older child or adolescent seeks out a drug knowing that he or she can produce an altered state. It's the sensation of altered mood, the effect it produces—*not* the substance itself—that we crave. This fundamental verity of drug use is often overlooked as society's attention remains fixated on the drugs themselves as the source of our problems.

Addiction Syndrome Disorders

It is common to describe specific drugs, activities, or objects as addictive (e.g., alcohol, gambling, and the Internet). This view implies that the cause of each problem is different (Shaffer, LaPlante, et al., 2004). Specific measures for prevention and treatment are therefore designed for particular forms of behavioral excess. Today, a commonalities approach to addictive disorders, the signature of our earlier work (Milkman, 2001; Milkman & Sunderwirth, 1987, 1998, 2009), is supported by research from both biological and social sciences.

There is an accruing body of biological research that points to common genetic underpinnings for a variety of addictive behaviors (e.g., Betz, Milhalic, Pinto, & Raffa, 2000; Potenza, 2001; Wise, 1996; Volkow, Fowler, Wang, Swanson, & Telang, 2007). Evidence from longitudinal twin studies shows a common *externalizing factor* underlying symptoms of impulsivity, sociability, and rebelliousness (Blonigen et al., 2005; Burt, McGue, Krueger, & Iacono, 2005; King, Iacono, & McGue, 2004). The disruptive or *externalizing disorders* consist of attention deficit hyperactivity disorder (ADHD), conduct disorder, and oppositional defiant disorder. When an identical twin is affected with an externalizing disorder, the other twin has a very high probability of manifesting a disorder from the same category. Also, genetics and environment have been shown to mediate the relationship between a particular pattern of brain wave activity (lower amplitude P300 brain waves) (Zukov, et al., 2009) and a range of externalizing disorders (e.g., see Hicks et al., 2007; Iacono, Malone, & McGue, 2003; Kendler, Prescott, Myers, & Neale, 2003; Patrick et al., 2006). Alcohol dependence, drug dependence, nicotine dependence, conduct disorder, and adult antisocial behavior are rampant in these diagnostic categories.

From a psychosocial perspective, personality and environmental risk factors are common across both chemical and behavioral expressions of addiction. Impulsivity, poor parental supervision, and delinquency, as well as various demographic risk factors such as poverty, geography, and peer groups, can influence the onset and course of both drug use and other risk-taking activities, such as gambling. Furthermore, when those in treatment for diverse substance abuse problems (e.g., drug dependence or driving under the influence) are studied for co-occurring disorders there are commonalities in other forms of psychopathology, such as increased rates of anxiety and depressive disorders (Shaffer, LaPlante, et al., 2004).

Other similarities across the range of hedonic dependencies (e.g., gambling, sex, eating, drugs, and alcohol) include:

- Common milestones in the progression of behavioral dysfunction (e.g., relationship, work, and economic problems);
- Dopamine malfunction, which plays a primary role in both drug and behavioral addictions;
- Parallel neurobiological consequences across addictive behaviors (e.g., neuroadaptation resulting in tolerance and withdrawal);
- Nonspecificity of object choice (i.e., it is common for people who are recovering from one pattern of addiction to "hop" to another); and
- Comparable patterns of emotional distress.

The upshot of these explicit commonalities is the emergence of a syndrome approach to addictive disorders. Although the specific objects of addiction show considerable variability, they share a cluster of signs and symptoms related to a common underlying condition.

> The current view of separate addictions is similar to the view espoused during the early days of AIDS diagnosis, when rare diseases were not yet recognized as opportunistic infections of an underlying immune deficiency syndrome. Our analysis of the extant literature reveals that the specific objects of addiction play a less central role in the development of addiction than previously thought, and it identifies the need for a more comprehensive philosophy of addiction. (Shaffer, LaPlante, et al., 2004, p. 367)

The foundational premise of this book is that our understanding of a broad array of hedonic activities is dramatically improved through a commonalities approach. Those who are concerned about prevention, treatment, and aftercare for addictive disorders will benefit from this perspective. The information contained herein may be compared to a broad-spectrum vaccine, effective across a range of disease agents. By way of analogy, in 2007 the World Health Organization (WHO) "convened the third meeting on 'Influenza vaccines that induce broad spectrum and long-lasting immune responses.' The objectives of the meeting were to review the current status of research in the area of influenza vaccine strategies targeting vaccines that are able to induce broad-spectrum and/or long-lasting immune responses and to provide cross-protection against divergent influenza virus strains" (WHO, 2007).

Addiction of all kinds is based on a "pathological usurpation" of the executive functions of the brain which includes motivation, memory, and decision making. "The key role in the development of these changes belongs to the mesocortical-limbic dopaminergic system. Types of addictive behavior based on agents other than psychoactive substances are linked with similar changes in the nervous system" (Ivilieva, 2012, p. 678). *Evolutionary mismatch* theories posit that potentially addictive behaviors were genetically enhanced during our hunter-gatherer ancestry (Davis, 2014). In the modern era of advanced technology, these key-to-survival behaviors become overexpressed.

> Similar to the manufactured purification of psychotropic plant-based substances, the reward impact of processed and hyper-palatable foods, with their high levels of sugar, fat, and salt, is much increased from foods produced in nature ... what was once beneficial and necessary for our survival has been altered and ultra-processed into edible products that may be disadvantageous and potentially addictive. (Davis, 2014, p. 129)

Similar arguments can be made for weapons of mass destruction and the destructive use of social media and internet propaganda.

Extent of the Problem(s)

"First, we have to be courageous enough to say, 'It's in my living room.'"
—Hoffman & Froemke, 2007, p. 33

The statistics on compulsive pleasure-seeking are astounding. The phenomenon of alcohol or drug dependence is so pervasive that addiction impacts 1 in every 4 families (Hoffman & Froemke, 2007).

Table I.1 shows prevalence data on just a few of the most common hedonic dependencies: alcohol, cigarettes, marijuana, the Internet, online pornography, gambling, and obesity.

Table I.1 Prevalence and Severity of Common Hedonic Dependencies

Drug or Activity	Prevalence and Severity of Outcomes
Alcohol	In 2014, 60.9 million people reported binge drinking in the past month, and 16.3 million reported heavy alcohol use (Center for Behavioral Health Statistics and Quality, 2015, p. 19). Approximately 15.1 million adults and 623,000 adolescents in the United States meet criteria for a diagnosis of Alcohol Use Disorder (National Survey on Drug Use and Health [NSDUH], 2015).
Marijuana	The most commonly used illicit drug in the U.S. in the past month is marijuana, which in 2014 was used by 22.2 million people aged 12 or older (Substance Abuse and Mental Health Services Administration [SAMHSA], 2015). According to the 2015 National Survey on Drug Use and Health, an estimated 44% of the U.S. population (age 12 and older) have tried marijuana at least once in their lifetime.
Psychedelics	In 2014, an estimated 1.2 million people aged 12 or older were current users of hallucinogens. This includes LSD, PCP, peyote, mescaline, psilocybin mushrooms, and "Ecstasy" (MDMA), representing 0.4 % of the population aged 12 or older. "The percentage of the population aged 12 or older in 2014 who were current users of hallucinogens was similar to the percentages between 2002 and 2013." (SAMHSA, 2015, p. 12)
Illicit Drugs	In 2014, 10.2 % of the population aged 12 or older (an estimated 27 million people) used an illicit drug in the past 30 days. The 2014 percentage was higher than the percentages of illicit drug use from 2002 to 2013. High percentages of illicit drug use are primarily driven by marijuana use and the nonmedical use of prescription pain relievers. 4.3 million people aged 12 or older reported current nonmedical use of prescription pain relievers (Center for Behavioral Health Statistics and Quality, 2015a).
Cigarettes	In 2014, 16.8% of adults in the U.S. were current smokers. (Centers for Disease Control; National Health Interview Survey, 1965–2014). Cigarette smoking is the most preventable cause of premature death in the United States, accounting for about 480,000 deaths per year (U.S. Department of Health and Human Services, [USDHHS], 2014). "In 2014, 66.9 million people aged 12 or older were current users of a tobacco product, including 55.2 million cigarette smokers. Across all age groups, tobacco use and cigarette user were lower in 2014 than in most years from 2002 to 2013" (Center for Behavioral Health Statistics and Quality, 2015, p. 1).
The Internet	2014 saw the biggest increase in time spent online in a decade, with Internet users spending over three and a half hours longer online each week than they did in 2013 (20 hours and 30 minutes in 2014, compared to 16 hours and 54 minutes in 2013) (Ofcom, 2015). About 73% of Americans go online on a daily basis; 21% go online almost constantly; 42% go online several times a day and 10%; go online about once a day; 13% of adults report not using the Internet at all (Bratskeir, 2015).
Online Pornography	It's estimated that 13% of internet searches are for pornographic material, with about 2/3 of those searches coming from people in the United States (Ogas and Gaddam, 2011). An estimated 40 million adults in the United States regularly visit Internet pornography sites. In 2007, global porn revenues were estimated at $20 billion, with $10 billion in the U.S. The Free Speech Coalition estimated both global and U.S. porn revenues have been reduced by 50% between 2007 and 2011, due to the amount of free pornography available online (Barrett, 2012).
Gambling	There are about 2 million gambling addicts in the United States (Jabr, 2013). People pumped $38.54 billion dollars into the U.S. casino industry in 2015 (American Gaming Association, 2016).
Food	Global data show that as of 2014, the U.S. is second only to China in terms of obesity rate; about one-fourth of severely obese men and one-fifth of severely obese women live here. Mean global BMI is 24.2 for men and 24.4 for women. Meanwhile, global prevalence of underweight is about 9–10% (NCD Risk Factor Collaboration, 2016). From 2011–2014, the prevalence of adult obesity was about 36% in adults (38% women, 34% men) and 17% in youth (no difference by sex) (Ogden, Carroll, Fryar, & and Flegal, 2015, p. 1).

Figure I.1 shows the extent of use of popular social networking sites (SNS). During the past 12 years, the use of SNS has grown exponentially. As reported by Facebook, as of March 2014, there were 1.28 billion active users on the site per month, and at least 802 million of these users logged into Facebook every day (Ryan, et. al, 2014). Facebook is the most popular SNS in the world.

Figure I.1 Active Users of Ten Popular Social Networking Sites (Ryan, Chester, Reece, and Xenos, 2014)

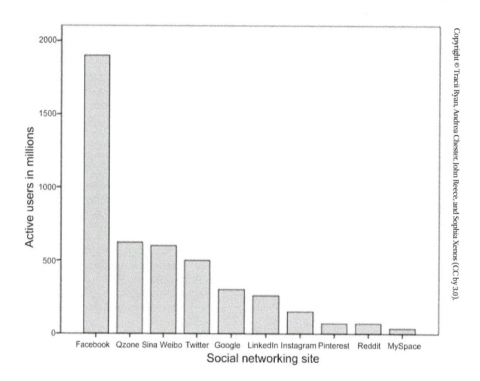

Positive Psychology and Natural Highs

When spider webs unite, they can tie up a lion.

—Ethiopian proverb

By approaching the age-old search for pleasure from an addiction syndrome perspective, we develop a more complete and helpful understanding of human compulsion and loss of control. Sound principles from psychology and sociology are integrated with emerging discoveries in brain science to present a positive approach to self-regulation of the need to feel good.

Since the discovery of endorphins (Hughes, 1975; Kosterlitz & Hughes, 1975), neuroscience has amassed conclusive evidence that the brain is a giant pharmaceutical factory that manufactures its own mind-altering chemicals. During the past decade, positive psychologists (those working in the field of positive psychology, defined below) have actively addressed the fundamental need to achieve pleasure and well-being without the debilitating fallout from *excessive dopamine backlash* (e.g., Cloninger, 2004; Milkman, 2001; Milkman & Sunderwirth, 1993; Peterson & Seligman, 2004; Seligman, 2002).

Based on a commonalities model, whereby hedonic pursuits are linked by altered brain chemistry, we developed a multidisciplinary definition of addiction inclusive of both drug and behavioral dependencies.

> *Addiction:* "Self-induced changes (psychology) in neurotransmission (biology) that result in problem behaviors (sociology)" (Milkman & Sunderwirth, 1983).

In light of the seemingly universal need to seek out altered states, it behooves researchers, educators, parents, politicians, public health administrators, and treatment practitioners to promote healthy means to alter brain chemistry. We have posited the concept of *natural highs* in order to promote awareness of the need to actively pursue changes in brain chemistry that lead to health and well-being (Milkman, 2001; Milkman & Hunter, 1987, 1988; Milkman & Sunderwirth, 1993).

> *Natural highs:* "Self-induced changes in brain chemistry that result in positive feeling states, health, and well-being for the individual and society" (Milkman & Sunderwirth, 1993).

Consistent with our definition, health practitioners and researchers agree that there is more to optimal living than freedom from biological aberration. The World Health Organization (1948) has defined health as "a state of complete physical, mental and social well-being and not merely the absence of disease or infirmity." This definition has not been amended since its origination more than 60 years ago. Realization of optimal health is the implicit goal of the burgeoning field of *positive psychology*, "the scientific and applied approach to uncovering people's strengths and promoting their positive functioning" (Snyder & Lopez, 2007, p. 3). Positive psychology embodies principles for cultivating strength of character (e.g., authenticity, persistence, kindness, gratitude, hope, and humor) and virtues (wisdom, courage, humanity, justice, temperance, and transcendence) as indispensable means for achieving happiness throughout the life span (Peterson & Seligman, 2004).

Our approach to hedonic dependencies seeks to create a more balanced view of human functioning. We examine both the positive and negative sides of pleasure. After exploring a broad range of destructive strategies to achieve feelings of well-being and wholeness, we present positive approaches to mood alteration and lasting happiness. The matrix of cognitive, emotional, and behavioral skills enveloped by the construct of natural highs include the ability to manage thoughts in the service of generating positive feelings and actions; the use of mindfulness skills to achieve peace of mind and connection with others; a positive program of nutrition and physical activity; and the realization of our individual areas of interest, passion, and ability.

Across the broad spectrum of society's efforts to prevent, intervene in, and treat hedonic dependency, the single most important remedial factor is the experience of intimacy characterized by a deep-seated sense of nurturance, trust, and support.

Critical Study: Resilience on the Garden Island of Kauai

Indeed, human connectedness—so difficult to measure—has been documented as the foundation for health and well-being. In her groundbreaking work, Werner (1989) published the findings of her 30-year study that underscore the vital importance of nurture and support. In 1955, all 698 children who were born on the Hawaiian island of Kauai participated in Werner's study, which followed their development at 1, 2, 10, 18, 31, and 32 years of age. While 422 were judged to have a supportive environment, 201 were considered at risk for developing some form of emotional or behavioral disorder later in life. These vulnerable youth had four of the following risk factors prior to their second birthday: perinatal stress, chronic poverty, parents' education level less than the eighth grade, family discord, or divorce. They constituted 30% of the surviving children on the island. Two-thirds of these children (129) did develop serious learning or behavioral problems by age 10 or had delinquency records, mental health problems, or pregnancies by the time they were 18.

More important, 1 of 3 did not! Seventy-two of these high-risk children grew into competent young adults who loved, worked, and played well. The research team was able to identify a number of factors that seemed to protect vulnerable children from poor adjustment. Their temperaments were characterized by high activity, low excitability and distress, and high sociability.

Their social circumstances were perhaps even more revealing. Kids who remained healthy had four or fewer children in their immediate family. Also, there were at least 2 years between the births of siblings. The at-risk children who succeeded had emotional support outside of their immediate family. They participated in extracurricular activities and had formed a close bond with one or more caretakers during the first years of life. Of paramount importance was the establishment of at least one genuine, caring relationship. Werner (1989) found that "the resilient children... had at least one person in their lives who accepted them unconditionally regardless of temperamental idiosyncrasies or physical or mental handicaps." She concluded that "all children can be helped to become more resilient if adults in their lives encourage independence, teach them appropriate communication and self-help skills and model, as well as reward acts of helpfulness and caring" (p. 106).

Nurturing healthy children by guiding them through critical phases of development has benefits throughout their lives. Natural highs depend on the positive resolution of specific psychological conflicts through caring, nurturing, and intimate human relationships. Otherwise, energy is directed to problems that were not effectively handled during childhood, often resulting in misguided attempts to reduce suffering.

From the perspective of object relations theory, addiction results from a failure in the separation-individuation process (e.g., Baker & Baker, 1987; Kohut, 1977). Due to the lack of reliable caretakers and the incapacity to make *transmuting internalizations* (incorporating a solid sense of self through exposure to and nurturance from genuine and caring others), the addict remains dependent upon external sources of tension reduction. Because comfort provided by external addictive agents cannot be internalized into the self, the process inevitably fails (Graham & Glickauf-Hughes, 1992). Treatment involves providing opportunity for healthy resolution of the need for separation-individuation through internalizing the soothing and resilient characteristics of the therapist or fellow group members.

During his ninth decade of life, Erik Erikson (1982) expanded upon the template he and his wife, Joan, had developed 40 years earlier for understanding how lessons from each of life's stages mature into multiple facets of wisdom that blossom during old age. As shown in Table I.2, positive attributes (e.g., hope, will, purpose) generated from the resolution of specific psychological conflicts culminate in a strong sense of purpose and meaning, even in the face of death.

Table I.2 The Completed Life Cycle of Natural Highs

Conflict and Resolution	Attribute	Attainment in Old Age
Old Age Integrity vs. Despair	Wisdom	Existential identity; a sense of identity strong enough to withstand physical disintegration
Adulthood Generativity vs. Stagnation	Care	Caritas, caring for others; and agape, empathy, and concern
Early Adulthood Intimacy vs. Isolation	Love	Sense of the complexity of relationships; value of tenderness and loving freely
Adolescence Identity vs. Confusion	Fidelity	Sense of complexity of life; merger of sensory, logical, and aesthetic perceptions
School Age Industry vs. Inferiority	Competence	Humility; acceptance of the course of one's life and unfulfilled hopes
Play Age Initiative vs. Guilt	Purpose	Humor; empathy; resilience
Early Childhood Autonomy vs. Shame	Will	Acceptance of the cycle of life, from integration to disintegration
Infancy Basic Trust vs. Mistrust	Hope	Appreciation of interdependence and relatedness

Source: Adapted from "Erikson in His Own Old Age, Expands His View of Life" by D. Goleman, 1988, June 14, New York Times, pp. 13–14.

Throughout the remainder of this book, after exploring the nature and causes (biological, psychological, and social) of the three basic patterns of behavioral excess—*arousal, satiation,* and *fantasy*— along with basic human needs for *intimacy, love, and belonging,* we delineate *natural highs* as positive means to cope with the inevitable *sturm und drang* (storm and stress) of being alive. Personal accounts highlight our vulnerability to cravings and addictions and how natural highs can become powerful allies for establishing enduring health and well-being.

We conclude our introduction to natural highs with some thoughts of Albert Hofmann, who is viewed by many as the father of the modern drug age. In April 2008, Hofmann, known for his discovery of LSD-25, died at the age of 102. Hofmann discovered the world's most famous hallucinogen on April 16, 1943, at the Sandoz research laboratory in Basel, Switzerland. He was isolating and synthesizing the unstable alkaloids of the ergot fungus and inadvertently ingested the drug. Hofmann viewed LSD as a sacrament for the modern age. He perceived that it had given him a sense of union with nature and of the spiritual basis of creation. Throughout the 60-plus years after his mind-shattering discovery, Hofmann believed that he had unveiled the potential antidote to the problems associated with consumerism, industrialization, and the vanishing sense of the divine. Although he remained saddened by the misuse of and consequent ban on LSD in most countries, he believed that the power of LSD is based on access to the radiance and sense of oneness with creation that could be accessed naturally, often during childhood, through communion with nature. His advice to those seeking a powerful altered state was simple: "Go to the meadow, go to the garden, go to the woods. Open your eyes!" ("Obituary: Albert Hofmann," 2008).

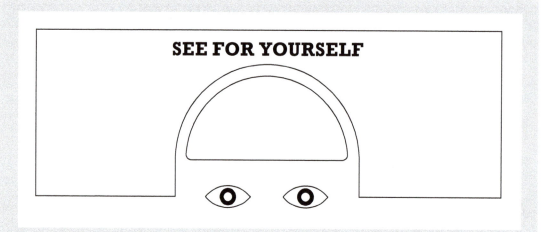

The Power of Addiction and The Addiction of Power. 2014. Gabor Maté. TED Talk. 18:46

 Dr. Maté discusses the commonalities approach to substance abuse and behavioral addiction, which are rooted in childhood suffering and loss. **https://www.youtube.com/watch?v=-mpbBAQvrKM**

Drugs Don't Cause Addiction. 2015. By Kurzgesagt – In a Nutshell. 5:51

 Animated video on how lack of connection and inhuman living conditions cause addiction. When these conditions are ameliorated for people (and animals) former addicts return to healthy lifestyles. **https://www.youtube.com/watch?v=ao8L-0nSYzg**

1

Addiction to Experience

Some to dance, some to make bonfires, each man to what sport and revels his addiction leads him.
—*Othello*, Act II, Scene 2

The Broad Scope of Addiction

In the drama of human excess, experience is the protagonist, and drugs or activities are merely supporting actors. We are compelled by repetitious urges to become energized, to relax, to imagine. These three citadels of consciousness are the beacons of compulsive behavior.

Recognition that the term *addiction* should transcend drug abuse emerged from the problem of categorizing so-called non-addictive and addictive drugs. By the late 1960s, it became clear that some people could become compulsively involved with marijuana and LSD, substances that seemed to have a relatively low potential for physical dependency. Meanwhile, some users (chippers) could maintain relatively casual relationships with opium derivatives such as heroin or codeine, customarily associated with rapidly increased tolerance and severe discomfort upon discontinuance. Scientific research during the past 20 years had shown that focusing on a physical versus psychological distinction is a distraction from the real issues.

> From both clinical and policy perspectives, it actually does not matter very much what physical withdrawal symptoms occur. Physical dependence is not that important, because even the dramatic withdrawal symptoms of heroin and alcohol addiction can now be easily managed with appropriate medications. Even more important, many of the most dangerous and addicting drugs, including

methamphetamine and crack cocaine, do not produce very severe physical dependence symptoms upon withdrawal. (Leshner, 2007, p. 43)

According to the National Survey on Drug Use and Health (NSDUH, 2015), nearly 7% of those aged 12 and older had used ecstasy at least once in their lifetime. Although nearly 60% of those who reported use acknowledge symptoms of withdrawal (i.e., fatigue, loss of appetite, depression, and trouble concentrating), about 23% did not meet the diagnostic criteria for abuse or dependence (National Institute on Drug Abuse [NIDA], 2007e).

Behavioral Addictions

Behavioral science research has developed the scientific underpinning for a syndrome approach to addictive behaviors (e.g., Cloninger, Svrakic, & Przybeck, 1993; Iacono, Malone, & McGue, 2003; Krueger et al., 2002; Legrand, Iacono, & McGue, 2005; Milkman & Sunderwirth, 1983, 1987, 1993, 1998; Shaffer, LaPlante, et al., 2004). Parallels have been drawn between traditionally held ideas about drug involvement and a host of pleasure-fueled activities far removed from the compulsive intake of food or drugs (Figure 1.1). People regularly describe themselves as "addicted" to seemingly harmless activities like aerobics or watching MTV. Media-coined disorders such as "chocoholism" (Ozelli, 2007) or "workaholism" (Oates, 1971) are widely accepted with an abundance of explanations. Endorphins, our internal opioids, are proposed as the "keys to paradise" for runners who push beyond "the wall."

Television, magazines, and newspapers have all jumped on the bandwagon of a commonalities approach to habitual behaviors. Of current notoriety is addiction to computer games such as *World of Warcraft* or *Second Life*. During the past two decades, the worldwide population of online users grew dramatically, with an estimated 5.9% to 13% exhibiting some form of disturbed behavior related to online pursuits (Morahan-Martin, 2001). Fifteen percent of university students in the United States and Europe reported that they knew someone who is addicted to the Internet (Anderson, 1999). In 2012 it is estimated that more than one billion people played computer games—nearly 15% of the world population (Kuss, 2013).

The Addictive Personality

The addictive personality is described in various scientific reports as impulsive, rule breaking, deviant, nonconformist, and depressed (e.g., Iacono et al., 2003; Jessor, 1998; Krueger et al., 2002; Legrand et al., 2005). Youngsters who later develop compulsive problem behaviors often experience difficulty in school and in their family relationships. Auto accidents, fighting, truancy, delinquency, and vicious struggles with parents are common. Perhaps the entire spectrum of antisocial behavior patterns provides some relief to youth who encounter genetic predisposition, familial inadequacy, poverty, bereavement, or geographic instability. Figure 1.2 shows the composite of risk factors that contribute to addictive patterns of behavior.

Who Is Most at Risk?

Scientists estimate that genetic factors account for between 40% and 60% of a person's vulnerability to addiction, including the effects of environment and gene expression and functions. Adolescents and other individuals with mental disorders are at greater risk of drug abuse and addictive behavior than the general population. Of course, parents and other family members who abuse alcohol or other drugs or engage in

Figure 1.1 **The Broad Scope of Addiction** Brain science provides scientific underpinning for a syndrome approach to addictive behaviors. The nucleus accumbens and pathways connected to it mediate natural rewards and are affected by mood-altering drugs.

Figure 1.2 **Risk Factors for Dependency** Genetic factors, including the effects of environment and gene expression, account for between 40% and 60% of a person's vulnerability to addiction.

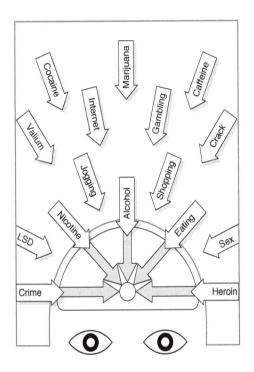

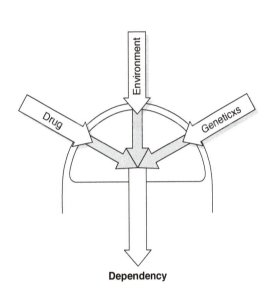

criminal activity increase children's risks of developing addictive problems. During adolescence, friends and acquaintances appear to have the greatest impact on the development of social problem behaviors (Kandel and Maloff, 1983). As with other mental or physical disorders, vulnerability varies from person to person. Generally, the more risk factors an individual has, the greater chance that partaking of risky behavior will lead to compulsion and loss of control. Protective factors (the other side of the coin) reduce a person's risk for developing addiction. Zhai et al. (2015) found that for adolescents there is a relationship between low self-esteem and negative coping. Correspondingly, Zavar et al., (2013) reported a significant association between low self-esteem and smoking, illegal drug abuse (e.g., heroin, pills, alcohol, and other substances). These results suggest that increasing self-esteem is essential for preventing emotional and behavioral disorders (Khajehdaluee, Zavar, Alidoust, & Pourandi, 2013, p. 1).

Table 1.1 shows examples of both risk and protective factors.

Table 1.1 Examples of Risk and Protective Factors

Risk Factors	Domain	Protective Factors
Early aggressive behavior	Individual	Self-control
Poor social skills	Individual	Positive relationships
Lack of parental supervision	Family	Parental monitoring and support
Substance abuse	Peer	Academic competence
Drug availability	School	Anti-drug use policies
Poverty	Community	Strong neighborhood attachment

Source: From "Drugs, brains, and behavior: The science of addiction" by National Institute on Drug Abuse, 2008, NIH Pub. No. 14-5605, p. 7.

Acquisition and Maintenance of Reward-Dependent Behavior

It is unnecessary to develop separate sets of principles to explain how drug use and other compulsive behaviors gain control over human life. Drugs, food, sex, gambling, and aggressive outbursts all give prompt, salient, and short-lasting relief to the people who indulge in them due to dopamine being released in the brain's reward center. In addition to sharing pleasure-inducing properties, both substance use and other mood-altering activities tend to produce an initial state of euphoria, which is then followed by a negative emotional state—that is, a high followed by a low. This post-euphoric discomfort gives further impetus to repetition of the rewarding activity. The old "hair of the dog" remedy of drinking to restore "normal" brain chemistry and relieve hangover symptoms is consistent with this idea.

As illustrated in Figure 1.3, Wikler (1973) developed a two-phase model for the origins and progression of narcotics addiction that is applicable to other compulsions as well. In the *acquisition phase,* the novice begins and continues a potentially compulsive activity because of pleasurable sensations brought about through the experience. We now know that this is the result of an increased concentration of dopamine in the reward centers of the brain (e.g., Milkman & Sunderwirth, 1998; NIDA, 2007a; Ozelli, 2007). The environment in which the desired feeling occurs becomes associated with a "rush" or sense of well-being. Thus, the pleasure setting becomes a composite of cues that stimulate craving for the need-satisfying activity. The alcoholic, for example, who has previously enjoyed the euphoria brought on by drink, cannot resist temptation when fate (usually self-orchestrated) delivers him or her to the neighborhood bar or an old friend's New Year's Eve party. This phenomenon is known as *conditioned desire* (Heinz, 2006). The human body eventually adapts to most novel stimulation by reducing the potency of its effect. The user soon needs more of the mood-altering activity to experience similar alterations in feeling. The addicted climber must increasingly seek out more difficult cliffs; the hooked skydiver compulsively finds more challenging and frightening drops.

In the *maintenance phase* of addiction, a person is no longer motivated by any sense of pleasure from the drug or other need-gratifying behavior. Rather, the repetitive activity now serves only to relieve the sense of despair and physical discomfort that is felt when the mood-altering action or substance is not present. The user can only "break even" by performing his or her tension-relieving activity. Without it, the addicted person suffers from a devastating combination of physical dependence and an even more complicated and stressful environment. The compulsive meditator, for example, increasingly seeks out quiescent relaxation to escape from stress that builds from increasing social isolation and decreased productivity at home and at work.

Figure 1.3 The Addictive Progression In the *acquisition phase*, the individual experiences pleasure as the result of hedonic (drug or behavior) activity. Without the activity, he or she experiences the "normal" state of mood. In the *intermediate state*, tolerance results in the need for more of the hedonic activity in order to achieve positive effects. In the *dependence state*, hedonic activity no longer evokes pleasure, only relief from the suffering brought on by withdrawal.

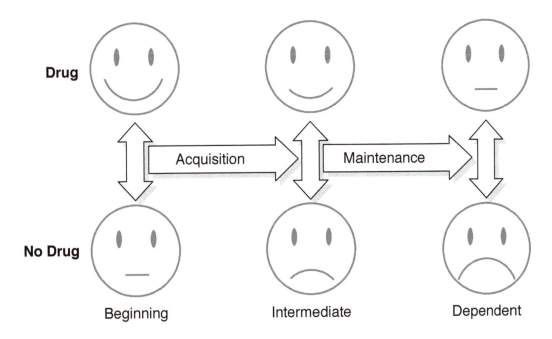

Wikler's two-phase model melds nicely with the incentive-sensitization theory of Robinson and Berridge (1993; Blum, 2012). There is a distinction between "liking" a substance and "wanting" a substance. The liking is present in the early stages when the person learns they can experience pleasure. Cues associated with drug use acquire "incentive salience" through their association with the drug's effects. Through Pavlovian conditioning the brain becomes attuned to stimuli associated with the drug. Over time, the user experiences less *liking* (pleasure), but continues to *want* (crave) the substance. Long-term drug abusers may continue to crave a substance even if they no longer particularly enjoy using it (due to tolerance). Robinson and Berridge link wanting substances to changes (e.g., increased sensitivity) in the mesolimbic dopamine system, which is involved in signaling the reward value of stimuli. The development of wanting through repeated use of the drug is an unconscious process, although it can activate a conscious desire for the substance and trigger drug-seeking behavior. Moreover, dysregulation of the dopamine system may lead to a spillover of "wanting" towards other targets, which would explain the co-occurrence of drug abuse along with compulsive gambling or hypersexuality (Robinson & Berridge, 2008).

Figure 1.4 shows how an initially rewarding or need-gratifying activity can progress into a persistent problem of substance abuse or other reward-seeking behavior. Life situations at point A lead to a need or desire to modify mood through drugs or other mind-altering behavior. At point B, the participant experiences pleasure or decreases discomfort as the result of mood alteration. Hence, at point C the user's thoughts (positive outcome expectations) and mood-altering behaviors are strengthened (reinforced) as the result of successful changes in mental state. Points A, B, and C constitute the mental and behavioral correlates of the acquisition phase of a problem dependency. At point D, the individual begins to experience negative consequences from the activity, such as getting fired, relationship problems, and so forth. If the person does not intervene on his or her own behalf, at point E he or she may increasingly rely on the temporary need-gratifying behavior to counter the increased stress brought on by the "rewarding" behavior pattern. At point F, there is an even further negative consequence from use, resulting in another escalation of stress and discomfort. At point G, the individual is faced with having to deal with the original life problems now compounded by overreliance on the addictive activity. Points D through G correspond to Wikler's maintenance stage, as shown in Figure 1.3 (Wanberg & Milkman, 2006).

As shown in Figure 1.4, an addictive pattern is evident when one becomes progressively less able to control the beginning or end of a need fulfilling activity. As reward-dependent behavior increasingly leads to harmful outcomes, the maintenance cycle is initiated with increasingly devastating consequences. Yet below the surface are more profound explanatory links. The spectrum of addictive behaviors is connected by a biochemical thread. Advances in scientific understanding of the reward centers of the brain (discussed in detail in Chapter 3) depart from moralistic explanations of addiction, that is, "lack of motivation, poor character." Science increasingly views the problem as rooted in aberrations of the brain (e.g., Leshner, 2007). It has become obvious that individuals can change their brain chemistry through immersion in salient mood-altering activities as well as through ingesting intoxicating substances.

Whether the behavior is sleeping too much, compulsive gambling, engaging in violence, desperately looking for sex, or relentlessly trolling the Internet, the neurochemical mechanisms at play parallel the ones for those addicted to drugs. Memory-linked reminders cue these addicts to the relief rewards, they experience cravings, and they repeatedly fail to change, even when these behaviors are clearly leading to self-destruction. "Scratching the itch feels good, but it produces a sore" (Smedley, 2015, p. 42).

As earlier stated, addiction is best defined as *self-induced changes in neurotransmission that result in problem behaviors*. Our discussion now turns to exploring each component of this definition: self-induced (psychology) changes in brain chemistry (neuroscience) that lead to problem behaviors (sociology).

Figure 1.4 The Mental-Behavioral Impaired Control Cycle

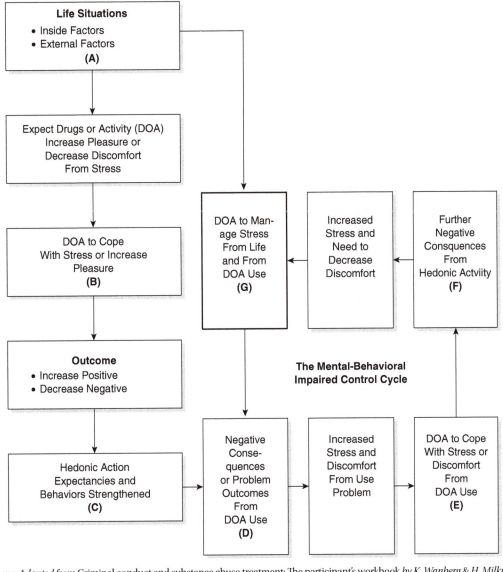

Source: Adapted from Criminal conduct and substance abuse treatment: The participant's workbook *by K. Wanberg & H. Milkman, 2006, Thousand Oaks, CA: Sage Publications.*

Drugs and Activities of Choice

Given that we may voluntarily alter our neurotransmission to achieve a desired feeling, why do only some of us become compulsively involved in this pursuit? After all, most people can safely become disinhibited by having a few drinks or occasionally experience some degree of mania at the racetrack without going off the deep end. Exposure to sexual imagery is rampant, yet most people do not squander their money and success on prostitution or pornographic pursuits. Along with genetic factors that predispose individuals to particular behavioral styles (e.g., Cloninger et al., 1993), learned patterns of coping with stress (internal and external) are common to most forms of addiction. The chronic absence of good feelings about the self provokes a dependence on mood-changing activity.

Whether internal or external in origin, a powerful way of coping with distress is to immerse oneself in an activity—a tension-relieving behavior—that provides psychological respite (Briere & Rickards, 2007). The climber, clinging to a mountain face with only a rope, pitons, and a tenuous foothold, while satisfying a primary sensation-seeking drive, has few moments to spare on self-derogation. The risk taker may figuratively bridge the crevasse of his or her inner turmoil by temporary surrender to something outside the self. Brian, a 32-year-old cocaine user, reported a particularly vivid dream that illustrates this point:

> I recall seeing my personality as a huge concave surface. It looked like a great ceramic bowl with irregularly spaced craters on an otherwise smooth surface. Somehow I could patch the holes with ultra-fine putty made of cocaine paste. The new shimmering surface appeared nearly unmarred. (Personal communication, December 2008)

The user's drug or activity of choice often depends on his or her style of coping with stress. In a research study at Bellevue Psychiatric Hospital in New York, Milkman and Frosch (1973) found a striking relationship between personality and drug of choice. Those who preferred heroin (or other narcotics) used passive withdrawal and reduced sensory stimulation as primary coping devices, e.g., Billie Holiday. In sharp contrast, amphetamine users were apt to confront a hostile or threatening environment with physical or intellectual activity, e.g., Benzedrine and the beat poets. People who used hallucinogens such as LSD reported that they characteristically relied on imagery, daydreaming, and altered thought processes to reduce tension e.g., "psychedelic art" by Pablo Amaringo or Alex Grey. The examples shown in Table 1.2 illustrate differences among compulsive users of heroin, amphetamine, and LSD in their management of self-esteem.

The key that opens the doorway to excess for the pre-addict is the good feeling that he or she learns to create, and repeatedly re-create, through self-determined activity. Unaccustomed to the wine of success, the novice experiences as a godsend any involvement that provides escape from the increasing sense of despair born of inner turmoil experienced in the "straight world." He or she not only delights in a reprieve from tension, but also experiences elevated feelings of self-worth for having discovered the ability to produce a pleasurable sensation. In "The Road to H: Narcotics, Delinquency, and Social Policy," Chein, Gerard, Lee, and Rosenfeld (1981) describe the addict's infatuation with self-determined mood change as a consequence of having achieved a strong state of tension reduction and pleasure at his or her own doing.

> In [heroin] addicts with strong craving … it is in large measure a psychic consequence of achieving a state of relaxation and relief from tension or distress through one's own activities, not through a physician's recommendation or prescription, but through an esoteric, illegal, and dangerous nostrum. We can observe an analogous phenomenon in people who win the Irish Sweepstakes; win on dice, cards, horses or numbers; or even in persons who park in no-parking zones without getting a traffic ticket. They feel important, worthwhile, and interesting; they feel a sense of pride and accomplishment. Such an illusory achievement is an important psychic phenomenon, particularly important when it stands out by contrast with the remainder of a person's life. (p. 111)

Table 1.2 Use of Various Drugs to Regulate Self-Esteem

Heroin	Amphetamine	LSD
How do you feel about yourself generally?		
Lousy. I don't like myself.	I think I'm all right, ya know.	I feel like a voyager in an awesome adventure.
What about your looks? Do you think you're good-looking?		
I don't like them and I don't know why.	I think they're all right. I'm satisfied. Yeah, I think I'm good-looking.	Sometimes I feel like an alien, like I'm a gorgeous being from another planet.
How do you compare with others your age?		
Right now I know I don't compare well. I can't control my desire for drugs. I can't do what I want to do… I can't be a man. I am not doing anything.	I don't think I'm as mature, serious, or business-minded as a 25-year-old should be. As a man, I'm all right. I'm big and strong and I try to be kind. I love women and I dig kids.	I don't compare myself to others. I just think about how I'm dealing with my own Karma so I can improve my chances now and in a future life.
What do you believe that other people think of you?		
That I'm a cop-out; some people would say degenerate.	I think others like me—some people would say they like me a great deal. They really do not say it, but I know they do. I make friends easily and people smile and they embrace me and make me feel like I'm not rejected.	They think I'm on a path of spiritual discovery. That I am in touch with some cosmic force that they would like to understand.
What kind of person would you like to be?		
I'd just be average and get along, say middle class. I want to be able to work and be middle class. I don't have goals of making a million or anything, just make a living.	I would like to be free of drugs. I would like to not even have to put a grape pop in my mouth if I didn't want to. Right now I'm taking vitamin D and taking grape ice pops. I'm playing with kids. I bought a yo-yo yesterday. I'm laughing a lot and enjoying life.	I would like to be in flow with the forces of the universe… to experience oneness with people and nature… to merge with the cosmos.

Source: Adapted from "On the preferential abuse of heroin and amphetamines," H. Milkman & W. Frosch, 1973, Journal of Nervous and Mental Disease, 156(4), 242–248.

Beacons of Compulsion

After studying the life histories of drug abusers, we have seen that drugs of choice are harmonious with an individual's usual means of coping with stress. The discovery of a need-fulfilling drug is usually a serendipitous event; the novice becomes infatuated because of the immediate reduction of stress achieved through the experience. Incipient addicts usually experience behavioral compulsion and loss of control before ever ingesting a psychoactive substance. Juvenile delinquency, persistent and vicious family struggles, and inability to adequately cope with everyday demands are common childhood precursors to drug abuse. Heroin users often show histories of passivity alternating with uncontrolled rage; stimulant users describe multiple episodes of life-threatening impulsiveness; those who rely on hallucinogens report that they regularly avoided problems through fantasy during prolonged periods of their childhood.

We repeatedly pursue three avenues of experience as antidotes for psychic pain. These preferred styles of coping—*satiation, arousal,* and *fantasy*—may have their origins in the first years of life. Childhood experiences combined with genetic predisposition are the foundations of adult compulsion. The drug group of choice—depressants, stimulants, or hallucinogens—is the one that best fits the individual's characteristic way of coping with stress or feelings of unworthiness. People do not become addicted to drugs or mood-altering activities as such, but rather to the satiation, arousal, or fantasy experiences that can be achieved through them.

For example, addicts whose basic motivation is satiation are likely to binge on food or television watching or to choose depressant drugs such as the benzodiazepines (e.g., Xanax). Psychologically, they are trying to shut down negative feelings by reducing stimulation from the internal or external world. The life of the satiation type of addict bears striking similarity to that of a child during the first year of life. The mouth and skin are the primary receptors of experience, and feelings of well-being depend almost completely on food and warmth. Khantzian (1997) explains how narcotics provide a pharmacologic defense against the user's own aggressive drives. Binge eating or excessive television watching may fulfill the same adaptive role by helping people quiet strong hostile impulses. On a biochemical level, the effect of satiation activities may be similar to that of opioids. Growing dependence on behaviors such as overeating and watching television may be analogous, though more subtle, versions of opioid addiction.

While satiation addicts try to avoid stimulation and confrontation, others actively seek it. The behaviors associated with the arousal mode of gratification include crime, gambling, risk taking, and use of stimulant drugs such as amphetamines or cocaine. These addicts seek to feel active and potent in relationship to their environment and people in their midst. They are often boastful about their artistic talent, intellectual skill, and sexual or physical prowess. Their vast expenditures of mental and physical energy are designed to deny underlying fears of helplessness. This posture is reminiscent of 2- and 3-year-olds coping with the world of giants in which they live. Asked, "Who is biggest or toughest?" they often reply, "I can beat up Daddy." They protect themselves through the defense of magical denial: "I am really not helpless and vulnerable; I am powerful and feared."

The third type of addict, the one who uses fantasy as the preferred way of dealing with the world, favors repetitive activation of right-hemisphere thinking (Pink, 2005). Thoughts become dreamlike with rapidly shifting imagery and illogical relations between time and space. This style of coping often includes preoccupation with day or night dreams; compulsive artistic expression; or various forms of mystical experience, sometimes expressed as a quest for the feeling of oneness or cosmic unity. People who rely on this style partially overcome their fears by creating fantasies in which they are effective and important. They may travel with extraterrestrials, encounter the Grim Reaper, or have their body entered by a supernatural entity. Religious fanaticism is another manifestation of this coping mode. These addicts favor hallucinogens (such as LSD), mushrooms containing psilocybin, or peyote.

Interestingly, the two basic types of chemical molecules present in nearly all hallucinogens—variations of indole and phenethylamine—are also found in many compounds that occur naturally as neurotransmitters. For example, dopamine and norepinephrine have the basic phenethylamine structure, whereas serotonin has the indole structure. The fantasy aspects of some artistic, romantic, or spiritual activities may be brought about by conversion of the brain's own indole or phenethylamine compounds into hallucinogenic variations of these chemicals.

Behavioral Excess and the Brain

Addiction covers a broad spectrum of compulsive pleasure-seeking activities with common neurochemical underpinnings. The root of craving lies in the brain's reward system, a network of neurons that become activated when we perform functions that help us to survive, such as eating or sex. The reward network includes a set of neurons found in the ventral tegmental area (VTA) of the brain, which connects to the nucleus accumbens and other areas such as the prefrontal cortex. Reward payoffs create conditioned responses (i.e., reward-seeking behaviors) that are subsequently evoked at the mere sight of food or a sexual object, or by the environment in which these activities occurred. Illicit drugs stimulate this pleasure circuit and can induce even greater feelings of pleasure than natural functions. Compulsive eaters, gamblers, and drug addicts may be unwittingly trying to compensate for an abnormal response to dopamine, the neurotransmitter that regulates reward-seeking activity. An irregularity or an inability to achieve satisfaction from "normal" amounts of dopamine may cause them to continuously dose themselves with a broad spectrum of pleasure-inducing acts (Delgado, 2007; Ozelli, 2007; Reuter et al., 2005). Here is our own take on how food may be used to satisfy an underlying craving for dopamine:

> You rummage through the kitchen cupboard, frantically seeking remaining squares of the Hershey bar that you started last night. ... Damn ... someone else must have eaten it. ... What about the M&M's? ... No luck either ... so you desperately hoe into a few tablespoons of peanut butter followed by a marshmallow chaser (finally, a dopamine rush).

Compounds that block opioid receptors can reduce the intake of sweets. Foods high in sugar are thought to stimulate the release of internal opioids, which create a pleasurable response. When opioid receptors are blocked, there is a corresponding reduction in the urge to consume sweets. It is known that some addictive drugs like heroin or morphine directly target these opioid receptors. A recent review shows that sweet foods can induce craving and that they can be equally, if not more, rewarding than drugs of abuse; moreover, some individuals use sweet foods as a way of altering their moods (Ahmed, Guillem, & Vandaele, 2013). Although addictive drugs undoubtedly cause much more powerful reactions in the brain, it is likely that there are neurochemical parallels between drugs and sweets (Society for Neuroscience, 2003).

In contrast to their commonality of depositing dopamine in the nucleus accumbens, the three types of addiction seem to involve different parts of the brain. Mood shifts are influenced by excitatory and inhibitory pathways in the limbic system, located near the middle of the brain. This system is associated with emotions and with sexual, feeding, and aggressive responses. As arousal decreases, moods may downshift from relaxation to tranquility and finally to a state of blissful satiation. Conversely, increases in arousal are accompanied by changes in experience that range from ordinary alertness to creativity, and ultimately to manic states.

While the limbic system appears to play a major role in pleasurable sensations connected with altered levels of arousal, the convoluted outer brain known as the cerebral cortex is an important determinant of mental content. Excessive activity in the cortex of the right hemisphere may help explain the uncontrolled imagery found in the fantasies of heroin users, mystics, and schizophrenics. Increased activity in the left cortical hemisphere may intensify sensations of perceptual clarity and mental alertness reported during high-risk activities that require an accurate and logical appraisal of one's options, such as rock climbing and skydiving.

As shown in Figure 1.5, the objects of addiction, whether substances (e.g., depressants) or behaviors (e.g., risk-taking), are fueled by combined activation of limbic and cortical systems. The "sphere of ordinary experience," in the center of the illustration, pertains to lower-intensity (healthful) activities (e.g., tennis) or substance use (e.g., drinking black tea) that also alter mood, albeit safely.

Figure 1.5 **Addictive States** While the brain's limbic system appears to play a major role in the pleasurable sensations of addiction, the cerebral cortex influences mental content. Its right hemisphere may be involved in fantasy experiences such as those achieved through LSD or other imagination-oriented activities. The heightened sense of reality experienced during compulsive risk taking or work may be linked to activity in the left hemisphere.

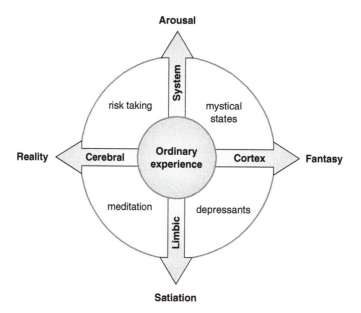

Mismanaging the Brain

The case of New York governor Eliot Spitzer (Hakim & Rashbaum, 2008), who resigned from office after being discovered as "Client 9" of a prostitution ring, exemplifies how a "limbic hijacking" can achieve governance over the cerebral cortex, which is designed to inhibit wayward aggressive, sexual, or other hedonic impulses (e.g., gambling, food, or drugs). Rather than attributing Spitzer's behavior exclusively to a sexual addiction, a more sophisticated explanation would include lifelong patterns of narcissistic self-inflation, sensation seeking, and extreme needs for power and control. Of course, these characteristics are the very ones that elevated Mr. Spitzer to the pinnacle of political success. An old proverb captures the biological determinants of Spitzer's situation: "When the penis goes to the sky, the brain falls to the ground" (source unknown).

While Spitzer may have fallen prey to the complications of extreme need for arousal, others may be waylaid by needs for satiation or fantasy. Advocates for mind-altering substances, for example, may rationalize drug use in terms of "mind expansion" or "spiritual discovery." When taken out of context (e.g., fasting or use of psychedelic plants during religious ceremonies), attempts to induce spiritual awakenings may lead to gross misunderstandings and perceptual inaccuracies. Consider the case of Pat, a college student who earnestly believed that her use of LSD would catalyze a spiritual bond with a complete stranger.

CASE EXAMPLE: User–Observer Discord

It was 1969 and I was in Philadelphia and I was in art school. It was an incredibly interesting time. The war was going on and there was a whole group of people that were being very experimental with some sort of light, sound, and electronic equipment—experiential kinds of things that are especially designed for drug taking.

So anyway, I got involved with these people. They called themselves "the group." We were just friends. And they were smart and really hip and for some reason I got in with these people and I didn't really have to do anything. I just kind of hung around. But for one of the gigs they were brought in by various colleges to put on these environmental kind of music light shows. So they brought me in because it became more and more holistic and experiential. I helped them design this one little tunnel of plastic that you go through where you get to feel everything. There are no visuals and all you do is feel various things.

Then there was this one experience that they wanted me to kind of get involved in, in the massage room. I think they only did this at one college. I don't think it was part of their normal thing. This was a Catholic college that hired them and I came with them on this one. It was wonderful. We set up and the whole gym was given over to a huge screen with this pulsing light show and music that went with it and this huge experiential sort of large snake that people went through. And then on the side in one of the classrooms we set up candles and all these mattresses on the floor and dropped acid [laugh]. So, all kinds of people started to come in. They came in one by one and the idea was that I would massage one person and that they would feel this, this inspiration, and basically—the whole notion was I felt, was that I was channeling the cosmic, loving, healing, energy of the universe. So, I came in and I was given a massage and I was on acid already.

Then I had my massage and I was very impressed and I felt very connected with all of the energy in the universe. So, I massaged numerous people as they came in. And then, a nun came in, one of the sisters. She was in full habit. She lay down on the mat and I was just, at that point—I was just feeling—oh this is just so beautiful. It's just all about love, basically, and God, and I just want to be nothing but the hands of God and the loving touch of the cosmos. So I just began, you know, with her neck. She was lying down. There was lovely music, our own lovely sort of music playing—candle light. I was very near her neck going down her shoulders and her arms and her fingers and down into her back. And then I kept going—it took me awhile—finally I got down to her low, low back and then just started without even thinking about it, just thinking and knowing and feeling that the entire human organism was just nothing but sacred.

So I was just beginning to massage her butt and really into it and tripping [laugh] and all of a sudden, all I know is she just got up and flew out of the room and I just didn't know what was going on, it was a real shock. She came back in very quickly, flipped on all of the fluorescent lights, and got out a razor blade, and started scraping up the wax that had hit the floor. At that point, everything was shut down. The whole experience came to a screeching halt [laugh] and we all basically had to pack up and go home.

But, my experience wasn't her experience of the whole thing [laugh]. It was, in retrospect, very funny, but it was very upsetting at the time. On the way back, we just kind of couldn't quite get it, but these are Catholics, after all [laugh].

Anyway, that's the whole story as I remember it. Basically, we were all tripping. … All of the people, you know, who put on the event. It was very cosmic. Really, my intentions were only of the purist nature, although it was quite naïve of me, I have to say.

Society and the Deviant Career

Differences in neurotransmission, influences from the limbic and cortical systems, and the effects of various brain enzymes all interact with powerful social forces that can push susceptible individuals toward activities that have a high dependency potential. Computer games, public lotteries, and telephone escorts are just a few examples of widely available escapes from routine existence. Advertising plays on the human quest for effortless, impersonal reduction of stress. There is an implicit promise that participation in activities with high dependency potential will diminish the discrepancy between actual self-concept and ideal self-concept. Tobacco and alcohol propaganda provide the most blatant examples of this phenomenon. A visual, ego-ideal fantasy is provided in association with the product, often accompanied by a verbal suggestion for indulgence: "Come to X-Brand country." In this context of promoted immediacy, the individual moves through a network of social interactions that may influence his or her reliance on particular channels of behavioral excess.

As illustrated in Figure 1.7, in the earliest phase of deviant identity, a child may possess a subtle yet identifiable characteristic that steers him or her in the direction of behavior outside the norms of mainstream culture. Consider the 2-year-old who enjoys his or her first taste of beer or the young boy whose nickname is "Lucky" or "Romeo" (i.e., who displays early characteristics). The young person may be valued conditionally so that parental affection depends on performance of expected behaviors (i.e., channelization). Further socially driven behavior occurs when an early sense of low self-worth is relieved through rewards associated with a specific activity. The dejected young person may begin to feel potent as a result of attaining external reinforcers such as drugs, money, or sex.

Although parental role models and styles of child rearing are viewed as important contributors to future coping patterns, adolescent adjustment is inextricably bound to peer influence. According to Kandel and Maloff (1983), the most reliable finding in drug research is the strong relation between one person's drug use and concurrent use by friends. The strength of peer conformity is symbolized by the varied dress rituals among subculture groups. Although members of a particular subculture (e.g., rockabilly, hip hop, punk, Goth, stoner) differentiate themselves by style of dress, taste in music, choice of drugs, types of crime, and so forth, there is a high level of horizontal conformity within each group. Ironically, strong needs for nonconformity result in more parochial and rigid adherence to the norms of a particular subculture (Figure 1.6).

If a person's channelization toward problem behaviors continues into early adulthood, opportunities for success diminish as he or she is increasingly imprisoned, both socially and personally, within a deviant role. The adolescent reaches a point of no return when the social and personal costs of changing lifestyles seem to outweigh the benefits. Imagine the difficulty of a 17-year-old high school dropout and long-standing street gang member suddenly attempting to become an athlete or college student. Eventually, the emerging deviant is labeled by those around him or her as a member of a deviant subgroup such as alcoholic, obese, or criminal. This stigmatization tends to further decrease the addict's sense of self-worth. The youngster may begin to enact socially expected roles such as being irresponsible, nonconforming, or impulse-ridden. The stereotyped individual thus becomes further engulfed in a pattern that restricts his or her life opportunities.

As the addict now drifts from stable family and love relationships, social settings are increasingly selected because of their potential for immediate gratification. The bar, sex parlor, discotheque, or video arcade may become important islands of alienated comfort. The progression of deviance can result in dramatic conflict with the environment. Heightened environmental demands and repeated personal failures require increasingly severe efforts to recoup self-esteem through excessive pleasure-seeking activity. The downward spiral of functioning may lead to a variety of social service interventions including hospitalization, incarceration, or both, often occurring on a cyclical basis. What social scientists have labeled as relapse may simply reflect another episode in the naturally oscillating course of the person's futile struggle to regain control. As shown in Figure 1.7, the "deviant career" is characterized by a progression of stages from childhood to old age.

Figure 1.6 Horizontal Conformity While mainstream conformity involves adherence to the norms of society at large, "nonconformist" subgroups also adhere to the standards of their group by conforming to the patterns of thought and action of the subculture to which they belong.

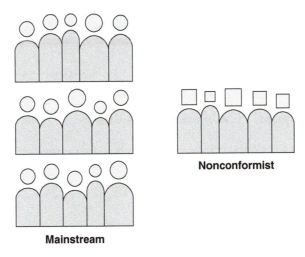

Nonconformist

Mainstream

Figure 1.7 The Deviant Career The process of becoming dependent on a hedonic activity may be conceptualized as a "deviant career." Novices advance through a series of socially influenced stages as they progress to full status in their offbeat professions. The negative effects from being marked or stigmatized (i.e., x, as shown in the figure) as an "addict" or otherwise deviant personality—fatty, junkie, criminal, alcoholic, and so on—may last throughout a person's lifetime.

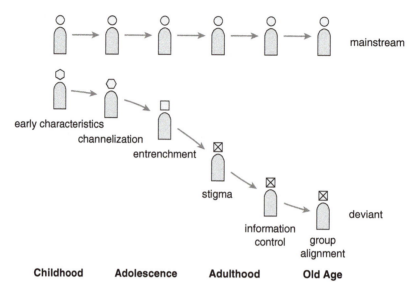

Source: Based on Goffman, E. (1963). Stigma: Notes on the management of spoiled identity. Englewood Cliffs, NJ: Prentice Hall.

Chapter Summary

This chapter sets the groundwork for understanding addiction as a broad spectrum of hedonic dependencies including overindulgence in food, sex, drugs, and risk-taking activity. A multidisciplinary definition of addiction, *self-induced changes in brain chemistry that lead to problem behaviors,* highlights the need to integrate information from psychology, neuroscience, and sociology to arrive at a deeper understanding of the ubiquitous craving for ecstasy. We attempt to manage life's inevitable storm and stress through activation of three primary experiential modes: arousal, satiation, and fantasy. Psychologically, one's chosen drug or pleasure-producing activity is harmonious with his or her characteristic style of coping with stress. The biological underpinnings of compulsive pleasure seeking reside in genetic predispositions that manifest in differential neurologic patterns within the brain. Sociologically, subculture provides the normative structure through which individuals can develop "careers" in a broad array of tension-reducing styles such as alcoholism, promiscuous sexual behavior, and compulsive gambling.

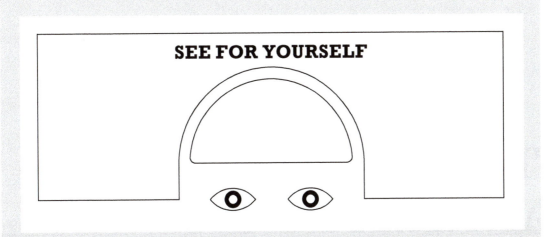

SEE FOR YOURSELF

Nuggets: Kiwi Bird Addiction. 2014. Alexander Katiraie. 4:57

Animated short about the diminishing rewards and eventual suffering in association with objects of addiction. **https://youtu.be/pkZXEf304ss**

Center for Behavioral Health Statistics and Quality. (2015). Behavioral health trends in the United States: Results from the 2014 National Survey on Drug Use and Health (HHS Publication No. SMA 15-4927, NSDUH Series H-50).

Retrieved from **https://www.samhsa.gov/data/sites/default/files/NSDUH-FRR1-2014/NSDUH-FRR1-2014.pdf**

CHAPTER **2**

The Many Faces of Substance Misuse

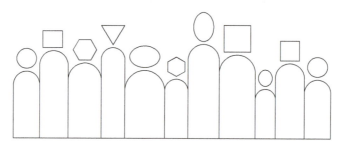

People think I do drugs because I'm self-destructive. But, if anything, I am averting suicide. I don't much like my life, but for some dumb reason, I want to be alive, because sooner or later, I figure it will work out. I should and could be in New York, taking steps toward making it work, but I've been trying that for years, and it's no longer feasible. I can't do it anymore. I give up. I surrender. The only thing keeping me from killing myself is drugs—and the fact that I can still run away.

—Elizabeth Wurtzel, *More, Now, Again,* pg. 23

This chapter explores some of the special populations of individuals who engage in substance misuse as a means of self-medication. A critical facet of addictive behavior is that people use drugs to deal with discomfort and lack of meaning. Given that there is almost universal awareness of the hazards associated with the myriad of licit and illicit drugs, why does such a high percentage of humanity knowingly place themselves in harm's way?

Substance vs. Suffering

Are drug and alcohol abusers dyed-in-the-wool hedonists? Are they covertly suicidal? Most likely, neither is true. Having been involved during the past four decades in the treatment of more than 1,000 patients with substance abuse problems, Khantzian (1997, 2001, 2012), at Harvard Medical School, has developed the "self-medication" model of addiction. According to Khantzian, an individual's vulnerability to substances is founded on what Carl Jung famously referred to as *spiritum contra spiritus*, i.e., spirituality can overcome spirits (alcohol)." This formulation implies that harmful involvement with mind-altering chemicals is related to our drive for comfort, connection, and wholeness. Drugs push aside suffering. Khantzian (2012) identifies four areas of human suffering that evoke dependence on alcohol, drugs or other objects of addiction: (1) emotions; (2) self-esteem; (3) relationships; (4) self-care.

The following quote from German poet Rainer Maria Rilke captures the essence of this perspective:

> *"Perhaps all the dragons in our lives are princesses who are only waiting to see us act, just once, with beauty and courage. Perhaps everything that frightens us is, in its deepest essence, something helpless that wants our love."*
>
> —Letters to a Young Poet (1903)

Is This a Good Idea?

Khantzian's "self-medication" construct is fundamental to a more humane and person-centered understanding of addiction.

Khantzian reminds us that the view of addiction as "pleasure-seeking" is a widely held misperception that contributes to the view that addiction should be managed in the criminal justice sector rather than be viewed as a disease or disorder. Anyone who treats individuals who suffer from addictive disorders recognizes that substance use is associated with shame, pain, chaos, and confusion for the addict. The notion that addictions are a manifestation of suicidal intent is another misguided perception ... Most people with addictions have dreams and aspirations for their future and look forward to the day they have sustained abstinence and stability in their lives. Khantzian reminds us to treat our addicted patients with the compassion, care, and understanding that they need to overcome their addiction (Brady, K., 2012, p. 279).

The propensity for self-medication is particularly evident in those who suffer traumatic life events. Sharp (2003) calls substance use and abuse "almost inevitable" for women and girls coping with abusive experiences. Although the co-occurrence of post-traumatic stress disorder (PTSD) and substance abuse is more common in females, a significant proportion of the male population is seen as abusing substances to cope with suffering resulting from traumatic life events.

Whether the focus of self-repair is a drug or an activity, understanding and compassion require consideration of the internal struggle from which hedonic dependency derives. In this chapter, we explore biological, psychological, and social mechanisms that underlie self-medication through the abuse of tobacco, alcohol, opioids, and inhalants. Obviously, our list could include all of the misguided avenues for comfort and survival, which constitute the entirety of this book, and topics too numerous to discuss or as yet unforeseen. Perhaps the underlying issue is unfulfilled needs for intimacy (personal and spiritual), a topic that is covered at length in Section V, "Craving for Intimacy." Our exploration of self-medication will begin with mental health issues that often co-occur with substance abuse. We will then consider subpopulations, such as women, adolescents, and senior citizens. We also address substance abuse among people in the military, those who are justice-involved, the homeless population, and among people whose professions are linked to a higher incidence of substance abuse and addiction.

Mental Health and Substance Abuse

For the concept of self-medication to apply, the substance user must have some sort of condition from which they seek relief. The modern world has no shortage of such conditions, as will soon become apparent. But before exploring these different conditions, it is worth mentioning the chicken-and-egg problem: *self-medication* implies that the condition (typically psychological in nature) came first, leading the person to adopt the use of substances to help ease the discomfort of the condition. In reality, it may be difficult to pinpoint which condition came first for a given individual. Moreover, it is quite possible that common factors (genetics, traumatic experiences, etc.) may denote a tendency for a person to develop both an addiction and another psychological condition. Once both conditions are present, they may reciprocally influence one another, leading to a worsening of both conditions. Although it is possible that one of the conditions preceded the other, the tendency for them to co-occur may be due to shared genetic vulnerabilities and common environmental risk factors. Sometimes, the same brain regions may be involved in mental illness as in substance use; both types of conditions might be considered as developmental disorders, given that they often emerge in adolescence or even earlier in life (NIDA, 2011).

According to NIDA (2012), as many as 4 out of 10 substance abusers have co-occurring psychological disorders. Individualized treatment approaches therefore strive to treat the entire person with all of their issues, rather than addressing an addiction separately. Thombs (2006) provides guiding principles for integrated treatment for those with both addiction and co-occurring disorders, including treating both the psychological disorder and the addiction with the same team of care providers and using psychotherapeutic medications as appropriate.

Figure 2.1 **Past Year Substance Use Disorder and Mental Illness Among Adults Aged 18 and Older, 2014.** According to these survey data, 39% of U.S. adults with substance use disorders had a co-occurring psychological disorder. (SAMHSA, 2015)

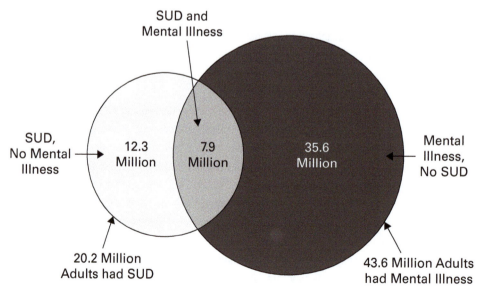

SUD = Substance use disorder.

Source: Substance Abuse and Mental Health Services Administration, Behavioral Health Trends in the United States: Results from the 2014 National Survey on Drug Use and Health, pp. 32. 2015.

There are numerous psychological conditions that co-occur with addiction, including personality disorders (such as antisocial personality disorder and borderline personality disorder), as well as more serious mental illnesses such as mood disorders (major depression and bipolar disorder), anxiety disorders (with post-traumatic stress disorder being the most common of these), and schizophrenia. Conditions such as eating disorders and attention deficit hyperactivity disorder (ADHD) may also co-occur with addictions. That serious mental illnesses sometimes co-occur with addictions is important. Given that altered neurochemistry has been linked to each of these conditions, treatment for either mental disorder or substance abuse must consider the role of brain chemistry in achieving stability and mental health.

Women

Several large-scale studies have shown that the prevalence rates of drug and alcohol use disorders are higher among men than women. A survey of more than 40,000 adults (Conway, Compton, Stinson, & Grant, 2006) showed that men are twice as likely as women to meet lifetime criteria for any drug use disorder—13.8% of men versus 7.1% of women. Twelve-month prevalence rates of alcohol abuse are almost three times as high among men as they are among women—6.9% of men versus 2.6% of women (Grant, Dawson, et al., 2004).

Women often use drugs differently, respond to drugs differently, and often have unique barriers to effective treatment. A frequent obstacle is not being able to obtain responsible child care or being prescribed treatment that has not been adequately tested on women. Women who are pregnant or have young children may not seek treatment or may drop out prematurely, fearing that authorities will take away their children. For treatment to be successful, women require increased levels of family or community support (NIDA, 2015a).

Although there are more men than women in treatment for substance use disorders (Figure 2.2), women are more likely to seek treatment for dependence on sedatives such as anti-anxiety and sleep medications.. Whereas men have historically been more likely to seek treatment for heroin use, the rate of women seeking treatment has increased in recent decades. By 2010, there were nearly equal numbers of male and female heroin users seeking treatment (Cicero et al., 2014).

Figure 2.2 Substance Use Disorder Treatment Admissions (All Drugs)

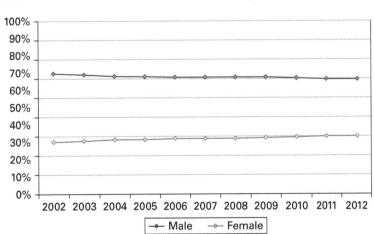

Source: Substance Abuse and Mental Health Services Administration, Treatment Episode Data Set (TEDS) 2002 - 2012. 2014.

Substance use disorders have been shown to progress differently for women than for men. Women often have a shorter history of abusing certain substances such as cocaine, opioids, marijuana, or alcohol (NIDA, 2015a). However, they typically enter substance use disorder treatment with more severe medical, behavioral, psychological, and social problems. This appears to be related to the fact that women show a quicker progression from first using the substance to developing dependence (Greenfield, Back, Lawson, & Brady, 2010).

About 60% of U.S. women have at least one drink per week, and among women who drink, 13% have more than seven drinks per week. Although fewer women than men drink, among the heaviest drinkers, women equal or surpass men in alcohol-related problems. Female alcoholics have death rates that are 50% to 100% higher than male alcoholics, including deaths from suicide, alcohol-related accidents, heart disease and stroke, and cirrhosis of the liver (National Institute on Alcohol Abuse and Alcoholism [NIAAA], 2005).

In terms of cigarette smoking, tobacco use poses a serious risk of death and disease for women. Women have been extensively targeted in tobacco marketing which is dominated by themes of social desirability, independence, and weight control. Smoking messages are conveyed through advertisements featuring slim, attractive, and athletic models. Annually, cigarette smoking kills an estimated 201,770 women in the U.S.

Lung cancer has surpassed breast cancer as the leading cause of cancer deaths among women in the U.S., almost certainly related to the fact that from 1959 to 2010, the risk of developing lung cancer increased tenfold for women. This is possibly due to early detection and improved treatments for breast cancer during the past 50 years. Female smokers are nearly 22 times more likely to die from chronic obstructive pulmonary disease (COPD), which includes emphysema and chronic bronchitis, compared to women who never smoked. Women who smoke often begin during teenage years in order to avoid weight gain and to see themselves as independent and glamorous. That cigarette smoking can fulfill these desires is reflected by tobacco advertising which portrays cigarettes as causing slimness and implies that cigarette smoking suppresses appetite (USDHHS, n.d.).

In regard to self-medication for co-occurring disorders, women are more likely to meet criteria for anxiety, depression, eating disorders, and borderline personality disorder, and men are more likely to meet criteria for antisocial personality disorder (Brady, Grice, Dustan, & Randall, 1993; Sinha & Rounsaville, 2002). For women, the onset of a psychiatric disorder is more likely to antedate the onset of the substance use disorder. This suggests that women are more likely to abuse substances as a form of self-medication (Kessler, 2004). In fact Gilman and Abraham (2001) found that after a 2-year follow-up period, women with a major depressive episode (MDE) were more than 7 times as likely as women without a MDE to have alcohol dependence. However, men with a MDE were not at higher risk for the development of alcohol dependence.

Females also use cigarettes as a form of self-medication. Research has shown that across gender, individuals with depression are more likely to smoke cigarettes and are less successful in smoking cessation attempts. This relationship appears to be particularly strong for women. Oncken, Cooney, Feinn, Lando, and Kranzler (2007) found that women with a history of MDEs were twice as likely to relapse to smoking at a 1-year follow-up as women without an MDE.

Multiple studies show that relationships among trauma, post-traumatic stress disorder, and substance use disorders are highly important for women. Sexual abuse in particular and early life stress in general appear to be more common in girls than in boys (Kendler et al., 2000). Also, women who were exposed to violence in adulthood tend to use substances to self-medicate their feelings of anger, guilt, anxiety, fear, and shame, which places them at increased risk for repeated victimization, thus perpetuating the cycle of victimization and substance use (Kilpatrick, Resnick, Saunder, & Best, 1998). In short, women's substance-using careers are far different from men's.

Explaining Sex Differences in Substance Abuse

Women and men differ in terms of their substance abuse patterns and vulnerabilities due to psychological, sociological, and biological factors. We've already mentioned above that women tend to self-medicate psychological distress; men, on the other hand, may be motivated more by arousal and sensation-seeking. For women, it may actually be the co-occurring psychological condition that leads them to treatment in the first place, compared to men who are more likely to seek treatment for substance abuse rather than mental illness. In terms of sociological factors, women seem to be more influenced by the legal status of substances. Thus, men may be more willing to use illicit stimulants such as cocaine or amphetamines, whereas women are more likely to use substances, like alcohol and legal opioids (Fattore, Melis, Fadda, & Fratta, 2014).

Perhaps the biggest factors contributing to sex differences in substance abuse are biological. Some of these factors relate to how substances are processed in the body. For instance, compared to men, women typically have lower levels of an enzyme involved in metabolizing alcohol; as a result, they do not process alcohol as rapidly as men. Women also tend to have a higher percentage of body fat, which means they have a lower volume of body fluid in which to distribute alcohol. As a result of these biological differences, women experience higher blood alcohol concentrations with similar drinking amounts, even if controlling for body weight (Lieber, 2001). This makes females more vulnerable to organ damage, notably liver disease and brain damage. Thus, lower levels of drinking are recommended for women than for men. According to NIAAA (2005), drinking more than seven drinks per week increases a woman's chances of abusing or becoming dependent upon alcohol; also, women who drink fewer than seven drinks per week but have four or more on any given day are more likely to develop alcohol abuse or alcohol dependence.

Other critical biological factors are hormones. From a growing body of evidence, there are several important lessons to learn. One is that female hormones such as estrogen and progesterone alter women's responsiveness to drugs; generally speaking, females tend to be more sensitive to the rewarding effects of several drugs, including cocaine, opioids, alcohol, and cannabinoids (such as THC, the primary psychoactive ingredient in marijuana; Fattore et al., 2014). Moreover, females' sensitivity to drug effects differ across their menstrual cycles; for instance, they report a greater subjective positive response to cocaine during the follicular phase when estrogen levels are high and progesterone levels are low (Evans & Foltin, 2006). The reasons for the changes in sensitivity to the drug's rewarding effects seem to be due to estrogen directly interacting with the dopamine reward pathway (Bobzean, DeNobrega, & Perrotti, 2014; and Fattore et al., 2014). Finally, female hormones interact with stress hormones, and stressors pose triggers for drug use and relapse (Bobzean et al., 2014).

Overall, data suggest that—although men are more likely to abuse substances—progression of substance abuse occurs more rapidly in women than in men. Once women go into treatment, their substance addictions are generally more severe than their male counterparts. They also report greater cravings and are more prone to relapse.

The case history of Bernice (below) is illustrative of a woman whose life has been fraught with guilt, depression, anger, and hostility in regard to current and past relationships. Her problems with alcohol are inextricably connected with a deep sense of disappointment regarding her feminine role. From a research perspective, women who have difficulty with their intimate relationships tend to drink more than others. Heavy drinking is more common among women who have never been married, are unmarried and living with a partner, or are divorced or separated. Also, a woman whose husband is a heavy drinker is more likely than other women to drink excessively (NIAAA, 2005).

CASE EXAMPLE: Bernice Self-Medicates with Alcohol

Bernice is a middle-aged housewife who lives with her husband and 23-year-old son. Many years of hidden drinking eventually became visible through a series of emergency hospitalizations. The present hospitalization was precipitated by a full night of solitary drinking after she felt rejected and insulted by a female friend. Bernice called her psychiatrist and asked to be treated for alcohol withdrawal symptoms. She said that she was frightened by the illusion of a young, dark-haired girl who appeared at the side of her bed. Bernice denied any connection between her vision of the young girl and her daughter, who died 10 years earlier. She saw her hospitalization as an escape from her husband's and son's anger and the feelings of loneliness she experienced at home.

Bernice was raised in a Midwestern city along with her sister, who is 5 years older. In her early childhood, Bernice felt coerced to conform to what she regarded as unreasonable parental expectations. Her early relationship with her mother is described as "OK," but as she grew older, the situation deteriorated dramatically. Bernice believes that her mother lived vicariously through her children. "She wanted me to do what she wanted to do." Her memory of her father is somewhat more pleasant. She describes him as an "intelligent, ingenious, fun-loving person … whose idealism causes him to be disappointed in people who don't live up to his standards." She also remembers that "he wished more from me than could be expected of a young child."

During early childhood, Bernice had only one female friend, a mentally ill foster child. Bernice was looked after by her sister, who resented this. Until Bernice was 15 years old, they occupied the same bed. Bernice recalls the physical closeness that she and her sister shared with displeasure, and describes resentment at being ordered about. Her teenage years were "ghastly," and most of her adolescent friends were boys. When her sister joined the military, Bernice was left to care for her mother who suffered from epilepsy. She has horrible memories of her mother being stricken with grand mal seizures, sometimes becoming injured or screaming from lack of oxygen. During this time, the relationship between Bernice and her mother was most stressed. Bernice felt the brunt of her mother's frustrations.

Bernice studied psychology in college, where she met her husband. Their courtship lasted about 2 years and was for the most part asexual. She had intercourse with her husband and one other man prior to marriage, and in 1950 became pregnant with her first child—out of wedlock. She and her husband went to great lengths to conceal the pregnancy from her parents until after they were married. The child was born brain-injured with a diagnosis of cerebral palsy.

At the time of the most recent hospitalization, Bernice associated her problem drinking with the agony of caring for her daughter, who required medication in the early hours of the morning. Bernice would remain awake reading and drinking vodka until her daughter was sedated. She continued drinking after her daughter's death and believes that she had been alcoholic about 3 years prior to that.

Bernice became disturbed at the thought of divorce. She recalled her doctor's warning that "he may have to divorce you in order to get you to stop drinking." She believed that her husband and son were angry at her for her drinking and that she could use alcohol to avoid their anger. Her marriage was further complicated by Bernice's concern about not having reached orgasm for the past year. She wondered whether this was alcohol related. She also experienced loneliness during her husband's absences from home when he travelled as a salesman.

At the onset of psychotherapy, Bernice had neither a strong sense of femininity nor a sufficient degree of positive self-regard. Early experiences with females were unusually stressful. Having internalized a rather strict set of parental expectations, Bernice was critical of others and of herself. The guilt engendered by a premarital pregnancy was considerable, but the feelings of worthlessness surrounding the mothering of her severely afflicted daughter were enormous. Bernice felt victimized, at the mercy of circumstances and people—her parents, sister, and daughter in the past, and her friends, husband, and son in the present. Drinking was the vehicle through which she had been able to cope. She became as helpless as the people to whom she dedicated much of her life. Like her mother, she commanded assistance from those who cared about her.

Through psychotherapy, Bernice began to assume personal responsibility for alcoholism, while she gradually revised the deep-seated view of herself as a victim. In-depth explorations of her feelings about femininity and motherhood were beneficial. In the context of a safe and caring relationship with a female therapist, she was able to disclose feelings of guilt, inadequacy, and failure. After one year of individual therapy, her husband participated in counseling with Bernice. The couple came to understand the relationship between Bernice's drinking and her husband's moods and absence. Although Bernice was the "identified patient," her husband also benefited from treatment. They committed to spend more time together in mutually satisfying activities. Bernice and her therapist explored her relationship with her son, specifically how she would cope with separating—if and when he left home. She began to realize that her intellectual skills qualified her for interesting and rewarding employment; she set a long-term goal to transform from a woman feeling inadequate and victimized to one who accepts the challenge of having a comfortable and responsible life without the use of substances.

Of particular benefit to Bernice was her therapist's use of Marlatt's (e.g., Marlatt & Gordon, 1985; Marlatt & Witkiewitz, 2005) relapse prevention strategy (this will be discussed in chapter 18, "Elements of Effective Treatment"). By systematically reviewing and exploring her typical thoughts and actions just before she began drinking, Bernice was able to understand the mental precipitants of previous relapses and to remain sober.

Substance Abuse During Pregnancy

Ideally, for the sake of the fetus, pregnant women would abstain from substance use. But this is not always the case. For one thing, a woman will not be immediately aware that she is pregnant: it usually takes at least a few weeks for pregnancy to become apparent. If the pregnancy is unplanned, then she may have engaged in substance use during that interim. Also, a woman who is addicted may have great difficulty resisting the urge to use substances while pregnant, even if she intends to abstain. Alcohol abuse during pregnancy is linked to Fetal Alcohol Spectrum Disorders, and an expecting mother's abuse of substances such as alcohol and opioids up until the time of birth often leads to Neonatal Abstinence Syndrome (NAS). According to NIDA (2012), infants born with NAS tend to have low birth weight and are more prone to feeding difficulties. They may also experience serious complications such as seizures, respiratory distress, or even death. Medication may be required to medically stabilize the infant.

Adolescents

Each year since the mid-1970s, the University of Michigan has conducted the Monitoring the Future survey, which is funded by NIDA. Large numbers of middle and high school students across the U.S. are surveyed about many different substances. The survey has consistently shown that teenagers most commonly use three substances: alcohol, marijuana, and nicotine/tobacco. The most recent findings show that tobacco and alcohol usage are at historic lows. Although marijuana usage is currently lower now than it was in the late 1970s, the use of this substance is on the rise. This increase in marijuana use is associated with a decreased perceived risk associated with its use (Monitoring the Future, 2015). This may reflect attitude changes that have occurred due to national dialogues about medical and legal marijuana that have occurred for over a decade. As more states within the U.S. consider legalization of marijuana for not only medical but also recreational use, this trend may continue to rise. Also on the rise is the use of e-cigarettes, as discussed in Chapter 6.

Adolescents with Co-Occurring Conditions

Adolescents with psychological issues—like their adult counterparts—are at elevated risk for developing substance abuse and addiction problems. However, the types of psychological conditions that teenagers experience may be somewhat different from those of the adult. Although adolescents with mood and anxiety disorders are at risk for substance abuse issues, other conditions more commonly seen in adolescents can also elevate risk. These include externalizing disorders such as conduct disorder, oppositional-defiant disorder, and ADHD (NIDA, 2012).

CASE EXAMPLE: Death of a Child Star

Mary "Anissa" Jones was the older of two children born to a Midwestern family. Her family moved to California shortly after her brother's birth. In dancing classes at age 4 and cast in a commercial at age 6, Anissa had the adorable good looks and charm of a Shirley Temple. At age 8, she was cast as "Buffy" in the 1960s wholesome, popular sitcom *Family Affair*. She rocketed to star status, but fame was fleeting. When she was nearly 14, the show was cancelled. It was the end of her acting career.

Anissa was fine with stepping out of the limelight. Between filming and making public appearances to promote the show and related merchandise, she was exhausted. Moreover, her personal life was rocky. The year before the show started, her parents had divorced, and it was bitter. Her mother was awarded custody of the children and tried to keep their father out of their lives. Anissa's relationship with her mother did not seem particularly loving. Although Paula was the ever-present stage mom, the relationship between mother and daughter did not seem to be particularly close. Anissa's earnings from the show were actually supporting the family, which may explain why Paula had Anissa audition for other roles after the show was cancelled. Anissa just wanted to be a normal kid who attended public school and had time to spend with her friends. With her acting career behind her, Anissa did exactly that; unfortunately, the peer group with whom she bonded were into the drug scene. Anissa joined in.

Her family life remained turbulent. After another custody hearing, Anissa's father won custody of his two children. Sadly, he died about a year later, and Anissa scattered his ashes over the Pacific Ocean on her 16th birthday. Custody reverted back to her mother, but Anissa tried living with her father's fiancé instead of returning to Paula. Her mother reported her as a runaway, and the police picked her up and took her to a juvenile center where she stayed several months. She ended up returning home to her mother and brother after release.

By the time she turned 18 and had access to her $70,000 trust fund from her sitcom earnings, Anissa was heavily involved in drugs. Her financial windfall allowed her to move out of her mother's house and into a rental apartment; she took her brother with her. The money also financed her drug habit. She was surrounded by friends and entrenched in the drug culture. Her life ended that same year after a night of heavy partying. The coroner's report revealed extremely high levels of barbiturates, along with PCP, cocaine, and Quaaludes in her system.

"Buffy's" story is a tragic one. Other former child stars have fallen into similar traps, although some manage to escape. But a teenager doesn't have to be famous in order to follow in these same footsteps.

Prescription and Over-the-Counter Drug Use: Pharming, Robo-Tripping, and Smart-Doping

There are some substance use patterns that occur more often in teenagers and young adults compared to those who have moved into their late 20s or beyond. One example of this is the habit of taking prescription drugs for purely recreational purposes—sometimes called "pharming", referring to the use of pharmaceutical substances. Lauby & Wheelock (2009, cited in Maguire & Schnurbush, 2016) describe how adolescents may engage in this activity at "pharm parties", where attendees will bring "Pilz" and pass them around. This can be a risky proposition because participants may mix substances or wash them down with alcohol, which can lead to potentially dangerous drug interactions. "Pilz" could include opioid pain medications, anti-anxiety medications, or ADHD medications.

Not everything served at a teen drug party need be prescription: over-the-counter (OTC) cold and cough medications may also be used in such settings. The term "Robotripping" refers to using Robitussin (or similar) cough syrups for the purpose of feeling high. Cough and cold medications (syrups and capsules) with names that include the abbreviations "DM" or "DXM" contain an opioid called dextromethorphan. Ironically, dextromethorphan was introduced as an alternative to codeine because in previous decades, codeine-containing cough syrups were abused; unfortunately, this replacement has abuse liability of its own. Although DXM is technically within the opioid family, it has rather different properties than most other opioids (working primarily by blocking NMDA glutamate receptors). When taken in excessive doses, DXM produces dissociative hallucinogenic experiences in which the person may feel separated from their body and the environment and can induce psychotic-like behavior or delirium. Taken in large quantities—and there are teens who will chug a bottle of syrup in a sitting—this substance can be dangerous because there's more in the syrup than just the DXM. Some of these medications are intended to treat additional cold symptoms besides just the cough, so there are often decongestants and analgesics in them. Decongestants can raise heart rate and blood pressure; if acetaminophen is included as a pain-reliever, excessive intake of the syrup can harm the liver (even in a single large dose). Unfortunately, adolescents may not perceive prescription and OTC drugs as risky because they are legal. Their easy accessibility makes them prime choices for earlier substance use experiences. King and Vidourek (2013, cited in Stanciu, Penders, & Rouse, 2016) reported similar percentages of male (7.7%) and female (6.3%) teenagers engaging in Robotripping, although females were more likely to be self-medicating as a stress-coping mechanism, whereas males were more likely to be using for purely social or recreational purposes. King and Vidourek's survey data also indicated that use of cold and cough medications was highest among Hispanic youth.

Another trend among teenagers and young adults is the non-medical usage of stimulant medications such as Ritalin and Adderall (prescribed for ADHD) or Modafinil (prescribed for sleep disorders) in an effort to try to enhance their cognitive function. This practice, sometimes called "smart doping" or "neuroenhancement," is most common in high school and college students. A review by Battleday & Brem (2015) assessed 24 studies looking at the effects of Modafinil. The studies varied markedly in their assessments, and the results were mixed; Modafil improved performance on some tasks, impaired performance on others, and sometimes had no effect compared to placebo. These mixed effects were sometimes obtained in the same study. It is possible that the effects of such a stimulant substance would differ in individuals who do not have a neurological reason for needing them, such that individuals with ADHD or sleep disorders might benefit whereas healthy, non-sleep-deprived individuals might not.

Arria (2017) reports that numerous studies investigating nonmedical use of prescription stimulants among college students indicate that these students have lower grade point averages than their non-smart doping counterparts. Moreover, nonmedical use of stimulants is correlated with problems with alcohol and cannabis use and more frequent class absences (Arria et al., 2013). Thus, there's not good evidence to support that these students are truly "getting ahead" of their peers.

Inhalants: How Stupid Can You Get?

Inhalants, which are volatile substances that produce breathable vapors, include paint thinners and removers, spray paints, deodorant, vegetable oil, gasoline, glues, and other aerosols. In addition, certain medical anesthetics found in commercial and household uses are abused. These include chloroform, ether, nitrous oxide (laughing gas), and aliphatic nitrites (NIDA, 2005a). Products that qualify as inhalants may include multiple components which are capable of producing a drug state if "huffed". Many of these components can have toxic effects on the brain and other organs if used repeatedly. Monitoring the Future data consistently shows that those who are most likely to use these substances are young teens. Because these substances are so easy to access, it should not be surprising that they may serve as first drug experiences for some youth.

Nitrites, which include cyclohexyl, amyl, and butyl nitrite, are often used to enhance sexual performance. Nitrites act much like Viagra by dilating blood vessels and relaxing muscles. Cyclohexyl nitrite is found in room deodorizers, while amyl nitrite is sometimes prescribed by doctors for heart pain. Both amyl and butyl nitrites are packaged in small bottles, and are referred to as "poppers." These inhalants are lesser known, compared to volatile solvents.

Inhalants and the Brain: One of the most dangerous as well as widely used inhalants is the organic aromatic compound toluene (found in gasoline, paint thinner, and correction fluid). It is used commercially to make TNT (trinitrotoluene), an explosive used in military bombs. Although quite different from TNT, toluene does a number on the brain not unlike that of TNT on a city. But first, let's see if we can explain why anyone would use inhalants such as toluene (pronounced "toll you wean," if you find your tongue getting twisted). Toluene and other inhalants (except nitrites) activate the brain's dopamine system. In fact the effects of toluene on the firing rate of dopamine neurons in the reward pathway are known to be about 100 times more potent than alcohol (Nimitvilai, et al., 2016). That should not come as any surprise at this point. The rapid high produced by inhalants resembles that of alcohol intoxication. This high is followed by drowsiness, lightheadedness, apathy, impaired functioning and judgment, disinhibition, and belligerence. The other short-term effects of inhalant abuse are too numerous to mention here, but include dizziness, slurred speech, increased lethargy, muscle weakness, and stupor. While long-term effects include weight loss, irritability, decreased coordination, depression, and withdrawal, the real bomb—figuratively speaking—is the damage to the brain. Much of it is damage to the myelin sheath, which insulates the neurons and significantly speeds neurotransmission. This insulating sheath is soluble in many organic solvents including toluene, which literally dissolves this protective layer.

Toluene's effects on the brain are shown in Figure 2.3. The brain actually shrinks in size with chronic toluene abuse. The neurons are destroyed in a manner similar to that of buildings in a city being destroyed by TNT. Since toluene affects nearly all areas of the brain, it is like a "dumb bomb," indiscriminately destroying everything it hits. This is really bad news, since the two areas we need to preserve are the hippocampus, for memory, and the frontal cortex, for cognition. Rosenberg, Grigsby, Dreisbach, Busenbark, and Grigsby (2002) have shown that inhalant abusers suffer more brain abnormalities and cognitive deficits than cocaine users. It is also believed that much of this damage by inhalants is irreversible.

Not all of the potential damage from long-term inhalant abuse is restricted to the central nervous system. Depending on the substance, damage can be produced to peripheral nerves that serve the body or in organs such as the liver or kidneys. The actual damage done by an inhalant depends on what is in the substance being sniffed. For instance, some gasoline contains lead, which can be harmful to organs such as the liver and kidneys, and benzene is a known carcinogen linked to leukemia. Regardless of the specifics of the inhaled substance, the potential for damage to the nervous system is there.

The danger of inhalant abuse does not require repeated use: inhalants carry an acute risk of death by anoxia. In the process of "sniffing" or "huffing," abusers can starve their brain and body of oxygen, essentially producing a lethal overdose (known as *Sudden Sniffing Death Syndrome*). Heart failure and death can occur within minutes after a prolonged "sniffing." Even if death does not occur, brain cells can die from oxygen starvation (hypoxia). In other words, a person doesn't have to abuse inhalants for long periods of time to start shrinking their brain (although they will do more damage the more they engage in this behavior).

Figure 2.3 Toluene's Effect on the Brain The brain shrinks in size. Brain images show marked shrinkage of brain tissue in a toluene abuser (B) compared to a non-abusing individual (A). Note the smaller size and the larger (empty) dark space within the toluene abuser's brain.

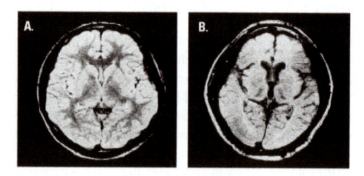

Compared with the brain of an individual with no history of inhalant abuse (A), that of a chronic toluene abuser (B) is smaller and fills less of the space inside the skull (the white outer circle in each image). Courtesy of Neil Rosenberg, M.D., NIDA Research Report (NIH 05-3818).

The Teenage Brain

It has been said that the brain of an adolescent is like a car with a full tank of gas, a sensitive accelerator, and no brakes (Steinberg, 2014). This analogy captures how the teenage brain is acutely sensitive to reward—related to developmental changes in dopamine—but lacks the proper impulse control from the frontal lobes to stop from engaging in reckless behavior. The majority of people who develop substance abuse issues start as teenagers, and this leads to numerous concerns. One concern is that use of substances during adolescence may result in substance abuse or addiction that would be carried through to adulthood. During the teenage years, engaging in drug use can alter one's life course, potentially for the long term: will the person finish high school, find employment, continue their education? Adolescent drug users may be unwittingly setting themselves up for later hardships.

Another concern is that early drug use could potentially alter the remaining maturation of the brain, inducing differential wiring of neural circuits which could lead to alterations in cognition, emotions, and behavior. There is a growing body of data from animal studies supporting the notion that alcohol and drug exposure during adolescence has a different effect on the brain compared to the same amount of exposure during adulthood. Spear (2016) reviews the effects of alcohol, nicotine, THC, cocaine, and other stimulants on adolescent brains in rodent models. Although there are some differences across substances, there tend to be common findings: adolescent substance exposure affects development of the frontal cortex, hippocampus, amygdala, and nucleus accumbens (although Spear notes that the effects on the brain do not seem to be exhaustively investigated—these are common targets where researchers would expect to find changes). Cognitive deficits (memory impairments, increased impulsivity) and anxiety-like responses may also be evident, and these behavioral changes can persist into adulthood. In some circumstances, animals exposed during adolescence are more likely to self-administer substances in adulthood.

In terms of treatment, NIDA (2012b) notes that adolescents have "unique needs stemming from their immature neurocognitive and psychosocial stage of development." This harkens back, in part, to the previously used analogy of the car with the full tank of gas, sensitive accelerator, and no brakes. At this particular stage of development, teens are very sensitive to peer and family influences, so enabling these influences to be a positive factor in an adolescent's substance abuse treatment can be helpful for the teen to attain sobriety.

Substance Abuse and Criminal Conduct

It is common knowledge that substance abuse and criminal conduct are "joined at the hip." Three primary drug related offenses are: (1) drug possession and sales; (2) offenses related to the compulsion to obtain and abuse drugs, e.g., stealing money; (3) offenses related to the drug abuse lifestyle, e.g., through association with other offenders and access to illegal markets such as prostitution or stolen property. Substance abusers are more likely to commit crimes of all sorts, including violent crimes, and it is common for individuals who commit crimes to have used alcohol or other drugs before, during, or after the offense. Statistics The total correctional population in 2008 was estimated to be 6,937,600, with 4,794,000 individuals on probation or under parole supervision. Drug law violations accounted for the most common type of criminal offense (Glaze & Herberman, 2013). In a survey of state and federal prisoners, BJS estimated that about half of the prisoners met Diagnostic and Statistical Manual for Mental Disorders (DSM) criteria for drug abuse or dependence, and yet fewer than 20% who needed treatment received it (Chandler et al. 2009; Mumola & Karberg, 2006). The juvenile justice system is also awash with substance abuse disorders. It is estimated that as many as 2/3 of justice-involved juveniles have a SUD and females who enter the juvenile justice system have even higher SUD rates. (McClelland et al., 2004).

Is This a Good Idea?

Untreated substance abusing offenders are more likely than treated offenders to relapse to drug abuse and return to criminal behavior. This can lead to re-arrest and re-incarceration, jeopardizing public health and public safety and taxing criminal justice system resources. Treatment is the most effective course for interrupting the drug abuse/criminal justice cycle for offenders with drug abuse problems. Drug abuse treatment can be incorporated into criminal justice settings in a variety of ways. Examples include treatment in prison followed by community-based treatment after release; drug courts that blend judicial monitoring and sanctions with treatment by imposing treatment as a condition of probation; and treatment under parole or probation supervision. Drug abuse treatment can benefit from the cross-agency coordination and collaboration of criminal justice professionals, substance abuse treatment providers, and other social service agencies. By working together, the criminal justice and treatment systems can optimize resources to benefit the health, safety, and well-being of the individuals and communities they serve.

Principles of Drug Abuse Treatment for Criminal Justice Populations–A Research-Based Guide (NIDA, 2014, p.1)

Senior Citizens

To some degree, senior citizens may be the invisible addiction sufferers in our culture. Typically we associate excessive substance use with teenagers and young adults. However, the population of people over the age of 65 has been growing as people live longer. As this subset of our society increases in number, so does the number among their ranks who suffer from addiction. It is sometimes easy for people in this age group to keep an addiction hidden: they may have already been widowed, children may be no longer living in their homes or even nearby, they are less likely to be working outside of the home, and they generally interact with fewer people than those in younger age groups. According to the National Council on Alcoholism and Drug Dependence (2015), 2.5 million adults aged 65 and older have problems relating to alcohol or other drugs. Widowers over 75 years of age are reported to have the highest rate of alcoholism in the U.S. Although alcohol is a commonly used substance among senior citizens, these folks also may have chronic health issues that have resulted in their being prescribed pain medications. Others may have prescriptions for anti-anxiety medications such as benzodiazepines. Thus, due to a combination of factors, senior citizens may have a number of living circumstances that contribute to addiction. Moreover, they may evade detection because behavioral changes like cognitive impairments, emotional changes, or balance and movement issues might be assumed to indicate age-related brain changes or neurodegeneration rather than a substance-related problem.

Not all seniors with addiction issues develop their problems during their later years. NIDA (2012b) reports that the "baby boomer" generation engaged in more drug use than prior generations, so perhaps it is not surprising that addiction issues within this population has risen. There are additional health concerns related to people who have been abusing substances for decades. For instance, due to harm reduction approaches such as needle exchange programs, IV drug addicts live longer than they might be expected. They are vulnerable to many of the same age-related health issues as other seniors, although they tend to develop these conditions at a younger age, say in their 40s rather than in their 60s or 70s (Ford, 2011). Among other things, long-time addicts may be prone to early-onset dementia. This may pose special concerns regarding available services for this population.

CASE EXAMPLE: Geriatric Substance Abuse

John is an older man in his late sixties and is a bit disheveled in appearance. He lost his wife of 25 years about five years ago. He is accompanied in the hospital emergency room by his landlady who reports that she found him earlier this evening trying to enter his apartment door. He was sweaty, his eyes where dilated, and his hands were trembling so badly that he could not get the key in the door. He kept calling her by another name and saying he was trying to get into his office to do some work. She knows he retired years ago, has lived in her apartments for several years, and knows her real name. His blood/alcohol level is low and his speech is not slurred. He can correctly identify himself, but also appears confused. He is unable to tell you the month or season. His nose and cheeks are red with tiny spider veins and his stomach distended and when he extends his hands out in front of him they are very tremulous. His demeanor is polite and apologetic to you and the staff. He tells you he has never had a problem with alcohol. He then admits to an occasional drink every now and then. He claims to have had a few drinks earlier today, but can't say exactly when. However, he is willing to come into the hospital for a brief stay if the doctors thought it was necessary.

Adapted from "Seven Case Studies of People with Substance Abuse Problems" originally published by The Josiah Macy Foundation in New York City. Retrieved, October 24, 2016 from http://www.cnsproductions.com/pdf/casestudies.pdf

Lots in Life

There are many populations and subcultures that are particularly vulnerable to addictive disorders, for example those disenfranchised by reason of age, race, ethnicity, physical or emotional handicap, poverty, etc. Among the most vulnerable populations are children of parents with active criminal conduct and/or SUDs. Additionally, some members of certain high stress professions, such as military service or emergency health workers, have distinct problems with substance abuse and other addictions. As shown above, individuals who commit crimes, whose lives are often interwoven with some form of impoverishment, are particularly vulnerable to SUDs. Because of the ready availably of pharmaceutical products and a false sense of empowerment over their ability of manage them, a subpopulation of impaired health professionals find their way into the throws of addiction. Below are two examples of groups of individuals whose lots in life have set the stage for battles with substance abuse and associated lifestyles: members of the armed forces and "street wise" addicts who "prescribe" illegal medications for a host of physical and emotional problems.

Patients in Uniform: Substance Abuse in the Military

Substance use disorders have long been a problem in the U.S. Armed Forces. The use of alcohol, including binge drinking, has been an accepted custom, serving as a means of building camaraderie and to reduce tension. Magnifying the problem is that alcohol is often sold inexpensively on military bases (Institute of Medicine, 2013). Griffin (2012) described how heavy drinking increases dramatically after active-duty soldiers return from deployment; for some, the return home is an opportunity to cut loose, for others it breaks up the tedium of a more routine life, and for still others, it is a form of self-medication for dealing with trauma experienced in war zones. Other substances can be abused as well. For instance, Bray, Olmstead, and Williams (2012, cited in *Substance Use Disorders in the United States Armed Forces*, 2013) report that misuse of prescription opioid drugs is a bigger problem in the military than among the civilian population.

Patients in the Street

A complicating feature of the drug scene is that addicts often appear to have more practical information about the effects of mind-altering drugs than the physicians who prescribe them. An old adage is, "The doctor who treats himself has a fool for a patient." Deep in the gutter of the treatment community, a group of patients prescribe and administer their own medications. Through rumor and experimentation, they discover illegal, mood-affecting drugs, which appear to magically induce enormous pleasure and also subdue undesired states. Through trial and error and various social influences, the novice learns to procure a host of substances that are known among street users to influence or improve painful emotions. Illicit drugs serve as prosthetic devices that temporarily reduce discomfort from feelings such as anxiety, rage, hurt, shame, and loneliness. Addicts select their drugs of choice based on an interaction among street mythology, the chemical action of the drug, and the nature of their particular cognitive and emotional state.

Based on observations and interviews with hundreds of addicts, Khantzian (1997, 2001, 2012) found that opioid users are particularly compelled by the anti-aggression and anti-rage action of narcotic drugs. Addicts' life histories reveal prolonged periods of uncontrolled rage and anger, replete with horrifying accounts of violent episodes that predate their drug experiences. The addicts themselves were often victims of unusual levels of aggression in their family, their community, or both. During treatment, opioid-dependent patients repeatedly explained their compulsion for narcotics on the basis of how it made them feel in relation to their anger. They frequently use such terms as mellow, soothed, normal, calm, and relaxed. Khantzian also found that patients who often appear hyper-aggressive, restless, or even assaultive in group therapy become more relaxed as they adjust to a therapeutic dose of methadone. Many patients who started their drug abuse with another type of drug switch to heroin as their drug of choice when they repeatedly experience uncontrolled fits of violence or rage under the influence of alcohol, sedatives, amphetamines, or cocaine.

In his 14-year history of experimentation, abuse, addiction, and drug-related crime, Philip became extremely knowledgeable about the commodities and characters in the drug world. In the following case study, we shall "inject" Philip's understanding of his progression from heroin use to addiction with an explanation of the biochemical substratum of his progressively disturbed functioning. His case illustrates how an individual with a substance a use disorder learned to regulate his physiology through a well-planned self-medication schedule. His skill reflects a high level of street knowledge of how to cope with the medical issues of dependence, tolerance, and withdrawal.

CASE EXAMPLE: Self-Medication and Recovery

Philip switched his drug of choice from cocaine to heroin after discovering heroin's soothing and anti-aggressive effects. When interviewed, he was 29 years old and had been in drug-free treatment for nearly 14 months. He had begun smoking pot and using amphetamines at 13 years of age and maintained a $100 to $200 per day heroin habit for 5 years, prior to his conviction and mandatory treatment. He supported his addiction primarily through the sale of marijuana and cocaine. In lieu of prison, Philip opted for placement at a residential drug treatment center after having been arrested for possession and attempted sale of 10 grams of cocaine.

Philip is the only male in a family of eight children. He felt "robbed" at the age of 9 when his father suddenly died of a heart attack while serving in the military. During adolescence, in the mid-1960s, he lived in a large metropolitan area where illicit drugs were readily available. He started experimenting with marijuana and amphetamines at the age of 13. At 15, he began to snort cocaine and would sell grams of coke to his friends and school contacts. He first sniffed heroin at 17, recalling that he was tricked by a friend who told him it was cocaine. He was initially angry because he had heard about the perils of heroin on the street. He ignored the warnings, however, as he enjoyed the soothing sensations brought on by the drug. He continued to use heroin, blocking from his mind any thoughts of becoming "strung out."

Through sniffing heroin, Philip brought about a temporary change in his neurotransmission, which was precisely the effect that he enjoyed. However, in a few hours the drug sensations wore off, and his level of neurotransmission returned to normal. Subjectively, he experienced a return to his customary state of loneliness and tense depression. He continued to episodically sniff heroin for the next 6 months when the drug was available and when inner distress and anxiety seemed unbearable. Although filling opioid receptor sites in the brain by the ingestion of heroin caused a corresponding decrease in neurotransmission, the brain would automatically initiate a self-regulatory process to reinstate normal neuronal activity.

When he first began to use heroin, Philip could be satisfied with an amount about the size of one match head. It would "nod him out" for about 6 hours. Between irregularly timed doses, which he ingested two to three times weekly, his functioning seemed unimpaired. In only a few hours, the drug sensations seemed to wear off and Philip could conduct his business as usual. He was able to eat and sleep regularly. Yet the immediate soothing effects that he derived from ingesting heroin were slowly being challenged by longer-lasting changes in brain chemistry. Although he continued to use heroin at the initial match-head level, the intensity of his feeling was being eroded constantly by these insidious chemical changes that attempted to return his neurotransmission to a "normal" level.

After several weeks, Philip noticed that he needed an increased amount of heroin to feel high. His required dose began to swell to two, three, four, and still more match heads. Even at higher doses, however, he began to recognize that he wasn't getting the same feeling of pleasure. He recalled that after about 6 months of frequent and escalating use, he woke up one morning "feeling shitty." Philip had become physically dependent on heroin and required it regularly just to feel normal. He was getting strung out.

About 2 months later, he allowed a crony to "geez" him with a hypodermic syringe. "Hitting up" was like nothing he had ever experienced before. It was "heaven...like everything in the world had just been taken care of." He quickly learned to self-administer the drug and began to use it on a daily basis. Without heroin, he would anticipate becoming sick. His thoughts became obsessed with when and how he was going to "do some stuff." He would attribute all unpleasant bodily sensations, even hunger, to the absence of heroin in his system. His body weight decreased from 150 to 118 pounds. When heroin wasn't readily available, Philip would use prescription narcotics. He knew a physician who, in exchange for cocaine, would allow him to browse through the PDR (*Physician's Desk Reference*) and pick out any drug he wanted. He would select Dilaudid to avoid being sick, but always preferred heroin, which didn't seem to have negative side effects like headaches or ringing in his ears. At this point in his addictive "career," his entire life began to revolve around not being sick. His dependence was so great that he could get "normal," but he couldn't get high. Philip was deeply entrenched in the maintenance phase of his habit. The chemical levels in his brain had changed so drastically that even large doses could not re-create the feelings of pleasure and calm, hallmarks of his initial use.

After 2 to 3 years of regular use, Philip recalls having to wake up every 3 to 5 hours to inject himself with heroin. When he was without the drug for more than 8 hours, his withdrawal symptoms would become very severe. He remembers his skin becoming blotchy; breaking out in cold sweats; shaking all over; getting cramps in his legs, back, and stomach; and sometimes vomiting. In the absence of the drug, his neurotransmission did not return to normal; rather, it became accelerated because of his chronic drug abuse. Somehow he would manage to get some heroin from a spoon into a syringe, then into a vein. Within about 30 seconds, he felt as if heroin were "filling all the gaps" in his body. Sometimes he would "jack off" with the needle by pulling up blood into the syringe and then injecting it back into his vein. For the most part, Philip found this practice repulsive and he did it infrequently. He remembered a female addict, however, who would sit, sometimes for 20 minutes, "pulling it up in the syringe. . . in and out."

During the lengthy maintenance period, Philip was nearly always obsessed with the functioning of his body. He recalls being regularly constipated from the effect of heroin on his digestive system. When several days passed without a bowel movement, Philip would interpret being constipated as "something wrong." His remedy was based on practical experience with a range of pharmacological effects. He would sit on the toilet, get some cocaine, and then "hit it up." By repeating this procedure at least twice per week, Philip was able to "clean himself out." After 5 years of living in this hellish state, Philip was ordered by the court to choose between jail and treatment for his drug problem at a therapeutic community (TC).

In this setting, drug addiction is traditionally viewed as a symptom of weakness in character, usually associated with alienating childhood circumstances. The addict chronically avoids dealing with conflict by withdrawing into a protective shell. This self-destructive pattern is interpreted as a response to feelings of incompetence and inadequacy. While using drugs to escape from stress, the addict denies personal problems and hides behind a criminal mask of toughness and superiority. Under the guise of sincere friendship and urgent need, addicts manipulate others to assist them in gratifying their infantile wishes.

The therapeutic community strives to provide a positive family atmosphere in which self-realization can occur. In a setting where drug inaccessibility is strictly enforced, addicts are given the opportunity to clarify their values and goals in life. They are expected to move toward the development of a greater sense of moral responsibility. These opportunities are possible largely because the addict has been removed from the environmental stimuli—drug access, recurrent stress, and drug-using friends—that have surrounded and fostered his compulsive drug-using behavior. Correspondingly, TC graduates are expected to eliminate drug use, learn adaptive responses to stress, and readjust to the outside world as comfortable and responsible citizens.

The new resident's involvement in the TC program is strongly influenced by his or her experience during the initial or "prospect" phase of treatment. Philip was tempted to "jump" several times, but each time a senior resident talked to him, and he decided to stay. He remembers feeling completely disoriented during the beginning of treatment when he was required to wear pajamas, work at menial chores, and sit in groups with fellow residents who "confronted each other whenever someone would hide out in their druggie attitude."

A hierarchical arrangement of leadership roles within the resident group is an integral part of the TC treatment approach. Residents take on increasing responsibility for operating the facility as they earn status as reliable and trustworthy members of the community. Conversely, verbal reprimands, role demotions, and increased work assignments are directed toward shaping and directing clients who have been observed to "slip."

As time went on, Philip began to realize the importance of being in treatment. In the beginning, he remembers feeling that it didn't matter how he acted; he would get accused, insulted, and questioned anyway. He felt "damned if you do, damned if you don't." He later understood that the purpose of frequent personal confrontations was to promote healthy responses to stress. "No matter what situation you were in, no matter what you tried to work out, you could always do it without stickin' a fucking needle in your arm." He remembers always being scrutinized and challenged by other members of the group about minute details of his demeanor. After several months of being constantly and thoroughly checked for his motives and attitudes, he noticed that he began checking himself. "All of a sudden you caught yourself like, I'm doing something wrong. I shouldn't be doing this.... [Y]ou started to feel guilt. For once you started feeling happy. You noticed the birds singing and the sun's shining, and they're gonna let us out in the park to throw the football around."

When positive experiences such as these occur, the result is often enhanced self-esteem and a corresponding reduction in alienated-alienating behaviors. Philip now regards having "stuck out" the therapeutic community as the best decision of his life. He views the TC as the only place where a hard-core drug abuser can have a chance at getting his life together. He feels that in the course of treatment, he came across many people who helped him to "clean up," but the person he thanks most is himself. After 14 months of complete abstinence, Philip reported that he reached a point where he made the decision to stay clean permanently. He realized that there was no way that he could continue doing heroin and be a normal human being, "and what I want to be is a normal human being, so I decided never to do it again."

Philip was hired as a counselor in the therapeutic community. He has been able to use his drug abuse and treatment experiences to guide others through the recovery process. At the time of this writing, he has been entirely drug-free for 16 years.

Chapter Summary

Khantzian's (1997, 2001, 2012) self-medication model of addictive behavior views the use of mind-altering chemicals as misguided attempts to cope with feelings of discomfort, lack of meaning, and a fragmented sense of self. An underlying theme in many drug-involved lives is unfulfilled longings for intimacy. The propensity to use drugs as means to create an illusion of closeness and capacity to escape from psychological pain is particularly evident in those who suffer from traumatic life events. In fact, substance abuse may be "almost inevitable" for women and girls whose lives have been shaken by abusive life experiences. A considerable proportion of males are also seen as abusing drugs to cope with traumatic life events. Khantzian's self-medication model is at the core of a more humane understanding of addiction.

The chapter begins with exploration of mental health issues that often co-occur with substance abuse. As many as 4 out of 10 people with substance use disorders have co-occurring psychological disorders. Factors unique to women, teenagers, and justice-involved clients are examined. Finally, the chapter discusses those whose lots in life, e.g., military duty, old age, and immersion in drug culture set the stage for substance abuse and addiction. Case histories are presented for: a woman hospitalized for alcohol dependence; a child sitcom star who died at the age of 18 after overdosing on multiple drugs; a man in his late 60s who lost his wife; and a heroin addict who treated the indirect effects of opioids with cocaine.

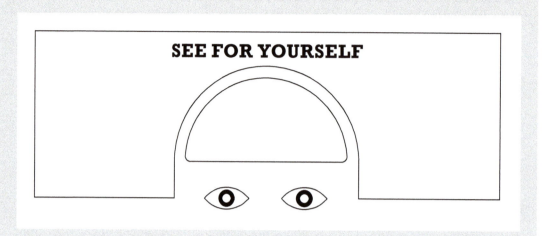

SEE FOR YOURSELF

"Alcohol as Escape from Perfectionism." 2013. Ann Dowsett Johnston. The Atlantic. Feature Length Article.

This piece is adapted from the author's book, *Drink: The Intimate Relationship Between Women and Alcohol.* The article explores the author's personal experience with alcohol dependence as a "successful" woman with high socioeconomic status. **https://www.theatlantic.com/health/archive/2013/10/alcohol-as-escape-from-perfectionism/280482/**

"Male Birds Poison Themselves to Appear Sexier—a First." 2014. Jason Bittel, for *National Geographic.* Brief Article.

This brief article presents an example of "self-medicating" in the animal world. **http://news.nationalgeographic.com/news/2014/10/141024-great-bustard-birds-mating-sex-animals-science/**

"Pot of Gold." 2014. Clip from *National Geographic*'s *Drugs, Inc.* Episode "PCP in DC." 2:55

Charisma, a PCP user, describes why she uses this drug to self-medicate and how it affects her. She is HIV positive and diagnosed with Bipolar Disorder. Charisma describes PCP as her "best friend," while acknowledging that the drug affects others very differently. **https://video.nationalgeographic.com/tv/drugs-inc/pot-of-gold**

3

Pleasure and the Brain

[W]hen each minute brain component has been located, its function identified and its interactions with each other component made clear—the resulting description will contain all there is to know about human nature and experience.

—R. Carter, 1998, p. 8

B efore discussing the powerful effects of drugs or activities on the mind, we will take some time to explain the basic design of the brain, which has been described as more complex than the entire known universe. First, it should be clear that the language of the brain is chemistry. Indeed, the brain is a giant pharmaceutical factory constantly manufacturing chemicals that result in moods such as fear, anger, shame, despair, joy, depression, mania, and any other mood to which the human species is subjected. However, in this chapter we are interested in how drugs manufactured outside the brain (possibly in your neighbor's RV) affect mood and behavior. To comprehend how these external chemicals affect the internal chemistry of the brain, we need to understand how the brain itself works. So prepare yourself for Neurochemistry 101.

Neurochemistry 101

Although the metaphor is not perfect, it is helpful to consider the brain as an electrochemical computer as well as a chemical factory (Milkman & Sunderwirth, 1993). Its 100 billion or so nerve cells, which constitute the brain's hardware, are able to store more information than all the libraries in the world combined. Each of these nerve cells (neurons) is in turn composed of three basic elements (Figure 3.1). The nucleus of the cell body (soma) constitutes a miniature brain within a larger brain. It is the soma that "decides" to transmit a message (an electrical impulse) from one nerve cell to the next, that is, to "fire." Or the soma may decide to ignore a message, that is, to "not fire." This is the only decision the soma needs to make, but it needs to make that decision very quickly. For example, you don't want to wait 5 minutes to remove the hand you unknowingly placed on a hot stove while the soma takes its time deciding to transmit the message to the next neuron and ultimately on to the brain. Like a computer, the soma is a "fast idiot." It has to make one of only two possible decisions, that is, to fire or not to fire. Connected to the soma is a long fiber, the *axon,* through which the message must travel on its way to the next neuron. The message is transferred from one of the many branches at the end of the axon of the sending neuron to one of a number of branches on the receiving cell. These branches on the receiving cell are called *dendrites;* each neuron may have up to 10,000 dendrites. If we consider the possibilities of interaction among the 100 billion neurons found in the human brain with 10,000 dendrites per neuron, we have the possibility of quadrillions of connections—different ways to send messages to different "receivers," with different results. Clearly, as we have said, the brain is the most complex entity in this universe.

Figure 3.1 The Neuron Neurons are made up of a cell body, an axon that transmits electrical impulses called action potentials, dendrites with receptors that respond to chemical signals (neurotransmitters, left blowup), and axon terminals that store neurotransmitter molecules in vesicles (membrane-enclosed sacs, right blowup).

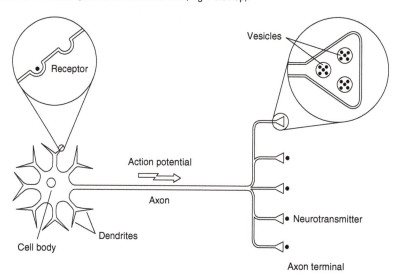

Incredibly, this process of communication between neuron and neuron is carried out without any direct physical contact between the two cells—as if this were all taking place in a city of trillions of people, all talking to each other on cellular telephones! Neurons are separated by a gap known as the synapse or synaptic junction. The message is carried from one neuron to the next by molecules known as neurotransmitters, which in our computer analogy may be considered as the software of the brain. Chemical changes that occur in these neuronal spaces determine how we respond to each "message." This process of communication between neurons, known as neurotransmission, is largely responsible for the brain functions that determine what we are as individuals including our personalities, intellect, and character. It is precisely because the neurons are separated by a synapse—in other words, they are not "hardwired"—that the brain ends up with nearly limitless options for neurotransmission, which results in the limitless complexity of the human species, with its limitless ability to "screw up."

We are our neurotransmission. What we are as human beings is reflected in the way our neurons communicate and form new pathways as well as utilize old ones. Crick (1995) summarizes the relationship between self and neurotransmission as follows:

> The astonishing hypothesis is that you, your joys, and your sorrows, your memories and ambitions, your sense of personal identity and free will, are in fact no more than the behavior of a vast assembly of nerve cells and their associated molecules. As Lewis Carroll's Alice might have phrased it, "You're nothing but a pack of neurons." (p. 3)

In order for us to understand the effect of drugs on the brain, we need to know how the brain works, and especially the role of neurotransmitters. Let us consider a very important neurotransmitter, norepinephrine (NE), which is found in a part of the brain known as the locus coeruleus (Figure 3.2). One of NE's primary functions is to produce arousal and excitability, including the fight-or-flight phenomenon associated with the release of adrenaline. The ability of NE to stimulate the fight or flight response is an evolutionary survival mechanism. The rise in NE levels in times of danger or stress results in an increase in adrenaline, which raises blood pressure and increases heart rate. This forces more oxygen-carrying blood into the muscles, which in turn enabled our prehistoric ancestors to fight if the attacker was a small bear or "run like hell" if it was a saber-toothed tiger. Sapolsky (1994), in his book *Why Zebras Don't Get Ulcers*, explains that zebras, unlike humans, don't activate their stress response, that is, release NE, until a lion (or your boss) actually appears. The rest of the time, they are munching grass on the savanna unconcerned that a lion, or an angry boss, may attack. Many of the illnesses present in modern society are due to the release of stress hormones and NE with the accompanying increase in blood pressure and blood glucose (among other effects), which over time may result in cardiovascular disease and diabetes. But let's leave these side issues and get back to brain chemistry.

Figure 3.2 Cross Section of The Human Brain The frontal cortex, major components of the limbic system, and locus coeruleus are shown.

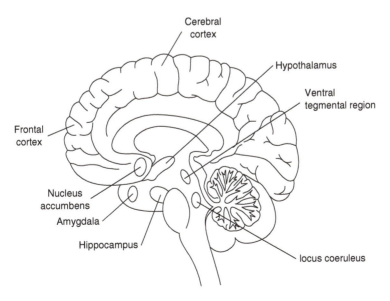

To understand how NE, as well as other neurotransmitters, is involved in communication between neurons, let us continue in Neurochemistry 101.

As we have said, the language of the brain is chemistry, and therefore the flow of information (impulse) from one neuron to the next must be chemical. This action is illustrated in Figure 3.3, indicating what occurs at a single synaptic junction between two neurons during the saber-toothed tiger episode. Chemical messages flow from the axon on the top (presynaptic) neuron, across the synapse to the dendrite of the postsynaptic neuron on the bottom, and then on to the soma of the postsynaptic neuron. As the impulse reaches the presynaptic terminal, specific channels open in the membrane of this neuron, which allows doubly charged calcium atoms (ions) to enter the cell. This in turn stimulates the release of the neurotransmitter—in this case, NE (illustrated by round dark molecules)—into the synapse. NE moves across the synapse, carrying the message to the postsynaptic neuron. Embedded in the outer membrane of this neuron are hundreds of complex chemicals (proteins) that act as receptors for NE. These receptors have specific shapes that exactly complement the shape of NE. This enables the molecules of NE to attach themselves to these receptors in much the same way that a key fits into a lock. In fact, the key must not only fit the lock perfectly but must also open the door. Just as many Cadillac keys will fit the ignition of Buicks but will not start the engines, the same is true of neurotransmitters and receptors.

Figure 3.3 Mechanism of Neurotransmission Signals are transmitted from presynaptic to postsynaptic neurons by neurotransmitters. An action potential in the presynaptic neuron causes vesicles to migrate to the cell membrane and release their neurotransmitter into the synapse (the space between adjacent neurons). The neurotransmitters diffuse across the synapse and combine with receptors on the postsynaptic membrane; this can open channels that permit ions (charged particles) to flow across the membrane. The postsynaptic neuron is said to be depolarized when positive ions enter the cell, and it will generate an action potential if a sufficient amount of depolarization occurs (see Figure 3.1).

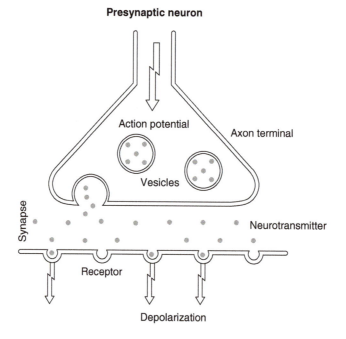

NE not only fits the locks but also opens the doors (ion channels) of the postsynaptic cell. Opening these cell doors allows certain ions (potassium, sodium, and chloride) to go in and out of this cell. If enough channels (doors) are opened and enough ions go in and out, the electrical nature of the receiving cell's outer membrane is altered (depolarized). This enables the message to be sent to the cell body (soma) of the postsynaptic cell, where it is processed with input from thousands of other cells, all undergoing the same process.

Before the membrane of the postsynaptic cell can fire (become depolarized and send its impulse down the axon), a critical number of the many receptor sites must be occupied by NE. The more molecules of this neurotransmitter (NE) that we can shove into the synapse, the quicker this critical number of sites will be occupied. Imagine trying to fill the holes of an egg carton by dropping ping-pong balls from 10 feet above. Many of the balls will not land in the holes of the egg carton. If we want to fill the carton quickly, we need to drop more ping pong balls in a given period of time. In the case of neurotransmission, the more molecules of NE released into the synapse, the sooner these receptor sites are occupied—and the more rapidly the neurons will fire, and the more aroused you will be and able to run from the saber-toothed tiger or your abusive boss. Just exactly how does this increase in NE neurotransmission bring this about?

The increased level of NE signals a region of the brain known as the *hypothalamus* to send messages to another region, the pituitary gland, which in turn causes the adrenal glands (adrenal cortex) sitting on top of the kidneys to produce *cortisol,* known as the stress hormone. Although long-term release of cortisol can result in serious physical and mental health problems, in emergency situations, cortisol enhances memory and immunity and decreases sensitivity to pain. For example, when meeting the tiger, you don't want to try to remember if he or she is "really bad," or begin to worry about catching a cold or suffering from a sore tooth.

Activation of this system, known as the hypothalamic-pituitary-adrenal (HPA) axis (Figure 3.4), accelerates the heart rate, which brings oxygen and other nutrients to the various parts of the body, increasing strength, and decreasing reaction time. Following the escape from the tiger, or your boss, you will be unable to sleep for many hours because the chemicals (NE) produced by this episode cascade back and forth across the synapse, keeping the rate of neurotransmission high, your eyes wide awake, and your brain pulsating.

Figure 3.4 Hypothalamic-Pituitary-Adrenal (HPA) Axis In response to stress, the hypothalamus secretes corticotrophin-releasing hormone (CRH) into a specialized blood supply that transports it to the pituitary gland where it stimulates the release of adrenocorticotropic hormone (ACTH) into the general circulation. ACTH, in turn, stimulates the adrenal cortex to release cortisol into the general circulation. Cortisol is a steroid hormone that decreases inflammation and mobilizes fuels.

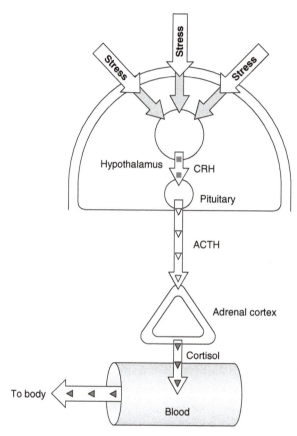

What makes neurotransmission so remarkable is the speed with which this seemingly very cumbersome and complex process occurs. It is like running a marathon race in which there are a thousand streams to cross. At each stream, the runner must gather rocks (neurotransmitters) from the first shore (presynaptic terminal) to build stepping stones to the next shore (postsynaptic terminal). The encounter with the tiger (boss) increases the number of "neuronal" rocks that are available on the shore where the runner arrives (presynaptic neuron); the more rocks available, the more rapidly will the runner be able to build a path to cross over the stream.

Of course, most activities in which we engage do not alter our consciousness to the level of arousal brought on by the attack of the tiger or serious confrontation with our boss. The tiger scenario should, however, give you some idea of how the mind and body can be energized, how mood can dramatically shift, and how the moment can be seized—all through the power of brain chemistry. It should be noted that this elevation of neurotransmission (i.e., mood) is brought about without resorting to stimulant drugs such as cocaine or methamphetamine. In today's society, we are often tempted to alter our mood by the use of drugs, which, as we shall see, can increase neurotransmission in certain parts of the brain that result in pleasurable experiences. Let us now turn our attention to the effect of drugs on the brain (Neurochemistry 102). It turns out that most of the mood alterations brought about by drugs are due to the role of a neurotransmitter known as dopamine (DA).

The Joy of Dopamine (DA) and the Reward Cascade

The most pleasure that life has to offer is an adequate
flow of dopamine into the nucleus accumbens.

—S. G. Sunderwirth

Understanding the joyful feelings evoked by brain chemistry begins with a search for a site in the brain responsible for this pleasure. The presence of a *pleasure center* in the brain was demonstrated by Olds and Milner (1954) at McGill University. They found that a rat with an electrode implanted into a certain region of the brain would continually press a lever in order to receive electrical stimulation. Routtenberg (1978) of Northwestern University later showed that, given a choice between a lever that delivered food for survival and one delivering brain stimulation, rats would forgo food in favor of the "reward" of brain stimulation. In other words, they chose ecstasy over survival. Rats, it seems, may become as addicted to an artificial (and ultimately fatal) paradise as humans.

In these experiments, the preference for "prolonged ecstasy" occurred only if the electrode was placed in a very small part of the brain, which Routtenberg (1978) referred to as the *reward center*. In recent years, the search for the specific site in the brain that regulates mood has led scientists to a complex array of neuronal clusters known as the *limbic system* (Figure 3.2). This region of the brain is believed to control emotions and is often referred to as the "reptilian brain," since we share this primordial brain with other living creatures.

Blum et al. (1991, 2012, 2013) has proposed a model for reward (pleasure) involving the interaction of several neurotransmitters with the various parts of the limbic system that compose the reward center. The release of dopamine into the nucleus accumbens, an important reward site, plays a major role in mediating our moods (Carelli, 2002). Although there are other reward sites in the limbic system, for simplicity we will limit our discussion to the action of dopamine on the nucleus accumbens. In Blum's model, which he calls the *reward cascade,* feelings of well-being, as well as the absence of craving and anxiety, depend on an *adequate supply of dopamine* flowing into the nucleus accumbens. Dopamine mediates the rewarding properties of both natural and drug-induced pleasures (Carelli, 2002). In humans, any imbalance that would lead to a deficit of dopamine would produce anxiety and a craving for substances (alcohol, cocaine, heroin, amphetamine, etc.) or activities (e.g., gambling, crime, promiscuous sex, hang gliding) that would temporarily restore this deficit. The levels of dopamine in the nucleus accumbens are increased with virtually every drug of abuse (Carelli, 2002).

A modified version of the reward cascade (Figure 3.5) helps us to understand this complex interaction of neurotransmitters. Let's start with serotonin, that ubiquitous neurotransmitter about which thousands of articles have been written. The introduction of Prozac and other selective serotonin reuptake inhibitors (SSRIs) has made serotonin (5-HT) a household word. In the hypothalamus, serotonin neurons stimulate the release of methionine enkephalin (or simply enkephalin), which in turn inhibits the release of GABA (gamma-aminobutyric acid) in the limbic system. (It seems that we have one more chemical to consider.)

What is GABA? The brain must have synapses that retard neurotransmission as well as increase it; otherwise we would be in a constant state of emotional turmoil even more than we are now. GABA is the neurotransmitter utilized by these inhibitory synapses; it's our own internal "Valium," regulating our mood through inhibition of the release of neurotransmitters such as dopamine and norepinephrine. "GABA is the major inhibitory neurotransmitter in the mammalian nervous system" (Hu & Quick, 2008, p. 309).

Figure 3.5 The Reward Cascade Serotonin neurons stimulate the release of enkephalin, which in turn inhibits the release of GABA (gamma-aminobutyric acid) in the limbic system. As GABA decreases, we can expect the release of dopamine to increase. In other words, the enkephalin has inhibited the inhibitor (GABA).

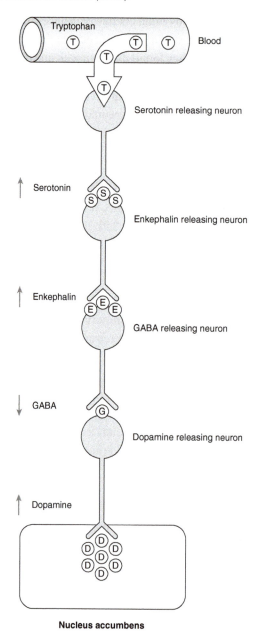

Nucleus accumbens

Now that we have struggled through these technical terms, let's see what they really mean in terms of our emotional state. As we follow the reward cascade, the most important concept to keep in mind is that an adequate supply of dopamine in the nucleus accumbens is necessary for feelings of well-being. Studies have shown that increased levels of dopamine in the nucleus accumbens can lead to increased pleasure and reward as well as decreased anxiety. As earlier stated, most drugs of abuse as well as certain activities increase the supply of DA in the nucleus accumbens (Blum, 1991; Carelli, 2002). Tables 3.1 and 3.2 summarize these effects. Figure 3.6 highlights common effects of drugs and certain activities on dopamine in the nucleus accumbens.

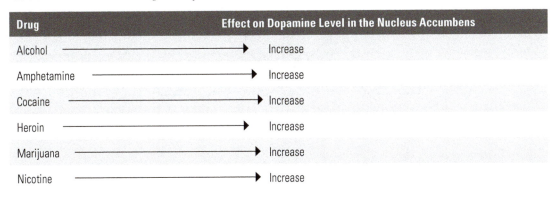

Table 3.1 Effect of Various Drugs on Dopamine Levels in the Nucleus Accumbens

Drug	Effect on Dopamine Level in the Nucleus Accumbens
Alcohol	Increase
Amphetamine	Increase
Cocaine	Increase
Heroin	Increase
Marijuana	Increase
Nicotine	Increase

Table 3.2 Effect of Various Activities on Dopamine Levels in the Nucleus Accumbens

Activity	Effect on Dopamine Level in the Nucleus Accumbens
Crime	Increase
Eating	Increase
Gambling	Increase
Hugs	Increase
Risk taking	Increase
Sex	Increase

Figure 3.7 illustrates where various drugs act on the brain to increase DA in the nucleus accumbens. It is now generally accepted that DA is the master chemical of pleasure and that the "high" from drugs is caused by this increase in DA.

How does the reward cascade work to produce this flow of DA into the nucleus accumbens? As we have said, the process is initiated by the neurotransmitter serotonin (5-hydroxytryptamine, or 5-HT), which is produced in the brain from the amino acid tryptophan and is enhanced by antidepressants such as Prozac. Once we have a supply of serotonin, what does this do for us? How does it help us not only to sleep, but in general to reduce feelings of anxiety and craving? In the hypothalamus, serotonin-releasing neurons impinge on enkephalin neurons, enhancing the release of enkephalin. In Figure 3.5, the up and down arrows indicate an increase or decrease, respectively, of the appropriate molecules. The primary function of enkephalin neurons in the brain is to inhibit the release of neurotransmitters from any neuron with which they interact; the more enkephalin released from these neurons, the more inhibition they exert on neurons on which they impinge (Figure 3.5).

Figure 3.6 Effects of Drugs and Activities on the Nucleus Accumbens Addictive drugs and compulsive problem behaviors share the common effect of increasing levels of dopamine in the nucleus accumbens.

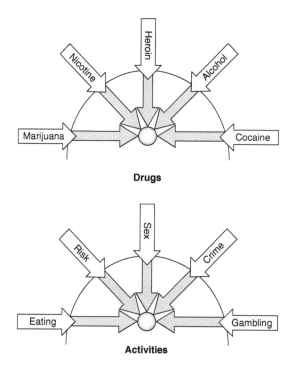

Figure 3.7 Action of Various Drugs on the Brain to Increase Dopamine Addictive drugs act on different sites in the brain with the common effect of increasing dopamine in the nucleus accumbens.

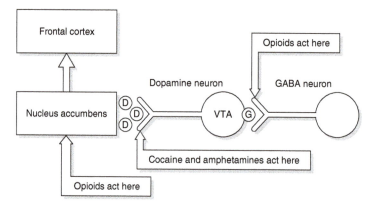

Now, how does GABA fit into this neurochemical puzzle? Conveniently, GABA-releasing neurons, as well as other neurons, have receptor sites for enkephalin molecules. As the number of these receptor sites occupied with enkephalin molecules increases, the release of GABA decreases. But GABA keeps the release of dopamine in check through another inhibitory synapse. Therefore, as GABA decreases due to either enkephalin increase or opioid ingestion, we can expect the release of dopamine to increase. In other words, the enkephalin has inhibited the inhibitor (GABA). This process works with the logic of a double negative and results in a positive increase in dopamine at the nucleus accumbens, which brings about a decrease in feelings of restlessness and anxiety as well as a general increase in feelings of well-being. Serotonin is the battery that starts the engine (reward cascade) that brings about enhanced dopaminergic neurotransmission.

Although serotonin starts the reward cascade engine, the real power behind the pleasure pathway is enkephalin, that internal opioid produced by our brains in response to both internal and external stimuli. It is this euphoric effect that has resulted in enkephalins and their cousins, the *endorphins*, being referred to as "the keys to paradise." Enkephalins and endorphins, although structurally different, are often grouped together under the generic name *endogenous* or *internal opioids*. These self-produced opioids are involved in the reward system, the regulation of mood, and the stress response (Nikoshkov et al., 2008). Much to our credit—and eternal regret—humankind has been able to find drugs (morphine) and even manufacture drugs (heroin) that have chemical structures similar to our own enkephalins (and endorphins) and, as we shall see later, can produce the feelings of euphoria even more intensely than our internal opioids.

For a drug to produce reward or pleasure, it must increase levels of dopamine in the nucleus accumbens. There are several ways that they can do this. One way would be to attach itself to receptor sites that are present in the brain. In other words, the drug just mimics compounds for which the brain already has receptors. For example, opioids can occupy the receptor sites for enkephalins, which are in the brain, and therefore activate the reward cascade. Milkman and Sunderwirth (1982, 1987, 1998) proposed that people could become addicted to activities as well as to drugs and that the brain chemistry associated with these activities was similar to that of drugs. We now know that many rewarding activities do increase the level of dopamine. Even the anticipation of reward increases the level of dopamine in animals. For example, Phillips, Stuber, Heien, Wightman, and Carelli (2003) at the University of North Carolina have shown that when rats encounter anything that they associate with past drug-taking (cocaine), dopamine levels "surge," which pushes the rats to seek more of the drug. In humans, similar encounters with drug contexts also produce dopamine surges and push the addict toward further drug-seeking activity.

The concept of conditioned craving has been picked up by the popular press. A *Newsweek* article entitled "Electronic Morphine" (Will, 2002) dealt with the problem of compulsive gambling by citing the case of an individual earning $35,000 a year who lost $175,000 during several years of gambling. This behavioral compulsion has become a serious problem with the increase in gambling opportunities that include online poker, other video games, service station pull tabs, and riverboat casinos. A recent automobile advertisement for the Lincoln LS had the following heading: "The Pleasure Neuron: Luxury May Be Habit-Forming, and We Have the MRIs to Prove It." This was followed by "I love this car." Dopamine is released, producing a feeling of well-being.

Clearly, the concept of the relationship between pleasure and dopamine release has reached the general public. The fundamental concept is that drugs or behaviors that elicit pleasure or reward are accompanied by an increase of dopamine in the nucleus accumbens. Table 3.1 shows the wide variety of drugs that cause an increase in dopamine in the nucleus accumbens, ultimately interpreted by the user as rewarding. Extra activity in the nucleus accumbens occurs when the person is involved in rewarding activities (Floresco, 2007). Activities or certain behaviors can mimic the neurochemistry of drugs of abuse. Activities as different as crime and eating have been shown to increase the level of dopamine in the nucleus accumbens. Table 3.2 shows the various activities that also bring about this increase. Obviously, hugging your child will not give you the same sensation as a line of cocaine. Although both are accompanied by an increase in dopamine in the nucleus accumbens, other pathways in the brain are also involved. To be sure, nothing in brain chemistry is simple. But in this chapter, let's stick to the effect of drugs of abuse on the brain and the *dopaminergic reward system.*

Table 3.3, adapted from the work of Di Chiara and Imperto (1988); Tanda, Pontieri, and Di Chiara (1997); and Joseph, Young, and Gray (1998), indicates the sites of action and the percentage increase in dopamine compared with controls (absence of drugs). It is clear that *amphetamine has the greatest influence* (900+%), followed by cocaine, heroin, and marijuana. Methamphetamine has an even greater effect than amphetamine. Although alcohol is not as powerful as a stimulant for DA release, as we shall see, the amount in which it is consumed in this country makes its use the second most serious drug problem in the United States, after nicotine.

Table 3.3 Site of Action of Drugs in the Reward Cascade and Percentage Increase in Dopamine in the Nucleus Accumbens

DRUGS AND DOPAMINE
Control: (Absence of Drugs)
Serotonin ↑ → Enkephalin*↑ → GABA ↓ → DA ↑
Amphetamine: Enhances release and blocks reabsorption of DA
Serotonin ↑ → Enkephalin*↑ → GABA ↓ → DA ↑↑ (900+%)[2]
Cocaine: Prevents reuptake of DA
Serotonin ↑ → Enkephalin*↑ → GABA ↓ → DA[1] ↑↑ (200+%)[2]
Nicotine: Stimulation of excitatory ACH receptors on DA cell bodies
Serotonin ↑ → Enkephalin*↑ → GABA ↓ → DA[1] ↑↑ (100%)[2]
Heroin: Increases DA through opioid receptors
Serotonin ↑ → Heroin (Enkephalin*)[1] ↑↑ → GABA ↓↓ → DA ↑↑ (160%)[2]
Marijuana:
Serotonin ↑ → THC (Enkephalin*)[1] ↑↑ → GABA ↓↓ → DA ↑↑ (130%)[2]
Prozac: Inhibits reuptake of serotonin
Serotonin[1] ↑↑ Enkephalin* ↓↓ → GABA ↓↓ → DA ↑↑
Morphine: Inhibits the inhibitor (GABA), therefore increasing DA
Serotonin ↑ → Mor (Enkephalin*)[1] ↓↓ → GABA ↓↓ → DA ↑↑ (60+%)[2]
* an opioid[1] site of action[2] % increase over control

Source: Di Chara, G. et al., Proceedings of the National Academy of Science, USA, 85, 5274–5278 (1988); Joseph, M. H. et al., Human Psychopharmacology. Vol. II S55–S63 (1996); and Tanada, G. et al., Science. Vol. 276, 2048–2050 (1997).

Addiction Is Not So Simple

Although there is much research support for the central role of the nucleus accumbens and dopamine malfunction in most forms of addiction, there is some controversy about dopamine's hegemony and evidence that other brain mechanisms are also at play.

> There is robust evidence that stimulants increase striatal dopamine levels and some evidence that alcohol may have such an effect, but little evidence, if any, that cannabis and opiates increase dopamine levels. Moreover, there is good evidence that striatal dopamine receptor availability and dopamine release are diminished in individuals with stimulant or alcohol dependence but not in individuals with opiate, nicotine or cannabis dependence. (Nutt, Lingford-Hughes, Erritzoe, & Stokes, 2015, p. 305)

> We suggest that the role of dopamine in addiction is more complicated than the role proposed in the dopamine theory of reward. We propose that dopamine has a central role in addiction to stimulant drugs, which act directly via the dopamine system, but that it has a less important role, if any, in mediating addiction to other drugs, particularly opioids and cannabis. Addiction is a complex mixture of behaviours and attitudes that vary from drug to drug and from user to user, and it is unlikely that a single neurotransmitter could explain every aspect of addiction. We foresee that addiction will be conceptualized as a multiple-neurotransmitter disorder in which the dopamine system is central to stimulant addiction but in which other neurotransmitter systems, such as the endogenous opiate or GABA systems, have important roles in other drug addictions. (Nutt, Lingford-Hughes, Erritzoe, & Stokes, 2015, p. 310)

Our brains are "plastic", meaning that they change based on experience. The dopamine system, like the rest of the brain, is not static. Stress hormones, triggered by adverse environmental conditions, can affect the sensitivity of this system. Moreover, the actual development of the brain, including neurotransmitter systems such as dopamine and the endogenous opioids, is influenced by early experiences. Thus, early experience may "prime" the brain for addiction.

Repeated drug use, another form of experience, leads to changes in the dopamine system, which ultimately affects both the function of the nucleus accumbens as well as the prefrontal cortex.

> [L]ike most humans, most laboratory rats will not drink alcohol to the point of physical dependence, let alone to the point of convulsions and death. Alcohol is simply not a very powerful reinforcer for laboratory rats; this is not surprising, as it causes only a modest 100% increase in extracellular levels of the reward transmitter dopamine. But what about intravenous cocaine or amphetamine, which drive extracellular dopamine levels many times higher? In the case of intravenous cocaine, I believe that quite limited initial self-administration of the drug is a sufficient condition for addiction, at least in laboratory rats. If given unlimited access to intravenous cocaine, rats or monkeys that learn to respond regularly for the drug

will, unless their veins or catheters fail, almost invariably take cocaine to the point of convulsions and death ... We did not food-restrict, prime, or shape these animals; we simply placed rats with jugular catheters for 4 h a day in chambers where accidental or intentional lever pressing resulted in intravenous injections ... Animals trained in the same way and given unlimited access to intravenous cocaine invariably continued to take the drug, with little variation in rate (except for periods of collapse and sleep), to the point of convulsions and death. (Wise & Koob, 2014, p. 255–256)

We've already mentioned that cravings are conditioned (learned) and can be elicited by cues (images of drugs or drug paraphernalia, environmental stimuli, etc.). These cues trigger an increase in dopamine in the nucleus accumbens, and in humans this is correlated with subjective ratings of drug craving. However, the release of dopamine in response to drugs is decreased after repeated use, suggesting development of tolerance to the rewarding effects of the substance. Unfortunately, there is a decrease in dopamine response to natural rewards as well, making it more difficult for a drug abuser to experience natural rewards and allowing the effects of the drug to overshadow other rewards. There are also changes in the function of the prefrontal cortex: this region will tend to be *hypo*active in the absence of drug or drug-related cues, but problematically *hyper*active in response to drug cues and stressful stimuli. The addicted individual is thus operating with a differentially sensitive reward circuit and an impaired behavioral control circuit, leaving himself or herself vulnerable to cravings for their substance. Volkow and Morales (2015) present an excellent review of the role of dopamine in reward and reward prediction.

Genes and Drug Abuse—Choose Your Parents Carefully

The idea that the synthesis, vesicular storage, metabolism, receptor formation, and catabolism of neurotransmitters are controlled by genes is well documented. Most importantly, polymorphisms of reward genes can disrupt the neurochemical events that culminate in neuronal release of DA within the mesolimbic reward circuitry. A breakdown of these neuronal events in the the brain reward cascade will eventually lead to DA dysfunction. DA neurotransmission is essential for an individual to experience of pleasure (reward) and the reduction of stress. DA dysfunction then can result in a deficiency in reward and a predisposition to substance-seeking in an attempt to ameliorate hypodopaminergic function (Blum et al., 2013, p. 4).

Not everyone responds equally to the same drug. There is considerable variation in the drug-induced pleasure of dopamine from one individual to another. Why is this true?

Studies of twins (e.g., Ferguson & Goldberg, 1997; Legrand et al., 2005) point to genes as the basis for the variance in the vulnerability of individuals to alcohol and drug abuse and dependence. Nikoshkov et al. (2008) assert that addiction has been shown to be linked to the reward sensitivity of the individual, and more specifically, that opioid abuse is correlated to some variability in the endogenous opioid systems mentioned earlier (enkephalins), which have a profound effect on pleasure. According to Uhl, Liu, and Naiman (2002), genes in the dopamine circuit are "likely candidates" for the variation in the susceptibility of individuals to drug abuse and addiction. To understand the genetic contribution to dopamine-seeking behaviors, let's continue in Neurochemistry 101 and see how dopamine is produced in the brain. Dopamine is produced from amino acids (either phenylalanine or tyrosine, both of which are present in foods such as meat). These amino acids are converted into dopamine by a series of reactions, each of which requires a special enzyme. Should any of these enzymes be deficient, the production of dopamine would be decreased. This would result in a decreased ability to experience pleasure. Individuals with this enzyme deficiency may be more prone to compensate for the resulting decrease in dopamine by choosing dopamine-enhancing drugs such as opioids, cocaine, or methamphetamine. Before leaving this section on dopamine, it is important to note that imbalances in dopamine have been implicated in disorders such as Parkinson's disease, schizophrenia, ADHD, and even anorexia.

Another example of the role of genes in substance abuse can be seen in the reward cascade (Figure 3.5). Tryptophan, found in many foods, is converted into serotonin (5-HT) by a series of reactions, each of which is catalyzed by an enzyme. An enzyme deficiency would result in a decrease in the production of serotonin. You will recall that serotonin starts the reward cascade, which results in the flow of dopamine into the nucleus accumbens. Therefore, any decrease in serotonin would result in a decrease of dopamine, with the resulting craving for drugs or hedonic activity to make up for this deficiency. Enzymes are proteins that are formed by the following scheme:

$$\text{Parents} \rightarrow \text{DNA} \rightarrow \text{RNA} \rightarrow \text{Proteins (enzymes)}$$

Since DNA is genetically determined by your parents, it is important to choose your parents carefully!

Current genetic research often emphasizes epigenetics, or how environment affects expression of genes (i.e., whether or not genes are actively being transcribed and producing proteins). It is now known that even two genetically identical individuals can have different gene expression, depending on their experiences and environment. For instance, environmental factors such as diet and exposure to stressful experiences can alter gene expression. Because parents are usually responsible for their children's early environment, and this environment may influence the child's gene expression, it really is important to choose your parents carefully!

Drugs to Fight Drugs

The history of using medication to combat drug abuse is not rosy. Aside from the traditional wariness from 12-step programs that pharmaceutical "band-aids" will likely result in substitute addictions, anti-addiction medication (although bursting with promise) does not have a great track record. Dating back to the late 1800s, both opium and cocaine were introduced as cures for alcoholism. Following the introduction of heroin as a "safe" replacement for morphine (although in reality, it is more potent than morphine), methadone to treat heroin addiction turned out to be highly addictive itself. The effects of Antabuse', highly touted for its ability to cause illness and vomiting after ingestion of just a small amount of alcohol, can be sidestepped by skipping the dose. Despite these problems and disappointing outcomes, there are currently more than 200 compounds being developed or tested by the National Institute on Drug Abuse to suppress the impulse, block the intoxication, or manage the withdrawal from psychoactive drugs (Interlandi, 2008).

Table 3.4 summarizes currently available medications approved by the Food and Drug Administration (FDA) for treatment of addictions. People looking for a quick fix to their substance abuse problems should be aware that medications are intended to be adjunctive to other treatments, rather than being a magic bullet. Moreover, data supporting the efficacy of these treatments tend to be mixed, and individual responses to these medications tend to be highly variable. The future of pharmacotherapy for addictions will likely be heavily influenced by the field of pharmacogenetics, which addresses why different people respond differently to drugs based upon genetics (Connery, 2015; Zindel & Kranzler, 2014).

Table 3.4 FDA-Approved Medications for the Treatment of Substance Use Disorders

Treatment/Drug Name	Used for	Action
Disulfarium (Antabuse®)	Alcoholism	Impairs alcohol metabolism; induces nausea, headache, dizziness if alcohol is consumed while on this medication
Acamprosate (Campral®)	Alcoholism	Agonizes GABA-A receptors and antagonizes glutamate receptors; helps treat alcohol withdrawal
Naltrexone (Revia®) (daily oral dose)	Alcoholism, Opioid dependence	Blocks opioid receptors, reducing feelings of pleasure associated with alcohol & opioid
Naltrexone (Vivitrol®) (monthly injection)	Alcoholism, Opioid dependence	Same action as oral naltrexone; longer lasting, generally better compliance
Methadone (Dolophine®, Methadose®)	Opioid dependence	Agonizes opioid receptors in brain; long-acting; serves as a replacement for opioids to prevent withdrawal and reduce craving
Buprenorphine (Subutex®) (sublingual tablet)	Opioid dependence	Partially agonizes opioid receptors in brain; similar effects as methadone, but fewer side effects;
Buprenorphine + Naloxone (Suboxone®) (sublingual film)	Opioid dependence	Partially agonizes opioid receptors in brain; similar effects as methadone, but fewer side effects; naloxone (an opioid antagonist) included to prevent misuse
Nicotine Replacement Therapy (patches, gum, lozenges)	Tobacco dependence	Agonizes acetylcholine receptors, just like nicotine in tobacco; decreases cravings and withdrawal symptoms
Varenicline (Chantix®)	Tobacco dependence	Partially agonizes acetylcholine receptors, replacing nicotine; decreases cravings and withdrawals
Bupropion (Zyban®)	Tobacco dependence	Atypical antidepressant that blocks reuptake of dopamine & norepinephrine; reasons for aiding with tobacco abstinence unclear

Sources: Compiled from Connery (2015), NIDA (2016), and Zindel & Krazler (2014)

In addition to a growing arsenal of pharmaceutical devices to treat drug addiction, researchers are focused on developing vaccines that will prevent intoxicants from affecting the brain. The vaccines' preventive action is predicated on "tricking" the body into creating antibodies normally used by the immune system to identify and neutralize foreign particles, usually bacteria or viruses. An anti-drug vaccine would prime the body to form antibodies against a specific substance; if the drug is then taken, the antibodies should attack the drug molecules in the bloodstream and prevent their passage into the brain. Vaccines have been created for several substances including cocaine, amphetamine, heroin, and nicotine, although only the cocaine and nicotine vaccines have been tested in human clinical trials with drug abusers. Unfortunately, the results obtained in humans are not as promising as those obtained in pre-clinical animal studies. As with pharmacotherapy, the response to immunotherapy varies greatly across individuals. Variables such as sex, genetic make-up, and whether individuals have previously formed their own antibodies to a drug appear to affect the ability of the vaccine recipient to achieve high blood levels of antibodies (Ohia-Nwoko, Kosten, & Haile, 2016).

Undoubtedly vaccines present progress in the treatment of addiction; however, they are not a "universal remedy," solving all the problems related to addiction. It seems that immunotherapy may be an opportunity for effective treatment of drug addiction if directed to adequate candidates for treatment. For other addicts, immunotherapy may be a very important component supporting psycho- and pharmacotherapy (Zalewska-Kaszubska, 2015, p. 6549).

Research into addiction vaccines continues, but it will likely be a number of years before a viable vaccine is available on the market.

Chapter Summary

This chapter lays the groundwork for understanding how drugs and activities modify mood by affecting changes in the reward centers of the brain. Beginning with an overview of how neurotransmission is the biological substratum for all aspects of our awareness including thought, perception, and emotion, the chapter moves to a discussion of how the HPA axis mediates the interaction between neurotransmission and the body's global response to stress. This provides a template for understanding how an emergency situation (or a perceived emergency situation) can release powerful chemicals throughout the brain and body, similar to the powerful effects of stimulant drugs. The reward cascade is then discussed as the unifying mechanism for a range of drugs and behaviors, through which dopamine arrives at the nucleus accumbens, thereby resulting in the subjective experience of pleasure. Genetics are then discussed in terms of individual differences in reward sensitivity, which may contribute to an individual's compulsion toward pleasure-seeking activity. The chapter concludes with a discussion of how pharmacological research is engaged in developing new compounds to stave off craving, reward activation, and withdrawal associated with various agents of addiction.

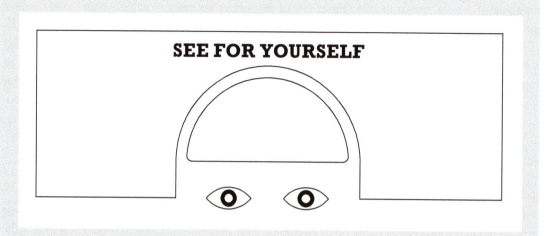

SEE FOR YOURSELF

From Saints to Sociopaths: Dopamine and Decisions. 2015. Dr. Nadine Kabbani. TEDxGeorgeMasonU. 21:34

This talk introduces dopamine as the reward mechanism in the brain. Dr. Kabbani relates dopamine to behaviors including eating, drug use, sex, and other "feel-good" behaviors. She goes on to discuss research that suggests that individuals with a specific gene that affects dopamine in the brain have been found to engage in more risk-taking and violent behaviors. Individuals who have the gene are more likely to end up in prison than those who don't, but there are powerful environmental factors that impact the outcome as well. For example, of the people who have the gene, those who had a consistent parent at home growing up were much less likely to engage in criminal behavior as adults. **https://youtu.be/J8w_0sZ97Bc**

"The Mystery of Risk." 2013. Peter Gwin. *National Geographic*. Brief Article.

This article explores dopamine's relationship to risk-taking behavior and motivation to seek novel experiences. The author distinguishes between people who are "adrenaline junkies," and those driven by dopamine, as well as compulsive risk-taking associated with addiction, and those who are motivated to take calculated risks such as explorers, wildlife photographers, and stunt performers. **http://ngm.nationalgeographic.com/2013/06/125-risk-takers/gwin-text**

DrugsLab YouTube Channel. 2016. BNN (A Dutch Public Broadcasting Association). 1:01

This YouTube Channel from the Netherlands features a group of young people who test out various drugs on film "in the name of science." The group describes their programming as an "educational YouTube channel about drugs." Each week, the group releases a new video depicting the use of a different drug, starting in September 2016. **https://www.youtube. com/channel/UCvRQKXtIGcK1yEnQ4Te8hWQ**

Nellie is Panicking Because of Salvia. 2017. DrugsLab. 16:10

In this episode, one of the hosts, Nellie, takes Salvia on camera. She and her co-host explain how the drug works in the brain before Nellie takes it and describes her experience. **https://www.youtube.com/watch?v= -GkSyWXWQX8**

SECTION II

Finding Relief and Letting Go

*I do not think that anyone completely understands its mechanism,
but it is a fact that there are foreign substances which, when present
in the blood or tissues, directly cause us pleasurable sensations; and
they also so alter the conditions governing our sensibility that we
become incapable of receiving unpleasurable impulses.*
—Sigmund Freud (1929/2005, p. 27)

Overview: Seeking Safety and Comfort

The goals of this section are to first illuminate neurochemical similarities between a range of satiating activities, including abusing opioid drugs, excessive drinking, unhealthy eating, and smoking cigarettes. In Chapter 4, "Feeling No Pain," we discuss the pursuit of satiation through pain-relieving chemicals and the phenomenon of rising addiction to opioids, including both legal prescription pain medications as well as illegal substances such as heroin. In Chapter 5, the question of how alcohol can trigger addiction is followed by a discussion of health benefits (cardiovascular) and potential risks (cancer) from moderate drinking. In Chapter 6, we examine the barroom setting, which we have dubbed "The Great Psychiatric Tavern," whereby a host of psychological and social needs are managed by a surrogate "mental health treatment" team. Chapter 7, "Nicotine: The World's Antidepressant," examines how cigarettes and other forms of nicotine ingestion is used worldwide as a misguided attempt to manage thoughts and feelings. Chapter 8, "Food/Mood Connections," analyzes how food may serve as a drug to alter mood and how eating disorders such as bulimia, anorexia, and binge eating may be conceptualized as addictions.

Metaphorically, growing up consists of finding the right substitutes for your thumb. From the cradle to the crypt, we discover various means—some socially approved, others highly disdained—for coping with the inevitable stress of walking through life's corridor. As infants, we have limited resources for dealing with repetitive swells of physical or emotional discomfort. Whether we survive depends on adult caretakers. We require proper nourishment, safety, and love. From the newborn's perspective, the universe is benign or malevolent depending on his or her experience with feeding and forming intimate emotional bonds. The nursling's knowledge that he or she will be lovingly fed allows baby to develop a basic trust in other human beings. As earlier stated, this perspective is embodied by *object relations theory* (e.g., Baker & Baker, 1987; Graham & Glickauf-Hughes, 1992; Kohut, 1977).

An infant's tension is reduced through the kind deliverance of food and touch. Misery and despair soon fade into gurgles and coos as the baby swoons in a state of blissful delight. Food, touch, and novelty become associated with love and the pleasures of being unshackled from disquieting physical sensations. A soothing influence appears from the outside world and suddenly baby feels better. A flailing state of alarm melts into passive euphoria. Like Sinbad on his magic carpet, the newborn simply forms a whimper and a wish and "zam-zam alacazam," a Shangri-La of nurturance and affection quickly unfolds: mother's breast, mommy and daddy's bed, a kiss, a caress, sumptuous creamy food. Behold, the *Garden of Eden*. All this for some rapid breathing, a few tears, and several whining screams. The infant soon discovers that a measure of tension can also be regulated through self-stimulation. Syllabic babbling, masturbation, and thumb sucking become important means for reducing stress. As Freud stated in *Three Essays on the Theory of Sexuality* (1905/1962),

> It is impossible to describe what a lovely feeling goes through your whole body when you suck; you are right away from this world. You are absolutely satisfied and happy beyond desire. It is a wonderful feeling; you long for nothing but peace—uninterrupted peace. It is unspeakably lovely: you feel no pain and no sorrow, and ah! you are carried into another world. (p. 47)

As adults, we repeatedly seek passage to the infant's heavenly retreat. Wistfully lamented by folk singers Peter, Paul, and Mary, "A million dollars at the drop of a hat/ I'd give it all gladly if life could be like that." Life's stressful and perilous journey is made more bearable by brief excursions into pleasurable moments that we have dubbed "substitutes for your thumb." Yet, as the poet John Milton sagely advised, "The mind is its own place. . . . It can make a heaven of hell or a hell of heaven." The same stimulus—whether a mood-altering drug or an activity like sex—can evoke paradise for one person and a fiery inferno for another.

An individual's unique combination of genetic characteristics and early childhood experiences determines his or her specific inclinations toward pleasurable activities. Some patterns emerge as early as the first year of life, while others are spawned during critical periods after many years of social learning and personal development. Quite naturally, need-gratifying behavior of any kind tends to be repeated because it continues to reduce conflict and tension. However, it is our biological adaptation to repeated mind-affecting stimuli—whether food, activities, or drugs—that requires increasing levels of exposure to achieve comparable feelings of pleasure. Any activity that produces salient alterations in mood (which are always accompanied by changes in neurotransmission) can lead to compulsion, loss of control, and progressively disturbed functioning.

Although the consequences of compulsive eating, TV watching, and repetitively abusing alcohol or other sedative drugs are obviously not the same, several commonalities exist. Subjectively, there develops an irresistible craving for food, drink, or activities that appear to lessen the impact of physically or psychologically arousing stimuli. Behaviorally, there are recurrent action patterns designed to re-create placid emotional states. Psychologically, satiation seekers reduce stress by adopting a stance of passive withdrawal from internal or external conflict.

Many today find soothing relief through electronic parent surrogates, for example, the Internet, DVDs, video games, and TV. Parents enjoy hours of relative calm as their children remain fixated on a plethora of computer-mediated images, interactive games, chat rooms, text messages, and music. For adults, soap operas, reality shows, and sitcoms provide temporary relief from unpleasant emotions, thoughts, or circumstances in daily life. Compulsive viewers eagerly await the times of day when they can watch the tormented lives of television characters who, in fantasy, become substitute members of their own family. Between episodes, reality show junkies, on some levels of consciousness, remain focused on an artificial, pre-scripted crisis. These agents of tension reduction are examined in Section IV, Mental Excursions.

A humorous example of how media can become addictive is taken from one of Greg Howard's "Sally Forth" cartoons:

> Listen Carol, just don't get yourself into the kind of trouble I did when I was on maternity leave. One day when I was nursing Hilary I turned on a soap opera just for fun. Within a week I was mainlining. I was doing four hours of soaps a day. Then I really flipped out and started to mix soaps and game shows. Finally, I had to quit cold turkey. It was awful! Do you know I still get occasional flashbacks from *General Hospital?*

We turn our attention now to soothing substances and the people who pursue them.

CHAPTER 4

Feeling No Pain
The Opioid Era

Among the remedies which it has pleased Almighty God to give to man, none is so universal and so efficacious as opium.

—Thomas Sydenham (c. 1650)

Nobody will laugh long who deals much with opium: its pleasures even are of a grave and solemn complexion.

—Thomas De Quincey, Confessions of an English Opium Eater (1821)

In France, a skinny man died of a big disease with a little name
By chance his girlfriend came across a needle and soon she did the same

—Lyrics from Prince's "Sign 'O' The Times" (1987)

Signs of the Times

Several pills taken from Prince's estate in Paisley Park after his death were counterfeit drugs that actually contained fentanyl, a synthetic opioid 50 times more powerful than heroin, an official close to the investigation said on Sunday.

The official, who spoke on condition of anonymity because of the continuing investigation, said many pills were falsely labelled as "Watson 385". According to Drugs.com, that stamp is used to identify pills containing a mix of acetaminophen and hydrocodone.

About a dozen tablets were found in a dressing room at Paisley Park, but the vast majority was in bottles of Vitamin C and aspirin that had been tucked inside a suitcase and bags, including one Prince often carried with him.

—Associated Press in Minneapolis, Sunday 21 August 2016[1]

The Opioid Epidemic

Prince Rogers Nelson was found nonresponsive in his home on April 21, 2016. The very brief autopsy report noted this was an accidental death due to fentanyl toxicity. He was one of literally dozens of opioid overdose victims who died that day, although he was the only one who had achieved worldwide fame. There are many unanswered questions about Prince's death. Did he start taking fentanyl for medical purposes? Did he obtain it through a prescription or through illegal means? News reports stated that people close to Prince had reached out for help from addiction specialists and that Prince had been treated in a hospital for possible opioid overdose just days before he died (Tarm & Forliti, 2016). We don't know how long Prince struggled with his opioid problem, but we do know that his case is all too common in the United States.

According to the *Centers for Disease Control*, fatal drug overdoses in the U.S. reached a new record in 2014 (CDC, 2016). Opioid overdoses account for more than 60% of those deaths, and there are actually more overdoses linked to prescription opioids such as oxycodone and hydrocodone than there are linked to heroin. On average, 52 Americans die daily from prescription opioid overdoses—which amounts to about 2 deaths every hour. Data from 2015 are not yet available, but don't expect the number of opioid-related overdoses to decrease: from 2013 to 2014, there was an increase of about 3,000 lethal opioid overdoses. It is thought that a significant number of these overdoses are linked to fentanyl. Originally available only by prescription, fentanyl is a synthetic opioid now being manufactured illegally. Compared to heroin, it is more potent yet less expensive to produce, making it a growing concern.

The current epidemic of opioid abuse is not the first in our nation's history. In the late 19th century, morphine and laudanum (a liquid of opium dissolved in alcohol) were freely available. In these days before aspirin, ibuprofen, and acetaminophen, people turned to opioid substances to cure all of their pains. It was not unusual to give morphine-containing medications to children or even infants. After the invention of the hypodermic needle, morphine injection kits could be purchased without prescription. According to Courtwright (2001), the majority of opium/morphine addiction cases in the 19th century U.S. were due to doctors prescribing or recommending these substances. By the time the early 20th century arrived, morphine and heroin (along with the stimulant cocaine) were seen as public problems, leading to passage of legislation to control trafficking and availability of these substances. For a number of decades, opioid use was relatively rare—until the late 1960s. Heroin popularity died again only to make a comeback in the 1990s (the era of "heroin chic") when more potent heroin was available and snorting or smoking, rather than injecting, became the trend.

The current problems with opioid abuse, however, are due in part to the increase in prescription opioid pain medications (CDC, 2016). The annual number of lethal overdoses of opioids has more than

---

1 Associated Press in Minneapolis, "Counterfeit Pills Found at Prince's Home Contain Powerful Opioid Fentanyl," The Guardian. Copyright © 2016 by Guardian News and Media Limited.

quadrupled since 1999. The number of non-lethal overdoses is even greater. No wonder this situation is viewed as a public health crisis. Our country is at the center of this crisis, given that the vast majority of the world's prescriptions for opioid pain medications are written in the U.S. Complicating the situation is that street opioids are often less expensive and more easily obtained (no prescription required), leading to some opioid abusers to switch from pills to heroin. NIDA (2014b) estimates that 1 out of 15 people using opioid pain medications for non-medical purposes will end up trying heroin within 10 years. The switch to "street" drugs risks legal complications, potentially bringing more negative consequences for the user.

Table 4.1 gives a select list of some common opioids, along with opioid antagonists. Some of these substances may be used medicinally or may be abused. Others on the list are intended to treat opioid addiction. This is by no means an exhaustive list of substances, as there are literally dozens of opioid compounds. A note about nomenclature: it used to be common to make distinctions between "opiates" (substances derived from the opium poppy, such as raw opium and its components morphine, codeine, and thebaine) and "opioids" (opiate-like substances). *Endogenous* opioids (enkephalins and endorphins) are produced naturally in the brain. *Exogenous* opioids are drugs which are synthetic (e.g., fentanyl) or semi-synthetic (e.g., heroin), yet work like opiates and endogenous opioids in the brain. Increasingly, the scientific literature refers to all of these substances as opioids, and for simplicity's sake, we will do so in this chapter.

Table 4.1 List of Opioid Substances

Substance	What It Is	History/Use
Opium	Secreted by Papaver Somniferum plant Medicinal use dates back millennia	Pain relief
Morphine	Major component of opium Isolated in early 1800s	Pain relief Available in U.S. without prescription from mid-1800s until 1914
Laudanum	Opium tincture, often containing alcohol Common patent medicine in 1800s	Pain Relief; used as "cure all"
Heroin	Chemically-Modified Morphine Several times more potent than morphine Marketed by Bayer Corporation in 1898	Originally marketed to treat pain and morphine addiction Still available as pain reliever (by Rx) in some countries Illegal in USA
Codeine	Component of opium 1/10 as strong as morphine	Pain relief, cough suppression
Loperamide (Imodium®)	Synthetic opioid Poor penetration of blood-brain barrier	Anti-diarrheal medication sold over-the-counter People taking this to try to get "high" at great risk for cardiac toxicity
Vicadin®	Hydrocodone with acetaminophen Similar potency to morphine	Pain relief; common Rx med Misuse associated with liver damage

OxyContin®	Oxycodone 1.5 times as potent as morphine	Pain relief; common Rx med Purdue Pharma changed formulation in 2011 due to misuse
Fentanyl	Synthetic opioid 50–100 times more potent than morphine	Pain relief, especially for chronic pain. Sometimes given in patch form or lollipops
Naloxone (Narcan®)	Opioid antagonist Carried by emergency responders	Treat opioid overdose (limited window of time) May not counteract fentanyl overdose (depends on fentanyl dose). Nasal spray or intramuscular injector.
Naltrexone (ReVia®, Vivitrol®)	Opioid antagonist Prevents "high" if opioids taken	Treat opioid addiction; ReVia® is given daily in pill form; Vivitrol® given as monthly injection
Methadone	Long-acting opioid Dose lasts approximately 24 hours	Treat opioid addiction; helps reduce withdrawals & cravings; serves as a replacement drug
Buprenorphine (Subutex®)	Partial opioid agonist Less potent than methadone	Treat opioid addiction; helps reduce withdrawals & cravings; Lower risk of overdose if abused or combined with other opioids
Suboxone®	Buprenorphine + naloxone Formula intended to decrease misuse	Treat opioid addiction Naloxone counteracts the opioid if injected or snorted

Compiled from Connery (2015) and Shaheen et al. (2009)

Is This a Good Idea?

FDA approves new hand-held auto-injector to reverse opioid overdose: First naloxone treatment specifically designed to be given by family members or caregivers

The U.S. Food and Drug Administration approved a prescription treatment that can be used by family members or caregivers to treat a person known or suspected to have had an opioid overdose. Evzio (naloxone hydrochloride injection) rapidly delivers a single dose of the drug naloxone via a hand-held auto-injector that can be carried in a pocket or stored in a medicine cabinet. It is intended for the emergency treatment of known or suspected opioid overdose, characterized by decreased breathing or heart rates, or loss of consciousness.

Figure 4.1 Auto Injectors

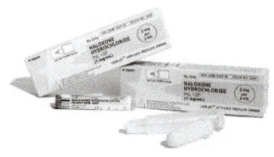

CVS announced it will add 12 states to its program to sell the opioid overdose antidote naloxone without a prescription, bringing the total to 14. Narcan nasal spray NARCAN° (naloxone HCl) is the first and only FDA-approved nasal form of naloxone for the emergency treatment of opiod overdose.

> Over 44,000 people die from accidental drug overdoses every year in the United States and most of those deaths are from opioids, including controlled substance pain medication and illegal drugs such as heroin .... Naloxone is a safe and effective antidote to opioid overdoses and by providing access to this medication in our pharmacies without a prescription in more states, we can help save lives.... While all 7,800 CVS/pharmacy stores nationwide can continue to order and dispense naloxone when a prescription is presented, we support expanding naloxone availability without a prescription and are reviewing opportunities to do so in other states. (para. 3, 5)

Retrieved September 9, 2016. **http://www.drugfree.org/news-service/cvs-will-sell-naloxone-without-prescription-14-states/**

The Chemistry of Calm: Opioids in the Brain and Body

The heroin rush is said to be king of the opioid-mediated sensations. Indeed, the quiet lethargy induced by heroin is reminiscent of the infant's calm, sleepy satisfaction after being breastfed. Are we then to assume that the world's most infamous narcotic and mother's milk have a chemical similarity? Is there an underlying biochemical thread that can explain the common reaction to these very disparate yet similarly satisfying substances? At first, even the suggestion of some commonality between milk and heroin seems ridiculous, even disrespectful. Yet these seemingly diverse substitutes for your thumb trigger similar changes in the brain's reward system. Similar biochemical principles may be used to account for progressive dependence on a wide spectrum of mood-calming activities—taking sedative drugs, listening to music, watching television, undergoing massage, or eating your grandmother's chicken soup—and yes, it is possible to develop a growing dependence on these chemically similar, though more subtle, versions of opioid addiction.

Let us go back to Neurochemistry 101 and the brain's endogenous (naturally-occurring) opioids. If our brains did not have *endogenous* opioids (endorphins and enkephalins), *exogenous* opioids (morphine, heroin, fentanyl, oxycodone, etc.) would not affect our moods and provide analgesia. Opioid drugs impersonate the endogenous opioids by binding and activating their receptors. As it turns out, opioids not only reduce pain, but also promote feelings of pleasure. Activating the brain's opioid system taps into the reward pathway (see Chapter 3), leading to an increase in dopamine in the nucleus accumbens. As a result, some individuals will be inclined to repeat taking opioid drugs, not only to renew analgesia (pain relief) but also euphoria. Besides activating the reward system, opioids also affect the amygdala and frontal cortex, key brain regions involved in emotional responses. Opioids help relieve negative emotion and induce calm. The user may even experience emotional detachment from pain, emotions, or aversive situations.

Opioid drugs like morphine, heroin, oxycodone, and many others, look similar enough to endogenous opioids that they bind and activate these receptors, increasing the overall activity of this neurotransmitter system. Drugs like naloxone and naltrexone are opioid receptor antagonists: they bind to opioid receptors but are not actually able to activate them. As a result, opioid antagonists block the receptors, preventing binding of opioids—both endogenous as well as exogenous. This is why naloxone can reverse an opioid overdose.

Figure 4.2 shows action at a synapse where endogenous opioids are released.

Figure 4.2 Action at an Opioid Synapse Under normal conditions, endogenous opioids are released by presynaptic neurons and occupy receptors on the postsynaptic neuron, causing activation of these receptors (left panel). In the presence of opioid drugs (middle panel), more receptors are activated because these drugs bind the same receptors, enhancing the message received by the postsynaptic neuron (more downward arrows). Naloxone (right panel) prevents opioids from binding with the receptors, blocking their signal.

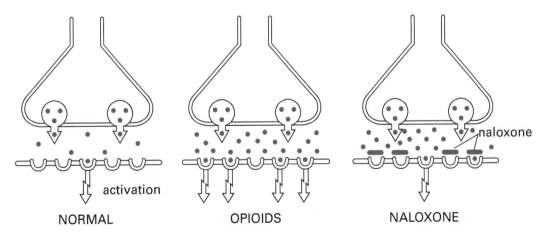

Figure 4.3 illustrates the distribution of mu-opioid receptors (commonly activated by opioid substances). Note that in addition to their presence in regions of the brain (influencing mood, pain perception, and pleasure), they are also expressed in portions of the spinal cord and in peripheral tissues (producing analgesia). Opioid receptors in the brainstem are linked to risk of lethal overdose. The presence of opioid receptors in the intestines influences gastrointestinal motility (leading to the side effect of constipation when opioids are taken continuously).

[Illustration from page 1255 of *New England Journal of Medicine* Volkow & McLellan 2016 article]

Figure 4.3 **Location of Mu-Opioid Receptors** Shown are the locations of mu-opioid receptors in the human brain, with high concentration in the thalamus, peri-aqueductal gray, insula, and anterior cingulate (regions involved with pain perception), in the ventral tegmental area and nucleus accumbens (regions involved with reward), in the amygdala (a region involved with emotional reactivity to pain), and in the brain stem (nuclei that regulate breathing). In the spinal cord, a high concentration of mu-opioid receptors is located in the dorsal horn. Mu-opioid receptors in peripheral terminals modulate the perception of pain, and receptors in the small intestine regulate gut motility.

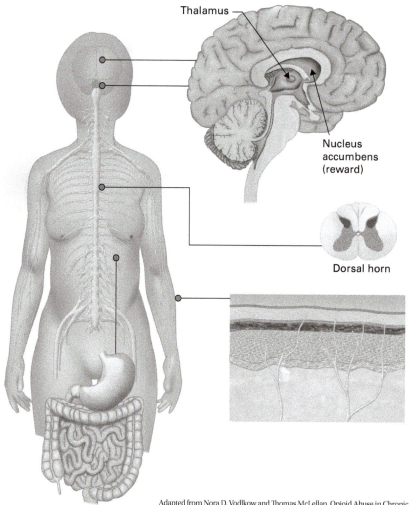

Thalamus

Nucleus accumbens (reward)

Dorsal horn

Adapted from Nora D. Vodlkow and Thomas McLellan, Opioid Abuse in Chronic Pain: Misconceptions and Mitigation Strategies. The New England Journal of Medicine, vol. 374, no. 13, ed. Dan L. Longo, pp. 1255. Copyright © 2016.

Although opioids are famous for producing strong physical dependence (more later), these substances—in a pure form—seem to be less toxic to the body than some other substances, especially compared to alcohol and tobacco. Nonetheless, there are risks associated with opioids. The most immediate risk is the potential for overdose; if the dose taken is high enough to severely suppress the respiratory center in the brainstem, coma or death can occur. Immediate medical attention is required if there is to be hope of reversing an overdose through the administration of Narcan', an opioid antagonist carried by many emergency responders, now available on prescription and non-prescription basis to families of known opioid abusers (see above: Is this a good idea?)

Other risks are linked to using street opioids. Unlike pain medications produced by pharmaceutical corporations, street opioids do not come with a listing of the bag's contents. Ingredients used to "cut" the drug may include harmful contaminants which can affect organs such as the heart, liver, lungs, or brain. Variations in purity also pose a problem: if a person has previously used a weaker cut of drug but ends up unknowingly obtaining a more potent batch, there is an elevated risk of overdose. Of course, if a person uses opioids by injecting them, there are risks associated with needle use; dirty needles—especially if shared between users—allow for spread of HIV, hepatitis C, and other infections. Advocates for harm reduction support the availability of non-prescription needle sales and needle exchange programs to make injecting drugs safer for those struggling with IV drug addiction, as well as the community at large.

Is This a Good Idea?

Needle Exchange Programs
There are currently 35 programs in California that provide syringe exchange services. Many have fixed locations, but others operate at various locations and times throughout the week. Northern California residents can check the San Francisco Bay Area Wide Syringe Exchange List for a detailed schedule of local exchange sites and times.

Pharmacy Syringe Access
Beginning January 1, 2015, any pharmacy in the state of California may sell an unlimited number of syringes to adults ages 18 and older without a prescription. Adults may also purchase and possess an unlimited number of syringes for personal use without a prescription.

Pharmacies are not required to sell syringes without a prescription, and many pharmacies are still learning about this change in law. The California Department of Public Health, Office of AIDS is encouraging pharmacies that participate in California's AIDS Drug Assistance Program (ADAP) to provide nonprescription syringe sale, and many have begun to offer the service.

Source: California Department of Health, Office of AIDS, 2015

Administer, Satiate, Repeat

When taken repeatedly, opioids tend to promote tolerance and can lead to a physical dependence. Dependence means that after repeated exposure to an event that disrupts neuronal activity in the brain, a person leans on that experience in order to feel "adjusted" or "normal." The brain contains regulatory mechanisms that maintain a relatively constant level of neurotransmission. Externally-induced variations in this level, which account for our mood swings, bring about a counteraction as the brain attempts to return neurotransmission to a normal level and maintain homeostasis. As a person continues to take *exo*genous opioids, brain cells decrease production of *endo*genous opioids, and the number and sensitivity of opioid receptors will also decrease. Translated, this means that the person's brain is making and using fewer of its own natural pain relievers because the person is supplying them from an outside source. Meanwhile, homeostatic mechanisms in other parts of the body kick in to help restore normal biochemistry: the liver produces more enzymes so that the drug can be metabolized faster. The result of these homeostatic processes is tolerance, which leads a person to increase the drug dose in order to get the desired effect.

The rate at which one becomes dependent is variable, depending upon the type of experience, amount of exposure (dose and frequency), and individual differences among users (including genetics, personality traits, environmental factors, etc.). Typically, the more potent the substance, the higher the dose, or the more frequently it is taken, the faster the rate of tolerance development. A user can become dependent on morphine in about a week by using a typical dose once daily. People naturally vary in terms of how much tolerance they have for a substance and how quickly they increase tolerance, and this is influenced by genes that encode for enzymes that metabolize drugs. According to a 2004 report by Stafford and colleagues (cited in Christie, 2008), individuals addicted to opioids can consume daily doses that are between 10s and 100s of times larger than a dose that would produce an effect in an opioid-naïve individual; in other words, the dose an addicted individual might take could easily kill a novice. However, tolerance is not permanent. During a period of abstinence, homeostatic mechanisms will bring the body's systems back toward where they were prior to the onset of opioid addiction; this can lead to overdose if a person resumes use of high doses after being "clean" for a while.

Tolerance is an interesting phenomenon in that drugs tend to produce more than one effect, yet tolerance to these different effects do not necessarily develop at the same rate. As mentioned above, opioids produce desired effects (analgesia and euphoria), but they also produce undesired effects (e.g., constipation). A bigger concern, however, is their suppression of the respiratory center located in the brainstem, which is critical for keeping the person alive. With repeated opioid use, tolerance to the desired effects develops faster than tolerance to the undesired effects. As a result, an opioid abuser risks overdose (severe, if not lethal, respiratory suppression) by escalating their drug dosage in order to get the physical or psychological relief they desire.

There is also evidence that at least a portion of the tolerance to opioids is due to Pavlovian (classical) conditioning and is controlled by the environmental setting where the drug is habitually used. Decades ago, Siegel and colleagues demonstrated this by repeatedly administering rats increasing doses of heroin to allow for development of tolerance. On the test day, rats were given a high dose of heroin (one which was lethal to 96% of heroin-naïve rats). Some of the heroin-experienced rats were given the test dose in the usual setting, while the others received it in a novel setting. Those rats that were injected in the unfamiliar environment were two times more likely to die of an overdose compared to rats that received the test dose in their usual environment. The authors argued that some of the homeostatic mechanisms that help counteract the effects of heroin are conditioned to the environment, leading to a loss of tolerance when opioids are used in unfamiliar settings (Siegel, Hinson, & Krank, 1982). That mechanisms of conditioned tolerance occur in humans addicted to heroin is supported by a study in which 54 patients who experienced non-lethal heroin overdoses were interviewed. About half (52%) of this sample reported injecting heroin in an unfamiliar surrounding (Gutiérrez-Cebollada et al., 1994). They are lucky to have survived.

Opioid tolerance poses another issue within the medical field: how can pain due to injury or surgery be managed in patients who are already hooked on opioids? Their tolerance means that they do not get pain alleviation from normal doses, and radically increased doses elevates risk of overdose. One alternative is use of dissociative anesthetic substances, such as ketamine, in hospital settings (Vadivelu, Kaye, & Urman, 2014).

Tolerance is only one problem associated with repeated opioid experiences. When prolonged participation in behaviors associated with the ingestion of opioids or release of endorphins is abruptly discontinued, a characteristic disturbance known as withdrawal (or abstinence syndrome) begins to occur. Withdrawal symptoms are the defining characteristics of physical dependence, which is fundamentally a biochemical process. Even addicted animals that have had the thinking portions of their brains removed, and babies who have inherited opioid dependence from their mothers, will experience acute physical withdrawal symptoms, without conscious awareness. These symptoms are experienced as the reverse of the drug's effects: instead of feeling euphoria and analgesia, the person will feel depressed and *hyper-algesiac* (that is, they will be extra sensitive to painful stimuli and may feel pain in the absence of external stimuli). They will also experience the opposite of constipation—severe stomach cramping and diarrhea. Add in cold sweats, temperature fluctuations, disrupted sleep, and other symptoms, and the person may feel like they are experiencing the worst case of the flu ever. Fortunately, withdrawal from opioids is not likely to be fatal, even though the person may *feel* like they are going to die. For some opioid abusers, the onset of withdrawal symptoms will prompt them to take the drug again because it is a sure (albeit temporary) cure. Some opioid abusers report experiencing withdrawal as a *violent death of their soul...*so even if physiologically, the experience is comparable to a bad flu, psychologically the addict experiences a kind of *personal hell*— no wonder withdrawal is often avoided at all costs.

The amount of subjective distress that occurs during withdrawal is very much a function of the user's expectations, beliefs, and life circumstance. Those who insist, for example, that they will endure incredible torment if they discontinue heroin will undoubtedly report acute psychological and physical suffering. Part of being "hooked" on a satiation experience—whether shooting heroin or excessive alcohol consumption—is the phenomenon of self-identification as an addict. The belief that "I need to have… [x, y, or z]" is no doubt influenced by the biological fact of dependence, but the intensity of subjectively perceived pain is very much influenced by psychology and circumstance.

Some opioid-dependent individuals may show seemingly incomprehensible desperation (to the outsider, at least) when they "need" their drug. This is illustrated by a recent trend in which opioid-addicted individuals resort to taking loperamide (Imodium', an over-the-counter antidiarrheal medication) to either alleviate the agony of withdrawals or to satisfy their craving for a high. Fortunately, there is a relatively small number of people who have done this because it is an extremely dangerous thing to do! The Food and Drug Administration (FDA) were informed of 48 cases of serious heart problems associated with loperamide between 1975 (when it came on the market in the U.S.) and 2015; more than half of the cases have been reported since 2010. Loperamide does not do a good job of getting to the brain (it has trouble crossing the blood-brain barrier), so in order for a person to feel a psychological effect of the drug, they have to take massive doses of it. This has toxic effects on the heart and can lead to sudden death, as in the case of 10 of the 48 individual cases reported to the FDA (FDA, Safety Communication, 2016a).

Tolerant satiation addicts can avoid becoming ill or physically distressed by maintaining a constant dose of their preferred drug or activity. Feeling high is a different story. To achieve pleasurable sensations, the addict constantly must increase the frequency or dose of the satiating experience. In the lingo of the street, "He can stay normal, but he can't get high." Some addicts continue their habits for months or years, resigned to the fact that they will no longer get high. They continue to want (crave) the substance even though they may not particularly like it any more. As soon as withdrawal symptoms begin, they will administer an accustomed dose and take pleasure in simply having achieved relief from the sufferings of abstinence—the only satiation the drug can still offer. Administer, satiate, repeat becomes a perpetual cycle.

A Monkey on Your Back

Although the origin of the phrase "you've got a monkey on your back" is unclear, since the mid-20th century it has been used to refer to opioid addiction. Who is going to be burdened by this metaphorical monkey? In other words, who is going to get hooked?

As is the case with other substances, most people who try opioids do not become addicted. That's the good news. However, according to recent survey data, about 1.9 million people in the U.S. have substance use disorders related to prescription pain killers, and about 586,000 people have substance use disorders involving heroin (SAMSHA, 2015). With regards to prescription opioid overdoses, the highest rate occurs in people between the ages of 25 and 54, with non-Hispanic whites being most represented. (CDC, 2014). Presently, it is more common for males than for females to die of prescription pain killer overdoses. But not all overdoses are lethal; emergency departments in the U.S. treat more than 1,000 people per day for prescription opioid misuse. According to NIDA, survey data from 2011 indicate that an estimated 23% of Americans (age 12 and older) who use heroin will develop dependence. Almost half of young IV heroin users reported that they abused prescription pain pills before transitioning to heroin. For some, the abuse of the prescription shifted from oral use to crushing the pills so that they could be either snorted or injected. This allows for the drug to reach the brain more quickly, producing a more rapid high, but it also increases the likelihood of compulsive drug use. For those that transitioned from prescription pain pills to heroin, it became easier and less expensive to acquire heroin (NIDA, 2014). With the rise in availability of fentanyl, which is far more potent than heroin, the same problem exists of people turning from the prescription medication to an illicit drug. Unfortunately, fentanyl is so potent that administering Narcan® is less likely to reverse on overdose of this substance compared to overdoses from other opioids.

CASE EXAMPLE: "Heroin" Overdose

Swanson and colleagues (2017) describe a lethal overdose of a 34 y/o white man, found slumped over and unresponsive in his vehicle with the engine still running. Responding paramedics determined he was dead. The contents in the console cup holder—a spoon, a syringe, and a baggie of brownish powder—explained that cause of death as a drug overdose. Given that the man had a history of heroin abuse, he likely thought that's what the baggie contained. But Swanson et al.'s analysis of his case reveals that he got more than he bargained for in that little yellow baggie. Chemical analysis revealed that the drug contained "caffeine, carfentanil, diphenhydramine [an antihistamine], fentanyl, para-fluoroisobutyryl fentanyl, furanyl fentanyl, heroin, hydromorphone, mannitol [often used as an artificial sweetener], 6-monoacetylmorphine (6-MAM), morphine, noscapine [an opium alkaloid], and quinine" (pg. 3).

Some of the substances in this non-pure substance are there simply as cutting agents, such as caffeine, mannitol, and quinine. Note that there are various types of fentanyl in the mix (all are about equally potent). More alarming is the presence of carfentanil, a fentanyl derivative that is said to be 10,000 more potent than morphine and 100 times more potent than fentanyl (Van Beaver et al., 1976). Carfentanil has no accepted human medical use, which is understandable: it's potent enough to tranquilize an elephant, which is its accepted veterinary usage.

Would a quickly administered Narcan injection have saved this man? Because this was such a potent opioid concoction, it likely would have taken multiple doses to do the trick. This case highlights the danger of street opioids and how someone who likely had a tolerance for heroin unwittingly overdosed due to the mixing of more potent opioids in with heroin. (Moreover, if he generally did not shoot up in his car, he would have been more prone to overdose due to loss of conditioned tolerance.)

The anonymous man depicted in this case study is not alone: heroin tainted with fentanyl has made headlines for several years, and heroin tainted with carfentanil has been spreading across the U.S.

Despite the statistics indicating that men are currently more likely to lethally overdose on prescription opioids, a 2015 study by Ailes and colleagues (cited by NIDA, 2015) indicates that women are more likely than men to obtain prescriptions for opioid pain medications. This may reflect differences in endogenous opioid systems between the sexes: women tend to have lower pain thresholds and report higher levels of pain (Wiesenfeld-Hallin, 2005). Women also have greater variability in their pain responses, which vary based upon hormonal fluctuations associated with menstrual cycles. McHugh and colleagues (2013, citead by NIDA, 2015a) report that women are more likely than men to self-medicate psychological distress by misusing prescription opioids. Men, however, are more likely to use illicit opioids such as heroin, and are more likely to do so by injecting. Females using heroin tend to be younger and influenced by sex partners who use drugs (NIDA, 2015a). Overall, then, there may not be large differences between males and females in terms of their tendency to use opioids, but the specific opioid, how they use it, and why they use it may vary across the sexes.

Of course, genetics also play a role in a person's vulnerability to use opioids, with about 40-50% of variance in opioid abuse linked to genetic variance, according to a review by Khokhar et al (2010). The gene most commonly linked to opioid abuse encodes for mu-opioid receptors; variants in this gene also influence how people respond to naltrexone treatment. Interestingly, this same gene has been linked to alcoholism. Additionally, genes that encode for specific liver enzymes involved in metabolizing opioids are linked to risk of opioid abuse. These types of genetic differences will influence how an individual responds to the pain-relieving and euphoria-inducing effects of opioids as well as how quickly they process such drugs and build tolerance to them.

Satiating effects of opioids may be particularly desirable to some individuals based on personality characteristics and negative life experiences. In a study with rats, Vazquez, Giros, and Dauge (2006) demonstrated that maternal separation shortly after birth elevates the risk of self-administering morphine later in life; however, this same form of deprivation did not seem to radically alter the risk of self-administering substances such as stimulants or alcohol. Other research demonstrates that these early experiences are affecting brain development, including the endogenous opioids in regions where they interact with the brain's stress response system (HPA-axis) as well as in the amygdala (Ploj, Roman, & Nylander, 2003). If we wish to generalize from animal research to humans, we must consider the possibility that abuse and neglect during childhood—both of which have been shown to increase the risk of substance abuse—may be influencing a person's risk for addiction by altering their brain chemistry in enduring ways. It is known that endogenous opioids play a role in mother-infant attachment (see Nelson & Panksepp, 1998, for a review), so it makes sense that unhealthy attachments—brought about through neglect or abuse in childhood—could increase a person's vulnerability to self-medicate with opioids. Schindler et al. (2009) describe heroin as "an emotional substitute for lacking coping strategies" (pg. 307). Their study compared attachment styles between groups of people who abuse opioids, cannabis, and ecstasy to non-substance abusers. The opioid users demonstrated fearful-avoidant and dismissing-avoidant attachment styles and had the least secure attachments of all of the groups. Cerda and colleagues (2014) argue that the development of positive attachments between parent and child can serve as a protective factor that deters opioid use in adolescence and young adulthood.

Getting off the Hook

One potential tool for helping a person get off of opioids is pharmacotherapy. The oldest form of pharmacotherapy for opioid addiction is replacement (agonist) therapy, with methadone as the first such drug developed and FDA-approved for that purpose. To some, it may seem reckless or contradictory to prescribe opioids to try to solve opioid addiction. Taking methadone, however, is not the same as injecting heroin. If used as directed (taken orally, in the prescribed dose), methadone will prevent withdrawal symptoms and help alleviate craving in people attempting to abstain from other opioids. Because it is taken orally, it will not produce a big "rush" to the brain like injected opioids, so the user should not feel high. The drug lasts longer, too, so the person maintains a level of opioids in their system that prevents unpleasant withdrawal symptoms. Buprenorphine is a similar, though less potent, medication, classified as a partial agonist. People may be on agonist treatment for years, whereas others may attempt to wean off of this treatment. Bell (2012) advises that agonist medications should not be seen as "cures" but rather as drug management programs that allow people to regain control over their situations. Compliant individuals whose lives were previously consumed with obtaining and using opioids can become functional with this sort of treatment.

Another pharmacological approach is antagonist therapy. The philosophy here is different: instead of replacing the opioid of abuse, the prescription medication will prevent the user from feeling pleasure from an opioid if they relapse. Anyone who uses an antagonist (ReVia˚, Vivitrol˚) as an aid to preventing relapse needs to go through detox first (get all of the abused opioid out of the system and through the withdrawals of abstinence). Opioid antagonists given to someone who is still physically dependent on an opioid will bring about sudden withdrawal symptoms.

A third category of prescriptions involves a combination of opioid agonists and antagonists. The most famous example of this is Suboxone®. This is really a replacement opioid, but with a twist: it includes an antagonist as a safe guard against abuse (which sometimes occurs in the case of methadone). If people try to take Suboxone˚ in any manner other than orally (say, by crushing the pills in order to snort or inject them), the antagonist portion of the formula will counteract the effects of the opioid in the medication. Essentially, the person is wasting their pills because they won't get high from them.

The evidence for the effectiveness of pharmacotherapy for opioid addiction is somewhat mixed. As reviewed by Connery (2015), agonist therapies appear to be generally more effective than antagonist therapies (e.g., naltrexone). Naltrexone tends to be associated with poor compliance, and there is an elevated risk of fatal overdose if antagonist use ceases and opioid use resumes. Bell (2012) notes that methadone tends to retain people in treatment longer, compared to buprenorphine; people taking buprenorphine are more likely to feel some symptoms of withdrawal compared to those on methadone. Importantly, it's relatively rare for heavy users of illicit opioids such as heroin to use only heroin. These individuals also tend to use alcohol, benzodiazepines (anti-anxiety medications), marijuana, or even cocaine. The agonist therapies do not seem to quell cravings or use of these other substances. For all of these medications, there are variations in individual responses, apparently influenced by genes that encode enzymes that metabolize opioids as well as opioid receptors. Those who do not feel an effect of methadone or buprenorphine are more likely to relapse.

Avoiding the Bait

National agencies such as the National Institute on Drug Abuse and the Centers for Disease Control see the epidemic of opioid abuse as a public health crisis, with so many cases of opioid abuse linked to prescription pain medications. There is consensus about the need to address not only prescription pain medications but also prescription treatments for ADHD. An important part of the focus will necessarily be placed on education. This needs to happen at multiple levels, including patients, prescribers, and producers of medications. Most states also have prescription drug monitoring programs (PDMPs)—databases that track names of both prescribers and patients. Information from these databases may be useful for identifying doctors who are inappropriately prescribing medications as well as patients who engage in "doctor shopping" to obtain multiple prescriptions for the same medication. Individuals identified through this reporting system could be subject to investigation and legal consequences. NIDA and other agencies are encouraging research into alternative medications with lower abuse potential.

The FDA recently took an unprecedented move by requesting Endo pharmaceuticals to take one of its pain medications (Opana ER) off the market because of the FDA's "concern that the benefits of the drug may no longer outweigh its risks" (FDA press release, June, 2017). Previously, Endo had reformulated the drug to try to reduce abuse risk (making it more difficult to snort or inject). But the FDA based their request on data indicating that the new formulation is still abusable through injection; moreover, the drug is linked to outbreaks of HIV, hepatitis C, and a blood clotting disorder. A month later, Endo agreed to pull their drug from the market. The drug was destined to disappear from pharmacies from the moment the FDA asked the company to stop making it because the federal agency has the power to enforce removal of a drug from the market by revoking their original approval.

Although public policy specialists are developing plans to fight the problem, individuals themselves must recognize the risk of opioids (and other substances) and avoid the bait. With regard to use of prescription opioids, doctors and patients can consider other options for pain management. Those with histories of opioid abuse or addiction should avoid prescribed opioid pain medications, even if they have been abstinent for a long period of time. For those seeking opioids to self-medicate psychological distress, pursuing natural highs, including positive social relationships with others, is generally a healthier and less expensive alternative (to which we will turn our attention in the final section of this book).

Chapter Summary

This chapter explores the phenomenon of addiction to opioids, including both prescription pain medications and illicit opioids such a heroin. These substances tend to promote fairly rapid development of tolerance, which may lead to a rapid progression of use and subsequent physical dependence. The mortality rate linked to these substances is largely due to fatal overdoses, although other risks of use include blood-borne illnesses linked to use of dirty needles and contaminants for users of street opioids. Presently, the U.S. is faced with a serious public health problem associated with over-prescription and abuse of opioid pain medications, which in some cases leads to people switching to street opioids when prescription opioids are no longer available. Opioid addiction is often a chronic, relapsing condition which can severely impair a person's ability to function in normal social, work, and school settings, resulting to impairments in quality of life. Prescription medications used to treat opioid addiction typically target opioid receptors and serve either as replacement drugs or as antagonists to prevent the person from feeling the effects of the drug. National efforts are underway to try to curtail opioid abuse.

The tolerant heroin addict can safely ingest a far greater amount of opium than the non-addict, for whom a large dose might cause coma or death from respiratory inhibition. Under increased internal or external stress, however, staying normal is not enough; the addict once again craves the feeling of getting high. At this point, he or she must again increase the opioid dose, either in frequency or in quantity. A common experience among addicts when they can do nothing more than stay "normal" is to construct their lives around "getting straight." They self-impose a period of abstinence, which usually involves an initial period of acute withdrawal and at least a few weeks of recuperative discomfort. Tolerance is lowered, and the satiation addict may once again experience the precious high, which for many stands out as the most salient experience of their lives. This often becomes a repetitive cycle.

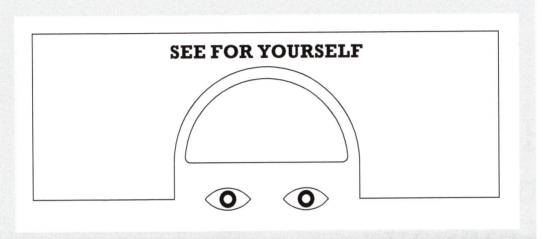

"A Twist On 'Involuntary Commitment': Some Heroin Users Request It." 2016. NPR: *All Things Considered.* 4:16

This piece opens up a controversy around court-mandated treatment, which some heroin users are requesting because of their desperation for treatment. **http://www.npr.org/sections/health-shots/2016/11/15/502029334/a-twist-on-involuntary-commitment-some-heroin-users-request-it**

Without Medical Support, DIY Detox Often Fails. 2017. Elana Gordon. NPR: Morning Edition. 3:51

This piece examines the extreme physical effects of heroin detox. Interviews with a former addict who experienced withdrawal from heroin as well as commentary from medical professionals are included. **http://www.npr.org/sections/health-shots/2017/07/03/533793801/without-medical-support-diy-detox-often-fails**

CHAPTER 5

Hey, What's in This Stuff, Anyway?

Alcohol, and not the dog, is man's best friend.

—W. C. Fields

To alcohol: the cause of and solution to all of life's problems.

—Homer Simpson

Introduction

There are many admonitions about the dangers of drink across time, place, and culture. Proverbs 23:29–35 in the Old Testament, for example, presents an insightful description of the progressive effects of alcohol, including those on the central nervous system:

> Who has woe? Who has sorrow? Who has strife? Who has complaining? Who has wounds without cause? Who has redness of eyes? Those who tarry long over wine, those who go to try mixed wine. Do not look at wine when it is red, when it sparkles in the cup and goes down smoothly. At the last it bites like a serpent, and stings like an adder. ... You will be like one who lies down

Source: https://commons.wikimedia.org/wiki/File:Ethanol-3D-balls.png.

in the midst of the sea, like one who lies on the top of a mast. "They struck me," you will say, "but I was not hurt; they beat me, but I did not feel it. When shall I awake? I will seek another drink."

The Old Testament also describes pleasure associated with alcohol: "Shall I leave my wine which cheers gods and men?" (Judges 9:13); "Mark when Amnon's heart is merry with wine" (2 Samuel 13:28).

This dichotomy was also prevalent in the Aztec city of Tenochtitlán, where drinking *pulque* (a very strong alcoholic beverage) was common practice, but public drunkenness was punishable by death (Escalante, et al., 2016).

The dual message of condemning excess while condoning moderation is at the heart of contemporary science and continued debate on this subject. In moderation, alcohol may have a beneficial effect, not only on the emotions but arguably on health as well (Klatsky, 2006). It is crossing that fine line, when use turns to abuse, that devastation begins to occur.

> Moderate alcohol consumption may have beneficial effects on health. These include decreased risk for heart disease and mortality due to heart disease, decreased risk of ischemic stroke (in which the arteries to the brain become narrowed or blocked, resulting in reduced blood flow), and decreased risk of diabetes.[39] In most Western countries where chronic diseases such as coronary heart disease (CHD), cancer, stroke, and diabetes are the primary causes of death, results from large epidemiological studies consistently show that alcohol reduces mortality, especially among middle-aged and older men and women—an association which is likely due to the protective effects of moderate alcohol consumption on CHD, diabetes, and ischemic stroke.[3]

[3]U.S. Department of Agriculture and U.S. Department of Health and Human Services. *2015–2020 Dietary Guidelines for Americans.* 8th ed., Appendix 9. Available at: **http://health.gov/dietaryguidelines/2015/guidelines/appendix-9/**

[39]U.S. Department of Agriculture. Scientific Report of the 2015 Dietary Guidelines Advisory Committee, Part D. Chapter 2, Table D2.3, p. 43. Available at: **http://health.gov/dietaryguidelines/2015-scientific-report/pdfs/scientific-report-of-the-2015-dietary-guidelines-advisory-committee.pdf**

Aside from seeking possible health benefits among middle aged men and women, why do so many people drink? Everyone has heard the statement, "Alcohol is a depressant." Are most people using alcohol as an anxiolytic, i.e., a drug to quell anxiety? Most people drink to feel better, to be more sociable and less sedate, not more so. Indeed, as we watch people who come to a cocktail party, we observe that after the first several drinks they seem to loosen up and become more relaxed. Rather than depressed, they appear to be more enthusiastic, animated, and expressive. As the party continues, and some guests are putting away their fifth or sixth drink, we notice a change in their behavior. Their speech becomes slurred, and they seem unable to comprehend simple concepts. If they drive, they are more likely to become involved in accidents because of delayed reaction time. Continued drinking may result in loss of consciousness.

How can we explain this apparent contradictory effect: initial excitation followed by sedation? The central nervous system has many checks and balances to prevent either chronic overstimulation or under-stimulation. Baseline levels of neurotransmission are maintained by the existence of the two types of synaptic connections mentioned earlier in Chapter 3. One type of connection is the excitatory pathway, which is responsible for increasing the state of arousal. Obviously there must be some means to regulate these excitatory connections, or everyone would be in a chronic state of excessive neural activity (which we commonly call seizures). The second type of connection is inhibitory, serving as a check on neuronal over-excitation. Alcohol works primarily by increasing inhibition; in low doses, the user will experience increased inhibition of pathways that are normally inhibitory (this is a phenomenon called disinhibition). As a result, a person's frontal lobes will be a little "looser" in terms of judgment, and the social lubricant effects of alcohol will be apparent. The drinker gets a little bit of a dopamine buzz, and this may be experienced as stimulating to the person. However, as drinking continues, more and more inhibition occurs in the brain, leading to sedative effects. Thinking and speech become slowed, and movement control becomes impaired. The stupor and slowed reaction time of excessive drinking set in, and the person is approaching the point of drowsiness. How does this seemingly benign beverage become the self-inflicted poison par excellence? In some ways, the answer may lie in the fact that not everyone who drinks, even excessively, becomes addicted. Historically, alcoholism was regarded as a sign of a weak or vicious personality. Consider these words from an 1897 temperance lecture, describing the behavior of someone under the influence of alcohol: *"But see that fiend incarnate with loathsome breath and oath-stained lips as he stumbles across the room to drag the dying wife from her last repose!"* (Craig, 1897, p. 446).

Inheriting Alcoholism

The contemporary perspective held by the National Council on Alcoholism, Alcoholics Anonymous, and the American Medical Association is quite different from the moral depravity explanation above. Alcoholism is regarded as a chronic and potentially fatal disease that pays little respect to strength or weakness of character. The disease concept, which has been invoked for other addictions as well, holds that addicts have inherited maladaptive biochemical responses to certain chemicals. Faulty genes can lead to the production of faulty enzymes that disturb the normal metabolism of substances; other faulty genes can change expression of neurotransmitter receptors which will alter a person's sensitivity to drugs. Both types of genetic differences can result in a pathological response to the drug, making the person vulnerable to addiction once they start using the substance.

Studies from the field of behavioral genetics have confirmed a heritable aspect of alcoholism. Identical twins, who share the same genes, are about twice as likely as fraternal twins, who share on average 50% of their genes, to resemble each other in terms of the presence of alcoholism. It has also been shown that 50% to 60% of the risk for alcoholism is genetically determined, for both men and women. Genes alone do not preordain that someone will be alcoholic; features in the environment along with gene–environment interactions account for the remainder of the risk (Crabbe, 2002; Heath et al., 1997; Heath & Martin, 1994; Kendler, Neal, Heath, Kessler, & Eaves, 1994; Prescott & Kendler, 1999).

To understand the theory of inherited alcoholism, consider the pathway by which alcohol is metabolized in the liver (Figure 5.2). In the first step, alcohol (ethanol) is converted to acetaldehyde using an enzyme called alcohol dehydrogenase (ADH). In the second step, acetaldehyde is then changed to acetate (acetic acid) and finally to carbon dioxide and water. The conversion of acetaldehyde to acetate requires another enzyme known as aldehyde dehydrogenase (ALDH). It is primarily *acetaldehyde* that is responsible for the negative effects associated with too much alcohol: nausea, vomiting, dizziness, and flushing of the skin. Disulfiram (Antabuse®) is sometimes prescribed (sometimes court ordered) to treat alcoholism. It works by inhibiting ALDH, delaying the body's metabolism of acetaldehyde into acetic acid. As a result, acetaldehyde will build up in a person's system if they drink while on disulfiram. The result is physical illness, intended to discourage the person from consuming alcohol again in the future.

Figure 5.2 **Metabolism of Alcohol** In the first step, alcohol (ethanol) is converted to acetaldehyde using the enzyme alcohol dehydrogenase (ADH) and the coenzyme nicotinamide adenine dinucleotide (NAD+). In the second step, acetaldehyde is changed to acetate and finally to carbon dioxide and water. The conversion of acetaldehyde to acetate requires aldehyde dehydrogenase (ALDH), as well as (NAD+).

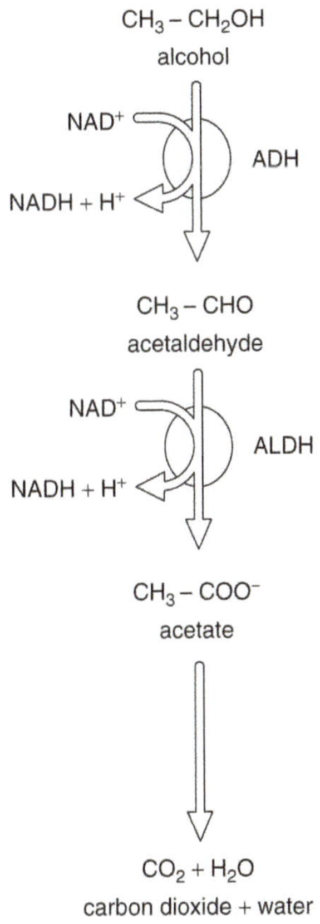

$$CH_3 - CH_2OH$$
alcohol

NAD^+

ADH

$NADH + H^+$

$$CH_3 - CHO$$
acetaldehyde

NAD^+

$ALDH$

$NADH + H^+$

$$CH_3 - COO^-$$
acetate

$$CO_2 + H_2O$$
carbon dioxide + water

Since enzymes (in this case ADH and ALDH) are involved in the metabolism of alcohol, alterations in their level would change the rate at which alcohol is processed. Habitual drinking will induce the liver to produce more of these enzymes, contributing to tolerance. Further, since the formation of enzymes ultimately depends on our genetic makeup, inappropriate drinking behavior may be partly explained by inherited irregularities of ADH, ALDH, or both. A number of studies show that certain individuals are at genetic risk for alcoholism because they metabolize alcohol differently from others. For instance, those who rapidly metabolize alcohol to acetaldehyde are more likely to feel the aversive effects of consumption: nausea, dizziness, and facial flushing. Genetic variants that promote this rapid production of acetaldehyde serve as a protective factor against heavy alcohol consumption. In addition, those who *slowly metabolize acetaldehyde* to acetic acid are those who are less likely to drink alcohol because they will be especially prone to suffering the negative effects of alcohol drinking when acetaldehyde accumulates in their bloodstream (Wall, Luczak, & Hiller-Sturmhofel, 2016). Ability to metabolize alcohol and acetaldehyde can vary across individuals, and certain genetic variants encoding for these enzymes tend to vary across ethnic groups.

In addition to genetic influences on metabolic enzymes, genes linked to several neurotransmitter receptors have been implicated in playing a role in risk for alcoholism. Some of these genes encode for receptors for GABA, opioids, dopamine, and other neurotransmitters. Interestingly, some of these genes may denote a risk for multiple addictions, such as a vulnerability to get hooked on both alcohol and opioids or both alcohol and nicotine.

Besides genes, there are experiential factors that increase one's ability to handle large amounts of alcohol. Before we blame our parents for all of our drug and alcohol problems, let us consider other factors besides "faulty" genes. The most obvious one is that addiction may be caused by the altered brain functioning resulting from excessive abuse of a substance (or behavior). Begley (2007) found that the brain exhibits plasticity and will rewire itself in response to challenges in normal neurochemistry caused by drugs or mind-altering activities. Even our thoughts, either positive or negative, can create changes in the brain.

According to Higley (cited by Heinz, 2006), a research scientist at the National Institute on Alcohol Abuse and Alcoholism, motherless rhesus monkeys (who grew up in the wild or in the lab) reacted less to drinks of high proof alcohol and other substances that affect the impact of the neurotransmitter GABA. As a result of stress-induced reduced sensitivity, these monkeys could drink huge quantities of alcohol, which they did when provided free access. Although genes play a decidedly important role in decreased sensitivity to the effects of alcohol, human studies have shown similar changes in people's brain chemistry as the result of loss and deprivation.

The Addictive Quality of Alcohol

Chronic ingestion of alcohol can cause neurochemical imbalances that are characteristic of alcoholism. This does not negate the concept of addictive disease, since many illnesses related to a genetic predisposition can also be worsened by environmental and behavioral factors. Diabetes, for example, is a disease whether it is inherited or environmentally induced. When the person with an alcohol use disorder faces potentially fatal consequences because of his or her uncontrolled behavior, altered biochemical processes may require the problem to be treated as a disease. The individual who alters his or her brain chemistry by excessive drinking is just as addicted as the person who happened to have "faulty" parents.

The concept of alcoholism as a disease—whether induced genetically, environmentally, or, more likely, through a combination of these factors—encourages us to examine the nature of alcohol's addicting power. Often we hear the comment that something (drug or other) is psychologically and not physically addicting. To invoke the notion of physically addicting, people are really getting at the notion of physical dependence. It is correct that some substances (such as opioids and alcohol) have a tendency to promote physical dependence, as evidenced by the development of tolerance and appearance of withdrawal symptoms. However, such a distinction is artificial and has no place in a sophisticated discussion on addiction. The distinction implies that the central nervous system (psychological addiction) is somehow separate from the rest of the body's functions (physical addiction), which it is not. Therefore, this is not a useful distinction.

Many theories attempt to explain the addictive quality of alcohol. A cursory look at the molecular structures of the substances that are most addicting leaves one with the feeling that alcohol does not belong in this group. As seen in Figure 5.3, alcohol is the only substance that does not contain the element nitrogen (indicated as N in the formulas). In addition, alcohol is by far the smallest of the molecules in Figure 5.3. Generally, one thinks of addicting molecules as those of moderate size (for example, cocaine) that contain nitrogen. Since alcohol is much smaller than the other addicting molecules and contains no nitrogen, scientists have looked to other factors that contribute to its addictive nature.

Figure 5.3 Chemical Structures of the Mind Benders Since alcohol is much smaller than the other addicting molecules and contains no nitrogen, scientists have looked to other factors that contribute to its addictive nature.

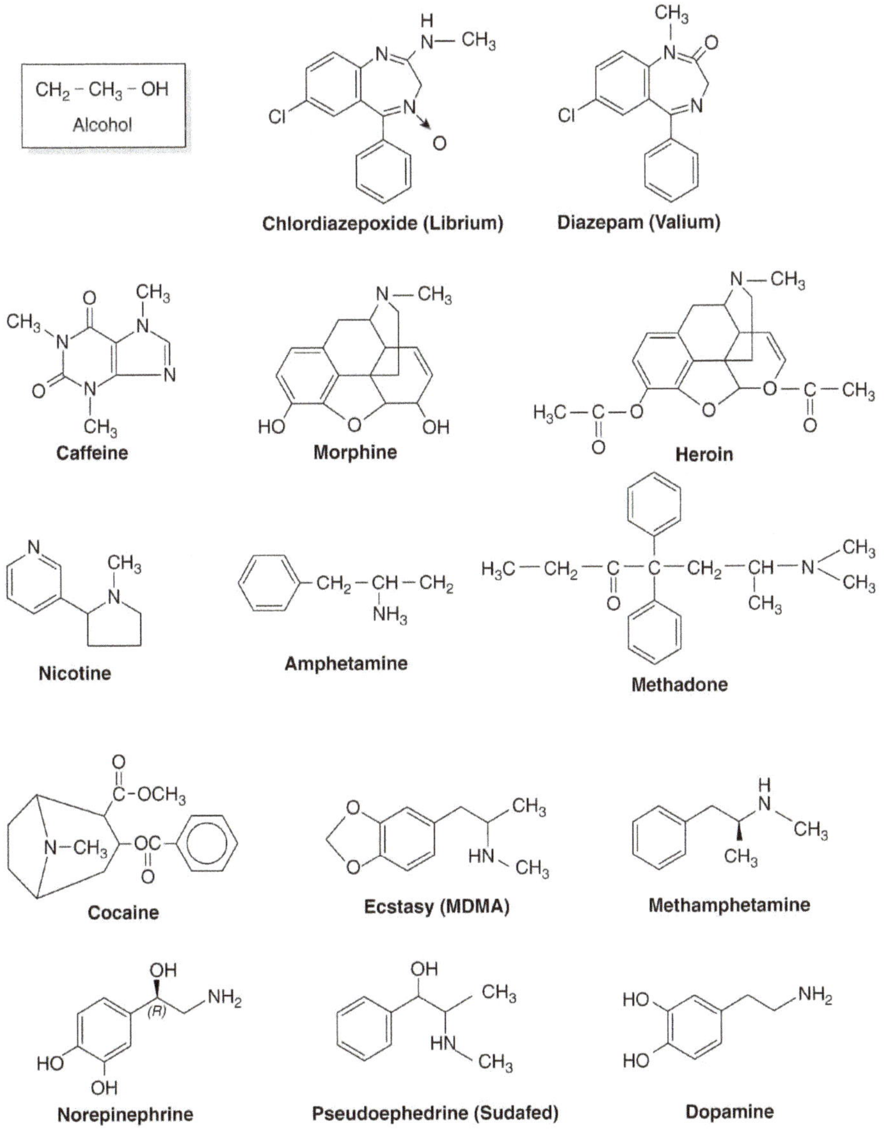

The answer to what makes alcohol addictive is still being feverishly researched. It turns out that it's complicated because alcohol is a messy substance! Most chemicals that we consider drugs have fairly specific ways in which they target the function of brain cells. For instance, a drug might bind and activate receptors for a specific neurotransmitter, increasing the activity of the receptors; or, conversely, a drug could bind and block receptors, preventing them from being activated by their own neurotransmitters. Whereas most drugs tend to target a relatively small number of neurotransmitters, alcohol seems to affect the functioning of several different neurotransmitter systems. Moreover, there are some data to suggest that metabolites of alcohol (either acetaldehyde itself, or an opioid-like metabolite produced by the synthesis of acetaldehyde with dopamine) may be responsible for some of the rewarding effects of alcohol (Soderpalm & Ericson, 2013). With so many potential targets, we will try to keep our discussion primarily focused on those which are currently identified as the major players in alcohol's chemical effects on the brain.

Neurotransmitter Regulation and Dysregulation

Heinz (2006) considers the effects of other neurochemicals involved in chronic alcohol ingestion—glutamate and GABA (gamma aminobutyric acid). These molecules influence our moods as well the uncomfortable and sometimes dangerous symptoms of withdrawal. Glutamate is the primary excitatory neurotransmitter in the brain, and when released from one neuron and detected by another one, it will encourage the receiving cell to fire. As a result, it increases overall neural activity. Any substance that enhances glutamate release from the presynaptic neuron will increase the rate of neurotransmission, which may result in arousal, depending on the neuronal pathways involved. GABA is the primary inhibitory neurotransmitter in the brain, and it does the opposite of glutamate: it decreases neural activity. In essence, GABA is the yang to glutamate's yin! It is the combined effect of alcohol on these two neurotransmitters, shown in Figure 5.4, which explains why alcohol is such a potent sedative.

Alcohol blocks glutamate from binding to its NMDA (N-methyl-D-aspartic acid, a type of glutamate) receptors. This creates a decrease in glutamate-induced neurotransmission resulting in decreased neural activity. Behaviorally, this can manifest as sluggish thinking, feelings of relaxation, sleepiness or even passing out. This is one of the reasons alcohol is often used for its calming effect in stressful situations. Alcohol also enhances the effect of GABA, resulting in a further decrease in neurotransmission (remember, GABA is an inhibitory neurotransmitter). Glutamate and GABA are the most widely-distributed neurotransmitters, found in virtually all major brain regions. So the combined effect of decreased glutamate and increased GABA which amplifies as consumption continues may be the drunken stupor, slurred speech, instability, impairment, and sleepiness characteristic of excessive alcohol consumption.

So we see how alcohol produces powerful states of sedation, but the human brain is not to be trifled with. The phrase "synaptic homeostasis" describes the brain's reaction to sustained attempts to achieve ecstasy by altering our "normal" neurotransmission. Consider the attempt, using alcohol, to achieve relaxation by blocking the binding of glutamate to NMDA receptors. For most moderate alcohol consumers, this works well. However, sustained heavy drinking alters the brain in a way that decreases the effect of the amount of alcohol that initially increased positive feelings. In order to counter this blocking of glutamate to NMDA receptors, the postsynaptic membrane creates more NMDA receptors. Also, neurons that release glutamate may increase how much of this neurotransmitter they release. Changes also occur within the GABA system: because of the excessive amount of GABA activity produced by repeated alcohol consumption, neurons decrease the number of GABA receptors they express, or the receptors may become less sensitive to alcohol. Neurons that release GABA also decrease how much GABA they release. More alcohol must be consumed to achieve the desired pleasure. After a while, alcohol is consumed mostly to not feel "crappy," and the hope of experiencing ecstasy is long gone.

Figure 5.4 Effect of Alcohol on Neurotransmission Alcohol excites inhibitory GABA neurons but inhibits excitatory glutamate neurons (left panel). Increased inhibition coupled with decreased excitation reduces neurotransmitter release (right panel).

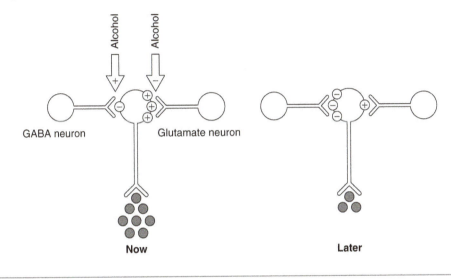

Alcohol also appears to affect several other neurotransmitter receptors, including the nicotinic type of acetylcholine receptors (which are responsible for nicotine's rewarding effects). The ability of alcohol to elevate dopamine levels in the nucleus accumbens is thought to be due, in part, to this effect on acetylcholine receptors, along with the possibly interaction of alcohol, or its metabolites, with opioid and glycine receptors (Soderpalm & Ericson, 2013). As stated earlier, alcohol is a messy substance, and it appears to influence many systems in the brain in rather complicated ways which contribute not only to the short-term effects of alcohol intoxication but also the long-term effects of alcohol dependence.

Harmful Effects on the Mind, Body, and Brain

Aside from understanding alcohol's relatively transient effects on excitatory and inhibitory neuro-transmission and potential health benefits from drinking in moderation (discussed below), a thorough risk–benefit analysis must also consider the dark side. Alcohol poses both acute risks as well as chronic risks, many of which can be very serious. Most people are aware—through either direct experience or by observing others—that a single episode of drinking can lead to seriously impaired judgment and poor behavioral control. This puts a person at risk for accidents, making it dangerous if the drinker drives under this condition. Alcohol's harmful effect on judgment is legendary, as evidenced by frequent connections with crime and violence. Binge drinking commonly leads people to experience nausea and vomiting, and hangovers the day after can add to the physically-punishing effects of over-imbibing. With high enough blood alcohol levels, individuals can pass out. It is also possible to suffer alcohol poisoning, which may result in an acute lethal overdose. Alternatively, an individual may continue to vomit after passing out, risking death by aspiration. However, if drinking in moderation (e.g., 1–2 drinks per day), people are likely to avoid many of these risks. Keep in mind that it's not just the number of drinks per day, but the rate at which they are consumed. A healthy person can process a standard drink every 60–90 minutes. An individual who consumes in moderation and at a normal rate of consumption (i.e., they don't "slam" their drinks) need not be overly concerned about acute risks of alcohol drinking.

One obvious problem with moderate drinking , as attested to by legions of neurologists, cardiologists, liver specialists, and mental health professionals, is that not everyone who attempts to have only one or two can actually do so, and therein lie many of the chronic risks associated with alcohol consumption. Alcohol can affect many organs within the body, so before drinking heavily—and doing so repeatedly—it is incumbent on people to run through a mental inventory of organs affected by alcohol and ask, "Am I going to need that organ later?" Generally, the answer is "yes"! In addition to the severe brain damage and associated dementia related to chronic and heavy alcohol consumption, one must also consider its effects on other systems of the body. The liver, for example, finds alcohol extremely alarming. Inflammation of the liver (hepatitis) can lead to scarring (cirrhosis) and eventual death through liver failure. Alcohol can damage the lining of the gastrointestinal tract, promoting internal bleeding and reducing the absorption of nutrients. Alcohol can also lead to inflammation of the pancreas. Heavy drinking can increase blood pressure and damage the heart muscle (cardiomyopathy). Chronic heavy drinking leads to dysregulation of the HPA (hypothalamic-pituitary-adrenal) axis, affecting a person's stress responses. Alcohol has also been linked to cancers of the mouth, throat, esophagus, colon, and breast. For many years, the mechanism by which alcohol promotes cancer was unclear, but researchers now believe that acetaldehyde (remember, that first breakdown product produced in alcohol metabolism?) is an important culprit (Eriksson, 2015)

For the heavy drinkers who develop physical dependence, there are medical concerns regarding cessation of drinking because of profound withdrawal symptoms if alcohol use abruptly stops. Recall that alcohol creates a great deal of neural inhibition by increasing the action of GABA (an inhibitory neurotransmitter) and decreasing the action of glutamate (an excitatory neurotransmitter) and that compensatory mechanisms try to counteract the effects of alcohol on these neuronal systems. If alcohol is no longer in the system, the brain's level of excitation will be *increased*, leading to a risk of seizures. In some cases, people may suffer lethal seizures and convulsions; according to Trevisan et al. (1998), about 5% of people who suffer *delirium tremens* (severe alcohol withdrawal) die from seizures. For this reason, medical supervision of alcohol withdrawal is highly recommended. During withdrawal, and persisting for weeks if not months, an individual's stress hormone system is elevated, promoting feelings of anxiety and dysphoria. Such feelings could prompt a desire to resume drinking.

Even moderate drinking carries health risks. Alcohol can disrupt sleep (especially suppressing rapid eye movement, or REM, sleep), and it can interact adversely with acetaminophen (Tylenol), antidepressants, painkillers, sedatives, and anticonvulsants. The interaction with acetaminophen is of special concern for your liver, as both of these substances pose a challenge to it; combining them makes it more likely that the liver will be harmed.

Finally, we should recognize that alcohol consumption during pregnancy poses risks for the unborn child. The timing and amount of alcohol exposure affect the severity of the damage done. More severe effects are seen with heavy drinking (either bingeing or regular heavy consumption). The first trimester of pregnancy seems to be an especially vulnerable time for producing the teratogenic effects categorized as Fetal Alcohol Spectrum Disorders (FASD). In the most severe cases, the infant will suffer extensive damage to brain development, along with alterations in head and facial features. The threshold for producing FASD is not known, so the National Institute on Alcohol Abuse and Alcoholism recommends complete abstention from drinking during pregnancy (NIAAA, 2016).

Alcoholism: A Reward Deficit Disorder?

George Koob (2013), director of NIAAA, has described alcoholism as a "reward deficit disorder," recognizing the negative emotional state that emerges with alcohol dependence. Although alcohol initially activates brain reward systems, repeated consumption activates what Koob calls an "anti-reward" system. This is brought about by the brain making adaptations to try to restore homeostasis. Part of the anti-reward system is the stress system involving the HPA-axis. Over time, tolerance to the rewarding effects of alcohol increases; meanwhile, the stress system activation increases, becoming sensitized with repeated cycles of intoxication and withdrawal. Together, decreased reward and increased stress responses create a negative emotional state marked by anxiety and dysphoria. This emotional state helps drive continued alcohol intake and is key to the negative reinforcing effects of alcohol. It's important to note that even after the worst of physical withdrawals have subsided in an individual trying to remain abstinent, the negative emotional state can persist for weeks or even months. This state can help prompt relapse.

Do I Have a Drinking Problem?

Surely, multiple biological events, as well as powerful psychological and social factors (discussed below), are related to alcohol's addictive properties. Whatever the constellation of causes (which may be different in each person), alcohol addiction remains one of the world's most serious drug problems. To complicate matters further, most people who abuse alcohol have difficulty in admitting that it presents a serious problem in their lives. The questions in Table 5.1 are suggested for people who want to take an honest inventory of their current relationship with alcohol. They are designed to enhance self-awareness, with the objectives of improved levels of personal and social responsibility. "Thus, a series of questions that circumvent denial have been devised that can identify most people with alcoholism. The list of questions in Table 5.1 provides the most useful single guide I know to the clinical interview" (Vaillant, 1983, p. 296).

Sobriety and the Brain: What If I Quit?

Let's suppose that you or someone you are trying to help wants to quit drinking. In addition to being mindful of all the psychological booby traps en route to health and well-being, we shall now examine the brain's reactions to getting sober. Case examples of Regis and Mike illustrate two primary neurobiological challenges to sobriety: *conditioned desire* and *conditioned withdrawal;* however, new medications are proving helpful.

Regis stopped drinking about 2 years ago with the help of a buddy who turned him on to AA. His girlfriend works as a waitress in the neighborhood bar and Regis picks her up after work on Saturday nights to spend some time together and to give her a ride home. He doesn't go inside the bar; rather, he waits in the car until the customers begin to leave. Once, after watching patrons becoming energized at the proverbial "last call for alcohol," Regis began to leap from his car, reacting to heavy sensations of scotch in his nostrils and throat.

Regis was experiencing *conditioned desire*. When in situations similar to the ones in which the person had always consumed alcohol, the "feeling of the need for alcohol becomes almost irresistible. Then, even after years of abstinence, consuming a single drink can set off a powerful longing to imbibe more and more" (Heinz, 2006, p. 57).

Table 5.1 Questions That Circumvent Denial

1. Do you occasionally drink heavily after a disappointment or a quarrel, or when the boss gives you a hard time?

2. When you have trouble or feel under pressure, do you always drink more heavily than usual?

3. Have you noticed that you are able to handle more liquor than you did when you were first drinking?

4. Do you ever wake up the "morning after" and discover that you could not remember part of the evening before, even though your friends tell you that you did not pass out?

5. When drinking with other people, do you try to have a few extra drinks when others will not know it?

6. Are there certain occasions when you feel uncomfortable if alcohol is not available?

7. Have you recently noticed that when you begin drinking you are in more of a hurry to get the first drink than you used to be?

8. Do you sometimes feel a little guilty about your drinking?

9. Are you secretly irritated when your family or friends discuss your drinking?

10. Have you recently noticed an increase in the frequency of your memory "blackouts"?

11. Do you often find that you wish to continue drinking after your friends say that they have had enough?

12. Do you usually have a reason for the occasions when you drink heavily?

13. When you are sober, do you often regret things you have done or said while drinking?

14. Have you tried switching brands or following different plans for controlling your drinking?

15. Have you often failed to keep promises you have made to yourself about controlling or cutting down on your drinking?

16. Have you tried to control your drinking by making a change in jobs, or moving to a new location?

17. Do you try to avoid family and close friends when you are drinking?

18. Are you having an increasing number of financial or work problems?

19. Do more people seem to be treating you unfairly without good reason?

20. Do you eat very little or irregularly when you are drinking?

21. Do you sometimes have "the shakes" in the morning and find that it helps to have a little drink?

22. Have you recently noticed that you cannot drink as much as you once did?

Source: Reprinted by permission of the publisher from The Natural History of Alcoholism by *George E. Vaillant, pp. 296–297, Cambridge, MA: Harvard University Press. Copyright © 1983 by the President and Fellows of Harvard College.*

A Related Phenomenon is Conditioned Withdrawal

Mike had been sober for the past 5 years. He had reestablished good relationships with his two children and his wife who had threatened to leave if he didn't "clean up his act." He worked as manager of several commercial buildings. Suddenly, when the buildings were purchased by another corporation, Mike found himself out of a job. His initial response was to seek assistance from an employment agency. As time went on, the agency couldn't open any doors for interviews and Mike started to feel desperate. Tension in his primary relationship began to build as his wife complained about finances and her fears that Mike would fall back into old habits. Just after his older daughter blurted out that he was "becoming a bum," Mike started to think about running down to the pub and downing a few beers. Suddenly, he began to sweat profusely and his hands began to shake. Although he hadn't drunk in years, he felt similar withdrawal effects as after months of binge drinking.

Neuroscience can explain conditioned desire and conditioned withdrawal by tracking the brain's reactions to prolonged and excessive use of alcohol. Although high tolerance to alcohol seems like a beneficial adaptation, it functions more like a curse. As shown in Figure 5.4, alcohol affects neural mechanisms that regulate GABA and glutamate. Figure 5.5 provides an illustration for our discussion of why withdrawal occurs.

Figure 5.5 Mechanism of Alcohol Withdrawal The low level of neurotransmitters in chronic alcohol abuse leads to a compensatory increase in the number of postsynaptic glutamate receptors (middle panel). Under these conditions, a normal amount of neurotransmitters (left panel), as would occur when alcohol is not present, stimulates more receptors and thereby causes hyper-excitation (right panel). Because chronic alcohol abuse has down-regulated, the brain's GABA receptors, the brain becomes hyper-excitable.

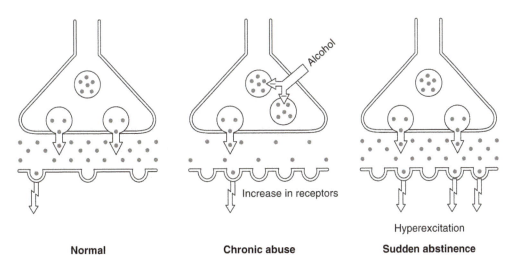

Regis's and Mike's symptoms are related to the brain's adaptation to chronic alcohol abuse, as described above when we discussed the effects of alcohol on the brain. To further elaborate, see Figures 5.4 and 5.5. Alcohol is shown blocking the binding of glutamate to NMDA receptors (Figure 5.4). To increase the probability of capturing glutamate, the brain compensates by increasing or sensitizing the number of NMDA receptors in the brains of those who chronically consume alcohol (Figure 5.5, middle). When alcohol use is suddenly interrupted (either through forced abstinence—e.g., jail—or voluntarily, by "going on the wagon"), the receptors continue to be more sensitive (Figure 5.5, right). This hyperactivity results in an overreaction to glutamate (no longer blocked by alcohol), which causes symptoms of withdrawal such as cramps, unstable blood circulation, tremors, and anxiety. These symptoms may occur when alcohol is withdrawn for a few days or even overnight. In addition, the excessive neural activity can produce seizures which can destroy large numbers of neurons, causing dementia or long-term damage to the neuronal system (Heinz, 2006).

NMDA receptors remain hypersensitive while GABA receptors continue to be undersensitive, resulting from the overactivity of GABA induced by alcohol ingestion (see Figure 5.4). These withdrawal symptoms can be treated with drugs such as chlormethiazole or a benzodiazepine, which bind GABA receptors in the absence of alcohol and with a deficit of GABA in the brain. Another medication acamprosate, is effective in suppressing the hyperexcitability of NMDA receptors and seems especially helpful for people like Mike who suffers from conditioned withdrawal. Heinz (2006) reports that that 30% to 40% of patients who take acamprosate during the first few months of abstinence remain dry for the first year after detoxification. Of course, this leaves a great deal of work for counselors and mentors who are vitally needed to transcend the limits of medical intervention.

Now back to Regis and his apparently conditioned desire. Just as in the case of compensating for excess activity of GABA and decreased activity of glutamate, the brain deals with another major factor in addiction—overstimulation of the reward center. To compensate for what it interprets as excessive bombardment from dopamine, the brain reduces the number of binding sites (called D2 receptors) on neurons that process dopamine. MRI studies show that when people with a history of alcohol dependence, like Regis, look at photographs of beer and wine, the regions of the brain that control attention are aroused more than in non-alcoholics (Heinz, 2006). The fewer D2 receptors available, the more attention is aroused by the sight of an alcohol-related image, and the more difficult it is for the individual to find satisfaction from anything besides alcohol, be it relationships, hobbies, or food. Some may desperately seek dopamine by switching to another drug or a behavioral addiction such as gambling or sex.

Although dopamine directs attention and desire, other neurochemicals—the endorphins—are intimately involved in the experience of pleasure. As discussed above, repeated overstimulation alters the system. Because alcoholics develop an increased number of binding sites for the endorphins, when they consume alcohol their neurons bind more endorphins, resulting in increased pleasure from drinking. Naltrexone is a drug that can considerably reduce the risk of relapse by blocking the receptor sites for the endorphins and causing a taste that ranges in quality from foreign to terrible. However, the need for psychosocial intervention is highlighted by the fact that by the second or third dose, the drink begins to taste good. Naltrexone might help to avert the first sip, but after the gate is open, all hell can still break loose.

Redeeming Alcohol: The Benefits of Booze

*[N]one seemed to think the injury arose from the use of a
bad thing, but from the abuse of a good thing.*
—Abraham Lincoln, addressing the Illinois Temperance Society, 1842

I have taken more out of alcohol than alcohol has taken out of me.
—Winston Churchill

One of the authors (Milkman) has an ongoing argument with his daughter about the concept of *natural highs*. She claims that there is no such thing as "unnatural" because everything that exists, including plastics, cocaine, atomic bombs, marijuana, and cigarettes, is derived from substances that exist here on earth. From her point of view, there is no valid distinction between "natural" and "unnatural" highs. Even synthesized drugs are "natural" because they are made from chemical elements, which are natural. Can one say, without being moralistic, that moderate consumption of alcohol, even to the point of feeling somewhat euphoric (without risk of harm), is not a natural high?

Following from our definition, that "natural highs are self-induced changes in brain chemistry that result in positive feeling states, health, and well-being for the individual and society," does moderate consumption of beer, wine, or spirits constitute an alcohol-mediated natural high? To be sure, there are vested interests in showing the bright or dark side of drinking. Presently, however, a preponderance of evidence accrued over the past 30 years (not without controversy) shows substantial health benefits from moderate consumption. Despite centuries of biblical, religious, moral, and medical objections to alcohol, what new evidence supports the proclamation of "health benefits"?

We shall begin our discussion of healthy drinking by defining what qualifies as reasonable or moderate consumption. First of all, what actually constitutes a drink? In the United States, "one drink" is usually defined as 12 ounces of beer, 5 ounces of wine, or 1.5 ounces of spirits. Each delivers about 12 to 14 grams of alcohol. Check your bartender's skills—he or she might pour a shot twice that amount—no doubt doing you a "big favor." The concept of moderation is even more slippery. In some studies, less than one drink per day is considered moderate, and in others, daily consumption of as much as three to four drinks qualifies (Dufour, 1999). The current consensus, in accordance with the U.S. Department of Agriculture and the Dietary Guidelines for Americans, is no more than one to two drinks per day for men and no more than one drink per day for women (U.S. Department of Health and Human Services [USDHHS], 2004).

Linking Alcohol and Health

Pathologists first discovered hints of the link between alcohol consumption and cardiovascular health about 100 years ago, noting that the large arteries of people who died of alcohol-related liver disease were remarkably "clean"—that is, free of arteriosclerosis (fatty plaque). According to Klatsky (2006), senior consultant in cardiology at the Kaiser Permanente Medical Center, a meta-analysis of 28 previously published studies on the relationship between alcohol intake and cardiovascular disease (CVD) showed that the risk of acquiring CVD went down as the daily amount of alcohol consumed went up from 0 to 25 grams (about 2 standard drinks). At 2 drinks, an individual's risk of a major coronary heart disease (CHD) "event"—either heart attack or death—"was 20 percent lower than for someone who did not drink at all" (p. 76). Furthermore, at a meeting of the American Heart Association in 2002, Klatsky and colleagues reviewed an updated analysis of 128,934 patients who had checkups between 1978 and 1985. They found that "those who had one or two alcoholic beverages a day had a 32 percent lower risk of dying from CHD than abstainers did" (p. 77).

Further, as presented in an article published by the Harvard School of Public Health (2008) entitled "The Nutrition Source: Alcohol and Heart Disease," it was discovered that "...more than 100 prospective studies show an inverse association between moderate drinking and risk of heart attack, ischemic (clot-caused) stroke, peripheral vascular disease, sudden cardiac death, and death from all cardiovascular causes" (p. 2). Table 5.2 summarizes the results of some of the largest studies.

Table 5.2 Results of Some Large Prospective Studies of Alcohol Consumption and Cardiovascular Disease

Participants	Duration	Association With Moderate Alcohol Consumption
Japan Collaborative Cohort Study for Evaluation of Cancer Risk cohort: 97,432 men and women aged 40 to 79 (Lin et al., 2005)	10 years	12–20% decreased risk of all-cause mortality in men and women who consumed less than 23 grams per day of alcohol; heavy drinking increased the risk of all-cause mortality
Kaiser Permanente cohort: 123,840 men and women aged 30+ (Klatsky, Armstrong, & Friedman, 1990)	10 years	40% reduction in fatal myocardial infarction; 20% reduction in cardiovascular mortality; 80% increase in fatal hemorrhagic stroke
Nurses' Health Study: 85,709 female nurses aged 34–59 (Stampfer, Colditz, Willett, Speizer, & Hennekens, 1988)	12 years	17% lower risk of all-cause mortality; an earlier report showed a 40% reduction in risk of CHD and 70% reduction in risk of ischemic stroke
Physicians' Health Study: 22,071 male physicians aged 40–84 (Camargo et al., 1997)	11 years	30–35% reduced risk of angina and myocardial infarction; 20–30% reduced risk of cardiovascular death
Cancer Prevention Study II: 489,626 men and women aged 30–104 (Thun et al., 1997)	9 years	30–40% reduced risk of cardiovascular death; mortality from all causes increased with heavier drinking, particularly among adults under age 60
Eastern France cohort: 34,014 men and women (Renaud, Gueguen, Siest, & Salamon, 1999)	10–15 years	25–30% reduced risk of cardiovascular death
Health Professionals Follow-up Study: 38,077 male health professionals aged 40–75 (Mukamal et al., 2003)	12 years	35% reduced risk of myocardial infarction

Source: Reprinted from The Nutrition Source, *Department of Nutrition, Harvard School of Public Health, "Alcohol and Heart Disease," http://www.hsph.harvard.edu/nutritionsource/what-should-you-eat/alcohol-and-heart-disease/index.html. Copyright © 2008 by the President and Fellows of Harvard College.*

Is Red Wine Better for You?

Nearly 200 years ago, an Irish physician made the observation that angina (chest pain) was less frequent among the French than the Irish and attributed the difference to the "French habits and mode of living" (Black, 1819). The comparatively low rate of cardiovascular disease in France, despite their reputed diet as rich in butter and cheese, has become known as the "French paradox." The view that health benefits derive from the chemistry of red wine is challenged by the fact that there are many other aspects of French lifestyle that may influence health outcomes. For example, the French diet, particularly for those who live in southern France, is similar to those of other Mediterranean cultures, which are also lower in heart disease.

Some studies suggest that red wine, especially when drunk with a meal, offers more health benefits than beer or spirits—that is, wine-drinking cultures fare better in terms of health (e.g., Rimm, Klatsky, Grobbee, & Stampfer, 1996; St. Leger, Cochrane, & Moore, 1979). Although it has been speculated that besides alcohol, red wine may contain health-augmenting substances, a Health Professionals Follow-up Study of 38,000 men carried out over a 12-year period showed that, independent of type of beverage (i.e., wine, beer, or spirits) or whether it was drunk with or without food, moderate drinkers were 30% to 35% less likely to have heart attacks than nondrinkers. Men who drank every day were at lower risk than those who drank once or twice per week (Mukamal et al., 2003). As in many aspects of health and nutrition, it appears that the jury is still out regarding red wine.

How does an ordinary person sensibly decide about how to manage alcohol, truly one of the world's amazing chemicals? Further evidence of alcohol's potential benefits to health are shown below:

- Moderate alcohol consumption, according to the *2015–2020 Dietary Guidelines for Americans*, is up to 1 drink per day for women and up to 2 drinks per day for men (USDA, 2015).

- Moderate alcohol consumption may have beneficial effects on health. These include decreased risk for heart disease and mortality due to heart disease, decreased risk of ischemic stroke (in which the arteries to the brain become narrowed or blocked, resulting in reduced blood flow), and decreased risk of diabetes (USDA, 2015).

- In most Western countries where chronic diseases such as coronary heart disease (CHD), cancer, stroke, and diabetes are the primary causes of death, results from large epidemiological studies consistently show that alcohol reduces mortality, especially among middle-aged and older men and women—an association which is likely due to the protective effects of moderate alcohol consumption on CHD, diabetes, and ischemic stroke (USDA, 2015).

- It is estimated that 26,000 deaths were averted in 2005 because of reductions in ischemic heart disease, ischemic stroke, and diabetes from the benefits attributed to moderate alcohol consumption (Danaei, G., et al., 2009).

- Expanding our understanding of the relationship between moderate alcohol consumption and potential health benefits remains a challenge, and although there are positive effects, alcohol may not benefit everyone who drinks moderately.

Although there seems to be an abundance of evidence showing that moderate alcohol consumption is protective for a variety of diseases, the jury is evidently still out on the subject of whether even moderate consumption confers the purported health benefits:

> Estimates of mortality risk from alcohol are significantly altered by study design and characteristics. Meta-analyses adjusting for these factors find that low-volume alcohol consumption has no net mortality benefit compared with lifetime absten-tion or occasional drinking. These findings have implications for public policy, the

formulation of low-risk drinking guidelines, and future research on alcohol and health. (Stockwell et. al., 2016, p. 185)

Hold the Press: What About Cancer and Other Potentially Fatal Outcomes?

So you no longer smoke, you eat fruits and veggies, exercise robustly, and gracefully pour one or two glasses of red wine each night. Just when drinkers were clapping their hands about how alcohol lowers the risk of heart disease, a major study conducted by the International Agency for Research on Cancer (IARC-WHO; Baan et al., 2007) throws a cat among the pigeons.

Although moderate drinking may improve coronary health, drinking even a small amount of alcohol daily could increase the risk of colon and breast cancer—two of the four major cancer killers. Based on findings from the European Prospective Investigation into Cancer and Nutrition (EPIC), which asked more than 480,000 Europeans about their drinking, those who drank over one drink a day (100 grams in a week) increase their chances of developing colon cancer by about 15%. For those who consume about four drinks daily, the risk is 40% higher. Apparently, the risk is dose dependent—the more you drink, the more your risk goes up (Baan et al., 2007). Regular consumption of more than one drink per day has been associated with an increased risk of breast cancer in women (Hamajima et al., 2002).

According to Rehm, head of public health and regulatory policies at the Ontario Center for Addiction and Mental Health, and his colleagues (Rehm, Patra, & Popova, 2007), alcohol is detrimental for more than 60 diagnoses. After smoking and obesity, alcohol consumption is the third-biggest cause of preventable death in the United States (R. N. Anderson, 2002). In 2002, the most recent year for which data is available, drinking caused 100,000 deaths—including more than 12,000 cancer deaths, comparable to the 13,674 killed in alcohol-related traffic accidents. The same data show that about 30,000 fatal heart attacks were prevented by moderate alcohol consumption. However, the evidence for alcohol preventing heart attacks is less reliable. Compared with teetotalers, those who drink moderately tend to exercise more, have better medical insurance, and have lower fat-to-muscle ratios, that is, they probably have had fewer heart attacks because of factors other than alcohol intake.

To Quit or Not to Quit?

Inevitably, some who are now considering abstinence are thinking that if they have already caused the damage, why not have some fun? To help you decide, there are additional data. Quitting seems to eventually reverse the added risk. In a study published in the *International Journal of Cancer,* Rehm et al. (2007) showed that the risk of head and neck and esophageal cancer decreased significantly within 10 years of giving up booze and was the same as that for nondrinkers after 20 years. Although even one or two drinks a day raised a woman's breast cancer risk, there was no increased risk for those who reported having a few drinks a week. So where is the tipping point, or put another way, what is the threshold for abuse?

Like many short-term pleasure/long-term pain puzzles, risk–benefit analysis will be different for each person. A person in his or her late teens or early twenties with very low risk of heart disease will probably suffer more damage from loss of judgment associated with drinking than gain any long-term cardiovascular benefits. On the other hand, a 50-year-old man with neither a personal history of alcohol abuse nor family history of cancer may enjoy distinct cardiovascular benefits from moderate consumption. Correspondingly, a younger woman with no cardiac risk and a family history of breast cancer would probably do better not to drink. Finally, in deciding whether to drink, you may want to ask, how important is alcohol to your lifestyle and how much benefit do you personally derive in terms of pleasure, anxiety management, and connections with others?

Other Sedating Substances: Benzodiazepines

Alcohol is not the only substance that amplifies GABA activity, thus producing large amounts of neural inhibition. Drugs which have been traditionally used either to induce sleep, treat seizures, or calm anxiety work on the same receptors as alcohol, although not as potently. Benzodiazepines are often given to individuals in medical settings who are going off of alcohol; because they have similar effects on GABA, they help control withdrawal symptoms, preventing life-threatening seizures. The intention is that the person will eventually be able to wean off of the benzodiazepine, rather than simply replacing one substance with another.

Benzodiazepines are sometimes prescribed for people with anxiety disorders and are another example of prescription medications that are sometimes abused. Like alcohol and opioids, these drugs can calm the negative emotions arising in the amygdala of the brain. Unfortunately, if taken daily, people may develop physical dependency on these substances; those who develop tolerance to benzodiazepines are at risk for withdrawal symptoms. Though not as likely to be fatal as alcohol withdrawal, there are cases where people have experienced lethal seizures when abruptly discontinuing benzodiazepines. Therefore, medical supervision and/or tapering off of these substances is wise if efforts are made to quit them. The risk for overdose, severe withdrawal symptoms, and seizures is exponentially increased when an individual combines alcohol and benzodiazepines to achieve altered states of consciousness.

Chapter Summary

Beginning with a short discourse on biblical admonitions about the abuse of alcohol, we move to a science-based discussion of why some people seem to be more vulnerable to alcohol than others. Aside from cultural and environmental influences, genetics are implicated because they bring about individual differences (metabolic and neurochemical) in how people react to the same drug. The addictive qualities of alcohol are discussed in terms of the drug's effects on glutamate, GABA, and the brain's internal opioids. A brief discussion of the many organ systems that are harmfully affected by alcohol is followed by an inventory designed to help the reader assess whether he or she is actually at risk for abuse or dependence (see Table 5.1). The chapter moves to a discussion of the psychobiological factors involved in drinking cessation, including conditioned desire and conditioned withdrawal. Although alcohol is clearly implicated in premature death, massive harm to communities and families, and a host of disease states, research during the past 30 years shows cardiovascular benefits for those who consume in moderation. However, some studies point to increased risk for certain types of cancer, even when drinking is done in moderation. A risk–benefit analysis is suggested for each person in consideration of age, sex, family disease history, and alcohol's perceived contribution (or lack thereof) to quality of life. The chapter concludes with a brief discussion of other sedating substances that work in a similar manner to alcohol.

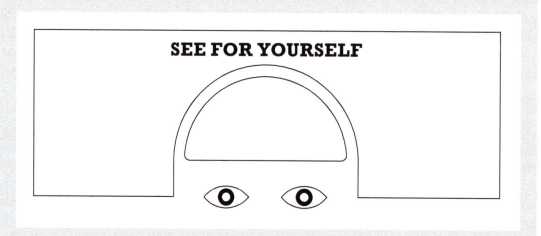

SEE FOR YOURSELF

The Truth About Alcohol. 2016. BBC Documentary. 58:00

Following a recent study of the effects of alcohol the UK dramatically changed its recommendations for safe drinking. For men, the recommended weekly limit was cut by a third to 14 units per week, equivalent to about seven pints of beer, bringing it in line with the amount recommended for women. So what is behind the change? Doctor Javid Abdelmoneim explores the science of drinking and the new evidence for the health risks of alcohol. Why do some people get drunk quicker than others? What is behind red wine's healthy reputation? Is a nightcap actually good for your sleep? Does lining your stomach work? And can alcohol actually make you eat more? **https://www.dailymotion.com/video/x4hc742**

How I overcame alcoholism. 2016. Claudia Christian. TEDx London Business School 14:43

Claudia Christian, a successful actress, shares her experience with Alcohol Use Disorder and the many treatment options she explored before finding success with the Sinclair Method. Christian explains the basic concept behind the use of opioid blockers such as naltrexone, and her personal experience with this treatment. **https://youtu.be/6EghiY_s2ts**

CHAPTER 6

The Great Psychiatric Tavern

Introduction

In general, men drink more than women. In recent years, however, these longstanding differences appear to be narrowing—not only in amounts consumed but also in alcohol related harms. In accordance with annual surveys conducted between 2002 and 2012, differences in measures such as current drinking, number of drinking days per month, reaching criteria for alcohol use disorder, and driving under the influence of alcohol in the past year, all narrowed for females and males (White, et. al, 2015). Many women are having "wine o'clock" most nights of the week.

Samantha rang in the big 3-0 with endless rounds of vodka tonics and overflowing flutes of bubbly. Wearing a bright blue dress that set off her strawberry-blonde hair, the single optometrist wove through the Manhattan bar with the grace of a slalom skier rounding gates, boisterously greeting friends as they arrived. Before she could finish a drink, another one would be placed in her hand. Samantha giggled, flirted, and danced to the beats of Lady Gaga and old-school Madonna until nearly sunrise, when she finally poured herself into bed. Nearly 63% of women ages 21 to 34 report binge drinking (Greenfield, 2009).

In the past 15 years, the percentage of women in the U.S. who drink alcohol has increased nearly 22%, while the percentage of adult men who drink has remained about the same. As females experience increased achievement and status in education and business, there has been an escalation and normalization of similar drinking habits that used to be male-dominated (Vestal, 2016).

In an analysis of four million people between 1948 and 2014 across 68 international studies "there was a clear and dramatic downturn in the male-to-female ratio of alcohol use" (Hamblin, 2016). Men born between 1891 and 1910 were 2.2 times more likely than women to drink alcohol, while within the population of people born between 1991 and 2000, that ratio fell to 1:1. Since alcohol abuse in men has not significantly decreased over time, the change of ratio is likely due to increased female consumption.

Table 6.1 below summarizes key points around excessive drinking among women and girls (CDC, 2011). A In 2015, 26.9% of people ages 18 or older reported that they engaged in binge drinking in the past month (SAMHSA, 2015). The National Institute on Alcohol Abuse and Alcoholism (NIAAA) defines binge drinking as a pattern of drinking that brings blood alcohol concentration (BAC) levels to 0.08. This typically occurs after 4 drinks for women and 5 drinks for men—in about 2 hours (NIAAA, 2004).

Table 6.1 Key Points: Binge Drinking Among Women and High School Girls

- Binge drinking is responsible for more than half of the estimated 23,000 deaths and 633,000 years of potential life lost among women and girls because of excessive alcohol consumption in the United States.
- In 2011, more than 13.6 million (12.5%) U.S. adult women binge drank (prevalence) an average of three times a month (frequency), and consume on average six drinks on occasion (intensity).
- The prevalence and intensity of binge drinking was highest among women aged 18–24 years.
- Women with household incomes ≥$75,000 had the highest binge drinking prevalence.
- In 2011, more than one in three high school girls reported drinking and one in five reported binge drinking; most high school girls who drank reported binge drinking.
- More widespread implementation of evidence-based interventions, such as those recommended by the Guide to Community Preventive Service and by the U.S.
- Preventive Services Task Force, would reduce binge drinking in states, as well as the health and social harms related to it.

Source: Centers for Disease Control (2013)

http://www.cdc.gov/vitalsigns.

The Substance Abuse and Mental Health Services Administration (SAMHSA), which conducts the annual *National Survey on Drug Use and Health* (NSDUH), defines binge drinking as 5 or more alcoholic drinks for males or 4 or more alcoholic drinks for females on the same occasion (i.e., at the same time or within a couple of hours of each other) on at least 1 day in the past month (SAMHSA, 2016).

Considering the recent escalation of female drinking, there is undoubtedly an increased prevalence of women who use the tavern as a kind of oasis—historically more exclusively populated by men—to satisfy a host of psychological and social needs.

A Stage for Letting Go

Throughout most of the world, there is an abundance of public and private settings in which the use and abuse of alcohol are fundamental to the needs and expectations of participants. A description of a brewery on an Egyptian papyrus dating back to 3500 BCE provides the earliest record of alcohol production (Fort, 1969). The first evidence of prohibitionist teaching (2000 BCE) is found in the writings of an Egyptian priest: "I thy superior forbid you [his student] to go to the taverns: Thou art degraded like the beasts" (King County Bar Association Drug Policy Project, 2005, p. 3). Today, taverns of varied design and diverse clientele exist in most societies, cutting across racial, ethnic, gender, social, religious, and geographic lines.

Although the typical bar or tavern serves as a center for relaxation, interpersonal encounters, and casual business negotiations, it is also a venue to observe and express deviant behavior. Throughout Western society, there exist many such venues. Small neighborhood bars cater to unmet psychosocial needs of community residents. Metropolitan centers supply a variety of clubs where there is an expectation of meeting strangers who may become friends, lovers, or brief sexual partners.

In a quasi-controlled environment (the bar), both men and women may sidestep ordinary social norms. They are free to become more aggressive or sexually disinhibited (Garland, Hughes, & Marquart, 2004). Patrons may tell dirty jokes, churn out lewd comments, and make sexual propositions. They may dress and act more provocatively or allow themselves proximate personal advances (K. A. Parks et al., 1998). The bar is a place of license—where deviance is acceptable, where "out of line" behaviors are permitted and even encouraged. For those who "play-within-the-rules," there is ample opportunity for unleashing libido and partially satisfying a host of unmet needs. When entering, bar patrons may shirk their ordinary social roles; upon leaving, they can dissociate from "being naughty." (Goffman, 1963).

There are many types of bar settings in contemporary society. Trendy places feature hip music, fusion food, and a medley of artistic devices ranging from exotic wood-sculpt backdrops to open-air cityscapes. Encounters with strangers are sometimes encouraged by adjoined knee-level tables with complementary cushioned seats. In contrast, the basic small town, belly-up bar, with café seating and standard recreation (e.g., pool or shuffleboard) is where most residents go to drink. Although atmospheres vary, the fundamental patterns of human behavior remain the same.

Tavern Mental Health Center

By way of analogy, the bar serves as a *mental health center* where people can express a sociability that would be unacceptable in ordinary discourse: exploring new relationships, release of tensions, and acting out impulses. People can also discuss everyday problems, forbidden fantasies, and deep-seated emotional conflicts. A striking parallel exists between the *psychiatrist* and the bartender. Each provides psychological counsel and administers pharmacologic remedies:

> Bartender (jokingly)—"What can I do you in for?"
> Client—"I'll have a beer. Doctors' orders."

In a typical neighborhood bar, the bartender [*psychiatrist*] conducts individual and group treatments [*psychiatry*], assisted by a team of service personnel [*health professionals: male and female nurses*] bouncers [*orderlies*], and other support services, e.g., taxis and Uber [*ambulances*].

Hospital administrators (owners and managers) provide various recreational activities while clients imbibe. Some of these devices include live music, dancing, darts, pool, television, arcade games, board games, lawn games, trivia, and open mics.

Available recreational devices parallel characteristics of the established clientele. Particularly in large cities, there is an ample supply of venues to satisfy needs *for arousal, relaxation, or fantasy.* Computerized games may satisfy wish fulfilling fantasies of conquering a host of villains. The karaoke bar attracts a diverse crowd of music loving patrons high on extraversion and sociability. "[It] is a culture unto itself: participatory, eclectic, convivial, habitual, and liberating. There is singing, drinking, camaraderie, and wish-fulfillment. Karaoke gives everyone a chance to be the star, if only for a night, if only for one song. Karaoke, which involves singing to a soundtrack in front of a live audience, has become a part of the culture of American bars..." Men and women have equal opportunity to perform (Lamb, et al., 1994). The down-home country western bar may suit the lovelorn romantic who is suffering through their last breakup.

The bar is essentially a for-profit business. "Therapeutic décor" is choreographed to elicit heightened emotional states, thereby stimulating increased alcohol consumption. In some venues, environmental cues combine dim light, increased noise, and overcrowding (where physical contact can hardly be avoided). Depending on current life circumstances, preexisting personality traits and social setting, alcohol may be used to enhance mood by increasing either depression or euphoria (Zinberg, 1984). The "well-medicated" patron reaches an "optimal" state of emotional reactivity, which furthers attraction and attachment to the barroom setting.

More affluent, "therapy" venues are artfully decorated and efficiently serviced. Fashionable servers deliver an array of powerful medications in a timely manner. Medication may be complemented by sumptuous meals, served with elegance and charm. In more pedestrian locations, "patients" are coaxed to heighten their dose levels through alluring devices such as "Happy Hour" and "buybacks" (a drink "on the house" for every few the patient buys). "Prescriptions" are self-selected based on the customer's psychological need or intention to provoke. "I'll have a screaming orgasm, zombie, between the sheets, climax, etc."

Personality and 'Bar of Choice'

It is possible to understand the characteristics of an individual's bar behavior by investigating his or her Myers-Briggs personality style: E (extraversion); I (introversion); N (intuition); S (sensation); T (thinking); F (feeling); J (judging); P (Perceiving). A humorous caricature might include the ESFP (extraverted, sensation seeking, feeling, perceiving) type who is flirting and making physical contact with everyone in range; meanwhile the INTP is secretly enamored by the ESFP, but decides to ignore them rather than talking to them, because for them, logic trumps feelings. Obviously, people will self-select their preferred pub based on personality style, therapeutic décor, like-minded clientele, recreational devices and featured music. In perhaps the largest study of music preference and personality, North (2008), studied the relationship between pop music culture and consumer behavior. Through analysis of 36,000 questionnaires in more than 60 countries, North compared preferred musical styles with personality types as measured by the *Big Five Inventory* (BFI) (John & Srivastava, 1999): (E) extraversion vs. introversion; (A) agreeableness vs. antagonism; (C) conscientiousness vs. lack of direction; (N) neuroticism vs. emotional stability; (O) openness vs. closedness to experience. The results showed (Collingwood, 2016):

- Blues fans have high self-esteem, are creative, outgoing, gentle, and at ease
- Jazz fans have high self-esteem, are creative, outgoing, and at ease
- Classical music fans have high self-esteem, are creative, introverted, and at ease
- Rap fans have high self-esteem and are outgoing
- Opera fans have high self-esteem, are creative, and gentle
- Country and western fans are hardworking and outgoing
- Reggae fans have high self-esteem, are creative, not hardworking, outgoing, gentle, and at ease
- Dance fans are creative and outgoing, but not gentle
- Indie fans have low self-esteem, are creative, not hardworking, and not gentle
- Bollywood fans are creative and outgoing
- Rock/heavy metal fans have low self-esteem, are creative, not hard-working, not outgoing, gentle, and at ease
- Chart pop fans have high self-esteem, are hardworking, outgoing and gentle, but are not creative and not at ease
- Soul fans have high self-esteem, are creative, outgoing, gentle, and at ease

Sanctuary

In addition to the phenomenon of drinking atmospheres matching the personality of participating clientele, the tavern serves an even more profound function for marginalized groups. For example, many in the GLBTQ community find "identity" bars as places of comfort, safety, and solace. The following commentaries attest to personal importance of the gay bar.

CASE EXAMPLE: Sanctuary

Rachel Maddow

Host of MSNBC's "The Rachel Maddow Show"

The year was 1990 when Rachel Maddow first appeared in a gay bar. At the age of 17 she paid $25 for a poorly forged fake ID. She was afraid of being caught for underaged drinking and scared of being recognized by someone who might know who she was. Rachel doesn't recall even ordering a beer; she just obsessively played pinball by herself, not talking to any of the clientele during the entire time she was there. The counterfeit ID was her ticket to become part of the gay community that she so much wanted to be a part of. "I wish I still had that terrible fake Arizona drivers' license — I think my alter ego from that ID (her name was Ann) would be 48 years old by now. I still have her same haircut."

Don Lemon: CNN Anchor

During the time Don Lemon was in college in the 1980s he and everyone else he knew that was gay, were deeply in the closet. Coming out in the South was a lot slower then, compared to how it is now. When with his straight fraternity brothers at LSU, they would frequent the Bengal on Highland Road. He would surreptitiously leave for the bars down the road. "One was named Xanthus, an 'alternative' bar where the bouncer was a girl named Big Hair. (By the way, Hair and I are still friends to this day.)"

Alison Bechdel: Cartoonist, Author of the Graphic Memoir "Fun Home"

When Alison Bechdel was in college, her first gay bar was called Satan's, in Akron, Ohio. She and her friends would drive about an hour and a half to arrive. She recalls "feeling like a total alien" when socializing in 'normal' places. "But that night, ... I experienced the profound existential relief, for once, of not being the only queer." A year later, in 1981, Alison moved to New York City. She routinely experienced anti-gay hostility on the street. She experienced being hassled for just holding hands. "But then you'd step past the bouncer at the Duchess, and you were home free. The bar had its own perils—no one ever paid the slightest attention to me there—but it afforded me the space to just be, with my guard down, and that was salvational."

Adapted from: 'My First Gay Bar': Rachel Maddow, Andy Cohen and Others Share Their Coming-Out Stories, NYT, June 22, 2016

Disinhibition and Violence

Many bars provide highly permissive environments that encourage childish fantasy and adolescent swagger. Garland et al. (2004) described patterns of behavior in a small-town- pub, populated by college students and locals. Male student patrons were classified as *jocks, frat boys,* and *wolves;* female patrons were dubbed *Madonnas* (showed up to please their partner; did not talk to others; never bought drinks for themselves) and *sheep* (arrived in groups, dressed provocatively); locals as *blue collar* and *professionals.* Jocks mostly huddled in all-male- groups, mulling over recent sporting escapades. Frat boys were recognizable by their style of dress: T-shirts and baseball caps with fraternity logos. As the evening progressed and more alcohol was consumed, frat boys became increasingly loud and aggressive toward female students, while "wolves" (a.k.a. "the wolf pack") crossed over physical boundaries in what would be considered elsewhere as "inappropriate touching."

The relationship between the actors in this seemingly provincial small-town venue projects a disheartening narrative concerning a larger problem of abusive sexual encounters. Bars are often places where the excess use of alcohol impairs judgment and lowers inhibition resulting in dangerous and unwanted sexual encounters. Consider "#MeToo".

> "... hooking up and the amount that close friends drink are tied to higher alcohol expectancies [belief in the benefits of intoxication] for both men and women, and these expectancies lead to their higher levels of drinking, which, in turn, increases one's risk for sexual assault." (Tyler, Schmitz, & Adams, 2015, p.19)

Flack and colleagues (2007) conducted a study of unwanted sexual experiences in a collegiate "hookup" culture. "Hooking up is typically although not always unplanned, with the often-implicit assumption of physical but not necessarily emotional intimacy and with no sense of commitment over time" (p. 153). One-time-casual-encounters often involve intercourse with no expectation of continued relationship. In a sample of 761 women students, approximately 50% reported at least one experience of unwanted sex with 70% reporting to have experienced unwanted sex in the context of a hookup (Garcia et. al, 2012). In a study of men and women who had engaged in uncommitted sex that included vaginal, anal, or oral activity, perceived levels of intoxication were reported: 35% were very intoxicated, 27% were mildly intoxicated, 27% were sober, and 9% were extremely intoxicated (Fisher, Worth, Garcia, & Meredith, 2012). Alcohol may also serve as an excuse—a defensive strategy to protect the self from having to justify hook-up behavior. The phenomenon of hooking up has become more accessible with the advent of mobile phone apps designed to match potential partners.

Mobile apps like Tinder and The Grade have made hookup culture prominent by making hooking up more accessible. Tinder is on-demand, instant gratification interaction with a potential partner: swipe through photos, see one that strikes your fancy, and "like" him or her. If he or she "likes" you back, the app connects you. The ease and low risk factor are two reasons the more than 50 million active users on Tinder check their accounts as much as 11 times per day (Drexler, 2015).

The Marketplace

Cloyd (1976) described the "marketplace bar" as a business establishment that "caters to young, usually single persons interested in meeting and possibly having sex with persons of a similar orientation" (p. 293). Based on observations conducted in 11 Midwest Metropolitan bars, Cloyd identified a 3-phase "pairing ritual" in the barroom setting:

1. *Initiation*—Interpersonal encounters are usually predicated upon approach-oriented body language and eye contact.

An individual may "raise their ante" by presenting themselves provocatively and using blatantly *open*-body-language to convey an *open* invitation. In response to such open provocative behavior, potential partners may size up the possibilities and assess whether "this is something they *can handle*."

2. *Squaring Off and Negotiations*—Of paramount importance is an individual's projected self-confidence as being someone who can fulfill the needs and interests of the object of his or her attention. Both parties may use alcohol to project more confidence.

3. *Disclosures and Settlements*—Members disclose their ultimate intentions, and the settlement of gains and losses occurs. An individual may unfold their prior commitment to a significant other or partner and decline. A person will either "get lucky" or "get shut down."

4. In some rougher settings, tempers may flare and fights may break out. Holes have been reported to be punched in bathroom walls, particularly around closing time. High alcohol consumption is a significant predictor of male aggression. "Those who were involved in male alcohol-related aggression (MARA) had higher levels of trait aggression, concern for social honour and expected positive consequences of aggression in bars than did those without such involvement" (P. Miller et al., 2014, p.136). Sometimes even support given by friends is not sufficient to assuage the deep sense of disappointment and ensuing rage. If this support is insufficient, the bouncer's job becomes "cooling the mark" (Goffman, 1967).

With so much sexual innuendo and opportunity for alcohol-fueled aggression, how can the bar function with any semblance of comfort and safety? As in most high-population psychiatric settings, this cannot always be guaranteed. Leonard, Quigley, and Collins (2002) found that in a randomly selected community sample, 25% of men and 12% of women had exposure to barroom aggression. In their study of bar aggression toward women, Buddie and Parks (2003) found that among females, more severe bar-related aggression was associated with heavier drinking, which correspondingly was related to "going to and leaving the bar with less known individuals and with talking to more people in the bar" (p. 1389).

In large measure, however, order in the "psychiatric tavern" is maintained by shared understanding of informal rules, enforced by a team of "mental health" specialists (i.e., bartenders, servers, and bouncers). In cases of serious or persistent infringement, violators are ostracized and forced to find a new subculture where they can try to belong (Garland et al., 2004).

Surrogate Family Atmosphere

Figure 6.2 Regression, Consolation, and Nurture at the Great Psychiatric Tavern

A magical movement of the hand introduces a magical substance, and behold, pain and suffering are exorcised, the sense of misery disappears and the body is suffused by waves of pleasure… [T]he ego is, after all, the omnipotent giant it had always fundamentally thought it was.
—Sandor Rado, "The Psychoanalysis of Pharmacothymia"

An intriguing similarity between the mental hospital and the tavern is the illusion of a familiar family setting. In atmospheres such as these, where childlike behavior is expected, staff become symbols of parental authority. An alluring server delivers the "milk of human kindness" in an atmosphere of heightened stimulation and increased vulnerability. The incipient "bar-patient" may develop amorous feelings toward the server who triggers the patients' libido or sexual fantasies. The bar-patient harbors secret wishes that the bartender—who symbolizes parental authority—would either cease to exist or at least temporarily disappear. Yet sexual intimacy is forbidden. When the mixture of intoxication and libido erode the client's dignity s/he is doomed to rejection. A hassled server will first avoid personal contact, and then limit service availability. Disorderly conduct may ultimately be reported to the bartender (symbol of patriarchal or matriarchal authority). Anxiety caused by the fear of being rejected is conveniently blunted through increasing doses of alcohol. When sex or aggression becomes seriously unbridled, the server, on orders from the bartender, may deliver the humiliating sentence, "You're cut off!" At this point, the wounded patron is denied service for the duration of the evening. More reprehensible behavior, based on a cumulative record of misconduct (or a single incident of poor impulse control) can result in the penalty of being *eighty-sixed* (thrown out). Such customers re-create oedipal disappointment. Ostracized or exiled customers experience unrequited love and reprisal at the hands of a surrogate parents.

Below the often cheerful and successful personas, e.g., happy-go-lucky, bon vivant, or pensive loner, chronic bar patrons may suffer from deeper feelings of worthlessness and despair. Equilibrium and composure depend on the firm guidance and external support of a professional-tavern-team. The bouncer (*orderly*), who represents a visible extension of paternal authority, must be vigilant and instantly available to quell primitive expressions of lust or rage that may surface during the intoxicated state. Overinflated projections of a powerful self barely soften the bludgeons of self-perceived failure and ineptness. Minor interpersonal confrontations can acquire the intensity of powerful sibling conflicts—rivalries that may even explode into fits of rage.

The "Therapist's" View

Those who have become dependent on the local pub often learn to repress their libidos and form amicable relationships with the bartender and staff. Day into night, these "socialized" patrons may look toward the barkeep for *attention* and *counsel*. Alcohol releases power and control fantasies while triggering repressed memories and forbidden impulses. The bartender performs a dual-role: provides psychoactive drugs and a reliable source of human connectedness. Patrons can discuss highly personal, often painful, life events. The following exemplifies the client-counselor relationship afforded by the psychiatric tavern.

Pauleen ... Bartender by Night... Psychiatric Nurse by Day

They could be looking directly at a mirror. Most bars have mirrors so you can look at your own reflection … I do it myself. I've sat down in bars when I'm by myself and I don't know the clientele or the bartender, so I will stick to the bartender—probably in fleeting moments—exactly as they do. And I can sit at the bar and look in the mirror, and let my mind wander … what they do when I'm on the other side of the bar. And of course, when you walk past there's an exchange of conversation, which can be short, depending on the business at the bar. When I walk away, you can see the customer drift off into fantasy. When I return, it gives them the opportunity to respond to their own thoughts. You might be a Christmas tree but s/he thinks that you are listening.

When a customer telegraphs potential volatility or emotional distress, the bartender becomes a crucial source of control. S/he signals the inebriated patron to regain composure using facial expressions, direct commands, or outright discontinuance of service. Pauleen recounts her experience as a bar disciplinarian: "There's the younger ones and the older ones. Some will tap on the bar... One thing I can't stand is whistling. If someone whistles, I just say, "I'm not going to serve you—I'm not a dog." So, I wait … if they whistle twice, I won't serve them for a little longer. And so, there you see. They've got to behave or leave. You train the client to your own pace because you're in control … You can always turn around and say: "You're the drunk and I'm sober."

Sometimes the "therapist" may discontinue the session and defer "treatment" until the following day. Like the hostage who develops a *Stockholm Syndrome* (feeling affection for one's captor), tavern regulars eventually feel gratitude and devotion toward the bartender. They murmur platitudes of respect, tipping lavishly, existing in drugged anticipation of a few sporadic moments with a longed-for confidant. At the close of the bar, taxis run ambulance from hospital to home.

Despite the watchful eyes of bar-staff, some patrons have a repeated history of acting-out bizarre impulses while intoxicated.

CASE EXAMPLE: Loss of Control

Roger is a successful young lawyer with a boyish face and contagious smile. He enjoys a lucrative corporate practice in a large metropolitan area. His favorite tavern is designed for the more impulse-ridden patron—servers allow physical contact, and the floor manager has been known to drink and share drugs with customers. One evening when Roger was feeling particularly alone—and very intoxicated—he quietly stood on the bar stool and urinated on the counter. He was immediately "cut off" and "eighty-sixed" from the premises.

Prior to the incident, Roger had a history of being unable to form intimate relationships with anyone but his mother. He was an only son, and when he was 6 years old his father died suddenly. Roger's mother assuaged her intense mourning by encouraging excessive physical contact and a deepening emotional dependence. The actualization of oedipal conquest left the young boy with a great sense of guilt. He had unconscious wishes for male domination, paternal reprisal, and ultimate forgiveness.

As a young lawyer, when trying a case, Roger would symbolically perform penance by impressing the judge with his sincerity and hard work; as an intoxicated tavernite, he yearned for punishment and pardon from a substitute father—the bartender. His wish-fulfilling choreography was so adept that the sympathetic manager, who also had been abandoned by his father early in life, reinstated Roger with full "treatment" privileges within 6 months of the dramatic incident.

What of the multitude of alcoholic patrons who establish long-term residence in the psychiatric tavern? Eventually, *regulars* understand that continued attempts to seduce servers destine failure and possible reprisal. Erotic or hostile impulses toward parental-figures (bartender and servers) gradually fade into feelings of affection and respect. Interpersonal relationships become centered on daily encounters between regulars and bar-staff. The function of the psychiatric-tavern merges with traditional family structure. Cohorts of alcohol dependent regulars develop tight bonds. Humor and wit become the currency for sibling-like affection and staff approval.

Drinking Games

Research shows that drinking games increase the per capita blood alcohol level (Clapp, 2008). Correspondingly, drinking games increase the risk of dangerous driving, unwanted sexual activity, and aggressive breakthroughs (i.e., verbal abuse or actual fights).

CASE EXAMPLE: The Game of Spoons

Figure 6.3 **"Spoons"** Drinking games increase the per capita blood alcohol level along with the risk of dangerous driving, unwanted sexual activity, and aggressive breakthroughs (i.e., verbal abuse or actual fights)

"Spoons" is a bar game that exemplifies the breakthrough of aggression in the absence of adequate external controls. A naive customer enters a tavern patronized by a cohort of well-established chronics. The newcomer becomes chatty, has a few drinks, and begins to enjoy a sparring camaraderie with several regular group members. Under the impression that the game is "fair," the newcomer is invited to partake in a drinking game known as Spoons. The novice is coaxed into watching a round and then participating themselves. Two of the regulars pull their bar stools to within a foot of one another. Each places the handle of a tablespoon solidly between their teeth with the ladle turned upright. To the crowd's delight, one forwardly head bows, inviting the other to play the spoon (a bop on the head with the mouth-held spoon). Amidst great *oooooohs* and *aaaahs*, the attacker twists their head up, musters maximum torque, and delivers the first ploy. Players alternate between bopper and bopped, while the crowd roots excitedly. After several playful bops, the newcomer is given an invitation to take a try.

> *"No harm can be done with a slight knock on the head ... The spoon is so close ... Go on, give it a try ... See who hits harder."*

The initiate takes up the dare: in hopes to please the crowd, to be a good sport, wanting to belong. S/he doesn't expect that a conspiring group member—would conceal a personal spoon—and blast an unmerciful bop, not by way of a mouth held spoon, but with the potent force of arm and hand.

The scheme is unraveled as a member of the group mischievously directs the unsuspecting *newbie* to the sight of three spoons placed on the bar.

> *"Now how many spoons do ya see there?"*

Amidst the cackles and squeals of an ecstatic crowd, it dawns on the *victim* that Spoons is one *dupe-trick* of a game. The newcomer's ability to handle humiliation and deceit will ultimately determine joining the fellowship of regulars, or finding another place to feel at home.

On college campuses, worldwide, there has been an explosion of drinking games. LaBrie et al. (2013) created a system for drinking game (DG) classification and reported differences between DG types. Having studied online survey results of 3421 college students (58% female), 100 distinct drinking games were identified and defined. Drinking games were then categorized into five mutually exclusive categories: (1) Targeted and Skill games; (2) Communal games; (3) Chance games; (4) Extreme Consumption games; (5) Even Competition games. Table 6.2 presents the categorization scheme and examples of games that fit each category. The findings provide a novel drinking game categorization scheme and an exploratory analysis of basic differences between game categories.

Table 6.2 Reported Drinking Games and Definitions

Game Category	DG Definitions and Examples					
Targeted and Skill games	This game type has a single loser (of 3 or more, no teams) who has to drink or a winner who sets to pick who drinks. These games usually involve some sort of skill or strategy to avoid personal drinking or target certain players to make them drink.					
	Apples to apples	Balls to the wall	Baskin	Beer hockey	BS	Catch phrase
	Celebrity	Chandeliers	robins 31	Darts	Drink driver	Eights
	Flip pong	Fuck you	Counting game	Jenga	Jeopardy	Kentucky
	Landmines	Montana	Hearts Moose	Numbers	Web	draw 1
	Questions	Spoons	3, 6, 9 Touretts	Thumper	Presidents	Quarters
	UNO	Zip-zap-zop		What the fuck	and assholes	Truth or dare
					Videogame drinking game	
Communal games	This game type has no official winner or losers. Everyone participates simultaneously following an agreed upon set of rules that dictate how much and when they will drink. All players drink in response to an agreed upon action, phrase, event, etc.					
	Movie drinking game	Never have 1 ever...	Spin the bottle	Song game	Drinking game to debate	TV drinking game
Chance games	This game type involves no (or very little) skill or strategy and each person drinks in turn. Often these games involve the rolling of dice, guessing of playing card values, or randomly drawing playing cards to see what action you or others must complete.					
	Beer slut	Candy land Fuck	Circle	Connections	Dice	Drinko
	Electricity	the dealer	of death	Horse races	Indian poker	Kings cup
	Let's get fucked up	High/low, black/red	3-Man	Shots and ladders	The good, the	Queens cup
	Ride the bus	7, 11, or doubles	1, 2, 3, drink beer	Suits	bad, the ugly	Pyramid
	Titanic	Tower	Poker		Mushroom	
			Up the river			

Extreme Consumption games	This type of game involves extreme isolated chugging episodes. Typically one or more standard drinks. Rules (if there are any) are simple and rarely progress beyond drinking a lot. drinking fast, or finishing your drink.					
	Beer bong Dizzy bat Shotgun(ning)	Bucket Drink the beer Shots	Edward 40 hands Drunk ball Waterfall	Chugging Case race Wine slapping	Century club power hour Frisbee challenge Wisest wizard	Cowboy face Keg stand
Even Competition games	This game type is defined by one versus one or team versus team competition where the losing side must drink as punishment. The winner(s) do not have to drink.					
	Baseball Civil war Taboo	Beer die Cranium Tic-tac-toe	Beer pong Flip cup Hit 'em up	Black out Foosball	Boat races Up chicken down chicken	Chess checkers Rock, paper, scissor

Closing Time

In a properly managed tavern, primitive expressions of anger or uncontrolled sexual altercations might still occur. The well-behaved chronic accepts medication beyond the point of disinhibition and impulsive acts (welcoming sedation and stupor). Like a dazed mental-patient, the heavily-intoxicated regular staggers from bar stool to toilet, and eventually home. The abrupt declaration of "Last call for alcohol" pierces through ethanol's cushion of befogged escape. Noise levels soar! Drunken conversations become louder and more intense. The vociferous flurry, just before closing, represents an emergent awareness that the sleep that follows will be on a pallet of loneliness, discomfort, and desperation. A notorious bar in Philadelphia, announces last call by shouting:

"IF YOU'RE NOT FUCKING THE HELP, PLEASE LEAVE!"

Is This a Good Idea?

Marijuana Clubs Approved in Colorado Senate
As of this writing, Colorado has a few dozen marijuana clubs, but they have no permits and sometimes operate underground. On Thursday, March 9, 2017, Colorado's Senate passed a first-in-the-nation bill expressly permitting marijuana clubs. Senator Bob Garner, a Colorado Springs Republican and sponsor of the bill believes that clubs can alleviate "problems…of people publicly using marijuana." There are complaints that Colorado's sidewalks and public parks have been inundated with pot smokers since the advent of legalized marijuana (Wyatt, 2017). Gov. John Hickenlooper has noted several issues of concern: (1) "…given the uncertainty in Washington…this is not the year to be out there carving off new turf and expand markets and make dramatic statements about marijuana; (2) "Smoking is bad for you;" he will likely veto the measure unless it is re-written to ban indoor smoking.

Chapter Summary

The "great psychiatric tavern" remains a stronghold for camaraderie and psychological support. As females experience increased achievement and status in education and business, there has been an escalation and normalization of drinking habits similar to the drinking patterns of males. The "white wine syndrome" has become an occupational hazard for professional women, particularly those between 21 and 24 years of age. Young professionals make use of the "businessman's lunch," which may continue after work, through dinner, and into the evening. Wine coolers (lower-alcohol mixtures of wine, fruit juice, and carbonated water) are consumed by increasing numbers of female bar-attendees.

It appears that the alcohol industry has taken an "If you can't beat 'em, join 'em" stand on the issue of health promotion. It is common knowledge that heavy drinking can lead to liver, heart, and kidney problems, and increase the risk of cancer. Wine and beer are being marketed as better choices than hard liquor, and reduced drinking is a becoming increasingly recognized as a healthier way to reduce stress.

For certain individuals, the bar can serve as a sanctuary, providing shelter and belonging. Across race, ethnicity, social status, sex, and gender identity, a multitude of neighborhood and metropolitan bars function as *informal psychiatric clinics*. These covert *mental health centers* provide relief for a plethora of psychological needs. For many, it serves as a place of license, where manifest behaviors, unacceptable in most segments of society, are tolerated or even condoned. On college campuses, worldwide, there has been an explosion of drinking games, with yet unknown consequences to health and wellbeing. Bars are often places where the abuse of alcohol impairs judgment and lowers inhibition resulting in dangerous and unwanted sexual encounters.

Caring communities are challenged to develop alternative means for gratifying the needs that have been previously met through tavern life. Atmospheres must be created in which surrogate family networks provide constructive measures for coping with internal conflict and social stress. The sense of adventure, spontaneity, relaxation, and human relatedness, all within reach at the bar, must be preserved, without the unwanted consequences of repetitive intoxication and loss of impulse control. In recent years, the alcohol industry has taken a proactive stand on the issue of health promotion. Wine and beer are being marketed as better choices than hard liquor, and reduced drinking is a becoming increasingly recognized as a healthier way to reduce stress.

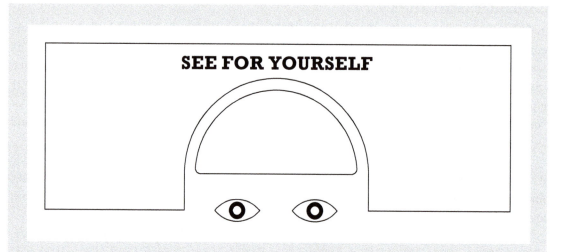

Star Wars Episode IV: The Bar Scene. What similarities do you see between the ideas discussed in 'The Great Psychiatric Tavern' and the bar scene for Episode IV of Star Wars?

https://www.youtube.com/watch?v=g6PDcBhODqo&feature=youtu.be

CHAPTER 7

Nicotine
The World's Antidepressant

If I cannot smoke cigars in heaven, I shall not go.
—Mark Twain

It is now proved beyond doubt that smoking is one of the leading causes of statistics.
—Fletcher Knebel

My smoking might be bothering you, but it's killing me.
—Colette

Tobacco is a dirty weed. I like it.

It satisfies no normal need. I like it.

It makes you thin, it makes you lean.

It takes the hair right off your bean.

It's the worst damn stuff I've ever seen.

I like it.
—Graham Lee Hemminger, Penn State Froth, 1915[1]

---

1 "Tobacco is a Dirty Weed," Froth, vol. 7, pp. 19. 1915.

Introduction

 ating back to at least 500 years ago, hookah is nothing new. Once just known as a Middle Eastern tradition, hookah has become increasingly popular in colleges, bars, lounges, clubs, and households. It seems like you can't go to any social setting without a hookah being present.

I was introduced to hookah in high school, hookah lounges almost never carded and they made us feel grown. When I got to college, students had them in their dorms, it was cheaper than cigarettes (another nasty habit I picked up in high school) and a different way to meet new people, and it seemed like a win/win situation to me. I came to my senses and decided to give up cigarettes, but didn't feel the need to do so with hookah. I mean it's herbal right? There was no way it could be as bad for me as cigarettes, plain tobacco soaked in molasses or honey and fruits, none of that stuff those cigarette commercials warn us about. So when I started hearing that smoking hookah was the equivalent of smoking 200 cigarettes (honestly? I just gave those up) I had to get to the bottom of it, and I didn't like what I found.

—Jelani Addams Rosa, *Why You Should Think Twice About Smoking Hookah*

Our consideration of need gratifying activities continues in this chapter with discussion of self-administration of nicotine, the active ingredient in the tobacco plant. By increasing the availability of dopamine (evoking pleasure) and acetylcholine (enhancing memory and mental alertness), nicotine and other ingredients in tobacco set the stage for rapid onset and extremely high rates of dependency. As shown in Table 7.1, tobacco is the crème de la crème of addictive drugs: it is one of the most widely used substances in the world, yet also the most damaging voluntary ingested substance the world has ever seen—an insidious weapon of mass destruction.

Table 7.1 Smoking Related Disease

Smoking leads to disease and disability and harms nearly every organ of the body.
- More than 16 million Americans are living with a disease caused by smoking.
- For every person who dies because of smoking, at least 30 people live with a serious smoking-related illness.
- Smoking causes cancer, heart disease, stroke, lung diseases, diabetes, and chronic obstructive pulmonary disease (COPD), which includes emphysema and chronic bronchitis.
- Smoking also increases risk for tuberculosis, certain eye diseases, and problems of the immune system, including rheumatoid arthritis.
- Smoking is a known cause of erectile dysfunction in males.

Smoking is the leading cause of preventable death
- Worldwide, tobacco use causes nearly 6 million deaths per year, and current trends show that tobacco use will cause more than 8 million deaths annually by 2030.
- Cigarette smoking is responsible for more than 480,000 deaths per year in the United States, including nearly 42,000 deaths resulting from secondhand smoke exposure. This is about one in five deaths annually, or 1,300 deaths every day.
- On average, smokers die 10 years earlier than nonsmokers.
- If smoking continues at the current rate among U.S. youth, 5.6 million of today's Americans younger than 18 years of age are expected to die prematurely from a smoking-related illness. This represents about one in every 13 Americans aged 17 years or younger who are alive today

U.S. Department of Health and Human Services (2014)

According to the World Health Organization: "Tobacco kills up to half of its users ... around 6 million people each year. More than 5 million of those deaths are the result of direct tobacco use while more than 600,000 are the result of non-smokers being exposed to second-hand smoke. Nearly 80% of the world's 1 billion smokers live in low- and middle-income countries (World Health Organization, 2015).

A Gift from the Gods, or the Devil?

> Huron Indian myth has it that in ancient times, when the land was barren and the people were starving, the Great Spirit sent forth a woman to save humanity. As she traveled over the world, everywhere her right hand touched the soil, there grew potatoes. And everywhere her left hand touched the soil, there grew corn. And when the world was rich and fertile, she sat down and rested. When she arose, there grew tobacco ... (Borio, 1993)

The tobacco plant is native to the Western hemisphere, and the use of its leaves to produce psychoactive effects dates back millennia to people living in South America. Early use of tobacco among these groups appeared to be both religious and social in nature (Gately, 2001). The first Europeans to encounter tobacco were members of Christopher Columbus' expedition. Rodrigo de Jeres and Luis de Torres were sent ashore at Cuba and given tobacco leaves as a gift by the island's inhabitants. Having observed the natives smoking, the men tried the practice. Columbus' party stayed in the New World for about three months, and de Jeres and de Torres were habitual smokers by the time the fleet set sail to return to Spain. Unfortunately for the first European users, smoking was frowned upon by the Spanish Inquisition: emanation of smoke from orifices, they thought, indicated demonic possession. De Jeres was forced to go "cold turkey" when the Inquisition imprisoned him for several years. Eventually, however, smoking tobacco was adopted by the aristocracy in Europe, and the habit became popular with many.

By the time Europeans settled in North America, smoking was an accepted practice and tobacco was an important crop. In those days, tobacco was smoked via pipes or cigars, specifically by men. The cigarette machine was invented in the late 19th century, allowing for mass and inexpensive production of a more compact product. America's relationship with tobacco became tumultuous in the 20th century. During the Prohibition movement, there were also anti-smoking leagues that grew with the rise in tobacco's popularity. Part of the public disdain seems to have been tied to smoke irritating non-smokers. It was also considered unacceptable for women to smoke, especially in public, as evidenced by the arrest of a woman for smoking on 5th Avenue in New York City

> 1904: New York City. A woman is arrested for smoking a cigarette in an automobile. "You can't do that on Fifth Avenue," the arresting officer says (Borio, 1993).

Numerous states banned the sale of cigarettes, and some business owners refused to hire smokers. Nonetheless, tobacco companies promoted their products and lobbied to get nicotine removed from the U.S. Pharmacopoeia in 1905. Their success in these efforts set the stage for the rise of nicotine addiction in the U.S. Marketing strategies and new products geared towards specific demographics increased the popularity of smoking, while nicotine's removal from the list of recognized drugs meant that tobacco products were not subject to regulation under the Pure Food and Drug Act (the law which created the

Food and Drug Administration). Over the next few decades, smoking rates rose, along with lung cancer deaths—which were extremely rare prior to 1900 (Borio, 1993).

Proctor (2012) traces the history of medical evidence regarding the hazards of smoking, noting that in 1912 Dr. Isaac Adler published the first medical monograph that suggested smoking (and alcohol consumption) may cause lung cancer. By the mid-1950s, however, the data were compelling: evidence from epidemiological studies, cell pathology, and animal experiments all pointed to cigarette smoking as a cause of cancer. Moreover, numerous carcinogens had been isolated from cigarette smoke. The smoking-cancer connection was clear to the tobacco industry, but they kept quiet about what they knew and tried to distract from reports made public by the medical community. Even after the Surgeon General's historical report on the hazards of smoking was released in 1964, the industry continued to deny that their products were deadly.

Today (as described above) it is undeniable that tobacco poses a serious public health threat. In the U.S., cigarette smoking causes an estimated 480,000 deaths, or about 1 of every 5 deaths, each year. This estimate includes approximately 42,000 deaths from secondhand smoke exposure (Centers for Disease Control and Prevention [CDC], 2014). Add up the deaths caused each year by alcohol, illegal drugs, motor vehicle accidents, firearms, and human immunodeficiency virus (HIV), and you still will not meet the number of deaths caused by smoking (Mokdad et al., 2004). We will return to specific health hazards, after exploring how nicotine is used and its effects on the brain.

Self-Administration: Choose Your Method

There is wide array of nicotine delivery products available on the market. Typically, we associate nicotine with cigarette smoking, although cigars, pipe tobacco, chew, and snuff have existed for hundreds of years. Chew and snuff allow nicotine to be absorbed through mucous membranes (in the mouth and nose, respectively), which means the user can get their "fix" without smoking, but they are less popular methods than smoking. Nicotine replacement products, intended to help people cease or at least curb their tobacco use, come in gums, patches and oral mists. Chantix® is a prescription medication that reduces nicotine cravings, without the potentially harmful effects of nicotine. More recently, electronic cigarettes (i.e., e-cigarettes), have been introduced into the U.S. Some cigarette smokers have self-prescribed these as a form of nicotine replacement therapy. However, it should be noted that these products were first developed in China and did not go through FDA-approval as a nicotine replacement therapy. Recent survey data indicate that teenagers are more likely to smoke e-cigarettes ("vape") than to smoke regular cigarettes; for instance, a little over 5% of 12th graders reported daily cigarette use, whereas over 15% of those same 12th graders reported vaping nicotine (Monitoring the Future, 2015b). Many people believe that vaping is healthier than smoking cigarettes, although we will return to that issue later.

Effects on the Brain

Nicotine is one of the active ingredients in cigarette smoke that partially accounts for the addicting power of cigarettes. As we discussed in Neurochemistry 101 (Chapter 3), the addicting power of tobacco is due to an increase of dopamine (DA) in the nucleus accumbens (NAc). Nicotine directly stimulates the flow of DA into the NAc (Figure 7.1). Nicotine also stimulates the release of the excitatory neurotransmitter glutamate, which triggers additional release of DA. But as we have seen, GABA in the ventral tegmental area (VTA) moderates DA release. The VTA initially enhances GABA release (producing calming effect) to moderate the increase of DA produced by nicotine. However, within a few minutes nicotine kicks in to inhibit the release of GABA (Mansvelder & McGehee, 2002). Inhibiting the DA-releasing inhibitor (GABA) results in high DA levels in the NAc. The combination of these effects, that is, (1) direct stimulation of DA release and (2) inhibiting the inhibitory effects of GABA on DA, results in an increase in DA in the NAc and an amplification of the rewarding properties of nicotine (Mansvelder & McGehee, 2002). GABA is one of a complex network of actors that promotes addiction to nicotine and may provide an important target for nicotine addiction treatment. It gets even worse. There appear to be substances in cigarette smoke that block the action of monoamine oxidase (MAO), which is our bodies' enzyme responsible for breaking down (destroying) DA (as well as serotonin and norepinephrine) in order to maintain neurotransmitter balance. So now it seems that smoking is a *triple-sided sword:* one to directly enhance DA, one to inhibit the DA inhibitor, and the third to block the DA destroyer (MAO). It would not be possible for the best pharmaceutical company in the world to design a more potent combination of drugs (nicotine and the unknown MAO inhibitors) to produce addiction. According to Hogg's (2016) review, the MAO-inhibiting components of tobacco leaves and smoke can produce effects similar to low therapeutic doses of some MAO-inhibiting drugs (which were the first generation of antidepressant medications). If a smoker ceases cigarette use, the levels of MAO will increase in the brain, which will enhance the breakdown of DA, serotonin, and norepinephrine in the brain. It might be expected that someone attempting to quit smoking will feel depressed during withdrawal.

It should be of no surprise that the Japanese name for a type of cigarette translates to "Short Hope."

Figure 7.1 Neurochemical Effects of Nicotine Nicotine activates inhibitory GABA neurons, stimulates dopamine-releasing neurons, and stimulates excitatory glutamate neurons (left panel). Each of these effects increases the amount of dopamine released in the nucleus accumbens (right panel).

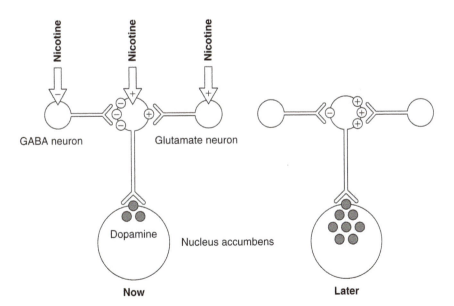

Mason sought to discover whether the enjoyable effects associated with smoking could be reduced in some way. When people use nicotine they may experience a sensation of reward, diminished anxiety, or a belief that they can focus more clearly or learn more easily. Researchers wanted to explore how a specific type of neuron that releases dopamine, a chemical that has been associated with pleasure, can prolong and intensify the pleasurable effects of nicotine. Although GABA inhibits those neurons, nicotine works against the ability of GABA to inhibit dopamine neurons after about 20 minutes, so the gratifying effects of nicotine are prolonged. (American College of Neuropsychopharmacology, 2007)

Even this is not the end of the nicotine story with its multitude of effects on the brain. Many smokers, quite aware that smoking is really stupid, will claim that smoking makes them temporarily smarter and more alert. Actually, this is probably true. It is known that the chemical structure of nicotine is similar to that of the neurotransmitter acetylcholine, which is involved in many brain functions including memory and mental alertness. Because of the similarity in chemical structure, nicotine can attach itself to and activate acetylcholine (cholinergic) receptor sites.

In fact, some evidence indicates that nicotine may increase cognition. Why not use it for treatment of the memory loss that almost inevitably accompanies aging, i.e., dementia including Alzheimer's? Not so fast: Ott and his colleagues (2004) have shown that mental functioning degrades 5 times faster in elderly smokers than in elderly nonsmokers. They also observed that those who smoked more declined faster (showed more cognitive deficits) than those who smoked less. This is especially significant as we observe an increase in the average age of the population in the United States and around the world.

Is Tobacco Addicting?

For many years, the tobacco industry denied that tobacco products were addictive. Any doubt that cigarette companies were ignorant of the addicting effects of nicotine should be dispelled by David Kessler's (2001) exposé of the tobacco industry, *A Question of Intent*. Kessler, who holds degrees in both law and medicine, led an investigation of the tobacco industry during his tenure as head of the FDA. Kessler reveals that the industry actively suppressed data about the addictive nature of nicotine—data collected by scientists working directly for cigarette companies. Attempting to disseminate information from such studies through conference presentations or submission to peer-reviewed scientific journals resulted in termination of employment accompanied by a required non-disclosure agreement. Unsurprisingly, people who were once industry insiders were reluctant to reveal what they knew, even if they felt the public had a right to know.

Data from outside of the industry clearly argue that individuals can become hooked on tobacco products. One indicator is the inability of people to cease smoking. Survey data indicate that tobacco is a difficult substance to quit with a very high relapse rate. For instance, Garvey and colleagues (1992) demonstrated that 87% of people attempting to quit smoking without any form of assistance relapsed within one year. But it didn't take a full year for most people to resume smoking: 32% relapsed within 3 days and 49% relapsed within the first week! Fortunately, relapse becomes less likely the longer a person has been abstinent; follow-up data with the same cohort of research participants indicated that, after attaining 10 years of abstinence, less than 1% relapsed each year (Krall, Garvey, & Garcia, 2002). The good news is that the number of former smokers exceeds the number of current smokers; the bad news is that nicotine is just as hard to quit as alcohol, heroin, or cocaine and can thus be deemed to be just as addictive (CDC, 2015c)

How Fast Can I Get Hooked?

DiFranza (2008) explored how nicotine addiction develops in novice smokers. He developed a stunning hypothesis: limited exposure to nicotine—as little as one cigarette—can change the brain, causing neuronal modifications that stimulate the craving to smoke. He considered the defining feature of addiction to be *loss of autonomy*, that is, that quitting requires an effort or discomfort. DiFranza developed the Hooked on Nicotine Checklist (HONC), now available in 13 languages (see Table 7.2), to operationally define symptoms of nicotine addiction. The HONC, which could easily be modified to fit most other hedonic dependencies, is a thoroughly validated measure of nicotine addiction.

The HONC was administered to hundreds of teenagers repeatedly over 3 years, and it turned out that rapid onset of addiction was very common. The most likely time for addiction to begin was the month after having the first cigarette. HONC symptoms could occur within the first weeks of smoking onset. "On average, the adolescents were smoking only two cigarettes a week when the first symptoms appeared.... A dozen studies have now established that nicotine withdrawal is common among novice smokers"—10% within 2 days and 25% to 35% within a month of having their first cigarette. In a large study of New Zealand youth, 25% had withdrawal effects after smoking 1 to 4 cigarettes (DiFranza, 2008, p. 84).

Table 7.2 The Hooked On Nicotine Checklist (HONC)

An answer of "yes" to any one of the questions indicates that addiction has begun:

Have you ever tried to quit smoking but couldn't?

Do you smoke now because it is really hard to quit?

Have you ever felt like you were addicted to tobacco?

Do you ever have strong cravings to smoke?

Have you ever felt like you really needed a cigarette?

Is it hard to keep from smoking in places where you are not supposed to, like school?

When you tried to stop smoking (or when you haven't used tobacco for a while):

- Did you find it hard to concentrate because you couldn't smoke?
- Did you feel a strong need or urge to smoke?
- Do you feel nervous, restless, or anxious because you couldn't smoke?

Source: J R DiFranza, et al., "Development of Symptoms of Tobacco Dependency in Youths: 30 Month Follow Up Data from the DANDY Study," Tobacco Control, vol. 11, no. 3. Copyright © 2002 by BMJ Publishing Group.

Why do People Smoke?

The drug nicotine appears to create craving and to suppress it: "[T]he direct immediate action of nicotine is to suppress craving and this action is magnified to an extreme because subsequent doses of nicotine provoke greater responses than the first dose" (DiFranza, 2008, p. 85). This phenomenon (sensitization), common to all addictive drugs, suggests that nicotine is addictive, not because it causes pleasure but rather because it suppresses craving. Apparently, nicotine, from the first cigarette, is sufficient to trigger a remodeling of the brain (DiFranza, 2008). This finding highlights the importance of anti-smoking campaigns.

Studies that show images comparing brain responses to the first dose of nicotine through the fifth dose given 4 days later, illustrate dramatic changes in brain function in areas such as the anterior cingulate gyrus (involved in a number of functions including emotional processing and vocalization of emotions) and the hippocampus (encoding memory). The response to the first dose is relatively limited, but brain activity is far more intense and widespread after the fifth dose. These findings indicate that the brain quickly becomes sensitized to nicotine, enabling addiction to begin after just a few doses (DiFranza, 2008).

Who Gets Hooked?

Other work by DiFranza and colleagues (2007) shows that the best predictor of adolescents getting hooked on nicotine is a feeling of relaxation produced by the very first puff from a cigarette. Although only a little more than 20% of first-time inhalers actually experience this sense of relaxation, 91% of those who do become dependent. The next best predictor of dependence found in their study was feelings of depression. Their data suggest that self-medication is a driving force in development of nicotine dependence for some individuals.

Nicotine's role as an antidepressant is further supported by the findings of McKee et al. (2011), who tested smokers in a laboratory where they were exposed to a stress-induction procedure. The stress induction increased smokers' craving ratings and feelings of negative emotions. It also made it more difficult for them to resist smoking during a 50-minute delay-to-smoke period after the stress-induction. Those who smoked sooner after the stress procedure tended to report greater satisfaction from the cigarette compared to those who were able to resist smoking until the end of the 50-minute delay. Other research (reviewed in Holliday & Gould, 2016) confirms that people with higher stress levels (unemployed individuals, military personnel currently deployed to active duty) are more likely to smoke compared to those with lower stress levels.

Data also indicate that the earlier a person starts smoking, the more likely they are to become dependent (Breslau et al., 1993; Hu et al., 2006). Kendler and colleagues (2013) investigated pairs of identical twins, all of whom were smokers. The researchers specifically studied twin pairs in which the age of onset of regular smoking began at least two years earlier in one member of each pair. The average age at which the early-onset twins became regular smokers was 14.8 years, whereas the late-onset twins became regular smokers at 21.1 years. The early-onset twins had more severe dependence and reported higher craving ratings than their later-onset twins.

Initiation of smoking at such an early age may alter adolescent brain development to increase vulnerability to become dependent. Holliday & Gould (2016) review animal research that addresses why this may be the case. It turns out that both the acetylcholine and dopamine systems go through marked changes during adolescence as a normal part of development. These changes alter sensitivity to reward and also influence learning. In rodent studies, adolescents show a greater increase in DA release in response to acute nicotine exposure and appear to experience enhanced reward, compared to adult animals given the same level of acute nicotine exposure. Further, chronic exposure to nicotine during adolescence changes the expression of acetylcholine receptors, increasing their sensitivity to nicotine; this does not happen when chronic nicotine exposure is initiated in adult animals. The changes in receptors can be long lasting, even when nicotine administration ceases. If human adolescent brains show similar responses to acute and chronic nicotine as those demonstrated in rodent models, this may explain why 90% of people who get hooked on smoking do so during adolescence.

Genetics also influence a person's vulnerability for getting hooked on nicotine. Several genes have been identified that elevate the risk of becoming dependent. Some of these are genes for acetylcholine receptors, to which nicotine binds to exert its effects. Although peers who smoke are an important risk factor associated with teen smoking, Johnson et al. (2010) demonstrated that peers matter less for those who have the greatest genetic risk associated with acetylcholine receptor mutations. This study highlights how genetic risk can interact with environmental factors to contribute to a person's vulnerability to developing nicotine dependency.

Additionally, a person's ability to metabolize nicotine is influenced by their genetics. Some individuals are fast metabolizers of nicotine, whereas others are slow metabolizers. Research shows that fast metabolizers are more likely to become dependent and smoke more cigarettes per day compared to slow metabolizers (Ray, Tyndale, & Lerman, 2009). This makes sense: if a person likes the way nicotine makes them feel but the drug is destroyed relatively quickly in the person's system, the person will need to re-administer the drug sooner than someone who is a slow metabolizer. Moreover, fast metabolizers seem to have more difficulty quitting smoking and are less likely to have a positive response to using nicotine replacement therapy.

Health Effects of Smoking

Figure 7.2 Woman and Lung

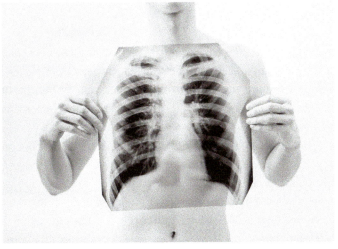

Copyright © 2015 Depositphotos/Kryzhov.

The truly devastating effects of smoking are not the multifaceted action of nicotine in the brain. Figure 7.3 (from the CDC) shows serious effects on the health of smokers in the United States. Obviously, lung cancer is the greatest hitter, followed by heart disease. In terms of health effects and deaths, cigarette smoking is the most serious drug problem in the United States today.

Figure 7.3 Annual Deaths from Smoking in the United States According to the CDC (2016), based on statistics from 2005-2009, of an approximate 480,000 annual deaths in the United States attributable to cigarette smoking, 29% were due to lung cancer and other cancers, 28% were due to cardiovascular disease (coronary heart disease and stroke), and 21% were due to pulmonary disease.

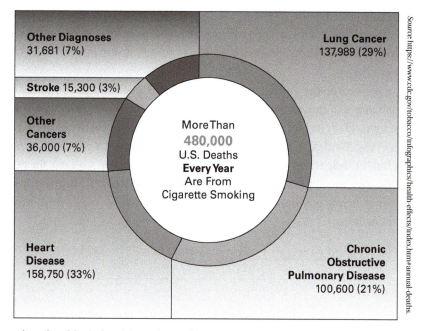

Source https://www.cdc.gov/tobacco/infographics/health-effects/index.htm#annual-deaths

Note: Average annual number of deaths for adults aged 35 or older, 2005–2009.

Tobacco is the most widely used drug of abuse and is responsible for more deaths and more financial expenditures due to health problems and lost productivity than all other legal and illegal drugs combined. Smoking is also the most preventable cause of death in the United States today. The deaths from cigarette smoking are not specifically due to the nicotine, but to the 200 known poisons, including approximately 70 carcinogens, in the tobacco smoke.

Many people do not realize that cigarette smoking has an immediate effect on a person's oxygen levels. Smoking tobacco allows for rapid absorption of nicotine across the lungs and into the bloodstream, allowing the drug to get to the brain within just a few seconds. But the smoke that goes along with the cigarette is a source of carbon monoxide (CO), and putting this into one's body decreases the flow of oxygen to muscles and organs. The reason for this is that oxygen is carried through our systems by attaching to hemoglobin in our blood. However, oxygen is not the only gaseous substance that will bind to hemoglobin—CO binds to it as well, and the strength of the CO-hemoglobin bond is about 200 times greater than the oxygen-hemoglobin bond. There's a twist here: once CO begins to bind to the hemoglobin, the binding affinity for oxygen will increase. So, there will still be some oxygen binding and being carried through the bloodstream. However, the stronger the bond between oxygen and hemoglobin, the harder it is for the oxygen to dissociate and diffuse into the tissues. This is essentially a double whammy effect that results in less oxygen being delivered to tissues (Sen, Peltz, Beard, & Zeno, 2010). (Figure 7.4 illustrates this effect.) Meanwhile, the binding between CO and hemoglobin is so strong that it can last for hours, meaning that lower blood-oxygen levels persist well beyond the length of time it takes to smoke a cigarette. It's not surprising, then, that non-smokers are usually better runners than smokers! On the plus side: ceasing smoking will increase oxygen-binding capacity of the blood within a matter of days. Although it's unlikely that a smoker would actually suffer CO poisoning (unless they smoke lots of cigarettes in a very short period of time), the elevated CO levels are thought to contribute to cardiovascular disease related to smoking.

Figure 7.4 Carbon Monoxide Poisoning Oxygen (dots) is carried in blood by hemoglobin molecules in red blood cells (circles). Oxygen is added to venous blood in the lung and the resultant arterial blood then delivers oxygen to the tissues (left panel). In carbon monoxide poisoning (right panel), less oxygen is added to the blood in the lung (smaller arrows between lung and blood) because CO displaces oxygen. Less oxygen is delivered to tissues (smaller arrows between blood and tissue) because the blood is carrying less oxygen and CO impairs the ability of hemoglobin to release oxygen. For these reasons, CO poisoning can lead to hypoxia (low levels of oxygen).

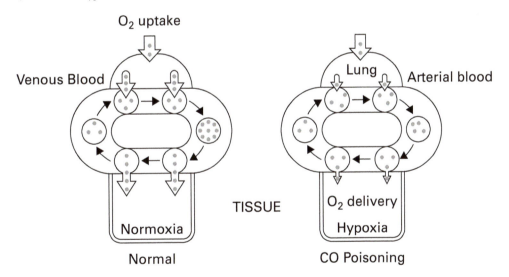

Nicotine itself is quite toxic in high doses, and it makes a very effective pesticide (Fishel, 2009). However, the major negative health effects of tobacco are due to smoking (and chewing) and not to the nicotine. The tars and toxins in cigarette smoke can lead to chronic obstructive pulmonary disease (COPD), a group of lung conditions that include bronchitis and emphysema. The smoke suppresses the function of tiny hairs (cilia) that line the airways to help remove debris and pathogens from our lungs. Over time, with chronic exposure to smoke, the cilia become paralyzed, making the person more vulnerable to lung infections. The walls of the lungs can thicken, making it difficult for oxygen to pass into the blood. Long-time smokers may end up using supplemental oxygen because their lungs are so impaired.

Smoking is responsible for most of the lung cancer in the world as well as cancer of the larynx, esophagus, bladder, kidney, pancreas, stomach, and uterine cavity. It is also a major cause of heart disease. Researchers now recognize that second-hand smoke increases the risk of cancer and pulmonary diseases; moreover, smoking during pregnancy poses risks to the fetus (CDC, 2015). Using chew tobacco instead of smoking does not eliminate cancer risk; instead, the person will have an elevated risk of oral cancer. Overall, three-fourths of the cancer cases in the U.S. are linked to tobacco.

A lesser-known but shocking health consequence of chronic smoking is Buerger's disease. This condition occurs when long-term, heavy smoking produces profound impairments in blood flow to the extremities. People with this condition may end up having toes or feet amputated because the loss of blood flow can lead to development of gangrene.

Other Means of Administration

E-Cigarettes

Given that e-cigarettes provide nicotine without cigarette smoke, one might assume that e-cigarettes must be safer than regular cigarettes or chewing tobacco. However, we don't really have enough data to evaluate the risks; instead of saying that "the jury is out," we must say that we don't yet have the longitudinal evidence required to deliberate the case. A recent review (Kaisar et al., 2016) highlights how little is known about the safety of these devices; however, what is known gives cause for concern. Data indicate that nicotine cartridges used for e-cigarettes can contain some degree of toxins. Furthermore, the vehicles (solutions in which the nicotine is dissolved, often called e-liquids) may be unsafe and contribute to lung disease. For instance, common e-liquids contain substances similar to antifreeze. There are also added flavorings, such as diacetyl; this chemical is normally used to give a popcorn flavoring to microwave popcorn but is also used in many e-cigarette cartridges (Allen et al., 2016). This substance has been demonstrated to produce lung damage through environmental exposure (among people who worked with flavorings in popcorn factories); because diacetyl causes irreversible lung damage, there is concern about people inhaling it directly into their lungs. Many young smokers bypass regular cigarettes and head directly for e-cigarettes, and some products are flavored to appeal to youth (e.g., Cupcake, Cotton Candy), raising further concerns about the safety of these products.

As shown in Figure 7.5, about 60% of teenagers who regularly use e-cigarettes report vaping flavor cartridges without any nicotine (USDHHS, 2016). Unfortunately, it may be years before enough data are accumulated to determine the long-term health effects of e-cigarettes.

Figure 7.5. Past Month Percentage of Teens that Use E-Cigarettes vs. Cigarettes by Grade Level

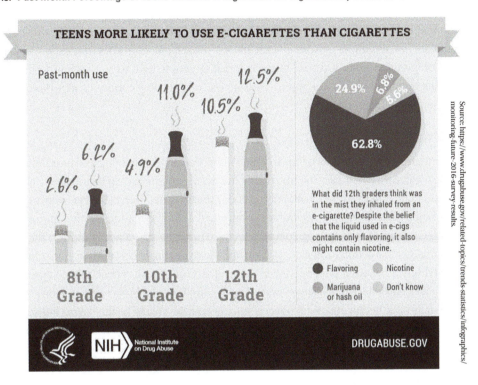

Hookahs or Waterpipes

(Other names: argileh, ghelyoon, hubble bubble, shisha, boory, goza, and narghile).

Hookahs are devices used for smoking tobacco by means of inhaling the smoke through a partially filled water bowl. Although it is commonly thought that hookah smoking carries less risk than cigarettes, some research suggests that waterpipe smoke "is as toxic as cigarette smoke" (Knishkowy & Amitai, 2005; Cobb et al., 2010).

Figure 7.6. Hookah

Copyright © 2009 Depositphotos/Aptyp_koK.

The charcoal used to heat the hookah contains many toxins, and the amount of time (and number of puffs) involved in hookah smoking greatly exceeds that of cigarette smoking. A hookah smoker might spend up to an hour in a smoking session, and they can achieve high levels of nicotine in their systems. Unfortunately, they are also achieving high levels of toxin exposure. Recent data reviewed by Kim and colleagues (2016) suggest that risks of cardiopulmonary disease, COPD, and cancer exist with hookah use. The air quality of hookah lounges can be assessed according to air quality scales used for rating air quality in populous cities. For people who frequent or work in these lounges, there is an elevated risk of health problems as air quality may reach unhealthy levels. Health concerns may exist specifically for hookah use, compared to other forms of tobacco: because people tend to smoke from a shared water pipe, passing the mouthpiece between them, there is a risk of spreading communicable diseases such as tuberculosis, hepatitis, and meningitis.

Legal Status of Tobacco Products

Earlier, we mentioned that the tobacco industry hid knowledge of the addicting and harmful nature their products from the public. Eventually the truth came out during congressional hearings in 1994 (typically called the Waxman hearings). Although initially testifying that they believed cigarettes were not addicting, executives of major tobacco companies ultimately admitted to both the addictive and harmful nature of their products. As a result of the hearings, concessions were made by the tobacco industry. These included numerous changes in marketing strategies: no more television and print ads, and no more marketing that is clearly aimed towards young people (rest in peace, Joe Camel!). Moreover, tobacco products were required to put warning labels on packages, and tobacco companies had to pay out millions of dollars for further research into the health effects of tobacco and to cover the cost of health claims linked to tobacco usage. Today, tobacco company websites feature copious amounts of information about the health risks of tobacco, although one cannot help but wonder if smokers actually read this information. To recoup lost money as a result of the concessions, U.S. tobacco companies began marketing more in undeveloped countries where there are fewer regulations.

More recently, there has been an expansion of FDA regulation over tobacco products. In 2009, the Family Smoking Prevention and Tobacco Control Act was passed, which allowed the FDA to regulate manufacturing, distribution, and marketing of tobacco products. The FDA's power was further extended in August, 2016; now, the FDA regulates virtually all forms of nicotine delivery, including e-cigarettes (USFDA, 2016b). People must be 18 in order to buy any nicotine products, and tobacco companies must receive approval from the FDA before they can market any product. FDA approval in this case is not the same as the approval the agency grants for therapeutic drugs: in the case of medication, pharmaceutical companies are required to demonstrate that their products are generally safe and effective. In the case of nicotine and tobacco products, however, approval from the FDA does *not* mean the products are safe—it merely indicates that the FDA is allowing them to be sold to adults with appropriate warnings attached to the product packaging.

Because tobacco is one of the oldest industries in the U.S., it is unlikely that tobacco will ever be prohibited in our country (not that prohibition of substances makes people stop using them anyway!). Cigarette smoking rates are lower now than they were in the 20th century, and this decrease is largely attributed to smoking education programs that warn about the health risks of tobacco products. With rising levels of e-cigarette and hookah use, longitudinal data are needed so that educational programs can be re-tooled to address risks associated with these products. Potential consumers—especially adolescents—need to be given accurate information if they are to try to make sound decisions about use of these products.

Smokers: Modern Day Pariahs?

B. Roberson

Most Americans are familiar with smoking bans: many cities and states have passed laws prohibiting smoking in public places, including businesses, restaurants, campuses, etc. Some housing rental agreements forbid tenants from smoking in their residences, and hotels may not offer prospective guests the option of "smoking or non-smoking" when someone makes a room reservation. Such bans reflect both the short-term irritation of non-smokers by environmental smoke as well as the long-term hazards linked to second-hand smoke. Everyone is healthier when no one is smoking.

But is it possible to go too far with bans? Some states allow employers to ban smokers—that is, to legally refuse to hire people who smoke. Job applicants would be subjected to drug testing, which many corporations use to screen out abusers of illegal substances such as marijuana, cocaine, or heroin. In this case, though, employers would also screen for nicotine; those who test positive for it would be denied employment unless they demonstrate that the nicotine is from a smoking cessation treatment (nicotine patches, gums). According to Huddle and colleagues (2014), the rationale for eliminating smokers from a company's workforce is often seen as an economic benefit for the employer: smokers have more sick days and higher health care costs compared to their non-smoking colleagues. Smokers also take more breaks during the day and may be seen as less productive. Smoker bans can occur within health care systems, and may be rationalized by hospitals who adopt such policies because smoking is antithetical to their mission of promoting health. Some employers think that smoking bans could help bring down the overall prevalence of smoking in society; if more employers refuse to hire smokers, then people will be forced to give up their unhealthy addiction in order to get a job. Smoking could potentially be "denormalized" (which may be equivalent to stigmatized).

Is it a Good Idea?

Some people will argue that it's one thing to say a person cannot smoke within the building at their place of business, but it's quite another to say a person cannot smoke at all—not even off-duty in their own homes. In other words, *smoking* bans seem reasonable to protect the rights and health of non-smokers, but *smoker* bans seem to violate the rights of individuals who do smoke. If employers can refuse to hire smokers, then couldn't they also refuse to hire drinkers or unhealthy eaters? After all, these individuals will also have elevated health care costs compared to co-workers who eat healthy diets and avoid harmful drugs. Huddle et al.'s (2014) review of the arguments surrounding smoker bans reveals that this sort of employment policy would likely disproportionately affect people from lower socioeconomic groups: smoking is more common among people who earn less than $35,000 per year, as well as among adults without high school diplomas. Preventing people from getting a job (which may also provide access to health insurance) seems to put them into a predicament that perpetuates their lower socioeconomic status. Another problem is that these policies typically affect new hires: smokers hired prior to the adoption of the policy probably will not be fired, although they will be strongly encouraged to quit. This creates a double-standard between new and old employees, based on a policy that Huddle and colleagues suggest is paternalistic.

Is This a Good Idea?

"On January 20, 2016, New Jersey Governor Chris Christie vetoed a bill passed with strong bipartisan support by his state legislature that would have raised New Jersey's minimum age of sale for tobacco products to 21. The veto is a setback in an otherwise accelerating movement toward dissemination of "Tobacco 21" laws as a new tool for reducing young people's access to cigarettes and e-cigarettes. In 2013, only 8 U.S. localities had adopted Tobacco 21 laws. By March 2016, at least 125 localities and the state of Hawaii had done so, and California was on the cusp of following suit. In September 2015, the first federal Tobacco 21 legislation was introduced (Tobacco to 21 Act, S. 2100)" … (Morain et. al., 2016).

Research data on the effectiveness of Tobacco 21 laws at reducing smoking is encouraging. Analysis of the effects of the law adopted in Needham, Massachusetts revealed a 47% reduction in the smoking rate among high school students, along with a reported decline in area retail tobacco purchases (Morain et.al. 2016). Should Tobacco 21 laws become required throughout the land? Research evidence points in that direction. The vast majority of smokers become initiated during adolescence, a period when the brain is more susceptible to becoming dependent on nicotine. Those who purchase cigarettes for teenagers are almost entirely under the age of 21. Thus, raising the sale age prevents older high school students from purchasing tobacco products for their peers. As of this writing, local and state efforts have succeeded in extending Tobacco 21 protections to more than 16 million Americans. "We believe the time has come to expand this effective, broadly supported approach to a much greater share of the population" (Morain et al., 2016).

Chapter Summary

This chapter discusses self-administration of nicotine, one of the active ingredients of the tobacco plant. When smoked in the form of cigarettes, nicotine is associated with one of the most dangerous health hazards known to humans. According to the World Health Organization: "Tobacco kills up to half of its users… around 6 million people each year." More than 5 million of those deaths are the result of direct tobacco use while more than 600,000 are the result of non-smokers being exposed to second-hand smoke. There is a broad array of nicotine delivery products including: cigarettes, cigars, pipe tobacco, hookahs, chew, snuff and e-cigarettes.

Recent survey data indicate that teenagers are more likely to smoke e-cigarettes ("vape") than to smoke regular cigarettes. Nicotine replacement products, intended to help people cease or at least curb their tobacco use, come in gums, patches, and oral mists. Although, for many years the tobacco industry denied that tobacco products were addictive, data from outside of the industry clearly show that individuals can become hooked on tobacco products. In fact, the brain quickly becomes sensitized to nicotine, enabling addiction to begin after just a few doses. That smoking serves as a form of self-medication is confirmed by known facts about its neurochemical mechanisms of action as well as from social science research on those who are more likely to smoke. People with higher stress levels (e.g., unemployed individuals, military personnel currently deployed to active duty) are more likely to smoke compared to those with lower stress levels.

As of August 2016, the Food and Drug Administration's authority has been expanded to regulate virtually all forms of nicotine delivery, including e-cigarettes. In the vast majority of municipalities throughout the U.S., the minimum age is 18 for purchasing any nicotine products. Tobacco companies must demonstrate that appropriate warnings are attached to product packaging. The final segment of this chapter explores several questions about nicotine regulation: Is it possible to go too far with smoking bans? Should there be a nationwide minimum age of 21 for purchase of any products sold for purpose of ingesting nicotine?

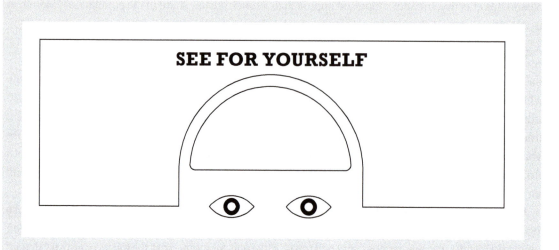

SEE FOR YOURSELF

Daily Smoking Prevalence. 2017. The Lancet.

Interactive model showing the percentage of daily smokers by countries worldwide.
http://www.thelancet.com/lancet/visualisations/gbd-smoking

The Real Cost. U.S. Department of Health and Human Services. Anti-Smoking Media Campaign.

The following link, designed by the Department of Health and Human Services for teenagers and adults, vividly portrays the toxic effects of smoking, and also strategies for quitting.
https://therealcost.betobaccofree.hhs.gov/taking-control.html

CHAPTER 8

Food/Mood Connections

I knew no other way than eating to alleviate the loneliness, to fill in the spaces where comfort and security could have been.

—Andie Mitchel, *It Was Me All Along: A Memoir*

No matter how hard I run this morning, nothing can take away the damage done. As I slip out of bed and do deep lunges across the floor to the bathroom, I promise myself to cut my calorie intake in half to 150 for the day and to take twenty laxatives. That should do something to help. But it's not the weight gain from the six ounces of yogurt that worries me. It's the loss of self-control. It's the fear that maybe I've lost it for good. I start sobbing now as I lunge my way across the floor and I wonder how many calories I'm burning by sobbing. Sobbing and lunging—it's got to be at least 30 calories.

—Portia de Rossi, *Unbearable Lightness: A Story of Loss and Gain (pp. 7–8)*

Introduction

Although being svelte is undoubtedly in vogue, and many who diet are quite healthy, much of the world is, in fact, dangerously rotund. Overweight and obesity are the fifth leading risk for global deaths. "Once associated with high-income countries, obesity is now also prevalent in low- and middle-income countries" (World Health Organization, 2016).

According to the World Health Organization (WHO), more than 1.9 billion adults, 18 years and older, were overweight in 2014. Of these, over 600 million—one-in-eight adults globally—were obese. The United Nations' goal, set in 2010, to halt the increase in obesity by 2025, will not be met if the current trajectory continues (The Economist, 2016).

"44% of the diabetes burden, 23% of the ischemic heart disease burden and between 7% and 41% of certain cancer burdens are attributable to overweight and obesity" (European Association for the Study of Obesity, 2013). The prevalence of obesity nearly doubled between 1980 and 2008. Global evidence shows an ever-expanding prevalence of obesity, generally defined as exceeding the average weight for one's height and age by 20%. "The ratio of undernutrition to obesity has reversed remarkably so that the prevalence of obesity is double that of undernutrition" (Popkin, 2011, pg. 233). As shown in Figure 8.1 below, the prevalence of obesity in the U.S. exceeds 20% of the population for every state.

Figure 8.1 Prevalence of Self-Reported Obesity Among U.S. Adults by State and Territory, BRFSS, 2015

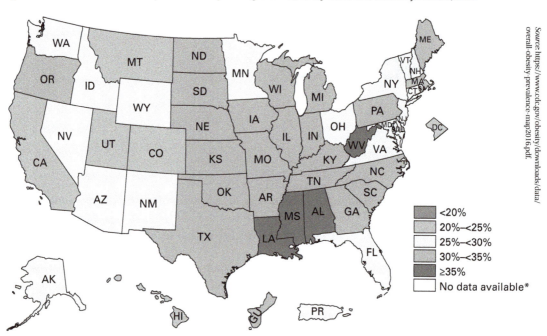

Source: https://www.cdc.gov/obesity/downloads/data/overall-obesity-prevalence-map2016.pdf.

Corresponding to the epidemic of obesity, most people in the U.S. would like to trim down. Nearly 90% of Americans believe that they are overweight and more than 35% say they want to lose at least 15 pounds (Grimm, 2007). As shown in Figure 8.2, there is a direct relationship between body mass and risk of disease. In fact, hundreds of millions of dollars are spent on appetite-suppressing drugs containing caffeine and amphetamine-related compounds. The diet-conscious purchase weight control and fitness guides with such regularity that at least one appears on the bestseller list each week; they maintain a torrid love affair with low-calorie foods and join health spas and self-help groups like Weight Watchers or TOPS (Take Off Pounds Sensibly) by the millions. A myriad of nutrition gurus including doctors, psychotherapists, and religious fanatics are enlisted to coach self-denial and impulse control.

Fortunately (or unfortunately, depending on your viewpoint), there is a tailor-made diet for every taste. Eating fads range from high-protein to high-carbohydrate diets, with obligatory emphasis on vegetables, fruits, and high-fiber foods. Some regimens emphasize eating certain foods at fixed times of the day; others stress not mixing particular foods. Recommendations and admonitions are often contradictory and sometimes bizarre: no salt, no milk products, lots of milk products, fasting, eating as much as you like, fruit juice only, no fruit juice, no meat, all meat, drinking vinegar, or even your own urine (e.g., Christy, 1994; Peschek-Böhmer & Schreiber, 1999)—you name it. Recently, the diet industry has been caving in to the healthy food consumption industry. "Consumers are looking for a more holistic, more health and wellness approach...the shift in food trends is toward fresher and more natural ingredients" (Hottovy, 2016).

The contemporary obsession with weight control—the svelte craze—is influenced, not only by overwhelming scientific evidence on the health burdens of excess weight, by also by the whims of Hollywood and Madison Avenue. Among movie stars and models, thinness is not only fashionable but an occupational necessity. Since *Playboy* began publishing in 1953, centerfold models have become progressively slimmer. Social class seems to play a role. Women from lower-class backgrounds, whose diets are more likely to be higher in fats and carbohydrates, are 6 times more likely to be obese than upper-class women. Studies of immigrants and their descendants show that as new generations move up the socioeconomic scale, obesity, especially among females, declines. A simple extrapolation from the body measurements of a child's Barbie doll reveals the tremendous social pressure toward slimness and form. As a symbol of femininity, Barbie is not a harmless toy—not with a physique that when translated into human terms measures 33–18–28½ (Katz, 2011). These dimensions are unrealistic for a living female!

Figure 8.2 Body Mass Index and Risk of Disease Relative risk of disease plotted against body mass index (BMI), calculated as (body mass in kg)/(height in meters)^2 or, alternatively, as (body mass in lbs. × 703.1)/(height in inches)^2. BMI values in the 20–25 range are considered desirable, those 25–30 are classified as overweight, and values over 30 are classified as obese. The relative risk of disease compares an individual's probability (corrected for age) of having a disease with that of the general population. The curvilinear relationship indicates that obesity markedly increases disease risk.

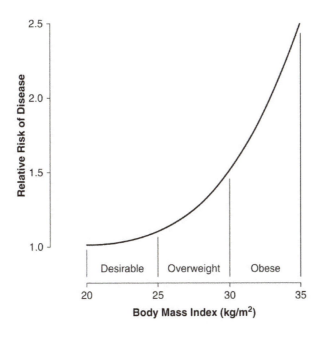

As in other compulsive disorders, overeating usually leads to progressively impaired functioning. While the psychological and social complications are severe—interpersonal anxiety, job discrimination, sexual and social limitations—the physical dangers are even more frightening. Obese people are at increased risk for high blood pressure, heart disease, diabetes, back and joint problems, and respiratory disorders. Fat men have a higher incidence of certain cancers, including those of the colon, rectum, and prostate. Overweight women are at a greater risk for developing malignant tumors of the ovaries and uterine lining, and after menopause, of the breasts. With stereotypic joviality, an obese person whose blood pressure began to soar as their weight reached nearly 300 pounds recalls their doctor's warning: "If you don't lose weight, I'll put you in a coffin with a shoehorn."

On counterpoint, there is an alarmingly high incidence of dangerously underweight individuals in today's *striving for slimness generation*. In some cases, dramatic weight loss may be attributed to a brain tumor, bowel disease, or glandular dysfunction.

However, as high as 1% of selected populations, primarily females, for no known biological reason appear to be starving themselves—sometimes to death. Of all psychiatric disorders, anorexia has the highest mortality rate, and it is also extremely resistant to treatment (Fields, 2011). We will discuss this matter below, first sugar!

Is Sugar the World's Most Popular and Dangerous Drug?

Figure 8.3 Gummy Bears

What if there is a drug that could boost mood, increase energy, is universally available, and can be ingested by mouth on a momentary whim? Furthermore, that chemical would mix well with about everything else that people eat or drink. When given to babies, it becomes a driving force behind the kinds of foods they will crave for the rest of their lives. And, there are no immediate negative effects. No visible intoxication; no staggering or slurring of words; no respiratory distress; no brain seizures or heart palpitations; and no observable detriments to work, love or play.

> More than anything, it makes children happy, at least for the period during which they're consuming it. It calms their distress, eases their pain, focuses their attention, and leaves them excited and full of joy until the dose wears off. The only downside is that children will come to expect another dose, perhaps to demand it, on a regular basis (Taubes, 2011).

> How long before parents would use this drug to persuade children to behave in accordance with their wishes; and how long before the drug would be used to insure happiness during times of celebration …football games, weddings, holiday parties, etc.? How long would it be before the less affluent people of the world would routinely squander their money on this ever-so-tasty delight, rather than on nutritious meals for themselves and their loved ones (Taubes, 2011)?

Historically, sugar is one of a number of "drug foods" that came out of the tropics and upon which nations built their empires beginning in the 16th century—join the party with tea, cocoa, chocolate, and tobacco. To make matters worse, it has been linked to all these products, i.e., rum is distilled from sugar cane, sugar is a critical ingredient of the American-blended tobacco cigarette (Camel was the first) and quickly became the nearly universal add-on to tea, coffee, and chocolate. Adding to the universal sugar frenzy, it was used to sweeten European spirits and wine in the 14th century, and in India as an additive in cannabis preparations. Opium based wines and spirits also contained sugar (Taubes, 2011). As to the question of whether sugar is in fact addicting, it induces the same type of responses in the brain's reward center as other highly addictive substances such as nicotine, heroin, cocaine, and alcohol; and it may promote tolerance and withdrawal. However, reviews from the field of neuroscience do throw some skepticism on the concept of sugar addiction; the phenomenon has been demonstrated in rat models under specific conditions (food-restricted schedules that promote bingeing when access to sugar is provided), but is not accepted as conclusive within humans.

It is obvious that excess consumption of sugar is psychologically addictive and is clearly linked to overweight. But the even darker side of the story is mounting evidence that excess consumption of sugar may be a factor in heart disease, diabetes, and cancer. Robert Lustig, an expert on childhood obesity (University of California, San Francisco School of Medicine), claims that sugar is a "toxin" or "poison"—"[It] should be thought of, like cigarettes and alcohol, as something that's killing us" (Lustig, 2009). Excess consumption has been linked to a disorder known as "metabolic syndrome," a serious health condition that affects about 23% of adults. It is a cluster of conditions—increased blood pressure, high blood sugar, excess body fat around the waist, and abnormal cholesterol or triglyceride levels—that occur together, increasing your risk of heart disease, stroke, and diabetes. Metabolic syndrome is closely linked to overweight, obesity, and inactivity.

Lustig puts forth a strong argument that high sugar consumption (including fructose) is causally connected to insulin resistance, which leads to the secretion of increased insulin, which promotes tumor growth, i.e., a person with metabolic syndrome has a greater probability of getting cancer (Taubes, 2011). It appears that many cancers rely on insulin to provide the blood sugar they need to grow and multiply. Insulin and insulin-like growth factor (and related growth factors) also provide the signal, in effect, to do it"

If sugar causes insulin resistance, excess consumptions likely causes some forms of cancer. More studies are needed to show a definitive link; however, the existing evidence appears to provide ample cause for "sweet vigilance."

Dr. Lustig's (2009; 2012) argument that sugar is toxic and the cornerstone of the obesity epidemic has been so powerful that at the time of this writing his YouTube video entitled "The Skinny on Obesity" has been seen by nearly 7,000,000 million viewers (link shown in See for Yourself).

Is This a Good Idea?

Tax on Sugary Soft Drinks

The question of whether sugar consumption should be regulated by the State is obvious. But is it the province of government to impose a "sin tax" on a set of widely enjoyed soft drinks?

For more than a decade, Coca-Cola, Pepsi, and other beverage companies have fought mightily against efforts to tax sugary sodas, defeating more than three dozen such proposals around the country.

But this month, voters in San Francisco, Oakland and Albany, Calif., as well as Boulder, Colo., stunned the industry by approving ballot measures in favor of soda taxes. Cook County, Illinois, followed a few days later, bringing a soft-drink tax to Chicago and surrounding areas. They are joining Berkeley, California, which passed a tax 2 years ago, and Philadelphia, which passed one in June, bringing the number of American communities with soda taxes to 7.

With that public momentum, a soda tax may be coming to a city near you.

Advocates say the recent sweep represents a watershed moment in the fight for soft-drink taxes. Once viewed as measures likely to find support only in largely health-conscious cities like Berkeley and Boulder, soda taxes have emerged as a bountiful revenue source for cash-strapped local governments to fund early childhood education, public safety, and reduce deficit reduction. Soda tax advocates say they believe more cities will now consider their own taxes on sweetened beverages to combat obesity and to finance local programs (O'Connor & Sanger-Katz, 2016).

Eating Disorders: Unhealthy Relationships with Food

Anorexia nervosa and bulimia are closely related eating disorders primarily found among middle- and upper-middle-class women who appear to be victims of fad and fashion. The core symptom of anorexia nervosa is a relentless pursuit of excessive thinness. Diagnostic criteria include self-imposed dieting; weight loss of at least 25% of the person's usual body weight; distorted perception of the body; cessation of menstruation; and no known medical illness to account for the weight loss. Approximately 50% of anorexics are also diagnosed as bulimic (M. J. Cooper, 2005; Hoek, 2006). The DSM-5 recognizes two subtypes of anorexia nervosa: the restricting subtype, which is more common, and the binge/purge subtype. (American Psychiatric Association [APA], 2013). Family and twin studies show that genetic factors contribute about 50% to the development of an eating disorder (Klump, Kaye, & Strober, 2001) and that anorexia shares a genetic risk with clinical depression (Wade, Bulik, Neale, & Kendler, 2000). It appears that genes influencing both eating regulation and emotion may be important contributing factors.

Research on the epidemiology of anorexia suggests an average prevalence of 0.3% (3 out of 1,000), with a much higher rate (up to 10%) in selected populations (e.g., achievement-oriented female high school or college students). Studies show that the condition largely affects adolescent females, with teens between 15 and 19 years of age making up 40% of all cases (Bulik, Reba, Siega-Riz, & Reichborn-Kjennerud, 2005; Hoek, 2006).

About 90% of people with anorexia are female (Lask & Bryant-Waugh, 2000). However, anorexia is not limited to a certain demographic. In March 2008, Rosemary Pope, a 49-year-old British senior university lecturer with a PhD in psychology and a professional background in health, died from anorexia (BBC News, 2008). It is notable, however, that conditions such as anorexia and bulimia are much more common in Western cultures, such as North America and parts of Europe. Just as the overeater seeks ecstasy through food, the person with anorexia seeks ecstasy through not eating. It is estimated that 1 in 100 females will develop anorexia sometime in her life, and 10% of these will die of it (Tyre, 2005). Anorexia nervosa also has a high rate of co-occurrence with other psychological conditions, such as depression and anxiety. In addition to possible genetic influences on neurotransmitter and hormonal systems and the social influence of body images portrayed in the media, development of anorexia has been linked to adverse childhood events, such as abuse and neglect.

Bulimia is a chronic dieting disorder usually associated with binge eating. Bulimics may be emaciated, of average weight, grossly obese, or anywhere in between. Experts disagree as to whether bulimia and anorexia are part of the same disorder. Characteristically, an individual with bulimia consumes an excessive amount of food in a short period of time. Binges are usually planned and may last from several hours to several days. Food tends to be eaten very rapidly, gobbled rather than chewed. It is often very sweet and high in calories. Eating usually occurs in a clandestine manner, in which the eater experiences a sense of loss of control and an inability to stop. Binging varies in frequency between individuals, from several times a month to several times a day. Many people who suffer from bulimia, which literally means pathologically insatiable hunger, begin to induce vomiting to prevent weight gain and to decrease sensations of physical discomfort. The binge-purge cycle often includes the use of such cathartic devices as laxatives, suppositories, or enemas for rapid evacuation of the bowels. This pattern of dietary chaos is often accompanied by periods of intense and sometimes excessive exercise, which may be interpreted as a form of penance for partaking of forbidden fruit (American Psychiatric Association, 1994). It looks like the "fobidden fruit" notion comes from an older version of the DSM. The DSM-5 was published in 2013. DSM-5 includes excessive exercise as a form of purging. Abuse of laxatives and excessive exercise to avoid gaining wait are behaviors that may also occur in individuals with anorexia.

Harvard researchers found binge eating disorder (BED) to be the most common eating disorder in the United States, even more prevalent than anorexia and bulimia combined (Hudson et al., 2007). People with BED share some traits with those suffering from bulimia; they consume large quantities of sugary, fatty foods in a single sitting, usually to the point of physical discomfort. They typically do this binging in private, and there is shame and guilt associated with the behavior. The BED sufferers differ in that they do not purge after their binges. Obviously, the problem is associated with the health hazards of obesity, a natural consequence of the disorder. Even when not gorging themselves, binge eaters are thinking about food, easily succumbing to their craving—a heavy price to pay for momentary ecstasy. In some very fundamental ways, compulsive eating is akin to addictions of all stripes, including gambling, sex, and drugs. In essence, the binge eater is using food as a drug. Although BED is more likely to occur in women than in men, the gender split is not as dramatic as it is for other eating disorders. The National Eating Disorder Association (NEDA) reports that about 60% of BED sufferers are female and 40% are male.

According to Leutwyler (2006), most people will over- or under-eat when confronted with stress. However, biology and personality types push some to the extremes. Anorexics tend to be "good students, dedicated athletes and perfectionists ... In contrast, bulimics and binge eaters are typically outgoing and adventurous, prone to impulsive behaviors" (p. 86). Depression, anxiety, and obsessive compulsive disorder often co-occur in each of these disorders. Each disorder is linked genetically and related to malfunction of the serotonin regulation system.

In terms of brain chemistry, people with anorexia or bulimia may have atypical levels of several different brain chemicals, for instance, abnormally low levels of serotonin. Serotonin at normal levels is associated with feelings of well-being. However, low levels may be associated with anxiety and obsessive thinking. Due to starvation, people with anorexia will have low levels of serotonin because they are ingesting very little food and especially avoid carbohydrates, which tend to be rich in tryptophan, an essential amino acid needed to produce serotonin. As a result, people with anorexia will have abnormally low serotonin. In addition to serotonin abnormalities, people with anorexia may have abnormally high levels of several other chemicals, including endorphins which may help ameliorate physical and psychological distress associated with starvation. Moreover, chemicals specifically involved in regulating appetite might be giving faulty signals in these individuals. For instance, a chemical known as CART serves as a satiety signal in the brain; when CART levels are elevated, appetite and eating should shut off. This chemical also affects the sensitivity of the mesolimbic dopamine pathway. Research by Stanley (2003) indicates that women with anorexia have abnormally high levels of CART (50% greater) than women without anorexia. Theoretically, abnormal CART levels could change how (or to what degree) anorexics experience hunger—as well as reinforcement from food, given that CART interacts with the mesolimbic dopamine system. Other data indicate deficiencies in ghrelin, a chemical that helps signal hunger (and which also influences sensitivity of the mesolimbic dopamine system). Other biochemical differences exist as well, some of which may not return to normal even if normal weight is recovered.

Do People with Anorexia Experience Different (Diminished) Hunger Signals?

Research points to numerous biochemical differences in anorexics, including deficiencies in chemicals such as ghrelin that triggers hunger, elevations in CART which triggers satiety, and higher levels of endorphins decrease pain sensations. Moreover, excessive exercise, which often accompanies anorexia, promotes elevations in adrenalin and noradrenalin and temporarily increases blood sugar level, decreasing immediate sensations of hunger (assuming that there was some degree of stored energy in some remaining fat tissue that could be broken down to use during exercise). Additionally, neuroimaging data indicate that brain tissue can shrink in chronic anorexia particularly in regions related to appetite, reward, and somatosensory processing (Titova et al., 2013). Such findings raise the possibility of cognitive dysfunction in these individuals as a result of nutritional deficiencies and brain impairments. Perhaps in chronic anorexics, these brain effects contribute to their distorted self-perception and inability to recognize they are dangerously thin. Is it possible that a state of starvation which many people would find extremely aversive and more-or-less unbearable is actually tolerable for the anorexic due to altered brain function and biochemical levels?

Regarding treatment, because of their normal weight, and their secretive and strange eating rituals, bulimics can be very difficult to identify. Anorexics, however, present the most obstacles to treatment because they view dramatic weight loss as positive, indicative of control over their life. When family, friends, or ill health directs a person with an eating disorder to seek help, cognitive-behavioral treatment (CBT), sometimes combined with medication, shows promise (M. J. Cooper, 2005).

The three main components of the CBT approach to eating disorders are the following:

1. Patients keep diaries of what, how, and when they eat and what prompted them to eat as they did;
2. Flawed perceptions about food and body image are identified (e.g., "I'm fat"), and with the help of the therapist, evidence against these ideas is listed and they are corrected; and
3. Strategies are developed to eliminate cues that reinforce abnormal perceptions (e.g., eliminating scales and mirrors).

Treatment outcomes for both anorexia and bulimia may improve when CBT is combined with Prozac, a serotonin reuptake inhibitor (Leutwyler, 2006). However, some data suggest that people with anorexia do not respond well to serotonergic drugs until they have regained a healthy body weight, although there are surprisingly few published studies on use of medications in anorexia patients. Part of the problem may be due to their already low levels of serotonin: most medications prescribed to elevate serotonin are reuptake inhibitors: they block the ability of nerve cells that release serotonin to take this neurotransmitter back inside. However, because anorexics are already deficient in serotonin, there is little gain in serotonin function. Moreover, serotonergic agents can suppress appetite; this may make sense as a treatment strategy for individuals with BED, but may be ill-advised for those with anorexia.

CASE EXAMPLE: Death of Drummer

Karen Carpenter was half of a musical duo who shot to pop music stardom in the early 1970s. Her older brother Richard was a musical prodigy who was extremely gifted at piano. He began composing in his teenage years and wrote many of the songs the duo recorded. Karen didn't discover her performing talents until high school, when she joined the marching band as a way of dodging gym class. She ultimately ended up playing drums, even though many people told her that boys, not girls, should be drummers. She was a quick study and seemed to have a natural talent for them.

The siblings performed in a couple of musical ensembles before finally landing a recording contract as The Carpenters. Karen, who considered herself first and foremost a drummer, was also the lead singer, and originally, she sang from behind her drum set, almost completely obscured from the audience. She was 5'4" and, although she was never obese, she had been considered pudgy since childhood. Ultimately, Richard and the band manager drew her out from behind her drum set and put her center stage to please their audiences: with the lead singer hidden, there was no focal point on the stage during the performance, which seemed weird to those watching. Out in front with only a microphone to conceal her, Karen became increasingly focused on her weight and appearance and began dieting.

Initially using a water diet, Karen shed about 25 pounds in 6 weeks. But food restriction didn't end there. Moreover, she developed purging tendencies and eventually developed a physical dependency on laxatives. She also took thyroid medication to increase her metabolism. After several years and dramatic weight loss, Karen was forced into treatment after collapsing onstage. The Carpenters went on hiatus for a while: Karen went to New York City and pursued psychotherapy for her anorexia (meanwhile, her brother pursued treatment for his Quaalude addiction). At one point, Karen was hospitalized due to dizziness and heart arrhythmia. Over the course of 8 weeks, she regained 30 pounds. She discontinued her psychotherapy and returned to California to resume her recording career with her brother and finalize her divorce.

Three months later and only a month before her 33rd birthday, Karen collapsed at her parents' home and was taken to the hospital where she died of cardiac arrest. Technically, at 108 lbs., her BMI was in a "normal range," but her years of self-starvation followed by rapid weight increase likely had weakened her heart. The coroner ruled her death as "emetine cardiotoxicity" as a consequence of anorexia nervosa. Emetine, better known as ipecac, is a liquid used medically to induce vomiting (intended for use when people swallow poison). Her family denied that Karen used emetine, although they acknowledged her laxative abuse. Her death in 1983 was perhaps the first high profile case of someone dying from an eating disorder, bringing the terms "anorexia nervosa" and "bulimia" into public awareness. Decades later, people mourn this gentle soul with a distinctive contralto voice—the self-described drummer who happens to also sing and who died many years too soon.

Eating Disorders as Addictions

The word "addiction" is not used extensively in the DSM-5. With regard to drugs and alcohol, problematic behavior would be assessed along the continuum of a "Substance Use Disorder" (SUD), with a minimum of at least 2 out of 11 symptoms required to warrant a diagnosis of a mild SUD. Four or five symptoms yields a diagnosis of moderate SUD, and 6 or more symptoms result in a diagnosis of severe SUD. The more criteria the person fits, the more extreme their SUD:

Table 8.1 DSM-5 Criteria for Substance Use Disorder (APA, 2013)

- Increased (amount, frequency) beyond intended use
- Unsuccessful attempts to control/decrease/stop
- Tolerance
- Withdrawal
- Failure to fulfill major obligations
- Continued use despite negative consequences
- Continued use despite knowledge of problems
- Repeated use in hazardous situations
- Spending excessive time using/obtaining/recovering from use

- Decreased time spent doing other things
- Craving

Eating disorders are categorized as completely different conditions, but one can make interesting comparisons between eating disorders and SUDS. For instance, consider the case of someone with BED. These individuals can be obsessed with food and have intense cravings. The amount of food consumed in binges can increase over time, and for some individuals, the frequency of binges can increase as well. The binge eater feels a loss of control once they start eating. Even though they feel guilt, shame, and depression over their behavior, they are unsuccessful at stopping it. Some binge eaters will ultimately develop health-related issues: obesity, diabetes, or other issues. However, many will continue to eat excessively even after they come to recognize these negative consequences. Binge eating can potentially involve excessive amounts of time, given that bingers may have eating sessions that last upwards of two hours; feelings of psychological distress or physical discomfort may follow, requiring them to "recover" from their misuse of food. These food abusers might not tick all the boxes for the diagnostic criteria, but they certainly hit many of them.

It may be obvious that people with bulimia, similarly, would fulfill many criteria. For the bulimic, efforts at purging may become more extreme and time-consuming as their condition progresses. Meule & Gearhardt (2014) provide an extensive comparison between food addiction and the DSM-5 criteria for SUDs. They argue that if one substitutes "food" for "drug" in the SUD criteria, four of these symptoms are empirically supported: increased consumption, unsuccessful attempts to control intake, continuance despite knowledge of problems (often psychological or health related), and craving. They further suggest that all the other symptoms (with the possible exception of repeated use in hazardous situations), are plausible for binge eating.

Fitting individuals with anorexia into the DSM-5 SUD criteria might seem a bit more difficult; however, there are still some parallels. The true anorexic is constantly avoiding food consumption, resulting in "dieting" taking over their lives. For an anorexic who exercises excessively to try to "purge" calories, the exercise itself may take up larger amounts of time. Gorwood et al. (2016) offer several models to explain anorexia, and one of their suggestions is that it is a starvation addiction linked to abnormalities in the reward pathways. Alternatively, these authors suggest that the disease is related to preserving mental homeostasis. Other models discussed in their review focus on specific biochemical abnormalities. We suggest that an integrated model is possible: biochemical abnormalities seen in anorexia are linked to abnormal reward responses regarding food; the behaviors involved ultimately help preserve mental homeostasis. This would fit with our definition of addiction as "self-induced changes in neurotransmission that result in problem behaviors." Figure 8.3 below illustrates Gorwood and colleagues' model regarding maintenance of mental homeostasis.

Figure 8.4 A Model of Anorexia Nervosa as an Attempt to Preserve Mental Homeostasis

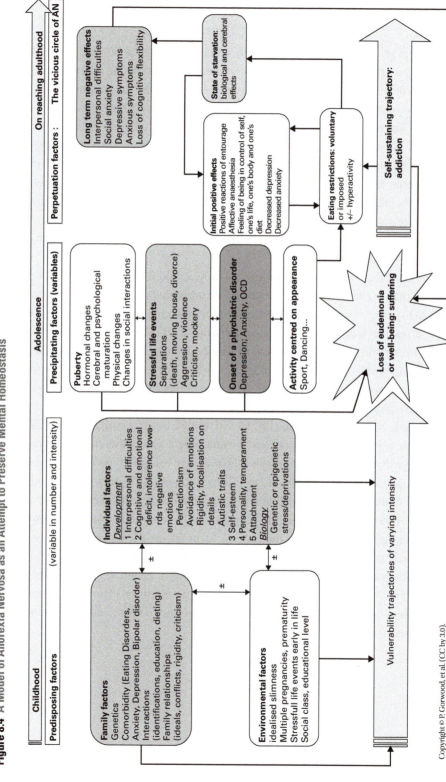

Eating and the Brain

According to Volkow (2013), food, sex, and drugs activate the same brain circuitry that evolved to ensure our survival. However, natural reinforcers, such as food and sex, take longer than drugs to activate the reward centers. Through the process known as classical conditioning, memory forges a link, not only between pleasure and the rewarding stimulus (in this case, food), but also with the surrounding environmental cues. Just like Pavlov's conditioned dogs that salivate to a sound (after repeating pairings of the sound and presentation of food), compulsive eaters (and drug addicts) develop a reflex to overindulge. In the case of eating, high-calorie foods, especially those high in fat or sugar, are more apt to trigger compulsive eating. For bingers, who usually overindulge in the privacy of their own homes, these settings can also serve as triggers for food cravings. In terms of evolution, the human hunter did not always have access to a ready food supply, so foods that stored a lot of energy (i.e., those that are high in calories) boosted survival. So today—whether trolling the supermarket or scanning our own fridge—we are magnetized by high-fat, high-sugar foods. Genetically, we are the same; however, environmentally, there is an abundance of rich food. In the case of eating, a genotype mismatch with our environment makes for a culture of obesity.

Had Pavlov been able to peer inside his dogs' brains when they salivated (conditioned response) to the sound (conditioned stimulus), he would have observed an increase in dopamine. This neurochemical messenger serves to alert us to information that will increase survival. It is activated by any promise of food, sex, and pleasure, as well as danger and pain. When people are shown foods to which they have been conditioned, there is a documented increase of dopamine in the striatum, which is the region of the brain involved in reward and motivation. The increase of dopamine occurs from just smelling or looking at food, the same type of neurochemical response that occurs when a drug addict sees a video of people engaging in any activity reminiscent of his or her drug of choice. The dopamine messenger impels the organism to action, an impulse that sheer willpower cannot easily overcome.

Volkow (2011) explains that in the brains of both drug addicts and the obese, there is typically a reduced number of D2 dopamine receptors. This may be either the result of compensation from overstimulation by dopamine (the brain's compensatory response to repetitive overeating or drug taking) or because these individuals have a naturally lower number of dopamine receptors leading to an addictive predisposition (i.e., predisposed to seek dopamine). Volkow found an inverse relationship between obesity and D2 receptors (i.e., the more obese a person was, the fewer D2 receptors he or she had). Obviously, the genes that control dopamine receptors are not the only biological mechanisms involved in obesity. Twin studies show that genetics plays a significant role in the risk of both addiction and obesity. However, manifestations of genetic influence range from differences in the efficiency of metabolizing certain foods (or drugs) to differences in our likelihood to participate in behaviors that are high in sensation or risk. In the case of obesity, some people may be inherently more sensitive to the neurochemical rewards associated with food.

Why Chocolate?

For many people, the better question is, "Why *not* chocolate?" After all, chocolate is the most commonly craved food. Generally, women are more likely than men to crave chocolate, and women in North America are more likely than those in other regions to crave it. According to G. Parker et al. (2006), the sight and smell of chocolate and the desire for sensory gratification are sufficient to trigger cravings. There is a distinction between craving chocolate and sweets versus the more general craving for carbohydrates. Chocolate also contains fat, as do ice cream, doughnuts, and cakes, whereas bread and pasta do not. Psychoactive ingredients in chocolate include amines (organic derivatives of ammonia): caffeine, theobromine, tyramine, and phenethylamine. However, their concentrations are so low, they would not have a significant psychoactive effect in human consumption. In addition, when comparing milk chocolate, dark chocolate, white chocolate, and cocoa powder, milk chocolate is preferred by the most people. Per Parker et al., if psychoactive substances were involved, then cocoa powder would satisfy craving and dark chocolate would be the most preferred.

However, chocolate might nonetheless be providing biochemical changes that affect its consumers. Rigamonti et al. (2015) demonstrated that both the consumption of chocolate, as well as the anticipation of consuming it, leads to increases in ghrelin (a gut hormone linked to increased appetite) as well as endocannabinoids in obese subjects. Endocannabinoids are our bodies' versions of THC-like substances. (THC, short for tetrahydrocannabinol, is the psychoactive ingredient of marijuana.) Rigamonti and colleagues note that their findings are consistent with responses in normal weight individuals. Ghrelin is known to affect the function of the mesolimbic dopamine pathway and may by disrupted in women with anorexia.

People consume chocolate with an expectation of mood elevation. In a lab study, Macht and Mueller (2007) demonstrated that consumption of palatable chocolate was associated with emotional eating (the researchers had induced negative mood states in their participants). Unfortunately, the mood elevation lasted only three minutes! Because the chocolate would need to make its way into the digestive system before it could be absorbed into the bloodstream and reach the brain, the mood elevation cannot be attributed to any drug-like properties of chocolate. These data may support the notion that orosensory qualities of chocolate are partially responsible for the substance's feel-good effects. But with effects that short, the only way to keep feeling better is to have another bite.

Some obese people have increased brain activity in response to mouth, tongue, and lip sensations—*orosensory pathways* to addiction. Similarly, some have lower sensitivity to cues of satiety (knowing that they have had enough), thereby rendering them more vulnerable to cravings triggered by environmental food cues. Orosensory effects provide positive feedback; ingestion causes negative feedback, with eating typically stopping when the negative effects (fullness in the stomach or satiety) outweigh the positive orosensory effects. The satiety mechanism is not always effective, however, as is evidenced by a "moreishness" factor (i.e., you want more) among chocolate cravers attempting self-restraint; craving is experienced during abstinence, and moreishness is experienced while eating (G. Parker et al., 2006). The effects of carbohydrates on the brain are discussed in the section on biology versus psychology further below.

Check Your Craving: CFQ-T-r (Craving for Food Questionnaire-Trait-reduced)

The following questions are scored on a 5-point Likert-type scale, with 1 indicating "Strongly disagree" and 5 indicating "Strongly agree." Higher scores are associated with higher levels of craving. Research indicates that high scores on the original CFQ-T (of which this is a shortened version) is correlated with BMI, disordered eating, and failures in dieting.

1. When I crave something, I know I won't be able to stop eating once I start.
2. If I eat what I'm craving, I often lose control and eat too much.
3. Food cravings invariably make me think of ways to get what I want to eat.
4. I feel like I have food on my mind all the time.
5. I find myself preoccupied by food.
6. Whenever I have cravings, I find myself making plans to eat.
7. I crave foods when I feel bored, angry, or sad.
8. I have no will power to resist my food crave.
9. Once I start eating, I have trouble stopping.
10. I can't stop thinking about eating no matter how hard I try.
11. If I give in to a food craving, all hope is lost.
12. Whenever I have a food craving, I keep thinking about eating until I actually eat the food.
13. If I am craving something, thoughts of eating it consume me.
14. My emotions often make me want to eat.
15. It is hard for me to resist the temptation to eat appetizing foods that are in my reach.

From Meule, Hermann, & Kubler (2014)

Obesity Around the Globe

Obesity is promoting an increasingly severe health crisis on the world's population (rich and poor nations alike), with almost 30 percent of the worldwide population either obese or overweight—shockingly, 2.1 billion people (Dunham, W., 2014). For most developing nations, obesity, leading to an explosive epidemic of diabetes and heart disease, has become a more serious health hazard than hunger. Mexico is a prime example of a developing nation in the throes of an obesity epidemic. In 1989, less than 10% of the Mexican population was overweight. National surveys conducted in 2006 showed that 71% of Mexican women and 66% of Mexican men were overweight or obese. As people migrate from rural to urban areas, obesity rates tend to increase, but the prevalence of obesity has grown in rural areas as well. In Mexico, Turkey, South Africa, and Jordan, more than half the rural women are overweight (Popkin, 2007).

The connection between poverty and obesity seems to provide the best explanation for these findings. Just as it is in the United States, obesity seems to be largely a problem of the poor. In all countries with a gross domestic product in excess of $2,500 per capita (which includes most of the developing nations excluding sub-Saharan Africa), obesity rates are higher for poor women. With increasing income, farm laborers and the urban poor tend to adopt habits associated with obesity (e.g., television watching and shopping in supermarkets), without educational and recreational counterpoints to control their weight. Compounding the problem is that inhabitants of the developing world (low income countries),many of which are in Latin America, Africa, South America, and South Asia, may carry a disproportionate amount of "thrifty genes" that evolved to help them survive famine by enabling more efficient storage of fat. The problem is that for people with these genes, body fat tends to accumulate around the heart and liver, increasing the risk of heart disease and diabetes. Figure 8.5 shows the expected increase in diabetes cases during the next two decades. In China, for example, nearly one-third of the population suffers from high blood pressure (Popkin, 2007).

Figure 8.5 World diabetes cases expected to jump 55% by 2035

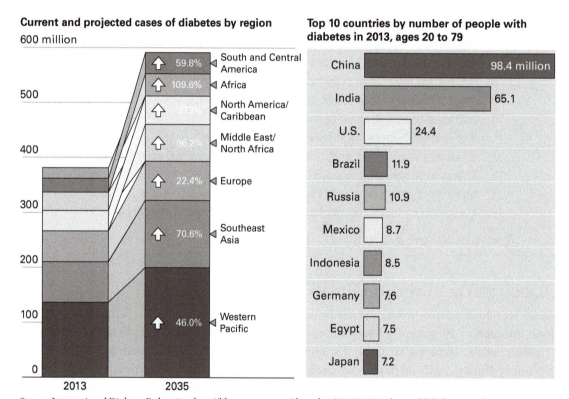

Source: International Diabetes Federation; http://blogs.reuters.com/data-dive/2013/11/15/the-world-diabetes-epidemic-in-charts.

Obesity in America

More than one-third (36.5%) of U.S. adults have obesity (Ogden, Carroll, Fryar, & Flegal, 2015). That is, their body mass index is equal to or greater than 30 kg/m^2. Obesity is clearly one of the most serious health problems in the United States today. Stand in any public place, especially an "All You Can Eat" buffet, and observe people, and you will be astonished at the number of overweight and obese men, women, and even children. Obesity is the major cause of many health-related disorders, especially diabetes and heart disease. It is also implicated in certain cancers, cardiovascular disease, osteoarthritis, gall bladder disease, hypertension, and even dementia.

Obesity in America began to rise precipitously in the 1980s (Figure 8.6). The "calories in" phenomenon is explained by sociologists as being the result of increasing demands of an overworked population for convenience foods (i.e., prepared, packaged products, and meals served in restaurants), usually higher in calories than home-cooked meals. Other forces include the Reagan administration's deregulation of controls on the agriculture industry and encouragement of farmers to increase production, consequently increasing calories available in the national food supply from 3,200 a day in 1980 to 3,900 per day in the year 2000 (Nestle, 2007). Furthermore, stockholder demands for higher short-term dividends on Wall Street pushed the food industry to expand sales by changing social norms such as increasing frequency of between-meal snacking, encouraging eating in bookstores, and serving larger portions.

According to Nestle (2007), a substantial rise in U.S. obesity rates during the past few decades was paralleled by increases in the availability of larger portion sizes, total calories, caloric sweeteners, and sugary soft drinks in the food supply. The apparent dip in three of these measures (calories, sugars, and sugary soft drinks) after 1998 may be explained by greater use of artificial sweeteners and the partial replacement of sugary soft drinks with beverages that are not sweetened with sugars.

Figure 8.6 Obesity in the United States The percentage of the U.S. population classified as obese plotted against year. The curvilinear relationship indicates that obesity rates are on the rise.

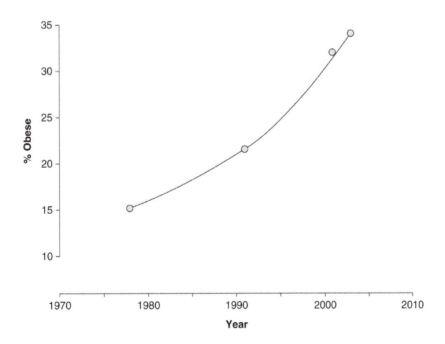

Biology Versus Psychology

A popular belief is that people become compulsive eaters because of unresolved childhood problems. Bruch (1961) explored this notion in her study of New York families during the Depression years. She observed that many mothers seemed to offer food to their children as a way of showing affection and devotion. Food became a means of appeasing the anxiety and guilt that these mothers felt about the material impoverishment that was imposed upon their children. The youngsters appeared to increase their demands for food as needs for gratification and security in other areas remained unfulfilled. Bruch reported that obese patients suffered from "conceptual confusion," which she could trace to early childhood experiences. They seemed to have difficulty in perceiving and forming appropriate responses to their emotional needs. A desire to be with another person, for example, might be confused with a desire to eat with another person. Psychotherapists have reported numerous case studies in which food is interpreted as a symbol of parental affection, a means of reducing internal conflict, or a passive expression of anger toward family members who are perceived as hostile and controlling. The obese person is trapped in a vicious circle: overeating originally relieves feelings of low self-regard, loneliness, and tension; however, the consequences of becoming overweight are even more intense feelings of low self-esteem, anxiety, and lack of belonging. In response, the person eats even more and becomes even more overweight.

Undoubtedly, many people suffer from obesity because of psychological distress. Research studies, however, do not support blanket acceptance of this interpretation for the majority of overweight people. The backgrounds of people challenged by obesity are no more psychologically disturbed than those of normal-weight people. More evidence appears to point to biological causes for obesity rather than psychological ones. Although overweight people are often depressed, it may well be that their suffering is the *result* of being overweight, rather than the *cause*.

Wurtman and Marquis (2006) describe a biological link between depression and obesity. Some depressed people who are also obese have a low level of the neurotransmitter serotonin. It is known that serotonin is manufactured in the brain from its chemical precursor, tryptophan, an amino acid that is found as a component of many foods such as milk. Consumption of foods rich in carbohydrates favors the transport of tryptophan over other amino acids from the blood into the brain. R.J. Wurtman and J.J. Wurtman (1989, 1995), J.J. Wurtman and Marquis (2006), and G. Parker et al. (2006) have made a strong case for people craving foods like spaghetti or cupcakes, rich in carbohydrates, to compensate for their brain serotonin deficiency. Since many carbohydrate snacks are high in calories and loaded with fat, obesity can easily result. Obese patients tend to overeat carbohydrates (especially snack foods like potato chips or cakes that are high in carbohydrates) to feel better. Interestingly, when opioids are not available, heroin addicts experience cravings for sweets. The release of B-endorphins in the hypothalamus may increase the pleasure of eating through an analgesic effect, which is reversible through administration of the narcotic antagonist naltrexone. In addition, sucrose has been shown to reduce crying in infants during hospital procedures, suggesting the release of endorphins (G. Parker et al., 2006).

Wurtman and Wurtman (1995) discovered that at meals, obese subjects consumed an average amount, about 1,900 calories per day with proteins and carbohydrates in balance. But for snacks, these carbohydrate cravers consumed an additional 1,000 calories per day in foods rich in carbohydrates. When asked to describe their mental state before eating, the subjects reported feeling anxious, tense, and unhappy. After snacking, they often reported feeling less tense and sometimes even relaxed. According to Wurtman and Wurtman, carbohydrates serve the same function for these people as antidepressant drugs: by increasing serotonin and thereby subduing depression, not only do they improve mood and diminish sensitivity to negative stimuli, they also ease the way to sleep. There is also the strong possibility that the act of eating releases endorphins, which further the sense of well-being and relaxation (G. Parker et al., 2006).

It is abundantly clear that there is a subset individuals who overindulge in snack foods like potato chips, cookies or cakes—all rich in carbohydrates and fats—to change the chemistry of their brain and improve their mood. The tendency to consume certain foods in a manner similar to compulsive drug use often results in overweight. The phenomenon is apparent in individuals who gain weight when: under stress; live in conditions of low sunlight during winter months; attempt to stop smoking; or experience discomfort in association with pre-menstrual syndrome (Wurtman & Wurtman, 1995, p. 477S).

Another biological factor contributing to obesity is the number of fat cells within one's body. Normal adults have anywhere from 30 billion to 40 billion fat, or adipose, cells. These cells swell or shrink like sponges to accommodate the amount of fat that is stored inside them. Fat cells appear in early childhood, but more develop later, especially during adolescence. In overweight people, the cells expand to hold more fat. Extra fat cells have been found only when a person is at least 60% above the ideal weight for his or her height and age. In obese adults, the amount of adipose tissue is often 3 times greater than what is found in people of normal weight. If an obese person diets, the fat cells will shrink in size, but their total number remains unchanged. Adipose cells release a hormone called leptin, which travels to the brain's hypothalamus and serves as a satiety signal, discouraging eating. Due to genetic reasons, some obese individuals have faulty leptin signals, so their brains do not read this satiety message. However, only a small percentage of obese individuals have mutations related to leptin, meaning that most obese people are struggling for other reasons.

It has also been posited that this adipose albatross manages to fix a "set point" for obesity (Paradis & Cabanac, 2008). The hypothalamus is thought to receive signals that urge further eating until shrunken fat cells are once again refilled. The person who manipulates his or her own weight to fall below the set point may feel irritable or depressed because of unanswered brain signals. The dieter often feels out of sorts until he or she regains every bit of missing cellular baggage. When a person uses an appetite-suppressant drug to lose weight, he or she may be artificially lowering the set point and briefly suppressing appetite. Once the diet medication is stopped, the person usually gains weight rapidly because the brain is once again receiving set-point messages in accord with a permanent repository of adipose tissue. What has been jokingly referred to as "the rhythm method of girth control" may very well have an underlying biological substratum.

A related handicap for overweight people is their relatively low rate of energy expenditure. How the body uses food as energy depends on two interrelated factors: (1) physical activity and (2) basal metabolic rate, or the energy required to maintain minimal body functions. In people of normal weight, basal metabolism accounts for roughly two-thirds of their energy expenditure. Because the metabolic rate is lower in fat tissue than lean tissue, the obese person's basal metabolic rate decreases as lean tissue is replaced by fat. To make matters even worse, basal metabolic rate further decreases when a person starts to diet. These factors work against the efforts of an overweight person to reduce and to maintain enduring weight loss. It may be the case that the formerly obese person can maintain a reduced level of body weight only if he or she consumes about 25% fewer calories than people who are normally at that level. The "used-to-be-overweight" people may never be able to return to a "normal" eating pattern.

While this chapter examines many of the factors that underlie the unhealthy use of food as a drug, Chapter 22, "Eating Yourself Fit," in the final section on natural highs, presents healthy strategies for taking charge of—while deriving pleasure from—one of the most enjoyable aspects of life besides sex: eating. Both activities ensure survival of the species.

Chapter Summary

Obesity is generally defined as exceeding the average weight for one's height and age by 20%. Once associated with high-income countries, obesity is a major health threat in low- and middle-income countries. 44% of the diabetes burden, 23% of ischemic heart disease, and between 7% and 41% of certain cancers are attributable to overweight and obesity. The prevalence of obesity in the U.S. exceeds 20% of the population for every state. For most low income nations, obesity, leading to an explosive epidemic of diabetes and heart disease, has become a more serious health hazard than hunger. The ratio of undernutrition to obesity has reversed so remarkably that the prevalence of obesity is double that of undernutrition. Obviously excess consumption of sugar is psychologically addictive and linked to overweight. However, recent evidence suggests that high sugar intake may be linked to life threatening conditions such as heart disease, diabetes, and cancer.

Weight management is a multibillion-dollar business—understandably so, when one considers that more than 1.9 billion people in the world are overweight (BMI 25 or higher) or obese (BMI 30 or higher). Anorexia nervosa and bulimia, closely related eating disorders, appear to be influenced by media portrayals of feminine beauty. However, family and twin studies show that biological factors contribute greatly to the development of obesity and eating disorders. In addition, anorexia shares a genetic risk with clinical depression. Genes influencing both eating regulation and emotion may be important contributing factors. Binge eating disorder (BED) is reported to be the most common eating disorder in the United States, even more prevalent than anorexia and bulimia combined. Eating disorders share many characteristics of substance use disorders and may be viewed as addictions.

Food, sex, and drugs activate the same brain circuitry that evolved to ensure our survival. Natural reinforcers such as food and sex, however, take longer than drugs to activate the reward centers. Regarding craving, chocolate is the most commonly craved food. This may be in part attributed to mouth feel (pleasurable mouth and tongue sensations), but also to the general phenomenon of carbohydrate craving, which among obese people appears to be neurochemically related to the same deficit found in compulsive drug users—a reduced number of dopamine (D2) receptors.

While psychological theories have traditionally considered the role of food in coping with stress, there is currently more evidence pointing to biological causes for obesity than psychological ones. There is a convincing case that overweight people crave foods like spaghetti or cupcakes, rich in carbohydrates, to compensate for their brain serotonin deficiency. Since many carbohydrate snacks are high in calories and loaded with fat, obesity can easily result. Another biological factor contributing to obesity is the number of fat cells within one's body. In overweight people, fat cells expand and increase in number to hold more fat. Extra fat cells have been found only when a person is at least 60% above the ideal weight for his or her height and age. In obese adults, the amount of adipose tissue is frequently 3 times greater than in people of normal weight. If an overweight person diets, their fat cells will shrink in size, but their total number remains unchanged. This creates a "set point" for obesity in that the person experiences strong cravings until the fat cells are once again expanded. The "used-to-be-overweight" person may never be able to return to a "normal" eating pattern.

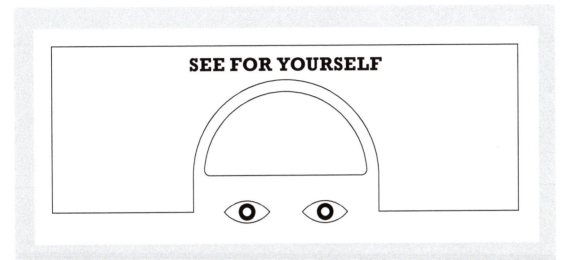

The Skinny on Obesity with Dr. Lustig

Robert H. Lustig, MD, UCSF Professor of Pediatrics in the Division of Endocrinology, explores the damage caused by sugary foods. He argues that fructose (too much) and fiber (not enough) appear to be cornerstones of the obesity epidemic through their effects on insulin.

http://www.uctv.tv/skinny-on-obesity

A Lifetime of Denial. 2008. Kate Hilpern. *The Guardian*. Brief Article

Article in response to Rosemary Pope's death, also discussing the prevalence of anorexia in older women and the challenges in treating the disease.

https://www.theguardian.com/lifeandstyle/2008/apr/29/ healthandwellbeing.health

SECTION III

The Thrill of Excitement and Risk

Security is mostly a superstition. It does not exist in nature, nor do the children of men as a whole experience it. Avoiding danger is no safer in the long run than outright exposure. Life is either a daring adventure or nothing.

—Helen Keller

Overview: What a Rush!

Our discussion of excitement and risk begins with three examples of thrill-seeking behavior: sex in an airplane, base-jumping from a tall building, and addiction to power. As disparate as these actions appear, they share similar biopsychosocial threads. In Chapter 9, "Stress Hormone Highs," we describe neurochemical mechanisms common to the array of thrill-seeking activities. The chapter discusses the trend toward "amping up" on highly caffeinated beverages, as well as more dangerous activities such as pathological gambling and autoerotic strangulation.

Chapter 10, "Rock Around the Clock," examines the wild stimulation produced by stimulant drugs and how "club drugs" have become part of a fast-paced, roller-coaster scene that combines extreme mind alteration with intense human contact.

Sex in an Airplane

Paul, a 58-year-old accountant, was returning home on a 12-hour flight from Singapore to Los Angeles after a 2-week vacation in Fiji with his wife and two children. He obtained a prescription of Ambien from his primary care physician to promote sleep on the long flight. He intended to combat the inevitable boredom and fatigue of the trip by downing two glasses of wine and taking the 10-milligram dose of Ambien about 7 hours prior to landing. His plan was to pass time more quickly and get sufficient rest to start work upon arriving home in Los Angeles.

About 10 minutes after swallowing the Ambien, he got up (he was sitting in the row directly in front of his wife and two children) and walked to the flight attendant station intending to ask for his second glass of red wine. Upon peering behind the curtain of the attendants' quarters he spotted a woman who appeared sexy, a bit tipsy, and older than her prime. Disinhibition quickly set in; he struck up a conversation about her tattoos. She confided that before her current career as a forest ranger, she was a dancer at gentlemen's clubs.

Both ripe for sexual adventure, the hitherto strangers began to touch erotically in the aisle behind the serving section. Consumed by the thrill, Paul invited her to join him in the bathroom, intending to escalate their sexual tryst. The two snuck into the flight restroom, undressed and carried out a variety of sexual acts, culminating in Paul reaching orgasm. He carried out this scheme without concern about the multiple risks of being discovered by his wife, his children, the flight staff, fellow passengers, or possible legal and health ramifications of having sex with a stranger in the bathroom of a commercial airline.

Jumping Off a Building

Robin and Brian ascend the 700-foot United Bank of Denver building, eager to jump off. Upon reaching the top, both fastidiously check their parachutes, making sure that everything is correctly rigged. Robin's father, who accompanies the duo, comments, "I'll bet you boys are feeling some butterflies now." His son replies, "We were scared yesterday and the day before … We're just in the groove … We're ready to go for it."

Robin steps out on the end of a scaffold that is being used to finish the building's construction. He begins the countdown—"Okay—four … two … three …" He turns to Brian and both begin to laugh.

Robin continues, "Boy that was great, wasn't it?" Then he resumes concentration, makes the proper countdown, and delicately steps off the edge. Time seems to stand still as Robin savors a sense of weightlessness and the dual feelings of fragility and power in the same instant. Exhilarated by the experience of total control, his life seems at once, supreme and valueless.

When the chute opens, he is pleased. He gracefully navigates his floating assemblage through a half circle, deliberately drifting to an urban clearing, descending near a stunned pair of middle-aged passersby. Wide-eyed, smiling, and invigorated with curiosity, one excitedly blurts out, "Jesus, what planet did you come from?" Robin's nonchalant reply: "Oh, you liked it, huh?"

Brian jumps. As soon as he lands, the two hop in the getaway car, driven by Robin's mother. The police arrive 4 minutes after the daring *fait accompli.*

In the aftermath, Brian and Robin become intoxicated by the wine of success. The pristine ecstasy of free fall is followed by group celebration, euphoria, and bliss.

The Party Seeks Power Entirely for Its Own Sake

Now I will tell you the answer to my question. It is this. The Party seeks power entirely for its own sake. We are not interested in the good of others; we are interested solely in power, pure power. What pure power means you will understand presently. We are different from the "oligarchies" of the past in that we know what we are doing. All the others, even those who resembled ourselves, were cowards and hypocrites. The German Nazis and the Russian Communists came very close to us in their methods, but they never had the courage to recognize their own motives. They pretended, perhaps they even believed, that they had seized power unwillingly and for a limited time, and that just around the corner there lay a paradise where human beings would be free and equal. We are not like that. We know that no one ever seizes power with the intention of relinquishing it. Power is not a means; it is an end. One does not establish a dictatorship in order to safeguard a revolution; one makes the revolution in order to establish the dictatorship. The object of persecution is persecution. The object of torture is torture. The object of power is power. Now you begin to understand me.—*1984,* George Orwell

Throughout the remainder of this section, we examine the psychological, biological, and social causes and consequences of deliberate participation in energizing, potentially dangerous, and sometimes even life-threatening activity. As in the above diatribe on *power,* the energy derived from control over others can be as seductive and addictive as any activity known to humankind. Some world leaders seem to feed off willful induction of conflicts—evoking high levels of stress in overlapping spheres of their personal and political lives. This characteristic is likely related to the exhilaration derived from "Stress Hormone Highs."

CHAPTER 9

Stress Hormone Highs

Introduction

Psychologists have long known that people perform most effectively when under some degree of stress. A moderate level of arousal tends to produce alertness and enthusiasm for the task at hand. When emotional excitement exceeds an optimal point, however, whether the evoked feelings are positive or negative, the result is progressive impairment of one's ability to function. Figure 9.1 shows the basic relationship between arousal and performance.

Figure 9.1 **Relationship Between Arousal and Performance: Yerkes-Dodson Law** Performance increases with physiological or mental arousal, but only up to a point. When levels of arousal become too high, performance decreases.

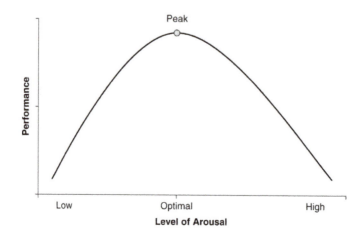

What is it about people like Robin and Brian that enables them to remain composed while most of us would literally become scared stiff under similarly arousing circumstances? In William James's classic, *The Varieties of Religious Experience* (1902), the author quotes Lutfullah, describing his experience when arousal becomes too intense, and adaptive coping is no longer an option.

> It was about eleven o'clock at night...but I strolled on still with two people... Suddenly upon the left side of our road, a crackling was heard among the bushes; all of us were alarmed, and in an instant a tiger, rushing out of the jungle, pounced upon the one of the party that was foremost, and carried him off in the twinkling of an eye. The rush of the animal, and the crush of the poor victim's bones in his mouth, and his last cry of distress, 'ho hai!' involuntarily re-echoed by all of us, was over in three seconds; and then I know not what happened till I returned to my senses, when I found myself and companions lying down on the ground as if prepared to be devoured by our enemy, the sovereign of the forest. I find my pen incapable of describing the terror of that dreadful moment. Our limbs stiffened, our power of speech ceased, and our hearts beat violently, and only a whisper of the same 'ho hai!' was heard from us. In this state we crept on all fours for some distance back, and then ran for life with the speed of an Arab horse for about half an hour, and fortunately happened to come to a small village ... After this every one of us was attacked with fever, attended with shivering, in which deplorable state we remained till morning. (Lutfullah, 1857, quoted in James, 1902)

Selye (1956, 1971, 1974) introduced the concept of getting high on our own stress hormones. When we become excited, through either anger or fear, the brain signals hormone-producing glands to release chemicals that prepare us for fight or flight. The adrenal glands produce cortisol, a chemical that increases blood sugar and speeds up the body's metabolism. Other messages to the adrenal glands result in the release of the amphetamine-like stimulant epinephrine (adrenaline), which helps supply glucose to the muscles and brain, and norepinephrine, which speeds up the heart rate and elevates blood pressure. Figure 9.2 illustrates the body's chemical response to stress.

The psychological by-products of a moderate biochemical emergency are noticeable increments in one's feelings of physical prowess and personal competence, often associated with strong sensations of pleasure. In many ways, the state of biological and psychological "readiness" produced by stress is mimicked by the effects of stimulant drugs. People may self-induce similar alterations of consciousness with amphetamine, methamphetamine, cocaine, or caffeine (two-and-a-half cups of coffee will double the level of epinephrine in the blood), or by engaging in activities that appear to be life threatening. Positive experiences—falling in love, riding a roller-coaster, or watching a thrilling movie—can evoke the same stress hormones as more troublesome flirtations with danger or drugs (Manhart, 2005). Apparently, our brains will not distinguish between a real and a manufactured dose of dopamine, so the stimulant seeker may quell his or her need for dopamine through high-risk activity or stimulant drugs—often both.

Figure 9.2 Stress Response In response to stress, the hypothalamus secretes corticotropin-releasing hormone (CRH), which stimulates the pituitary gland to release adrenocorticotropic hormone ACTH into the general circulation. ACTH stimulates the adrenal cortex to release cortisol. The hypothalamus also stimulates the adrenal medulla to release the catecholamines, epinephrine and norepinephrine, into the general circulation. Catecholamines mobilize stored fat and make the heart beat faster and stronger.

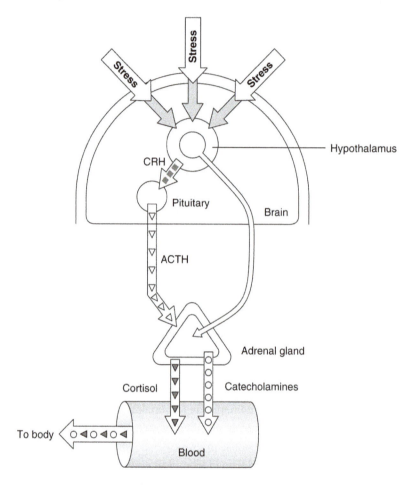

Wake Me Up! Caffeine Buzz

Caffeine is the most popular psychoactive substance in the world, with approximately 80% of the population in the United States, including children, consuming it each day (Reissig, Strain, & Griffiths, 2008). And coffee is just the beginning. Other common sources of caffeine include tea and carbonated beverages. In 2006, an estimated 500 new brands of energy drinks were released worldwide (Reissig, et. al, 2009). With enticing names like Jolt, AMP, Monster, and Rockstar, what teenager or young adult wouldn't be tempted to "hit the can"? In fact, that is a slogan of some "energy drinks" proudly displayed in grocery stores, gas stations, and even drink dispensers on college campuses. Brands have even begun to mimic "the illicits" with names like XTC and Cocaine. The energy drink industry is rapidly expanding. In 2012, worldwide sales were estimated to be over $12.5 billion U.S., an increase of 60% from 2008 (Zucconi et al., 2013).

Caffeine in the Brain

Caffeine is in a different class of stimulants compared to the nicotine found in tobacco products or the major stimulant drugs, such as cocaine, amphetamine, and ecstasy (which will be discussed in our next chapter). Caffeine affects the brain by blocking receptors for a neurochemical known as adenosine. When adenosine levels increase, sleepiness increases. Caffeine promotes wakefulness by binding adenosine receptors and preventing this chemical from promoting sleep.

Caffeine lovers may report feeling a buzz from their substance. Some of that may be related to increased arousal. Caffeine does not seem to elevate dopamine levels in the nucleus accumbens—a characteristic of many other psychoactive drugs, especially substances such as cocaine and amphetamine. However, caffeine indirectly helps increase dopamine activity because antagonism (blockade) of adenosine receptors has been shown to increase the number of dopamine D2/D3 receptors in this region (Volkow et al., 2015). Thus, there are more receptors available for dopamine to bind. Overall, the stimulant effects of caffeine are less potent than those of major stimulants. Nonetheless, there can be consequences to continued, heavy caffeine use.

Caffeine Risks

Caffeine is legal and available almost anywhere, and we tend to view it as harmless. Although caffeine is generally less harmful than many drugs people use regularly, it is not without risks. For instance, high intake of caffeine can elevate heart rate and blood pressure, along with promoting heart arrhythmias. Excessive intake can increase anxiety, which is problematic for people with such conditions. Caffeine users who have trouble falling asleep should first assess their daily intake of caffeine; if intake is high and/ or occurs late in the day, sleep may be delayed. In such cases, individuals would do better to decrease caffeine usage before resorting to sleep aids. Coffee, more so than other forms of caffeine intake, can promote unpleasant stomach and intestinal symptoms.

Acute, high doses of caffeine can produce "intoxicated" states, as described in DSM-5 (APA, 2013, pp. 503–504). Besides physical symptoms of gastrointestinal distress, elevated and/or irregular heart rate, muscle twitching, flushed face, and increased urination, the defining characteristics of caffeine intoxication are restlessness, nervousness, psychomotor agitation, and a rambling flow of thoughts. Individuals may be in a state of excitement, seemingly "bouncing off the walls" with their high energy and incessant talking. The degree of symptoms must be extreme enough to interfere with normal functioning to be considered an intoxicated state.

The Food and Drug Administration has issued a warning about individuals acquiring pure caffeine from chemical supply companies and using it to spike their beverages. This statement notes that "[a] single teaspoon of pure caffeine is roughly equivalent to the amount in 28 cups of coffee" (FDA, 2015); thus, it would be rather easy to accidentally overdose on this substance. In 2011, nearly 1,500 adolescents visited hospital emergency rooms due to negative symptoms of caffeine use. Even if a person does not lethally overdose, high levels of caffeine intake can promote sleeplessness and anxiety. Athletes who rely on heavily caffeinated sports drinks should take heed of these findings.

Caffeine Benefits

Despite its potential risks, caffeine seems to have some benefits. In the short-term, it is helpful in alleviating headache pain, which is why it is sometimes used in over-the-counter pain relievers such as Anacin and Excedrin. It has also been shown to enhance performance on some cognitive tasks (Chen, 2014). Caffeine may also have long-term benefits. Chen reports several studies that indicate lower risk of developing some neurodegenerative disorders, such as Alzheimer's Disease and Parkinson's Disease, thus preventing cognitive decline and impairments in motor function. There are likely multiple reasons why caffeine provides these long-term benefits, including effects on growth factors, glia (supporting cells in the brain), and the blood-brain barrier. For those who prefer their caffeine in the form of coffee, recent data even support increased longevity, with moderate consumption linked to decreased risk of death from a number of illnesses (Gunter et al., 2017; Park et al., 2017).

Daily Caffeine Usage: An Addiction?

Although caffeine is considered a mild psychostimulant, consuming it daily, even in low doses, can produce dependence. Juliano and colleagues (2012), developed the Caffeine Withdrawal Symptom Questionnaire (CWSQ). People withdrawing from caffeine may feel physically sick, including headache, fatigue, stomach distress, and flu-like symptoms. They also will likely experience psychological symptoms, such as decreased alertness, difficulty concentrating, low motivation, lack of interest in social interaction, and mood disturbances (such as being irritable or depressed). These researchers have demonstrated that higher CWSQ scores are positively correlated with craving ratings. Figure 9.3 shows caffeine withdrawal ratings for daily and non-daily consumers. If you're curious about your "habit" check out your symptoms after a day or two of non-use.

Figure 9.3 **Caffeine Withdrawal Ratings for Daily and Non-Daily Coffee Consumers** Bars represent the difference scores between the baseline and abstinence assessment points for each of the CWSQ factors. Significant differences between daily and non-daily coffee consumers are indicated by asterisks. (Adapted from Juliano et al, 2012).

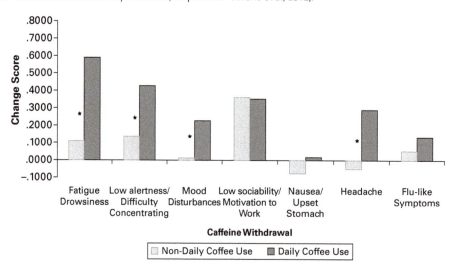

Some daily consumers experience adverse effects due to regular use but are unable to stop using—a typical sign of an addiction. Although somewhat rare, some seek treatment for caffeine dependence, as described in the case study below. Meredith and colleagues (2013) suggest that problems related to excessive caffeine use may be much more widespread than realized, given the prevalence of caffeine withdrawal and how commonly caffeine is used across the globe.

CASE STUDY: Mr. C., Grocery Employee

Fifty-one-year-old Mr. C. worked at a grocery store, stocking shelves on the night shift. He sought treatment for his caffeine dependence at the recommendation of his doctor due to sleep problems. Previous attempts at decreasing usage had failed due to withdrawal symptoms (headaches) and cravings. Although Mr. C. rationalized his caffeine usage by saying that it allowed him to stay alert while working overnight, he admitted to sometimes riding the bus to the store in the middle of the night to satisfy cravings when he wasn't working. His relationship with caffeine began at the age of 8 (drinking tea); at age 12, he transitioned to his beverage of choice: caffeinated soda. At intake into the program, he was consuming 2 liters per day of Diet Pepsi Max, plus additional diet colas; his daily caffeine intake was nearly 500 mg (depending on the strength of the coffee brewed, this would be equivalent to 3–5 cups of coffee/day). Over the course of 6 weeks of treatment, Mr. C. successfully quit all forms of caffeine intake, exceeding his original expectation of being able to cut his consumption in half. At a 6-month follow-up, he was still caffeine "abstinent" despite occasional cravings.

The American Psychiatric Association includes caffeine as one of the classes of substances which, when used excessively, can be a diagnosable substance use disorder, per the DSM-5 (APA, 2013). However, numerous substances have specific diagnostic classifications, such as Alcohol Use Disorder, Cannabis Use Disorder, Inhalant Use Disorder, etc.; this is not the case with caffeine. The diagnostic manual does include Caffeine Use Disorder as a "condition for further study," which means that in the next edition of the DSM, caffeine use disorder might have its own diagnosis.

Do You Agree?

In response to an in-class admission to being "a caffeine addict," one of the authors of this text received the following comment on the end-of-semester teaching evaluations: "This course would have been better if the professor had a real addiction." Do you think that caffeine addiction is a real phenomenon, or do you agree with the student who wrote the comment? Does the concept of caffeine addiction fit with the definition of addiction offered in this book?

Caffeine usage is so common that consumers may find it odd that non-consumers even exist. Efforts have been made to try to delineate differences between those who use and those who don't. The data are mixed in terms of demonstrating personality traits that are correlated with caffeine usage. Gurpegui and colleagues (2007) linked higher caffeine consumption with impulsivity, along with research tying caffeine dependence to sensation-seeking (discussed later in this chapter). Gurpequi et al.'s data fit with these earlier findings in that their study correlates heavy caffeine consumption with novelty-seeking. On the other hand, Hewlett and Smith (2006) report no differences between caffeine consumers and non-consumers with regard to impulsivity. These researchers state that caffeine non-consumers may be a small portion of the population who experience aversive symptoms related to caffeine usage and therefore avoid use. Hewlett and Smith did find, however, that those who use caffeine are more likely to smoke cigarettes and drink alcohol than those who do not use caffeine. The general findings that high caffeine usage correlates with sensation and novelty seeking support a primary concept of this book: "The user's drug of choice is harmonious with their characteristic means of reducing stress."

Do Energy Beverages (EB)Work?

While the jury is not in on the benefits and liabilities of EBs, there is considerable evidence for caution. It is important to consider both the short and long term effects of these increasingly used beverages. Measurable physiological effects occur immediately after the first dose. In one study, 15 healthy adults aged 18–40 years of age consumed 2 cans (500 mL) of a popular EB containing 1,000 mg. of taurine and 100 mg. of caffeine, as well as vitamins B5, B6, and B12, glucuronolactone, and niacinamide, daily for 1 week. The effects of the EB on their blood pressure, pulse, and electrocardiogram (ECG) were measured. The key findings were: 1) within 4 hours of EB consumption, maximum systolic blood pressure increased by 8% and 10% on day one and 7, respectively; 2) Diastolic blood pressure, measured within 2 hours of consumption, resulted in a maximum increase of 7% and 8% on day 1 and 7, respectively; 3) Heart rate increased by 8% on day 1 and 11% on day 7 (Steinke et al., 2009). Although these kinds of transient elevations in blood pressure and heart rate are not likely to cause problems in healthy consumers, those prone to high blood pressure may be pushing the envelope. It is recommended that patients with hypertension should avoid consumption of this type of drink (Steinke et al., 2009).

Regarding long-term effects, there are no long-term studies of the combined effects of caffeine, taurine, and glucuronolactone, and other additives to high energy drinks. It is known, however, that EBs may serve as a gateway to other forms of drug dependence and thereby exacerbate the risk for heart disease. Norway, Denmark, and France have prohibited the sale of Red Bull, in part due to a study where rats were fed taurine and exhibited bizarre behavior, including anxiety and self-mutilation (NBCNews, 2010). It is still controversial whether caffeine can cause hypertension and coronary artery disease, although questions about its safety in patients with heart failure and arrhythmia have been raised (Frishman, et al., 2003).

Sports coaches and family medicine practitioners should address (provide guidance about) the effects and risks of EBs with populations that may be at risk. Table 9.1 provides guidelines regarding safe consumption of sports drinks (SDs) and energy beverages for athletes and non-athletic consumers.

Table 9.1 Recommendations Regarding Energy Beverage Consumption

For the non-athlete consumer:
- Limit your consumption of EBs to no more than 500 mL, or 1 can per day
- Do not mix EBs with alcohol; this can mask intoxication and may be extremely dehydrating
- Rehydrate with water or an appropriately formulated SD after exercise or intense physical activity
- If you experience an adverse reaction to an EB, report it to your health care professional or organization
- If you are being treated for hypertension, avoid using EBs
- If you have a serious underlying medical condition, including coronary artery disease, heart failure, or arrhythmia, consult with your physician before using EBs

For the athlete participating in exercise lasting ≤1 hr.:
- Do not use EBs
- SDs appear safe, but we recommend against EBs while exercising because of the possibility of dehydration, elevation of blood pressure, and lack of equivocal benefits vs water or SDs

For the athlete participating in exercise lasting ≥1 hr:
- Do not use EBs. SDs containing carbohydrates and electrolytes help prevent dehydration and restore important minerals lost through perspiration, and they produce better hydration than water
- EB = energy beverage; SD = sport drink

Source: Energy Beverages: Content and Safety (p. 1039). John P. Higgins, MD, MPhil; Troy D. Tuttle, MS; and Christopher L. Higgins, BHMS (ExSc). Mayo Clin Proc. 2010; 85(11):1033-1041

There are few studies on the energizing effects of the extra ingredients usually consisting of guarana, taurine, ginseng, or ginkgo biloba. Caffeine, however, has been amply studied, as coffee is a mainstay of societies around the globe (Scholey & Kennedy, 2004).

Ingestion of either caffeine or glucose (sugar) causes a brief increase in cognitive performance (Reissig et al., 2008; Scholey & Kennedy, 2004). The effects are especially apparent when it is used in situations of fatigue or boredom. However, much of caffeine's effects are due to consumer expectations and psychological effects related to the setting in which consumption occurs (Childs & de Wit, 2008). Childs and de Wit studied whether the energizing effects of coffee and energy drinks are exclusively due to caffeine, or if one's sense of increased vigor is also related to taste and expected outcomes. They found that indeed caffeine does improve mood and mental energy (e.g., reaction time), but expected effects also play a large role in subjective experience. Decaffeinated coffee also caused an increase in subjective alertness in people when they were made to believe they had consumed the caffeinated counterpart.

A study by Scholey and Kennedy (2004) looked at the effects of caffeine and glucose in a created "energy drink" along with three comparison beverages: (1) only the caffeine, (2) only glucose, and (3) only the herbal flavorings (ginkgo biloba and ginseng). They found that the drink they had concocted with both the caffeine and sugar produced the most cognitive improvements and mood changes. The study showed that energizing effects are largely due to a combination of glucose and caffeine, but the drinks require a good amount of caffeine in order to bring about changes in performance. Table 9.2 shows the amounts of caffeine per specific types of energy drinks and other caffeinated beverages.

Table 9.2 Caffeine Content of Beverages and Other Products

Energy Drinks	Caffeine Content, mg	Sodas	Caffeine Content, mg
5-Hour Energy	207	Coca-Cola, 12-oz can	35
Amp, 8 oz	72	Coca-Cola, 20-oz bottle	58
Amp, 16 oz	143	Coca-Cola Zero, 12-oz can	34
BAWLS Guarana, 8 oz	50	Coca-Cola Zero, 20-oz bottle	57
BAWLS Guarana, 16 oz	100	Diet Coke, 12-oz can	47
Full Throttle, 1 6 oz	197	Diet Coke, 20-oz bottle	78
Monster, 16 oz	160	Diet Pepsi, 12-oz can	36
Monster, 24 oz	240	Diet Pepsi, 20-oz bottle	60
No Fear, 8 oz	87	Dr Pepper, 12-oz can	42
No Fear, 16 oz	174	Dr Pepper, 20-oz bottle	70
NOS, 16 oz	260	Mountain Dew, 12-oz can	54
Red Bull, 8,4 oz	80	Mountain Dew, 20-oz bottle	90
Red Bull, 12 oz	114	Pepsi, 1 2-oz can	38
Red Bull, 16 oz	152	Pepsi, 20-oz bottle	63
Red Bull, 20 oz	190	Pepsi MAX, 12-oz can	69
Red Bull Energy Shot	80	Pepsi MAX, 20-oz bottle	115
Rip It, 16 oz	200	Vault, 12-oz can	71
Rip It Shots	100	Vault, 20-oz bottle	118
Rockstar, 8 oz	80	**Other**	
Rockstar, 16 oz	160	Arizona Iced Tea, black, 16 oz	32
Rockstar, 24 oz	240	Arizona Iced Tea, green, 16 oz	15
Rockstar 2X, 12 oz	250	Black tea (brewed),[a] 8 oz	55
SPIKE Shooter	286	Coffee-flavored ice cream,[a] 8 oz	58
		Coffee (brewed),[a] 8 oz	85
		Coffee (brewed),[a] 16 oz	170
		Espresso shot,[a] 1 oz	64
		Excedrin Extra Strength, 2 pills	130
		Hershey's Kiss, 1	1
		Hershey's milk chocolate bar	12
		Hot chocolate,[a] 8 oz	9
		NoDoz Maximum Strength, 1 pill	200
		Stay Alert gum, 1 piece	100
		Vivarin, 1 pill	200

[a]*Average values; individual brands may vary.*

Source: Center for Military Psychiatry and Neuroscience at the Walter Reed Army Institute of Research, 2012.

Question: How Much and What Type of Caffeinated Beverages are Right for You?

According to the Mayo Clinic (2014), up to 400 milligrams (mg) of caffeine a day is the safety cutoff for most healthy adults. That equates to roughly the amount of caffeine in four cups of brewed coffee, 10 cans of cola, or two "energy shot" drinks. As shown in Table 9.2, actual caffeine content in beverages varies widely, especially among energy drinks.

One fad that has spread across America along with the burgeoning hype of the energy drink is the combination of energy drinks with alcohol. Anyone who has been to a bar in the past 5 years has surely seen or even tasted a Red Bull and vodka or a Jägerbomb (Jägermeister and energy drink). These beverages are particularly dangerous in that the caffeinated beverages are stimulants and the alcoholic beverages are depressants. The stimulant effects of the energy drinks mask (but do not reverse) the intoxication effects of the alcohol and can prevent a person from realizing how drunk he or she really is. The energy drink may also falsely imply to the person that he or she really is not impaired, but once the stimulating effects wear off, the depressant effects of the alcohol remain and could possibly cause vomiting or respiratory depression. Finally, both alcohol and caffeine are dehydrating, although some recent studies challenge the diuretic effect of caffeinated beverages (Kovacs Harbolic, retrieved 2.28.17). The body's ability to metabolize alcohol is disturbed when dehydrated, increasing toxicity and the severity of a hangover (Brown University Health Education, 2008).

Recent data indicate that those who choose to mix energy drinks with alcohol are prone to drinking alcohol in the first place. They are more likely to drink heavily and tend to have expectations that consuming these mixed drinks will either off-set sedative effects of alcohol or increase the rate at which they become intoxicated. Thus, the appeal of caffeinated alcoholic beverages may be specific to a subset of consumers. Mixing energy drinks with alcohol is popular among college students and young adults. One study found that 27% of college students reported that they had mixed alcohol and an energy drink at least once in the previous month (Davidson & Odle, 2015).

Stress Intoxication

Hans Selye (1956, 1971, 1974), who is regarded by many as the grandfather of all modern stress researchers, was acutely aware of the intoxicating correlates of fight-or-flight reactions. He pointed to "stress-drunkenness" (i.e., loss of judgment and decreased impulse control) as causing more overall harm to society than the universally acclaimed demon of demons, alcohol, and all other psychoactive drugs combined.

What is even more incredible than this seemingly outrageous claim by Selye is that much of the stress-drunkenness is deliberately self-induced. "Skydiving is the most fun you can have with your clothes on," proclaims Robin Held (personal communication, June 1986), who dives not only from buildings but also from smokestacks, mountain cliffs, airplanes, and bridges. "The greatest joy is being in such a dangerous situation that you nearly wet your pants," says a private detective who seeks out dangerous assignments for thrills. Eric, a young man in his early twenties, goes to the most savage, bloodthirsty movies in town because he "loves to be scared." These seemingly outrageous claims have been repeated many times over by "adrenaline junkies" who are addicted to a wide variety of risk-taking activities.

What is so attractive about risk taking and fear-inducing situations? These dopamine-triggering activities give our brain a dopamine-mediated high, and the individual wants that feeling to remain (Manhart, 2005). In terms of brain chemistry, risk-taking produces the same mind-altering escape from depression, stress, or fear of nonbeing as the use of powerful stimulant drugs. Whether through skydiving, gambling, or cocaine, self-induced changes in neurotransmission may well lead to the familiar path of compulsion, loss of control, and continuation in spite of harmful consequences.

Figure 9.4 is a simplified representation of the neurochemical pathways associated with the brain's reward system. As previously discussed (see Chapter 3), in order to produce drug-like feelings of pleasure and euphoria, the activity, drug, or behavior must increase dopamine in the nucleus accumbens. In addition to increasing the levels of cortisol and norepinephrine, stress hormone highs, such as from gambling, dangerous sexual liaisons, and skydiving, increase the level of dopamine in the nucleus accumbens.

Figure 9.4 Neurotransmission and the Experience of Ecstasy To produce drug-like feelings of pleasure and euphoria, the substance or behavior must have the ability to increase dopamine in the nucleus accumbens.

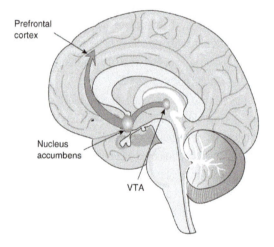

Addiction: The Brain out of Balance

Addiction is a by-product of the brain's ability to restore neurotransmission to a baseline level (homeostasis) following "self-induced changes." Consider the person who engages in either cocaine ingestion or a risk-taking behavior (skydiving). As the level of dopaminergic neurotransmission shifts into overdrive, the brain's homeostatic restoring mechanism prepares for action. Continued cocaine or behavior-induced alteration of dopamine levels brings about changes in enzyme (adenylate cyclase) levels, which decrease the effectiveness of dopamine neurotransmission by lowering the number of three-way combinations necessary of neurotransmission to occur: neurotransmitter, receptor, and enzyme.

As the abuse continues, dopaminergic cells begin to decrease production of both adenylate cyclase and dopamine. Because the dopamine remains in the synapse, there is no reason to make more. Adenylate cyclase decreases to restore baseline neurotransmission, which is being upset by an increase in the aforementioned three-way combination. The abuser then experiences an escalating need for increased activity, drug dose, or behavior. At some point, the person becomes dependent on the activity or drug just to feel normal. The earlier dose of cocaine no longer excites. The fast drive around the mountain becomes routine. To experience an elevated mood, s/he must use more of the drug (or activity) or an even more potent type of drug such as crack cocaine. Removal of the drug or cessation of the behavior produces a feeling of dysphoria from a deficiency of dopamine in the nucleus accumbens. This deficiency results from a decrease in the adenylate cyclase needed for neurotransmission as well as the dwindling supply of dopamine. Also, the number of dopamine receptors and their sensitivity have become altered during the time of substance abuse.

Correspondingly, the abuser of opioids experiences alterations in brain chemistry that have the potential to produce addiction. Interestingly, not everyone who uses drugs or engages in mood-altering behavior becomes addicted. It is believed that many of those who do may be attempting to compensate for a genetic or environmentally induced deficiency of dopamine in the nucleus accumbens. It is important to keep in mind that any drug or activity repeated specifically for pleasure has the potential to become addicting.

The Up and Down Game

The repeated pairing of opposite emotional experiences, and their underlying physiological counterparts, may be the sustaining force behind many forms of human compulsion. Per R. L. Solomon (1980), the same principle that produces alcoholics and drug addicts can be used to account for chronic daredevils, Coca-Cola addicts, and sexual compulsives.

R. L. Solomon's (1980) opponent-process theory of motivation posits that every event in life that exerts a potent effect on mood or feeling also triggers an oppositional biochemical process. When first attracted to a pleasurable experience induced through drugs or activities, people are motivated by the dominant sensations of euphoria or well-being. Mood-altering behavior is often sustained, however, because people seek to avoid the unpleasant effects that have been set in motion by the opponent process. In some addictions—for example, running—the initial experience of pain is followed by a highly pleasurable reaction, probably related to the release of endocannabinoids (Fuss et al., 2015). As shown in Figure 9.5, the opponent process leads to a waving pattern of mood alterations, which varies among people in terms of frequency and intensity. Some people seem to exist on a constant roller-coaster of mood change, seeking pleasure and avoiding pain, while others remain emotionally bland with only minor ripples in how they feel.

In some patterns of behavioral excess, a person may continue an experience that is no longer pleasurable because of a growing aversion to the sensations brought about through stopping it (i.e., opponent unpleasant state). In the case of extended risk taking, for example, chronic thrill seekers may increasingly seek to avoid the unpleasant feelings associated with lowered enzyme and neurotransmitter levels by seeking out new and more dangerous activities. In the case of satiation activities (e.g., opioids, TV addiction), euphoria is soon replaced by the anticipation of depression, anxiety or pain from withdrawal. Thrill seekers often exhibit more drug and alcohol abuse, and more gambling and risky behaviors such as drinking and driving, than the average person (Gupta, Derevensky, & Ellenbogen, 2006).

Figure 9.5 Opponent-Process Model of Addiction This figure shows the standard pattern of mood alteration based on opponent-process theory. The upper graphs (experience) depict an individual's subjective experience of pleasure in the initial and chronic phases of drug use or other mood-altering activity. The initial experience is the algebraic sum of the immediate biological effects of the mood-altering activity and the body's homeostatic response to neurochemical changes. Since the brain has not yet adapted to the neurochemically mediated high, a heightened sense of pleasure is experienced. After chronic mood alteration, homeostatic effects become so large that the pleasure-oriented activity can only return the user to his or her baseline state (before the beginning of chronic use). In the absence of mood-altering activity, the individual's subjective experience is significantly below baseline (i.e., withdrawal or suffering).

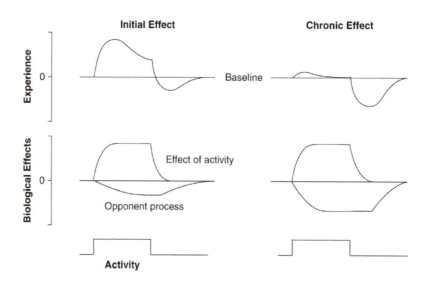

Although there are obvious differences in withdrawal symptoms from the diverse array of pleasure-inducing activities, Glassman, Jackson, Walsh, Roose, and Rosenfeld (1984) proposed that the same brain mechanism may account for the experience of craving, which is common to all addictions. Whether people are trying to kick alcohol, cigarette, or opioid addiction, they experience similar changes in brain chemistry, which create craving for drug use. According to Glassman et al., all these addictions are characterized by an excess of norepinephrine, which is concentrated in a small area of the brain called the locus coeruleus. A person may subdue biochemical excitation in this area of the brain by using cigarettes, alcohol, or opioids. During withdrawal, however, the locus over-fires, producing too much norepinephrine, which results in the common experience of craving.

The fact that stress elevates the level of norepinephrine in the brain may account for the increased craving and frequency of addiction relapse during periods of duress or conflict. Glassman's model may also help to explain the high frequency of dual addictions, as in the upper-downer cycle of cocaine-heroin dependence, and the various combinations or switches among risk taking and alcohol, cigarette, and opioid abuse.

Problem and Pathological Gambling

Pathological gambling is considered an impulse control disorder characterized by persistent and recurrent gambling behavior; preoccupation with gambling; loss of control; "chasing" losses; and continued gambling despite problems in personal, family, or vocational pursuits that worsens over time

(American Psychiatric Association, 1994, 2000). Gambling is readily available almost anywhere, with lotteries, casinos, sports betting, slot and poker machines, and especially the online casinos that are overwhelming the Internet (Gupta et al., 2006). "[A]round two million people in the U.S. are addicted to gambling, and for as many as 20 million citizens the habit seriously interferes with work and social life" (Jabar, 2013, p. 28).

DSM-5 includes gambling disorder as a "Non-Substance-Related Disorder," appearing alongside substance use and addictive disorders. The symptomology parallels that of substance use disorders, including "needs to gamble with increasing amounts of money in order to achieve the desired excitement" (tolerance), "is restless or irritable when attempting to cut down or stop gambling" (withdrawal), and "has jeopardized or lost a significant relationship, job, or educational or career opportunity because of gambling" (negative consequences; APA, 2013, p. 585–589). The DSM specifies 9 criteria, with a minimum of 4 which must be demonstrated over a 12-month period of time in order to warrant diagnosis. Further, manic episodes must be ruled out as an alternative explanation for the impulsive behavior. Like those with other types of addictions, pathological gamblers will engage in this behavior as a way of "medicating" negative emotional states such as depression or anxiety. They will lie to others to hide how much money and/or how often they gamble, and they are often mentally preoccupied with gambling (akin to the craving experienced by a drug abuser). This preoccupation, along with "chasing losses," are the most commonly reported symptoms. To acquire money for gambling, individuals may resort to criminal activities (theft, embezzlement, etc.) or may seek financial assistance from other people to help them out of dire circumstances.

Pathological gamblers seem to be particularly prone to cognitive errors. Scales, such as the Gamblers' Beliefs Questionnaire (GBQ; Steenbergh, et al., 2002) and the Gambling-Related Cognitions Scale (GRCS; Raylu & Oei, 2004) have been developed to tap into these thought patterns. Among other characteristics, "illusion of control" has been identified as a problematic thought pattern common among problem or pathological gamblers. Cognitive distortions are correlated with severity of gambling issues, such that those showing more distorted thinking have more severe gambling problems (Cunningham et al., 2014). MacKay and Hodgins (2012) report this same sort of relationship between thinking and gambling among Internet gamblers.

Personality characteristics common in problem gamblers include competitiveness, disinhibition, impulsivity, above-average intelligence, and high energy. Adolescents show a higher rate of problem gambling than do adults, and adults that do have severe gambling problems often begin their gambling as adolescents (Gupta et al., 2006). Adolescents and adults with gambling issues specifically deviate from normative samples in impulsivity, distractibility, over activity, self-indulgence, and difficulty adapting to group norms (Gupta et al., 2006). Compulsive gamblers often find themselves in financial distress, emotional and physical demise, and dealing with impaired interpersonal relationships (LaPlante & Shaffer, 2007).

Problem gambling is more prevalent in persons seeking treatment for substance addictions and other psychiatric issues (Nelson & Oehlert, 2008). In a large epidemiologic study ($N = 43,093$), Morasco et al. (2006) examined medical disorders and health service utilization associated with problem and pathologic gambling. They assessed self-reported medical diagnoses and past-year medical services used. Their research showed that compulsive gambling is associated with many adverse health consequences.

Pathologic gamblers were more likely to have been diagnosed with tachycardia, angina, and cirrhosis and other liver disease. Gambling severity was also associated with higher rates of medical utilization, with pathologic gamblers more likely than low-risk individuals to have been treated in the emergency room in the year before the survey. The authors conclude that "a lifetime diagnosis of pathologic gambling is associated with several medical disorders and increased medical utilization, perhaps leading to a burden on healthcare costs in the United States" (p. 976). The DSM-5 reports the lifetime prevalence of gambling disorder as relatively rare, affecting between 0.4 and 1.0% of the general population (APA, 2013). However, a recent phone survey of 2,963 respondents in the U.S. suggests the rate is higher, with 6.8% of males and 2.5% of females meeting 3 or more diagnostic criteria for problem gambling (Barnes, et al., 2015). This same study also reports higher levels of problem gambling among those of lower socio-economic status; Blacks (8.8%) had higher rates than Hispanics (5.8%) or Whites (3.7%).

A variety of conditions can commonly co-occur with gambling disorder, including depression, bipolar disorder, anxiety disorders, and personality disorders. Co-occurrence of substance use/abuse with problem gambling is also common and may help escalate the gambling problem. Barnes and colleagues (2015) report that dependence on alcohol, tobacco, or marijuana is correlated with higher risk of problematic gambling. In some cases, it may be helpful for us to imagine a gambler sitting in a casino, where free alcoholic beverages are often provided as long as the person is gambling. The alcohol consumption may further impair the individual's ability to control their impulses to bet and make appropriate judgments about when to quit. A study by Markham et al. (2012) suggests that this could be a factor. Their survey data indicate that for non-problem gamblers, alcohol consumption is negatively related to gambling; however, for problem gamblers, alcohol consumption is positively correlated with gambling. Those with more severe gambling problems gambled longer and drank more than those without gambling problems.

Gambling is thought to activate the same neurochemicals that drugs and other risky behaviors causing excitement and physiological arousal (A. Wexler & S. Wexler, 1992). Depending on timing, venue, and win-or-lose outcomes, gambling can be stimulating, tranquilizing, or pain-relieving, sometimes all experienced during one episode. The withdrawal symptoms from pathological gambling are similar to drug withdrawals, following the opponent-process model as presented above. Because compulsive gambling can be assumed to entail a high degree of ongoing stress over time, overstimulation of the hypothalamic-pituitary-adrenal (HPA) axis would be expected to increase vulnerability to a host of medical and psychiatric conditions, including damage to the reproductive organs, disordered menstrual cycles, suppression of growth hormone, irritable bowel syndrome, diabetes, depression, phobias, and panic attacks (Englert, 2003).

Brain imaging data further support the similarities between compulsive gamblers and drug addicts. Both groups tend to have lower than typical prefrontal cortex activity (which could lead to decreased impulse control and impaired judgements). Further, they may have naturally lower levels of activity in the reward pathway, fitting with the idea of a "reward deficiency." However, when exposed to cues related to gambling, they experience high activation in the mesolimbic pathways, compared to control participants. (van Holst et. al, 2010)

Research shows that as exposure to gambling increases in the community, so does the rate of pathological gamblers and the availability of self-help groups. More chapters of Gambler's Anonymous can be found in areas where gambling is legal and therefore more accessible and socially encouraged (e.g., where the ads read, "Buy a lottery ticket for the one you love"). Individuals of lower socioeconomic standing tend to spend greater proportions of their income on gambling (Shaffer, LaBrie, LaPlante, Nelson, & Stanton, 2004).

CASE STUDY: The Gambling-Addicted Casino President

In March of 2001, the highest-ranking casino executive ever to confess to being a compulsive gambler was banned from New Jersey casinos for 5 years. New Jersey gaming regulators voted unanimously to strip the casino key license of Gary DiBartolomeo, 46, for lying about his gambling activities to his employers and licensing authorities. DiBartolomeo, by establishing himself as a player development executive who could charm high rollers, artfully landed a $362,000-a-year job as president of Caesars Atlantic City. He ultimately succumbed to the lure of the blackjack tables and roulette games that he so skillfully managed.

As a condition of his license renewal, he was warned by regulators to quit gambling, but on dozens of occasions he violated the restrictions. While playing in casinos in Nevada, Connecticut, Mississippi, the Bahamas, and Monte Carlo, he bet up to $1,500 per hand and lost $389,000 in an 18-month period. One time he recruited a fellow Caesars worker to act as his "alter ego" to play blackjack with DiBartolomeo's money as DiBartolomeo supervised the bets. Tearfully, DiBartolomeo described himself before the gaming commission as "the David Copperfield of deception." He called compulsive gambling the demon inside of him.

Shop 'til You Drop

Shopping, a seemingly benign arousal activity, may achieve the status of a mood-altering addiction, characterized by powerful mood swings from intense arousal to blissful satiation, often followed by depression and remorse. Although compulsive shopping is not included in DSM-5 under the category of Substance-Related and Addictive Disorders, Andreassen (2014, p. 198) argues that shopping disorder is best understood from an addiction perspective, characterized by "being overly concerned about shopping, driven by an uncontrollable shopping motivation, and to investing so much time and effort into shopping that it impairs other important life areas." Jung & Yi (2014) identified three types of compulsive buyers: 1) "excitement seekers" (motivated to relieve boredom); 2) "escape seeker" (shops to relieve negative emotions); and 3) "low affect management buyer" (whose impulsive buying is not tied to emotional extremes). This latter category actually made up the largest group (around 45%) of Jung & Yi's sample. The authors suggest that motivations for shopping may have important implications for treatment.

In the case study below, Karen, a Los Angeles–based writer and single mother of two school-aged children, reminisces about her uncontrolled passion for clothes.

CASE EXAMPLE: Compulsive Shopping

Sometimes I go for months without buying anything; however, I recently went through a major binge in which I bought a Dior suit (at half price, $130), a dress and suit ($268), and ski pants and a parka ($240). All in about one week. I had some extra money because my father sent me some, but I should have used it to pay off part of my credit card debt. So I started thinking about this behavior and my inability to control it. I know the experience—when I see something I like, and I try it on, and it looks good on me, I get a euphoria that I love. It's seeing myself in the mirror looking good; there's also an aspect of costume to it—wearing many different kinds of clothes is like playing lots of different roles, being different people. I began my clothing fascination with the images of women in comic books when I was 8–10 years old. There was a comic series about Katy Keene the Pinup Queen; these comics were full of pictures of clothes. I cut them out and filled two large scrapbooks with the pictures. When I woke up in the morning and it was time to get dressed, I would look in the scrapbook and try to put together an outfit from my own clothes that resembled something in the book. It usually meant wearing a red blouse to try to copy a red strapless evening gown. I wished I could have all those numberless outfits for every kind of fantasy occasion. And in fact, one of Katy's two boyfriends (the other was a tall, rich blond) was K. O. Kelly, a red-headed freckle-faced boxer who looked a lot like my last boyfriend, John.

For 3 years, a friend and I owned and ran a small dress shop. There, I was able to buy clothes on a grand scale for the shop, and we had a rule that whenever we marked anything down, one of us could take it for herself if she wanted. Every Saturday when I worked in the shop, after I closed up, I pulled everything I liked off the sale rack and tried it on—everything I liked, I took home. I built an enormous wardrobe that way. When we sold the shop, for months afterward, I dreamed of being in the shop and being able to have all the clothes I wanted. And it was after we sold the shop that I started to go on clothes-buying binges. Before having the shop, I had always been very frugal about buying clothes, as about everything.

The first time John and I broke up, I was devastated. I couldn't sleep properly for months, and for the first few weeks I went 2 nights out of 3 hardly sleeping at all, and then the third night I would fall into a sort of coma from sheer exhaustion. Getting through every day was a struggle, trying to keep my feelings under control and maintain an appropriate demeanor at work. One day, about 4 or 5 weeks after we broke up, I dropped the kids off to see a movie at a shopping center. I was going to kill time till the movie was over, browsing. I saw some wonderful clothes in a store window; I went in and started trying things on, and in 20 minutes I had picked out $500 worth of clothes and shoes. I put a deposit on them and came back the next day and paid for them all. After trying them all on and picking them out, I floated out of the store on a cloud. It was my first happy moment after breaking up with John, and it was a heady, euphoric high.

The notion of shopping to elevate mood is so familiar in our culture and tied to the tongue-in-cheek concept "retail therapy" (Schmich, 1986), implying that shopping has therapeutic value. Unfortunately, the initial high experienced in connection with the newly acquired symbols of self-love soon fades into what has become known to psychologists as "buyer's remorse." Shopping euphoria turns to depression and feelings of unworthiness. After the binge, buyers confess that they didn't discriminate among purchases. They find that they bought clothes that are all the same, or that don't seem to match at all. In either case, they do not seem to use what they buy; sometimes they return all the purchases, only to go off on another binge. Some addicts fear embarrassment that they will be recognized by shopkeepers as "binge-purge" shoppers. They maintain their composure simply by keeping the items around, much as a young child clings to a security blanket. For some compulsive shoppers, financial hardship may follow if they are charging purchases they cannot actually afford.

McElroy et al. (1994, cited in Mueller et al., 2007) suggested that maladaptive preoccupation with shopping or actual maladaptive purchases are indicated by irresistible impulses to buy or frequently purchasing of items one cannot afford or does not need. Shopping may extend to involve more time than is actually needed. The purchasing behavior can result in marked psychological distress or interfere with social or occupational functioning or may produce financial hardship. These criteria are considered distinct from impulsive, excessive buying that could occur during mania or hypomania in individuals with bipolar disorder.

A number of conditions can co-occur with compulsive shopping, such as OCD, eating disorders, depression, anxiety, and substance abuse. Mueller et al. (2007) also found a link between compulsive shopping and hoarding; hoarders who are compulsive shoppers tend to have greater problems with compulsive buying and greater incidence of co-occurring psychological conditions—in particular OCD, mood, anxiety, and eating disorders. These authors suggest that those compulsive shoppers who are also hoarders may need special treatment considerations to address their problematic behavior.

Autoerotic Fatalities

Perhaps the most extreme and bizarre example of the relationship between opponent processes and human compulsion is drawn from a growing body of literature on autoerotic fatalities. Each year, a small, yet significant, number of people, primarily males, accidentally die during voluntary participation in dangerous sexual practices. "Autoerotic deaths are defined as accidental deaths that occur during individual, solitary sexual activity in which some type of apparatus that was used to enhance the sexual stimulation of the deceased caused unintentional death. In the Western countries, the incidence of these deaths is of approximately 0.5 deaths per million inhabitants per year (Sauvageau, 2014, p. 1).

For certain individuals, the preferred or exclusive mode of producing sexual excitement is to be mechanically or chemically asphyxiated to or beyond the point at which consciousness or perception is altered by cerebral hypoxia (diminished availability of oxygen to the brain). Nevertheless, other individuals for whom this is not the preferred means for enhancing sexual arousal repeatedly self-induce a state of cerebral hypoxia to the degree where consciousness or perception is sufficiently altered so as to produce sexual excitement (Dietz, 1983).

In a more or less typical case (e.g., Sheehan & Garfinkel, 1987; Uva, 1995), a 15-year-old boy was referred for psychiatric care after he told the police of his practice of suspending himself with a rope and ejaculating while hanging. The boy would repeatedly hang himself from the clothes rod in his closet by lifting his feet from the ground, and he learned to place a towel around his neck, under the rope, to prevent marks or bruises. He reported that he would hang for one-half to 2 minutes and nearly always ejaculated while suspended. The frequency of self-hangings increased from once every 2 weeks to four times a week. The boy said that he repeatedly engaged in this bizarre practice because he wanted to anger his mother and because it relieved his depression and temporarily made him feel good.

Of people who describe themselves as "bondage practitioners," many use hanging or strangulation in their sexual practices. Sexual excitement is apparently heightened for some people when they engage in sexual acts in which they might be caught breaking a social custom or religious taboo. For such people, risk-taking is more than simply spicing an already tasty dish; it can be the major component of the entire sexual act, as in widely practiced sadomasochistic sex rituals, with or without the aid of mechanical props or psychoactive drugs. Rupp (1973) concluded that autoerotic asphyxia is carried out by large numbers of individuals who arrive at this practice independently of one another.

Am I a Speed Demon?

To be sure, a thrilling adventure such as skydiving, mountaineering, or white-water rafting would elicit squeals of delight from some and shrieks of horror from others. According to Manhart (2005), the difference in the reactions may be explained by individual differences between people's dopamine systems (i.e., how much dopamine people have access to and how readily it can be used to transmit messages between neurons). When we consider that (1) a mild to moderate level of arousal tends to help people perform at their maximum effectiveness, (2) people are aroused to different degrees by the same stimuli, and (3) optimal performance is usually accompanied by enhanced self-esteem, then it becomes clear that some people thrive on excitement while others become disoriented and emotionally disturbed by it. When skydivers—who may represent a broad spectrum of high-risk adventurers—are interviewed about the thrill of free falling, the common response is, "Skydiving is the most enjoyable sport imaginable," with nearly universal agreement that the greatest feelings of excitement and pleasure are experienced during free fall.

The subjective experience of boredom has been linked to the need for excess excitement (Gosline, 2007). Boredom, however, is not a one-dimensional concept; it is derived from many things including level of attention and emotional factors. A person more susceptible to this trait has a higher need for excitement, variety, and novelty, and usually requires a constant and changing supply of stimulation to achieve his or her optimal level of arousal (Gosline, 2007). Stimulants such as caffeine and amphetamines reduce fatigue and inattention during monotonous tasks as well as decrease reported boredom. Those who are predisposed to boredom have a higher rate of depression and drug addiction, as well as decreased performance in school and work. They are also at increased risk for anxiety, anger, aggressive behavior, and lack of interpersonal skills. Risky behaviors may be used to provide "false refuge" from these negative experiences. But thrill chasing often leads to self-destructive behaviors like gambling, drugs, and crime. Better ways to achieve optimal dopamine levels include: a challenging job or course of study, or finding new interests, skills, and hobbies could satisfy some of the need for thrills. In Chapter 23, we examine exercise as an important means to achieve stimulation and arousal in the service of improved mental and physical health outcomes. Chapter 24 explores meaningful engagement of talents as a primary means to sidestep boredom and wasted energy.

Consistent with our discussion on the factor of boredom, Farley (1986) identified a "type T" or thrill-seeking personality. According to Farley, thrill seekers opt for excitement and stimulation whenever they can find it, through intense physical or mental activity, or both. Farley postulates that a combination of genetics, early childhood experience, and nutrition contribute to the development of a thrill-seeking disposition. Under positive environmental conditions, a type T might channel his or her propensity for risk to the benefit of society, as exemplified by heroes such as Charles Lindbergh or Martin Luther King.

In the negative case, however, a type T predisposition may lead to pointless self-destruction or even the bizarre criminal behavior of a serial killer like the infamous Ted Bundy.

Farley (1986) divided his type T individuals into two categories, positive and negative. A positive risk taker will use the need for the rush to create, invent new things, explore new places, or start his or her own businesses. A negative thrill seeker will use the rush in unfavorable ways such as compulsive gambling or criminal activity. Often, a person with a type T personality will fall into both categories; the person will have aspects of each element in his or her personality. Risk takers often deny that they are participating in risky behavior, as they often see their fate as in their control.

In terms of general characteristics, Farley (1986) describes type T people as creative, risk-taking extroverts who prefer more sexual variety than average. Their artistic preferences tend to be experimental; they are more likely to be juvenile delinquents and reckless drivers. In the mental arena, type Ts are creative thinkers who have a talent for transforming one type of mental representation into another. They may shift from abstract to concrete thinking and tend to form images into words more easily than other people. Farley finds that biology is the major determinant of the type T personality, but socialization decides whether the individual will become a preserver or destroyer. Underlying the constitutional predisposition for the thrill-seeking personality may be a low level of physiological excitability

According to Zuckerman's (2007) research on the biological basis of sensation seeking, numerous studies point to low levels of monoamine oxidase (MAO) as a biochemical determinant of the risk-taking personality. As mentioned in Chapter 3, this enzyme plays a vital role in the regulation of excitatory neurotransmission in the brain. The less of this enzyme a person has, the more dopamine flows into the nucleus accumbens and the more likely the individual is to seek out exciting, daring pastimes (Manhart, 2005). Perhaps sensation seekers require higher levels of external stimulation to evoke a substantial change in their already high rate of excitatory neurotransmission.

As we discussed earlier in Chapter 1, Addiction to Experience, Milkman and Frosch (1973) conducted a study of the relationship between personality and drug preference. Subjects who preferred amphetamine as their drug of choice were similar in many respects to both Zuckerman's biologically based sensation seekers and Farley's type T thrill seekers. When rated according to their responsiveness to external stimuli, which included noise, light, sound, and pain, amphetamine users appeared to be less responsive than normal and significantly less sensitive than those who preferred narcotics as their drug of choice. The "speed freaks" observed by Milkman and Frosch appeared to use stimulant drugs as a means of putting themselves in closer touch with environmental stimuli—stimuli that they would ordinarily find dull or uninteresting because of their "thick-skinned" reactions to sensory cues. In terms of personality characteristics, Milkman and Frosch found that amphetamine users fit Farley's description to a "T."

> The amphetamine user is characterized by active confrontation with his environment. While the heroin user feels overwhelmed by low self-esteem, the amphetamine user utilizes a variety of compensatory maneuvers. He reassures and arms himself against a world perceived as hostile and threatening via physical exhibition of alienated symbols of power and strength. Identification with radical political groups further serves the need for active expression of hostility. Promiscuity and prolonged sexual activity may be the behavioral expression of

needs to demonstrate adequacy and potency. High-level artistic and creative as-pirations are usually unrealized self-expectations, bordering on delusional gran-diosity. Such beliefs often lead to compulsive and unproductive behavior. Active participation in hand crafts, music, drawing, or physical labor is striking in nearly all of the amphetamine users studied. To maintain his tenuous sense of self as a potentially productive individual, the amphetamine user deploys many defenses. Denial, projection, rationalization, and intellectualization are characteristically observed. Equilibrium is maintained at the cost of great expenditures of psychic and physical energy. (p. 244)

More recently, personality traits of internalizing and externalizing behaviors (keeping emotions in or expressing them in negative ways) have been associated with the user's drug of choice (Hopwood, Baker, & Morey, 2008). Those who prefer psychostimulants tend to have higher tendencies for sensation seeking and disinhibition. Those addicted to stimulant drugs tend to behave more impulsively and take more risks (White, Lejuez, & de Wit, 2007).

After more than a decade of clinical observations on the personality characteristics of cocaine and more recently methamphetamine users it appears that they are much like their predecessors, the sensa-tion-seeking amphetamine users of the late 60s and 70s. Each generation of speed demons seems to cope with underlying feelings of helplessness via the energizing effects of stimulant drugs. The arousing quali-ties of stimulants serve the users' needs to feel active and potent in the face of an environment perceived as hostile and threatening. Massive expenditures of psychic and physical energy are geared to defend against underlying fears of vulnerability, passivity, and inadequacy.

Interestingly, animal data support the relationship between sensation-seeking, differential levels of basal dopamine (and corticosterone) levels, and tendency to self-administer stimulant drugs such as cocaine and amphetamine. Rats that are prone to actively explore novel environments (an animal trait thought to be akin to novelty-seeking) share several traits with their human sensation seeking coun-terparts, including the tendency to self-administer stimulant drugs such as cocaine and amphetamine, compared to rats who avoid exploration of novel environments (A. Meyer et. al, 2010). It appears that sensation seeking may be viewed as a stable personality characteristic, with biological underpinnings. M.E. Miller et al., (2015, p. 435) define the trait as the "seeking of varied, novel, complex, and intense sensa-tions and experiences, and the willingness to take physical, social, legal and financial risks for the sake of such experiences." The author findings of the relationship between sensation seeking and drug of choice are consistent with the aforementioned preferences of novelty seeking rats for stimulant drugs and the Milkman and Frosch (1973) finding that amthamine abusers are "active-confrontational" types. In fact Miller et al. (2015, p. 439) found that among adult males there was a significant association between SS (Sensation Seeking) and preference for amphetamine. "Participants with increased Total, Disinhibition, Thrill and Adventure Seeking, and Experience Seeking scores had significantly greater odds of choosing d-AMPH [amphetamine] over placebo..."

The style of coping is reminiscent of a phase of early childhood development that culminates around the middle of the second year of life. During this stage, described by Mahler (1967) as the practicing period, "the freely walking toddler seems to feel at the height of his mood of elation. He appears to be at the peak of his belief in his own magical omnipotence which is still to a considerable extent derived from his sense of sharing in his mother's magic powers" (p. 749). The child seems to delight in flooding his or her senses while moving with reckless abandon through an environment fraught with diversity, difficulty, and danger. The fearless conduct is of course little more than a behavioral facade to compensate for continuous threats to a sense of self-importance or personal safety. As Reich (1960) explains, "The need for narcissistic inflation arises from a striving to overcome threats to one's bodily intactness." If early traumatizations are too frequent, the primitive ego defends itself via magical denial: "It is not so, I am not helpless, bleeding, destroyed. On the contrary, I am bigger and better than anyone else" (p. 220).

Those who thrive on courting danger appear to have carried this primitive style of coping into the adult realm. They win admiration and approval from witnesses by appearing to be tougher and more daring than everyone else. As described by Tom Wolfe in *The Right Stuff* (1980), both heroes and psychopaths have the uncanny ability to tread on the brink of disaster while maintaining their calm; they can function with wit and poise even when confronted with gargantuan distress. Brigadier General Chuck Yeager, one of America's original astronauts, appears to fit Wolfe's criteria for a fearless person. He is said to have hidden the fact that he had broken several ribs during a reckless midnight horseback ride so that he could crawl into a tiny X-1 rocket and allow himself to be ejected from the belly of a B-29, flying at 26,000 feet, to become the first man to travel faster than the speed of sound.

Other far less esteemed yet equally fearless members of our society attain the ignoble title of psychopath. As originally described in psychiatrist Cleckley's classic work, *The Mask of Sanity* (1941), psychopaths are generally quite intelligent. Their charm is undoubtedly more compelling because they lack visible tension or anxiety. Yet they are basically incapable of genuine affection or love and have no respect for the truth. They are characteristically unreliable, taking senseless risks even after having been punished for similar acts. The psychopath does not seem to learn from unpleasant past experiences and lacks the capacity for genuine remorse or shame. He is usually male—in three cases out of four—and has great facility for blaming others for his inappropriate or criminal actions. He seems unable to appreciate or foresee how others will react to his behavior. Cleckley portrays the psychopath not as deeply vicious, but as unable to take seriously the threat of disaster or harm and respond accordingly.

Following Farley's (1986) concept of the type T personality, psychopaths may be viewed as the black-sheep cousins of respectable adventurers. Both may be cut from the same biological cloth; they differ primarily in their early childhood experiences with parents and other socializing influences.

At the time of being interviewed, Detective Daril Cinquanta had been with the Denver Police Department for 17 years. He had been involved in more than 3,000 felon arrests without ever shooting a suspect. Detective Cinquanta is regarded by both criminals and responsible citizens as a law enforcement hero and champion of justice. He attributes much of his success as a crime fighter to his ability to understand the mentality of the people that he arrests. Coming from a lower-social class background himself, Cinquanta is known among criminal adversaries for his cunning and fearlessness. He purposely cultivates the image of a maniacal daredevil to inspire as much fear as possible in his foes.

In the following case example, Cinquanta communicates the deep sense of pleasure and mental exhilaration that he derives from the excitement and risk of being a professional crime fighter.

CASE EXAMPLE: Officer Cinquanta—Type T Hero

We had a series of armed robberies in north Denver where somebody was robbing fast food restaurants with a sawed-off shotgun. We didn't have anything on this until one robbery when we got a surveillance photograph and it shows this Chicano male with a mask on. The only thing you can see is the shave line on his neck, that his wrists are hairy and his eyebrow … and he's got a sawed-off shotgun. … One morning during this rash of robberies, a little girl gets killed at McDonald's at 38th and Irving. … [G]uy comes in, hits the place and shotguns this little girl—kills her in the robbery.

Well, I knew this guy. I just **had** to know him. I developed a suspect from his eyebrow. I went through my pictures and I figured out who it was . . . and then I directed an informant of mine who had done time with him—who was a friend of his—to make contact with him … and one day [the suspect] admitted to him that he killed the girl in McDonald's. … So then my informant corroborates. He says, "God damned, he admitted it; said he shot her because she was ugly!" I go, "Jesus Christ!" He [informant] says he's [suspect] all strung out, doing dope and paranoid. So I figured the only way I'm going to do this guy is to follow him to his next robbery. I need to get some physical evidence; we need to make him surface that shotgun or the shoes he wore because we had a shoe print from the counter he jumped over at McDonald's. … I convinced Command to let me follow this guy 24 hours a day and live with him.

And we did. On the 14th day he, guess what? He commits an armed robbery. … Well, he tried to hit a Pizza Hut first, and we were moving in on him when he abandoned it because he saw a police car go by. … [H]e had the mask down and he was just getting ready to pull the gun and go in the back door. … He went back to the car. So then he cruised around. … This is after 8 hours—we followed him 8 hours the last day until he picked his target. So he picks this gas station and he got down by a dumpster, his partner parked about 100 feet away … and he pulled the mask down and got his gun out of his sock. He had a .25 and put the gloves on and then went around to the gas station.

As he was going around, I ordered that we move in. We had two teams coming around from opposite directions. Well, I was right behind him when they confronted him. He panicked … he had the gun … he turned around and I was going to do him and said "Drop it!" He leaped between two fences, between a lumber yard and the back of the station … and he raised the gun … and one of the detectives shot him.

It was exciting … it was wonderful … I loved it. … [I]t's just unbelievable … the exhilaration.

Some of the same qualities that distinguish Detective Cinquanta as a successful crime fighter have apparently gone astray in the people that he apprehends. Whether the game is "cops and robbers" or the Web-based *World of Warcraft*, children derive primal pleasure from both sides of the chase. The thrill of conquest or danger is undoubtedly connected with the excitement that one experiences when the senses become flooded by survival cues. Sensation seeking appears to be a trait common to the entire spectrum of adventurous personalities—cops, criminals, coke addicts, and Casanovas included. Zuckerman (1994, 2007) developed the Sensation-Seeking Scale (SSS) to measure an individual's desire to engage in risky or adventurous activities, seek new kinds of sensory experiences, enjoy the excitement of social stimulation, and avoid boredom. Table 9.3 offers a sample of items from the SSS and a scoring procedure.

Table 9.3 Am I a Sensation Seeker?

Each item contains two choices. Choose the one that best describes your likes or feelings. If you do not like either choice, mark the choice you dislike the least. Do not leave any items blank.

1. A. I have no patience with dull or boring persons.

    B. I find something interesting in almost every person I talk to.

2. A. A good painting should shock or jolt the senses.

    B. A good painting should provide a feeling of peace and security.

3. A. People who ride motorcycles must have some kind of unconscious need to hurt themselves.

    B. I would like to drive or ride a motorcycle.

4. A. I would prefer living in an ideal society in which everyone is safe, secure, and happy.

    B. I would have preferred living in the unsettled days of history.

5. A. I sometimes like to do things that are a little frightening.

    B. A sensible person avoids dangerous activities.

6. A. I would not like to be hypnotized.

    B. I would like to be hypnotized.

7. A. The most important goal of life is to live to the fullest and experience as much as possible.

    B. The most important goal of life is to find peace and happiness.

8. A. I would like to try parachute jumping.

    B. I would never want to try jumping from a plane, with or without a parachute.

9. A. I enter cold water gradually, giving myself time to get used to it.

    B. I like to dive or jump right into the ocean or a cold pool.

10. A. When I go on a vacation, I prefer the comfort of a good room and bed.

    B. When I go on a vacation, I prefer the change of camping out.

11. A. I prefer people who are emotionally expressive, even if they are a bit unstable.

    B. I prefer people who are calm and even-tempered.

12. A. I would prefer a job in one location.

    B. I would like a job that requires traveling.

13. A. I can't wait to get indoors on a cold day.

    B. I am invigorated by a brisk, cold day.

14. A. I get bored seeing the same faces.

    B. I like the comfortable familiarity of everyday friends.

Scoring: Count one point for each of the following items that you have circled: 1A, 2A, 3B, 4B, 5A, 6B, 7A, 8A, 9B, 10B, 11A, 12B, 13B, 14A. Add your total for sensation seeking and compare it with the norms below:

0–3 Very low

4–5 Low

6–9 Average

10–11 High

12–14 Very high

Source: This is an arbitrary sampling of items and not the full Sensation-Seeking Scale, which can be found in M. Zuckerman (1994), Behavioral expressions and biosocial bases of sensation seeking. *New York: Cambridge University Press. Also see M. Zuckerman (2007),* Sensation seeking and risky behavior. *Washington, DC: American Psychological Association.*

Your Sensation Seeking Drive

The people who score high on the SSS are more likely than others to enjoy risk in their work and play. High-sensation types are more probable candidates for variation and experimentation in their patterns of drug use and sexual practices; they tend to behave more fearlessly when confronted with such common phobic situations as heights, snakes, or darkness; they take more risks when gambling; and they report driving at higher speeds than low-sensation seekers. They are more likely to engage in such dangerous sports as parachuting, motorcycle riding, or scuba diving. Zuckerman and his colleagues have found that compatibility in sensation seeking is also a meaningful predictor of marital adjustment. Per one happily married team of underwater adventurers, "The couple that dives together, thrives together."

Question: How might Hitler's alleged abuse of stimulant drugs add credence to the "addiction to arousal" model of this book? Check out his mannerisms in Figure 9.6.

Figure 9.6 Adolf Hitler's Manic Mannerisms May be Attributed to his Crystal Meth Abuse.

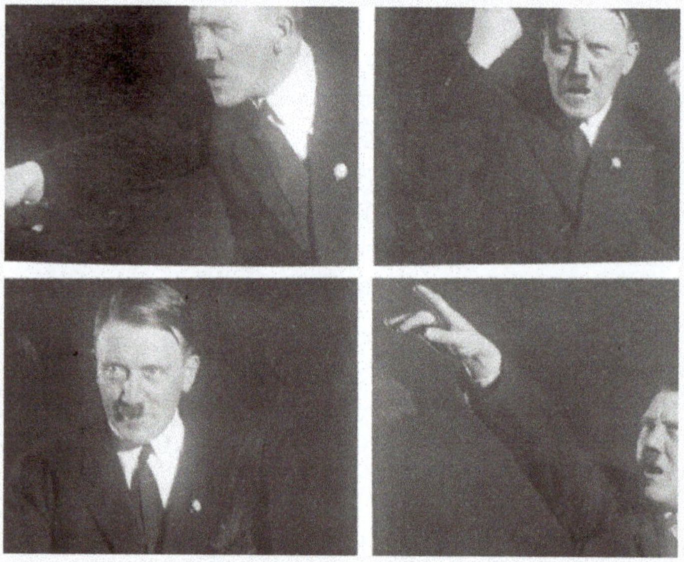

Copyright © Heinrich Hoffmann (CC BY-SA 3.0) at https://commons.wikimedia.org/wiki/File:Bundesarchiv_Bild_102-10460,_Adolf_Hitler,_Rednerposen.jpg.

Chapter Summary

This chapter begins with a description of the relationship between arousal and performance. People perform most effectively when under some degree of stress. A moderate level of arousal tends to produce alertness and enthusiasm for the task at hand. This may account for the universal use of the stimulant caffeine, found in coffee, and increasingly used as an ingredient in a slew of "energy drinks." When emotional excitement exceeds an optimal point, even when the evoked feelings are positive, the result is progressive impairment of one's ability to function.

Selye introduced the idea that people could alter consciousness though chemical changes associated with stress. The psychological by-products of a moderate biochemical emergency are noticeable increments in one's feelings of physical prowess and personal competence, often associated with strong sensations of pleasure. In many ways, the state of biological and psychological "readiness" produced by stress is mimicked by the effects of stimulant drugs. In addition to increasing the levels of cortisol and norepinephrine, pleasure derived from fear-inducing activities, such as gambling, dangerous sexual liaisons, and skydiving, increases the level of dopamine in the nucleus accumbens. However, to maintain the intensity of an elevated mood, the sensation seeker must escalate his or her use of the drug or activity. Cessation of the drug or behavior produces a feeling of dysphoria mediated by neurochemical changes in the brain.

The repeated pairing of opposite emotional experiences, and their underlying physiological counterparts, may be the sustaining force behind all forms of human compulsion. According to R. L. Solomon's opponent-process model of mood oscillation, the same principle that produces alcoholics and drug addicts can be used to account for daredevils, Coca-Cola addicts, and promiscuous sex junkies. Mood-altering behavior is often sustained because people seek to avoid the unpleasant effects that have been set in motion by the opponent process. Compulsive shopping and autoerotic fatalities are presented as examples—one relatively benign (shopping), and the other lethal—of opponent-process dynamics.

Pathological gambling exemplifies a mood-altering activity that triggers neurochemical messages similar to those induced by stimulant drugs. Personality characteristics of gamblers parallel those of other sensation-seeking types (e.g., competitiveness, disinhibition, impulsivity, above-average intelligence, and high energy). Because compulsive gambling often entails a high degree of ongoing stress over time, over-stimulation of the HPA axis is likely to increase vulnerability to a host of medical and psychiatric conditions. In fact, research shows that compulsive gambling is associated with many adverse health consequences.

The chapter concludes with a discussion of the psychological and neurochemical characteristics of sensation seekers and the related factor of propensity toward boredom. A person more susceptible to becoming bored has a higher need for excitement, variety, and novelty and usually requires a constant and changing supply of stimulation to achieve his or her optimal level of arousal. By themselves, sensation seeking and escape from boredom are neither positive nor negative. The important question is how these fundamental human needs may be channeled and developed for the mutual benefit of the individual and society. Finally, readers are invited to examine their own sensation-seeking needs through a self-assessment instrument, Zuckerman's Sensation-Seeking Scale (Table 9.3). National Geographic videos are suggested in See for Yourself, which add depth to our understanding of the relationship between stress and illness ("The Science of Stress") and the use of drugs and personality ("Hitler's Drug Use Revealed").

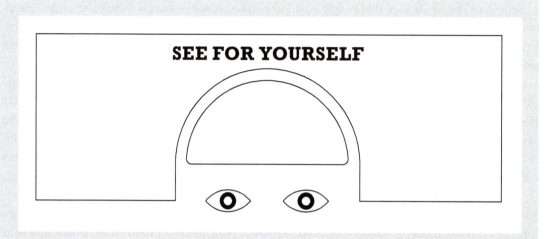

Hitler's Drug Use Revealed. 2013. National Geographic: Nazi Underworld Series. 44:56

Professor Nassir Ghaemi claims: "It's not whether Hitler was an amphetamine addict or not – it's that Hitler had bipolar disorder and amphetamines made it worse." **www.youtube.com/watch?v=IaWTDzR1mRI**

Crystal Meth in Nazi Germany. National Geographic. 2:57

This brief clip discusses the Nazis' prolific use of a form of crystal meth as well as a medical explanation for Hitler's anxiety and drug dependence. **http://www.nationalgeographic.com.au/videos/hitler-the-junkie/crystal-meth-in-nazi-germany-3407.aspx**

The Science of Stress. 2013. National Geographic. 55:50

Explores toxic and beneficial effects of stress comparing animal exposures in nature and human experiences in society. Examines immediate and long term effects of stress on the brain, immune and cardiovascular systems. **https://www.youtube.com/watch?v=ZyBsy5SQxqU**

How to Make Stress Your Friend

TED talk (Kelly McGonigal, 2013) explains how the harmful effects of stress can be remediated by healthy attachment. 14:28

https://www.youtube.com/watch?v=RcGyVTAoXEU

CHAPTER 10

Rock Around the Clock

Meth, 'Bath Salts,' Coke, Ecstasy and the Club Scene

Now I'm losing touch with reality and I'm almost out of blow

It's such a fine line; I hate to see it go

Cocaine, runnin' all around my brain
— "Cocaine," by Gary Davis; additional lyrics by Glenn Frey and Jackson Browne

Introduction

This chapter explores the psychosocial underpinnings and neurochemical effects of illegal stimulants, including methamphetamine, cocaine, MDMA ("Ecstasy"), and synthetic cathinones (sometimes called "bath salts"). Although cocaine and amphetamines have limited medical use, the psychological, social, economic, and health damage associated with illegal use of these drugs is enormous. Our discussion begins with methamphetamine, a powerful stimulant that has moved from biker gangs and all-night raves to just about every nook and cranny of society. Then we discuss the more recently developed "bath salts" before covering cocaine, the oldest of these stimulating drugs. The popular "club drug," Ecstasy, is discussed along with other substances associated with the club scene: GHB, Rohypnol, and ketamine.

Methamphetamine—Speeding to Hell

Amphetamines have been around since the early 20th century and were originally made from the extract of the *Ephedra vulgaris* plant. Methamphetamine (ice, meth, speed, crystal, and scores of other slang names ranging from dummy dust to zoom) is a chemically-modified version of amphetamine that is especially potent. Meth's increased potency is not linked to its direct effects on the brain, but rather its ability to reach the brain more readily than amphetamine. Meth has seeped into commonplace venues across the United States. Meth users can be found in dingy basements, prisons, middle-class suburbs, million-dollar homes, urban gay communities, on the job, and at all-night raves (Jefferson, 2005; Moore & Miller, 2005; Owen, 2007). The drug affects all levels of society, from the homeless to professionals such as doctors, lawyers, accountants, and designers (Jefferson, 2005; Ladika, 2005; Owen, 2007). Often linked with sex, meth produces a feeling that the user can last longer and longer. It is also linked with risky sex practices in both the straight and gay communities (Halliburton, 2005). During the early phases of use, there is a sense of enhanced concentration and alertness, personal empowerment, and increased capacity for work—or criminal activity.

Because tolerance and dependence are rampant in the meth community, criminal activities, are frequently relied upon to support powerful habits. Identity theft is generally considered a relatively low-risk crime with light penalties for first-time offenders. Using the Internet, it remains quick, anonymous, and nonviolent. So, meth addicts often turn up as suspects in Internet crime rings across the country. After stealing bank account and credit card information, cybercriminals send in meth-addicted cronies to extract the stolen money from accounts (Acohido & Swartz, 2005).

Meth is easily manufactured in homes, barns, pickups, and SUVs using a common cold remedy, and easily available chemicals such as anhydrous ammonia and lithium batteries. The manufacturers of homemade meth are not professional chemists (not even close), and with highly flammable substances, explosions and flash fires are rampant (Falkowski, 2003). Noxious waste from the manufacturing process is often dumped haphazardly, potentially posing environmental threats, and harmful chemical residues can remain in the environment (in walls, for instance) for long periods of time, requiring clean-up by "Haz Mat" (hazardous material) teams when meth lab locations are found. The Patriot Act, signed in 2006, attempted to reduce the availability of over-the-counter cold medicines that contain pseudoephedrine (the active ingredient in Sudafed used to manufacture meth) by requiring them to be placed behind the pharmacy counter and only sold in limited amounts to people after identification is shown. A log is kept of the amount and date they were purchased (Bren, 2006). The restrictions on readily available components of the drug have made an enormous impact on the amount of "mom-and-pop" labs, resulting in a drastic decrease in the number of labs seized in the United States (Zernike, 2006). But the demand for the drug remained unchanged, so the supply started coming in from Mexico. "Mexican ice" is crystallized and more potent than the product manufactured in the mom-and-pop labs, increasing probabilities for addiction and overdose.

Figure 10.1, *Southwest border drug seizures,* shows the relative rise, since 2009, of Mexican smuggled methamphetamine and heroin into the U.S. in the wake of the Patriot Act and declining cross border delivery of marijuana. Apparently, the widespread availability of 'Made in the U.S.A.' pot, with increased potency and quality control, has reduced the demand for imported Mexican strains.

Figure 10.1 Southwest Border Seizures

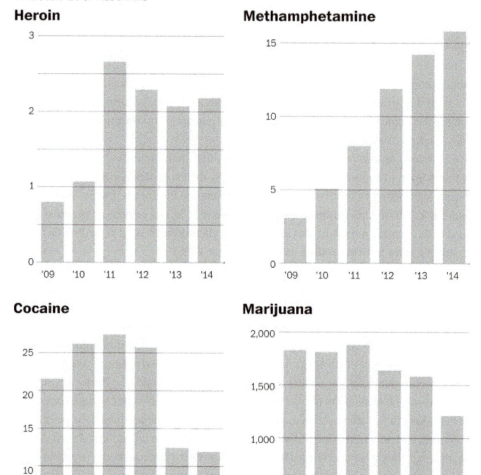

Source: https://www.washingtonpost.com/apps/g/page/
world/southwest-border-drug-seizures/1543.

Table 10.1 presents a summary of the health effects and possible treatment options for the abuse of methamphetamine (NIH, 2018)

Table 10.1 NIH Methamphetamine Summary Chart

Street Names	Commercial Names	Common Forms	Common Ways Taken	DEA Schedule
Crank, Chalk, Crystal, Fire, Glass, Go Fast, Ice, Meth, Speed	Desoxyn®	White powder or pill; crystal meth looks like pieces of glass or shiny blue-white "rocks" of different sizes	Swallowed, snorted, smoked, injected	II**

Possible Health Effects	
Short-term	Increased wakefulness and physical activity; decreased appetite; increased breathing, heart rate, blood pressure, temperature; irregular heartbeat.
Long-term	Anxiety, confusion, insomnia, mood problems, violent behavior, paranoia, hallucinations, delusions, weight loss, severe dental problems ("meth mouth"), intense itching leading to skin sores from scratching.
Other Health-related Issues	Pregnancy: premature delivery; separation of the placenta from the uterus; low birth weight; lethargy; heart and brain problems. Risk of HIV, hepatitis, and other infectious diseases from shared needles.
In Combination with Alcohol	Masks the depressant effect of alcohol, increasing risk of alcohol overdose; may increase blood pressure and jitters.
Withdrawal Symptoms	Depression, anxiety, tiredness.

Treatment Options	
Medications	There are no FDA-approved medications to treat methamphetamine addiction.
Behavioral Therapies	Cognitive-behavioral therapy (CBT) Contingency management or motivational incentives The matrix model 12-Step facilitation therapy

Meth has become so steeped in our culture that a popular cable television show, *Breaking Bad*, provided a fictional view of manufacturing, dealing, trafficking, and use of an extremely pure version of meth with a signature blue color made by high school teacher Walter White (alias "Heisenberg"). The show captures the desperation, greed, and violence related to this substance. Whether used to party, or to enhance capacity for sex, work, or crime, the usual aftermath of abusing methamphetamine is incredible hardship and suffering.

Consider Haley's description of how her experience with methamphetamine became so degrading that it is a wonder she is alive and capable of functioning as a college student.

CASE EXAMPLE: Haley's Meth Run

I found myself sitting in a dirty hotel room, and my friend was clearing a spot off the night stand to do a line. The drug in front of me is not what made me nervous but how to actually snort the line without a bill or straw and not look like a fool. I was so nervous of being judged by my new "hard-core" friends; all I wanted was for them to like me. I was a college student in my sophomore year, [I had a] full-ride scholarship, volunteered at a hospital, coached volleyball, and got good grades; I did not fit in with them. After a few more lines, we were off on our way to a party, but I was the only one with a license and a clean record and don't forget, the nice car, so I was going to be the driver. A few more nights like this soon led to partying on the weekends—Friday through Sunday, not just one night. During all this, I tried to keep a job, managed to get through the semester with only a couple bad grades, but I figured I had the time to waste.

Meth is a dirty and disgusting drug, but for some reason it had an appeal to me. Basically, getting high consisted of sitting around on couches and passing the pipe around all night long. One person played video games all night and his girlfriend cleaned; I did not know what to do, so I just sat there and clenched my jaw. The high lasted all night no matter what I did. I was not able to get to sleep until the next night. This habit turned into an every-other-weekend thing and quickly progressed into every weekend. I actually had a group of friends now for the first time that were like big brothers, or so I thought. So, I continued to party with them and felt special that I was always with the main man, the dealer. Looking back, I know I was mistaken. I was the one with the car, the money that I saved up from scholarships, and the fact that I was a girl [fed their] hopes they could persuade me to have sex with them or do other things for them.

I ended up finding another meth dealer through someone else that was supposed to have better stuff. I hung out with this dealer one night and his friends, got high on meth, and it was the night before college was starting for the semester. I allowed a guy to sleep on my couch for only one night because he was about to get evicted, but he didn't leave for a year. I continued to hang out with this boy because his friend was a dealer and he knew plenty of others. My meth use then quickly progressed from 2 or 3 days in a row to pretty much every other day and sleeping only every third day. I began to lose so much weight and I loved it! Losing the weight almost became a motivator to keep using. At the depths of my addiction, I was snorting a gram in one line multiple times a day as well as smoking it and swallowing it in toilet paper or empty vitamin capsules. My $10,000 savings account was diminishing faster than I could even find my next bag, even though it was everywhere, at all times of the day and night.

I had to move out from where I was living so that I could smoke freely in my own apartment and stay up all night every night without anyone saying anything. After a couple more moves and apartment deposits later, I was running out of money, but still managed to find meth. I saved money by going to the food bank to get food instead of spending it on groceries. At this point I had to drop out of school for the semester and had lost 35 pounds in just a couple months. It was hard enough to do simple tasks like driving a car when you have not slept for 4 days, let alone try to go to school and maintain a 3.5 average; I was in big trouble.

I decided to tell my mom in hopes I could clean up for a while, but in all actuality, I was not ready to stop. I looked good, I was skinny and attractive and having so much fun living the life of the drugs and partying, but I gave recovery a try. I had no idea how hard it was going to be to come off of meth. My body craved food so much, things like sweets and junk food. I was basically living off of Gatorade because I knew I needed something in my body so I could at least function. Nighttime was the worst, horrible nightmares all night long, and I was always so tired. I had to take a nap after breakfast, get up and eat lunch, then go back to sleep and do it again for dinner and go back to sleep. The thing was, though, that even being so tired, when you fall asleep you feel like you are dying. It's hard to describe because I have never felt anything like it before, but you dream that something is on top of you like a huge brick and you can't move or breathe. Sometimes you don't even dream it but it wakes you up and you actually can't move and it happens multiple times throughout the night. It was so scary to wake up and feel suffocated and stuck to the ground. I would have to force my arm to twitch to pull out of it, and it was so hard to get a body part to move.

This sucked so badly and I was putting back on all the weight I had just lost so I started to use again, figuring all I had to do was hide it. The thing was that this time meth was not as available, only crack. I hated crack. It was only a 30-second intense high, but it was more intense than anything I had ever felt. It numbed my throat and made me gag every time and the comedown starts in 2 minutes. The comedown honestly makes you want to scream and pull your hair out or even kill yourself. The only way around it is to do more, which just starts the cycle over. I hated this drug so much but did it multiple times.

When I finally got back to meth, I wanted to try shooting it up. It was a whole new feeling, different than snorting or smoking either of the two drugs. With coke, you get an intense rush that makes your head buzz and ring; you can barely see or stand up for a good 2 minutes. With meth, it sends a hot rush through your chest that feels like fire is oozing from your lungs, throat, and whole body. It made my chest get all red and my body shake, making it hard to walk. You are almost too high, so all you can do is just sit there and feel the effects until it calms down a little.

That night or the next, I don't remember, I ended up in the emergency room and I thought meth was to blame. Going into the hospital and having them draw blood from an arm with bruised veins due to the drug sent a rush of guilt, anxiety, fear, and shame. I didn't know what they would do to me, knowing I am a drug user. It ended up being related to other health causes from prolonged use of meth and on top of it I was pregnant. Now I really needed to clean up. My boyfriend went to jail to help himself, and I was all alone on the journey to get clean and raise a healthy baby. I managed to stay clean for 4 months until I lost the baby as my body was not healthy enough to support another life, barely my own. It was tough to get through the loss of my child and more so to realize I had to move on with my life, get away from the scene. To this day, it is still hard to think about, to write about, and to stay away from...

Synthetic Cathinones: Not Your Grandma's Bath Salts!

Figure 10.2 Bath Salts

The newest form of stimulants on the illegal market is synthetic drugs similar to cathinone, the active ingredient of the khat plant. Authorities in the U.S. became aware of these substances after an increase in the number of calls to poison control centers rose dramatically in 2009 (Leger, 2012). These substances are commonly called "bath salts" because they resemble the small, crystal-like products that one might purchase at Bath and Body Works; some were sold in packaging actually labeled "bath salts," along with a phony warning stating "not for human consumption." Make no mistake: they are not made of soap, actually are intended for human consumption, and you should not soak in a tub with them! These substances are extremely potent amphetamine-like drugs that have been linked to many adverse effects. It is not unusual for "bath salts" to be a mix of several different stimulant substances; the potency and subjective effects of the drug experience will vary, depending on the mix of compounds. Components could include chemicals such as methylone, mephedrone, and MDPV (methylenedioxypyrovaleraone), the latter of which has been associated with many adverse psychological effects (Spiller et al., 2011, cited by Lehner & Bauman, 2013).

Originally, "bath salts" were referred to as "legal highs" because there were no laws on the books to prohibit them. Users found them in convenience stores and head shops, alongside energy supplements, and selling for about $30 per ounce. That changed when Congress passed the Synthetic Drug Abuse Prevention Act in 2012, which made these chemicals Schedule I substances. Of course, that didn't stop the illegal manufacture and sale of them on the street or over the Internet. The names of the products have also changed; although users, clinicians, and researchers still typically refer to them as "bath salts," the drugs have also been sold under the names "plant food," "glass cleaner," and other misnomers.

An even more potent, second-generation synthetic cathinone known as "gravel" (or "flakka") hit the streets a few years back. Containing a substance called α-PVP, gravel is so potent that it is known on the street as "$5 insanity": dealers would charge $5 for the first ounce of this substance that tends to promote crazy behavior in its users. Florida was hit particularly hard by the flakka trend, and there are numerous adverse reports documenting the bizarre and sometimes dangerous behavior associated with the "excited delirium" it produces. Users may experience hallucinations, paranoia, incoherent speech, and seemingly super-human strength. The users' body temperatures can rise to 105 degrees, which may explain why users may strip off their clothes.

Synthetic cathinones have a reputation for being "zombie" drugs because media reports suggesting that violent attacks involving assailants eating their victim's faces were caused by these substances (such as the strange case of Rudy Eugene in Miami). Although these links may have been premature and incorrect, the drug's reputation for inducing crazed behavior remains. The worst of the flakka scourge appears to be over, per a March 4, 2016 *Sun Sentinel* article. This is likely due to China, a major source of "bath salts," clamping down on manufacturing and trafficking. But if you ever see a naked, paranoid, incoherent, aggressive person running towards you, suspect that the person is high on synthetic cathinones rather than a reanimated corpse. Table 10.2 summarizes known facts about synthetic cathinones.

Table 10.2 Facts about Synthetic Cathinones

- Synthetic cathinones, more commonly known as "bath salts," are drugs that contain one or more synthetic (human-made) chemicals related to cathinone. Cathinone is a stimulant found in the khat plant.
- Synthetic cathinones are marketed as cheap substitutes for other stimulants such as methamphetamine and cocaine, and products sold as Molly (MDMA) often contain synthetic cathinones instead.
- People typically swallow, snort, smoke, or inject synthetic cathinones.
- Much is still unknown about how all of the chemicals in synthetic cathinones affect the human brain.
- Synthetic cathinones can cause:
  - nosebleeds
  - paranoia
  - increased sociability
  - increased sex drive
  - hallucinations
  - panic attacks
- Intoxication from synthetic cathinones has resulted in death.
- Synthetic cathinones can be addictive.
- Behavioral therapy may be used to treat addiction to synthetic cathinones.
- No medications are currently available to treat addiction to synthetic cathinones.

Source: NIH (2016). National Institute on Drug Abuse. What are synthetic cathinones?

Effects of Stimulants on the Brain, Mind, and Body

Cocaine, meth, Ecstasy, and synthetic cathinones are substances with high abuse potential because they have very powerful effects on the brain's reward pathway. Let's start with cocaine, which in terms of its mechanism of inducing stimulation, is the simplest of these substances.

Cocaine–"Gift of the Gods." In the early 16th century, when Francisco Pizarro encountered the Quechua (usually referred to as the Inca) people of present-day Peru, he found that royalty used the extract of a local shrub known today as *Erythroxylon coca*, or simply the coca plant. This was the first contact of Europeans with this drug, which was soon to become one of the most widely abused drugs in the world. In Peru, the extract of the coca plant was considered to be "the gift of the gods" and was used in religious ceremonies as well as for medicinal purposes. The use of cocaine was initially banned by the Spanish conquerors, but they soon learned that the enslaved natives could not work the gold mines in the rarified air of Peru without the stimulation of coca leaves that were distributed several times a day to the workers. The returning conquistadors called the drug "the elixir of life." They introduced the coca leaf to Europe, where it soon became used in a fashionable social beverage.

Sir Arthur Conan Doyle depicted fictional character Sherlock Holmes as a cocaine user, and doctors even prescribed it as an antidote to morphine addiction. Cocaine was readily available in the late 19th and early 20th centuries either over the counter or in beverages such as Coca-Cola, which was introduced in 1886. It was claimed to be a brain tonic and a cure for nervous affliction. A typical serving of Coca-Cola contained about 60 mg of cocaine. Today Coca-Cola contains only the name "coca," not the drug.

Crack is Wack

Figure 10.3 Crack is Wack

Arguably NYC's most famous street art (Keith Haring, 1986), on a handball court at 128th Street and 2nd Avenue. The mural was inspired by the crack epidemic and its effect on New York City. Crack is cocaine base that has not been neutralized by an acid to make the hydrochloride salt. This form of cocaine comes in a rock crystal that can be heated and its vapors smoked. The term "crack" refers to the crackling sound heard when it is heated.

—NIDA (2008) InfoFacts: Crack and Cocaine

Cocaine is found in the coca plant as the freebase form where it constitutes about 1% of the leaf. After being extracted, the paste is treated with hydrochloric acid. This forms cocaine hydrochloride, an organic salt. This is the form in which it arrives in the United States, as a white powder. Cocaine can be extracted from the leaves in hot water to make coca tea, a popular beverage in Peru. Cocaine becomes dangerous when extracted and concentrated to form pure cocaine hydrochloride. This form is usually snorted since it is not sufficiently volatile to smoke. The hydrochloride salt may be converted to "crack" by a general chemical reaction (acid plus base) learned by every beginning student of chemistry. Treatment of the acid salt with any household base, such as ammonia or sodium bicarbonate, releases the hydrochloric acid to form the volatile "freebase," known as crack, which, once extracted with ether and dried, can be smoked to give a much faster high than can be obtained by snorting. Sounds easy, right? Actually, it is very easy for anyone in a chemistry laboratory equipped with an exhaust hood. The problem arises when inexperienced "chemists" evaporate the ether extract to get the pure cocaine. Ether is very volatile and flammable, and many serious accidents have resulted from igniting the ether during extraction. The comedian Richard Pryor suffered severe burns while attempting to evaporate the ether extract with a flame. The Inca of Peru were also able to "freebase" cocaine by using calcium oxide as the base to remove the hydrochloric acid.

Compulsion and Loss of Control

Women living in inner cities have tended to show more dependence on crack cocaine than any other illegal drug (Lejuez, Bornovalova, Reynolds, Daughters, & Curtin, 2007). When one thinks of the crack environment, images of dirty run-down houses, prostitution, or homelessness come to mind. These stereotypes are in part due to the fact that there is more research on crack use in the inner cities (i.e., lower-income areas). Impoverished settings and cocaine abuse have been associated with other high-risk behaviors such as nonuse of condoms, trading sex or sexual acts for drugs, crime, homelessness, and the contraction of HIV through unprotected sex or the sharing of needles (Lejuez et al., 2007). However, the use of crack extends well beyond the lower socioeconomic bracket. In November 2013, Rob Ford, Mayor of Toronto admitted using crack. When Ford made his admission, he told reporters it probably occurred "in one of my drunken stupors" about a year ago. His public apology is shown in the Canadian Broadcasting Corporation video (2013) (See for Yourself).

As described below, Vivian's struggle began when she was 17 and had graduated high school, while she was living with her parents in a middle-class neighborhood; she began with a strong appetite for powdered cocaine.

CASE EXAMPLE: Vivian's Cocaine Nightmare

For over 4 years, I lived deep in the darkness of cocaine and crack. I started getting deep into powdered cocaine at age 17 when I still lived at my parents' house, right after I graduated high school. I would stay awake all night drawing twisted demons and demented aliens. I would do it in the bathrooms everywhere, including gas stations I would stop off at on the road to a party. I often missed out on the socializing and brawls at parties because I was holed up in the bathroom or a back room all night snorting a teener [1.75 grams of cocaine] with a couple other people. I ended up getting kicked out of my house and living in my car for a month, all the while scraping up change for gas because all my money I made at work went to purchasing the drug. After losing my home and then my job, I ended up attempting rehab and got clean for a few months. I was not yet ready to quit though, and soon found a new group of people who enjoyed the drug.

With my compulsive need to have some coke in my pocket and share with everyone else (that way I was the "cool" one, the life of the party), I soon became a fixture in a dingy apartment on the rough side of town. I would spend days, sometimes even weeks at a time awake on the drug, rarely seeing the light of day. We would go through 8-balls [3.5 grams of cocaine, or 1/8 of an ounce] like there was no tomorrow. If I was sick of sharing with other people, I would get in my car, snorting a line, drawing some messed up stuff, then getting paranoid and driving to a new spot, doing a line, drawing macabre things, getting paranoid, and the cycle would continue for 14 to 16 hours. I would be missing for weeks at a time, only because I was in the apartment and no one that really loved me knew where I was or how to get ahold of me. Pretty soon my dealer ran out of supply and we needed to find a new one quick.

This is when I met up with a hard-core, New York–raised crack pusher that knew how to run the game and was not the least bit apprehensive to put someone in their place. I ran with this crowd for about 10 months, hanging out in more dingy apartments, snorting while driving my car, and isolating myself from everyone I knew before this crowd. It was at this time that I got introduced to smoking crack. I had always passed up crack, preferring the powdered coke and the rush I got from it. That was, until I tried crack. I had been up for 16 days straight off cocaine at that point, and the dealers had run out of powdered and were passing around three crack pipes filled to the max. In my desperation of coming off my powdered high, I went ahead and started hitting up the pipes. Talk about a crack high. I still believe if you looked up crackhead in the dictionary you would see a picture of me that night. It was a whole new rush.

From the next day on, I was chasing that dragon, trying my hardest to get to that insane, discombob- ulated, euphoric state that I was in that night. I kept smoking crack after that. I would stay in dark, dirty apartments for days and weeks at a time still, but now I would be peeking under doors while my pal was checking out the blinds. I would be tweaking, or searching the floors and couches and any place I could possibly think of to find a piece of crack I just knew I had dropped. I would pride myself on showering every day, but I wore the same clothes over and over, only washing my undies in sinks and blow-drying them or wearing them soaking wet. I thought I was so great because I still kept up my hygiene (or so I thought), but my clothes were always dirty, my teeth were half-assed brushed, and all I did all day was sit in smoke-filled cracked-out spaces, searching for, begging for, and needing more. I cringe to think about how disgusting some of the places were that I was spending my time, and even more when I think about what I had become. I would smoke it everywhere, even in the car while driving; I just needed the rush so bad.

I remember on one New Year's Eve I was speeding, trying to get back to "home base" to pick up the main guy for a kilo run, and I lit up the crack pipe in my car. Glancing over, I saw that I was staring in the eyes of the police officer driving next to me. He slowed down, got behind me and I knew I was toast. The ironic thing was that I was not scared about getting busted by the cops, not scared about the paraphernalia and drugs in my car. I was terrified that if I got sent to jail and this huge drug deal did not go through because my car was not there, then I would be dead by the main guy. He would take me out in the blink of an eye for messing up the transaction.

Cocaine and the Brain

The prefrontal cortex, in control of long-term memory and higher-level thinking, has been shown to be affected by the continued use of cocaine (Ikegami et al., 2007), especially when the use starts in adolescence (Santucci, 2008). The disruption in the cortex could explain the errors in judgment frequently displayed by addicts (Ikegami et al., 2007). The use of cocaine in adolescence, a developmentally critical period for the cortical areas of the brain, is especially detrimental, as research has shown that it can be more addicting than if it was started in adulthood (Brenhouse & Anderson, 2008; Santucci, 2008).

Connections between different parts of the brain increase throughout childhood and well into adulthood. As the brain develops, the fibers connecting nerve cells are wrapped in a protein [myelin] that greatly increases the speed with which they can transmit impulses from cell to cell. The resulting increase in connectivity—a little like providing a growing city with a fast, integrated communication system—shapes how well different parts of the brain work in tandem. Research is finding that the extent of connectivity is related to growth in intellectual capacities such as memory and reading ability (NIMH, 2011).

Briefly stated, cocaine produces its high by increasing the availability of guess what, our good friend, dopamine (along with serotonin and norepinephrine). No surprise there. When dopamine is released from the presynaptic neurons (Figure 10.4) of the dopamine-producing nerve cells in an area of the brain known as the ventral tegmental area (VTA), it causes a flow of dopamine into the reward center, the nucleus accumbens, where it produces the expected high (Ikegami, Olsen, D'Souza, & Duvauchelle, 2007). After activating the cells of the nucleus accumbens, dopamine is transported back into the presynaptic VTA cells by transporter proteins. Cocaine blocks these transporters, which prevents dopamine from being reabsorbed. Since it stays in the synapse, it can be used repeatedly, and to continually activate the neurons of the nucleus accumbens, giving the user the intense high characteristic of cocaine use.

> Cocaine increases levels of the natural chemical messenger dopamine in brain circuits controlling pleasure and movement. Normally, the brain releases dopamine in these circuits in response to potential rewards, like the smell of tasty food. It then recycles back into the cell that released it, shutting off the signal between nerve cells. Cocaine prevents dopamine from recycling, causing excessive amounts to build up between nerve cells. This flood of dopamine ultimately disrupts normal brain communication and causes cocaine's high. (National Institute on Drug Abuse [NIDA], 2016)

Obviously, cocaine, like most drugs of abuse—even caffeine—exerts its major effect on the brain. Because of the intense high associated with the drug, addiction can start during even a single binge episode. It has been shown by Ciccocioppo et al. (2004) that a single cocaine binge can establish cue-induced, long-term drug-seeking behavior in rats. Once addicted, the user finds him- or herself in a continuing spiral of increased usage to reach the previously obtained high and foremost to avoid the effects of withdrawal. These effects include severe depression, with the resulting intense craving to resume using. Prolonged usage can produce paranoia, especially among crack users, who may become aggressively paranoid. Dopamine activity in the brain of people expecting a cocaine high is stimulated when they see a conditioned stimulus, meaning if they see a place where they used the drug, their dopamine levels will surge in their reward center and they will expect the cocaine or crack rush (Ikegami et al., 2007).

Figure 10.4 Cocaine in the Brain The number of neurotransmitters in a synapse depends on the balance between the rate at which neurotransmitters are released into the synapse (from vesicles) and the rate at which they are removed from the synapse by the reuptake pump (left panel). By blocking the reuptake pump, cocaine increases the concentration of neurotransmitters, which in turn occupy more receptors and cause hyperexcitation (right panel).

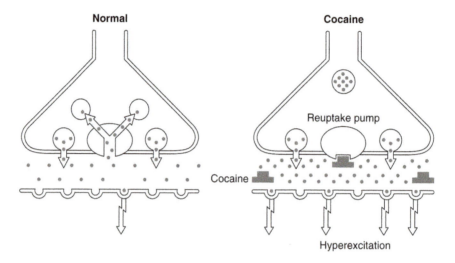

Cocaine works by blocking reuptake of several key neurotransmitters: dopamine (DA), serotonin (5-HT), and norepinephrine (NE). Thus, these neurotransmitters stay in the synapse longer, allowing them to engage in more binding to receptors. The following activity may be used to illustrate the principles of neurotransmission that underlie the brain's (and consequently the mind's and body's) dysfunctional response to cocaine.

ACTIVITY: Cocaine in the Brain

There are eight volunteers. One person represents cocaine, three represent the presynaptic neuron, three represent the postsynaptic neuron, and one person represents a beautiful sunrise. A container (clear bowl or glass) of small packages of sugar symbolizes the synaptic vesicle, which contains many molecules (the sugar packets) of the neurotransmitter dopamine. The six people who represent the neurons arrange themselves in two lines of three with a 3-foot space between them (the synapse). The perception is a beautiful sunrise.

	Beautiful Sunrise					Cocaine			
pre	1	2	3	synapse	post	4	5	6	synapse

At one end (presynaptic terminal)—triggered by sensations from the sunrise—person #1 makes a motion and taps person #2 on the shoulder, who taps #3, who is standing at the synapse. Then #3 reaches into the synaptic vesicle and takes out one of the sugar packets (dopamine) and moves it across the synapse, giving it to person #4 who then taps #5 who taps #6 who exclaims, "Whoa!"—waving his or her hand in ecstatic delight (showing a natural sense of joy that might come from seeing a beautiful sunrise).

When #4 sends the message on, he or she hands the neurotransmitter (sugar packet) back to #3, who replaces it in the synaptic vesicle. Then #1 at the presynaptic neuron starts the process again. Practice this one to two times until it runs smoothly.

In comes cocaine ... The message comes in normal fashion; that is, #1 taps #2 and so on. The dopamine (sugar packet) crosses the synapse; however, this time when #4 attempts to give it back to #3, cocaine steals the sugar and hands it back to #4 (blocks the reuptake of the dopamine), and #4 sends the message in the usual fashion by tapping #5. As soon as #4 taps #5, #4 *attempts* to return the sugar packet to #3 but *again cocaine takes it and hands it straight back*. At this point, #6 is saying, "*Whoa! Whoa! Whoa!*" very fast (excess dopamine).

Person #3 is just sitting there with the remaining sugar packets in the synaptic vesicle (the container), and *he or she doesn't need them anymore*. So #3 *empties the cylinder* and dumps the sugar packets (dopamine) on the floor. The police officer (person who facilitates the exercise) then removes the cocaine, and the neurotransmitter (sugar packets) can no longer be accessed from the cylinder. Withdrawal comes when the cocaine is no longer available, and the pleasure derived from the excess dopamine is absent because the supply of dopamine has been depleted. This leads to *cocaine withdrawal.*

With some slight modifications, the same model could be used to explain withdrawal from other drugs like caffeine, methamphetamine, Ecstasy, or nicotine.

Table 10.3 presents a summary of the health effects and possible treatment options for the abuse of cocaine (NIH, 2016).

Table 10.3 NIH Cocaine Summary Chart

Street Names	Commercial Names	Common Forms	Common Ways Taken	DEA Schedule
Blow, Bump, C, Candy, Charlie, Coke, Crack, Flake, Rock, Snow, Toot	Cocaine hydrochloride topical solution (anesthetic rarely used in medical procedures)	White powder, whitish rock crystal	Snorted, smoked, injected	II**

Possible Health Effects	
Short-term	Narrowed blood vessels; enlarged pupils; increased body temperature, heart rate, and blood pressure; headache; abdominal pain and nausea; euphoria; increased energy, alertness; insomnia, restlessness; anxiety; erratic and violent behavior, panic attacks, paranoia, psychosis; heart rhythm problems, heart attack; stroke, seizure, coma.
Long-term	Loss of sense of smell, nosebleeds, nasal damage and trouble swallowing from snorting; infection and death of bowel tissue from decreased blood flow; poor nutrition and weight loss from decreased appetite.

Other Health-related Issues	Pregnancy: premature delivery, low birth weight, neonatal abstinence syndrome.
	Risk of HIV, hepatitis, and other infectious diseases from shared needles.
In Combination with Alcohol	Greater risk of overdose and sudden death than from either drug alone.
Withdrawal Symptoms	Depression, tiredness, increased appetite, insomnia, vivid unpleasant dreams, slowed thinking and movement, restlessness.

Treatment Options	
Medications	There are no FDA-approved medications to treat cocaine addiction.
Behavioral Therapies	Cognitive-behavioral therapy (CBT) Community reinforcement approach plus vouchers Contingency management, or motivational incentives The matrix model 12-Step facilitation therapy

Source: "NIH Cocaine Summary Chart," Facing Addiction in America: The Surgeon General's Report on Alcohol, Drugs, and Health. 2016 by US Department of Health and Human Services.

Cocaine and the Heart

Even recreational cocaine use increases the risk of sudden heart attack and stroke. Frequent use is associated with higher blood pressure, stiffer arteries, and thicker heart muscle walls; effects that have been documented to persist long after the intoxication has worn off—hence cocaine has been dubbed "the perfect heart attack drug" (American Heart Association, 2015). Satran et al. (2005), identifies increased risk of fatal coronary aneurysms as another negative health effect of cocaine. Consider the landmark death of Len Bias, first round draft choice of the Boston Celtics basketball team.

> In life, Len Bias was basketball's next great hope, contender for a crown that went instead to Michael Jordan. In death, he became a trigger for the war on drugs. Bias' 1986 cocaine overdose helped sparked a panic, stoked by false rumors and a high-stakes political campaign, that culminated in a law that swept thousands of low-level drug offenders—most of them young and black—into prison. Thirty years later, America is still reeling from the impact.
>
> The new law established mandatory minimum drug sentences, provisions that exacerbated racial disparities, led to an explosion in prison populations and helped lay the groundwork for grievances that erupted in anti-police riots in Baltimore last year and in Ferguson, Missouri, in 2014. Those effects are now fueling a bipartisan reform effort. "The law that flowed from this completely destroyed the federal justice system and tarnished the reputation of the whole American justice system," said Eric Sterling, who as a young congressional aide helped draft the legislation and has since worked to unwind its effects.

Source: NBC News (2016). 30 Years after Basketball Star Len Bias' Death, Its Drug War Impact Endures

Is This a Good Idea?

Should the potentially fatal effect of illicit drugs play a significant role in determining penalties imposed by the criminal justice system for possession or sale? (view See for Yourself video).

Prenatal Effects of Cocaine

Not only does cocaine have profound effects on the adolescent and adult brain, but pregnant women who use cocaine (including "crack") may cause severe damage to the fetus. "Prenatal cocaine exposure has been associated with numerous behavioral phenotypes in clinical populations, including impulsivity, reduced attention, alterations in social behaviors, and delayed language and sensory-motor development" (McMurray et al., 2015, p. 80).

Meth, Ecstasy, and Bath Salts

Amphetamines (including meth and Ecstasy) and synthetic cathinones also block reuptake of excitatory neurotransmitters (e.g., dopamine, serotonin, and norepinephrine), but they are more powerful than cocaine because they have an additional mechanism by which they produce their effects. These chemicals can increase release of these neurotransmitters, as well. Consequently, high levels of these molecules stay in the synapse, producing long-lasting effects.

As we well know, major stimulants can be extremely harmful to the user, yet they are quite popular. If you don't understand why, go back and review Neurochemistry 101 ("Pleasure and the Brain," Chapter 3). They produce profound feelings of euphoria (DA effects), along with wakefulness and energy (NE effects). The resulting euphoria produced by amphetamines lasts longer (from 8 to 24 hours for meth) compared to that associated with cocaine, which lasts 20 to 30 minutes (NIDA, 2007a). These chemical disruptions in the brain cause an initial rush of euphoria followed by increased concentration, alertness, and energy, and a decrease in appetite and need for sleep (Falkowski, 2003).

The long-term use of these substances can produce brain damage. To some degree, we can think of the potent effects of these drugs as essentially "burning out" brain cells, possibly the most serious health problem from chronic abuse of major stimulants. Studies have shown that most of these substances damage neurons in several parts of the brain, including the frontal cortex, which is responsible for cognitive functioning and decision-making capacity. It also is known to damage cells in the striatum. Damage to these cells could lead to movement disorders resembling Parkinson's disease and tardive dyskinesia. Cadet, Ordonez, and Ordonez (1997) have shown that methamphetamine not only damages neurons but destroys them through a process called *apoptosis* (Figure 10.3).

Figure 10.5 Neurotoxic Effects of Methamphetamine Possibly the most serious health problem from chronic methamphetamine abuse is damage to the neurons of the brain.

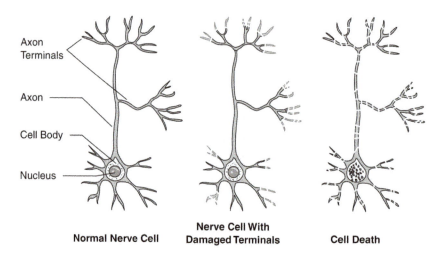

Normal Nerve Cell   Nerve Cell With Damaged Terminals   Cell Death

In experiments using rodents (mice), Cadet et al. (1997) showed that neuronal death was also prominent in the frontal cortex and hippocampus, which is utilized in the formation of long-term memory. There is also extensive damage in the striatum (Figure 10.4).

Figure 10.6 Human Brain Areas Corresponding to the Mouse Brain Areas Damaged by Methamphetamine The figure shows that neuronal death is prominent in the frontal cortex and hippocampus.

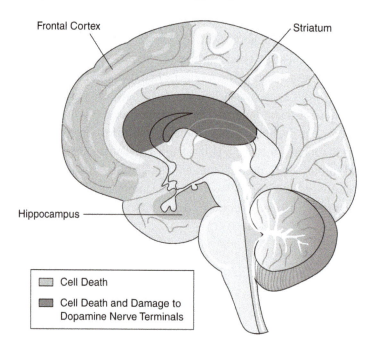

Cell death in the frontal cortex, which is involved in cognition and reasoning, is especially troublesome for young adults since during adolescence this area is still undergoing rapid change. Immature development makes this part of the brain especially vulnerable to apoptosis. It is obvious that this combination of damage to cell terminals and death of neurons in the young adult would result in permanent brain damage.

Another serious consequence of meth usage is damage to the nerve endings of dopamine-producing cells due to overstimulation. This injury persists for at least 3 years after drug intake has ceased. This damage to dopamine-producing cells is like that caused by Parkinson's disease and may be responsible for the addicting aspects of methamphetamine usage. These earlier claims regarding the effects of methamphetamine on the brain have been confirmed by Chang et al. (2002) using a technique called perfusion nuclear magnetic imaging (pNMI), which measures blood flow into important brain regions.

Whereas cocaine and meth are prone to damaging dopaminergic cells, Ecstasy (and possibly some synthetic cathinones) appear to have stronger effects on serotonergic cells. Since the late 1980s, Ecstasy has been linked to damaging serotoninergic cells in rats (Commins et al., 1987). A review by Vegting, et al. (2016) summarized multiple studies conducted on neurotoxic effects of Ecstasy. They conclude that heavy usage of Ecstasy does decrease binding of serotonin transporters in the brain, but there is uncertainty as to whether this truly reflects neurotoxicity. Data indicate that levels of these transporters recover over time.

A particularly concerning effect associated with major stimulants is drug-induced psychosis: hallucinations, delusions, and bizarre behaviors that manifest like schizophrenia. Chronic use of cocaine, meth, and cathinones have been shown to produce this condition; in the case of potent "bath salt" mixtures that include MDPV or α-PVP, a single dose may be sufficient. It can take a period of days after the drug has worn off before the psychotic behavior completely subsides, and the individual may be treated with sedatives and antipsychotic medications during this interim to help them recover.

As described above in the tragic death of Len Bias, major stimulants can produce many negative effects on other organs, including the cardiovascular system. Serious effects from usage include rapid and irregular heartbeat and increased blood pressure resulting in irreversible damage to small blood vessels in the brain, which in turn may result in strokes. Damage can also be induced in the kidney, lungs, and liver. Users may experience hyperthermia and dehydration; this is especially true of Ecstasy and "bath salts."

Although we don't usually have the ability to peer into people's brains to see damage produced by stimulant drugs, we can often see tell-tale outward signs via chronic users' physical deterioration (which NIDA refers to as a meth-a-morphosis). Individuals tend to lose copious amounts of weight and appear to "age" rapidly—looking much older than they really are. Additionally, they may have "meth mouth" and numerous skin lesions (the latter linked to sensations of bugs crawling on the skin, which the person feels compelled to pick at). Figure 10.5 shows these phenomena.

Figure 10.7 Physical Effects of Methamphetamine Abuse: "Meth Mouth" and Skins Wounds Indicative of "Crank Bugs"

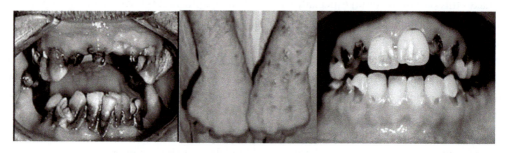

An interesting but morbid observation has been made about the corpses of meth abusers: scavengers such as coyotes don't like to eat them! Seventeen-year-old high school student Daniel Jeffrey Martin of Phoenix, AZ, took 2nd place in a 2009 NIDA-sponsored science fair with a project entitled "The Effect of Methamphetamine on Carnivore Scavenging." He used autopsy reports of corpses found out in the desert to demonstrate a negative relationship between levels of meth and the degree to which carnivores consumed the remains: the higher the level of drug in the system, the less carnivores fed upon them. Daniel suggested that scavengers can detect the toxin in the body and therefore avoid ingesting them. Of course, if only the humans had avoided ingesting the toxins first hand, there would likely be fewer corpses in the desert.

When it comes to these toxins (street drugs), the adage "buyer beware" applies. Because their products are illegal, dealers do not label the contents of their packaging (whereas legal pharmaceuticals are required by the Food and Drug Administration to provide truthful labeling of their drugs' contents). All street drugs bear a risk of potentially being tainted or "cut" with other substances. Because the effects of these substances are so similar, "bath salts" might be passed off as meth or Ecstasy. But because purity of street drugs can vary from batch to batch and dealer to dealer, the user cannot be confident of what they're really buying and using, making it harder for users to fully gauge the risk they are undertaking for their dopamine surges.

Club Drugs (Ecstasy, Ketamine, GHB, and Rohypnol)

Ecstasy (MDMA)

Ecstasy—"Meth's More Glamorous Chemical Cousin"—is the street name for MDMA—short for 3,4-methylenedioxymethamphetamine. Because the drug is so rarely referred to by its real name, many people may miss the fact that it is chemically related to meth. So far as major stimulants are concerned, this drug has a different reputation compared to those of cocaine and meth. Ecstasy has generally been associated with the "club" scene and those who use it may do so primarily within social contexts compared to those who use cocaine and meth. Ecstasy has been called the "hug drug" because users sometimes feel more socially connected to others while under the influence. In addition to its stimulating properties, Ecstasy evokes reactions similar to those associated with hallucinogens (e.g., mescaline, psilocybin). This is not surprising, given that in addition to its stimulant qualities, MDMA is chemically like mescaline, the hallu-cinogenic component of the Peyote cactus.

Ecstasy is judged as the most popular club drug among youth now. When all-night dance festivals, or raves, became popular in the mid-1980s, countries around the world saw a dramatic increase in Ecstasy's use (Diamond, Bermudez, & Schensul, 2006). Although extremely popular in club settings, the use of Ecstasy is much more widespread (Rivas-Vasquez & Delgado, 2002). In the 1990s, as raves moved to mainstream bars, clubs, and other venues, the use of MDMA began to seep into well-trafficked urban venues frequented by more mainstream and minority clientele.

In a study focusing on the effects of rap music and the rise in mainstream Ecstasy use, Diamond et al. (2006) found that the number of songs promoting MDMA use increased as it was finding popularity in ur-ban areas throughout the United States. Of the 69 songs they studied, the most common scene described was the use of MDMA at a club or party. Ecstasy was also largely promoted as a sex-enhancing love drug. Many of the songs focused on men giving women the drug, making them less inhibited and more willing to perform risky sexual practices. Interestingly, the rise of Ecstasy as a sexual enhancer coincided with the introduction of Viagra, both of which make it more feasible to maintain sexual arousal.

Ecstasy produces euphoria, increased energy and happiness, heightened sensations and sexual desire, and emotional openness (Diamond et al., 2006). On the romantic plane, advocates for Ecstasy believe that the drug promotes feelings of closeness and intimacy. More recently, Ecstasy has been marketed as "Molly" which is most often falsely advertised as "pure ecstasy." As shown below, Molly presents serious dangers to those who buy into the widespread hype.

MDMA as Synthetic Love?

As William Shakespeare wrote in his Sonnet 29,

> Haply I think on thee, and then my state,
>
> Like to the lark at break of day arising
>
> From sullen earth, sings hymns at heaven's gate;
>
> For thy sweet love remember'd such wealth brings
>
> That then I scorn to change my state with kings.

What if there was a synthetic drug that mimics the action of the suspected neurochemical Aphrodite? Ecstasy's reputation as the "love drug" or "hug drug" may lead one to conclude that this is synthetic love. Ecstasy (MDMA) is less potent and differs only slightly in chemical structure from the psychedelic MDA, the 1960s' version of the "love drug." In *The Marriage of the Sun and Moon*, Weil (2004) describes his observations of how people react to MDA.

> Such experiences confirm in a powerful way the sense of well-being. It feels as if nothing is threatening, and, in fact, things in the external world behave differently. This theme carries through to interpersonal relations. When people feel well, centered, unthreatened, and aware of their own strength and loveliness, they are able to drop many of the usual barriers that develop in groups. It is common in

group MDA experiences for people to explore mutual touching and the pleasures of physical closeness. Participants may feel very loving toward one another, but the feelings are not explicitly sexual because MDA tends to decrease the desire for orgasm. For many people the experience of enjoying physical contact and feeling love with others in the absence of a specific hunger for sex is unique and welcome. (Some people do use MDA to heighten sexual experience.) (p. 178)

Ecstasy combines some of the hallucinogenic effects of mescaline with the stimulant effects of amphetamine. Those who endorse Ecstasy cite case histories where MDMA was used as a tool in psychotherapy, triggering insight and releasing patients from emotional injury.

Mathew Klam (2001) described his first experience with the popular drug. All of a sudden, as if with the blink of an eye, in one moment of exhale, he felt happy and clear. It was not as if he had taken a drug…he felt neither "stoned" nor like in a daydream. He explained that MDMA didn't disrupt the basic sense of who he was; he barely even felt strange. There were none of the perceptual alterations that are characteristic of being high on LSD. Sensations (e.g., music, touch) just seemed to sound and feel extraordinarily good. "With Ecstasy, I had simply stepped outside the worn paths in by my brain and in the process, gained some perspective on my life. It was an amazing feeling" (Klam, 2001, p. 69).

Should I Try Ecstasy?

Many advocates for MDMA believe, "Nothing that can make you feel so good could be bad." There is an abundance of anecdotal evidence for the drug's capacity to bring out beauty and love. And then there is the scientific perspective. As described earlier in this chapter, research has shown that MDMA may cause irreversible or at least long-term damage to dopaminergic and serotonergic neurons. There is also a decrease in the gray matter in several parts of the brains of users, which can be associated with memory and cognitive deficits. However, some of this research has been contradicted by other scientists. So what are we to believe?

The conflicting data do show damage to serotonin-releasing neurons, although the extent of this damage is controversial. However, other effects on health that seem to be substantiated are dehydration, hypertension, brain swelling, hyperthermia, and heart and kidney failure. Considering the potential damage to the brain and the rest of the body, repeated, frequent use of Ecstasy appears to present considerable risk. R. K. Siegel (1986), a psychopharmacologist at UCLA, finds that under high doses people may become insane rather than ecstatic. Recently, there is renewed interest among psychotherapists to use Ecstasy as a tool to aid psychotherapy, but clinicians are administering doses of the drug under supervision, in their offices. Clients will ultimately receive only a few doses of the drug, presumably lower than what would be taken recreationally making it a different undertaking than social use at a club or party. Nonetheless, there are reasons for caution, as outlined in reviews by Parrott (2007, 2014); both positive emotions (euphoria and feelings of connectedness) and negative (anxiety) moods may be elicited, and some clients may be distressed by the anxiety. Additionally, clients may feel a "crash" several hours later, once the drug has worn off.

The case of Legba provides a vivid example of the inane and irrational quality of one user's Ecstasy experience.

The Case of Legba

Legba had a sheltered childhood. He grew up in a picturesque house surrounded by trees, with a church just a stone's throw away. One night he found his way to a local rave and feverishly danced under Ecstasy's blissful spell for hours on end. At 5 in the morning, when everyone else had gone, Legba had nothing to do but to go home. Still feeling wired, sleep seemed far away. The only living thing around was Chippie, the family bird, who was quietly nestled in its cage. Legba's spirit was lifted by the feeling that his love for Chippie was being reciprocated. He reached into the cage and began to hug Chippie. The bird responded as if Legba was a dangerous creature and began clawing and biting. As there was nothing left to snort, smoke, or swallow, Legba gave up, right there in his mom's kitchen, and went to bed.

Adapted from Klam (2001).

Molly

If you Google "Molly," many blogs refer to the drug as "pure" MDMA, the active ingredient in Ecstasy. The hype is that Molly was originally developed as a pure drug to treat depression and now it is finally available to energize and bring rapturous euphoria to the dance club and music festival scene. Actually, the drug called Molly is most often a toxic mixture of lab-created chemicals, according to the U.S. Drug Enforcement Administration (DEA). According to the DEA, 13% of the Molly seized in New York state in the last four years actually contained any MDMA, and even then it often was mixed with other drugs. The drugs frequently found in Molly are methylone, MDPV, 4-MEC, 4-MMC, pentedrone and MePP (substances commonly used to make "bath salts").

The target group for Molly is sometimes first-time drug users; youth between the ages of 12 and 17, as well as traditional rave, electronic dance music fans who may think they're getting MDMA.

Figure 10.8 Club Scene

Although it's most often found in a capsule or powder, Molly can take many forms, e.g., applied to blotting paper, like LSD, and in injectable forms. It is particularly dangerous because of the toxic mix of unknown chemicals; kids often have no idea of what or how much they are taking. In sharp contrast to MDMA and other illegal drugs that have known effects, the chemicals for these synthetic drugs keep changing, and they're manufactured irrespective of how they affect the user. Almost all the chemicals in Molly are sold online from laboratories in China and are then cut with other substances in the U.S. Taking Molly is much like playing Russian Roulette (Griffin et al., 2015).

GHB, Rohypnol ("Roofies"), and Ketamine

These are considered "newer" club drugs and are often used in "clubbing settings" (preclub bars, in-club spaces, dance music festivals, after-parties) (Moore & Miller, 2005, p. 5). According to users' self-reports, they are effective as tools to enhance sociability, dancing, and good times (Moore & Miller, 2005; G. A. Parks, 2005). Many claim to use only a few times per month, returning to "real life" during the weekdays and feeling secure in their knowledge and capacity to manage possible dangers.

Gamma hydroxybutyrate (GHB) is a depressant drug that comes in liquid or powder form (Office of National Drug Control Policy [ONDCP], 2008). The liquid form has been used as a "date rape drug" by offenders slipping the colorless, odorless liquid into unaware victims' drinks. Weightlifters sometimes use this drug for its supposed muscle-building effects. GHB was originally investigated in the 1960s for potential anesthetic use and was used for sleep disorders, depression, anxiety, and symptom relief of alcohol and opioid withdrawal (Sumnall et al., 2008). It has only recently become self-administered for nonmedicinal purposes. Euphoria, relaxation, disinhibition, and increased sensuality are some of the attractive effects of the drug. Individuals taking the drug to enhance a club experience will attend to the effects of the drug that are compatible with this. On the negative and extremely dangerous side, GHB has been shown to produce drowsiness, nausea, unconsciousness, seizures, severe respiratory depression, and coma. In addition, GHB has increasingly become involved in poisonings, overdoses, date rapes, and fatalities.

Rohypnol is a tranquilizer that is a legal prescription drug in numerous countries outside of the United States (ONDCP, 2008). This depressant drug is often consumed orally or snorted after the pill form has been crushed down to a powder. It has sometimes been used in sexual assaults because it has a sedating effect.

Rohypnol, GHB, and ketamine are central nervous system depressants. Lower doses of Rohypnol can cause muscle relaxation and can produce general sedative and hypnotic effects. In higher doses, Rohypnol causes a loss of muscle control, loss of consciousness, and partial amnesia. When combined with alcohol, the toxic effects of Rohypnol can be aggravated. Of an estimated 106 million emergency department (ED) visits in the United States during 2004, the Drug Abuse Warning Network (DAWN) estimates that 1,997,993 were drug-related. DAWN data indicate that MDMA was involved in 8,621 ED visits, GHB was involved in 2,340 visits, Rohypnol was involved in 473 visits, and ketamine was involved in 227 visits (SAMHSA, 2008).

Ketamine is an animal tranquilizer that became popular in the 1980s (ONDCP, 2008). Large doses tend to cause dissociative states and hallucinations, much like the effects of PCP (both are discussed in greater detail in Chapter 12). Users may perceive sights and sounds differently from when in a sober state, and they often feel as if they are disconnected from their bodies and uncoordinated. The effects tend to last for an hour or less and can cause respiratory depression and irregular heartbeats. Ketamine comes in both liquid and powder form, and it is often injected, taken orally (i.e., in drinks), smoked, or snorted.

Combining Drugs

Most club drugs (including MDMA) are used in combination with other drugs, be it more club drugs, alcohol, or marijuana (Sumnall et al., 2008). Parks (2005) found that ketamine was used most often for stress reduction, relaxation and escape, at home, with others, or at raves. GHB has a popular reputation as a club drug consumed with the intent to enhance sociability, dancing, and the overall clubbing experience.

However, Sumnall et al. (2008) found that GHB was primarily used in the privacy of homes, rather than at clubs. Sumnall's group found that GHB was typically used along with alcohol to settle down from the negative feelings brought on by uppers (e.g., insomnia), or to enhance sex. GHB has been reported to produce heightened touch and sensory experiences as well as less inhibition around sexual contact. Both Rohypnol and GHB have been used to "spike" drinks of others in an attempt to make them more compliant.

Drug Concerts: The New Drug Scene

The most popular drugs in a club or rave setting include MDMA (Ecstasy), ketamine, GHB, LSD, and Rohypnol. Raves got their start in Europe in the 1980s as secret parties for members of a youth subculture (McCaughan, Carlson, Falck, & Siegal, 2005), and they soon spread to the United States through such ports as Chicago, New York, and Detroit (Ter Bogt & Engels, 2005). Although the rave scene of the late 20th century has largely disappeared, a considerable number of high school students continue to attend. A study by Palamar et al. (2015) found that one out of five students (19.8%) reported ever attending a rave, and 7.7% reported attending at least monthly. Females and highly religious students were less likely to attend. Hispanics, students residing in cities, students with higher income, and those who go out for fun multiple times per week were more likely to show up. Rave attendees were at least two times more likely than non-attendees to report use of an illicit drug other than marijuana. Table 10.4 shows prevalence rates for use of club drugs among high school students.

Table 10.4 Prevalence Rates for Various Drugs Associated with the Club Scene

Monitoring the Future Study: Trends in Prevalence of Various Drugs for 8th Graders, 10th Graders, and 12th Graders; 2016 (in percent)*				
Drug	Time Period	8th Graders	10th Graders	12th Graders
GHB	Past Year	–	–	0.90
LSD	Lifetime	1.20	3.20	4.90
	Past Year	0.80	2.10	3.00
MDMA	Lifetime	[1.70]	[2.80]	[4.90]
	Past Year	[1.00]	[1.80]	[2.70]
Ketamine	Past Year	–	–	1.20
Methamphetamine	Lifetime	0.60	[0.70]	1.20
	Past Year	0.40	[0.40]	0.60
Rohypnol	Lifetime	0.90	1.00	–
	Past Year	0.50	0.50	1.10

Data in brackets indicate statistically significant change from the previous year.
Source: NIDA (2016). Club Drugs.

Music festivals remain popular venues for large gatherings where drug taking occurs. Table 10.5 shows the results of a study conducted by DrugAbuse.com (2015) which calculated the percentage of various drugs mentioned in Instagram posts about top music concerts and festivals.

Table 10.5 Top Concerts and Festivals by Substance

Top Concerts & Festivals by Substance
% of posts mentioning substance and event

Alcohol		Marijuana	
1 Chili Cook-Off	90.26%	1 Marley fest	82.04%
2 Summerfest	87.02%	2 Camp bisco	25.11%
3 Glastonbury	69.01%	3 Bonnaroo	25.05%

MDMA/Molly/Ecstacy		Mushrooms	
1 Electric Daisy Carnival	42.99%	1 Burning Man	7.42%
2 Ultra Music Festival	37.68%	2 Bonnaroo	5.99%
3 Camp Bisco	21.00%	3 Camp Bisco	2.81%

Cocaine		Crack cocaine	
1 Coachella	12.39%	1 Burning Man	3.85%
2 Mad Decent Block Party	11.76%	2 Bonnaroo	3.73%
3 Lollapalooza	10.67%	3 Glastonbury Festival	3.72%

DMT		LSD	
1 Burning Man	7.22%	1 Burning Man	5.64%
2 Electric Daisy Carnival	0.90%	2 Ultra Music Festival	2.61%
3 Life in Color	0.81%	3 Camp Bisco	2.60%

Opioids		Pills	
1 Mad Decent Block Party	5.88%	1 Electric Daisy Carnival	0.47%
2 Lollapalooza	5.63%	2 Tomorrowland	0.36%
3 Holy Ship!	5.49%	3 Lollapalooza	0.29%

Mescaline		General drug terms	
1 Burning Man	0.48%	1 Camp Bisco	14.94%
2 Camp Bisco	0.43%	2 Tomorrowland	14.57%
3 Electric Daisy Carnival	0.33%	3 Burning Man	9.14%

Instagram Posts Collected March 2015

drugabuse.com

[Electric Daisy Carnival] EDC and Ultra were the epicenters of MDMA posts, with 42.99% and 37.68% of those festivals' posts mentioning the popular party drug.

Coachella took top billing for cocaine-related posts, with 12.39% of posts mentioning this addictive stimulant. General drug terms (such as "tripping" and "drugs") were most common in posts from Camp Bisco (14.94%) and Tomorrowland (14.57%). When it came to posting about psychedelic drugs such as mushrooms and LSD, Burning Man was the top festival for both. The weeklong Nevada event was also the top festival for posting about crack cocaine, DMT, and mescaline. (Drugabuse.com, 2015, para. 15)

Concerts and Drugs

Question: Is harm reduction at music festivals helpful?

The Lightning in a Bottle Music Festival, held over Memorial Day weekend in California, took extra steps to try and reduce negative outcomes for concertgoers who used drugs by partnering with harm-reduction organizations like DanceSafe. This group offers drug testing and tries to educate people at electronic music festivals and nightlife venues about potential warning signs connected to drug use, like heat stroke and dehydration, since these are the main reasons people die or become seriously ill from MDMA at music festivals. DanceSafe also hands out water.

Lightning in a Bottle also offered help to anyone going through a difficult experience while on psychedelic drugs like acid or mushrooms.

Not everyone thinks harm reduction is a good idea. Some people think trying to make drug use safer is just a way to promote drugs rather than keep people from using them altogether. By making it a little bit safer, they say, you are giving people the green light to go ahead and do something that could harm them.

Few would argue against the idea that knowledge—including a person knowing what's really in the powder they bought at a concert—is always better than ignorance. But we don't know how much that information actually influences people to change course when they find out they got swindled. Does finding out they've bought bath salts and not Molly keep them from taking the product they just spent money to get? We also don't know if these harm-reduction programs have prevented any overdoses or deaths, or if anyone has been more likely to use drugs when they know an aid station is there to help if something goes wrong. In the end, the only way to ensure good health is to stay away from drugs offered at these concerts.

Will harm-reduction programs at concerts help people make smarter decisions about their health, or encourage risky behavior?

Chapter Summary

Methamphetamine has seeped into commonplace venues across the United States. Whether used to party or to enhance one's capacity for sex, work, or crime, the usual aftermath of abusing methamphetamine is incredible hardship and suffering. Besides addiction, serious effects from meth usage include rapid and irregular heartbeat and increased blood pressure resulting in irreversible damage to small blood vessels in the brain—which in turn may result in strokes. Possibly the most serious health problem from chronic methamphetamine abuse is damage to the neurons of the brain. The intense and long-lasting euphoria (8–24 hours) produced by methamphetamine results from profuse release of dopamine from the presynaptic neuron in combination with meth's ability to block reuptake of DA from the synapse, thereby strengthening the overall effect. In addition, meth facilitates the release of norepinephrine, which accounts for the sleeplessness and hyperactivity experienced during the high.

The newest form of stimulants on the illegal market is synthetic drugs similar to cathinone, the active ingredient of the khat plant. These substances (marketed as "bath salts") are extremely potent amphetamine-like drugs. It is not unusual for "bath salts" to be a mix of several different stimulant substances; the potency and subjective effects of the drug experience will vary, depending on the mix of compounds. An even more powerful, second-generation synthetic cathinone is "gravel" (or "flakka"). Known on the street as "$5 insanity," dealers would charge $5 for the first ounce of this substance that tends to promote psychotic behavior. Body temperatures can rise to 105 degrees, which may explain why users may strip off their clothes.

Cocaine exerts its effects on the brain by increasing the amount of dopamine flowing into the nucleus accumbens. There is general agreement that maturing "crack" babies exhibit attention deficits, irritability, and aggression. Cocaine interferes with the normal growth of dendrites, especially around the part of the brain involved in learning and attention. This is especially problematic among young adults whose brains are not completely developed. Effects on health include brain damage, addiction, euphoria followed by depression, increased blood pressure, increased risk of heart attack, coronary aneurysms, and compromised immune systems. The cocaine scene is still going strong, despite the efforts in the 1980s and 1990s to reduce the use of powdered cocaine and crack by increased international surveillance, police work, and criminal sanctions.

With the decline of raves, music festivals have become common meccas for widespread use of the class of psychoactive substances known as "club drugs." These in include MDMA (Ecstasy), ketamine, GHB, and Rohypnol. Many blogs refer to the club drug "Molly" thought to be "pure" MDMA, the active ingredient in Ecstasy. The hype is that Molly was originally developed to treat depression and now it is finally available to energize and bring rapturous euphoria to the dance club and music festival scene. Actually, Molly is most often a toxic mixture of lab-created chemicals. Each of the club drugs has its own negative effects and perceived benefits. As with all the mind-altering drugs and activities discussed so far, the risks far outweigh the wished-for "benefits."

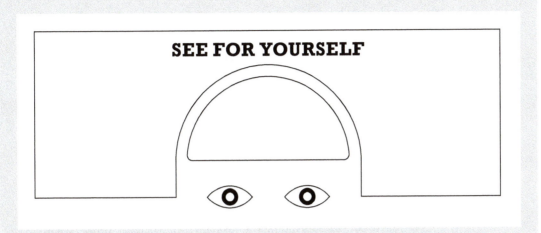

SEE FOR YOURSELF

How a basketball player's drug overdose led to today's mandatory minimums. 2015. America Tonight. Joie Chen. Al Jazeera. 4:55

Discusses how the apparent cocaine related death of Len Bias sparked mandatory minimum sentence laws that resulted in the long-term incarceration of thousands of nonviolent drug offenders. **http://america.aljazeera.com/watch/shows/america-tonight/articles/2015/11/5/how-a-basketball-players-drug-overdose-led-to-mandatory-minimum-laws.html**

How the Brain Responds to Methamphetamine. 2016. National Institute on Drug Abuse. 2:41

NIH video explains how dopamine and the reward center are co-opted by methamphetamine.**https://www.drugabuse.gov/videos/reward-circuit-how-brain-responds-to-methamphetamine**

Molly Hits Seattle's Rave Scene. 2014. National Geographic: Drugs, Inc. 2:35

MDMA, or "Molly," is a dance-inducing drug that's popular on the rave scene. National Geographic shows how users experience MDMA in powderedform.**http://natgeotv.com/ca/drugs-inc/videos/molly-hits-seattles-rave-scene**

Commonly Abused Drugs Charts. 2016. National Institute on Drug Abuse.

NIDA presents summary charts of the major drugs of abuse. **https://www. drugabuse.gov/drugs-abuse/commonly-abused-drugs-charts**

Mayor Rob Ford won't step down despite crack use. 2013. Canadian Broadcasting Corporation. 6:32

Mayor of Toronto admits smoking crack cocaine. **http://www.cbc. ca/news/canada/toronto/mayor-rob-ford-won-t-step-down-despite-crack-use-1.2415533**

SECTION IV

Mental Excursions

When I examine myself and my methods of thought, I come to the conclusion that the gift of fantasy has meant more to me than my talent for absorbing positive knowledge.

—Albert Einstein

I like nonsense, it wakes up the brain cells. Fantasy is a necessary ingredient in living. It's a way of looking at life through the wrong end of a telescope. Which is what I do. And that enables you to laugh at life's realities.

– Dr. Seuss

Overview: Imagination—The Quintessential Human Trait

Fantasy may be described as the ability to reproduce elements from prior experience (e.g., faces of persons, snatches of dialogue, objects in the universe) presently unavailable to our senses, and to reshape these into new and complex forms (J. L. Singer, 1976). The purpose of this section is to explore the gift of fantasy as an essential means for experiencing pleasure, understanding the world, and enhancing survival. The human proclivity for imagination, however, carries the same abuse liability as our needs for arousal and satiation.

Our ability to create mental events, which stand as intermediaries between biological impulse and instinctual reactions, may be the single most important difference between humans and all other life on earth. We not only forecast the weather and visualize tomorrow's clothing, but we can also imagine our own death. The ability to project ourselves into future environments and to appreciate the likely consequences of intended actions has undoubtedly enabled the prolific survival of the human species. However idyllic, bizarre, improbable, or grotesque, imagination usually reflects a response to psychological need. Fantasies are spoken about, privately savored, or preserved as forms of art.

The interplay between our internal mental experience and information from outside sets the stage for individualized representations and interpretations of the world. The development of self-concept, cognitive styles, emotional reactivity, and behavioral responses are, in part, determined by fantasy and imaginative thought.

Without forming fantasy images of our own, we may be engaged in attending to others' fantasy expressions. *Receptive fantasy* is the concentration on thoughts or pictures that have been produced from outside ourselves—for example, watching television, reading a novel, being at a concert, or going to an art gallery. *Active fantasy* is the production of images and thoughts that emerge spontaneously from one's own psyche. These may be highly representational and reality oriented, such as a person visualizing how to approach his or her employer, or they may be abstract and unrealistic, such as imagining the creation or destruction of the universe. Figure IV.1 illustrates the distinction among three distinct categories of visual fantasy: realistic, unrealistic, and abstract.

Figure IV.1 Continuum of fantasy images Fantasies range from representational and reality oriented to unrealistic and abstract.

REALISTIC

UNREALISTIC

ABSTRACT

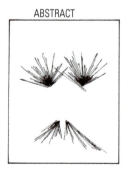

Exploration of the child's use of fantasy in fairy tales and storybooks sets the stage for understanding the adaptive function of imagination. Religion and myth play similar roles in providing guidelines for ethical and responsible living within a context of family, community, and culture. The function of dreams is explored in terms of enhancing one's capacity to solve problems and to reduce stress. Each of the three chapters in this section is predicated on the adaptive, survival nature of fantasy, thereby associating it with both pleasure and high potential for abuse.

Chapter 11, "Virtual Reality and Electronic Bogeymen," focuses on the emergence of virtual reality as an important element of the media age. Virtual reality gaming is where a person can experience being in a three-dimensional environment and interact with that environment during a game. Younger consumer groups (under 18 years of age) appear to show the greatest interest in virtual reality. Video games are the key drivers of virtual reality hardware with a global audience of 58.9 million virtual reality users and production of 38.9 million virtual reality devices (Gaudioisi, 2016). The global market for virtual reality hardware is estimated at $8.9 billion in 2017 and $12.3 billion in 2018. *World of Warcraft* and other competitive battle games including DotA 2, accounted for approximately 25% of the $100 billion digital games market in 2017. In some cases, eSports viewership surpasses many popular sports (Foye, 2016). League of Legends is identified as market leader, hosting over 100 million monthly active users. Virtual reality (VR) gambling wagers are set to rise 800% in the next five years driven by "high rollers" who play simulated gambling games in a 3-D Las Vegas type environment. The total amount of bets from VR gambling is predicted to grow from just over $58.5 million in 2016 to just under $520 million by 2021 (Foye, 2016).

World of Warcraft, prolific in the genre of "massively multiplayer online role-playing games," or MMORPGs (pronounced "morepegs"), are examined in terms of how players escape into imagination to combat their enemies. *Second Life*, which continues to be the most popular virtual reality world, is discussed as an "engine of creativity" where residents own the intellectual property inherent in their creations ("Virtual Online Worlds," 2006). These "pixelated worlds" have brought countless hours of excitement, creativity, and peace of mind to millions of players. Unfortunately, some have become entrapped in a web of compulsion, loss of control, and continuation despite harmful consequences (i.e., they have become addicted).

Chapter 12, "Fantasy and the Drug Experience," examines how certain drugs may be used to activate the imagination, for better or worse. Lysergic acid diethylamide, LSD-25, is discussed as a pharmaceutical wonder, first synthesized on April 16, 1943, by Albert Hofmann, a chemist working for Sandoz Labs in Basel, Switzerland. In the 65 years following his discovery, Hofmann took a lot of LSD. He credited the drug with providing him with a sense of "union with nature and the spiritual basis of all creation" ("Obituary: Albert Hofmann," 2008). Many others, some creative geniuses, have held similar opinions. Hofmann died on April 29, 2008, at the age of 102, still mourning the unfulfilled promise of his "problem child," which he regarded as "a sacrament for the modern age: the antidote to the ennui caused by consumerism, industrialization, and the vanishing of the divine from human life" ("Obituary: Albert Hofmann," 2008). In the past 15 years, brain science has reopened the doors for exploring the use of psychedelics (e.g., LSD, psilocybin, mescaline, ayahuasca, DMT, MDMA) as tools for unraveling the stranglehold of mental disorders (e.g., obsessive compulsive disorder [OCD], severe anxiety in terminal cancer patients, posttraumatic stress disorder) (D. J. Brown, 2007).

Chapter 13, "Compelled by Fantasy," explores how the boundaries between fantasy and reality may become blurred and cross over into destructive action. Born from intense psychological need, destructive fantasy fuels a host of compulsive problem behaviors ranging from wanton sexual acts to terrorism on a global scale. Fanaticism in belief and behavior is examined as a primary human response to unfulfilled psychological and social needs. Many researchers now believe that terrorism is not a manifestation of mental illness but rather a "rational choice" to meet political and religious objectives (Schaefer-Jones, 2007). Variations of the widespread apocalyptic fantasy (world destruction followed by heaven on earth) are examined as misguided and highly dangerous manifestations of the basic human capacity for wish-fulfilling fantasy.

Electronic Media Everywhere

Images and ideas from our surroundings are the psychic nutrients for our fantasies. There is a constant interplay between a person's spontaneous production of thoughts and images and the incredible array of external stimuli to which we are exposed. Television, which dominated the world of electronic media until the 1990s, has been joined by a vast array of information delivery systems: video players, audio media (e.g., Spofify, podcasts, etc.), video games (both console-based and handheld), computers, cell phones, personal digital media players (PDMPs), personal digital assistants (PDAs), and handheld Internet devices (Brooks-Gunn & Donahue, 2008).

In 2005 a typical 8- to 18-year-old in the United States lived in a home with three TVs, three video players, three PDMPs e.g., two video game consoles, and a personal computer (Roberts, Foehr, & Rideout, 2005). Shocking as it may seem, by 2010 a typical 8- to 18-year-old in the U.S. would spend the equivalent of more than a full work day using media—more than 7.5 hours, except that they use media seven days a week instead of five. Since youth tend to use two or more media concurrently, they are actually exposed to more than 10½ hours of media content during that period. "And this does *not* include time spent using the computer for school work, or time spent texting or talking on a cell phone" (Rideout, Foehr, & Roberts, 2010, p. 11). Many teenagers spend more time engaged with electronic media than with any other element of life, including sleep.

Electronic media devices coexist with basic print (e.g., magazines, paperbacks, and newspapers) and other informational devices (e.g., billboards, graffiti, shopping mall displays, and movies). Together, they bombard the public with information ranging from intellectually stimulating, practical, and aesthetically pleasing, to whimsical, violent, horrifying, and obscene. The content of visual productions (e.g., YouTube, virtual reality, tattoos, pornography) and acoustic presentations (e.g., songs, slam poetry, political and religious propaganda) exists on a continuum, from representational and easily understood, to highly abstract (see Figure IV.1).

The Child's Use of Fantasy

The basic function of fantasy is to explore our relationship to the world. As children we begin to develop specific mental pictures of who we are, which become a kind of personal identity, uniting our past experiences to our intended actions. By imagining, we can work through painful memories and sufferings or formulate models of enchantment through which we will soar to blissful heights with our lovers, family, or friends. The emergence of innovative ideas from the reshaping of a multiplicity of past events, in a sense, becomes a vast additional source of knowledge.

According to Greenspan (1985), between the ages of 18 and 38 months, the child begins to create an internal world of ideas, symbols, and representations. He or she learns to abstract the functional properties of objects and form mental representations of the outside world. These are not only visual, but also multisensory and interactive images. For example, if a 2½-year-old thinks of "mother," the internal image is of smell, touch, voice, actions, feelings, and interactions, as well as past and present subjective experiences.

From 2 to 4½ years, single repetitive play (e.g., doll drinks from a cup) evolves into "the grand epic drama." For example, "the doll drinks from the cup, goes to sleep, is awakened, spanked for spilling the milk and then spanks the mommy doll back, and finally is in love and cuddling" (Greenspan, 1985, p. 151). Thus, fantasy is used to internalize a template for managing the emotional themes of life, that is, "dependency, pleasure, curiosity, assertiveness, aggression, protest, anger, self-limit setting and by age 3–4 empathy and consistent love" (p. 151).

If for any reason the child is not sufficiently practiced in the use of fantasy and pretend play (parents may be made anxious by the use of fantasy in emotionally relevant contexts-(e.g., separation or divorce), deficits or constriction in representational capacity can occur. As a result, the child (and later the adult) may become limited to a pattern of restricted and concrete thought. "Many adults are more frightened by the representation of a theme, such as sexuality or aggression, than the behaving or acting out of the same theme" (Greenspan, 1985, p. 151). Drug abuse and other forms of hedonic escape may serve the purpose of providing "false refuge" for those who lack internal means for managing the "emotional themes of life" (i.e., those who have a poorly developed capacity for fantasy). According to Singer and Kolligian (1987), moderate use of imagination is necessary for adaptive living. Singer's research with overeaters and drug abusers reveals their impoverished fantasy lives. These individuals may react by responding primarily to external stimulation. The outside world seems to cry out for sensory encounters, namely food, sex, or drugs. Similarly, children who do not partake of imaginative play tend more toward fighting, delinquency, and antisocial acts.

Whereas fairy tales largely provide guideposts for children to master the tasks of growing up, religion and myths provide ethical prescriptions for conduct in the adult world. The adaptive function of imagination, however, far exceeds that of helping to establish meaning, purpose, and patterns of conduct in an often confusing existence. Fantasy affords us an internal system for reducing stress. We can diminish tension through the imagined gratification of physical or psychological cravings or needs. By creating alternative mental environments, we are temporarily released from internal conflict or from tension in the outside world. Parents longing for the return of their college-bound children may find solace in their fantasy of having a joyous Thanksgiving reunion. Because of these intense reward capabilities, we regularly rely on fantasy solutions to everyday problems in living.

The interplay of *receptive* and *active* forms of fantasy is best understood by examining imagination in one of its simplest forms: the child's experience with the fairy tale. In its pure form, the fairy tale helps children to understand the inner pressures and concerns entailed in growing up. It offers both temporary and permanent solutions to pressing difficulties. Bettelheim (1976), renowned for his expertise on the meaning and importance of fairy tales, describes how children may benefit from enchanting stories:

In order to master the psychological problems of growing up—overcoming narcissistic disappointments, oedipal dilemmas, sibling rivalries, becoming able to relinquish childhood dependencies, gaining a feeling of selfhood and self-worth, and a sense of moral obligation—a child needs to understand what is going on within his conscious self so that he can also cope with that which goes on in his unconscious. He can achieve this understanding, and with it the ability to cope, not through rational comprehension of the nature and content of his unconscious but by becoming familiar with it through spinning out daydreams—ruminating, rear ranging and fantasizing about suitable strong elements in response to unconscious pressures ... Fairytales have unequaled value because they offer new dimensions to the child's imagination which would be impossible for him to discover as truly on his own. Even more important, the form and structure of a fairy tale suggests images to the child by which he can structure his daydreams and then give better direction to his life. (p. 7)

Examination of *The Tale of Peter Rabbit* (Potter, 1902/1991) sheds light on youngsters' use of fairy tales to cope better with the fears and impulses of childhood. The story has sold more than 40 million copies worldwide. Beatrix Potter's now-classic story begins,

Once upon a time there were four little Rabbits and their names were Flopsy, Mopsy, Cottontail and Peter... "Now my dears," said old Mrs. Rabbit one morning, "you may go into the fields or down the lane, but don't go into Mr. McGregor's garden. Your father had an accident there; he was put in a pie by Mrs. McGregor. ..."

Flopsy, Mopsy and Cottontail, who were good little bunnies, went down the lane to gather blackberries. But Peter, who was very naughty, ran straight away to Mr. McGregor's garden and squeezed under the gate! (pp. 5–6)

Peter did not understand the value of portion control and was beginning to learn a lesson about giving carte blanche to wayward impulses.

But round the end of a cucumber frame, who should he meet but Mr. McGregor! ... Peter got frightened and ran but got caught by the large buttons on his jacket in a gooseberry net. ... Peter gave himself up for lost and shed big tears; but his sobs were overheard by some friendly sparrows who flew to him in great excitement and implored him to exert himself. (Potter, 1902/1991, p. 10)

Freud believed that only by struggling courageously against what seems like overwhelming odds can one succeed in wringing meaning out of life. This is an essential message of most fairy tales.

Peter had a very tough time running away from Mr. McGregor. He was frightened and cried, lost his clothes, and became wet and cold before he ran into a white cat who was staring at some goldfish. "Peter thought it best to go away without speaking to her; he had heard about cats from his cousin, Little Benjamin Bunny" (Potter, 1902/1991, p. 19). This is perhaps the most moving and essential part of the story. Young Peter must learn to take the advice of others—vicarious learning—to avoid making similar mistakes. Recall his father who was turned into rabbit pie.

Finally, Peter slips by Mr. McGregor, but not before he has a glance at what happened to his clothes: "Mr. McGregor hung up the little jacket and the shoes for a scarecrow to frighten the blackbirds" (Potter, 1902/1991, p. 23). Perhaps this is a symbol of crucifixion and a last reminder that death may be a penalty for impulsive behaviors.

When Peter got home, he was not feeling well. His mother put him to bed and gave Peter a dose of chamomile tea, one tablespoonful to be taken at bedtime. But Flopsy, Mopsy, and Cottontail had bread and milk and blackberries for supper. The good children were rewarded for their good behavior. Peter, on the other hand—whose nerves were undoubtedly shot—was mildly "medicated" and ordered to rest.

It is self-evident that when a young child becomes riveted by this enthralling tale, he or she inadvertently internalizes schemas (scripts) for impulse control and vicarious learning. The next time you have the chance to read *The Tale of Peter Rabbit* to a young child, notice how seriously he or she attends to every detail.

Religion and Myth

Be it Buddhism, Christianity, Hinduism, Islam, or Judaism, modern religion provides allegorical counsel for child, adolescent, and adult questions about life and death. Throughout the world, groups of people accept as truth ideas, concepts, or images that appear to violate the laws of nature. Beliefs in the supernatural are generally accepted as truths within a practicing group and regarded as myths or false beliefs by outsiders. These shared stories and legends become so ingrained that entire cultures may be guided by their meaning.

The organization of beliefs, rituals, and images that collectively purport to explain the meaning of life for a specific group may be considered a religion. For example, a large segment of the people in India share a set of beliefs, rich in imagery, depicting incredible supernatural events. To a Westerner, the stories enveloped by the religion of Hinduism are understood as fascinating myths. To the religious Hindu, the causes of the supernatural events in these widely shared stories are attributed to gods.

Religion and myth, fairy tale and fable, folklore and legend collaborate to form intricate systems of informal social controls over human impulse and action. Whereas the law provides direct mandates for correct action, shared parables usually enhance survival by providing internalized road maps for correct action. In the story of Abraham and Isaac (common to Judaism, Christianity, and Islam), Abraham subjugates himself to a power (God) that supersedes individual will or self-love. Clearly, Abraham's willingness to sacrifice his only son promotes respect for a force mightier than personal volition. A group's survival is enhanced if its members can be guided by symbols that encourage cohesiveness and allegiance to a shared set of values and leaders.

Even atheist communism uses symbolism to instill shared cultural beliefs. During a trip to mainland China, one of the authors (Milkman, 1981) asked his tour guide to explain China's position if Russia and the United States were at war. The guide offered the following parable:

> It is for you to decide who is China, Russia, or the U.S.
>
> There sits a large clam on the beach with its shell wide open.
>
> A seagull moves in to devour the flesh.

Now the clam closes its shell on the seagull's beak.

The seagull cannot escape and the clam cannot release its grip.

A fisherman comes by and takes them both.

Figure IV.2 Clam, Bird, Fisherman

When one considers the audacious awakening of China (a.k.a. "the sleeping giant") during the early part of the 21st century, the guide's parable seems prophetic. Culturally shared parables like "the seagull and the clam" have great psychological impact, with the power to influence the course of human life. In effect, symbols (memes) become the "social transmitters" of cultural understanding.

Hindu stories are probably the richest in imagery of all living religions. The Hindu religion has survived for thousands of years despite repeated conquests from foreign powers who brought with them different religious beliefs. According to the Hindu faith, men are often unable to combat the powers of evil. In situations such as these, the Hindu god Vishnu temporarily returns to help the people on earth in their struggle against the evil person or situation. Thus through symbol, there develops a mental preparedness, or cognitive schema, to emulate Vishnu in the struggle for group cohesiveness and survival.

One of Vishnu's more interesting reincarnations is as Narasinha, who comes to the earth to free the world from the powers of a demon king who had obtained a promise from the god Brahma. The promise consisted of an immunity that would prevent the demon king from being killed by man or beast, by day or by night, inside or outside his house, in heaven or on earth. Instead of using this miraculous safeguard from death to help the people, the demon king became so depraved that he forbade worship of all other gods and demanded the worship of himself in their place. He even attempted to kill his own son, whom he found doing obeisance to Vishnu. The demon king finally created so much misery for the people on earth that Vishnu returned in the form of Narasinha, the man-lion. He immediately attacked the demon king, took him to a doorway of a house at twilight, held him on his knees, and tore out his heart.

The story of Narasinha illustrates the concept that good will triumph over evil despite all odds to the contrary (i.e., through perseverance, success will follow—recall the sparrows' message to Peter Rabbit). Also, consider the power of visual imagery in this story. Narasinha is usually pictured as the half-man, half-lion hybrid holding the demon king on his knees. Combination creatures are not only found in other avatars of Vishnu, but are also common in mythology throughout the world. For example, the Olmec people, who lived in the land occupied by present-day Veracruz in Mexico, believed that they were descendants of a mating between a jaguar and a goddess. Much of the art of the Olmecs depicts people as were-jaguars, hybrids of men and jaguars. The centaur of ancient Greek mythology is a hybrid of a man and a horse, while the Roman griffin has the head and wings of an eagle and the body of a lion.

As depicted in "Reflections on an Indian Train" and Figure IV.3, fantasy is a powerful wish-fulfilling device for easing life's heavy burdens.

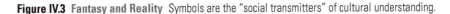

Figure IV.3 **Fantasy and Reality** Symbols are the "social transmitters" of cultural understanding.

Reflections on an Indian Train

(Where the solution is the problem and its genesis)
The people are so poor and so many
Only fantasy can fulfill their desire
Where there is little to possess
Detachment becomes a virtue
When horror is normal
Shock abounds
If the self is so neglected
The gods are even more mighty

When the senses are so assaulted
Pleasure becomes a vice
Where life is chaotic
Ritual provides relief
Where death lurks in each corner
Preservation of life becomes a fetish
Where substance is remote
The gimmick is fascination
Where nurturance is so sparse
The feminine is worshipped
When life is compensation
Rationalization is a savior

— H. Milkman (1980)

In the folklore of seafarers, mermaids symbolize the sailor's ultimate dichotomy: rescue by a gorgeous companion (wish) from the nightmare death at sea (fear). The last stanza of an old English sea shanty, "Married to a Mermaid," supports this view:

We lowered a boat to find him; we thought to see his corpse,

When up to the top, he came with a shock, and said in a voice so hoarse,

"My ship mates and my mess mates, oh, do not weep for me,

For I'm married to a mermaid at the bottom of the deep blue sea."

Science and Religion

Whether called hybrid creatures, omnipotent deities, or just plain superstition, there appears to be a basic human drive to believe in something transcendent, incomprehensible, and otherworldly, beyond the reach of scientific explanation. Even people who claim to be atheists are prone to magical thinking. Scott Atran (2002), an anthropologist at the National Center for Scientific Research in Paris, presented college students with a wooden box that he said was an African relic. He told them that if they had negative sentiments toward religion, the box would destroy whatever they placed inside. When instructed to put their pencil in the box, the nonbelievers had no problem. Next came their driver's license—most did, but with considerable hesitation. When he told them to put their hand in, however, few complied.

Why do we believe in the supernatural beyond all reason? According to anthropologists, religion exists in virtually every culture on earth, with common notions of an afterlife and belief in the power of prayer to change the course of human events (Henig, 2007). This is certainly true in the United States, where about 60% of the population report that they believe in the devil and hell, 70–80% believe in angels, and 92% believe in a personal God (Henig, 2007; HuffPost Live, 2013)

Atran (2002) posits a biological explanation for the belief in God. He regards the god concept as an evolutionary by-product of a complex neurological matrix for survival, yet with no functional value of its own. In architecture, this may be compared to the V-shaped structure formed between two adjacent rounded arches, or the empty triangular space beneath a staircase. Stephen Jay Gould (1997, 2002), the famed evolutionary biologist at Harvard, coined the term "spandrel," borrowed from architecture to describe a human trait that has no adaptive value—like the triangular space beneath a staircase that could remain neutral or be made functional by using the area for a closet or storage cabinet. So, if God is a spandrel, what is the evolutionary value of the neurologically mediated cognitive structures from which it derives?

The hardships facing early humans favored the development of certain cognitive tools that increased the probability of survival: (1) the ability to recognize creatures that might cause harm, (2) the capacity to develop causal explanations for natural events, and (3) recognition that there are other beings that have minds of their own. Anthropologists refer to these propensities respectively as "agent detection," "causal reasoning," and "theory of mind". From an evolutionary perspective, one need only to fill in the blanks or connect the dots across time, place, and culture to show how religion is a universal by-product of these protective neuropsychological devices.

Elkind (1970) noted some remarkable parallels between four basic elements of religion and four stages of a child's intellectual growth. First, every religion has a concept of a god, a deity that is permanent and immortal across all time and space. This parallels the child's understanding of the *permanent object* by the end of the first year of life. There develops the belief that people or things no longer available to the senses will remain present.

Second, by the age of 2 the child attains the ability to create, comprehend, and employ symbols. For example, anything that floats can become a toy boat. This is paralleled by the presence of *religious symbols* that stand for elements of pious belief (e.g., wine and bread in Christianity, the Torah in Judaism, and head coverings in Islam).

Third, religion carries a set of *rituals*, whether kneeling, standing, or rocking during prayer, or taking Holy Communion. This is paralleled by the development of rules that children adopt at about the age of 6 or 7 when they enter the "age of reason." Children can play scripted games or create structures and rules to play by on their own.

Finally, during adolescence there is a propensity to consider ideal life circumstances and fact-challenging propositions (e.g., a world without poverty or war). Similarly, all theologies provide *idealistic visions* and urge their adherents to live according to the highest standards of conduct (e.g., compassion and right actions in Buddhism; the Ten Commandments in Judaism, Islam, and Christianity).

The implication of these parallels is that our developmental modes of thought provide a predisposition for comprehending the primary elements of religion, which also parallel the four basic elements of science: conservation, symbolism, ritual or experimentation, and theory. From this perspective, religion and science represent alternative means of applying our four basic modes of thought, neither one right or wrong.

Einstein (1937/1956) had a similar idea (Figure IV.4):

> All religions, arts and sciences are branches of the same tree. All these aspirations are directed toward ennobling man's life, lifting it from the sphere of mere physical existence and leading the individual towards freedom. (p. 7)

Figure IV.4 Branches of the Same Tree All these aspirations are directed toward ennobling man's life.

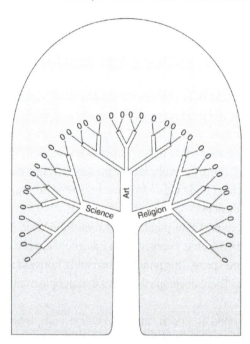

Personal Fantasy

On an individual level, the images of politicians, deities, prophets, or movie stars become internalized as guiding factors in personal life. We identify or put ourselves in the place of the darlings of our time and shape our behavior through vicarious experience of their lives. Idolizing, or overidentification with highly visible members of a community, is yet another vehicle for patching the self from without. In some cases, the fantasy of being *like* one's chosen idol unconsciously ensures the wish to be *liked by* that idol and to experience some measure of the idol's success. How many articles of clothing are sold every day carrying the logo of a famous sports figure or team? It is not at all unusual for members of a social group to mimic the dress and look of their media heroes. Lady Gaga, Tom Brady, Angelina Jolie, Caitlin Jenner, Beyonce, Brad Pitt, Taylor Swift, Kanye West, Blac Chyna, and George Clooney each has his or her share of look-alikes, not to even mention the millions of sports fans who walk around with T-shirts or hats symbolizing their athlete heroes.

Some individuals form pathological identifications with their heroes and antiheroes. Mark Chapman reasoned that he murdered John Lennon "because he loved him." In a letter to the *New York Times,* he wrote that the answer to the murder could be found in J. D. Salinger's *The Catcher in the Rye* (Holden, 2008). John Hinkley's attempted murder of President Reagan involved his fantasy identification with Travis Bickle, a psychotic assassin (played by Robert DeNiro) in the movie *Taxi Driver*. Columbine-style copycat murders may remain an enduring feature of U.S. culture (Nizza, 2007).

Based on 132 five-hour interviews and survey data from 18,000 people in Britain and America, Kahr (2008) unveils the results of his comprehensive research into their sexual fantasies. In *Who's Been Sleeping in Your Head: The Secret World of Sexual Fantasies,* Kahr not only reveals the ubiquity of sexual fantasy (9 out of 10 people have them), but also reports on the common occurrence of people having such lurid fantasies as doing disgusting things in front of strangers, or relaxing by thinking about extreme sexual violence toward unsuspecting strangers. Kahr explains his findings to mean that people use fantasy to rewrite unpleasant childhood memories, sometimes to wreak revenge on absent or abusive adults or to redress harm by sanitizing unpleasant memories. Rather than viewing sexual fantasy as a sign of troubled relationships, Kahr sees them as a kind of safety valve for blowing off dangerous steam. As shown in the case example below, the benefit of wish fulfillment is a strong element of the fantasy experience.

CASE EXAMPLE: Wish-Fulfilling Dream

Dr. Saul's (not his real name) dream illustrates how a powerful fantasy, accessed after awakening from sleep, can be an effective tool for coping with stress. Prior to the dream, Dr. Saul was engaged in a fierce bureaucratic struggle at work. He perceived institutional attempts to crush a professional goal of his that symbolized 15 years of research and academic concentration. He was considering abandoning his project and resigning from work. The dream began with the visualization of a theater marquee that featured the film *Holocaust From the Side of the Germans*. Dr. Saul awakened with full recollection of his dream and wrote the following verbatim report:

Last night before I went to sleep I was feeling persecuted by several people, primarily faculty and other associates with whom I've recently had some rather unpleasant business dealings. I had a vivid dream of Nazi persecution in which I saw a billboard that read, "Holocaust From the Side of the Germans, shown in cinema vérité."

The dream was extremely lucid and portrayed huge German armies engulfing relatively small groups of Jews who were armed with primitive jousting instruments: long sticks with hatchets tied on the ends. The weapons were modifications of the stickball bats I used as a child in the Bronx. In my adolescent bursts of power, I reveled in the thrill of hitting a rubber ball a distance of more than three sewers.

I recall the feeling of becoming so irate about having to defend my right to exist as a free human being that I, along with hundreds of others, lunged into ferocious battle with the German tormentors. My whole being shrieked in an exhilarated frenzy as I maimed and killed German soldiers, helter-skelter, all the time thinking that I would most probably die.

Miraculously, I survived the episode and was amazed at how nicely the Germans behaved toward the Jews the following day. Suddenly the Jewish people were walking in peace among Nazis, albeit a temporary state of tranquility.

I awakened with a distinct feeling of rejuvenation along with the conscious thought that I had acted heroically. I was true to myself and my people by successfully opposing the sadistic tormentors. As soon as I woke up, I pondered how I could create this wonderful dream again. That morning I met with the college president, who gave me complete freedom to carry on with my project.

Clearly the dream fantasy was a symbolic representation of what the dreamer was experiencing in waking life. He was of Jewish descent and felt exposed to hatred like what he had learned about the Jewish experience in Nazi Germany. Upon waking, he reported a sense of increased vigor, optimism, and heightened commitment to pursue his academic goals. The tension of the past week had suddenly dissipated. The vivid dream fantasy served to channel an aggressive impulse that might otherwise have been expressed through self-punishment (e.g., alcohol abuse) or self-defeating hostility toward his employers. Instead, he would stand up to his opponents and ask the college president to intervene.

Daydreams or night dreams are augmented by fantasy objects in our midst. In *The Movies on Your Mind* (H. R. Greenberg, 1975), psychoanalyst Greenberg shows how cinema preferences may be used as diagnostic interviews, much like the Rorschach inkblot test. In analyzing his patients, Greenberg discovered that most were at least "moderately addicted" to the cinema and that movie associations were an effective route to the unconscious. A patient's ruminations about a particular movie may give invaluable insight into his or her childhood conflicts, troubled present, or anxious premonitions about the future. Greenberg cites the example of an adolescent with a school phobia who reported that his favorite film was *King of Kings*.

> He especially enjoyed the part where the Roman soldiers pounded the nails into Jesus' hands. I discovered that his cranium was jammed with homosexual and masochistic fantasies: he avoided school because of a tremendous fear—and hidden wish—that a gang of local bullies would beat and rape him. In his daydreams, he would show a Christ-like forbearance and pity for his tormentors, so that they would give up their evil ways and worship, rather than despise him. (p. 4)

Certainly, *King of Kings* helped this young man to validate his persecutory beliefs and to organize his underlying fears and wishes. Greenberg finds that those most prone to movie mania are rigid, inhibited types who characteristically avoid any close interpersonal contact. Individuals such as these become intolerably anxious when faced with the spontaneity of a personal encounter and only feel alive as vicarious participants in adventures of their movie heroes.

Summary

Our ability to create mental events that stand as intermediaries between biological impulse and instinctual reactions may be the single crucial difference between humans and all other life on earth. This overview examines the gift of fantasy as an essential means for experiencing pleasure, deriving meaning, and enhancing survival. The human proclivity for imagination, however, carries the same abuse liability as our needs for arousal and satiation.

The interplay between our internal mental experience and information from outside sets the stage for individualized representations and interpretations of the world. The development of self-concept, cognitive styles, emotional reactivity, and behavioral responses are all, in part, determined by fantasy images and imaginative thought. Since youth often use two or more media concurrently, they are actually exposed to more than 10½ hours of media content each day. Many teenagers spend more time with electronic media than they do participating in any other element of life, including sleep.

If the child is not sufficiently practiced in the use of fantasy and pretend play, deficits or constriction in representational capacity can occur. The child, and later the adult, may become limited to a pattern of restricted and concrete thought. Drug abuse, delinquency, and various forms of hedonic escape may provide "false refuge" for those who lack internal means for managing the "emotional themes of life."

Whereas fairy tales largely provide guideposts for children to master the tasks of growing up, religion and myths provide people with ethical prescriptions for how to conduct themselves within the boundaries of cultural norms. The adaptive function of imagination, however, far exceeds that of helping to establish meaning, purpose, and patterns of conduct in an often-confusing existence. Dreams and reverie are examined as adaptive means to reduce tension and to channel impulses that might otherwise result in stress, emotional discomfort, and negative behavioral outcomes. Although fantasy affords us an internal system for reducing stress, when imagination is more satisfactory than direct action, we begin to tread on the road to harmful consequences. With each experience of pleasure or removal from pain, the probability of seeking out an imaginary solution increases. Our work, love, and play may progressively falter as the result of an increasing reliance on imaginary pleasures.

CHAPTER 11

Virtual Reality and Electronic Bogeymen

Bogeyman: An imaginary person or monster that causes fear or is invoked to cause fear, especially in children.

—Encarta (online dictionary)

Look at it, every day more lusers than users, keyboards and screens turning into nothing but portals to Web sites for what Management wants everyone addicted do, shopping, games, jerking off, streaming endless garbage.

—Thomas Pynchon, *Bleeding Edge*

Introduction: Evolution of Electronic Media

In Western culture, the gods of science and technology have developed synthetic tools for fulfilling wishes and satisfying unmet needs. The 21st century has seen the emergence of electronic media beyond our wildest dreams. Television, which dominated the "pixilated world" through the mid-1990s, has been assailed by a throng of electronic media devices and features including smartphones, iPads, video games, instant messaging, interactive multiplayer video games, virtual reality sites, Web social networks, and e-mail (Brooks-Gunn & Donahue, 2008). The impact of massively multiplayer on-line role-playing games (MMORPGs) is of significance during adolescence, when one considers that the primary developmental task is to form a coherent sense of self. The possibility of substituting cyberspace personas for face-to-face interaction may facilitate peer group interactions, yet some players may suffer the aftershock of failure to develop the capacity for genuine closeness. "In other words, he could put on a new identity like a new suit of clothes, becoming someone who walked on water, healed others, and cast lightning bolts, in stark contrast to his daily experience of himself as inadequate" (Allison, von Wahlde, Shockley, & Gabbard, 2006, p. 381).

As examined in the next section, *craving for intimacy* is a root cause of suffering and addictive behavior. If fantasy relationships take precedence over direct human contact for some people, how does this phenomenon affect primary needs for love and belonging? Our discussion of virtual reality begins with the evolution of three great waves of electronic media: television, video games, and MMORPGs.

In *Four Arguments for the Elimination of Television,* Mander (1978) presented the most scathing indictment of Filo Farnsworth's monumental 1927 invention: TV.

- First, TV is limited as a source for gathering information, compromising other, more vital forms of human interaction and experience (Figure 11.1).

- Second, TV is foremost a political device. By regulating the information that people receive and therefore what they think, TV is used for social control and human domination. The enormous human capacity for identification and modeling has been a means of steering human actions in every civilization. A cogent example was the Soviet satellite system until the 1990s. It spanned ten time zones with high priority given to the broadcast of socialist achievement and the rhetoric of Soviet philosophy.

- Third, TV produces a hypnotic-addictive effect because of the neurophysiologic responses of human beings to the television signal. By introducing a device that renders viewers passive they become unable or unwilling to attend to many of their own best interests and needs of society.

- Fourth, TV has only a very limited capacity to improve one's understanding of life. It characteristically reduces complex issues into overly simplistic representations of reality. The mentality derived from TV programming tends to be materialistic, devoid of meaning, and lacking in real-life experience.

By the early 1980s, we progressed to the second level of the media revolution. Rossel Waugh (2006) describes video games as a new and more advanced stage in our addiction to media. Scripts were parallel to the basic dramatic themes of cartoons, Westerns, space fantasies, or murder mysteries. However, whereas television requires passive observation with occasional lapses in concentration, video games require full attention and active participation. The games graphically play out fantasy confrontations with fundamental anxieties of life: conquest and defeat, pursuit and flight, heroic struggle, envelopment and escape. Participants enjoy fantasy experiments with anxiety-provoking or life-threatening situations in a limited and safe way. The clear majority of people who play video games use them for enjoyment and relaxation, with no problems of compulsion or loss of control. Yet, for some, the use of interactive video technology is dangerously enthralling because it provides fantasy reprieve from problems in living. The bizarre, yet true, case example below illustrates how a young man improvised a scheme for using video images and cocaine, combined with biofeedback, to inundate his nucleus accumbens with desired spurts of dopamine.

Figure 11.1 **Information at the Expense of Experience** TV viewing compromises more direct forms of interaction and human experience.

CASE EXAMPLE: Virtual Sex

A 30-year-old Los Angeles cocaine user reported that he was no longer satisfied having sexual intercourse with "biological units." A career musician, familiar with electronics, he developed a biofeedback contrivance that could register changes in penile erection and transmit the information to an Apple computer. He would mechanically masturbate via an automatic vacuum device, developed to provide sexual stimulation for people who could not masturbate because of spinal injury. The penile biofeedback would program the computer to project increasingly explicit pornographic footage, excerpted from a database of 400 films. The whole experience was augmented by repeated and heavy use of cocaine.

Through this synthetic orgy, he was able to manifest ecstatic states that corresponded to rewarding surges of dopamine delivered to the pleasure centers of his brain.

Source: David Smith, MD, June 1992, personal communication.

In the more mundane world of basic video game attraction, the desire (for some, the compulsion) to play can be explained from a cognitive-behavioral perspective. In terms of operant conditioning (behavioral component), when an action is followed by reward, the probability of that behavior recurring will increase. Video games provide a series of intermittent (variably timed) prizes that are contingent upon positive outcomes (i.e., successful maneuvers are registered via points, lights, noises, and free replays). In terms of addiction, if using an intoxicant results in a deposit of dopamine in the nucleus accumbens (the reward), the behavior will increase in frequency.

In the cognitive domain, fantasies of empowerment may be even more compelling than the rewards associated with skill development and competitive success. The pre-scripted drama of escaping danger and conquering hostile or alien forces is both exciting and compelling. Fears associated with technology, natural disasters, and wars diminish through the fantasy of controlling negative, potentially tragic situations. For example, the wish-fulfilling fantasy of surviving a military invasion or even a nuclear holocaust contributes to the compulsion to play. The 1980s produced such prolific games as *Missile Command* (civilization is defended by using an antiballistic missile system to protect six major cities), *Space Invaders* (where the object is to attack aliens—strange creatures from outer space that threaten our moon base), and *SCRAM* (in which players use their home computers to build and control a nuclear power plant and control a meltdown).

Although there is much pleasure in the fantasy of vanquishing evil, a major disadvantage of video games is that they constrain imagination. Like other "pre-scripted toys," the player is restricted by limited play options. In the simplest form of pre-scripted devices, dolls have been programmed to shoot, cry, burp, or wet (or even talk like Donald Trump!), making it difficult for the child to invent alternatives. Nonetheless, the pre-scripting ploy is beneficial for manufacturers. The initial appeal of the game is high, but boredom and abandonment quickly set in. In short measure, players look for a similar play object, only with a slightly modified script. Therefore, at the onset of the 21st century, we have progressed to the third level of human–media interaction: massively multiplayer online games.

Massively Multiplayer Online Games

In Massively Multiplayer Online Games (MMOGs) the action occurs in common virtual space that permits hundreds of gamers to play simultaneously. Participants can communicate, collaborate and establish relationships (Griffiths, Davies, & Chappell, 2003). The game is perpetual and anyone can connect to virtual worlds at any time (i.e., it is a constant universe) (Safko & Brake, 2009).

Three types of MMOGs predominate; Massively Multiplayer Online Role Playing Games (MMORPGs), Massively Multiplayer Online First Person Shooter (MMOFPS) games, and Massively Multiplayer Online Real-Time Strategy (MMORTS) games (Kuss & Griffiths, 2012). In MMORPGs, the game revolves around the character chosen by the gamers who choose their own cast, thus defining their skills and role in the game. Missions completed allow for chances to improve and to gain valuable objects that differentiate gamers (Shin, 2012). MMOFPS games are usually skill-based action games as they primarily utilize the person's reaction time and attention skills. These games offer many opportunities to compete individually or in teams. In MMORTS games, troops/teams develop their specialty areas with other players to gain high status in the name of an important figure of the virtual world (Rice, 2006).

Massively Multiplayer Online Role-Playing Games: These are developed worlds with intense visual and auditory components (Cole & Griffiths, 2007). Players have the capacity to control the movement of their characters, engage with the environment, network with fellow gamers around the world, and experience new situations that are not possible in real life (Calleja, 2007). Millions of people are attracted to the fulfilling rise of status and power for their character and the authority to create their character or avatar by themselves. Thanks to the progress of third-generation games such as *Second Life* and *World of Warcraft (WoW)*, video and online gamers are increasingly moving from single- and dual-player games to "massively multiplayer" systems where thousands of players can interact simultaneously—just as the acronym says (Bainbridge, 2007).

The increasing popularity of these online games has exceeded the motion picture industry in terms of dollars spent. In 2006, "gamers" forked out $2.1 billion on virtual goods and services (Greenemeier, 2007). People are spending and making real-life money in accordance with their characters' role. According to Greenemeier, hard-core gamers tend to see their virtual property and goods as status symbols; some report feeling social pressure to have a significant amount of money put into these alternative lives. Unlike the popular view, research has shown that most players are not adolescents, but adults (Bainbridge, 2007; Cole & Griffiths, 2007).

Players use online games to create characters through which they feel free to explore new people, objects, and surroundings. The resounding themes of social interaction, working on a team, mastery and manipulation of characters, status building, and exploration are common. According to Bainbridge (2007), "Virtual worlds are creating a very new context in which young people are socialized to group norms, learn intellectual skills, and express their individuality" (p. 475). Not only are these games entertaining, but they are also used for escape and opportunities not found in everyday life (Bessiere, Seay, & Kiesler, 2007). Players may use their avatars (movable three-dimensional images used to represent humans or other conscious beings in cyberspace) to express their ideal selves, or aspects thereof. This enhances a sense of personal power by creating a representation of who they see themselves as or who they would like to be. Gamers are connected to their online persona psychologically, socially, and emotionally. They can use the anonymity of the Internet to manifest wish-fulfilling fantasies and to explore aspects of themselves not available in the real world (Bessiere et al., 2007).

Virtual-world gamers tend to find emotional satisfaction by being able to select environments and life events compatible with desired moods. If a player is missing excitement, the games will create it for him or her. If the player is experiencing too much excitement, the game can be used to calm the self with peaceful imagery and friendly interactions. If a player feels intellectually under stimulated, he or she can find interest in a game's strategic challenges. Similar to addicts who choose drugs that coincide with their natural means of coping (Milkman & Frosch, 1973; Milkman & Sunderwirth, 1983, 1987, 1998), players choose games that correspond with their attitudes and emotional states (Calleja, 2007). Thrill seekers will likely seek out exciting, arousing, action-packed games, while those who relish shutting down may select calming or stress-reducing scenarios.

As evidence of the breakthrough of virtual reality into the mainstream culture, high-profile adult cartoons such as *The Simpsons* and *South Park* have caricatured MMORPG influence. In episode 1817, Lisa Simpson tells her mother, Marge, who has become consumed with a game very similar to *WoW*, "You're like Christopher Columbus. You discovered something millions of people already knew about." Marge finds the online game *Earthland Realms* and spends every waking minute playing it, even staying up all night the first time she is introduced to it.

South Park, on the other hand, really likes to push buttons as it depicts the four main characters, Cartman, Stan, Kyle, and Kenny, becoming so immersed in *WoW* that they stop taking care of themselves. In this Season 10, Episode 8 program (entitled "Make Love, Not Warcraft") the boys become extremely overweight and full of pimples as they no longer feel the need to do anything but play; they eat, consume high-sugar energy drinks, and stay inside on the computer (huddled in Cartman's basement, each at his own computer terminal) rather than going outside to play with their other school friends. In an ironic twist, the show depicts the "creators" of *WoW* sitting in a meeting room, astonished at four newer players who have increased 50 levels in 3 weeks. One exclaims, "Oh my God, they must have no lives at all!" And indeed these four boys have given up everything in order to band together and destroy the man behind the powerful character they are trying to get rid of because he keeps killing everyone. When they succeed, after spending weeks of nonstop playing, by killing the evil character, they wonder what they are to do next. An obese, zit-filled Cartman replies that they can finally play outside because that guy's character will no longer kill them. In another bit of social commentary, the reason why the boys succeed in killing the evil player is because Stan's father, desperate for some interaction with his son, joins the game and sacrifices his avatar to help the boys win their fight.

Some of the top online games include *World of Warcraft, Second Life, Starcraft, Runescape, Halo,* and *Lord of the Rings Online.* Our focus here is on *WoW* and *Second Life* because they are two of the most popular MMORPGs. *Second Life* and *World of Warcraft* have different underlying purposes. *Second Life* avatars are usually depicted as the identities of the humans behind the game, while *WoW* refers to the people playing as surreal warring characters, so the players are slightly more distanced from the game than their *Second Life* counterparts (Bainbridge, 2007).

World of Warcraft

WoW is a game that allows a person to take his or her virtual character on quests, fight monsters, build skills, and interact with other players as well as computer-controlled characters. The rewards from successful quests include in-game money, items, status, and increased levels, which in turn allow the player to become more skilled and powerful. The character can develop noncombat skills in what are known as professions. Professions allow the character to create or enhance items such as weapons. The quests in the game get more complex as the player moves up through the levels, and it takes an increasing number of people teaming up to succeed. By triumphing in a quest, a player is rewarded with goods, gold, experience, or reputation. Reputation, or status as it is called in other areas, is a very important and complex part of the game. Increased reputation allows for price reduction from in-game merchandise vendors, more access to restricted parts of the world, and the ability to purchase special items.

One die-hard *WoW* aficionado explains his attraction to the game this way:

> *World of Warcraft* offers a sort of second reality for me to dwell in. I can band together with others and accomplish great and daring missions, gain friendships, and feel more powerful than I do in everyday life. I think I am so hooked on cyber games because they give me an escape from the lonely aspect of life and I have a place where I can feel welcome no matter what, even wanted, and in this other reality I am powerful. It's great to have a way to unwind at the end of the day and get my mind off whatever is bothering me. I get excited if I know the workday is almost done and I can go home and play for an hour, to settle down. If it's a bad day at work, I might play longer, just to make sure I don't bring the rotten feelings into my relationship.

Second Life

One of the main points of attraction is that this online world is created by the residents. Everything in the *Second Life* "metaverse" is constructed by its inhabitants, and there is always plenty to find and do. A person can shop, play, eat, party, gamble, have sex, and even wed in *Second Life.* There are nightclubs and strip clubs, and many people profit by working in or selling these services such as escorting, prostituting, and stripping. Not only do the residents create the world, but they also create the character they want to be. They can make their avatars realistic and similar to themselves, or they can make them fanciful, changing their gender, ethnicity, and the like. Although most people feel they have found a place that is more accepting and tolerant than in "real life," people still bring their real-life attitudes and biases to the game.

Residents of *Second Life* own the intellectual property inherent in their creations. Players can determine whether the inventions, architecture, or other materials that they conceive of can be copied, modified, or transferred. In accordance with these property rights, residents actively buy, sell, and trade their creations in Linden dollars (the in-world currency), which can be exchanged for real money, that is, real-life currency ("Virtual Online Worlds," 2006).

Boellstorff (2008), an anthropologist, used an ethnographic approach in studying the virtual world of *Second Life*. For 2 years he lived among the residents, participated in everyday activities, and spoke with avatars about their experiences. He found this virtual reality to have subcultures, its own economy, and even its own celebrities. A virtual newspaper would often report on real-life events, or real-life musicians holding virtual concerts. He saw that many people found relationships, friendships, family, and sexual experiences. They were able to experiment with their creativity, sexuality, gender fantasies, and social well-being. Boellstorff found both kindness and cruelty, just as one would find in the real world. He speaks of "griefers," or people who deliberately set out to annoy or harm others. Conversely, altruism was also generously displayed, as he witnessed many acts of sharing or giving away items as well as avatars helping one another with explanatory texts.

Second Life is not merely a game. Its seemingly unlimited capacity engulfs participants in different realities and has enormous potential as an educative tool. Peter Yellowlees (cited in "Virtual Online Worlds," 2006), a professor of psychiatry at the University of California, Davis, has used *Second Life* to create a virtual mental hospital. Psychiatric residents walk through a hospital ward. Suddenly, a picture on the wall flashes the word "shitface." Unexpectedly, the floor morphs into a path of stones above the clouds, and the screen on an in-ward TV changes from a normal political speech to a prominent politician shouting, "Go ahead and kill yourself, you wretch!"

Yellowlees was able to create a window into the mind of a person suffering with schizophrenia, exemplifying the versatility of virtual reality in the realm of education. He leases an island in *Second Life*, for $300 per month, where he built a clinic that is a virtual replica of the one in Sacramento where his students practice. Yellowlees's students are given avatars so they can attend his lectures in *Second Life* and experience the psychiatric symptoms of the disorder that he is presenting ("Virtual Online Worlds," 2006).

Online Game Addiction

As with any substance or action that produces a change in neurochemistry of the brain, the Internet can become addicting. Research has shown that people can lose control of their lives after becoming involved so deeply with games, chat rooms, or even online shopping (Young, 2004). Many online players will skip basic needs such as sleeping and eating, even ignoring work and school so that they can keep playing these games. Young reported that nearly 6% of Internet users have symptoms of addiction, while many more fit the category of abuse.

What distinguishes Internet addiction from drug addiction? If, unrelated to school or work, a person experiences one or more of the following patterns, he or she may be suffering from abuse of or dependence on the Internet, just as if the object were alcohol or any other intoxicant:

- Preoccupied with the Internet
- Using the Internet for increasing periods of time
- Tried unsuccessfully to control or cut back use
- Feel irritable and depressed when attempting to control use
- Staying online longer than planned
- Lying to close people about use
- Using the Internet to escape or cope with problems
- Continuation despite harmful consequences

According to Young (2004), Internet addicts can indulge themselves for 40 to 80 hours per week with sessions running up to 20 hours. Thus, the compulsion to use tends to disrupt sleep, adversely affect work, and impair school performance. Other problems involve lack of proper exercise, poor eating habits, and weakening of the immune system. Some addicts also suffer physical disability due to carpal tunnel syndrome.

Perhaps the most damaging aspect of Internet addiction, however, is the impact it has on relationships (Young, 2004). Long-term relationships can be harmed or even destroyed when a person becomes compulsively involved in a cyber affair. Why would a person go online and cheat on his or her real-life partner with someone the person has never met and most likely never will? It appears that in the virtual world, people can interact with less inhibition and more honesty, revealing themselves more fully and quickly, which in turn leads to an intimacy that might not be achieved for months or years in a real-life relationship. Some indications that a significant other may be pursuing a cyber affair include a change in sleep patterns, the need for privacy with the computer, responsibilities being ignored, getting caught in lies, changes in personality, a loss of interest in sex, and decreased interest in maintaining the relationship.

Internet abuse and addiction is an area of concern across high schools and colleges throughout the United States (Young, 2004). Of course, even if the Internet addict isn't having a cyber affair, it's rather off-putting for their partners, family, and friends when online activities are chosen over spending time with loved ones. There are other negative consequences, as well. According to Young, approximately 58% of the student population may be experiencing some compromise of their school performance due to their use of the Internet. They report poor study habits, failed classes, and lower grades. It is not surprising that a youthful college student can get entrapped, as free and unlimited access to the Internet and computers is the status quo. With students often leaving home for the first time, the newfound freedom can result in excessive online gaming, shopping, and dating.

A third crisis in Internet abuse is related to employees abusing the Internet while at work. According to Young (2004), "employee abuse of the Internet during work hours results in lost productivity, negative publicity, and possible legal liability" (p. 410). About 70% of companies provide access to the Internet, and while 64% of these have taken corrective action against Internet abuse, 30% have actually fired employees for their online activities (Young, 2004). Employers lose billions of dollars annually from on-line misuse. In addition to loss of productivity, companies lose revenue from negative publicity. When a company receives bad press from employee Internet abuse, consumers lose confidence. Finally, under the Americans with Disabilities Act it is illegal to terminate employment when the company itself provides the user with a "virtual intoxicant." Wrongful termination lawsuits are increasingly filed under this pretense as companies are attempting to crack down on the unproductive surfing of the Net during paid time.

According to Cole and Griffiths (2007), excessive online interaction negatively affects social development, lowers self-esteem, makes for social inadequacy, and often creates more social anxiety. The games are socially interactive, but this is at the expense of creating and maintaining social interaction with other real-life humans. Although computer games are available to a great number of players at any one time, only one person needs to be at an isolated computer to partake. Individuals often become obsessed with their virtual selves, seeing them as a true part of themselves at the expense of responsibilities such as school, work, and relationships. People go to *Second Life* and *World of Warcraft* to create an ideal self, to experiment, to sell their creations, even to seek social and emotional interaction (Melby, 2008). Some may believe they are more social than usual because they talk to many people online and reveal more personal things to the other avatars. In reality, being excessively online takes away from face-to-face contact. Gamers often consider their online friends to be better than or as good as their real-life friends.

While men tend to engage in virtual reality to improve their self-perception of higher status and success, women are more apt to prefer the social aspects of these games. More research on pathological computer use is taking place, and such use is now being seen as a problem. In South Korea, for example, there are nearly 50 treatment centers specializing in this area (Mears, 2007).

Internet Addiction: It's Complicated!

Over 20 years have passed since compulsive internet use was first proposed as a behavioral addiction (Young, 1996). Concepts related to this phenomenon continue to emerge, as this is a very active topic of research. Recently, researchers recognized two different types of Internet addiction: Generalized Internet Addiction (GIA) and Specific Internet Addiction (SIA) (Brand, Laier & Young, 2014; Brand, Young, & Laier, 2014). GIA is indicated when a person spends excessive amounts of time on the Internet doing a variety of things, often switching from one site to another, having multiple browser tabs open, and traveling down cyber rabbit holes when they should be spending their time doing other things. SIA is indicated when the individual uses the Internet as a convenient way of accessing stimuli or situations that they are already drawn to and could seek out in other ways. For instance, someone with SIA may already be a compulsive shopper, gambler, gamer, or consumer of pornography; if their Internet access were cut off, they would still be able to access fabulous sales, exciting games of chance, intriguing role playing games, or images of naked people—they would simply have to personally interact with a "supplier" (store clerk, casino employee, etc.) to gain access to their desired activity. Thus, the GIA individual spends way too much time on the Internet simply frittering away their time, whereas the SIA individual's online activities reflect their natural proclivities. IA researchers suggest that this distinction may be helpful in guiding treatment. Like other behavioral addictions, imaging data indicate that pre-frontal cortex circuits are affected (Brand, Young, and Laier, 2014).

Other conditions may co-occur with Internet addiction. For instance, young people with atten-tion-deficit hyperactivity symptoms (even if they don't have an ADHD diagnosis) are more prone to Internet addiction than those without such symptoms (Yoo et al., 2004). Wu and colleagues (2016) report that Internet addiction is linked to depression as well as a lack of social support.

In recent years, there has been a lot of publicity about the problem of Internet addiction in Asia—so much so that we may tend to see this region of the world as having the highest incidence of this problem. However, Cheng & Li (2014) completed a meta-analysis of studies conducted in 31 nations around the world. Overall, they found the global prevalence rate to be about 6%, with the highest prevalence actually occurring in the Middle East (10.9%), rather than Asia (7.1%). Their investigation correlated higher rates of Internet addiction in nations where people reported lower levels of life satisfaction; they also point to the environmental factors of pollution and commute time as being positively correlated with levels of Internet addiction. These data highlight that it's not simply an issue of countries having high levels of computer and Internet availability; environmental and psychological factors are key risks for developing Internet addiction.

Can Someone Die from Internet Addiction?

Consider this North Korean couple as reported in the *New York Times*

SUWON, South Korea—Neither had a job. They were shy and had never dated anyone until they met through an online chat site in 2008. They married, but they knew so little about childbearing that the 25-year-old woman did not know when her baby was due until her water broke.

But in the fantasy world of Internet gaming, they were masters of all they encountered, swashbuck-ling adventurers exploring mythical lands and slaying monsters. Every evening, the couple, Kim Yun-jeong and her husband, Kim Jae-beom, 41, left their one-room apartment for an all-night Internet cafe where they role-played, often until dawn. Each one raised a virtual daughter, who followed them everywhere, and was fed, dressed and cuddled—all with a few clicks of the mouse.

On the morning of Sept. 24 last year, they returned home after a 12-hour game session to find their actual daughter, a 3-month-old named Sa-rang—love in Korean—dead, shriveled with malnutrition.

In South Korea, one of the world's most wired societies, addiction to online games has long been treated as a teenage affliction. But the Kims' case has drawn attention to the growing problem here of Internet game addiction among adults.

South Korea Expands Aid for Internet Addiction, Choe Sang-Hun, New York Times, p.4, May 28, 2010.

Is the Internet Good or Bad?

Internet activity reflects the profound drive toward survival and self-realization present in all humankind. Through identification, imitation, and observational learning, young people are gaining the skills to manage the technology of the future. In response to the criticism of the computer's limited interactional capabilities, as evidenced by such innovations as *World of Warcraft* and *Second Life,* we are witnessing an increased development of software that provides opportunities for chance, paradox, ambiguity, intimacy, and humor. There appears to be no turning back. The line between virtual and actual reality has become so blurred that a clear distinction is no longer possible.

In a special issue of *The Future of Children*[1] entitled *Children and Electronic Media,* Subrahmanyam and Greenfield (2008) explore the question of whether online communication has made teenagers more isolated and emotionally damaged or whether it actually strengthens their social connections. The authors conclude that although we are just in the early days of this type of research, positive effects overshadow the negatives. They find that children and youth primarily use Internet tools to enhance communication with people they already know. In the past few years, even though some children and youth have continued to interact with people that they don't know—in chat rooms, bulletin boards, or online multiplayer games—communication with strangers has declined. Such communication tools, however, should not necessarily be construed as negative. Although the new means for social interaction can provide a platform for bullying and predation, Subrahmanyam and Greenfield dispute the notion that the Internet is the cause of the problem. Rather, the negative behavior is simply being transferred to a new context—from offline to online. In an important sense, the Internet may have become the latest scapegoat for more basic problems in Western culture. As we are so immersed in the new digital age, it is not surprising that juvenescence zealously embraces a symbol that distinguishes it from earlier times. The key challenge is for parents to be knowledgeable and aware of inappropriate Internet involvement and to provide guidance for their children.

Heavily influenced by science, perhaps the most eagerly anticipated video game of all time has come of age. *Spore,* which first appeared on the commercial market in September 2008, was developed by Will Wright, best known as the creator of *The Sims* ("Will Wright on Creating 'The Sims' and 'SimCity,'" 2000), in which players run the lives of a virtual family. *The Sims* is the best-selling video game franchise in history, with sales exceeding $100 million. *Spore* is designed to simulate the process of evolution. Players start with single-cell microbes that can evolve into intelligent, multicellular creatures capable of building civilizations, colonizing the galaxy, and populating new planets (Zimmer, 2008). More recently (2018), Wright unveiled a new game called Proxi, a simulation based around creating an artificial intelligence from your memories and then building a world out of them. *Spore,* possibly the mother of all future video games, may symbolically point to a new branch of the evolutionary tree. In terms of human evolution, it is entirely conceivable that natural selection and mutation may favor humans with the kind of neural networking (i.e., computer-friendly brains) that can thrive in the computer age.

Smartphones: Portable Electronic Addiction Devices

To coin an analogy, smartphones are to cell phones as heroin is to morphine: more potent and more abusable. Indeed, Taneja (2014) indicates that smartphones are more likely to be used excessively compared to basic cell phones.

Table 11.1 highlights some of the specialized lingo associated with smartphone addiction.

Table 11.1 Know Your Phone Addiction Symptoms! (adapted from Taneja, 2014)

Symptom	Translation
Communifaking	Pretending to be on the phone; to look important; or to avoid engaging with others
FOMO	"Fear of missing out," which compels the phone addict to keep their devices with them at all times and frequently check messages, social media, news, etc.
Nomophobia	Fear of no access to one's mobile phone (due to dead battery, poor reception, forgetting or misplacing one's device, or "ridiculous" rules about not using phones in certain settings)
Ringxiety	A form of auditory hallucination where cell users think they hear their phones ringing when they really aren't
Textiphrenia	A form of hallucination where cell users detect a message alert (often a vibration) when there is none
Textiety	Obsessive texting

Students who cannot divorce themselves from their phones during class have become the bane of college instructors. Campbell (2006) reported that both students and college instructors find texting in class to be rude. Excessive smartphone users might see their behavior as "victimless," but the behavior can be quite distracting to their classmates as well as their instructors. Moreover, students tend to overestimate their abilities to parallel process information. Research demonstrates that in-class phone use is associated with lower grades (for two examples of several such studies, see Bjornsen & Archer, 2015, and McDonald, 2013). The dangers of phone use can be greater in other situations, such as driving a car. Most states in the U.S. have laws against texting while driving, although that doesn't seem to stop some people. According to the National Highway Traffic Safety Administration, 13% of all fatal automobile crashes in 2014 involved drivers distracted due to cell phone usage (U.S. Department of Transportation, 2016).

CNN recently reported poll results from Common Sense Media that showed that 50% of teens in the U.S. think they are addicted to their phones (Wallace, 2016). However, smartphone addiction is not limited to the U.S. Below is the case of a Hungarian student who displays numerous symptoms consistent with cell phone addiction (Kormendi et al., 2016).

CASE EXAMPLE: Annette

This 18-year-old business school student was referred into counseling by her mother (with whom she lived); the mother had recently seen a talk about excessive cell phone usage and thought her daughter fit the description. Although Annette recognized that she used her smartphone a lot, she made no plans or efforts to decrease usage. Checking her phone intermittently throughout the day (approximately every 15 minutes), her average weekly usage was estimated to be about 6-7 hours of total time spent using the phone. This usage was primarily texting and social media, although she also used the phone to play music. Annette reported distress if she somehow did not have her phone, stating that she "borrows or steals one from one of her friends" so she doesn't have to be without access. She acknowledged that she chose communicating via her phone over interacting with her friends in person. For example, she described taking a beach holiday with a group of people, but on the trip she actually spent about half of her time in the apartment using her phone rather than hanging out with her friends on the beach. Annette had a fervent desire to make friends, but stated that these friendships didn't last long (often 2–3 weeks) and were typically shallow relationships. Her phone usage seems to be linked to a fear of losing friends if she doesn't engage in frequent contact via her phone. Her therapist considered Annette to have social anxiety, along with mild depression. The therapist also believed there was an underlying fear of intimacy within Annette that was tied to dissatisfying relationships between the young woman and her parents. Her parents had separated many years before, and her relationship with her father was especially shallow. Both parents had histories of depression, and the father had once attempted suicide. Although Annette did not describe phone use as making her feel good, it was an apparent source of negative reinforcement for her: her anxiety would build up, only to be relieved (briefly) by engaging in phone usage. Annette was in counseling for 2 years but never gave up her excessive phone usage.

A review by De-Sola Gutierrez, Rodriguez de Fonseca, F., and Rubio (2016) provides an overview of the smartphone addict. Those with the greatest problems are around 14 years of age. Females are more likely than males to be hooked on their devices, and these young women are using the phones primarily for social connectedness and social approval. A 2013 study (cited by De-Sola Gutierrez et al.) indicates that there is a greater risk of developing excessive cell phone use when one's first phone is obtained prior to age 13. This finding is reminiscent of data linking earlier age of substance usage to higher risks of drug addiction. Takao's 2014 study (also cited by De-Sola Gutierrez et al.) linked personality traits such as extraversion, neuroticism, and low openness to experience with excessive cell phone use. There may be a tendency for people to equate cell phone addiction with Internet addiction, although emerging research suggests that's an overly simplistic view. Internet addiction is more likely to be associated with introversion and depression, whereas cell phone addiction is more commonly associated with anxiety and extraversion. Nevertheless, there are some overlaps among the conditions, such as negative impact on sleep and muscle/joint issues (especially in the hands and wrists).

Special Treatment for Technology-Based Addictions

Treatment offered to people with behavioral addictions linked to computers or cell phones pose different issues compared to people who have substance addiction. It is feasible that an alcoholic or an opioid addict could aspire to total abstinence, but this isn't reasonable for compulsive Internet or smartphone users. These inventions are so fundamental to our lives at this point that the only reasonable goal is to get people to cut down drastically and learn to control their usage.

Dr. Kim Young, who developed the first treatment program for this condition, has developed a specialized form of cognitive-behavioral therapy known as CBT-IA©. She has also trademarked the term "Digital Detox,"™ a component of her program for electronics abusers that requires them to relinquish their devices when they enter treatment. Access to the devices are earned back, and the clients learn to use them as intended—as useful tools to make life more convenient rather than beacons of compulsion.

There are numerous people who seem to have strong attachments to their phones, even if they wouldn't qualify as addicts. Clinicians who treat technology addictions often recommend loved ones take vacations without their electronics and learn to reconnect with one another.

Chapter Summary

This chapter traces the evolution of electronic media from the invention of TV in 1927 through the emergence of interactive video games to the development of massively multiplayer online games at the onset of the 21st century and into the age of the smartphone.

In Massively Multiplayer Online Role-Playing Games (MMORPGs), players create three-dimensional online characters (avatars) with whom they explore new people, objects, and environments. The themes of social interaction, working in a team, mastery and manipulation of characters, status building, and exploration are common. *Second Life* and *World of Warcraft* (*WoW*) are examined as preeminent examples of online role-playing games with different agendas. While *Second Life* avatars are usually realistic manifestations of the humans behind the game, *WoW* involves surrealistic warring characters, thus permitting more emotional distance than that of their *Second Life* counterparts.

From a sociological perspective, virtual worlds are creating a new context in which young people are socialized to group norms, learn intellectual skills, and express their individuality. Not only are these games entertaining, but they are also used for escape and to explore opportunities not found in everyday life. Players may use their avatars to express their ideal selves, or aspects thereof, thus augmenting their sense of personal power. Gamers are connected to their online personas psychologically, socially, and emotionally. They can use the anonymity of the Internet to manifest wish-fulfilling fantasies and to explore aspects of themselves not available in the real world.

The evolution of cell phones to smart-phones allows for even greater access to online activities. Cell phones may have originally seemed like the quintessential modern convenience, allowing us to link to others whenever or wherever we need to—a particularly handy gadget in an emergency. But now cell phones are seen more as necessities rather than luxuries, and the advent of smartphones with mindboggling apps have changed how mobile phones are used. Between Facebook, Instagram, Tinder, newer and newer online apps, smartphones are to cell phones as heroin is to morphine.

Fascination and enthusiasm for online activity morph into abuse and dependence when the medium becomes a vehicle for harmful consequences. Online players may skip basic needs such as sleep and eating, or ignore work and school so that they can keep playing. Nearly 6% of Internet users show patterns of dependence, while many more fit the category of abuse. Symptoms of Internet addiction include, but are not limited to, preoccupation with the Internet, increasing periods of activity, lack of success at cutting back, and continuation despite harmful consequences.

Internet addiction is particularly damaging when virtual relationships substitute for real-life intimacy. Another area of concern is the toll it takes on students who compromise their academic standing as the Internet becomes a pervasive element in their lives. A third crisis involves employees who abuse the Internet while at work.

Has online communication made teenagers more isolated and emotionally damaged, or has it strengthened their social connections? Although we are still in the early days of the Internet revolution, some research suggests that "the positives outweigh the negatives." At its worst, the Internet can have negative effects on social development and self-esteem as well as contribute to social inadequacy and increased levels of social anxiety. On balance, Internet activity reflects the universal drive toward survival and self-realization. It has enormous potential as an "engine of creativity," a tool for enhanced learning. It is conceivable that natural selection may ultimately favor individuals with neural networking designed to thrive in the computer age.

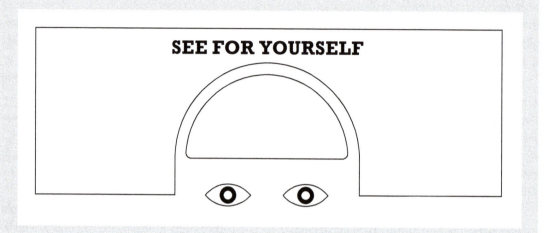

China's Web Junkies: Internet Addiction. 2014. The New York Times Op-Docs. 7:12

This short Op-Doc delves into a residential treatment program for teens thought to be addicted to the Internet in China. **https://youtu.be/jqctG3NnDa0**

Internet-addicted South Korean children sent to digital detox boot camp. 2015. ABC News Australia. 2:04

South Korea reportedly has one of the highest rates of Internet addiction in the world. This brief news clip features a treatment program for Internet addiction where teens engage in social activities at a residential center. **https://youtu.be/YuT_RAugJu0**

What you need to know about internet addiction. 2015. Dr. Kimberly Young. TEDxBuffalo. 17:03

Dr. Kimberly Young is the founder and director of the Center for Internet Addiction Recovery, and launched the first study on internet addiction in 1995. In this talk, Dr. Young discusses various types of Internet addiction, delving into problems people incur when addicted to fantasy experiences such as *Second Life*. She compares treatment plans to combatting overeating—clients are prescribed "digital diets" and learn to manage their "digital nutrition" to moderate Internet use for healthy habits. Dr. Young further discusses the impact of technology use in young children, and what we can do to combat the negative consequences of Internet addiction. **https:// youtu.be/vOSYmLER664**

Note

1. A collaboration of the Woodrow Wilson School of Public and International Affairs at Princeton University and the Brookings Institution.

12

Fantasy and the Drug Experience

Were it not for the motion and color play of the soul, man would suffocate and rot away in his great passion, idleness.

—Carl G. Jung

I went to a place of total aloneness—the you've-got-to-walk-this-valley-by-yourself deep awareness of separation from the universe, and the realization that there really was nothing at all you could hold on to. Fortunately, this state is a hair's-breadth away from the place next to it, in which there was only one thing and I was a part of it.

—James Fadiman, *The Psychedelic Explorer's Guide*

Remember what the dormouse said,
Feed your head, Feed your head

—from "The White Rabbit" by Grace Slick

Figure 12.1 Fantasy and the Drug Experience

Introduction: The "Trip" Begins

When Hernán Cortés entered Mexico in the early 16th century, he found the inhabitants involved in religious ceremonies that included use of psychedelic plants. The Aztecs were especially known for using magic mushrooms (*Psilocybe mexicana*). The Nahuatl (language of the Aztecs) name for the mushrooms was *teonanactl*, which means "flesh of the gods." The inhabitants of Mexico as well as the southwest United States also used the peyote cactus in their religious ceremonies. Mescaline, the active ingredient of the peyote cactus (*Lophophora williamsii*) buttons, was named after the Mescalero Apaches who ingested the buttons as part of their religious ceremonies. Natives of the Amazon River basin have long used ayahuasca ("the spirit vine"), a brew made from hallucinogenic plants, for their rituals.

Some researchers have suggested that humankind's relationship with these mind-altering substances played an important role in the development and evolution of religions (Miller, 2013). To this day, these substances are still used by some practitioners for spiritual purposes. Recently, there has been a resurgence in interest in using these substances for spiritual exploration. Consider that in recent years, hallucinogenic "tourism" has emerged; participants pay hundreds, or possibly thousands, of dollars to experience guided sacred healing ceremonies involving hallucinogenic plants. Many of these experiences are hosted in South America, where use of such substances is legal. However, there are a few places in the U.S. where interested people may partake—although engaging in this activity typically requires a person to join the church which engages in these practices. Years ago, Native American churches were granted exemptions from prosecution for using peyote and hallucinogenic mushrooms for their religious practices, due to the 1st Amendment of the U.S. Constitution.

Psychedelic research began in 1897 when the German chemist Arthur Heffter isolated mescaline, the primary psychoactive compound of the peyote cactus. As noted in Chapter 1, in 1938 the Swiss chemist

Albert Hofmann isolated the active ingredient in LSD (lysergic acid diethylamide) from compounds that he derived from ergot, a fungus that grows on rye grass. Five years after Hofmann created the drug, he accidentally ingested a small amount of the compound and experienced the first recorded "trip" with LSD:

> My surroundings ... transformed themselves in more terrifying ways. Everything in the room spun around, and the familiar objects and pieces of furniture assumed grotesque, threatening forms. They were in continuous motion, animated, as if driven by an inner restlessness. ... Even worse than these demonic transformations of the outer world were the alterations that I perceived in myself, in my inner being. Every exertion of my will, every attempt to put an end to the disintegration of the outer world and the dissolution of my ego, seemed to be wasted effort. A demon had invaded me, had taken possession of my body, mind, and soul. (Hofmann, 1980, p. 12)

In 1958, fifteen years after his fateful "trip," Hofmann was the first to isolate psilocybin and psilocin—the psychoactive components of the Mexican "magic mushroom," *Psilocybe mexicana* (D. J. Brown, 2007).

The modern drug epidemic is thought to have begun when a small group of antiestablishment intellectuals—notably Jack Kerouac, Alan Ginsberg, and William Burroughs—called for a consciousness revolution through the use of what they referred to as "mind expanding" drugs. The natural hallucinogenic compounds derived from mushrooms and cacti were soon displaced by LSD, a synthetic hallucinogen, free of the uncomfortable side effects associated with peyote and magic mushrooms (nausea, discomfort, and dizziness). Beginning in the mid-60s, Timothy Leary became the iconic high priest of LSD, long remembered by his signature phrase, "Turn on, tune in, and drop out." When the Controlled Substances Act of 1970 was passed, hallucinogenic substances—including LSD—were placed at Schedule I, denoting that in the U.S. government's eyes, these substances posed an elevated risk for abuse or dependence and had no accepted medical use. As a result, relatively little research has been done on these substances, especially in the U.S., since the 1970s. However, interest has recently been renewed in hallucinogens as potential therapeutic agents.

> In clinical research settings around the world, renewed investigations are taking place on the use of psychedelic substances for treating illnesses such as addiction, depression, anxiety and posttraumatic stress disorder (PTSD). Since the termination of a period of research from the 1950s to the early 1970s, most psychedelic substances have been classified as "drugs of abuse" with no recognized medical value. However, controlled clinical studies have recently been conducted to assess the basic psychopharmacological properties and therapeutic efficacy of these drugs as adjuncts to existing psychotherapeutic approaches. (Tupper, Wood, Yensen, & Johnson, 2015, p. 1054)

Hallucinogens and the Brain

Hallucinogens are a complex and diverse class of drugs, generally consumed orally. Scientifically, there are two broad classes of hallucinogens: 1) psychedelics, which are further divided into two basic chemical groups, *tryptamines* (e.g., LSD, DMT, and psilocybin) and *phenethylamines* (e.g., mescaline and MDMA), and 2) dissociatives (such as PCP, ketamine, and a few other substances, which are addressed in a later section). In terms of chemical structure, tryptamines have more than one carbon ring, whereas phenethylamines have only one (DuPont & Ford, 2000). The chemical makeup of mescaline, psilocybin, and LSD is similar in structure to our brain's own neurotransmitter, serotonin (Figure 12.2)—which all hallucinogenic drugs share a common capacity to inhibit (DuPont & Ford, 2000).

Because of the structural similarity between LSD and serotonin, it is not surprising that scientists believe that LSD as well as the other plant-derived hallucinogens act on serotonin receptors in three brain regions (Passie et al., 2008). One is the *cerebral cortex*, which is involved in cognition, perception, and mood. The other two are located in the brainstem: the *locus coeruleus*, an area that becomes activated during panic attacks, agoraphobia, and other anxiety disorders (DuPont & Ford, 2000) and the *raphe nuclei*, involved in sensory inhibition and REM sleep (Passie et al., 2008). Notably, most of the brain's serotonin-releasing neurons arise in these brainstem areas, so a substance that affects these regions has the potential to have a large impact on overall brain function. Consciousness is understood as a complex interaction among the cortex, thalamus, and striatum; serotonin-releasing neurons originating in the brainstem project to these regions. The most prevalent theory of the mind-altering and hallucinogenic effects of psychedelics involves disruption of this network by activation of the serotonin 5-HT$_{2A}$ receptors (D. J. Brown, 2007). MDMA (Ecstasy) is also chemically classified as a phenethylamine, and is chemically similar to mescaline; however, its action in the brain is substantially different from the other drugs discussed in this section. In contrast to most psychedelics, MDMA does not directly affect the 5-HT2A receptors; rather, it causes dopamine, serotonin, and norepinephrine to be released from their storage sites in neuron endings and blocks their reuptake (D. J. Brown, 2007; Nichols, 1997; go back to Chapter 10, "Rock Around The Clock" for a refresher on MDMA, if needed).

Figure 12.2 Structure of Serotonin and Selected Hallucinogens Hallucinogenic drugs are much like the neurotransmitter serotonin in their molecular structure as well as where and how they act on the brain.

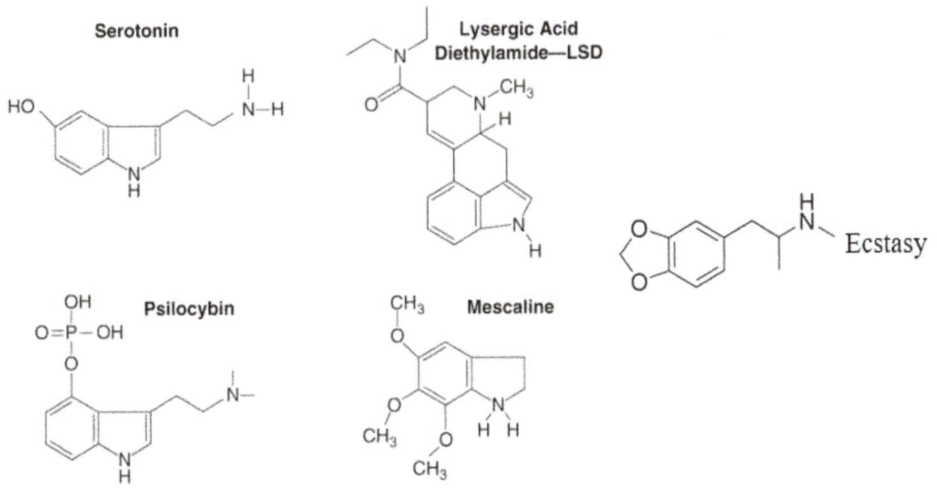

LSD

LSD is a clear or white, odorless, water-soluble material synthesized from lysergic acid, a compound derived from the rye fungus. LSD is initially produced in crystalline form. The pure crystal can be crushed to powder and mixed with binding agents to produce tablets known as microdots or tiny squares of gelatin called "window panes." More commonly, it is dissolved, diluted, and applied to paper or other material (NIDA, 2001). LSD is the most potent mood- and perception-altering drug known; oral doses as small as 30 *micro*grams can produce effects that last 6 to 12 hours. The long-lasting effects of LSD have recently been linked to the drug's ability to bind to serotonin receptors for long periods of time (Wacker, et al., 2017). The effects of hallucinogenic drugs vary greatly from one person to another and within any person, from one episode to another. Moreover, set and setting are important: "set" refers to the person's mindset (expectations for the experience, along with personality traits), and "setting" refers to the environment and context in which the drug is taken (Leary et al., 1963, cited in Hartogsohn, 2016). The most common effects of LSD are perceptual distortions (Figure 12.3).

Figure 12.3 Perceptual Distortions The effects of hallucinogenic drugs vary greatly from one person to another and within any person, from one episode to another. The most common effects of LSD are perceptual distortions.

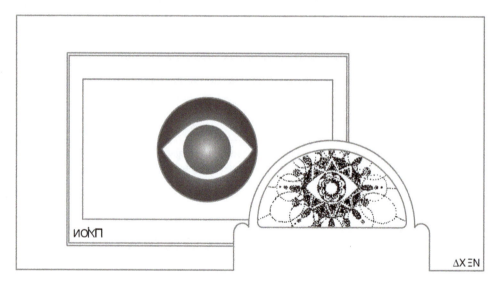

The overall effects of LSD are unpredictable, ranging from euphoria, mania, and creative genius to panic and depression. Objects may lose their boundaries and merge, faces become distorted, stationary objects may seem to move, and perceptions become more salient. Users may attach great significance to previously unattended-to objects or events, and they may perceive reality on multiple levels (for instance, "seeing" individual molecules of an object or "seeing" the entire universe). Users may also experience synesthesia, a mixing of sensory experiences (such as "hearing colors" or "seeing sounds"). The sense of time and normal relatedness is dramatically altered and personal identity seems to become fragmented or lost, thus giving way to mystical experiences or frightening delusions. In 1976, while under the influence of a psychedelic drug, Alex Grey had a vision of Christ ascending in an atomic mushroom cloud looking down at a fiery city. Four years later he painted *Nuclear Crucifixion*, a representation of that vision, which he later interpreted as signifying that "Christ stood for what is good in us, and that the same brutality and ignorance that murdered Jesus could someday be responsible for a nuclear war." (as cited by Grey, 2015). (View image on See for Yourself link).

The experience of LSD is sometimes compared to "watching a theater in the mind." The user may experience being in two mental worlds simultaneously, where bizarre perceptual distortions are witnessed by another part of the psyche that remains anchored in the "real" world. LSD commonly produces such novel perceptional distortions as this one: "My cheeks became gills and suddenly a dorsal fin formed from my spine while my fingers became webbed for surviving in water." Trips commonly include perceptions of floating in a void, moving between planets or clouds, or somehow being able to travel within one's own body (DuPont & Ford, 2000). Figure 12.4 represents the common LSD experience of witnessing two worlds simultaneously. In other words, the man viewing himself in the mirror knows he is "tripping."

Recent imaging data provide a glimpse of what is happening on a global level in the brain while under the influence of hallucinogens. Through the use of psilocybin, activity of the brain's default mode network (DMN) is suppressed. Carhart-Harris and colleagues (2014) describe the DMN, known to be involved in self-awareness and metacognition, as a "central *orchestrator* or *conductor* of global brain function" and note that "psychedelics alter consciousness by *disorganizing* brain activity" (p. 6). Some therapists see this as a way of tapping into the unconscious mind (Grof, 1996). Dating back to some of the earliest research conducted in the 1960s, modern day use of psychedelic drugs became associated with the attainment of spiritual experiences:

> Perhaps the most influential and rigorous of these early studies was the Good Friday experiment, conducted in 1962 by Walter Pahnke, a psychiatrist and minister working on a Ph.D. dissertation under Leary at Harvard. In a double-blind experiment, twenty divinity students received a capsule of white powder right before a Good Friday service at Marsh Chapel, on the Boston University campus; ten contained psilocybin, ten an active placebo (nicotinic acid). Eight of the ten students receiving psilocybin reported a mystical experience, while only one in the control group experienced a feeling of "sacredness" and a "sense of peace." (Telling the subjects apart was not difficult, rendering the double-blind a somewhat hollow conceit: those on the placebo sat sedately in their pews while the others lay down or wandered around the chapel, muttering things like "God is everywhere" and "Oh, the glory!") Pahnke concluded that the experiences of eight who received the psilocybin were "indistinguishable from, if not identical with," the classic mystical experiences reported in the literature by William James, Walter Stace, and others.
>
> – *The Trip Treatment* by Michael Pollan

Repeated or long-term LSD use leads to tolerance, including tolerance to psilocybin and mescaline, because these drugs produce their effects through the same brain mechanism (5-HT$_{2A}$ receptors); this phenomenon is known as cross-tolerance. LSD has been demonstrated to produce rapid tolerance, in that a person taking it daily develops tolerance within 3–4 days. However, if the person stops taking LSD, within just a few days, the tolerance will be lost. This is thought to be a rare occurrence, given that most hallucinogen users do not partake on a daily basis; the full-blown "trip" is intense and rather incapacitating in terms of allowing for normal function, and most people cannot carry out daily responsibilities under these conditions. Repeated use of psychedelics will not produce tolerance to substances such as marijuana and amphetamine, as they do not target serotonin receptors.

Other long-term effects are persistent psychosis and occasional "flashbacks." The psychosis is characterized by distortion of reality as well as the inability to think rationally. Some users experience long-lasting psychotic states including dramatic mood shifts, visual disturbances, and hallucinations, a rare condition that DSM-5 calls Hallucinogen Persisting Perception Disorder (APA, 2013, p. 531).

Despite the tendency to produce rapid tolerance, LSD does not seem to promote development of physical dependence: abrupt discontinuance of usage does not lead to a withdrawal syndrome marked by illness. Addiction to these substances is thought to be rather rare. The greatest risks associated with use are considered to be behavioral—users may have "bad trips" or inadvertently hurt themselves due to perceptual and thought distortions (such as jumping out of a window in the mistaken belief that they can fly). Risk of long-lasting psychotic states may be elevated for those who are at risk for schizophrenia due to family history.

Figure 12.4 Experiencing Two Worlds The experience of LSD is sometimes compared to "watching a theater in the mind."

Is This a Good Idea?

Filmed in the Netherlands, Drugslab is described as an educational YouTube series about drugs. Rens Polman, Nellie Benner, and Bastiaan Rosman, take the drugs viewers with them to try. In the name of science their alleged purpose is to show you what the effect of drugs are on the human body. The project purports to provide information about safe methods of use, safe doses, the effects, the risks, and very useful do's and don'ts when high on drugs. In the episode cited below, the hosts demonstrate the do's and don'ts about taking the powerful, short acting drug, Salvia. Should this information be provided to the public? Is it accurate? What are the dangers?

Nellie is Panicking Because of Salvia. 2017. DrugsLab. 16:10

In this episode, one of the hosts, Nellie, takes Salvia on camera. She and her co-host explain how the drug works in the brain before Nellie takes it and describes her experience.

https://www.youtube.com/watch?v=-GkSyWXWQX8

Dissociative Drugs

Two other mind-altering drugs, PCP (phencyclidine) and ketamine, were originally developed in the 1950s and 1960s to be used in surgery as general anesthetics. They are often referred to as hallucinogenic because they bring about feelings of detachment from reality and distortions of space, sounds, sight, and body image. Because of these effects, which are not true hallucinations, PCP and ketamine are known as "dissociative" rather than hallucinogenic drugs. The dissociative effects can be extreme enough that people feel disconnected from their bodies, as if they are viewing themselves from the outside. Some users feel that they may have travelled to another dimension. People can be very disconnected from reality while under the influence of these substances.

PCP—"Zombie" an Accurate Description

Known by such street names as *zombie, dummy dust, angel dust, boat,* or *peace,* PCP acts on the brain by blocking the NMDA subtype of receptors for the neurotransmitter glutamate. These receptors are involved with the way we perceive pain, as well as in emotion and cognition, which affects our ability to learn and to remember. Users may seem unresponsive to pain and may feel superhuman, allowing them to engage in potentially dangerous physical feats. The effects on glutamate receptors will impair memory for events. The rush from PCP is caused by the increase in the release of the neurotransmitter dopamine into the nucleus accumbens. Generally, these effects are felt within minutes and last several hours or even days. Even after a year of abstinence, the user may experience memory loss and depression. PCP also has effects on other parts of the body besides the brain. These include elevated body temperature, increased heart rate, and dangerous increases in blood pressure.

Ketamine: Looking for the K-Hole

A less violent chemical cousin of PCP is ketamine (used at parties, raves, and music festivals, as discussed earlier in Chapter 10, "Rock Around the Clock"), known on the street as *K.* It was developed in 1963 to replace PCP in surgery and is used in human anesthesia as well as in veterinary medicine (hence its other nickname, *cat valium*). Although its effects are similar to PCP, ketamine's are milder and of shorter duration. It has been used as a "date rape drug." Since it is tasteless and odorless, it can be slipped into drinks to bring about amnesia in its victims. The victim may not remember the resulting sexual assault.

Users of ketamine sometimes state that they are looking for the "K-hole"—the point where they reach the "out-of-body" experience and are generally completely non-functional. Some describe the K-hole as a near-death experience. Although some people find these experiences frightening, others deliberately seek them out with high doses of ketamine.

In comparing the abuse liability of psychedelic hallucinogens to that of dissociative hallucinogens, the dissociatives would rate as the substances posing greater concern about people potentially becoming "hooked" on them. Psychedelics seem to have little impact on the mesolimbic reward pathway, which lowers their reward value. In general, LSD and similar substances do not seem to promote craving or compulsive drug seeking (NIDA, 2016). Further, data show that psychedelics are not self-administered by laboratory animals—with the exception of MDMA. Mice, rats, and some species of non-human primates have been shown to self-administer MDMA (see Fantegrossi, Murnane, and Reissig, 2008, for a review). This should not be surprising, given that MDMA impacts dopamine, whereas LSD does not. It may be that psychedelic substances such as LSD and psilocybin have a rather select appeal to a subset of humans who are interested in mind expanding and mystical experiences. On the other hand, numerous studies have demonstrated that lab animals will self-administer ketamine (for instance, see Venniro, Mutti, & Chiamulera, 2015 or De Luca & Badiani, 2011) and PCP (Campbell, Thompson, & Carroll's 1998 study is an early example). These substances have been shown to have an indirect effect on the dopamine reward pathway, so it is understandable that abuse liability for these substances is higher. Chronic abuse of ketamine has been associated with bladder damage, which may result in blood in the urine and incontinence (Chen et al., 2011).

Given the ability of the Internet to provide far reaching information about the multifactorial nature of psychoactive drugs, it is not surprising that a website (Erowid) has emerged as the go-to reference.

> People who are interested in psychoactive cacti, ketamine, and LSD are generally unfazed by strangeness. Any such person will likely know of Erowid, as will most toxicologists and many E.R. doctors. When the site launched, in 1995, it served as a repository of drug-culture esoterica, drawing just a few hits a day. Today, Erowid contains highly detailed profiles of more than three hundred and fifty psychoactive substances, from caffeine to methamphetamine. Last year, the site had at least seventeen million unique visitors.
> —*The Trip Planners*, Emily Witt, 2015

Dextromethorphan (DXM): Cough Syrup Anyone?

The amount of dextromethorphan found in a single dose of cough syrup is not harmful. However, abuse can occur when taken in higher doses. Use of these substances for recreational purposes occurs mostly in teens and young adults. Carter et al. (2013) gave ascending doses of DXM to healthy, drug-experienced volunteers and found that the effects of DXM change in a dose-dependent manner. At lower (but above therapeutic) doses, effects are more alcohol-like. As doses increase, the effects resemble those of classic hallucinogens, such as LSD or psilocybin. At high doses, it produces effects similar to ketamine and PCP, including distorted perception, dissociative hallucinogenic effects, and memory impairment. This shouldn't be surprising, given that DXM produces its effects the same way that PCP and ketamine do—by blocking NMDA glutamate receptors. As reviewed in Stanciu et al. (2016), there are cases of individuals who develop dependencies, as shown by increased tolerance, cravings, and withdrawal symptoms when use ceases. Therefore, not everyone who uses is simply "Robotripping" at a pharma party.

The risks of DXM are significant. At high doses, it elevates sympathetic nervous system activity, elevating heart rate, blood pressure, and breathing and inducing sweating. Irregular heart rate and fever can ensue. Vision may by blurry and involuntary eye movements (nystagmus) may occur. The person's balance and movements are impaired, along with slurred speech and impaired judgement and cognitive functions. Particularly notable is the "excited delirium" produced at higher doses, consisting of "paranoia, disorientation, aggression, hallucinations, delusions of supra-natural abilities such as flight or telepathy and insensitivity to pain" (Stanciu et al., 2016, pg. 375). Many abusers may experience nausea, vomiting, and diarrhea. In some cases, high doses induce coma. Some of the liver and cardiovascular-related risks linked to Robotripping are tied to other substances besides DXM contained within the syrup, as mentioned in our discussion of adolescent substance trends in Chapter 2, "The Many Faces of Substance Misuse."

When DXM is taken with other substances the risks are increased. When taken with Ecstasy, there is the risk of potentially fatal toxic reactions. Stanciu and Penders (2015, cited by Stanciu et al., 2016) note that some cases of death occurring in emergency rooms related to DXM are due to sudden cardiac or respiratory failure associated with people, brought in by law enforcement, experiencing excited delirium; the use of restraints further escalates the user's extremely elevated "fight-or-flight" (sympathetic nervous system) responses, sometimes with fatal results.

Can Hallucinogens Heal?

Before 1972, there were close to 700 studies that focused on the psychiatric healing properties of psychedelic drugs (Pollan, 2015). The research suggested that the psychedelics could be of significant value in helping alcoholics abstain, soothing anxiety in terminal cancer patients, and reducing symptoms for some difficult-to-treat psychiatric illnesses like obsessive-compulsive disorder (OCD). Grof (1975), for example, in his work with terminal cancer patients, showed that LSD combined with psychotherapy could be of great benefit in fostering peace of mind and inspiring spiritual beliefs.

> The individual comes to realize, through these [perinatal] experiences, that no matter what he does in his life, he cannot escape the inevitable; he will have to leave this world bereft of everything that he has accumulated and achieved and to which he has been emotionally attached. The similarity between birth and death—the startling realization that the beginning of life is the same as its end—is the major philosophical issue that accompanies the perinatal experiences. The other important consequence of the shocking emotional and physical encounter with the phenomenon of death is the opening up of areas of spiritual and religious experiences that appear to be an intrinsic part of the human personality and are independent of the individual's cultural and religious background and programming. In my

experience, everyone who has reached these levels develops convincing insights into the utmost relevance of the spiritual and religious dimensions in the universal scheme of things. Even hard-core materialists, positively oriented scientists, skeptics and cynics, and uncompromising Marxist philosophers suddenly became interested in a spiritual search after they confronted these levels in themselves. (Grof, 1975, pp. 95–96)

Between 1972 and 1990, however, due to the legal backlash against the psychedelic subculture, there were no human studies on the use of psychedelic drugs (D.J. Brown, 2007).

In 1990, things started to change as the FDA began to reopen the doors to psychedelic drug and medical marijuana research. Current studies are under way in the United States, Switzerland, Israel, and Spain that focus on psychedelic treatments for cluster headaches, OCD, severe anxiety in terminal cancer patients, and posttraumatic stress disorder (D. J. Brown, 2007). The beneficial therapeutic effects of the psychedelics are thought to result from activation of the $5HT_{2A}$ receptors, causing the number of these receptors expressed on the surface of neurons to decrease (downregulate). The neurochemical effects of psychedelics somehow change the way subjects perceive pain and distress, thereby producing cognitive changes that evoke new insight—the ability to see the world differently—and thus reducing anxiety and raising the threshold for pain (D. J. Brown, 2007). According to Strassman (2001), who investigated the effects of DMT (dimethyltryptamine) on 60 human subjects, psychedelics may be therapeutic insofar as they elicit mental processes known to be useful in the therapeutic context, including transference, enhanced symbolism, heightened suggestibility, controlled regression, and increased contact between thoughts and emotions. According to Blewett and Chwelos (1959, described by Das et al., 2016), individuals may come to a state of "self-realization," "self-understanding," and "self-acceptance" that helps in the therapeutic process. In the case of treating addiction and psychological conditions such as depression and anxiety, some of the benefits may be related to the spiritual qualities of users' experiences. It is not unusual for people to describe hallucinogenic drug experiences as "life changing" when those experiences include feelings of spiritual connectedness with a higher power (God or the Universe)—as described in the "Good Friday" experiment above. Perhaps it is not surprising that such substances might help people re-evaluate their lives and inspire long-term changes.

Even MDMA and ketamine are being researched for potential therapeutic benefits, despite their reputations as being drugs of abuse. Recent review articles discuss the use of MDMA to treat PTSD (Amoroso, 2015) and potentially substance abuse (Jerome, Schuster, & Yazar-Klosinski, 2013). Ketamine has been shown to produce rapid antidepressant effects (see Zhu et al., 2016 for a review, with an accompanying warning about neurotoxic and cognitive risks). It should be noted that such use is generally conducted during 1 or 2 therapeutic sessions; clinicians are not handing over prescriptions of these substances to be taken on a daily basis as they would with Prozac, Effexor, or other prescription medications. The use of the substance occurs in a directed session with the therapist, who utilizes the traditional notions of "set and setting" with regard to how people react to these substances. Hopefully, use in this manner would avoid the potential for neurotoxic effects that have been demonstrated for MDMA and ketamine.

Can Psychedelic Users Treat Their Own Psychological Issues?

In recent years there has been "buzz" about a practice known as microdosing, which involves taking small doses of a hallucinogen (often LSD) to improve one's sense of well-being, such as alleviating depression or enhancing creativity. The doses taken are *very* low—often 1/10 of a dose that would typically induce hallucinatory experiences—yet they allow the person to feel "different" without being disabled by vivid perceptual distortions. As of yet, there are no peer-reviewed scholarly sources available regarding this practice; nearly all of the information about it is found on the Internet. A January 2017 article from *Business Insider* notes the lack of scientific studies and how what is known about microdosing at this point relies on anecdotal accounts. Dr. James Fadiman, a psychologist and former researcher of psychedelic drugs (who, as an undergraduate, was a protégé of Richard Alpert, a.k.a. Baba Ram Dass) is perhaps considered the best authority on microdosing. Fadiman collects accounts of people who have practiced microdosing, and his 2011 book entitled *The Psychedelic Explorer's Guide: Safe, Therapeutic, and Sacred Journeys,* includes a chapter on the topic. One enthusiast, turned on by Fadiman's book, has written her memoir about her month of microdosing. In the afterword of her account, she writes, "I began this experiment as a search for happiness … I came to realize that happiness, though delightful, was not really the point. The microdose lessened the force of the riptide of negative emotions that so often sweeps me away, and made room in my mind not necessarily for joy, but for insight." (Waldman, 2017, Kindle locations 3548-3350). Of course, without controlled scientific studies, we cannot be certain that the effects experienced by someone like Ayelet Waldman are not a placebo effect. However, she reports having been through years of psychotherapy and a "shit-ton" (her word!) of psychiatric medications without ever finding relief for her mood swings (which had been attributed to Bipolar 2 at one point and Premenstrual Dysphoric Disorder at another). Perhaps in years to come, well-conducted scientific research will be done on the topic. In the meantime, LSD remains an illegal drug to those who choose to microdose, so users should be aware that they are risking potentially harsh penalties for what may or may not be a placebo effect.

Chapter Summary

Plant-derived hallucinogenic drugs have been used by ancient societies for centuries. Many of these societies, such as the Aztecs of Mexico as well as Native American tribes, used mushrooms and peyote cactus buttons in their religious ceremonies to create visions, which they believed enabled them to communicate with their gods. Some researchers have suggested that the evolution of religion is associated with mind altering substances.

LSD was synthesized by Albert Hofmann, a Swiss chemist who experienced the first "acid trip." In 1958, fifteen years after his fateful discovery, Hofmann isolated psilocybin and psilocin—the psychoactive components of the Mexican "magic mushroom." Beginning in the mid-60s, Timothy Leary became the iconic high priest of LSD, long remembered by his signature phrase, "Turn on, tune in, and drop out."

The chemical makeup of mescaline, psilocybin, and LSD is similar in structure to our brain's own neurotransmitter, serotonin, which all hallucinogenic drugs share a common capacity to inhibit. LSD affects the cerebral cortex, raphe nucleus, and locus coeruleus, resulting in short-term effects such as rapid mood changes and overstimulation of sights, sounds, and smells. The most prevalent theory of the mind-altering effects of psychedelics involves disruption of brain networks by activation of 5-HT$_{2A}$ receptors.

The experience of LSD is sometimes compared to "watching a theater in the mind." The user may experience being in two mental worlds simultaneously where bizarre perceptual distortions are witnessed by another part of the psyche that remains anchored in the "real" world. Other mind-altering drugs are PCP (phencyclidine) and ketamine.

Current studies are being conducted in the United States, Switzerland, Israel, and Spain that focus on psychedelic drug treatments for cluster headaches, OCD, severe anxiety in terminal cancer patients, and posttraumatic stress disorder. Psychedelics may be therapeutic to the extent that they elicit mental processes known to be useful in the therapeutic context.

Recently, there has been an upsurge in the non-medical (hence illegal) practice of "microdosing" where users take lesser amounts of a hallucinogen (often LSD). The doses taken are very low—often 1/10 of a dose that would typically induce powerful psychedelic experiences—yet they allow the person to feel "different" without being disabled by vivid perceptual distortions. As of yet there is no scientific evidence on the efficacy or safety of this practice.

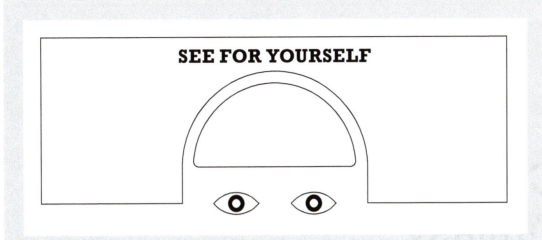

Psychedelics: Lifting the Veil. 2016. Robin Carhart-Harris. TEDx Warwick. 16:25

Dr. Robin Carhart-Harris discusses imaging data relevant to LSD's effects on the brain and the usage of psychedelic drugs to treat intractable depression in this TED talk. **https://www.youtube.com/watch?v=MZIaTaNR3gk**

Magic Mushrooms and the Healing Trip. Sky Dylan-Robbins. *The New Yorker.* 6:59

Impactful video of cancer patient's use of psilocybin to face "existential distress" and the possibility of death. **http://www.newyorker.com/tech/elements/video-magic-mushrooms-healing-trip**

Nuclear Crucifixion by Alex Grey:

https://www.google.com/#q=nuclear+crucifixion

13

Compelled by Fantasy

Our normal waking consciousness, rational consciousness as we call it, is but one special type of consciousness, whilst all about it, parted from it by the filmiest of screens, there lie potential forms of consciousness entirely different.

—William James

Every person should have their escape route planned. I think everyone has an apocalypse fantasy, what will I do in the event of the end of the world ...

—Simon Pegg

Introduction

When imagination is more satisfying than direct action, we find ourselves on a slippery slope. With each experience of pleasure or removal from pain, the probability of seeking out an imaginary solution increases. Our work, love, and play may progressively falter as the result of an increasing reliance on imaginary pleasures. Hence, those who compulsively fantasize may suffer the same perils as their "rushing" (arousal) or "laid back" (satiation) counterparts: compulsion, loss of control, and continuation despite adverse consequences.

This chapter explores how fantasy is often an integral part of extremely harmful behavior, for the individual, his or her family, the community, or even human survival. "Religious addiction" is examined as a destructive preoccupation with religious constructs. The Heaven's Gate cult is discussed as a delusional religious belief system—shared by many—which led to mass suicide. The Columbine massacre demonstrates how innocent lives were sacrificed at the hands of the fantasy-driven behavior shared by two high school misfits. Sadomasochistic sexual fantasy is explored through the eyes of a male homosexual prostitute. Deeper into the vortex of the destructive fantasy is Ted Bundy's confessed addiction to pornography and the connection between fantasy and serial murders. Finally, terrorism is examined in terms of fantasy as a means to allay the devastating anxiety resulting from collision of the will to survive and the immutable fact of death.

Father Leo Booth (1991) first defined religious addiction:

> "I define religious addiction as using God, a church, or a belief system as an escape
> from reality, in an attempt to find or elevate a sense of self-worth or well-being. It is
> using God or religion as a fix. … " (p.33)

According to Vanderheyden (1999): "A person who is religiously addicted chooses consciously or unconsciously to avoid pain and feel good by finding a sense of esteem through rigid faith practices and services within a spiritual setting" (p. 294). The validity of the concept may be questioned as there is a remarkable lack of research on the condition. Oddly, individuals with religious backgrounds seem more apt than psychologists to write about this phenomenon.

Arterburn and Felton (1991) write that religious addiction "intensifies as the abusive behaviors and toxic beliefs provide less and less relief. Addicts get hooked on the false hopes, mood alteration, and ability to distort reality. Those who fall deepest into the addiction deny reality altogether" (p. 103). These authors emphasize the person's sacrifice of their entire lives—families, friends, home, professions, money, sanity, etc.—as the key to religious addiction, which is also characteristic of many individuals who develop substance dependence.

Religious addiction is not recognized in the DSM-5. If diagnosed by a clinician, a person with problematic religious behavior might be labelled with "scrupulosity disorder"—a behavioral condition sometimes considered a subtype of obsessive-compulsive disorder (Abramowitz et al., 2002, cited in Miller & Hedges, 2008). Scrupulosity is marked by obsessive guilt and preoccupation with religious beliefs; the compulsive aspect involves extreme involvement in religious practices, such as prayer, confession, religious services, rituals, feasting, fasting, etc. The behavior eventually becomes maladaptive as it consumes more and more of the person's time and energy and affects their relationships with others. The religious addict may stand in judgment of others (including family and friends) whose behavior conflicts with the religious addict's dogma. They may attempt to convert loved ones and coworkers. They may be so engrossed with their practices that the only way a loved one could gain access to their time would be to join the religious group.

According to Miller and Hedges (2008), somewhere between 5–55% of patients with OCD (about 1% of the population) show symptoms of scrupulosity. If viewed through the lens of OCD, the religious addict's views promote feelings of guilt and accompanying anxiety. The compulsive behaviors (praying, engaging in rituals, etc.) help alleviate these—though only temporarily. Essentially the individual is using fantasy and religious practices to escape from negative psychological states, whereas someone with a drug addiction would use a substance.

Booth (1998) considers one of the primary characteristics of religious addiction to be abuse. Spiritual leaders are in a position to abuse their followers in a variety of ways (psychologically, physically, and financially). The addict's behavior can be controlled by the leader, the church organization, and the doctrine. This could involve controlling a person's relationships, including their sexual relationships and behavior.

Followers tend to yield their thinking to the leader and the doctrine, relinquishing control over their own lives. Just as a drug may damage a person's body and mind, a religious leader or organization can damage an obsessed follower. While there is a tendency to speak of religious addiction as an affliction of the followers, Vanderheyden (1999) suggests that the leaders themselves may be addicts as well. Regardless of whether the addict is the leader or a follower, the writings of Booth (1998), Vanderheyden (1999), Arterburn and Felton (1991), and Taylor (2002) make it clear that religious addiction is not confined to "cults," the label that has been applied to groups such as Heaven's Gate. Nor is religious behavior indicative of addiction. While many people are spiritual, most are not consumed by their spirituality. Multitudes drink alcohol but are not alcoholic!

One could review the DSM criteria for substance use disorders and note symptoms that seem to apply to those whose lives revolve around religion in a maladaptive way: increasing time spent engaging in use (such as attending services multiple times per week); being consumed by activities within the organization (e.g., moving into communal housing, etc.); negative consequences (which could be physical, social, financial, or vocational); withdrawal (feeling dysphoric when not with the group or engaged in religious activities); and craving (urge to participate in activities).

Shared Delusions

Fantasy may become integrated with the lives of those around us and form a symbiotic system in which the parties involved reap mutual benefit from a shared alteration of reality—separate from traditional forms of religious or spiritual dogma. The French term *folie à deux* (a madness shared by two) describes a rare psychiatric syndrome in which a symptom of psychosis (particularly a paranoid or delusional belief) is transmitted from one individual to another. The same syndrome shared by more than two people may be called *folie à trois, folie à quatre, folie à famille,* or even *folie à plusieurs* (madness of many). Some psychiatric classifications refer to the syndrome as a "shared psychotic disorder" (American Psychiatric Association, 2000). Periodically certain groups profess belief in a metaphysical force calling them to commit mass suicide or homicide or both. From a psychiatric standpoint, this may be referred to a shared delusional disorder. The example of Heaven's Gate shows how idiosyncratic, bizarre, and compelling group fantasies can become (Bearak, 1997).

Heaven's Gate: Shared Delusion Guides Group Suicide

Heaven's Gate, a religious group begun in the 1970s, believed that the earth was about to be "recycled" (wiped clean) and that the only hope for survival was to leave immediately via suicide. These individuals lived within the Rancho Santa Fe mansion, had cut off nearly all ties with family and outsiders, and worked solely for the purpose of the group (either doing website design to raise money to pay the Rancho Santa Fe rent or doing work within the commune to make meals, maintain the commune, etc.).

Those who joined Heaven's Gate were "all in" for their cause: education, professions, and relationships outside of the group were no longer a possibility as long as they stayed. Sexual relationships, even within the group, were forbidden. Outsiders would likely argue that castration as a way of helping control sexual urges is a rather large sacrifice, topped only by the final sacrifice of "exiting their vehicles" (which to outsiders, clearly seems like death rather than "graduating" from their earthly classroom). In preparing to ascend to The Evolutionary Level Above Human, the students had to get away from all earthly "addictions," such as sex, substances, wealth, etc.

The group believed that one of the paths to survival before "recycling" was through extreme hatred of this world and by using their "human" bodies as "vessels" designed to help them on their journey. The death scene included corpses of 21 women and 18 men. Most were found with small pieces of paper containing the suicide recipe: "Take pudding or applesauce and mix it with phenobarbital, drink it down and relax." In preparing to kill themselves, members drank citrus juices to ritually cleanse their bodies of impurities. In accordance with their "prescription," the suicide was accomplished by ingestion of phenobarbital mixed with vodka. Plastic bags were secured around their heads to induce asphyxiation. Members were found lying neatly in their bunks, their faces and torsos covered by a square, purple cloth. Each carried a $5 bill and three quarters in his or her pocket. All 39 were found with their hair closely cropped, dressed in identical black shirts and sweat pants, brand new black-and-white Nike "Cortez" athletic shoes, and armband patches reading "Heaven's Gate Away Team." The suicides were conducted in shifts, and the remaining members of the group cleaned up after each prior group's death.

Shortly after the suicide/exit of Heaven's Gate members, the *Los Angeles Times* printed an article which included information from an interview with the ex-husband of Judith Rowland, who eventually adopted the name "Jwnody" within Heaven's Gate. Judith was an early follower of Ti and Do, at a time when they were using the monikers "Bo" and "Peep" and calling their group Human Individual Metamorphosis ("HIM"). She was introduced to them by her mother and left to travel the country seeking converts for the group in 1975. The note to her husband at the time she abandoned him and their two children stated that she was ill with cancer and expected to only live for a couple of months. Leaving was explained as sparing him and the children from the stress of her impending death. A month later, Judith sent another letter, telling her husband she didn't love him anymore and that he needed to move on. In part, the letter said, "I am doing the 'FATHERS' work. I have given Him my life and in return he has given me mine... My love is the FATHER now" (Kelley & Wilson, 1997). Judith's ex-husband recalled that before leaving home, she was moody and depressed. In letters sent to friends months after she left home, Judith (then going by "Fleece") wrote reverently about Bo and Peep. Apparently, the two, their belief system, and their way of life fulfilled Judith's emotional needs. Why else would she stay with them for 22 years and "exit" with Do and the others?

Jwnody, considered one of the intellectual leaders in the group, wrote a number of essays addressing their belief system, how others may see them, and how they saw others. Neither Do nor his followers were oblivious to the fact that outsiders ascribed the word "cult" to their group. As quoted by Zeller (2014) Jwnody wrote: "Just who are the real occultists? Where are there more meaningless rituals performed than in the church, e.g., baptism, burial ceremonies, marriage ceremonies, genuflection, crossing oneself, kissing the Father's ring...? And who, in reality, are the number one promoters of idolatry?" (Kindle location 1608). Although this criticism was lodged at Christianity, the group was critical of other belief systems as well. Fellow "student" Stmody wrote, "But Buddha's message ... is mainly ritual and myth that keep people sidetracked, hooked on the 'drug' of spirituality" (Zeller, 2014, Kindle location 1614). By pointing the finger at people of other beliefs as being "hooked," members of Heaven's Gate seem to have been denying that their behavior and beliefs fit within the same mold.

We might legitimately ask: What is going on neurologically within a religious devotee? Once again, the answer may be dopamine! In a neuroimaging study, Ferguson and colleagues (2016) did brain scans on devout religious believers (young adult Mormons who had done 1.5–2 years of missionary work). During the scan, the participants were exposed to religious and non-religious stimuli. The religious stimuli, such as scriptures and quotes, were such that the participants later reported that when inside of the scanner, they were "feeling the spirit." The results show that, compared to non-religious stimuli, images that evoked spiritual feelings activated the nucleus accumbens (the reward center), along with the prefrontal cortex (which attends to rewarding stimuli). Interestingly, Ferguson and colleagues cite data from Comings et al. (2000), who have linked dopamine receptor polymorphisms to spiritual transcendence. Perhaps the religious addict and the drug addict have related patterns of brain activation, supporting the notion that "gods" can serve as drugs.

Besides a lack of research on the topic of religious addiction, there's little public discussion of this concept as well. Given the First Amendment of the U.S. Constitution guarantees freedom of religion, this is a sensitive issue in the U.S. Religious beliefs may be so central to a person's identity that many people may deem them "off limits" for criticism. As a result, the concept of religious addiction may remain controversial.

What Do You Think?

If a person is a religious addict, what are they "hooked" on? Is it the religious leader, the other members of the group, the belief system itself, or the whole package?

Reb and VoDKa

Unfortunately, suicide is but one violent outcome of collaborative fantasy. The infamous team of Eric Harris and Dylan Klebold (aka Reb and VoDKa) unveiled the horrendous power of fantasy to affect innocent lives. Together they annihilated 12 classmates and a teacher as well as killing themselves. In the aftermath of the Columbine shootings, investigators put together a retrospective formulation of how and why the event occurred. Shockingly, the pair had been planning the attack for at least a year, as indicated by Harris's signature in Klebold's yearbook from their junior year as well as entries in Harris's journal. These statements were relatively vague at first, but over the months that followed, plans emerged that encompassed even the minutest details of the event, including what they would be wearing. Fantasies about using explosives gave way to building them; desires for weapons progressed to acquiring and practicing with them. As devastating as the attack was, Harris and Klebold had aspired to much greater devastation— blowing up the school—but, fortunately, their large bombs failed to explode. The FBI ultimately deemed the assault on Columbine a terrorist attack, intended to be more devastating than the Oklahoma City bombing (Cullen, 2009). From a fantasy perspective, this was their own personal apocalypse.

Duggan, Shear, and Fisher (1999) described the boys as "bright young men who became social outcasts at their suburban Denver high school, and then built their own internal society by plucking strands from the pop whirlwind of cyberspace and fantasy games, the sound track of American youth and the netherworld that glamorizes Nazi symbols and terrorist violence" (p. A1). Harris was a fan of the video game *Doom*, and using special software he created new levels filled with monsters to be killed, which he distributed on the Internet using an AOL Web site.

Klebold and Harris left behind a trail of fantasy productions that in hindsight were solid clues to the horrific event. These included writing death poetry for their English class, making a video entitled 'Hit Men for Hire' featuring hateful threats and depictions of gun violence towards people who oppress others, and shouting murderous slogans that were posted on the AOL Web site. Harris's ramblings on his AOL member profile provide a glimpse into the mind-set of the killers: "Man has ruled this world as a stumbling, demented child king long enough. … As his empire crumbles, my precious black widow shall rise as his most fitting successor" (Duggan et al., 1999, p. A1).

Most people will say that anyone who perpetrates such an attack must be mentally disturbed. From a biochemical perspective, we might speculate that neurochemical imbalances may have played a role: serotonin dysregulation has been linked to both interpersonal violence and suicidal behavior (Rosell & Siever, 2015). When he died, Harris had Luvox (an SSRI antidepressant) in his system—a prescription he had been on for over a year–in his system. After Harris's death, FBI profilers argued that he was a psychopath (Cullen, 2005). Klebold was posthumously diagnosed as depressed, although he never was diagnosed as such during life. The journal he left behind spoke of wanting to die, and a bottle of St. John's wort (an herbal remedy purported to treat depression) was found in his room after he died (Klebold, 2009). Seemingly, Harris was hell-bent on killing massive numbers of people and was willing to die to accomplish this mission; on the other hand, Klebold was suicidal and willing to kill people in pursuit of his own death.

From a psychological perspective, wish-fulfilling fantasies of ultimate power—their journals alluded to being "god-like" with their final actions—merged with a hateful disdain for people in general and a perceived justification for "sweet" revenge; these fantasies were strengthened through ongoing validation and approval from each other. Their friendship was so close and insular that they linked their home computers into a mini network. Mutual support for perpetrating violence, admiration of Hitler, and use of technology to broadcast dark intensions (e.g., how to build pipe bombs) were repeatedly played out in fantasy scripts. These mental "intoxicants" served to compensate for profound feelings of insecurity, lack of intimacy, and intense anger. Eventually, the months of ardent fantasy gave way to acting out the plan, which in their minds was their ultimate reward.

Facilitator-Assisted Fantasy

Case material from a self-referred client whom we shall call Bill illustrates how sadomasochistic sexual fantasies can be facilitator assisted. At the age of 30, Bill made a living as a male prostitute whose clientele mostly included middle-aged homosexual men. Bill was often contracted to act out various sexual fantasies. Most of the staged scenarios involved some form of make-believe domination of the client. Bill describes his relationship with his primary repeat client, followed by his overall perspective on the type of relationships he has had with other customers.

CASE EXAMPLE: Facilitator-Assisted Fantasy

The primary repeat client with whom I deal has a very interesting fantasy in which he is symbolically powerful and powerless, super-stud and super-slut, lady of great refinement, and common slut. The evening starts out with him in a supra-masculine, Nazi, black leather motorcycle type outfit. He is a physically imposing and very handsome man and one would expect him to be quite dominant in sex (inserter) or play (master, whipper, etc.). However, this is only a preliminary posturing … [W]hen he makes contact, visual, verbal, or physical, with a potential playmate, he immediately switches to a very feminine role. He becomes a refined lady who wants to be used and abused; to be whipped on his "pussy" (his anus) … to have clamps put on his shaved "titties."

He has done this frequently, while being restrained in stocks or slings in front of a large public audience (30–100 people) or at an S&M bar. In the privacy of my bedroom he likes to change into full female undergarments and beg me to fuck his "pussy." I find myself unable to be aroused by either his fantasy or his submission and so I talk dirty, make up fantasies for him and bring him to a climax with my hand on his "clitoris" (penis) and a vibrator in his anus.

Other typical fantasies also center on sexual domination. The clients almost always (more than 90%) want to feel as though I want to "use" them to get off (climax or not, but I have to be apparently desirous of the contact and the "use" of them). They may want me to be the hot young stud in which case I "talk high school" and dominate or they may want me to be 25–30, in which case I develop scenes with older men for them to visualize while I dominate them sexually. Some also want me to be the helpless boy-stud that they take advantage of. So they are the oppressor; but even when they are the aggressor and nominally dominant, they give me the control almost always because the whole point for them is to succeed in giving *me* pleasure.

In addition to prostitution, Bill conducted a lucrative "phone sex" business where he received credit card payments for acting out sexual fantasies. Phone sex is commonly advertised on late-night TV and in local newspapers. Internet porn sites feature webcam access to interactive sexual fantasy. Similar to how drug dealers cater to the pharmaceutical needs and whims of a steady drug-using clientele, phone and Internet sex dealers dispense fantasy. Interestingly, a popular fantasy script for Bill and other operators is usually a run of sexy verbiage with a general theme of the caller being dominated. One man, for example, enjoys having his operator describe a scenario where he is diapered and repeatedly spanked. Like drugs, phone sex can provide temporary relief from loneliness, anxiety, and fear.

The fantasy of being punished for one's wrongdoing, while at the same time being attended to and sexually desired, is wish-fulfilling for the consumer. For Bill, the short-term psychological payoff of acting out his own sexual and interpersonal wishes, while earning money for self-maintenance, outweighed considerations of personal risk or legal culpability. In the years that followed, Bill was diagnosed as HIV positive.

Violent Sexual Fantasy and Serial Murder

That a vicious killer has an addiction to violence seems like some sort of an "excuse" to diminish the vileness of their deeds. However, at least in some cases, this concept may provide insight into unimaginable criminal actions.

Consider the case of Ted Bundy, the "poster boy" of U.S. serial killers. Bundy is believed to have killed at least 35 young women and girls in the 1970s. In his final interview (the night before his execution by electrocution in Florida), Bundy explained that he initially had a pornography addiction, which progressed to an addiction to violent pornography. Eventually, the porn was no longer satisfying, and he felt compelled to act on these fantasies. So, he progressed to stalking, assault, and ultimately murder. This description seems to fit with the phenomenon of tolerance, as does the escalation in the rate of killing. Occasionally, Bundy would "binge" by killing more than one person on a given occasion. In between kills, an anxious state, akin to withdrawal, would develop, along with a craving to repeat the behavior. In his final interview, Bundy stated:

> "...once you become addicted to it—and I look at this as a kind of addiction—like other kinds of addiction—I would keep looking for more potent, more explicit, more graphic kinds of material. Like an addiction, you keep craving something which is harder, harder, something which gives you a greater sense of excitement, until you reach the point where the pornography only goes so far. You've reached that jumping off point where you start to wonder if maybe actually doing it will give you that which is beyond just reading about it or looking at it."

Skeptics may rightfully point out that Bundy's words should be taken with a grain of salt, given that the man fit the criteria of "psychopath" (see Hare's Psychopathy Checklist), although this designation is not included in the DSM-5. Instead, Bundy likely would have been diagnosed with Antisocial Personality Disorder (Samuel & Widiger, 2007), a condition recognized by the American Psychiatric Association in the DSM. Frequently, "psychopath" and "antisocial personality" are conflated, which is understandable given overlap of some of the traits. While not all antisocial personalities are psychopaths, most psychopaths would qualify as antisocial (psychopaths are considered to be devoid of empathy, while antisocials, who are not psychopaths, are often capable of empathy for their victims and remorse regarding their criminal actions).

Antisocial individuals can be very manipulative, charming, and deceptive. Critics of Bundy's claim to having been addicted often argue that he tried to "buy time" towards the end of his life by offering confessions to more murders (although this approach did not result in a stay of execution as he likely hoped). On the other hand, one could play the devil's advocate by noting that the "compulsion" to engage in murder described by Bundy is not unique to him. Other serial killers have described their desires in a manner that fits the notion of craving, and statements made about how killing made them feel indicate that they found killing to be their greatest—and possibly their only—source of pleasure.

The notion that sexual serial killing resembles an addiction and is linked to pornography addiction that predates the escalation of the behavior to assault and murder has been previously noted (Leyton, 1988, cited in G.T. Blanchard, 1995). The addictive behavior progresses through phases of voyeurism, then rape, then murder (Hickey, 1991, cited in G.T. Blanchard, 1995). To elaborate:

> At all levels of sexual addiction, a self-loathing exists. The increasing mood alteration provided by criminal excitement and risk propel the offender to newer and more intense sex crimes that serve as an escape from his chronic dysphoria. For the sexually addicted lust murderer, a snowball effect develops in which there is no limit to the forms of violence that may unfold. (G.T. Blanchard, 1995, p. 63)

This sort of addict is compelled by both fantasy and excitement motivations. Ultimately, the act of killing, more so than the sexual assault that accompanies it, becomes the source of pleasure that overshadows other possible rewards. The killer discovers that holding the ultimate power over another individual is pleasurable to them.

Many serial predators can carry on "normal" lives while keeping their behavioral addiction a secret. Carlisle (2014), a clinical psychologist who spent over 20 hours interviewing Bundy, emphasizes that fantasy, dissociation, and compartmentalization were key for the Jekyll-and-Hyde type of behavior demonstrated by Bundy. The dissociation and compartmentalization help the person engage in the behavior, whereas the fantasy fuels it. Eventually, the lines between fantasy and reality break down—it's not that the serial killer fails at "reality checking" the way that someone with schizophrenia would. Rather, the predator needs to make fantasy become reality because the fantasy by itself is no longer satisfying. Having antisocial or psychopathic traits may make it easier to cross the line from fantasizing about rape and murder to perpetrating it: lack of empathy, disregard for social rules, and a lack of concern about others is part of the psychological package of psychopathic personalities.

Besides co-occurring personality disorders, several well-studied serial killers, including Ted Bundy, John Wayne Gacy, and Jeffrey Dahmer, had alcohol abuse issues. Instead of viewing their alcohol abuse as simply a comorbid condition, however, it provided a release of inhibition, making it easier for these individuals to kill by impairing their impulse control. There is also an overlap of risk factors for both substance abuse and Antisocial Personality Disorder, including childhood trauma, depression, and attachment issues (G.T. Blanchard, 1995). Perhaps the common risk factors "prime" individuals for potential pathology, and the reliance on fantasy as a means of escape and excitement guides the direction of the compulsive behavior.

The average person looks at the behavior of Bundy and thinks "that guy couldn't have been 'right' in the head!" A review by D. Smith and colleagues (2016) summarizes the findings of several neuroimaging studies which support that view. One brain difference is poor prefrontal cortex function in violent antisocial individuals. You may recall from discussions in previous chapters that the prefrontal cortex is also impaired in those with substance abuse issues. According to data reviewed by Smith et al. (Table 13.1), impairment in prefrontal function is even greater in the antisocial individuals than those with drug abuse.

Table 13.1 The Results of Damage to Certain Areas of the Brain Found By Neuroimaging

Modality	Findings
MRI	Individuals with APD had more violent crimes and reduced pre-frontal gray matter compared to drug dependent, psychiatric and healthy controls
SPECT	Decreased prefrontal activity in adolescents and adults who attacked others and destroyed property
SPECT	Patients with dementia had decreased blood flow to the frontal lobes
PET	Forensic psychiatric patients with violent behaviour had decreased frontal cortical blood flow or metabolism compared with controls
CT	Veterans with prefrontal injury had increased violent activity compared with non-frontal lobe head injury

Abbreviations: CT (computed tomography); PET (positive emission tomography); SPECT (single photon emission computed tomography)
Table adapted from: Smith et al., 2016, pg. 582.

Interestingly, the neurotransmitter serotonin has been linked to aggression (both homicidal and suicidal). Low levels of serotonin are associated not only with violent behavior, but also depression, anxiety, eating disorders, and numerous addictions. However, lest we assume we can "cure" someone addicted to violent behavior by simply giving them Prozac, we should give careful consideration to other risk factors that helped contribute to this destructive behavior.

Other neurochemical balances may exist in these offenders. Perhaps it should not surprise us that researchers have also linked psychopathy to dopamine dysregulation (see Yildirim & Derksen, 2015, for a review). The compulsive behavior, impulse control issues, and differential sensitivities to reward and punishment seem to be linked to dopamine dysfunction.

Finally, it is notable that the behavior of serial killers seems analogous to many symptoms associated with substance use disorders, as described by the DSM-5. We've already alluded to tolerance, withdrawal, and craving. But consider that someone like Bundy would also spend excessive time obtaining, using, or recovering from use (think of the time spent trolling for and acquiring victims, engaging in the violent acts, discarding of the bodies, and time spent revisiting deceased victims), decreased time spent doing other things, and failure to meet obligations. During one point in his "career" as a killer, Bundy was enrolled in law school, but he had lost such control over his killing that he was not spending much time in classes (Fagg, 1989). His dangerous behavior would also seem to fit the criterion of repeated use in hazardous situations, given the risk posed by abducting women in public places. Rationalizations for addictive behavior are not part of DSM diagnostic criteria, but they are commonly seen among substance abusers. Similarly, Bundy had his excuses for taking the lives of others. He saw the women he took as objects, rather than people, and sometimes objects get stolen. One of the most chilling statements he made in an interview was "What's one less person on the face of the earth anyway?" (Michaud & Aynesworth, 1999, Kindle location 5986)

The Terrorist Mind-Set

> Man's socio-genetic evolution is about to reach a crisis in the full sense of the word, a crossroads offering one path to fatality, and one to recovery and further growth. Artful perverter of joy and keen exploiter of strength, man is the animal that has learned to survive "in a fashion," to multiply without food for the multitudes, to grow up healthy without reaching personal maturity, to live well but without purpose, to invent ingeniously without aim, and to kill grandiosely without need. (Erikson, 1964, p. 227)

As discussed in Chapter 11, Internet access allows for widespread availability of fantasy experiences that may be shared by two, three, or even hundreds of people. In this section, we discuss the use of fantasy by terrorists as a primary means to cope with harsh realities of abject poverty and social inequity. In fact, by providing scripted images of the martyr's glory, in heaven and on earth, the Internet has become a major recruitment tool for terrorists around the globe. The World Trade Center and Pentagon attacks of 2001, the Madrid bombings of 2004, and the London suicide bombings of 2005—all of these incidents were carried out by individuals considered to be terrorists. What is their psychological makeup?

Thoughts of genocide by suicide provide comfort to those who subjectively experience inexorable psychological pain. Ideas of death leading to martyrdom are strengthened by images of glory and reprieve from misery. When wish-fulfilling suicidal fantasy (religious piety, defeat of the enemy, and reward in the afterlife) becomes primary for a particular ethnic group, violence can occur on an enormous scale.

Is terrorism a kind of *folie à plusieurs*, where legions of mentally disordered people are attracted by the magnetic effect of a "war of terror"? Not likely. Unlike schizophrenia, the majority of terrorists do not suffer from biological aberrations characteristic of severe mental disorder. According to Goertzel (2002), "Terrorists think rationally, but they think within the limits of belief systems that may be irrational" (p. 98). They have strongly held beliefs that they defend with great emotional fervor. Terrorists do not see their actions as a means of war against a particular nation or ethnic group; rather, they see themselves as fighters of freedom who are protecting their religion (Goertzel, 2002; Harris, 2002).

Ferracuti (1982) highlights the importance of fantasy in the terrorist mind:

> Terrorism … is fantasy war, real only in the mind of the terrorist. Fantasy war, of course, is only partial war, real for only one of the contestants who then adopts war values, norms, and behaviors against another, generally larger group, trying to solve through strength a conflict based on legitimate or illegitimate grievances. (p. 137)

Some of the hypocrisies of these fantasy wars include claiming the power of life and death over non-combat citizens and engaging in criminal activities while declaring their lawfulness. Terrorists perceive themselves as different from and superior to others because they belong to a group with intense ideological, cultural, and political beliefs. They view terrorist actions as a revolutionary struggle of the oppressed (Harris, 2002). Their enemies are dehumanized as mere props, in that they are perceived as not having independent wills and thoughts. According to Harris (2002), rehabilitation from terrorist ideology would require an immense mental adjustment. The objects of attack need to be transformed back into real people with real feelings and wills. When surrounded with others that hold similar views, fanatical ideas become validated and more likely to become firmly held beliefs. Harris claims that history abounds with people unable to see themselves as others see them, unable to recognize the horror they are causing others.

In the mind of the terrorist, martyrdom is the ultimate reward for acting on fanatical beliefs. Harris (2002) states that, by attacking the World Trade Center, the collective fantasy of radical Islam was brought to life. There could be no better proof that God was on the side of radical Islam and that the end of the reign of the Great Satan (America) was at hand. A small group of devout Muslims, men whose wills were absolutely pure, as proven by their martyrdom, brought down the mighty towers created by the Great Satan. Suicide to the radical Islamist is not a means to an end but an end in itself, as it leads to martyrdom. Martyrdom for the terrorist consists of transcendent glory, magical powers, and the infamous 72 virgins who will greet them when they arrive in heaven.

Sociocultural Origins of Terrorism

How are the radical viewpoints of fundamentalist religion propagated? Fundamentalist beliefs (based upon religious scriptures that reveal the supernatural as the literal truth of God's message) can be described (as can other human traits, e.g., intelligence) by a distribution ranging from least rigid and open-minded to the most exclusionary and dogmatic. Through religious schools, terrorist media, and even conversation on the street, the absolute ideologies of radical Islam or a myriad of other "radical" ideologies, are spread to children who would otherwise lack opportunities for schooling, jobs, or obvious future direction (Harris, 2002). In some quarters, religious training promotes an institutionalized view that suicide and mass murder followed by paradise is a plausible solution, fulfilling the need for escape from earthly hopelessness and ego annihilation.

> In the many circles of hell that exist for young men in Pakistan, the lowest is found at Dabaray Ghara, on the outskirts of Peshawar. It is an expanse of pits, dug out of the sunbaked earth, in which several thousand men, mostly refugees from Afghanistan, make bricks. It is the hardest of labor because it takes place outdoors, no matter how hot or cold, pays next to nothing and is literally backbreaking.
>
> You see children as young as 4 or 5 in the pits, except they are not playing. They are making bricks. ... Bakhtiar Kahn began working in the pits when he was 10. He is now 25 or 26. He isn't sure, because nobody keeps close track; time passes, that is all. He works from 5 in the morning until 5 in the afternoon, making 1,000 bricks a day, six days a week, earning a few dollars a week. He is thin, he wears no shirt or shoes and he cannot believe that a foreigner is asking about his life. ... "Life is cruel," he says [w]hich is not unusual and helps explain why Peshawar's youth are tinder for Islamic extremism. (Maass, 2001, p. 48)

Based on interviews with scores of religious zealots including the Bajrang Dal in India, the Jewish Underground in Israel, Hamas in Palestine, and violent fundamentalist Christians in the United States, Stern (2004) describes the sociocultural roots of terrorism:

> My interviews suggest that people join religious terrorist groups partly to transform themselves and to simplify life. They start out feeling humiliated, enraged that they are viewed by some Other as second class. They take on new identities as martyrs on behalf of a purported spiritual cause. ... What seems to happen is that they enter a kind of trance, where the world is divided neatly between good and evil, victim and oppressor. ... [A] sense of transcendence is one of many attractions of religious violence for terrorists, beyond the appeal of achieving their goals. (pp. 281–282)
>
> The ecstasy is very much of a sexual character: "call out in joy ... a wedding to 'the black-eyed' awaits your son in paradise," proclaims the last will of a Hamas suicide bomber to his mother. (p. 54)

In Silke's (1998) exploration of the relationship between terrorism and mental illness, he found no evidence for increased levels of mental disorder within the terrorist population. This validates older research in which terrorists on average are found to be psychologically healthier than violent criminals in prisons for non-terrorism-related crimes (Rasch, 1979). If psychopathology can't adequately explain the psychological foundation of a terrorist, what mechanism is responsible for driving a seemingly normal person to extreme acts of violence toward others?

The segue into terrorism appears to be more social than psychological. In his paper "Terrorism, Suicide Bombing, Fear, and Mental Health," Palmer (2007) uses a social learning model to explain how madmen are created from average people. The terrorist's environment may include individuals, groups, and even larger entities like his or her nation or religion that reinforce extremist and violent beliefs. Observations of praise for martyrdom or dedication to the terrorist organization become reinforcing to the outsider. Upon joining a radical group, the bonds and pressures from fellow terrorists become key factors in the continuation and escalation of violent activity. Close-knit connections and strong levels of commitment are accomplished through a focus on developing and maintaining small groups (replicating the family unit) with a central leader who delivers orders from the top. Fellow members replace each other's real family and relationships outside the group. Members will do and act in accordance with what the "family" wants or values. Thus, the terrorist organization can influence its members to take their own lives, willingly, for the cause of their supposed brethren.

Armageddon: The Ultimate Fantasy

Occasionally, a completely irrational precept is embraced as gospel by a powerful constituency of society. In such cases, the adverse consequences of fantasy dependence may reach catastrophic proportions. For example, the history of the Aztec people of Mexico reveals the destruction of an entire civilization in relation to a bizarre and destructive belief. The Aztecs believed that the sun needed to be nourished by human hearts. They felt compelled to feed the sun with thousands upon thousands of human hearts ripped from the bodies of sacrificial victims. What started as a well-contained ritual sacrifice degenerated into compulsive genocide when 75,000 humans were sacrificed in a 15th-century ceremony at El Templo Mayor (the Great Temple). The necessity of purging neighboring cultures to obtain sacrificial victims led to a state of war with victimized groups. When Cortés began the conquest of Mexico, surrounding civilizations were thus eager to join him in the destruction of Tenochtitlan, the Aztec capital.

A fundamentalist belief within Western culture has the earmarks of a devastating social intoxicant. The theology of Armageddon is described in Revelation, the last book in the New Testament, traditionally attributed to John. According to contemporary fundamentalist interpretations, Revelation predicts that before Christ returns to earth to establish his second kingdom, a last great battle between the forces of good and evil will occur. As told in Revelation 9:2–6,

> He opened the shaft of the bottomless pit, and from the shaft rose smoke like the smoke of a great furnace, and the sun and the air were darkened with the smoke from the shaft.
>
> Then from the smoke came locusts on the earth, and they were given power like the power of scorpions on the earth;
>
> They were told not to harm the grass of the earth or any green growth or any tree, but only those of mankind who have not the seal of God upon their foreheads; they were allowed to torture them for five months, but not to kill them, and their torture was like the torture of a scorpion, when it stings a man.
>
> And in those days men will seek death and will not find it; they will long to die, and death will fly from them.

Armageddon, the worst time on earth, will be preceded by an exceedingly troubled period referred to as the Tribulation. Believers explain current world unrest as evidence that we have entered this period. Those who have accepted Christ into their hearts will "in the wink of an eye" experience Rapture. During the Rapture, those who are aligned with the forces of good, namely fundamentalist Christians, will be brought to heaven and protected from the destruction below. There is a fundamentalist bumper sticker that reads, "Caution, in case of Rapture this vehicle will be unmanned." Armageddon theology is explained in *Late Great Planet Earth* (Lindsey, 1970), which is reported to have sold more than 10 million copies.

Some have used Armageddon theology as a defense for the use of nuclear weapons. They believe that the Bible identifies such entities as the Soviet Union, North Korea, China, or Iran with the Antichrist or Evil Empire and the precipitator of the final battle between good and evil—Armageddon. Of course, those who are on the side of good need not fear a nuclear holocaust (Armageddon) because it is God's will that the Evil Empire be destroyed.

One of the signs of the imminence of Armageddon is that people will wear the "mark of the beast," which is said to be the number 666. Revelation 13:16–17 explains, "Also it causes all, both small and great, both rich and poor, both free and slave, to be marked on the right hand or the forehead, so that no one can buy or sell unless he has the mark, that is the name of the beast or the number of its name."

The "mark of the beast" is interpreted by some as the symbolic representation of our credit card culture. When the Antichrist gains control of the earth, no one will be able to participate in any commerce without the "mark" on his or her American Express, Visa, MasterCard, or other "beastly" credit-charging device.

The apocalyptic fantasy in which "nuclear winter" is attributed to the will of God may be construed as denial of the horrific result of addiction to nuclear power . Like the addict who insists that he can control his drinking, militant leaders insist that we can control the world's most devastating intoxicant. Part of the report rushed to President Truman in 1945, after the earliest nuclear test explosion, reads as follows: "It lighted every peak, crevasse and ridge of the nearby mountain range with a clarity and beauty that cannot be described but must be seen to be imagined. It was the beauty the great poets dream about but described most poorly and inadequately ... Then came the strong, sustained, awesome roar which warned of doomsday and made us feel that we puny things were blasphemous to dare tamper with the forces heretofore reserved to the Almighty" (General Thomas Farrell, 1945, quoted in "The Manhattan Project: An Enduring Legacy," 1999).

"Heretofore reserved to the Almighty" and today reserved for the leaders of nuclear-armed countries— no wonder there is so much inclination to attribute this awesome power to a superior being. Yet the fantasy that it is God's plan to arrange for Armageddon permits a mystical rationalization for the continued development of nuclear armaments. Armageddon theology serves as a denial mechanism for those who will not take responsibility for the fact that, like lemmings, we are rushing headlong toward the precipice of world destruction. Indeed, we have far exceeded the thresholds of compulsion and loss of control when a war between the nuclear powers could mean a Third World War every second.

Another example of how biblical prophesies have been used to justify violent actions may be found in rhetoric for the Islamic State (Wood, 2015). An anti-Messiah, known in Muslim apocalyptic literature as Dajjal, will come from the Khorasan region of eastern Iran and kill a vast number of the caliphate's fighters, until just 5,000 remain, cornered in Jerusalem. Just as Dajjal prepares to finish them off, Jesus—the second-most-revered prophet in Islam—will return to Earth, spear Dajjal, and lead the Muslims to victory.

> "Only God knows" whether the Islamic State's armies are the ones foretold, Cerantonio said. But he is hopeful. "The Prophet said that one sign of the imminent arrival of the End of Days is that people will for a long while stop talking about the End of Days," he said. "If you go to the mosques now, you'll find the preachers are

silent about this subject." On this theory, even setbacks dealt to the Islamic State mean nothing, since God has preordained the near-destruction of his people anyway. The Islamic State has its best and worst days ahead of it. (Wood, 2015)

Fundamentalist teachings, which may be operative (among some factions), in religious states like Israel or Iran, are by no means prerequisite for developing a nuclear arsenal. The philosophy of mutually assured destruction (MAD) served as secular justification for the massive post WWII arms race between the U.S. and Russia. Nuclear weaponization is often justified by the perceived need to survive in a hostile world.

North Korea: A Nuclear State

In July 2017, the U.S. and South Korea conducted a ballistic missile drill in response to North Korea's test launch of a missile reportedly capable of reaching Alaska.

THIRTY MINUTES. That's about how long it would take a nuclear-tipped intercontinental ballistic missile (ICBM) launched from North Korea to reach Los Angeles. (Bowden, 2017).

In the words of its state-run television, the test demonstrated that North Korea is now "a full-fledged nuclear power ... capable of hitting any part of the world." Blind adherence to the "Juche philosophy," the 1950s' political ideology espoused by the late president Kim II Song, is at the core of the current crisis. This guiding philosophy places commitment to the state above all else. The unwavering allegiance demanded of all citizens has evolved into the equivalent of a totalitarian religion. When your body dies, "immortality" is achieved so long as the community perseveres. Today there are an estimated 40,000 statues of the late founding president throughout the country. His godlike status is further attested to by the requirement that every household display portraits of Kim and his son and successor Kim Jong II, who died in 2011, leaving Kim II Sung's grandson, Kim Jong Un as the current nuclear-obsessed ruler (Blumberg, A., 2017). Like his father and grandfather, Kim is the "anointed defender of all Koreans, who are the purest of all races" (Bowden, 2017).

Terror Management

A group of social scientists has undertaken the noble task of examining the root causes of terrorism, perhaps shedding light on a possible corridor to peace. *Terror management theory* (TMT) (Greenberg, Pyszczynski, & Solomon, 1986; Pyszczynski, 2004; Solomon, Greenberg, & Pyszczynski, 1991) takes the position that the two common elements of human consciousness are fear of death and will to survive (Pyszczynski, 2004). In terms of evolutionary psychology, humans, early on, developed intellectual means to manage the potentially terrifying knowledge of death by developing worldviews that provide means for attaining immortality in either a literal or symbolic sense. Beliefs in literal immortality, which are nearly universal, pertain to the notion that death is not the end of existence; rather, some part of us will live on, in heaven, through reincarnation, merging our consciousness with God, or the attainment of enlightenment. Cultures also provide us with symbolic immortality, which pertains to the belief that by being part of something more important and enduring than ourselves (i.e., families, nations, ethnic groups, and nations), we can access immortality (e.g., North Korea).

We need others to agree with and validate our cultural worldview (CWV) in order to develop our self-concepts and to maintain faith in our immortality. When we encounter others, who view the world differently, this threatens our faith and ignites existential anxiety (i.e., fear of death). Historically, people have vanquished opposing worldviews by ignoring their proponents as savages, converting them to their own ideologies, or simply exterminating them (Pyszczynski, 2004).

More than 250 TMT studies conducted in more than 13 countries (including the United States, Israel, Iran, and Japan) provide support for the TMT hypothesis that when the existence of a cultural group is threatened—such as during the 9/11 attacks on the World Trade Center or due to nuclear development in Iran—people become more fervently invested in their cultural worldview (Pyszczynski, 2004). Increasing faith in one's CWV tends to reduce death anxiety. Correspondingly, reminding people of death's inevitability leads to a broad range of attempts to maintain faith in their means for immortality. Convincing "evidence" of some form of an afterlife reduces the effects of "mortality salience" and provides a boost to self-esteem. According to Pyszczynski (2004), TMT studies show that reminders of mortality trigger a yearning for structure, thus evoking acceptance of quick and easy answers to complex problems.

By controlling the political agendas of "fearmongering," people become more amenable to open-minded thinking, which can lead to growth, change, and improvement. Zunes (2017) offers a rational view of how the encouragement of strategic non-violent civil insurrections may be the most potent weapon against religious or political extremism. The greater the understanding of non-military alternatives in struggling for justice, the less the appeal of violent extremism for those who feel oppressed. The greater the understanding of nonviolent alternatives to countering religious extremism, the less the appeal of military intervention and repression which tends to breed still more extremism. Indeed, recent history has shown that the most successful path to democratic change, of advancing social justice, of empowering civil society, of ousting dictatorship, of challenging both secular and religious extremism is through the power of strategic nonviolent action. The popular mobilization of the masses in large-scale civil insurrections has proven itself more effective and far less costly than military action in challenging violence from both the state and armed extremists. Given how all nations seek security, non-military means must be encouraged. Given that all faith traditions seek justice, the power of nonviolent civil resistance needs to be better understood.

The challenge for humanity is to demonstrate that there are, in fact, options to rigid adherence to a CWV designed to protect immortality. A cognitive shift along the lines of this basic question should be the target of a worldwide sociological intervention.

Chapter Summary

This chapter explores how fantasy is often an integral part of extremely harmful behavior, for the individual, the community, or even human survival. Fantasy may become integrated with the lives of those around us and form a symbiotic system in which the parties involved reap mutual benefit from a shared alteration of reality. The topic of religious addiction is discussed in terms of how individuals and groups may adhere to rigid and escalating faith practices, sometimes leading to self-destruction or violence toward others. The Heaven's Gate cult is examined in terms of how a shared delusional system can lead to mass suicide. The Columbine massacre demonstrates how innocent lives may be sacrificed at the hands of fantasy-driven behavior.

Case material from a man that earned money as a male prostitute illustrates how sadomasochistic sexual fantasies can be facilitator assisted. The theme of most of his paid sexual encounters was the acting out of various sexual acts that involved some form of make-believe domination of the client. The fantasy of being punished for one's wrongdoing, while at the same time being attended to and sexually desired, was a wish-fulfilling fantasy for many of his homosexual male customers.

The question of how addiction to serial murder and sexual violence may be supported by escalating fantasies is examined through the case of the "poster boy" of serial killers, Ted Bundy. In his final interview, Bundy proclaimed that he initially had a pornography addiction, which progressed to an addiction to violent pornography. Eventually, the porn was no longer satisfying, and he felt compelled to act on these fantasies. Research findings from various neuroimaging techniques designed to study brain functioning in violent individuals are also discussed.

Finally, terrorism is examined as a psychological state, grounded in the mind's capacity to utilize fantasy to allay the terrifying anxiety resulting from juxtaposition of the will to survive and the immutable fact of death. The theology of Armageddon is explored as a fundamentalist belief that has the earmarks of a devastating social intoxicant. Related prophesies that justify the actions of ISIS are discussed. The quest for immortality is also discussed in terms of how secular societies, e.g., North Korea, may construe blind adherence to the State as a means of transcending death. Last, terror management theory is used to explore the root causes of terrorism, possibly shedding light on how to improve human chances for survival.

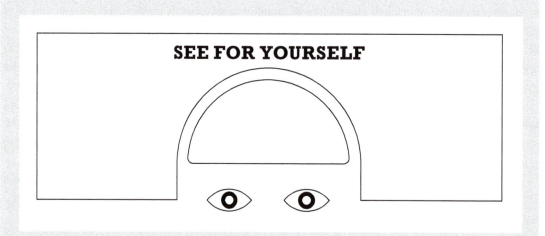

Do's Final Exit. 1997. HeavensGateDatabase. YouTube. 1:28:55

Do and his Heaven's Gate "students" who were preparing to "exit their vehicles" videotaped exit statements—farewell messages to family, friends, and the world in general. Do's exit lasts over 1.5 hours, and those of the students is just under 2 hours. **https://www.youtube.com/ watch?v=wdGXDQ_8bSA**

Student Exit Statements. 1997. HeavensGateDatabase. YouTube. 1:56:29

https://www.youtube.com/watch?v=wHz9it70TdI

The Heaven's Gate Website. 1997.

The Heaven's Gate website still exists at heavensgate.com. According to Kelley and Wilson, 1997, it is maintained by two ex-members who were asked to do so. **www.heavensgate.com**

Exploring the Mind of a Killer. 2009. Jim Fallon. TEDTalks. 7:05

In this TEDTalk, neuroscientist Jim Fallon discusses imaging and neuro-chemical data that may help explain how killers operate differently. **http://www.youtube.com/watch?v=u2V0vOFexY4**

What ISIS Really Wants. 2015. Graeme Wood. The Atlantic.

This in-depth article by journalist Graeme Wood provides invaluable insight into the ideological foundations of the Islamic State.
https://www.theatlantic.com/magazine/archive/2015/03/what-isis-really-wants/384980/

SECTION V

Craving for Intimacy

To love is to receive a glimpse of heaven.
—Karen Sunde

All you need is love
Love is all you need

—The Beatles

Overview: The Importance of Human Connection

Never Once

India is filled
with many
exceptionally beautiful women
who don't desire me
I verify this
every single day
as I walk around
the city of Bombay
I look into face after face
and never once
have I been wrong

—Leonard Cohen

Source: Leonard Cohen, "Never Once," Book of Longing, pp. 162. Copyright © 2006 by HarperCollins Publishers. Reprinted with permission.

L oneliness is not a healthy human condition. The brain needs connections with other people in order to maintain health of mind and body. Maslow (1954–1970), in his renowned hierarchy of human needs, recognized love and belonging as essential to developing positive self-esteem en route to realizing our full potential.

Inadequate bonding affects blood pressure and the incidence of heart disease (Hawkley, Masi, Berry, & Cacioppo, 2006). It has also been shown that quality time spent in meaningful relationships is a factor that enhances the brain's healing process, which leads to a greater life expectancy (Ornstein & Sobel, 1987).

There is a growing body of evidence that heathy attachment not only improves mental health, but improves the body's resistance to a host of stress-related illnesses (McGonigal, 2013).

Today, the importance of attachment, the strong emotional bond that forms between children and their caregivers, is perhaps the most rigorously studied area of developmental psychology. It is widely believed that the nature of the evolving relationship between the child and his or her caregivers is a critical feature of personality and social development, one that has a lifelong influence on the child's mental and emotional growth (e.g., Ainsworth & Bowlby, 1991). "Parenting practices have been found to have an effect on children's substance abuse, school problems, academic success, behavioral problems, social competency, ego resiliency, ego control, depression, and employment in adulthood" (Schwartz, Thigpen, & Montgomery, 2006, p. 41). Satir (1972) describes the impact of the family:

> Any infant coming in[to] the world has no past, no experience in handling himself, no skill by which to judge his own worth. He must rely on the experiences he has with people around him and the messages they give him about his worth as a person. For the first five or six years the child's self-esteem is formed by the family almost exclusively. After he starts school other influences come into play, but the

family effect remains throughout his adolescence. Outside forces tend to reinforce the feelings of self-worth or worthlessness that he learned at home. The high self-esteem child can weather many failures in school among peers. The low self-esteem child can experience many successes and yet feel a gnawing doubt about his own value. (p. 24)

Children need the knowledge that their feelings and emotions are valid. Satir found that families and their constituent members thrive when provided with what she referred to as the *Five Freedoms:* (1) the freedom to see and hear what is here and now, rather than what was, what will be, or should be; (2) the freedom to think and know what one thinks and knows, rather than what one should think and know; (3) the freedom to think and express what one feels, rather than what one should feel and express; (4) the freedom to want and to choose what one wants, rather than what one should want; and (5) the freedom to imagine one's own self-actualization, rather than playing a rigid role or always playing it safe (Satir & Baldwin, 1983, p. 163).

While supervising a child's behavior with appropriate limit setting promotes strength and resiliency, manipulation and psychological control may increase drug use and delinquent behaviors (de Kemp, Scholte, Overbeek, & Engels, 2006). Lack of parental support is directly related to depression in early adolescence. Parental disinterest and lack of support are correlated with a child's self-perception as unworthy and a quest for other means of finding support and comfort. De Kemp et al. (2006) confirmed earlier studies, finding that many facets of mental health and psychological well-being are adversely affected by inappropriate parental controls:

> Parenting is directly related to the intensified delinquent behavior of early adolescents ... Psychological control appeared to be related to an increased frequency of delinquent behavior. Controlling an adolescent's behavior by manipulation and guilt induction may contribute to feelings of insecurity and frustration. The use of psychological control is especially detrimental in early adolescence, during which young people firmly define themselves as connected to—yet separate from—their significant others. Repeated exposure to psychological intrusion increases the risk for developing internalizing as well as externalizing problems. As a means of relieving the negative atmosphere created by guilt induction, a youth might act out aggressively. (p. 505)

Blanchard and Lyons (2016) found that "[p]rimary psychopathic traits in men related to controlling mothers and avoidant attachment, whereas in women they related to uncaring fathers and both anxious and avoidant attachment" (p.56). In a study of adolescent children of veterans diagnosed with PTSD, Marsanic et al. (2014) found that externalizing and internalizing problems were related to lower levels of parental care and impaired parent-child bonding. "Internalizing symptoms were associated with family dysfunction, while externalizing symptoms were associated with paternal overcontrol/overprotection, and low maternal and paternal care" (p.295).

This section explores the basic struggle for human relatedness, which, when mismanaged in childhood or unsatisfied later in life, can result in internal distress and dysfunctional relationships. Disruption of the fundamental needs for love and belonging is closely aligned with seeking wholeness and connection through drugs, promiscuity, and other forms of unhealthy attachment.

Chapter 14, "Love or Addiction?," examines the agony and ecstasy of romance in terms of the neuro-chemical underpinnings of infatuation, desire, and loss of control. The psychology of love is revealed as a dynamic interplay of arousal, relaxation, and fantasy. Obsessive and tormenting love is a miscarriage of our natural attraction toward people who evoke feelings of safety, pleasure, and the possibility to procreate. In Chapter 15, "Cannabis—Reefer Madness Revisited," marijuana is examined as prototypical of various drug involvements whereby powerful cultural influences combine with innate longings for closeness and belonging. Chapter 16, "Romantic Sex Fantasy," examines the monumental demand for novel, no-strings-attached sexual stimulation through fantasy and paid companionship.

Together, these chapters are designed to provide readers with an expanded view of a broad spectrum of activities that deliver partial satisfaction, often at great cost, of life's greatest challenge and most precious gift—intimacy.

> *For one human being to love another, that is perhaps the most*
> *difficult of all our tasks, the ultimate, the last test and proof,*
> *the work for which all other work is preparation.*

—Rainer Maria Rilke

14

Love or Addiction?

Baby, please, let me begin
Let me be your heroin

—Aimee Mann, "High on Sunday 52"

Oh, can't you see?
You belong to me
My poor heart aches
With every step you take

—The Police, "Every Breath You Take"

I want you to want me
I need you to need me
I'd love you to love me
I'm begging you to beg me

—Cheap Trick, "I Want You to Want Me"

I'm hooked on a feeling
I'm high on believing
That you're in love with me

—Mark James, "Hooked on a Feeling"

Introduction

Some dyed-in-the-wool romantics describe the insatiable craving for an elusive, unattainable, yet tantalizing lover as a "jones." A jones means that you've got a habit—a bad habit. Eventually, it might even do you in. As with uncontrolled dependence on heroin, no matter how much you get, you always want more. Like an infant who has been abandoned by its mother, you fall to pieces when "mamma" won't give you a "fix." Freud (quoted in Reynaud et al., 2010, pg. 261), observed the similarity between love and drugs: "The Soma Elixir (a love potion) is perfectly in line with this most important intuition, that all our inebriating spirits and our stimulating alkaloids are merely a substitute for a single substance, yet to be discovered, the same that the intoxication of love procures."

We can all catch a glimpse of ourselves in this grim, shadow side of romance. In proper proportion, the majestic clockwork of love—a synchronized blend of arousal, satiation, and fantasy—gives rise to life's most fulfilling experiences. By nature, we become impassioned by elements that create or sustain life. But all too often the delicate process goes amiss: angels transform into devils, joy becomes jealousy, and heaven changes to hell. The nightmare of tormenting love is nothing but a miscarriage of our natural attraction toward people who evoke feelings of safety and pleasure. And so it is with all addictions; they are self-destructive outgrowths of adaptive, life-enhancing behaviors.

Infatuation and the Legend of St. Valentine

According to Slater (2006), romantic love is panhuman: it proliferates in almost every culture on earth and has been embedded in our brains since Pleistocene times. In a study of 166 cultures, evidence of romantic love was found in 147 of them. Indeed, the phenomenon of infatuation is so powerful that some people compulsively attempt to re-create the experience, time and time again. In fact, some researchers hypothesize that romantic love is rooted in our quest to recapture our earliest infantile experiences with intimacy, that is, the feeling at mother's breast, the look of her face, the caring and gentle touch (Slater, 2006). The usual failure of such pursuit leads some people toward a repetitious and seemingly compulsive search for intimacy.

In simplest terms, falling in love means thinking about another person all the time. Peele and Brodsky (1975) were the first to suggest that romantic love could be an addiction; they referred to people in all-consuming relationships as "interpersonal addicts." In *Love and Limerence: The Experience of Being in Love*, Tennov (1979) describes the symptoms of romantic love, which she collectively calls *limerence*. In limerence, there is constant thought about one person, to the exclusion of all others, usually as a possible sex partner. When for some reason the prospective lover is not readily taken, romantic sentiments are further intensified. Obsessed suitors are able to achieve some degree of solace through rich and elaborate fantasies of lovemaking and courtship. If the "chosen" shows even the slightest inclination toward amorous reciprocation, feelings of elation are likely to follow. For a state of true limerence, at least the potential for mating must exist, tinged with an umbra of uncertainty or doubt about the future of the relationship. Therefore, the answer to the age-old question is, yes—do play "hard to get."

A brief excursion into the legend of St. Valentine, the unofficial patron saint of romance, illuminates Tennov's portrait of limerence. During his reign, the Roman Emperor Claudius Gothicus (Claudius II) issued a decree that all Roman citizens must worship and pay homage to the 12 Roman gods. The monk Valentinus is said to have been a man of learning and a devout Christian. He refused to forsake his religion and was arrested for secretly marrying Roman soldiers when Claudius had forbidden it. Disobedience of this sort was considered a crime analogous to treason and punishable by death. Valentinus was kept in prison until the date of his scheduled execution.

During his captivity, Valentinus met a beautiful young woman named Julia, who, like love itself, was completely blind. She was the daughter of the jailer, who recognized Valentinus as a learned man. The jailer appealed to Valentinus to provide Julia with an education. She was delighted by Valentinus's teachings and cherished his accounts of nature and God. Julia confessed to Valentinus that each day she prayed for sight so that she could discover all the beauty that he had described. Valentinus is said to have assured her, "God does what is best for us only if we believe in Him." As the story goes, they sat quietly in prayer when suddenly the prison cell was enveloped by a brilliant white light. Julia's shrill voice pierced the air. "Valentinus, I can see," she shrieked, "I can see!"

On the eve of his death, Valentinus wrote a note to Julia urging her to remain close to God, even in his absence. He signed it, "From Your Valentine." His death sentence was carried out the next day, February 14, 270 AD, near a gate that was later named Porta Valentia, in his honor. He was buried at what is now the Church of Praxedes in Rome. According to the legend, Julia planted a pink-blossomed almond tree near his grave, which has endured as a symbol of abiding love and affection.

Undoubtedly, if Tennov (1979) could have observed the legendary courtship, she would have concluded that indeed a strong state of limerence had occurred. Julia, the blind child of a watchful father, presumably had little opportunity for intimate male contact. Valentinus, even though he was a prisoner, was as close as she might ever come to an attainable lover. Admittedly, the probability of actualizing a sexual relationship was quite remote, but Julia's blindness might have intensified her romantic fantasies. Valentinus, knowing that he was to die, might well have telegraphed his natural desires to be wanted and loved. Of course, the slightest hint from Valentinus that Julia's affection might be reciprocal would fuel her desire even more. Finally, the impending execution—particularly when we consider that Julia must have prayed for Valentinus's life, and on some level must have believed that God would spare him—most definitely meets Tennov's criterion of uncertainty regarding the future.

In some sense, the abrupt curtailment of Julia's short-lived romance was a blessing in disguise. Had Valentinus's sentence been commuted to life imprisonment, Julia might have encountered an even more difficult predicament. She would have continuously longed for the love of her life—the unattainable soul mate that helped her to see beauty in nature and affirmed her faith in God. The limitations of her childhood, coupled with the incomparable joy that she experienced with Valentinus, would etch a permanent imprint on her psyche. The fleeting moments of pleasure that she could extract from periodic visits to his cell would only enlarge her desire and prolong her suffering. Indiscretion would surface, as rationality would eventually dwindle to a mere silent observer. The folly of love would progressively erode her happiness, and eventually she would reach the same tortured state that many of us have endured—feeling desperately entrapped in love's crushing grip. Her behavior might well have been characterized by compulsion, loss of control, and continuation despite harmful consequences.

We can all identify with Julia's hypothetical plight. The combination of psychological need and social pressure "to be in love" is so great that we compulsively hang on, even after the game is over. In the short run, having a lover, no matter how problematic the relationship, serves to deflect the ubiquitous existential concern, "I am afraid to face my life and death alone." Objectively, it is not whether two people stay together, but *how* they stay together, that separates genuine intimacy from love addiction. In a healthy love relationship, both members strive to enrich and fulfill their lives through intense, mutual involvement. The love addict, despite a multitude of protestations to the contrary, cares little about the well-being of his or her partner. Romance junkies demand or beg for approval and affection in an escalating cycle of disappointment and reprisal. Eventually, harmful consequences result, including deterioration of work, social, or health functions. Alcohol, for example, may be used as a temporary stopgap for feelings of anger and despair. Unfortunately, most demoralized lovers who take refuge in the womb of spirits cannot honestly echo the famous boast attributed to W. C. Fields, "It was a woman who drove me to drink and I haven't had the decency to thank her."

Those who become addicted usually lack confidence in their ability to cope without some form of support, either real or imagined, from a love object. Klein and Liebowitz (1979) of the New York State Psychiatric Institute proposed the term *hysteroid dysphoria*—a chronic and intense form of lovesickness— as a category of mental disturbance. The disorder, which they observed with surprising frequency in the course of their psychiatric practice, is characterized by depression, depletion of energy, and increased appetite in response to feelings of rejection. Conversely, when a romantic figure shows even minimal signs of approval, hysteroids react with increased energy and euphoria. People who suffer from this disturbance seem to fall in love more easily than others, and with less discretion. Their moods are marked by great sensitivity to even the slightest sign of disapproval, particularly from people in whom they have made romantic investments.

If you seem to have more than an academic interest in this syndrome, then perhaps you may be questioning your own propensity as a love addict. Fear not; nearly everyone has a similar reaction: "Is that me?" Don't forget, however, that you can have mild, moderate, or severe degrees of love dependence, as with addiction to food, drugs, or alcohol, and the symptoms are remarkably the same. If your relationship meets three or more of the criteria listed below, then love may be your Achilles' heel.

- Denial. Your friends and family say you're in a bad relationship, but you don't agree.
- Immediacy. You require frequent emergency "pow-wows" with your lover in social and business situations.
- Compulsion. You've broken up (seriously) at least twice, yet you always make up.
- Loss of control. You often feel powerless to control your feelings or behavior with regard to your lover.
- Progression. Over time you suspect that your relationship has been on a downward spiral.
- Withdrawal. You become depressed and experience physical disturbance (loss of sleep or altered eating and drinking patterns) when distanced from your lover.

What Kind of Fool am I?

These lyrics were crooned back in the 1960s in a song about a man who is unable to truly fall in love, which captures one variety of relationship dysfunction. Love addiction can manifest in a variety of ways, from people who are constantly seeking the excitement of new relationships (and thus cheating on their current partners), to people who stay in destructive relationships no matter how bad they get. Some individuals with love addiction feel compelled to start a new relationship almost as soon as their last one ends—and may have scoped out a replacement partner for just such a situation. Other love addicts are drawn to the emotionally unavailable partner, a situation practically guaranteed to result in rejection. Still others will swear off of relationships once they have been "burned" by the person they thought was "the one." All of these patterns show dysfunctional approaches to relationships.

People's expectations about relationships are fueled, at least to some degree, by media—television, movies, music, and literature (Sussman, 2010). Media depictions promote unrealistic portrayals of romance: people fall in love "at first sight," jealousy is depicted as humorous or endearing rather than potentially destructive, couples are incredibly good looking, and the sex is always phenomenal. Even music inundates us with depictions of romance, many of which are not particularly healthy. In a content analysis of the 100 top songs (Billboard magazine's rankings for the years from 1958 – 1998), it was found 81% had lyrics based upon the theme of love (Dukes, Basel, Borega, Lobato, and Owens, 2003). Songs from the rhythm/blues (96%) and rock (82%) genres were the most likely to have love-related lyrics, with rap/hip hop songs being less likely to have love-themed lyrics (although the rap/hip hop genre still came in at 59% of their top-rated songs related to love). Such depictions may lead you to think that if you're not in a relationship—or if your relationship isn't as intense as what is depicted in media—you aren't normal. Mary-Lou Galician (2009), writes extensively about romantic myths portrayed in the media. She is on a mission to promote media literacy, particularly with regard to intimate relationships. Her "get real!" mantra is intended to alert people that media distorts our perceptions of relationships, promoting unrealistic expectations that then lead to feelings of dissatisfaction when their own relationships do not match what they see in the media.

But regardless of media influences, some individuals may be more prone than others to fall victim to a toxic bite from the love bug. Gender does not seem to play a role (Hatfield & Sprecher, 1986, cited in Sussman, 2010), although female love addicts may be more likely to engage in stalking (Purcell, Pathe, & Mullen, 2001, also cited in Sussman, 2010). Surprisingly, there seems to be little formal research on the personality factors linked to love addiction, with the exception of attachment styles. Hazan and Shaver (1987) applied Ainsworth and colleagues' (1978) concepts of secure and insecure (with insecure types including both anxious-ambivalent and avoidant) attachment styles to relationship patterns in adult romances. Their survey findings demonstrate that "anxious-ambivalent subjects experienced love as involving obsession, desire for reciprocation and union, emotional highs and lows, and extreme sexual attraction and jealousy" (Hazan and Shaver, 1987, p. 515). A study by Feeney and Noller (1990) supports these findings; their data show that anxious-ambivalent types scored higher on emotional dependence on one's partner, reliance on one's partner, and obsessive preoccupation, among other measures. Feeney and Noller further note that anxious-ambivalent attachment and limerance are related. There were also some parallels between anxious-ambivalent and avoidant types in this study, with these two attachment types scoring similarly on several measures, including unfulfilled hopes and self-conscious anxiety.

What is the significance of anxious-ambivalent attachment styles in relation to love addiction? Perhaps you learned in your Psychology 101 class that people's attachment styles form early in life, based upon interactions with their primary caregiver (often mothers); these styles are thought to form a "template" for future relationships. Those who form anxious-ambivalent attachment styles often received inconsistent parenting, whereby the caregiver is either non-responsive to their offspring's emotional needs or overprotective and smothering. The child is never really certain how the caregiver will respond and whether they can be relied upon. Rather than developing security and independence, the child is distressed by abandonment and can be clingy but angry when reunited with the caregiver. This pattern can be transferred to relationships with others, including friends and romantic partners (the topic of attachment is readdressed in Chapter 20, which addresses healthy relationships.).

Some of the interpersonal behavior patterns of those with anxious-ambivalent attachment styles are manifested in people with Borderline Personality Disorder (BPD). As Dozier and colleagues (2008) point out, dysfunctional early relationships are a fundamental concept related to development of BPD. Such individuals typically have patterns of stormy relationships: adoration can turn to hatred if the BPD individual feels rejected or "dissed" by the love interest. People with BPD also tend to fear and avoid abandonment by friends, family members, or loved ones. Thus, it seems that love addicts and borderline personalities share at least some characteristics. It is somewhat surprising, then, that there's relatively little published research on love addiction and personality types or traits. This may be due to a relative lack of peer-reviewed literature on love addiction in general. Online resources for 12-step groups, such as Love Addicts Anonymous, provide information about "types" of love addicts and personality patterns (See for Yourself).

The Internet is plentiful with websites for treatment centers for people with love addiction. However, sources for this online information are not always well-documented, making it appear anecdotal in nature. To make the situation even more complicated, there are those who argue that the phrase "love addiction" should be avoided. For instance, relationship therapist Thomas M. Greaney (2015) wrote an article for *Addiction Professional* in which he argued "love addiction" (and "sex addiction") is an inflammatory term that promotes stigmatization due to negative stereotypes associated with the terms "addict" and "addiction." Greaney recommends that "intimacy disorder" be used instead because it is more compassionate and helps people with these issues avoid self-stigmatization which may negatively impact their self-image and internal dialogue about their behavior. From a diagnostic standpoint, neither "intimacy disorder" nor "love addiction" are contained within the DSM-5.

What Do You Think?

Besides the controversy about the appropriate terminology to use regarding "love addiction," there's the issue of what exactly it means to be a love addict. In other words, what exactly is the person addicted to? This question is raised in a commentary by Jenkins (2017) who points out that the object of the addiction could potentially be the love addict's partner (or would-be partner), the physical contact with the partner (sex, kissing, hugging, etc.), or the actual attachment (relationship) itself. What do you think is the hook for the love addict?

Face It, You're Addicted to Love

Fisher and colleagues (2016) suggest that love is a "natural addiction" that can manifest in both a positive and a negative form. The positive form harkens back to our earlier evolutionary history, when pair-bonding promoted reproduction and survival of the species. For romantic love to be a "positive addiction", the affection must be mutual and the relationship healthy. Conversely, the "negative addiction" version is characterized by one-sided feelings (the love object does not reciprocate the lover's feelings); there may also be socially inappropriate behavior (jealousy, stalking, invasions of privacy, etc.), and the relationship can have toxic elements such as physical and/or psychological abuse. The notion that there can be a "positive addiction" conflicts with most conceptualizations of "addiction", which emphasize negative consequences (problem behaviors) result from the compulsive activity.

Fisher's view of love itself as an addiction (that can manifest in either beneficial or destructive ways) fits with what Earp and colleagues (2017) refer to as a "broad view" of love addiction. In this sense, the addiction is simply a desire that can be temporarily satisfied but will return later. On the other hand, a "narrow view" of love addiction necessitates that the love relationship actually causes problems for the person. Compared with the vast majority of people who would classify as love addicts under the broad view, only about 5–10% of our population would classify as love addicts under this narrow view (Timmreck, 2010, cited in Earp et al., 2017).

For those who repeatedly struggle in out-of-control relationships, there are a number of choices for getting help. One option is individual psychotherapy. People with love addiction are prone to depression and anxiety, either between relationships ("withdrawal") or when relationships turn sour; this option makes sense as a way of providing the person with better insight and coping skills to help manage their own feelings. Such treatment can help address attachment issues as well as problems related to personality disorders such as BPD, if pertinent to the individual case. If the person's partner is mutually interested in saving a troubled relationship, couples therapy may prove helpful. The couple can learn better communication skills and work on building appropriate interpersonal boundaries (e.g., no more spying on your partner's text messages or listening in on phone calls).

There are also a number of self-help groups based on the 12-steps of Alcoholics Anonymous. Formed in 1970s and 1980s, these groups include LAA (Love Addicts Anonymous), SLAA (Sex and Love Addicts Anonymous), SAA (Sex Addicts Anonymous), SA (Sexaholics Anonymous), and SCA (Sexual Compulsives Anonymous). In general, such groups do not discriminate between sex addicts, love addicts, and "sexual anorexics" (people who are so fearful of intimacy that they avoid relationships, despite longing for one). Sexual anorexics are reminiscent of a character from Thomas Pynchon's 1967 novel *The Crying of Lot 49*. The man is a member of *Inamorati Anonymous* (IA) and explains that "An inamorato is somebody in love. That's the worst addiction of all." (Pynchon, 2012, Kindle location 1224). IA members have sworn off of love and have adopted identities as "isolates" (people without relationships). Unlike other support groups, IA never holds meetings because it defeats the purpose for isolates to get together! Members help keep one another from falling in love, in the same way that an AA sponsor would talk an alcoholic out of taking a drink. Hopefully, the inamorato will kick the love habit completely. This satirical approach, however, runs counter to the goal of real-life relationship self-help groups. Ultimately, individuals with sex addiction, love addiction, or sexual anorexia are supported in the quest to build healthy relationships. Guidelines vary across groups, with some discouraging use of pornography, as well as any form of sex outside of marriage (including masturbation), so check the fine print in their 12-step guidebooks!

Fisher et al. (2016) provide suggestions for dealing with romantic rejection and the pains of withdrawal from an addictive romantic relationship. Just like people with substance addictions, love junkies can be triggered by stimuli; therefore, it's a good idea to get rid of signs of the ex-lover (photos, notes, belongings) and avoid contact with the ex to help prevent cravings. Love addicts in recovery also need to work on re-connecting with other natural rewards, such as spending time with family or friends, engaging in exercise, and partaking in "self-expanding" activities (sports and hobbies). These natural rewards, and how they can be helpful for someone in recovery, will be readdressed in more depth, in later chapters, i.e., "Natural Highs."

CASE EXAMPLE: Ethlie: Screenwriter, Journalist, and "Affection Deficit Disorder" Sufferer

Boy crazy but straight-laced as a teenager, Ethlie didn't develop love addiction issues until college, although she had a history of wanting boys who were essentially out of her league (guys who dated cheerleaders, rather than "Deathly Ethlie," the teacher's pet). It wasn't until years later that she realized she was drawn to unattainable men, seeing them as "challenging" rather than "impossible" to attain. Initial rejection by popular, attractive boys reaffirmed how "valuable" they were—it would just take some time to win them over. Her school-girl fantasies were of a pure romantic love: picture Sir Gawain, legendary knight of King Arthur's Round Table.

Her family life was dysfunctional, though not abusive. She did not have a close relationship with her father, a Milltown-sedated WWII veteran who was pathologically jealous of Ethlie's mother—possibly because she had cheated on him with numerous men. Ethlie blames her "affection deficit disorder" (her coinage) on her mother. As a young child, Ethlie was not aware of her mom's infidelities, but her mother sent other messages that shaped Ethlie's views about relationships. She kept telling Ethlie that she needed a man to take care of her, to complete her. Further cause for blame arose when her mother slept with a young man whom Ethlie fancied. Ethlie caught them together, which prompted her mother to explain how unsatisfying she found her marital relationship. This trauma occurred just before Ethlie entered college.

Turning to diet pills, marijuana, and alcohol to cope and simultaneously seem cool, Ethlie was determined to lose her virginity. She lost it to a writing partner who subsequently humiliated her in public. Of him, Ethlie says, "… this was one of the nicer guys" (Vare, 2011, Kindle location, 429). In college, she didn't enjoy sex but saw herself as the holder of a valuable commodity that guys wanted. She also lacked personal boundaries, impairing her ability to say "no." After graduating from college *summa cum laude* (at age 19, no less!), she got a job as a topless dancer. The attention she got from men fed her attention-starved psyche. Drinking and drugging continued, and she added criminal activities such as theft to her repertoire.

She kept score of her conquests (which eventually reached triple digits), and she got into some dicey relationships. She married several times. Her second husband was a pathologically jealous and physically abusive cocaine dealer; she took his extreme behavior as an indication that he loved her intensely. Their arrest for drug possession landed them both in jail and led to the annulment of their 9-day marriage. In her third marriage, both she and her husband were guilty of infidelities. The death of a lover led her back to snorting cocaine. She describes herself as a teenager in a mature woman's body, cultivating the "MILF" image before the term was ever coined. Most of the men she was involved with during this phase were either married or much younger than she was.

Eventually Ethlie hit her rock bottom. She writes: "You notice the similarities in your bad choices, like the repeating pattern in cheap wallpaper. You also have no buffer against the agony of withdrawal. I pined for a manic-depressive actor. Longed for a junkie tour manager. Yearned for a bisexual trust-fund baby. Went ballistic over a misanthropic physicist. Contemplated suicide over a married writer ... and then another married writer. And then I reluctantly turned myself in to a tough-love therapist, mostly because I did not actually want to die over this" (Kindle locations, 518–521).

Ethlie's story highlights a couple of key points: (1) the line between love addiction and sex addiction may seem blurred and confusing, and (2) love addiction is a serious condition that can kill someone. But it also emphasizes that people can recover from this condition. She has written her memoir to provide hope to others with "affection deficit disorder."

Neurochemistry of Romance

While the language of love is undoubtedly poetry, the language of the brain where love abides is chemistry. We respond chemically to other human beings. In fact, romantic attachment has been attributed in part to *oxytocin*, a hormone first released when the baby is nursing and in subsequent love connections throughout life. It has been postulated that those suffering from autistic spectrum disorders may have an oxytocin deficiency (Slater, 2006).

The understanding of the function of oxytocin has expanded dramatically over the years from a simple peptide adept at inducing uterine contractions and milk ejection to a complex neuromodulator with a capacity to shape human social behavior. Decades of research have outlined oxytocin's ability to enhance intricate social activities ranging from pair bonding, sexual activity, affiliative preferences, and parental behaviors. The precise neural mechanisms underlying oxytocin's influence on such behaviors have just begun to be understood. Research suggests that oxytocin interacts closely with the neural pathways responsible for processing motivationally relevant stimuli. In particular, oxytocin appears to impact dopaminergic activity within the mesocorticolimbic dopamine system, which is crucial not only for reward and motivated behavior but also for the expression of affiliative behaviors. (Love, T., 2014)

At the level of the neuron, our synapses are stirred by a lover's furtive glance. Love itself has become a legitimate target for neurochemical analysis. And why not? Through the use of positron-emission tomography (PET) and magnetic resonance imaging (MRI), scientists can now take pictures of the brain at work. It has been shown that emotion-laden events trigger the release of neurotransmitters that affect particular regions of the brain. In anxious people, for example, neurochemical activity increases in the right brain hemisphere. Altered neurotransmission in people with severe depression or schizophrenia has been the focus of intensive brain research for the past three decades. Some neuroscientists have now turned their attention to the study of positive feeling states. Anthropologists at Rutgers University recruited subjects who claimed to be "madly in love" for an average of 7 months (Fisher, Aron, & Brown, 2005). Each was shown a neutral photo and one of his or her beloved. MRI data showed that love lights up the *caudate nucleus*, which is home to a rich network of dopamine receptors.

What excited Fisher most was not so much finding a location, an address for love, as tracing its specific chemical pathways. ... [Fisher came to think of] dopamine as part of our own endogenous love potion. In the right proportions, dopamine creates intense energy, exhilaration, focused attention, and motivation to win rewards. It is why, when you are newly in love, you can stay up all night, watch the sun rise, run a race, ski fast down a slope ordinarily too steep for your skill. Love makes you bold, makes you bright, makes you run real risks, which you sometimes survive and sometimes ... don't. (Slater, 2006, p. 35)

More recently Fisher (2016) reported that in a reanalysis of her imaging data, activation was also found in the nucleus accumbens—just as we might expect, given its role in natural rewards and addiction. Additional imaging studies have found comparable results (see Acevedo & Aron, 2014, for a review).

Writing for *Scientific American Mind*, in an article entitled "Affairs of the Lips," Walter (2008) unravels the neurochemistry of kissing. We all know that a "good" kiss can enhance a relationship and that a "bad" kiss can destroy what may have initially been perceived as a possible long-term commitment. A "good" kiss should produce an increase in oxytocin, which is involved in social bonding, and a decrease in cortisol, which should decrease stress. Hill and Wilson (2007, cited in Walter, 2008) compared the levels of oxytocin and cortisol in college male–female couples before and after kissing and while talking and holding hands. The researchers were surprised to find that only the males in the study experienced a rise in oxytocin after kissing. The females experienced a decrease in oxytocin after kissing or talking while holding hands. Perhaps females need more than a kiss to feel emotionally connected, or maybe need contact over a longer period of time. As expected, the level of cortisol dropped in both sexes no matter the level of intimacy. Kissing also boosts blood pressure and increases pulse rate. Unfortunately, rationality decreases as emotional intensity increases—a classic example of the amygdala dominating the cortex. According to Winslow and Insel (1991, cited in Reynaud, Karila, Blecha, and Benyamina, 2010), release of oxytocin (which can occur in a variety of social interactions, including sexual contact), increases the dopamine signal in the mesolimbic reward pathway.

According to Liebowitz, author of *The Chemistry of Love* (1983), a substance known to biochemists as phenethylamine or PEA is released in the brain when we fall in love. The PEA molecule, which is considered an excitatory amine, bears striking structural similarity to the pharmaceutically manufactured stimulant amphetamine. Liebowitz regards the accelerated use of PEA, which occurs during infatuation, as the key to feelings of excitation, exhilaration, and euphoria.

Those with a romantic nature may take some offence at reducing perhaps life's greatest pleasure to a molecular underpinning. However, advancing brain science will not be slowed by the sentimental reins of romance. No matter how mystical we perceive love to be, we are now aware of its neurochemical aspects. Indeed, remarkable biological parallels exist between pathological drug use and the unhealthy need for affection. Becoming dependent on love may be described as a dynamic process with two distinct biochemical phases: infatuation and attachment.

Infatuation is usually an experience of heightened energy and feelings of euphoria. According to Liebowitz (1983), the initial period of psychosexual attraction produces increased concentrations of the neurotransmitter-like substance phenethylamine (PEA). The brain responds to this chemical in much the same fashion as it would to amphetamine or cocaine; infatuated lovers seem to experience boundless energy, elation, and a remarkable sense of well-being. They have no problem in "painting the town red," then going to work, then going out the following night and doing it all over again. [Note: although PEA has colloquially earned a reputation as a love chemical, there's relatively little peer-reviewed research on this substance—probably because it isn't particularly well understood. However, research does suggest that it is involved in helping increase dopamine release (Sabelli et al., 1976). Sabelli (2002) wrote "PEA increases emotional warmth, intellectual attention, affection, sexuality, and feelings of physical energy when a person is in intrapsychic and interpersonal harmony" (p. 102) and went so far as to describe PEA as the neuromodulator of psychic energy (literally libido). But the link to PEA and love tends to go cold after that. Because it is accepted that PEA plays a role in increasing dopamine release, it is reasonable that it may play a role in dopamine-mediated rewards.

After a brief time, however, the speedy feeling appears to reach a maximum level, and lovers begin to recognize that their relationship is on a plateau. The romance remains exciting, yet the remarkable sensations of invigoration and euphoria appear to be dwindling. In chemical terms, the pleasure of falling in love is derived not from increased production of PEA, but rather from steady increases in the rate of PEA production. When PEA acceleration reaches zero, that is, when increments in the rate of chemical reward have stopped, the honeymoon is over.

At this juncture, one of two possible biochemical processes becomes operative: amphetamine-like withdrawal, or a shift to an endorphin-mediated relationship. In the attachment phase, long-term lovers can make the transition from zooming around in the fast lane to enjoying cuddles and quiet evenings at home. But recall the chemistry of contentment. The prolonged love-swoon is, after all, an opioid-mediated experience. If one member of the relationship is a "dyed-in-the-wool" arousal type, he or she may seek excitement from people and places outside the relationship. The pair bond may dissolve as one or the other partner subjectively experiences boredom, stagnation, and depression.

In their review of the dopamine reward system's link to romantic love and pair-bonding, Acevedo and Aron (2014) highlight overlaps in brain activation linked to both emotional attachments and substance addiction. Citing Siegel (1999), who suggested that nurturing attachment plays a critical role in brain development, Acevedo and Aron suggest that a lack of such attachment in childhood impacts the brain's dopamine, opioid, serotonin, and oxytocin systems. Such changes may denote a susceptibility to "self-sooth" through substances due to faulty emotional regulatory systems. In essence, the substance addiction is a form of attachment disorder. They further suggest that close relationships are important in helping people overcome addictions of all types.

Finally, it's worth mentioning that part of the risk for love addiction may be genetic and linked to dopamine receptors. As reviewed in Reynaud et al. (2010), one variant of the gene for the dopamine D2 receptor is correlated with very low levels—and another variant with very high levels—of sexual desire. Thus, to some degree, a person's level of sexual yearnings is linked to their genes, which the person has no control over. Interestingly, the same polymorphism that promotes intense sexual desire is also linked to sensation-seeking and drug addiction. In a study by Emanuele et al. (2007, cited in De Boer, Van Buel, & Ter Horst, 2012), variants in the dopamine D2 receptor gene was linked to "Eros," a loving style characterized by intense physical attraction and emotional connection to one's partner. Perhaps it should not surprise us that our old friend dopamine once again appears to play a role in this rewarding, potentially compulsive, behavior.

Love and Death

It is love's unequaled capacity to profoundly influence each of the three pleasure planes—arousal, satiation, and fantasy—that qualifies it as the pièce de résistance of the addictions. While the human inclination toward intimate pairing affixes a territory within which mating can occur, it also holds the trigger to the most primitive impulses on earth. An instant of reflection on love's hearty contribution to homicide and suicide reminds us of the horrifying consequences of uncontrolled passion.

Poetry, the language of love, is often used to express the agony and ecstasy of life's most exalted emotion. In "Porphyria's Lover," Robert Browning (1888) encapsulates a man's compulsion to murder his sweetheart, aspiring to preserve forever his moment of ecstasy.

> Be sure I look'd up at her eyes
> Happy and proud; at last I knew
> Porphyria worshipp'd me; surprise
> Made my heart swell, and still it grew
> While I debated what to do.
> That moment she was mine, mine, fair,
> Perfectly pure and good: I found
> A thing to do, and all her hair
> In one long yellow string I wound
> Three times her little throat around,
> And strangled her. No pain felt she;
> I am quite sure she felt no pain.

Edgar Allen Poe writes of his morbid obsession upon the death of his wife, in "Annabel Lee:"

> For the moon never beams without bringing me dreams
> Of the beautiful Annabel Lee,
> And the stars never rise but I feel the bright eyes
> Of the beautiful Annabel Lee.
> And so, all the night-tide I lie down by the side
> Of my darling, my darling, my life, and my bride,
> In her sepulcher there by the sea,
> In her tomb by the sounding sea.

"Annabel Lee" follows Poe's favorite theme: the death of a beautiful woman (J. Meyers, 1992), which Poe (1849) has called "the most poetical topic in the world."

The addictive quality of romantic attachment becomes painfully obvious during periods of actual or anticipated separation. As in the examples of Browning's "Porphyria's Lover" and Poe's "Annabel Lee" above, sudden or prolonged absence can cause paranoid thoughts and deranged conduct. Forlorn satiation types may become as pathetic as any heroin junkie who suddenly finds himself without a fix. Love addicts may survive for years, completely undetected, so long as there is a constant drug supply. However, they may cheat, lie, steal, or kill—even for a minimal dose—to avoid the dreaded pain of withdrawal.

Some people become so dependent on the rush of increased concentrations of excitatory neurochemicals that they encounter severe depression, fatigue, and lethargy as their rate of neurotransmission begins to level off. Marazziti and Dell'osso (2008), at the University of Pisa, Italy, found neurochemical similarities between love and obsessive-compulsive disorder (OCD). They measured serotonin levels in the blood of people who had fallen in love in the last 6 months and admitted to obsessing about this love object for at least 4 hours per day. When compared with people suffering from OCD, they found the levels of serotonin in both groups were 40% lower than normal. Interestingly, variants in serotonin 5-HT$_{2A}$ receptors have also been linked to love obsession (Emanuel et al., 2007, cited in De Boer, Van Buel, and Ter Horst, 2012). Serotonin-enhancing drugs like Prozac may alleviate some of the negative feelings associated with obsession, but one's ability to fall in love and stay in love may be jeopardized.

Prozac might have been a godsend in the highly publicized and extremely bizarre love affair of Burton Pugach and Linda Riss. Upon learning that Riss, his ex-lover, had recently become engaged, Pugach hired a thug who threw lye in her face, disfiguring and eventually blinding her. Interestingly, low levels of serotonin are also associated with impulsivity and violence. We speculate that Pugach's depression was related to low levels of serotonin (Krakowski, 2003). Pugach was released after serving 14 years in prison for the assault, and then the couple married. The story of their twisted romance, detailed in the case study that follows, was recorded in newspapers and magazines throughout the United States and was also made into a documentary film (*Crazy Love,* 2007).

CASE EXAMPLE: Mr. and Mrs. Pugach

It was early in morning on Monday, June 15, 1959 when Linda Riss, a recently engaged 22-year-old woman answered the doorbell as she was leaving for work. There was a voice that called out "Package for Miss Linda Riss" (Fass, 2004). Upon opening the door to receive what she thought might be a gift from Larry Schwartz, her new fiancé, she was stunned by a flash of light and the feeling of a burning liquid, streaming across her face. Her first thought that it was hot water, but it turned out to be burning lye, which would instantly leave her blind in one eye and after years of painstaking surgery, rendered her completely blind, scarring her scalp and cheekbone on the right side of her face. Even though her attacker appeared to be a stranger, she immediately surmised that the person responsible for the horrific incident was her ex-boyfriend, Burton Pugach, an influential, cunning, and manipulative Bronx lawyer.

After more than a year of courtship, Ms. Riss was growing weary of a never-ending string of promises from Pugach that he would soon be divorced. Tired of waiting, she figured that divorce was not in the cards, so she tried to avoid contact and break off the relationship. Pugach, who later admitted that he was "obsessed," became increasingly violent. He carried a gun and would wait for her in the bushes outside her apartment after work. Once he hired a surrogate to throw a rock through her window and threatened to kill her if she refused to see him. When she called the police, they would dismiss her, claiming that because he was a lawyer they were helpless to act. Despite the ominous situation, she decided of marry Larry Schwartz, a cheerful 23-year-old with a career in uniform rentals. Riss viewed Schwartz as the ideal remedy for her trials with Pugach's venom and intensity.

During the party for her engagement with Schwartz, Linda Riss received the last and perhaps the most prophetically violent phone call. "If I can't have you", Pugach told her, "no one else will have you… And when I get through with you, no one else will want you" (Fass, 2004, p. 4). The morning after the engagement party, the hitman, Joe Louis Harden, *aka* "Heard," showed up at her apartment blasting her with the life-changing lye. According to Pugach, he just hired Heard to beat her up. Even now, Pugach insists that he would never have ordered such an attack…"I didn't even know what it was [lye]…They say love is a form of insanity, that you lose rationality" (Fass, 2004, p. 4)

Having served 14 years in prison, Pugach became eligible for parole, which was granted on March 21, 1974. Although a condition of his parole was that he could neither meet nor speak with the victim, he figured out a way around those stipulations. Upon his release, he was interviewed by local TV stations. Burton Pugach proposed to Linda Riss over the nightly news! After several months, a friend of Linda arranged for a double date and in August of that same year the two met for the first time since the trial.

According to Pugach, there were several factors that might account for Riss's decision to marry the man who maimed her: the counsel of a fortuneteller; her Christian belief in forgiveness; her conviction that the police were to blame because of their failure to heed her pleas for help; a fear that someone else would 'grab him up' because he was such a 'good catch.'

After 3 decades of marriage, Pugach insisted that Riss was very much in love with him. "Well, love might be a little too strong," Linda laughingly replied. In fact, after having been married for 30 years, the couple appeared like other long-term relationships. There had been ups and downs, like when Pugach had been convicted several years earlier for having harassed yet another woman with whom he was romantically involved. Over the years, the couple developed a dark-joke routine about their fateful connection. Linda who, at the age of 67, had a remarkably good complexion, responded to compliments by saying, "Lye is good for the skin but bad for the vision." With a wry smile, Pugach responded to the question of whether his wife still holds a grudge: "She doesn't throw it in my face" (Fass, 2004, p.4).

For readers who are thinking "WTF?" upon learning that Linda Riss married and stayed with Burton Pugach until she died in 2013, here are some speculations about why she did so. The lye attack left her blind (impairing her ability to work and support herself) and physically scarred (potentially limiting her options for marriage partners). So, marrying Burt provided a means of support. Perhaps she also felt that he owed it after what he did to her. It's also possible that his determination to pursue her after he was paroled may have convinced her his love was "real." In the world of love addiction, it could be argued that she was a co-dependent to her love-addict husband. She even served as a character witness for him when he was tried for harassment in 1997; the accuser in the case was a woman with whom Pugach had been having an affair for five years (Fox, 2013).

Mr. and Mrs. Pugach's craziness may be an extreme version of the prototypic "whirlwind romance" where the couple enacts wildly fluctuating changes in brain chemistry. Yet describing love in terms of its properties of arousal, relaxation, and fantasy doesn't capture what many regard as a "spiritual quality." When you gaze into your lover's eyes and all of infinity opens before you, you are one with your partner and at one with the world around you, as if time itself has stopped. Aesthetics explode—art, nature, theater, and music become backdrops for your courtship.

It would seem that there must be yet another chemical mediator, even more potent than dopamine, PEA, oxytocin, or endorphin, to account for these transcendent experiences. In fact, Liebowitz (1983) postulates that there is an additional, albeit not yet discovered, neurochemical factor, shorter in duration than the psychedelic drugs, yet similar in effect, that is responsible for the spiritual wonders of love. Liebowitz suspects that there is a psychedelic version of PEA that endows transcendent love with its mystical quality. As William Shakespeare wrote in his Sonnet 29,

> Haply I think on thee, and then my state,
> Like to the lark at break of day arising
> From sullen earth, sings hymns at heaven's gate;
> For thy sweet love remember'd such wealth brings
> That then I scorn to change my state with kings.

Chapter Summary

Romantic love is panhuman: it proliferates in almost every culture on earth, embedded in our brains since Pleistocene times. The nightmare of tormenting love is nothing but a miscarriage of our natural attraction toward people who evoke feelings of safety and pleasure. Love junkies may be prone to stormy and dysfunctional relationships due to attachment issues related to early childhood.

Tennov (1979) describes the romantic love people seek as *limerence*. Limerence occurs when thoughts are dramatically focused on one person and there is uncertainty about the future of the relationship. Love is a psychological and social need of humans, and a healthy love is one in which both members are mutually involved in the relationship. Love junkies, on the other hand, demand attention and hang on even when harmful consequences follow. They tend to follow a repeating pattern of finding support from one love object, then moving on to the next. Some characteristics of love addiction include denial, immediacy, compulsion, loss of control, progressive problems, and withdrawal. The compulsion to find and be in love can become unmanageable, painful, and insatiable.

Using MRI data from people who were "madly in love," Fisher et al. showed that love lights up the caudate nucleus and nucleus accumbens, which is home to a rich network of dopamine receptors. According to Fisher et al., the increased availability of dopamine is the neurochemical basis for why, "when you are newly in love, you can stay up all night, watch the sun rise, run a race," and so forth. Variants in dopamine receptors can influence people's sexual desire. Hill and Wilson found that after kissing, males had increased levels of the hormone oxytocin, which is important in the formation of secure bonding and attachment; however, females showed a decrease in the same hormone. Both males and females showed a decrease in the stress hormone, cortisol, after kissing or talking while holding hands.

Excitatory neurochemicals are released while one is falling in love, perhaps reason for the intense feelings of excitement, exhilaration, and euphoria when romance is in full-bloom. The roller-coaster ride of heightened energy and euphoria one experiences when falling in love will reach a maximum level after some time, and love can either go to an endorphin-mediated relationship or an amphetamine-like withdrawal, which at some point will need to be replaced with a new experience of falling in love. Love addicts experience severe depression, fatigue, and lethargy when the neurochemical whirlwind of romance begins to level off.

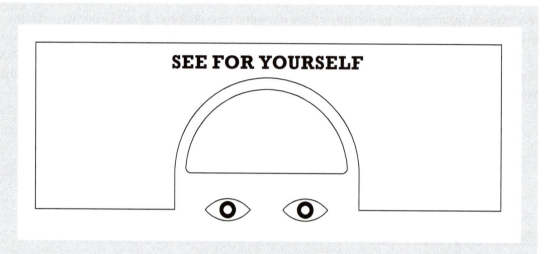

SEE FOR YOURSELF

Love Addicts Anonymous: This website provides anecdotal descriptions of various types of love addiction as well as links to the basic tenets of the 12-Step Recovery model for love addiction.

http://loveaddicts.org/kindsofloveaddicts.html

Intense, Passionate, Romantic Love: A Natural Addiction? How the Fields That Investigate Romance and Substance Abuse Can Inform Each Other. Helen E. Fisher, Xiaomeng Xu, Arthur Aron, and Lucy L. Brown. Front. Psychol., 10 May 2016

Thorough review article on love addiction: **https://doi.org/10.3389/fpsyg.2016.00687**

MDMA Therapy for Couples. 2015. *NatGeoTV.* 3:45

This clip briefly discusses the history and current use of MDMA before providing an example of a couple who used MDMA in couples therapy to process a cancer diagnosis. **https://www.youtube.com/watch?v=vlH7fnua1M0**

The Case for Using Drugs to Enhance Our Relationships (and Our Break-Ups). 2013. Ross Anderson. The Atlantic. Feature Length Article.

This piece discusses the use of biotechnology in the context of human monogamy. Including details about the evolutionary science of love, the author questions whether the use of drugs enhances bonding or disrupts maladaptive brain processes regarding love and partnership. **https://www.theatlantic.com/technology/archive/2013/01/the-case-for-using-drugs-to-enhance-our-relationships-and-our-break-ups/272615/**

Genesis, Lady Jaye, and the Pandrogyne. 2014. Brendan Baker and Nick van der Kolk. NPR. 14:39

This radio interview with artist Genesis P-Orridge delves into the Pandrogeny Project, an effort underwent by Genesis and his late wife, Lady Jaye, to use cosmetic surgery to become "absolutely integrated together through love." The pair completed many surgeries to appear more similar, describing their partnership as a "third being." **http://www.npr.org/2014/06/20/323955434/genesis-lady-jaye-and-the-pandrogyne**

CHAPTER 15

Cannabis—Reefer Madness Revisited

Boy, that gal means trouble
You ought to put her down
Get hip, take care
Look out, beware
Of sweet marijuana brown

—Barney Bigard, "Sweet Marijuana Brown," 1945

But I would not feel so all alone
Everybody must get stoned

—Bob Dylan, "Rainy Day Woman," 1966

If you don't like my fire, then don't come around
'Cause I'm gonna burn one down, yes I'm gonna burn one down

—Ben Harper, "Burn One Down," 1995

Introduction

Humans have had a long-term relationship with the cannabis plant. It is one of the earliest cultivated plants, with human use of hemp fibers (from the plant's stalk) dating back to about 6,000 BC (Earleywine, 2002). Hemp fibers are good for making fabrics, paper, and ropes and are still used for these purposes today. Historical records of cannabis for medicinal and psychoactive use appear a bit later but still date back millennia. Given that hemp seeds are edible and a source of nutrition, there are multiple reasons why humans cultivated this plant.

In terms of U.S. history, cannabis plants were raised for hemp fibers by colonists dating all the way back to Jamestown; it was an important cash crop for them. Medicinal use of cannabis was recognized as well. Cannabis oil was included in the U.S.P. (Pharmacopeia of the United States) from 1850 until 1941 (Earleywine, 2002). In the 19th and early 20th centuries, it was not unusual to see patent medicines that contained

tinctures of cannabis (cannabis oil in an alcohol solution). Reasons for medicinal use then were very similar to reasons for medical use now, including pain, sleep, seizures, and psychological issues (anxiety and depression).

Recreational cannabis use in the U.S. prior to the hippie generation of the 1960s and 1970s was not particularly common, although there were smoking dens in major cities in the late 1800s. In the early 20th century, there was an overall push for drug restrictions, including opioids, cocaine, alcohol, and cannabis. There were also negative stereotypes surrounding recreational cannabis; smoking marijuana was primarily associated with "fringe" groups, and some states had already passed laws against the substance. Its popularity increased among non-conformists during Prohibition. Use of the term "marijuana" as opposed to "cannabis" became more common during the 1930s and was related to anti-Mexican sentiments. The Federal Bureau of Narcotics was formed in 1930, and its director, Harry Anslinger, claimed that marijuana was dangerous and its use was on the rise. The 1936 propaganda film *Reefer Madness* was made during this era in an effort to stir anti-marijuana sentiment among the public. The ludicrous script and bad acting depicted young, straight-laced people becoming sex-crazed and violent after using marijuana: they play rollicking jazz music, have casual sex, attempt to rape people, engage in fights, and create other mayhem. The film became a cult classic in the 1960s and 1970s because of its outlandish claims of the harmful psychological effects of marijuana. This type of ridiculous treatment of a serious issue does a disservice by sensationalizing risks without addressing actual negative health effects of marijuana.

The anti-marijuana sentiment culminated in the Marihuana Tax Act of 1937, which taxed cultivating and selling of cannabis products. The federal law did not make possession and use of marijuana outright illegal—the federal government left that responsibility to individual states. At the time, some physicians still prescribed cannabis medicinally; under the Tax Act, growers, doctors, and pharmacists would have to pay the tax. How much they paid depended on whether they had registered and paid an annual fee and whether the person to whom they sold the substance had also done so. Some vocal members of the American Medical Association spoke out against the Act, but it passed anyway; soon thereafter, cannabis was removed from the Pharmacopeia. The law was eventually struck down in 1969 due to *Leary v. the United States* (yes, the same Timothy Leary of LSD fame). The Supreme Court ruled that complying with the federal law required individuals to incriminate themselves in illegal activity at the state level—which violates our Constitution's Fifth Amendment. However, the following year, Congress passed the Controlled Substances Act, and marijuana was established as a Schedule I substance, deemed to have no accepted medical use and a high risk of abuse. (Schedule I substances are not even legally permissible by prescription.) Despite legalization in 30 states and the District of Columbia for medicinal use and legalization in 8 states plus the District of Columbia for recreational use, marijuana remains illegal at the federal level.

A Weed by Any Other Name

Marijuana is the most widely used illicit drug in the United States and has held that position for decades. It can be taken orally, mixed with food, smoked in concentrated form as hashish (more common in Europe), smoked in rolled cigarettes (i.e., "joints," "doobies," or "fatties," the most common form of consumption in the United States), or smoked in pipes ("bongs") and occasionally hollowed-out cigars ("blunts"). Rolled cigarettes that combine marijuana and tobacco are called "spliffs." But that's not all! In Colorado and other states where cannabis is legal for medical and/or recreational use, there are at least a dozen different types of products available, including buds/flowers, edibles, potables, topicals (lotions, creams, sensual lubricants), various oils (for cooking, vaping, or dabbing), and even more (including suppositories!). There are numerous slang terms for marijuana flowers, including "pot," "weed," "reefer," "Mary Jane," "ganj," "grass," "herb," "kush," and too many others to list here. Accompanying all of the nicknames is a subculture based around cannabis. In states where cannabis is legal, there is a money-making industry tied to it: the capitalistic dream of enterprising weed growers.

Law makers, law enforcement, health care providers, and many others are keeping a watchful eye on the shifting cannabis culture and its impact on communities—for better or for worse. For instance, at least two Colorado mountain towns have seen increases in fake identification cards, which underage people have tried to use to buy recreational marijuana (Auslander, 2016; Renoux, 2016). The fake IDs have been seized from both locals and marijuana tourists and are purchased online and sent through the mail from far-away places such as China and the Philippines. Another example of potentially unforeseen effects relates to a 46% increase in emergency room and hospital admissions, [involving the possible use of marijuana among out-of-state residents], after legalization of recreational marijuana compared to the three years prior (Wong & Clarke, 2015, cited in Finn & Salmore, 2016). Data also indicate an elevated risk of overdose among children in states where cannabis has been legalized (NAS, 2017).

How popular is cannabis? According to the National Survey of Drug Use and Health (SAMHSA, 2016), about 22 million Americans had used marijuana in the past month, with use more common among adolescents and adults and more common in males than females. However, a national telephone survey conducted by Yahoo News and Marist University found that nearly 35 million Americans are regular users of marijuana, using at least 1–2 times per month. The seemingly large difference in reported numbers of users may be due to participants in the Yahoo/Marist survey being more open to responding, given that the study was not being conducted by a federal agency. The bottom line: marijuana smokers are almost as numerous as cigarette smokers (Ingraham, 2017).

Why Do People Use?

Why does pot retain its enormous popularity, pushing the boundaries of government regulation? Essentially, marijuana aficionados expect positive effects and have a less negative view of potential problems. Gaher and Simons (2007) investigated users' and nonusers' appraisals of the "benefits" of relaxation and tension reduction, facilitation of social and sexual contexts, and enhancements of mind and perception. They found that cannabis users anticipated positive outcomes in each of these domains while forecasting fewer and less frequent problems (i.e., less harmful consequences as the result of use) than nonusers.

Osborne and Fogel (2008) found people use marijuana in what they consider to be appropriate social contexts for two purposes: either to become more relaxed to enjoy the activity or to become more focused on the activity so that they could better enjoy it. Especially for adult users, marijuana had predominantly a social function. Almost half of the participants reported that a primary motive for using the drug was enhancing social contact. Many of the participants said that the drug "brings people closer together" and creates camaraderie between users. It appears that facilitation of a sense of intimacy along with relaxation and pleasurable cognitive and perceptual shifts are alluring aspects of this powerful plant. Given all the positive propaganda for the "pot scene" and testimonials from the drug users themselves, why would someone not want to use marijuana?

Tidal social forces appear to be far more powerful determinants of contemporary pot culture than an individual's attitudes about the benefits or risks of using marijuana. Zinberg (1984), presents compelling evidence that social setting is a primary (perhaps the major) determinant of an individual's choice to use an intoxicant. Drug use is intimately related to large social influences such as media, war, and massive environmental change (Halperin & Bloom, 2007; Zinberg, 1984). The success of marijuana festivals and marijuana rallies give some insight into the steadfast and growing popularity of mass social gatherings tied to marijuana. In addition to the huge turnout at music concerts and festivals (where pot is implicitly condoned), consider the major marijuana festivals where cannabis is openly celebrated. According to *Rolling Out* (Shropshire, 2017), the following annual events top the list as 10 of the biggest cannabis competitions, festivals, and parties:

- The Cannabis Cup: This world-famous contest for innovative strains takes place five or six times a year, in six different cities: Amsterdam, Los Angeles, San Francisco, Denver, Seattle, and Clio, Michigan.
- 4/20 in Denver: Civic Center Park
- HempFest, Seattle: One of the largest marijuana festivals in the world; more than 200,000 people attended the most recent event.
- Hash Bash: Ann Arbor's yearly marijuana celebration since 1971.
- Marijuana Business Conference & Expo: More than 1,000 professionals and investors come to the Las Vegas conference in November from more than 30 states and 10 countries.
- Oregon: Oregon History 420Bus Tour: The tour visits multiple locations throughout the Portland area that are significant to Oregon's marijuana movement.
- High Times Southern California Cannabis Cup – San Bernardino, California
- Thrive Cannabis Conference – Miami
- World Medical Cannabis Conference and Expo – Pittsburgh
- New England Cannabis Convention – Boston

Modern Cannabis ≠ Hippie Pot

Despite human's long-term relationship with the cannabis plant, marijuana remains one of the most poorly understood psychoactive substances. This seems ironic, given the prevalence of its use. There are at least two reasons for this: (1) it is a Schedule I substance in the U.S., making it extremely difficult to get permission to do research; and (2) the cannabis plant itself is very complex, with more than 100 cannabinoids in the plant, plus other components called terpenoids (which affect smell, taste, and quite likely the psychoactive properties of the plant as well). Most of the cannabinoids in the plant (called phytocannabinoids) are not well understood due to a lack of research, although THC (short for delta-9-tetrahydrocannibinol, to which the psychoactive effects are attributed) and CBD (short for cannabidiol, to which many medicinal effects are attributed) are the most abundant and most commonly studied. Their structures (which are extremely similar to one another) are shown in the Figure 15.1 below (Mechoulam, Peters, Murillo-Rodriguez, & Hanus, 2007).

Figure 15.1 Chemical Structures of THC and CBD

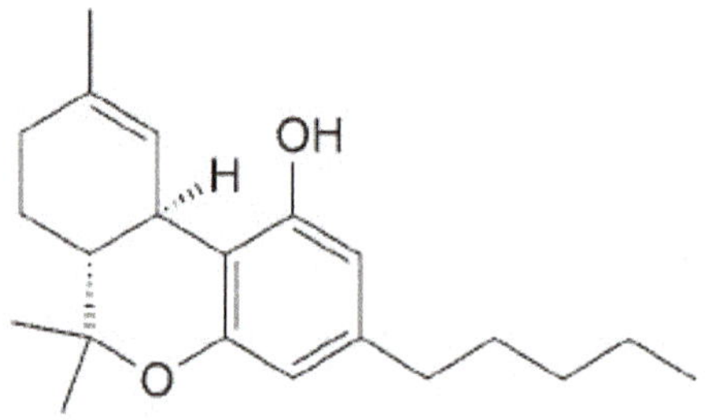

THC (1) 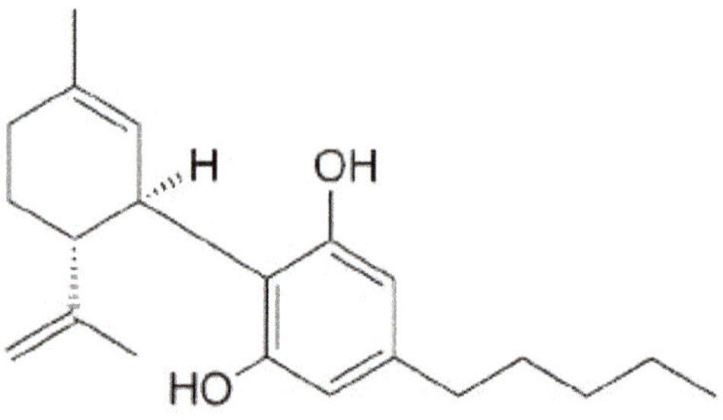   CBD (2)

If one wants to do research with marijuana, in the sense of actually administering it to human participants or animal subjects, the researcher needs federal approval (from the National Institute on Drug Abuse and the Drug Enforcement Agency), and they need marijuana supplied from the government (Gupta, 2013). That's a rare event. Moreover, the marijuana supplied by the feds tends to differ from what's in dispensaries, being much less potent; this greatly limits how well the results generalize to real world cannabis use (Vergara et al., 2017).

But it gets more complicated because "cannabis" is not a single type of plant. Although there is some disagreement among sources, generally three subspecies are recognized: *Cannabis sativa, Cannabis indica,* and *Cannabis ruderalis*. But if a person is actually buying marijuana in a dispensary, they have a choice of dozens of strains of marijuana, often hybrids of different cannabis plants (usually sativa and indica). Strains often have catchy names, such as "Purple Haze," "Strawberry Cough," "Girl Scout Cookies," "Bubba Kush," "Durban Poison," and "Trainwreck," to name just a few. The relative amounts of different components such as THC and CBD vary, depending upon the strain. Over the course of decades, cannabis horticulturists have selectively bred plants to either increase or decrease THC and CBD levels, depending on whether the purpose is to get "high" (recreational use) or to treat a medical condition. What effect the user gets is based not just on the percentage of these cannabinoids but on the ratio of THC to CBD: CBD counteracts some of the effects of THC (Mechoulam et al., 2007). Of course, this generalization about active chemicals in the plants ignores other cannabinoids (more than 100) as well as terpenoids in the plant which are minor constituents and have not been particularly well-studied. Thus, the effects of "marijuana" differ from one strain to another, depending on the combination of the different chemicals in the plant. To borrow a common disclaimer from automobile commercials, "actual mileage varies" when it comes to cannabis.

You may have heard that sativa-based strains generally have higher THC levels, whereas the indica-based strains are reputed to be CBD-rich. However, this is both simplistic and confusing. There are multiple research groups focused on studying the genetics of cannabis plants. Dusfresnes, Jan, Bienert, Goudet, and Fumagalli (2017) describe the sativa/indica distinction as informal and point out the lack of precision because it may refer to differences either in the morphology (tall with narrow leaves for sativa, short with wide leaves for indica) or the chemical properties (psychoactive effects produced by plants normally grown in equatorial regions for sativa, or relaxing effects for those originating in Central Asia) of cannabis plants. Strain information available at dispensaries indicates whether plants are sativa, indica, or hybrid; interestingly, high levels of THC can be found in all types of strains. It all becomes very dizzying, even when you're not actually partaking in weed. Cannabis researchers at the University of Colorado – Boulder avoid these distinctions, opting instead for "broad-leafed marijuana", "narrow-leafed marijuana," and "hemp" varieties. (Vergara, Kane, & Pauli, 2017).

Now here's where modern marijuana becomes even more interesting and confounding: THC levels in many of the currently-available cannabis plants are far in excess of what was used by the flower children of the 1960s and 1970s. Weed of the hippie generation typically had about 2% THC content, but later generations are being exposed to more potent pot. Figure 15.3, from ElSohly et al. (2016), shows the trend in increasing THC content based on assessments of samples of marijuana seized by the Drug Enforcement Agency (DEA). Note that by the 1990s, THC content had crept up to about 4% on average, but now in the 2010s, THC content of about 12% is considered to be typical.

The situation is actually more extreme, however, than ElSohly and colleagues depict in their study based on illegal marijuana. One can easily find buds in dispensaries that have THC content approaching 30% and some strains with even greater THC levels. Of course, this is just considering the plant matter itself. Many cannabis products (such as oils, waxes, and "shatter") are actually extracts from the plant with quite high THC concentrations of 75% or more. If the abuse liability of cannabis proves to be similar to other substances (alcohol, cocaine, opioids), then there is a legitimate cause for concern: more potent substances generally have higher abuse liability.

To add yet another wrinkle to this complicated situation, there is the consideration of *how* the marijuana is used, with the most basic distinction being smoking vs. eating. When smoked, marijuana reaches the brain extremely quickly, within a matter of seconds. When consumed (say, in the form of gummies, brownies, or cookies), it takes much longer for the substance to hit the system. In addition, the effect is somewhat different because marijuana absorbed through the gastrointestinal tract undergoes first-pass metabolism by the liver—meaning that some of cannabinoids undergo transformation before reaching the brain. Ironically, the first-pass metabolism of THC actually results in an equally (or possibly more)

Figure 15.2 Increasing Levels of THC Content from Illegal Marijuana

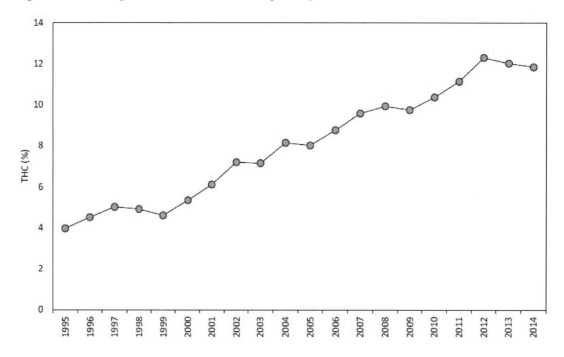

potent and longer-lasting metabolite known as 11-hydroxy-delta-9-THC (Halldin et al., 1982, cited in Dinis-Oliveira, 2016) that passes into the brain more readily than THC itself.

The "high" from an edible will take quite a bit longer to achieve (often ranging between 30 to 90 minutes for onset) but it will last longer. Unfortunately, edible novices have been known to experience negative effects due to overconsuming—either by failing to recognize what constitutes a single "dose" or by becoming impatient when the effects don't kick in right away and subsequently consuming more. The problems related to edibles are highlighted in the case below.

Case Example: Maureen, Cannabis Tourist

Maureen Dowd, a newspaper columnist, came to Colorado to experience marijuana post-legalization. She's not the only person to have done so, nor is she the only one to have a negative experience. She writes: "Sitting in my hotel room in Denver, I nibbled off the end [of a cannabis-containing caramel chocolate bar] and then, when nothing happened, nibbled some more ... What could go wrong with a bite or two? Everything, as it turned out" (Dowd, 2014). Still feeling nothing, she decided to order dinner (complete with wine) through room service and watch movies on the television. About an hour after eating too much of the chocolate bar (but before room service arrived), she felt the effects kick in; to say that she didn't enjoy them would be a gross understatement. She describes herself as having trouble recalling where she was, but the overwhelming effect was one of paranoia. Early in the experience, she feared opening the door for room service, afraid that they would call the police on her. Then, things got worse: "As my paranoia deepened, I became convinced that I had died and no one was telling me." (Dowd, 2014). The horrible experience lasted through the night. The next day, she learned how she managed to eat too much—the packaging did not indicate that the entire bar was actually 16 doses, not 1 or 2!

Since Maureen's experience, and others like hers, the State of Colorado has passed legislation requiring better labelling and packaging of cannabis products to make dosing more obvious. Cannabis-containing candies are now required to have "THC" stamped on them so that they will not be mistaken for ordinary chocolate bars or gummy bears. Maureen's case highlights problems with edibles. In some cases, there have been deadly outcomes, due to people inflicting harm on themselves or others in extremely cannabis-intoxicated states.

A final note about eating cannabis: don't expect potent effects from simply eating raw buds or leaves. The phytocannabinoids in the plant exist primarily in their acid forms: THCA and CBDA. Heating the plant through smoking (or baking it into edibles) drives the conversion of THCA into THC and CBDA to CBD.

Effects on the Brain

Just like other substances, marijuana would not have a psychological effect on us if our brains did not have a system that the chemicals could tap into and use. It turns out our brains make chemicals called endocannabinoids, short for "endogenous cannabinoids." The first discovered is known as *anandamide*, derived from "ananda", the Sanskrit word for "bliss." Research focuses on two types of cannabinoid receptors, CB_1 and CB_2. The distributions of these receptors differ, with CB_1 receptors found primarily in the brain and CB_2 found primarily in the periphery of the body, especially in the immune system. It turns out that, despite their structural similarities, marijuana's two primary cannabinoids have different effects on these receptors: THC is a partial agonist at receptors, whereas CBD serves as an antagonist at them (Mechoulam et al., 2007). In other words, THC partially activates the receptors, but CBD prevents activation of the receptors by anandamide or THC. These opposite effects on cannabinoid receptors helps explain why CBD counteracts some of the effects of THC.

The endocannabinoid system is the rebel of the neurochemistry world, violating the "rules" of neurotransmitter function. If you recall back to Neurochemistry 101 (in Chapter 3), we told you that neurotransmitters are released from synaptic vesicles of a presynaptic neuron, cross the synapse, and bind to receptors on a postsynaptic neuron. The receptor binding allows the neurotransmitter to send its message, either exciting or inhibiting the postsynaptic cell. Endocannabinoids, however, work the system in reverse. They are made and released as needed, not stored in vesicles. Once made, these fatty molecules pass through the neuron's membrane and out into the synapse, where they diffuse backwards across the synapse and bind to receptors (either CB_1 or CB_2) on the presynaptic cell. This backwards use of the synapse is called "retrograde messaging." Figure 15.4 illustrates how retrograde messaging occurs. Endocannabinoids do not appear to send their own messages—rather, their job is to modify the messages of other neurotransmitters by decreasing their release. This appears to be a way for the postsynaptic cell to "adjust" the signal coming from the presynaptic cell. Endocannabinoid signaling has been shown to adjust release of GABA, glutamate, and some other neurotransmitters. When marijuana is smoked or consumed, THC and CBD are going to bind to the same receptors that endocannabinoids use and either act in place of them (as THC does) or oppose them (as CBD does). CBD does not seem to be as well understood as

THC, but it actually has a weak binding affinity for CB receptors (Mechoulam et al., 2007), meaning that it has less interaction with CB receptors compared to THC.

Figure 15.3 **Retrograde Messaging** Endocannabinoids (open circles) released by the postsynaptic neuron combine with CB receptors on the pre-synaptic neuron. This reduces the amount of neurotransmitter (closed circles) released into the synapse.[1]

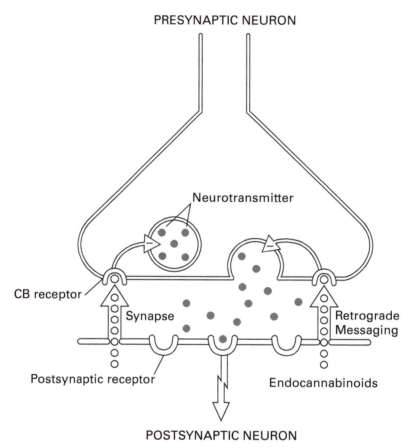

As shown in Figure 15.4, CB_1 receptors have not only been found in the cerebellum, hippocampus, and neocortex, but also in the nucleus accumbens (reward), basal ganglia (movement), hypothalamus (temperature regulation, appetite), amygdala (emotion), spinal cord (pain), central gray (analgesia), brain stem (sleep, arousal), and the nucleus of the solitary tract (nausea, vomiting) (Nicoll & Alger, 2004). It is of note that, despite being some of the most widely-distributed receptors in the nervous system, cannabinoid receptors are absent in the respiratory center of the medulla, presumably explaining the lack of lethal overdoses of THC (Julien, Advokat, & Comaty, 2008). Many drugs that produce lethal overdoses (for instance, alcohol, sedatives, inhalants, and opioids) produce their lethal effects because they suppress the respiratory center through neurotransmitter systems such as GABA and endogenous opioids. The lack of

---

1 Mahmoud A. ElSohly, et al., Changes in Cannabis Potency Over the Last 2 Decades (1995–2014): Analysis of Current Data in the United States. Biological Psychiatry, vol.79, no. 7. Copyright © 2016 by Elsevier B.V.

cannabinoid receptors in this region helps explain why there are not documented lethal overdoses due to marijuana alone. But that does not mean there are no risks associated with this substance—as we will discuss below. Moreover, THC has been shown to be toxic in dogs, so be careful about leaving marijuana edibles around the house where pets can access them; in fact, even second-hand smoke could make a dog ill (Fitzgerald, Bronstein, & Newquist, 2013).

The wide-spread distribution of cannabinoid receptors explains why marijuana has such profound effects on behavior. The endocannabinoid system is thought to play a key role in brain development: early (prenatal and neonatal) and during adolescence (reviewed in Viveros et al., 2012). Thus, there are legitimate concerns about prenatal exposure due to maternal use during pregnancy as well as adolescents beginning use before brain development is complete. The endocannabinoid system has been shown to affect the function of the dopamine system and is thought to play a role in substance abuse and addiction—even with regard to substances other than marijuana (Trigo & Le Foll, 2017). CBD may also be affecting the deactivation of anandamide, perhaps by inhibiting its degrading enzyme; other research suggests that effects on CB receptors are just part of the story; for instance, data indicate that CBD can affect other neurotransmitter systems, such as serotonin, endogenous opioids, and adenosine (as reviewed in Mechoulam et al., 2007). More research into CBD, THC, and other cannabis components is clearly needed in order to better understand the effects of marijuana on the brain and body.

Figure 15.4 Marijuana's Effect on the Brain

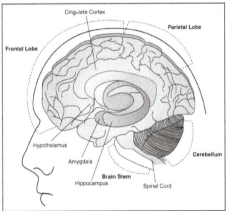

When marijuana is smoked, its active ingredient, THC, travels throughout the body, including the brain. To produce its many effects, THC attaches to sites called cannabinoid receptors on nerve cells in the brain, affecting the way those cells work. Cannabinoid receptors are abundant in parts of the brain that regulate movement, coordination, learning and memory, higher cognitive functions such as judgment, and pleasure.

Source: Marijuana Abuse. 2005 by National Institute on Drug Abuse.

Brain Region	Functions Associated With Region
Brain regions in which cannabinoid receptors are abundant	
Cerebellum	Body movement coordination
Hippocampus	Learning and memory
Cerebral cortex, especially cingulated, frontal, and parietal regions	Higher cognitive functions
Nucleus accumbens	Reward
Basal ganglia	Movement control
Substantia nigra pars reticulata	
Entopeduncular nucleus	
Globus pallidus	
Putamen	
Brain regions in which cannabinoid receptors are moderately concentrated	
Hypothalamus	Body housekeeping functions (body temperature regulation, salt and water balance, reproductive function)
Amygdala	Emotional response, fear
Spinal cord	Peripheral sensation, including pain
Brain stem	Sleep and arousal, temperature regulation, motor control
Central gray	Analgesia
Nucleus of the solitary tract	Visceral sensation, nausea and vomiting

Short-Term Effects

The stereotype of a "spacey" pot smoker is grounded in reality. Marijuana has negative effects on cognitive functions, such as memory, attention, and thinking processes. It also has negative effects on psychomotor speed and manual dexterity. It should be obvious, therefore, that driving while under the influence is very hazardous. Research evidence supports increased risk of motor vehicle accidents related to cannabis use (NAS, 2017).

Long-Term Effects

There has been a veritable explosion of cannabis-related research in recent years. Besides the sheer volume of information, some of the data are conflicting, making it difficult to draw conclusions. Fortunately, the National Academy of Sciences (2017) recently published a *magnum opus* document that reviews the extensive body of research. The NAS conclusions are summarized by "weight-of-evidence categories," recognizing that not all evidence is equal. Weight-of-evidence designations range include conclusive, substantial, moderate, limited, and no/insufficient evidence.

Table 15.1 represents a compilation of much (though not all) of the data summarized by the NAS report regarding long-term physical and psychological health consequences.

Table 15.1 Consequences of Long-Term Cannabis Usage

Effect	Level of Evidence
Worsening of respiratory symptoms, More frequent or chronic bronchitis	Substantial
Low birth weight in infants born to mothers who smoked during pregnancy	Substantial
↑ risk of schizophrenia or other psychosis	Substantial
↑ mania/hypomania	Moderate
↑ risk of depressive disorders, suicidal ideation, suicide attempts, suicide completion	Moderate
↑ risk of anxiety disorders or ↑anxiety symptoms	Limited
Impaired social functioning	Limited
Impaired academic achievement, low income and/or unemployment	Limited
Pregnancy complications, ↑ incidents of neonatal ICU admissions	Limited
Later negative outcomes in children whose mothers used during pregnancy (includes cognitive effects, risk of addiction, SIDS)	Insufficient

Conclusive findings are those for which "there are many supportive findings from good-quality studies with no credible opposing findings. A firm conclusion can be made, and the limitations to the evidence, including chance, bias, and confounding factors, can be ruled out with reasonable confidence." Substantial evidence denotes "several supportive findings from good-quality studies with very few or no credible opposing findings. A firm conclusion can be made, but minor limitations, including chance, bias, and confounding factors, cannot be ruled out with reasonable confidence." Moderate evidence relates to "several supportive findings from good-to-fair-quality studies with very few or no credible opposing findings. A general conclusion can be made, but limitations, including chance, bias, and confounding factors, cannot be ruled out with reasonable confidence." Limited evidence indicates that "there are supportive findings from fair-quality studies or mixed findings with most favoring one conclusion. A conclusion can be made, but there is a significant uncertainty due to chance, bias, and confounding factors." Finally, the designation of no/insufficient evidence is reserved for "mixed findings, a single poor study, or health endpoint has not been studied at all. No conclusion can be made because of substantial uncertainty due to chance, bias, and confounding factors." (See pp 7–8 of the 2017 NAS report for these definitions.)

The NAS report does not support a link between cannabis smoking and increased risk of head, neck, or lung cancers. Previously, there was conflicting information in the literature on this issue. There is limited evidence to support an association between cannabis smoking and cardiovascular disease and prediabetes. Curran and colleagues' (2016) review article points out that data on the effects of long-term cannabis use on cognition and IQ are conflicting, which can at least partly be attributed to lack of control over types/potency of cannabis used. Whether the cannabis is THC-rich or CBD-rich will make a difference, but quasi-experimental designs do not allow for that sort of control.

Tolerance, Withdrawal, Abuse, and Addiction

Is it likely that someone would get hooked on marijuana? In previous decades, marijuana was considered to have a low to moderate risk for abuse or dependence—and it's a point sometimes mentioned by advocates for legalization when making their case. However, given that marijuana is generally stronger now than it was in earlier decades, this may be outdated thinking. Indeed, data indicate that the number of people going into treatment for cannabis use disorders has increased over time. Surveys show that about 17% of patients seeking treatment for substance abuse were there for marijuana-related issues, although the prevalence varies by age group: cannabis accounts for nearly 2/3 of the admissions for substance use disorders among those who are under the age of 18, but only for about 5% of those aged 35 or older (Budney, Roffman, Stephens, & Walker, 2007). It is estimated that about 9% of people who try marijuana will get hooked (Lopez-Quintero et al., 2011), and the risk for frequent smokers is even higher. Specifically, regular smokers who began before the age of 18 are between 4 and 7 times more likely to develop a cannabis use disorder (NIDA, 2017). The incidence of dependence can be up to 30% in those who are regular smokers (Hasin et al., 2015, cited by NIDA, 2017). The case study below, originally reported by Levin and Kleber (2008), briefly describes a man who struggled to get off of marijuana.

Case Example: "Mr. A."—Successful Businessman & Daily Stoner

This 42-year-old man had smoked marijuana daily for about 20 years. If he stopped using (which he never successfully did for more than a few days), he experienced insomnia and irritability—withdrawal symptoms that prompted him to resume use. He sought treatment because his usage was causing problems at work and home. Marijuana was clearly Mr. A.'s drug of choice; he used no other drugs except for having an occasional alcoholic drink. He smoked 3–6 joints on weeknights after getting home from work, but on weekends and vacations, he increased his usage. His wife was frustrated at having a husband who sat spaced out in a chair all evening, disconnected from her and their children. Mr. A. was aware of other risks associated with his marijuana usage, such as the possibility that getting busted would end his career. Therefore, he was cautious about buying and didn't drive under the influence because he feared getting stopped or having an accident.

Treatment initially involved once-a-week sessions. Mr. A. seemed a bit resistant to change at first, going 3 weeks without decreasing his marijuana usage. Interestingly, his doctor prescribed Marinol (dronabinol), an FDA-approved synthetic THC in pill form that is intended to treat nausea in cancer patients. The doctor's intention was to use Marinol as a substitute substance in the same way that methadone is used to substitute for opioids. After 4 months, Mr. A.'s marijuana usage had decreased by 75%. The clinician prescribed an anti-seizure medication at bedtime; after another month, his patient completely stopped using marijuana. The last step of the process was to discontinue the Marinol by tapering the dosage over a period of 5 weeks. Ultimately, Mr. A. was able to get completely off of Marinol and has remained off of marijuana, although he still takes the anti-seizure medication to help with sleep at bedtime. He reported feeling healthier and that his marriage has improved as a result of quitting pot.

The use of cannabis-based prescriptions as replacement medication for marijuana is not widely reported in the literature. Besides this case study, there is a randomized, double-blind, placebo-controlled study (by Levin et al., 2011, cited by Marshall, Gowing, Ali, & Le Foll, 2014) and another study involving Nabiximols (an aerosol THC/CBD combo) reported by Allsop et al. (2014; cited by Marshall et al., 2014). In their review of pharmacotherapy for marijuana dependence, Marshall and colleagues ultimately conclude that "[t]here is moderate quality evidence that completion of treatment is more likely with preparations containing THC compared to placebo," and that such preparations are of "potential value;" however, due to limited evidence, use of "THC preparations should be considered to still be experimental" (Marshall et al., 2014, p. 22).

Like many other substances, repeated, frequent use of cannabis promotes tolerance. One of the hallmarks of addiction is the presence of negative physiological and psychological effects upon removal of the drug. The occasionally proclaimed view that marijuana is non-addicting is contradicted by observed withdrawal effects. Kouri, Pope, and Lukas (1999) found that long-term marijuana users who were unsuccessful at quitting became more aggressive during withdrawal than did former users who managed to stop using without much difficulty. Haney, Ward, Comer, Foltin, and Fischman (1999) found that chronic users experience other withdrawal symptoms such as anxiety, stomach pain, and irritability. Budney, Hughes, Moore, and Novy (2001) showed that during abstinence and while living at home, marijuana smokers experienced sleep difficulties; decreased appetite; and increased anger, aggression, and irritability. These studies on withdrawal effects clearly indicate that, contrary to earlier opinions, marijuana use can be associated with drug dependence. A review by Budney and colleagues (2004) suggests that withdrawal symptoms occur in more than 50% of heavy users (those who use daily or are dependent) and that the incidence is likely higher among those seeking treatment for cannabis misuse.

The CUDIT-R, a common assessment used to try to assess whether a person has a problem with cannabis use (Adamson et al., 2010), appears in Table 15.2 below. The numerical values for the answers are summed to determine a total score; *scores above 13 indicate a concern about abuse, whereas those above 23 indicate concerns about dependence.* Keep in mind that this test by itself is not a definitive diagnostic, but it can be helpful by allowing people to assess their own levels of use and negative impacts in their lives.

Table 15.3 provides a succinct summary of the short-term vs. long-term effects of cannabis on the brain, which helps explain not only how long-term cannabis use can lead to tolerance effects that may accompany dependence, but also negative effects on cognitive processes.

Table 15.2 The Cannabis Use Disorder Identification Test - Revised (CUDIT-R)

Have you used any cannabis over the past six months?   YES / NO

If YES, please answer the following questions about your cannabis use. Circle the response that is most correct for you in relation to your cannabis use *over the past six months*

1. How often do you use cannabis?

Never	Monthly or less	2-4 times a month	2-3 times a week	4 or more times a week
0	1	2	3	4

2. How many hours were you "stoned" on a typical day when you had been using cannabis?

Less than 1	1 or 2	3 or 4	5 or 6	7 or more
0	1	2	3	4

3. How often during the past 6 months did you find that you were not able to stop using cannabis once you had started?

Never	Less than monthly	Monthly	Weekly	Daily or almost daily
0	1	2	3	4

4. How often during the past 6 months did you fail to do what was normally expected from you because of using cannabis?

Never	Less than monthly	Monthly	Weekly	Daily or almost daily
0	1	2	3	4

5. How often in the past 6 months have you devoted a great deal of your time to getting, using, or recovering from cannabis?

Never	Less than monthly	Monthly	Weekly	Daily or almost daily
0	1	2	3	4

6. How often in the past 6 months have you had a problem with your memory or concentration after using cannabis?

Never	Less than monthly	Monthly	Weekly	Daily or almost daily
0	1	2	3	4

7. How often do you use cannabis in situations that could be physically hazardous, such as driving, operating machinery, or caring for children:

Never	Less than monthly	Monthly	Weekly	Daily or almost daily
0	1	2	3	4

8. Have you ever thought about cutting down, or stopping, your use of cannabis?

Never	Yes, but not in the past 6 months	Yes, during the past 6 months
0	2	4

This scale is in the public domain and is free to use with appropriate citation:

Adamson SJ, Kay-Lambkin FJ, Baker AL, Lewin TJ, Thornton L, Kelly BJ, and Sellman JD. (2010). An Improved Brief Measure of Cannabis Misuse: The Cannabis Use Disorders Identification Test – Revised (CUDIT-R). *Drug and Alcohol Dependence* 110:137-143.

On the Plus Side: Medicinal Effects

The National Academy of Sciences, (2017) extensive review included therapeutic effects, using the same designation for weight-of-evidence categories as those used for harmful effects of cannabis. Table 15.3 presents a partial summary of their conclusions. For full details of the evidence, readers are encouraged to explore the full 400-plus page report, which may be available for free through their library's subscriptions.

Table 15.3 Therapeutic Effects of Cannabis—Partial List

Effect	Level of Evidence
↓ chronic pain in adults	Conclusive
↓ nausea in chemotherapy patients	Conclusive
↓ MS patients' reports of muscle spasticity	Conclusive
Help short-term sleep issues related to pain, fibromyalgia, MS, and obstructive sleep apnea	Moderate
↑ appetite and ↓ weight loss in HIV/AIDs patients	Limited
Improving Tourette's syndrome symptoms	Limited
↓ anxiety associated with PTSD and social anxiety	Limited
Treating cancer	Insufficient
Treating epilepsy	Insufficient

Perhaps the biggest surprise of the National Academy's assessment is the *insufficient evidence* to support the use of cannabis for treating cancer and epilepsy. Currently, these are two of the commonly heralded uses for medical marijuana.

Not Really a Drug, Not Really Legal

When the Marihuana Tax Act of 1937 was passed, there were vocal members of the American Medical Association who opposed it. Some doctors had been prescribing cannabis to patients for a variety of reasons, and they recognized that this new legislation would mean that this substance could no longer be used for medicinal purposes due to the high tax levied on it. However, in the past couple of decades, there has been renewed interest in using marijuana for medical purposes, especially relief from pain. In 2005, Canada became the first country in the world to approve a cannabis-based painkiller derived from marijuana for those suffering from multiple sclerosis.

The Food and Drug Administration of the U.S. is not likely to consider marijuana a drug because cannabis in its plant form is not purified for controlled dosing. For any substance to be approved as a drug by the FDA, a New Drug Application must be filed and non-human research with at least two species must be conducted that demonstrates that the drug is safe; appropriate dosing and routes of administration need to be determined. Research on healthy humans is then required to further verify safety before clinical trials progress with patients. In the case of cannabis, specific components need to be extracted from the plant (or synthesized) and prepared to be delivered in precise doses. Ultimately, the FDA requires that the drug be demonstrated to be generally safe and effective; in other words, the drug should not be toxic and should show significant results for its purported use. Presently, the FDA reports that marijuana has not been demonstrated to be generally safe and effective.

However, the FDA has approved cannabis-related pills that are legal: Cesamet (a.k.a., nabilone, a Schedule II THC-like synthetic, currently with no generic available on the market) and Marinol (a.k.a., dronabinol, a Schedule III synthetic THC). These products are approved for medical use by a prescription, meaning that the FDA has agreed that they are generally safe and effective for specific medicinal purposes, such as appetite stimulation for people with HIV/AIDS and anti-nausea for chemotherapy patients. Thus, some federal officials have argued that there's no need to use an illegal substance—marijuana—for medical purposes given these legal, government-approved products. However, while some insurance companies do cover Cesamet and Marinol on their prescription plans, others do not. These drugs are more expensive than medical marijuana, which makes them less appealing to some patients. Moreover, according to Prus (2017), many people who seek relief from medical cannabis generally prefer actual marijuana to Marinol. Prus suggests that cannabis may be more effective and better tolerated. This makes sense, given that neither Marinol nor Cesamet contains a CBD component (or other cannabinoids and terpenoids found in marijuana), so the effects are not going to be the same. It may also be easier for patients to control their dosing by smoking marijuana rather than swallowing a pill, and the effects will obviously be more immediate. Overall, many advocates for medical marijuana do not see Cesamet and Marinol as viable options for patients.

Recently, some physicians have begun speaking out about the medical benefits of cannabis. For instance, Dr. Sanjay Gupta, chief medical correspondent for CNN, reversed his opinion and has become an advocate for medical marijuana. Part of his changed opinion was due to reviewing medical evidence for the efficacy of marijuana for conditions like seizures and pain. He did a historical review of research conducted prior to the 1970 Controlled Substances Act and determined that "[n]ot because of sound scientific evidence, but because of its absence, marijuana was classified as a schedule I substance" (Gupta, 2013). Adding to his judgment is another important fact: there are no known lethal overdoses of marijuana, which stands in stark contrast to the average of 2–3 deaths per hour due to opioid overdoses.

Although more than two dozen U.S. states have legalized medical marijuana, those state laws run counter to the federal ban on such usage. The U.S. Supreme Court (Mears, 2005) ruled that the federal law supersedes the state laws and that users of medical marijuana could be arrested. The Obama administration seemed to waver at times on this issue, although an August, 2013 memo by then-Deputy Attorney General James M. Cole, depicted a "hands off" policy with regard to prosecuting offenses within states with legal marijuana—provided that state laws were consistent with federal priorities laid out in the memo, such as keeping marijuana away from minors, not allowing diversion of marijuana outside of the regulated system or to other states, and that regulation of the market did not help black market marijuana enterprises. However, if state enforcement was not sufficient to ensure this, then the federal government could seek to challenge the state's regulatory structure and prosecute individuals or businesses who are in violation with federal priorities (Cole memo, 2013).

It seems that the country as a whole may be changing its views on legality of cannabis, with 60% of Americans favoring legalizing marijuana use (Swift, 2016). The push to change marijuana's status also may be gaining momentum within Congress. Four members of the U.S. House of Representatives (from Alaska, California, Colorado, and Oregon) formed the Congressional Cannabis Caucus, a bipartisan group aimed at changing the *status quo* of federal marijuana laws. As quoted in *The Washington Post*, Rohrabacher, one of the caucus members, stated "The federal government's decades-long approach to marijuana is a colossal, cruel joke, and most Americans know it. Not only have incalculable amounts of taxpayers' dollars been wasted, but countless lives have been unnecessarily disrupted and even ruined by misguided law enforcement" (Ingraham, 2017). In order to address conflicts between federal and state marijuana laws, Rohrabacher has introduced the Respect State Marijuana Laws Act of 2017 (H.R. 975). This legislation would protect individuals and businesses from being prosecuted for marijuana offenses at the federal level if they abide by marijuana laws within their own states. Additional bills have been introduced into Congress by other U.S. representatives to specifically address marijuana's status on the Controlled Substances Act. These proposals include a bill to remove marijuana from Schedule I (H.R. 1227), a bill to lower marijuana from Schedule I while removing CBD from the federal definition of cannabis and allowing for CBD itself to be unscheduled (H.R. 715), and a bill moving marijuana to Schedule III (H.R. 2020). Advocates of marijuana should be aware that this is not the first time bills have been introduced into the House that would change marijuana's legal status, and to date, none of them has passed. Recently, the DEA (Drug Enforcement Agency), the federal department responsible for enforcing the Controlled Substances Act, declined petitions to reschedule marijuana. Their decision was said to be based on recommendations from the Department of Health and Human Services as well as the FDA, whose official stance is that marijuana has not been proven to be safe and effective. Although the body of data addressing marijuana's medicinal use and safety is growing, the DEA states that presently the evidence is not sufficient to change the legal status of marijuana (Wallace, 2016).

Is This a Good Idea?

It has been estimated that in the U.S., 91 people die each day from drug-related harm. In this context, Attorney General, Jeff Sessions, asked Congress to assist in rescinding the legal constraints on federal prosecution of medical marijuana dispensaries which have been protected since 2014. Sessions wrote in a letter to lawmakers that the legal controls which prohibit the Department of Justice (DOJ) from cracking down on medical marijuana dispensaries (As of 2018 medical marijuana is legal in 30 states and Washington, D.C.) impair DOJ's ability to combat the "historic drug epidemic" and apprehend nefarious drug traffickers.

Science Calls Out Jeff Sessions on Medical Marijuana and the "Historic Drug Epidemic." Scientific American, June 14, 2017.

Herbal Weed: Maybe Just Say "No!"

There are synthetic THC-like substances (often called synthetic cannabinoids, or SCBs) that are far more potent than THC. These substances are illegal (Schedule I) substances in the U.S., but that doesn't stop them from being sold on the streets. Sold under names such as "Spice," "K2," and other names, they were originally billed as "legal highs" because when they first hit the streets, there were no laws on the books that covered them (until 2012). SCBs are often sprayed on plant material (dried parsley, for instance) and sold as "herbal weed." That may sound safe, but don't be misled! Because of the high potency of these substances, negative effects occur. The most common negative effects seem to be psychotic-like symptoms such as paranoia and hallucinations; people also may experience panic, elevated heartrate, irregular heartbeat, and high blood pressure, leading them to call poison control centers or go to a hospital emergency room. Other users may lay motionless in the middle of a public sidewalk; if conscious, their faces may look "glazed," leading passers-by to describe them as "zombie-like." A recent spate of cases in Brooklyn, NY, highlights the danger associated with these substances (Santora, 2016). Ford and colleagues (2017) provide a review of SCBs that reveals these substances are not only more potent than marijuana but are far more toxic; the toxicity can affect the nervous system and cardiovascular system, as well as the gastrointestinal tract and urinary tract (for instance producing kidney damage). Besides a greater risk of producing psychotic symptoms compared to cannabis, SCBs can produce seizures (whereas medical marijuana is sometimes used to treat seizures). At least 20 deaths have been attributed to SCBs over the past few years. Overall, the physical, psychological, and dependence risks of SCBs exceed those of cannabis, providing good reasons to avoid these substances.

As pointed out by Santora (2016), some of these potent "marijuana-like" substances were originally synthesized by pharmaceutical companies but ended up on the streets after clandestine chemists figured out how to synthesize them. Such is the case with AMB-FUBINACA, which was created by Pfizer but is now sold on the streets under such names as "AK-47" (which is also the name of a cannabis strain) and "24 Karat Gold." That's how "K2" and "Spice" found a street market, but in the case of those chemicals—originally created in the 1990s—the actual chemical formulations and synthesis information were published in chemistry journals by the research scientists who developed them. Academic chemists didn't recognize that underground drug labs would start producing and illegally selling the molecules they had originally synthesized in their lab but hadn't thoroughly tested for their effects and safety (McCoy, 2015). Interestingly, these SCBs don't look similar to real THC in terms of their chemical structure. Nonetheless, they are able to activate cannabinoid receptors more effectively than THC, which at least partially explains their greater potency compared to cannabis (Ford et al., 2017).

The Need for More Research

If one were listing substances that require more extensive and up-to-date research, cannabis would surely top the list. As discussed above, there is so much diversity among cannabis strains that marijuana is not a single, specific substance—especially given the myriad chemicals inside of the plant. Add to that the variety of ways in which cannabis can be used, and it is even more difficult to say for certain what the effects, risks, and benefits are. The notion that marijuana is unlikely to produce dependence is a notion that is perhaps better suited to 1970s pot than 2017 pot. A current concern among members of the medical community is that legalization is happening more rapidly than the effects of legalization can be assessed (Furlow, 2017).

Fortunately, in their mammoth 2017 report on marijuana, the National Academies made four recommendations for the future: (1) address gaps in research regarding both short-term and long-term effects of marijuana, including both positive (medicinal) as well as negative (harmful) effects; (2) improve the quality of research so that evidence is conclusive; (3) improve surveillance such that agencies capture real world data, such as information about youth exposure, incidences of negative consequences (hospital visits, accidental poisonings, accidents, etc.), and information about chemical composition of cannabis products; and (4) address research barriers to make it easier for researchers to study cannabis, such as providing research-grade cannabis and enabling funding for research (NAS, 2017). Hopefully, these recommendations will be followed, giving us the information we need to advise public policy and medical use in the future, as well as address abuse and addiction concerns.

The State of Colorado has taken the need for more research very seriously with the creation of the Institute for Cannabis Research (ICR for short, officially housed at Colorado State University–Pueblo) and an annual ICR conference is held there. The inaugural conference occurred in April of 2017 and brought together researchers, advocates, and other concerned parties not only from around our nation but from around the world. The conference attracted "rock star" level researchers of the cannabis world, including Raphael Mechoulam, the "father of cannabis research," who led the discovery of isolating THC from marijuana (Gaoni & Mechoulam, 1964). Because cannabis use isn't going away, we need to be proactive in promoting valid research. Many of the ICR conference presentations focused on CBD and its potential medical benefits. There are legitimate reasons to explore these benefits of cannabis, but much of the research thus far has focused on negative effects due to marijuana's federal status as an illegal substance and its long-standing status as a recreational substance that can result in misuse, abuse, or even dependence. Research is needed to address all sides of the issue: medical vs. recreational, beneficial effects vs. harmful effects, etc.

Finally, there may be other considerations that come into play in the future: the sustainability of the marijuana industry itself. What many people in the general public do not consider is the cost and logistics of growing cannabis. In general, growing any crop costs money, but it's even more costly for cannabis due to required licenses at multiple (state and city) levels. Then, there's the fact that grow operations are usually inside of greenhouses in order to protect the plants from outside elements as well as from thieves. State laws (at least in Colorado) require that grow operations are secure, meaning fully enclosed and able to be locked. Now, add in the lighting and watering systems needed for optimal growth, plus protecting the plants from pests, mold, fungus, and potential cross pollination between strains. Perhaps it shouldn't be surprising that a typical price for an eighth of an ounce of marijuana flower is around $30.

Interestingly, there is a biochemical researcher in Canada who is considering ways of generating cannabinoids from yeast, which would require less space and reduce cost (Hiatt, 2017). If the means of production proves viable, this provides more flexibility in production of medicinal products than the cannabis plants themselves. For instance, a variety of different cannabinoids besides just THC and CBD could be generated and then combined in different ratios in a more precise manner than cultivation of the cannabis plants allows. The goal is ultimately to provide better cannabinoid-based treatment for patients. It is unclear how many years away the researcher's dream is from being realized and what place his products would hold in the marketplace. However, his approach highlights something about cannabis that may be missed by many people in the general public: this is a high-tech industry!

Is This a Good Idea?

Consider this testimonial by the late Carl Sagan, world famous for writing popular science books and for cowriting *Cosmos: A Personal Voyage*, seen by more than 600 million people in over 60 countries, making it one of the most widely watched PBS programs in history (Svetkey, 1997). The following account was written for publication in *Marihuana Reconsidered* (Grinspoon & Sagan, 1971). Sagan was in his mid-thirties at that time. He continued to use cannabis for the rest of his life.

There is a very nice self-titrating aspect to cannabis. Each puff is a very small dose; the time lag between inhaling a puff and sensing its effect is small; and there is no desire for more after the high is there. I think the ratio, R, of the time to sense the dose taken to the time required to take an excessive dose is an important quantity. R is very large for LSD (which I've never taken) and reasonably short for cannabis. Small values of R should be one measure of the safety of psychedelic drugs. When cannabis is legalized, I hope to see this ratio as one of the parameters printed on the pack. I hope that time isn't too distant; the illegality of cannabis is outrageous, an impediment to full utilization of a drug which helps produce the serenity and insight, sensitivity and fellowship so desperately needed in this increasingly mad and dangerous world.

Chapter Summary

Marijuana is the most controversial of the illegal drugs and is the most widely used illicit drug in the United States. The NIDA-funded Monitoring the Future Study showed that a surprising number of school-age kids had used marijuana at least once in the year prior to being surveyed. Zinberg presented compelling evidence that social setting is a primary determinant of an individual's choice to use an intoxicant. Drug use is intimately related to large social influences such as media, war, and major environmental change. Tidal social forces seem to be greater determinants of pot culture than one's attitude regarding the benefits or risks of using marijuana.

Those in favor of unrestricted use claim that marijuana is beneficial in appropriate social contexts for two primary purposes: (1) it helps users become more relaxed to enjoy the activity; and (2) it enhances their enjoyment by making them more focused on the activity. Many adult users report that a primary motive is to enhance social contact. They believe that it "brings people closer together" and creates camaraderie between users. Facilitation of a sense of intimacy along with relaxation and pleasurable perceptual shifts are alluring aspects of this drug.

Despite the enjoyable aspects of marijuana use and widespread endorsement of looser government controls, there is substantial evidence that chronic marijuana usage has negative effects on memory, learning, and cognition. There is some dispute regarding how long these effects last. One of the most deleterious effects of cannabis smoking is its impact on the lungs. A link between cannabis use and psychotic symptoms seems to be increasingly clear. Once thought to be rare, cases of marijuana abuse and dependence seem to be on the rise, which may be related to increasing potency of cannabis. Potential consumers should be wary of substituting synthetic cannabis for real marijuana, given the great potency of synthetics and their increased risk of negative effects.

On the plus side, data strongly support the use of marijuana for treating pain and in believing nausea associated with chemotherapy for cancer patents.. Future research is needed to clarify its efficacy at treating seizures disorders and cancer. If effective, cannabis-based treatments may be preferable over traditional treatments that have negative side effects.

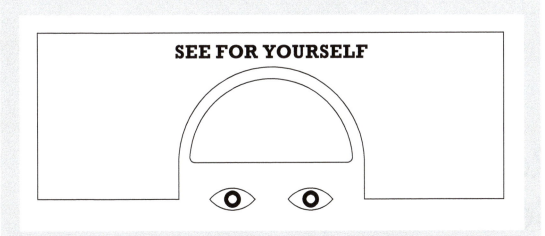

SEE FOR YOURSELF

The Martha Stewart of Marijuana Edibles. 2017. Lizzie Widdicombe. The New Yorker. Feature Length Article.

This article examines the emerging gourmet edible industry and the challenges of regulating quality in the recently legalized world of recreational marijuana. **https://www.newyorker.com/magazine/2017/04/24/the-martha-stewart-of-marijuana-edibles**

How Marijuana Works. 2011. *Drugged*. National Geographic. 4:28

This clip includes footage and interviews of people smoking marijuana, coupled with animation showing how the drug affects the lungs, circulatory system, and brain. **https://www.youtube.com/watch?v=Kg8wrzmIdyI**

George Carlin on Drugs and Marijuana. 1997. Jon Stewart and George Carlin. George Carlin: 40 Years of Comedy. 7:11

George Carlin discusses his use of marijuana in his creative work and his views on drug use. **https://www.youtube.com/watch?v=oj5Sd3BRm_I**

CHAPTER 16

Romantic Sex Fantasy

A library is a place where you can lose your innocence without losing your virginity.

— Germaine Greer

Of the delights of this world, man cares most for sexual intercourse. He will go to any length for it—risk fortune, character, reputation, life itself.

— Mark Twain

The modern sex industry is primarily designed for (i.e., is intended to satisfy the sexual desires of) heterosexual men (Wosick-Correa and Joseph, 2008). This makes it difficult to adequately assess the experiences of non-heteronormative populations. For example, Pilcher (2012) argues that when it comes to women as sexual agents, as consumers of sex, "we have no language for talking about power and desire outside of [heteronormativity]" because "the necessary conventions of consumption and performance that would indicate what female sexual agency in commercial sexual encounters would look like have not evolved very far" (p. 535). The waters become even murkier when considering queer experiences. Nevertheless, this chapter is intended to consider the entire range of sexual fantasy experiences, including not only multiple sexualities, but also the various ways in which sexual desires are pursued and fulfilled.

Sex Bars

One of the most common avenues through which people seek to fulfill sexual desire is through patronizing strip clubs or other sex bar facilities. Most sex bars cater to a heterosexual male clientele, with the euphemistic "Gentlemen's Club" by far the most prevalent type. In these establishments, needs for sensation seeking, sexual arousal, and intimacy are routinely handled by a cadre of fantasy lovers. In terms of money, the exchange between dancers and patrons occurs on three levels: selling of drinks, table dances, and private performances (Brewster, 2003). Sexual interaction occurs in three distinct spaces: the stage, the floor, and the private room (Forsyth & Deshotels, 1997). The club's public performance areas are usually the dancer's first encounter with "paying clients" and her opportunity to size up future economic gains. Performances are time-framed around a set of musical songs. Dancers use "impression management" techniques (Goffman, 1959) by dressing in various costumes and performing certain erotic movements to arouse a client's sexual fantasy (Brewster, 2003).

Emboldened by the club's explicit license for sexual pursuit, patrons may indulge in any manner of erotic fantasy. At center stage, stimulation is primarily visual, with interludes of close-up, one-on-one interaction, as strippers make special maneuvers for attentive customers. Stage-side customers usually tip when they are personally addressed, by conveying rolled-up dollar bills to the forbidden ecstasy beneath a dancer's G-string.

If attraction is consummated, the provocative female may be invited to perform more private and intimate dances at café-style tables. "Lap dances" are often the prelude to more isolated settings where the level of touch and intimacy is further advanced. Activities such as these allow for limited sexual pleasure; they conjure feelings of intimacy and romance, without the interpersonal demands, anxiety, guilt, and fear that often accompany sexual encounters.

These strip clubs, the "Gentleman's Clubs," reproduce societal scripts of heteronormative power relations, with the female as (sexual) object; but other kinds of clubs do exist which challenge (to a certain degree) those scripts. At male strip clubs, men dance for a predominantly heterosexual female audience, performing many of the same functions as the female dancers described above. In these environments, however, the women are sexually active (even aggressive) rather than passive, pursuers rather than pursued, objectifiers rather than objectified (Montemurro, 2001; Peterson & Dressel, 1982). Indeed, these clubs are often seen as evidence of "women's sexual freedom," representing "one place in which women can show themselves as actively desiring" (Smith, 2002, pp. 68, 83). However, while sexual aggression on the part of women might be liberating within the confines of a male strip club, the same aggression by patrons of lesbian clubs can be seen as simply reinforcing "the heteronormative ideals of the female body as sex object" (Pilcher, 2012, p. 532).

Male stripping also benefits from being more socially acceptable, performed in more respectable venues and presented as something you could take your grandmother to, which leaves female stripping as the "dirty" or "sleazy" counterpart (Tewksbury, 1993). While female strippers surrender much of their sexual agency when they are on stage, the same is not generally true for male dancers. Because heteronormativity reserves the role of "sex object" overwhelmingly for women, for a man to fully occupy that role would "relegate [him] to a subordinate masculinity," borderline femininity (Liepe-Levinson, 2002, p. 184). The role of the male stripper is thus "masculinized," with dancers never completely giving up their power and domination (Tewksbury, 1993, p. 179).

Figure 16.1 Arousing Sexual Fantasies Dancers use "impression management" techniques, dressing in various costumes and performing certain erotic movements to arouse a client's sexual fantasy. Does the image below suggest a male or female dancer?

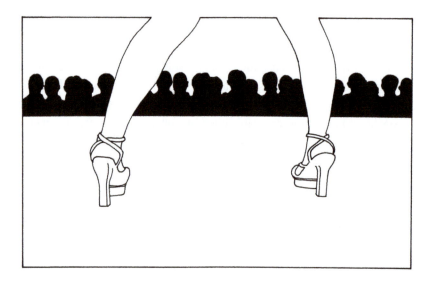

Who Attends and Why

The predominant motive for infrequent or intermittent attendees at a strip club may be the sexual "turn-on" sometimes with the underlying idea of having a sexual encounter outside the club (Ronai & Ellis, 1989). But sexual arousal and having sex outside the club are not the underlying motivating factors for those with more stable bonds to the sex club atmosphere. For many, the need to be intimate, to be seen close up, to feel recognized, to feel attracted by and attracted to another human being, are the driving human forces. In fact, the predominant source of income for women who sometimes earn nightly pay in excess of $1,000 at the Gentleman's Club is simply providing conversation to a mostly male clientele who seek comfort, closeness, friendship, and companionship. Intimacy-for-pay seems a fair price to those who struggle with profound loneliness and lack of belonging. In Chapter 20, "Maintaining Close and Intimate Relationships," we offer concrete examples of how needs for intimacy can be met by consciously orchestrating more fulfilling and meaningful relationships within the contexts of marriage, family, and friendship. Loneliness is a condition brought about by a lack of intimacy in our lives. The solution is to promote healthy alternatives to the purchase of closeness at erotic dance clubs. Table 16.1 summarizes a broad spectrum of motives for strip club attendance.

Several researchers have recognized the importance of intimacy and companionship among club "regulars" (e.g., Erickson & Tewksbury, 2000; Forsyth & Deshotels, 1998). Enck and Preston (1988) characterize the dancer–patron relationship as "counterfeit intimacy" where the posturing of words, facial expressions, and body movements mimic genuine romance. Price (2000) describes "monetary regulars" (sugar daddies) as patrons who appear to have a very strong commitment to "their girl," and Ronai and Ellis (1989) note that "some regular customers acted as if they were involved in a long-term serious relationship with a dancer ... forgetting the businesslike nature of the bar setting" (p. 287). Egan (2003) comments further that regular customers ... form both emotional and erotic bonds with their dancers, viewing themselves as "more than costumers." These men view themselves as "lovers" and/or "boyfriends" of the dancer they come to see on a regular basis and on whom they spend copious amounts of money (up to $50,000) on services and gifts (ranging from roses to breast implant surgery and cars) (p. 109).

Men who find continued club refuge usually experience varying degrees of conflict in their pursuit of sexual and emotional intimacy. Disinhibited by alcohol (and sometimes other drugs), patrons interact with nude (or nearly nude) women without concerns of commitment, need to perform, or rejection. Based on her experience as both a dancer and an ethnographic researcher, Egan (2003) offers a psychoanalytic perspective on the symbolic nature of the stripper–patron relationship:

> Sex workers in general and exotic dancers in particular occupy a more complex site than do most women in the matrix of desire, fantasy and power. Like other women, they become objects in the symbolic in order to sustain the male ego and his position within the phallic function. However, exotic dancers also occupy a unique position in that their bodies are sought out in the market as objects of desire and as such it is their job to recognize men and make them feel desired and desirable. Moreover, it is their job to become screens for male fantasy, quelling male anxiety of the unknowability of the feminine. (p. 112)

Women also patronize strip clubs; indeed they are doing so with increasing frequency, and have an even greater variety of reasons for attending than do their male counterparts. Heterosexual women might attend with their male partner, either to monitor his activities or with the intent of having a shared erotic experience. They might also go to the club as part of a group, just for fun as part of an evening out with friends; others, perhaps with the intent of exploring their sexual curiosity (Wosick-Correa & Joseph, 2008). Bisexual or lesbian women might also attend, like heterosexual men, to satisfy sexual desires. Researchers have found that, regardless of their reason(s) for attending, women often have much different experiences than men do, and are even treated differently by the dancers. Wosick-Correa and Joseph (2008) found that female patrons are not considered profitable by the dancers, and are consequently ignored, unless they are with men, i.e., "sitting next to her boyfriend's wallet" (p. 207). In other ways, women are afforded glimpses of the dancers that men are never allowed, through a process known as *sidestaging*. For example, the layout of a club can often force female patrons and dancers together (e.g., in a shared bathroom); as a result, they may have informal chats, discuss the male patrons, etc. But this commiseration "reinforc[es] the notion that women are not fully considered to be customers" (p. 209). Thus, female patrons can be rendered marginal, peripheral. While this marginalization might be inconsequential for most heterosexual women, it has more meaningful implications "for those women who wish to fulfill same-sex desires and retain their sexual subjectivity," as "they are forced to interact and actually consume differently" (p. 213).

A study of women who attend lesbian strip clubs found that said clubs are viewed approvingly by their female patrons as women-only spaces, where women can bond with other women and make new friends, and where they are free from male harassment (Pilcher, 2012). Indeed, not all of the women at one lesbian club watched the erotic entertainment, or even if they did "it was not always the primary reason they gave for visiting" (p. 530). Furthermore, the nature of a lesbian club increases the chances of customers finding a romantic partner from amongst the other patrons. Another interesting element to note is the dancers' range of personas. Their stage acts can embody masculine/domineering or more traditional feminine roles, an acknowledgment of the fact that what the female patrons find erotic varies from person to person. These clubs can thus provide a space for homosexual women to escape stereotypes and experience the many possible appearances (and ways of being) of lesbian women, from the "femme" to the "butch," and others in between.

Overall, sex bar recreation bears similarity to a widely used sex therapy treatment technique known as sensate focus. The basic premise is that apprehension during sexual interaction interferes with sexual excitement and pleasure. In females, anxiety blocks the lubrication and swelling phase; in the male, it suppresses erection. The goal of treatment is to reduce tension and to restore confidence. This may be achieved by promoting sexual enjoyment while minimizing the demands associated with arousal and intercourse. Couples are instructed to avoid having intercourse or orgasm, while actively appreciating the erotic sensations of non-demand sexuality.

Table 16.1 Motives for Strip Club Attendance

- Most men, especially regulars, recognize that sexual activity is available at other venues of the sex industry and state that they go to clubs to "relax."

- Strip clubs provide a different atmosphere from work and home where male sexuality is accepted by women and sexual experiences are offered without pressure, with some degree of safety.

- There is a permissive sexualized atmosphere compared with other spaces where sexual disinhibition may cause difficulty.

- The presence of nudity and the opportunity to talk allow for the creation of fantasies that are stimulating to customers.

- Clubs provide safe opportunities for interactions with women without the risk of rejection.

- Clubs serve as a site for the return of adolescent fantasy; dancers become the high school girl that got away.

- Visits are intertwined with men's concerns about losing a youthful body; reinvigorating the sexual response allays concerns over loss of masculinity.

- The fantasies of sexual possibility and interpersonal intimacy are alluring.

- One can be rid of his everyday persona, with its many demands and frustrations, and given a new script from which to play a different part. There is a fetishization* of the new role, that is, a fantasy self, as well as a fetishization of the dancer.

- Patrons do not desire a real physical relationship (that they could easily obtain by paying sex workers at other venues) but rather a realistic fantasy of such a relationship.

- Many men claim to be committed to monogamy and choose strip clubs because they would neither be expected nor tempted to have sexual contact with the dancers.

- Encounters are secret and interactive, sexualized but not sexual, seen as guilt-free romantic encounters, outside of committed relationships.

- Nonsexual liaisons and relationship building with strippers provide opportunity for newness and excitement as committed relationships evolve from passionate to affectionate.

- Visiting the club, even when undetected, is a means of enacting vengeful fantasies toward the spouse or significant other. The partner would be hurt by being excluded from a sexualized relationship.

*Fetish: an object, idea, or activity that a person is irrationally obsessed with or attached to (Encarta Online Dictionary).

Effects and Consequences for Dancers and Clientele

Many see the potentially empowering effect that stripping can have for the women performing. From this perspective, stripping provides women the opportunity not only to feel desirable on a grand scale, but also to exert their desirability, and their femininity, for economic gain. Based on interviews with 22 female strippers, Barton (2002) found that these women initially derive feelings of empowerment from being sexually liberated, generating substantial income, and being told they are beautiful. Toward the latter stages of the stripper's career, however, these "benefits" are eventually countered by feelings of being emotionally drained and feeling worse about their bodies, their sexuality, their intelligence, and ultimately their identity in the social world. This liability is highlighted by radical feminists who emphatically condemn the sex service industry, arguing that it reproduces and reinforces societal power dynamics. Strip clubs in particular are seen as places where patriarchy and heteronormativity combine, resulting in the construction of women as "ubiquitously available sex objects" (Pasko, 2002, p.64). And indeed, within most strip clubs men (clients as well as management) wield considerable power over the female performers (Pilcher, 2009). The exercise of this power over the performers can range from requiring them to pay management a daily commission, to verbal abuse, to coercing them into performing sexual acts (Chapkis, 2000).

Another line of thought highlights the fact that a stripper's role is not always explicitly sexual, but often involves providing emotional support for their customers. Hartley (1997), a self-proclaimed "hard core" stripper, explains how being an effective "sex therapist" is an important dimension of her self-identity:

> Through my experiences stripping, I learned many valuable lessons. I learned that my body was attractive to many different men, even though I am many inches and pounds away from any magazine model. I found that the majority of heterosexual men will follow sexually if the woman will only lead, and that men feel victimized around sex just as women do, only in different aspects of the sexual dance. I realized that, as a committed feminist, I had to be open to men's pain and see it [as] equally valid to women's. I discovered that a woman who is willing to talk about sex honestly and show her body can get men to listen, learn, and be better lovers with their partners. Finally, I learned that to be eternally mad at men's sexual "nature" was as useful as being mad that water is wet. Anger inhibits intimacy and shared pleasure, to the detriment of all involved. I seek in my work to defuse anger so that the pleasure I invoke can work its healing magic. (p. 61)

Indeed, no matter where they are in the continuum from empowerment to degradation, many strippers claim they derive a positive sense of purpose from their therapeutic role:

> Vivienne happily described herself as the resident therapist at the Velvet Lounge. She, like other dancers, felt that an important part of her job was talking to customers about their wives, girlfriends, and families and being supportive and caring. For the most part, dancers expressed enjoyment of this aspect of the job as long as the customer treated them with respect. Indeed, Vivienne feels that this part of the job is not really "work."

As Vivienne herself put it, "You strive toward being able to go in there and not have to dance and make as much money as you possibly can. To dance the least and make the most, I think that's the goal. To get paid strictly for talking, strictly for being a companion because there's no real work in that." (Barton, 2002, p. 596)

However, researchers have also found some negative consequences of this emotional labor. Highlighting the fact that dancers contrive and perform their relationships within the club, leaving their "true" selves at the door, studies have shown that this often leads to struggles with identity and intimacy outside of the club (Deshotels & Forsyth, 2006; Pasko, 2002). The need to construct a "false intimacy" with customers (Pasko, 2002, p. 49) can hinder dancers in their attempts to establish or maintain genuine intimacy in their personal lives. However, this effect seems to apply almost exclusively to female strippers. Male strippers are able to avoid this negative consequence because they generally do not perform the same emotional therapy role as their female counterparts; rather, male strippers' interactions with customers are much more limited, both in terms of length and depth (Tewksbury, 1993).

CASE EXAMPLE: "Intimacy" at the Gentlemen's Club

Nicky, a master's degree candidate in counselling psychology (by day) and a popular stripper (by night), describes how the need for intimacy is the major driving force for many of her paying customers:

I have personally experienced the phenomenon of men seeking intimacy without sexuality. Dean is an excellent example. I met him during a convention in Denver. All he wished [for] was companionship and a dinner partner. He explicitly expressed that he had no desire to have me dance or disrobe for him. Dean is not alone; many men I have met are seeking intimacy beyond physical sexuality. Initially, the erotic component may be what draws them in, being that it is socially acceptable in a patriarchal society, where masculinity is valued. However, the men I have encountered, who return to the same club and the same woman for years, are not ultimately interested in the sexual aspect of the environment. They seek companionship and intimacy. I know of numerous men who have developed long-term relationships with entertainers that transcend the immediate suggestion of the environment. These men come to talk to the entertainers. They ask the women about their lives and families. They ask for advice and express concerns. They want someone who will listen to their triumphs and disappointments. They want someone who will empathize and connect with them.

Often, these men want a woman to whom they can give gifts and celebrate holidays. It is an interesting situation which can be interpreted in many ways. Perhaps this woman is similar to a wife without strings attached or commitments or pressures. Maybe some of these men want to do something good for someone else, take care of someone. Maybe they want to be important in someone's life. I believe the motives are complex, fluid, and derived from numerous sources. They may change day to day within the context of each individual man's experience. However complex the motives are for engaging in such behavior, it is clear to me that these patrons seek something much different from the surface content.

Another phenomenon I have noticed with other entertainers and myself is that of patrons taking entertainers to the private dance area and paying the usual price for each song ($20–$30), except wanting to sit and talk to the women instead of having them disrobe and dance. They may desire other non-erotic activities as well, such as giving or receiving a backrub or engaging in prolonged eye-contact. A regular client of mine, Adam, has prolonged eye-contact as his favorite activity. He enjoys receiving some dances and some conversation, but frequently desires that we gaze silently into each other's eyes for at least 5 minutes at a time.

Another interesting point to note is the concept of "skin hunger," the idea that people who are deprived of appropriate physical contact with others crave any sort of physical contact. This need may be misinterpreted as sexual desire. I believe that this may be especially true for males in our culture. It is not socially acceptable for most men to receive nurturing touch and care. I have found examples of this phenomenon with men who continually attempt inappropriate physical contact with me.

For some men, having their primary intimate relationship with an entertainer in an adult establishment can be a negative or damaging experience. I have known many men who become obsessed with an entertainer, putting unhealthy amounts of time, energy, and money into this largely one-way relationship. Conversely, I have also known many men who have benefited from such one-way relationships.

Henry is a man who has been married for 20 years. He loves his wife, yet he has not been able to achieve the level of intimacy with his wife to share certain personal aspects of himself. Henry has several entertainers to whom he has become appropriately close. With the women, he is safe to share ideas, fears, and thoughts that he is not comfortable doing with his wife. Rarely does Henry allow an entertainer to dance for him. When one does, it is almost never one of those he sees regularly. Henry's relationship with me and his other favorite entertainers reminds me in some ways of counseling relationships. The entertainers self-disclose appropriately, but do not return the same openness displayed by Henry. The relationships between Henry and each of these women [are] characterized by warmth and respect from both parties. These relationships differ, of course, from psychotherapy in numerous ways, the most salient being the fact that Henry also likes to be entertained with alcoholic beverages, light and humorous conversation, and watching the on-stage entertainment taking place in the room.

Frederick is another example of how intimacy in a gentlemen's club can be beneficial. Frederick desired a relationship with a woman, but had gone through a bad marriage and in general, lacked social skills and confidence related to dating. He also felt cynical about women and relationships due to his divorce. He met an entertainer in a club who was warm, accepting, kind, and patient. He began coming to the club to see her once every one or two weeks. He paid her to dance for him, but mostly to spend time talking with him. After awhile, Frederick quit visiting the club. Several months later, he sent "his" entertainer a letter (at the club). He thanked her for spending time with him, making him feel good, being genuine, and giving him the courage and hope to begin dating.

The Allure of Prostitution

Some men go beyond the wish-fulfilling fantasies of the strip club, seeking pleasure, intimacy, and physical contact with prostitutes. Prostitution exists at all levels of society, from back-alley slums to brothels and upscale escort services. A study of one metropolitan area found that johns (male customers) traveled an average of 10 miles from their homes for sexual services (McCutcheon, Mustaine, & Tewksbury, 2016). Women at various sex venues are readily solicited as surrogate lovers; they may be available for minutes or hours, a given evening, as weekend partners, or even as long-term, live-in companions.

Prostitution is one of the world's oldest professions (Ramirez, 2008) and has existed in just about every culture. Today, it is a lucrative business, with the state of Nevada alone bringing in around $50 million in revenue each year. Brothels are legal in Nevada in counties with fewer than 400,000 residents. Cities such as Las Vegas attract the gamblers, but often vacations include a trip north or south to brothel businesses. Nevada has become more lenient with their laws regarding prostitution, as brothels can now advertise in areas outside of the county where they are based. The old-fashioned word-of-mouth advertising has been surpassed by billboards, Internet ads, telephone book listings, and radio and television commercials. Various kinds of prostitution rings have been uncovered, ranging from the high-end "D.C. Madam" operation to a "brothel on wheels" in South Beach, Florida (Skipp & Campo-Flores, 2008). This limousine bus was a custom conversion with leather benches and a full-service bar, with prices ranging from $10 for a "stand-up" dance to over $100 for access to a special curtained-off VIP area. Then, of course, there are the women who are termed "street workers." These girls and women, as their title implies, work the streets in seedy areas of cities across the world.

Deborah Palfrey was the backbone of an elite, sophisticated, alleged prostitution ring (Hosenball & Conant, 2007). Her escort service catered to a wealthy, upper-class, male clientele by hiring powerful elite women. This business ran under the name Pamela Martin & Associates and employed women who worked white-collar jobs as paralegals, lawyers, college professors, and even military professionals. These were not just young women, new to the world of prostitution; rather, they ranged in age from 23 to 55. Another high-end escort service, the Emperor's Club VIP, was busted with New York governor Eliot Spitzer's fall from grace. This type of elite escort service caters to a wealthy clientele and operates in cities all over the world. Clients shell out anywhere from $5,500 an hour to $31,000 a day (Campo-Flores & Smalley, 2008).

There are some important lifestyle differences between high-end escorts, indoor sex workers, and women who operate from the street. The "commercial sex" of indoor workers (i.e., those who work in spas or massage parlors, or for escort services) allows for the service providers to set some psychological boundaries between their job and their personal lives (Sanders, 2005). These women are more likely to be aware of the dangers in selling their bodies. Escort service workers tend to have some control over selection of their customers and the settings in which prostitution occurs (Sanders, 2005). In contrast, street-working prostitutes tend to have polydrug-using habits, experience more violence in their work and home lives, and are usually under the thumb of a pimp or partner. Street workers are exposed to far more violence, from verbal abuse to assault, rape, and murder. Their mortality rates are up to 40 times the national average. Studies have found that these women are more likely to have experienced sexual and physical abuse as children. The average age of introduction into prostitution in the United States is around 13 to 14 years old.

Why is paying for sex so widespread? Plumridge, Chetwynd, Reed, and Gifford (1997) studied the motives of men who frequented massage parlors. Subjects were from 23 to 78 years old. Many were married or in serious relationships. Their professions ranged from white collar, to blue collar, to self-employed. Although a small percentage acknowledged looking for "kinky" sex, most claimed they just wanted "normal" services such as vaginal intercourse, fellatio, and masturbation. The men taking part in the study had been purchasing sex for some time; that is, none of them were first-timers. All asserted that the main reason behind purchasing sex was pleasure. Many viewed prostitution as an exciting step out of the monotonous sex they had with their wives or lovers. While there was almost universal appreciation of having sex with no strings attached, "the men argued that paid sex was not just a social contact, it was represented as emotional" (Plumridge et al., 1997, p. 174). It was not the same as love to these men, but they experienced some emotional attachment. Perhaps the most interesting finding of this study was that these men all truly believed in reciprocal and mutual feelings on the part of the prostitutes with whom they had sex.

This search for romance and tenderness, for someone who acts less like a prostitute and more like a partner, has been referred to as the "girlfriend experience" (Milrod and Monto, 2012). Similarly, in studying online reviews of male escorts by their male customers, Tewksbury and Lapsey (2016) found that the most sought-after quality in an escort is a "degree of friendliness and creation of a sense of genuineness to the relationship," i.e., the girlfriend experience. However, research shows that most prostitutes do not get enjoyment from their work and do not experience romantic feelings toward the people they service. As street solicitation is more common and is different in character from "indoor" prostitution, these results may not be generalizable to clients obtaining services from street workers.

Many of those who pay for sexual services may be seeking an outlet for repressed, or otherwise unfulfilled, desires that have no place within the heteronormative world of strip clubs. Brothels are places for "deviant" behaviors and/or queer expression (Read, 2013). Apart from, or in addition to, sexual acts, Read documented cases of men wanting to be dominated or humiliated, dressed in women's clothing, or wrapped in saran wrap, among many others. As spaces of "fluid sexualities, heteroflexible performance, and negotiations of power" (Read, 2013, p. 471), customers have access to a more complete sexual (or non-sexual) experience, unrestrained by societal norms.

Some motives for paying for sex are unique to homosexual men. The "straight masculine" experience, for example, involves a prostitute who is straight looking or straight acting, and provides for the customer "a way of exerting power and/or having a nearly taboo form of sexual encounter" (Tewksbury & Lapsey, 2016, p. 7). Additionally, in what is known as "body worship," clients seek simply to "view, admire, touch, stroke, and find ways to admire the strength and physical power" of a male escort who has a "superhero physique" (p. 8). Thus, even in the world of prostitution, exchanges do not necessarily involve actual sexual activity. As with strippers, prostitutes and escorts often see their job as that of "fantasy performer, sex therapist, even doctor" (Read, 2013, p. 478).

The Role of Technology

Increasingly, people are using the Internet to satisfy their sexual desires, in lieu of or in addition to the more "traditional" avenues described above. Access to the Internet is now nearly ubiquitous, and it provides users access to an entire world of sexual possibilities and choices. Often, cyberspace is used simply as a starting point, a convenient way to initiate some of the previously discussed activities. For instance, due primarily to the anonymity that the Internet affords its users, online sex work has all but replaced the street scene (Bimbi, 2007); it is by far the easiest way for sex workers and their clients to find one another.

Internet pornography is perhaps the most widely recognized intersection of technology with sexual fantasy, but it is still not widely or well understood. In a study of hundreds of popular pornographic Internet videos, Klaassen and Peter (2015) found that both men and women are objectified in the videos, but in different ways. While women are more likely to be treated as simply instruments for men's pleasure, the men in the videos are more likely to be dehumanized in that their faces are rarely shown. Men are generally depicted as dominant and women as submissive, but violence and nonconsensual sex are rare. The researchers also found that amateur pornography contains more gender inequality at the expense of women than professional pornography (Klaassen & Peter, 2015). Some of these findings run contrary to long-held assumptions, and the content of gay online sexually explicit material has only recently begun to be analyzed (Downing, Schrimshaw, Antebi, & Siegel, 2014).

The Internet also provides a means for sexually diverse and marginalized groups to surpass the limitations of traditional approaches and instead find or create spaces for realizing their specific sexual fantasies and desires, spaces that are "simultaneously private and public" (Karim, 2014, p. 53). In short, cyberspace has increasingly become a safe haven for asserting non-heteronormative sexualities, for expressing those diverse erotic desires and practices.

Chapter Summary

In this chapter, we have explored diverse ways in which people seek out their sexual, and not-so-sexual (intimate), fantasies and considered a broad range of sexual fantasy experiences, including not only multiple sexualities but also the many ways in which sexual desires are pursued and fulfilled.

The "Gentlemen's Club" is by far the most common sex bar facility. Clients' needs for excitement, closeness, and intimacy are satisfied to some degree by fantasy lovers. While typical heteronormative clubs reproduce societal scripts of male/female power relations, a growing set of male strip clubs challenge those scripts. In environments that cater to female sexual fantasy, women are sexually active (even aggressive) rather than passive, pursuers rather than pursued, objectifiers rather than objectified. While sexual aggression on the part of women might be liberating within the confines of a male strip club, the same aggression by patrons of lesbian clubs can be seen as simply reinforcing "the heteronormative ideals of the female body as sex object."

Several researchers have recognized the importance of intimacy and companionship to club "regulars." The dancer–patron relationship functions as a sort of "counterfeit intimacy" where words, facial expressions, and body movements imitate genuine romance. Sex bar recreation resembles a widely used sex therapy treatment technique known as sensate focus, the basic premise being that apprehension during sexual interaction gets in the way of sexual excitement and pleasure. The goal of treatment is to reduce tension and restore confidence. The sex club atmosphere is free of performance expectations and associated anxiety.

Sex club dancers initially experience feelings of empowerment from being sexually liberated, generating a good income, and being told they are beautiful. However, in the latter stages of their career, these "benefits" are eventually countered by negative feelings about their bodies, their sexuality, their intelligence, and ultimately their identity. Even so, many strippers say they get a positive sense of purpose from what they see as their therapeutic role in helping men feel better about themselves.

Some men go beyond the wish-fulfilling fantasies of the strip club, seeking excitement and intimacy by having sex with prostitutes. There are some important lifestyle differences among high-end escorts, indoor sex workers, and women who operate from the street. The "commercial sex" of indoor workers allows them to set some psychological boundaries between their job and their personal lives. In contrast, street-working prostitutes tend to have multiple drug-use habits, experience more violence in their work and home lives, and are usually under the thumb of a pimp or partner.

Only a small percentage of sex customers in massage parlors or other indoor commercial venues acknowledge looking for "kinky" sex. Most claim interest in "normal" services such as vaginal intercourse, fellatio, and masturbation. Many view prostitution as an exciting alternative to boring sex with their wives and lovers. Repeat customers believe reciprocal and mutual feelings are felt by their paid sex partners. In fact, most prostitutes do not enjoy their work and do not experience romantic feelings toward the men they service.

The Internet plays an increasing role, not only in providing anonymous access to massive troves of pornographic images and videos but also in facilitating encounters between sex workers and their clients. The Internet also provides a means for sexually diverse and marginalized groups to surpass the limitations of traditional approaches and instead find or create spaces for realizing their specific sexual fantasies and desires, spaces that are "simultaneously private and public."

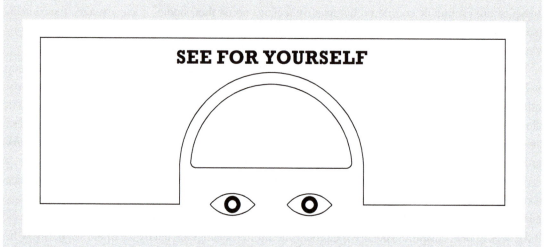

SEE FOR YOURSELF

Thank You, Princess. 2015. Brendan Baker & Nick Van Der Kolk. Love + Radio. 48:31

In this podcast interview, Ceara Lynch, a self-described "Humiliatrix," discusses her lucrative ten-year career in the world of sexual fetish. **http://loveandradio.org/2015/03/thank-you-princess/**

Sex Addiction. 2011. Taboo. National Geographic. 4:40

This clip introduces Janice, a woman who identifies as recovering from sex addiction. **http://channel.nationalgeographic.com/taboo/videos/sex-addiction/**

How One Man Recovered From His Internet Pornography Addiction. Alexander Rhodes interviewed by Robin Young. NPR. 9:28

Founder of a porn recovery platform and former internet pornography addict discusses his personal experience recovering from addiction and the supports his organization currently provides. **http://www.wbur.org/hereandnow/2016/08/30/internet-porn-addiction**

SECTION VI

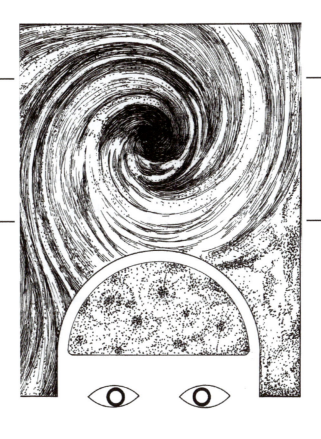

Journey To Oblivion

CHAPTER 17

The Voyage of Hardship and Suffering

Obsessed by a fairy tale, we spend our lives searching for a magic door and a lost kingdom of peace.
—Eugene O'Neill

Drugs will turn you into your parents.

—Frank Zappa

Drugs are a waste of time. They destroy your memory and your self-respect and everything that goes along with your self-esteem.

—Kurt Cobain

All the perfect drugs and superheroes wouldn't be enough to bring me up to zero.
—Aimee Mann, "Humpty Dumpty"

Introduction: The Disease Concept of Addiction

In 21st century America, we take the disease model of addiction for granted. A hundred years ago, however, that was not the case. Addiction was viewed as a moral weakness. It wasn't that alcoholics or drug abusers simply made bad choices—they were often seen as bad people. Today, this is not the case. Although there are some addiction specialists who disagree with the disease concept, the notion of addiction as a moral failing has been abandoned.

The concept of addiction as a progressively incapacitating disease (i.e., a "journey to oblivion") originates from a series of lectures presented by Jellinek (1952) at the Yale Summer School of Alcohol Studies in 1951 and 1952. On the basis of a questionnaire study of more than 2,000 male alcoholics, Jellinek formulated his four-phase concept of alcohol addiction. He distinguished between two categories of alcoholics: "alcohol addicts" and "habitual symptomatic excessive drinkers." The disease concept applies only to alcohol addicts who, after a variable period of problem drinking, lose control over their alcohol intake. Excessive drinkers, on the other hand, may pathologically use alcohol to relieve conflict for many years, yet the phenomenon of loss of control never becomes part of their drinking history.

In the first phase of alcohol addiction, which Jellinek (1952) called the "pre-alcoholic symptomatic phase," the prospective alcoholic begins to experience an inordinate amount of tension reduction through drinking and drinking-related activities. Generally, within a period of 6 months to 2 years, Jellinek's typical subject begins to use alcohol nearly every day to relieve stress. Although his tolerance for alcohol exceeds that of his peers—that is, he can drink a good deal more than they before reaching a desired level of intoxication—his excessive drinking remains relatively inconspicuous and undetected.

The rather sudden emergence of alcohol-related blackouts marks the second, "prodromal phase" of alcohol addiction. A blackout may be understood as a period of intermediate memory loss, whereby a person who imbibes as few as 2 ounces of absolute alcohol may carry on a reasonable conversation or complex pattern of activity without a trace of memory of it the following day. The blackout period is indeed intermediate in that the drinker experiences normal memory functions before and after the lost interval.

Soon after the onset of blackouts, the drinker begins to understand, in some very vague manner, that his pattern of drinking is different from that of others. He begins to sneak drinks at social gatherings and becomes preoccupied with when and how to get high. At this point, the prodromal drinker may be observed to gulp drinks while increasing guilt leads to more obvious signs of covering up. The incipient alcohol addict may, for example, conspicuously avoid any reference to alcohol, pro or con, during conversation. Depending on the drinker's physical and psychological condition, as well as the nature of his social network, the prodromal period may persist for anywhere from 6 months to 4 or 5 years.

The next stage of alcohol addiction, which Jellinek (1952) referred to as the "crucial phase," is marked by loss-of-control drinking. The addict appears to lose the faculty of making rational choices about how much to consume. Any level of consumption, even the taste of one drink, seems to trigger an irresistible demand for alcohol that continues until he is either too drunk or too ill to consume any more.

Loss of control often comes into play when people respond to conflict or stress by succumbing to drink. Before drinking, the alcoholic may appear sensible, affable, and emotionally intact. During this phase, he begins to rationalize his unseemly drinking by creating easily detected alibis (i.e., transparent excuses for drinking), attempting to convince himself that he has good reason to become intoxicated. He minimizes the extent of his disturbance by drawing attention to irresponsible actions among friends and associates.

At this point, alcoholism begins to bring about warnings and reprisals from family, friends, and business associates. The drinker, now thoroughly entrenched in the crucial phase of alcohol addiction, progressively withdraws from his usual social environment. He becomes noticeably more aggressive, with more frequent and penetrating feelings of desperation and remorse. He loses contact with most of his "straight" friends. Flurries of overcontrol (going on the wagon) alternate with episodes of alcoholic debauchery. The addict attempts to regain control by altering specific aspects of his behavior: He may change the times, beverages, or locations that have characterized his past drinking. His entire behavioral repertoire becomes markedly alcohol-centered, as drinking becomes his most salient need. Support from family and friends dwindles to a pittance, while sexual drive and nutritional prudence are negligible when compared with the need to consume alcohol. The drinker may now experience the first of a series of alcohol-related hospitalizations resulting from accidents or physical illness.

The crucial phase begins to terminate when the addict becomes so demoralized and confused by the conflict among outside pressures, inner needs, and his growing dependence on alcohol that he begins each day by steadying himself with a drink. Intoxication, however, usually remains restricted to the evening hours. The crucial- phase alcoholic may succeed in retaining his employment through many years of compulsive, loss-of-control drinking, although family life usually deteriorates dramatically.

The final or "chronic phase" is marked by prolonged periods of intoxication, colloquially referred to as *binges*. At this stage, the alcohol addict may drink with characters who are morally and intellectually inferior to his customary clique. His thinking and physical functioning begin to show dramatic signs of impairment. Tolerance for alcohol is diminished (half the amount previously required may be sufficient for intoxication and stupor), while indefinable fears and physical tremors begin to emerge. These symptoms of withdrawal appear as soon as alcohol is no longer present in the body. Consequently, the drinker "controls" them through continuous consumption. A relatively small percentage (approximately 10%) of alcoholics experience full-blown psychotic symptoms, such as hallucinations, delusions, or both.

Finally, the need for alcohol looms so large that the addict can no longer maintain any pretense that he has control over his drinking. According to Jellinek (1952), many alcohol addicts (approximately 60%) develop vague spiritual desires as they begin to call upon a higher power to rescue them from the alcoholic abyss. At this point, the addict has spontaneously become amenable to treatment for the disease (Figure 17.1).

Figure 17.1 Jellinek's Disease Model of Alcoholism The disease concept applies to "alcohol addicts" who, after a variable period of problem drinking, progressively lose control over their alcohol intake.

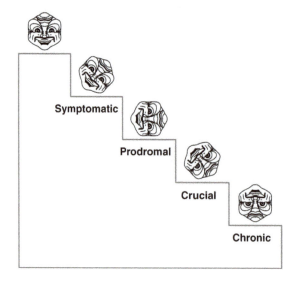

The case example of John, a former addict, now a licensed alcohol and drug counselor, provides a personal account of one man's progression through Jellinek's (1952) phases of addictive disease. As illustrated by John's story, the disease model describes a general pattern, a progression of addictive behavior. The specific events of each person's journey, however, are unique to his or her genetics, sociocultural background, and current life situation.

CASE EXAMPLE: John's Story—Journey to Oblivion and Back

Raised by both parents, I remember having a great early childhood of security, serenity, and happiness. At the age of 12, my life slowly began to change as I became aggressive and progressed to become the bully of bullies.

Pre-alcoholic Symptomatic

At the start of high school, I was introduced to drugs and alcohol and I really liked them. I began by sneaking drinks because I was underage and still living with my parents who did not approve. I did not have to get angry, sad, or frustrated anymore. I didn't have to feel anything. It started out with sneaking some here and there, then quickly progressed to a weekend thing, pretty much every weekend, then my use went to three or four times a week—plus the weekend. Most of the time I was relying on alcohol to soothe those feelings I didn't want to be feeling. I saw my tolerance was well above my peers, as I would be finishing off my second beer when they were just getting through their first.

Prodromal

During my sophomore year in high school, the blackouts started. I didn't try to hide my excessive drinking because I was always a jerk so I never cared who saw me. I was aware of the difference in my drinking from others, but I didn't think much of it. I isolated from anyone who was straight, turning to the streets, hanging around gangs and experimenting with more and bigger types of drugs, which triggered a lot of warnings from the judicial system.

Crucial/Chronic

Life took a drastic turn as my family was falling apart. My parents divorced, and I was overwhelmed with sadness and anger from seeing my mom suffer. I drank and used even more because the pain and anger were so extreme. Looking back, the first genuine experience that the game began was when I was drunk and found my dad and beat him pretty badly. I got a juvenile domestic violence charge, which I tried to fight. I claimed I was not in a relationship with my dad, but because it was family, the courts considered it a relationship and so the charge stuck.

I would say I was going to quit and not drink for a month or two, but then I would flip around and drink and use cocaine for weeks at a time. I was never officially in a gang, but members of my family were involved in the northside gangs and I was good pals with many members of a southside gang. The more we drank, the more eager we were to stir up some drama in the streets. One time we were real intoxicated and we went and shot at some guys from a gang on the westside. They found out pretty damn quick who we were, and about 3 hours later we were kicking it at my friends' and the members from the other gang came by and did a drive-by. A few of my pals got injured, shot in the leg, what have you, and I was sitting next to my partner Louie and my cousin was on the other side of him. Louie was shot in the neck, my partner, my friend, he died.

There were lots of drunken fights, [and] almost every single one ended in gunfire. At this time, I was selling lots of drugs and always had guns on me. If we were shot at, we had to retaliate, and sometimes we were the aggressors. There were a couple times that I blacked out, only to wake up to hear that I had beaten up some good friends so badly that the damage in the friendships was irreparable. It felt horrible, and still to this day it feels that way, to not even remember doing something so brutal to people that I was so close with.

When I was incarcerated, I drank even more than I had been. My kidneys would be in so much pain if I didn't drink that no matter what I took, aspirin, whatever, it didn't help the pain. Only alcohol would relieve the intensity of it, but this helped me justify my drinking at the same time. I witnessed many stabbings, both in prison and on the streets. In prison, hooch (slang for alcohol made in prison) often goes hand-in-hand with power. The more *items* (a.k.a. drugs and alcohol) you could trade or swap for the more power you would get, the more comfortable you could live, and the more options you could have. I was in the hole multiple times, but luckily never for being caught with hooch. The hole is a small cell that you sit in 23 to 23½ hours a day locked down in nothing but your underwear, and the showers are brought to you. You have to wash your hair while handcuffed; it's basically jail inside of jail.

Recovery

I was put in the south end of Buena Vista, known for its nickname as Gladiator Camp because everybody in there is in there for a gang charge or a murder charge. There is lots of politics in prison and it's a dog-eat-dog world. There are lots of perpetrators preying on others to survive. One time I observed a little Chicano kid, 18 or 19 years old, come in and mouth off to a big African American guy. The African American guy was drunk and horny and raped the little Chicano in the shower. A couple days later, after the boy got out of the infirmary, the African American tried to say he had only done it because he was drunk but the Chicano went up to this huge guy and started pounding him in the face. [H]e ended up stabbing the big guy to death, stabbed him over 40-some times, but the whole situation was blamed on the alcohol. I started to hate everything that alcohol stood for.

At that point, I became truly aware that my life had become unmanageable and I started to ask God for help. It may not seem like a big thing to others, but by denying myself my second parole I gave myself the life I am living today. I knew if I was released at that time that once I got out, I would be right back in … back in the alcohol, the drugs, the violence. It means a lot to me that I stayed in jail almost another 6 months until a bed in a rehabilitation center opened up, because at that point I was able to start living. When I got out of the horrible clutch of that alcohol and drug addiction, I was able to get on the path I am now.

I entered into rehab complemented with Alcoholics Anonymous. I completed the rehab program and have maintained my sobriety since. I still go to AA meetings and I am fond of the group I found. I am now happily married, and have two beautiful daughters. I am grateful to say that the trials and tribulations I have been through made me the man I am now, motivated and determined to stay away from the life I once led. But that experience provided me with a path to help others, and I've been counseling adults and adolescents for the last 6 years.

Since Jellinek's (1952) early formulation more than half a century ago, the disease model for alcoholism has been embraced by Alcoholics Anonymous, the National Council on Alcoholism, the National Institute on Alcohol Abuse and Alcoholism, and the American Medical Association. Alcoholism is now widely accepted as a disease when loss of voluntary control over alcohol consumption is the cause of an individual's social, psychological, and physical dysfunction. In short, an alcoholic may be thought of as a person who cannot always control when he or she starts or stops drinking. His or her life becomes unmanageable, with or without the bottle.

In the past three decades, the disease concept, originally formulated for addiction to alcohol, has been enlarged by treatment practitioners to include a slew of potentially addictive agents such as gambling, sex, and eating, as well as a plethora of addictive substances including cocaine, amphetamines, and opioids (e.g., Donovan, 2005; Lesieur & Blume, 1993; Schneider & Irons, 2001). Like cancer, addiction is viewed as a potentially fatal disease that may be triggered by a variety of causes. Among the many substances associated with addictive disease are 1) alcohol; 2) the sedative hypnotics, including the barbiturates (e.g., Seconal and Tuinal) and the benzodiazepines (e.g., Valium and Librium); 3) opioids (e.g., heroin, morphine, fentanyl, oxycontin); 4) the central nervous system stimulants, including methamphetamine and cocaine; and 5) the hallucinogens, including LSD, PCP, and 6) marijuana. Addictive substances may be used separately or in various combinations. Alcoholism has a high rate of co-occurrence with cigarette addiction as well as addiction to various other drugs (Crabbe, 2002). The process behind this co-occurrence has proven to be heavily influenced by genetics (Edenberg & Foroud, 2006).

Michael's escalating struggle with cocaine exemplifies how the disease model for alcoholism may be applied to millions of cocaine (or other drug) addicts in the United States today.

CASE EXAMPLE: Cocaine and Addictive Disease

Michael began to engage in "recreational" use of cocaine nearly 4 years ago. Although he seemed to enjoy coke somewhat more than his friends, he limited his use to parties and what he considered to be weekend treats. After several years, he began to rely on cocaine as a source of energy for business and school obligations. About 2 years ago, he found himself working on three separate, yet highly demanding projects: completing course requirements for a college degree in creative writing; editing the advertising section of a commercial newsletter; and devising a business plan to open and operate a coffee shop with several of his friends. He rationalized that he needed cocaine daily to muster sufficient energy to complete each task. Michael realized that his drug problem was becoming severe when he found that he was using more cocaine even after his school obligations were completed. In what may be described as the prodromal phase of cocaine addiction, he began to make up excuses for why he needed to get high. Each time there was any sort of business or advertising deadline, he would rationalize that he needed cocaine to help him get through.

Michael agreed with his therapist that he was in the loss-of-control or crucial phase of cocaine addiction when he spent $10,000 in 3 months solely to purchase the drug. He repeatedly experienced an irresistible urge to buy just a moderate amount, allegedly to help him cope with some temporary business stress. When the coke was gone, he would purchase more and more, until he either ran out of money or could find no more coke. Like the crucial-phase alcoholic, Michael would alternate between flurries of complete abstinence and cocaine debauchery.

According to the disease model, as in other medical illnesses (e.g., diabetes), a person may have a genetic predisposition for a disorder, yet may circumvent most of its complications by avoiding the substances or activities that trigger its symptoms. For example, a person who has a genetic predisposition to skin cancer may be able to dodge most of its harmful consequences by avoiding undue exposure to the sun. Similarly, a person who is predisposed to drug addiction may avoid the disease by abstaining from all mind-altering drugs.

The Downward Spiral of Addiction

As discussed in Chapter 3, "Pleasure and the Brain," there is a huge array of drugs or activities that can increase dopamine in the pleasure centers of the brain. The allegorical story of a "Journey to Oblivion" captures the essence of the addictive process.

Journey to Oblivion

What are the conditions of a trip to oblivion? The voyage is destined for hardship and suffering. It can begin anywhere in time and space. The universe abounds with capsules for transport. One blurs the senses with lightning velocity. Another creeps slowly, leaving trails of combustion. The passenger sleeps through much of the way, while observers mark progress via symbols of change. A robot pilot is strong at the helm. Only mutiny can adjust the ship's scattered course. A guard must be posted or the android returns. The traveler remains altered by this sojourn in hell.

Figure 17.2 Journey to Oblivion "What's up! China, Apache, roofies, monkey, flakka … what you need?" (21st-century drug dealer).

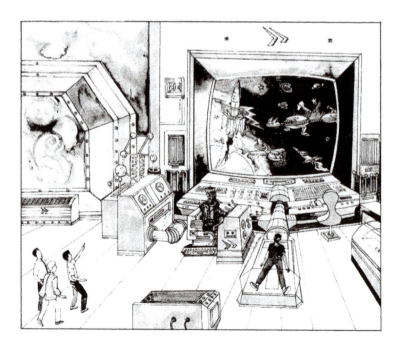

Capsules for Transport: Licit and Illicit Drugs

Cigarettes and alcohol, both legal drugs, continue to be of primary concern. In 2014, 139.7 million Americans aged 12 or older reported current use of alcohol, 60.9 million reported binge alcohol use in the past month, and 16.3 million reported heavy alcohol use in the past month. The percentage of adolescents aged 12 to 17 who were current alcohol users was 11.5% (Center for Behavioral Health Statistics and Quality, 2015a, p. 19). Regarding cigarettes, among the 55.2 million current cigarette smokers aged 12 or older, 32.5 million were daily cigarette smokers. About 292,000 adolescents aged 12 to 17 smoked cigarettes every day, which represents about one fourth (24.1%) of adolescents who were current smokers." (Center for Behavioral Health Statistics and Quality, 2015a, p. 16). According to the National Institute on Drug Abuse (2016), the prevalence of past-year drug use among 12th graders for alcohol was 58.2%; for marijuana, 34.9%; for Ecstasy (MDMA), 3.6%; amphetamines, 7.7%; cough medicine; 4.6%, and inhalants, 1.9%. As discussed in Chapter 4, "Feeling No Pain, The Opioid Era," on average, 52 Americans die daily from prescription opioid overdoses—which amounts to about 2 deaths every hour (CDC, 2016). Appendix B presents some of the emotional, behavioral, and physical consequences associated with an array of widely abused psychoactive drugs, with special attention to opioids. The information is by no means exhaustive. Interested readers are advised to consult SAHMSA, NIDA, and NIH online resources.

Behavioral Addictions

After a moment of reflection, it becomes obvious that any stress-reducing activity—whether ingesting a psychoactive substance, eating junk food, or gambling excessively—may be subject to compulsive overuse and the escalating consequences of loss of control. In fact, the disease concept may be applied to the entire spectrum of compulsive problem behaviors. As we have shown throughout this book, the distinction between internally and externally induced alterations of mood, thought, or behavior is arbitrary and misleading. Activities that evoke sensations of arousal, satiation, or fantasy bring about alterations in brain chemistry and patterns of compulsive behavior much like the symptoms traditionally associated with psychoactive substances. Arousal, satiation, and fantasy may be regarded as psychological systems, vulnerable to attack by multiple agents of addiction. As in viral and bacterial infections, the specific disease carriers may differ widely in origin and structure, and yet the consequences of foreign invasion may be virtually identical in terms of symptoms, prognosis, and treatment. Each of the behaviors shown in Table 17.1 may become an agent of addiction, subject to compulsion, loss of control, and continuation despite harmful consequences.

The dimension of *religious extremism and cults* transverses all levels and may be used to short-circuit the usual course of an addictive process. A multitude of recovering addicts seem to strengthen their resolve by leaning on the pillars of religion or spiritual practice. Members of Alcoholics Anonymous (AA), for example, usually proclaim a renewed faith in a higher power, who aids them in maintaining sobriety. Yet religion may be a double-edged sword. Consider the tragic example of The Order of the Solar Temple (OTS), started by Joseph Di Mambro and Luc Jouret in 1984, which had a primary goal of assisting humanity through the transition of preparing us for the Second Coming of Christ as a "solar god-king," who would further unification of Christianity and Islam. Following the October 1994 murder of a 3-month infant, who Di Mambro identified as the antichrist, at the group's headquarters, an inner circle of 12 members performed a ritual last supper. This was followed by mass suicides that took place in two villages in

Western Switzerland and in Morin Heights, Quebec. Fifteen members committed suicide with poison, 30 were killed by bullets or smothering, and 8 by other causes (Lewis, 2006).

In the most recent context, millions of people throughout the world are plagued by the epidemic of religious extremism. To be sure, the widespread belief in Armageddon (the site of the ultimate battle between God and Satan) across many religious faiths supplies a rationale through which contemporary religious fanaticism may result in untold hardship and suffering. The phenomenon of fantasy addiction was examined in detail in Section IV, "Mental Excursions."

Table 17.1 List of Behavioral Addictions

- Drug ingestion—Includes major psychoactive drugs and marijuana, alcohol, and nicotine

- Eating—Includes overuse of particular foods, for example, sugar

- Sex—Includes autoeroticism, pornography, and varieties of sadomasochistic activities

- Gambling—Includes numbers, horses, dogs, cards, and roulette

- Activity—Includes work, exercise, and sports

- Pursuit of power—Includes spiritual, physical, and material power

- Media fascination—Includes TV, Internet, and other electronic media devices

- Isolation—Includes sleep, fantasy, and dreams

- Risk taking—Includes excitement related to danger

- Religious extremism and cults—Includes groups using brainwashing or other techniques of psychological restructuring

- Crime and violence—Includes crimes against people and property

- Bonding-socializing—Includes excessive dependence on relationships or social gatherings

- Institutionalization—Includes excessive need for environmental structure, such as prisons, mental hospitals, and religious sanctuaries, and institutional use of psychoactive medication

The Passenger Sleeps

When children are asked if they would like to be addicts when they grow up, invariably they respond with a combination of disdain and perplexity. There is no way that they want to be hooked on anything, and besides, how could you have ever come up with such a goofy question? Yet statistically, 5% to 10% of all grade-school children will eventually become dependent on alcohol or drugs; if we include food and other behavioral compulsions such as gambling or sex, the figure easily exceeds 20% (see Table I.1, Section I "Prevalence and Severity of Common Hedonic Dependencies"). Nobody wants to be dependent on anything, yet the number of people who develop pathological habits is huge. How do people reconcile the difference between what they value in the morning of their life and what they do in the afternoon and twilight hours?

Those who suffer from hedonic dependencies insulate themselves from the glaring discrepancy between their natural inclination toward well-mindedness and the depraved lifestyle of addiction. As if they have fallen into a deep sleep, space trippers become oblivious to a multitude of observers imploring them to take heed of their compulsion and loss of control. In the face of massive evidence to the contrary, they continue to believe in their capacity to maintain adequate functioning. Reverend Joseph L. Kellermann (1970) describes alcoholism as "a merry-go-round named denial," in which the alcoholic, together with a regular cast of supporting actors, enacts a predictable scenario: there is a group composed of family or friends that unwittingly protects the afflicted from the harsh reality of his or her desperate plight. Whatever the vehicle for transport, the addict's support system usually includes three unintentional contributors to the avalanching predicament: an *enabler,* a *victim,* and a *provoker.*

The *enabler* is a character who is available to bail the addicted darling out of any crisis that might ensue from the demanding journey. This support person might be a professional, such as a physician or counselor, who helps the addict to "get by" with irresponsible behavior. He or she may also be a friend who fills in, on the job or at home, when the journey to oblivion takes a wild turn.

The part of the *victim* is played by the boss, employer, or supervisor who saves the addict's job when he or she cannot perform the expected duties. The victim picks up the tab for irresponsible conduct because love or concern for the addict prevents them from initiating proper consequences or disciplinary action at home or in the workplace.

Finally, the *provoker*—usually the girlfriend or wife of a male addict—is the person who seeks to control the alcoholic's life by crying, nagging, bargaining, blackmailing, and so on. S/he alternates among the roles of counselor, physician, parent, and spouse as the addict vacillates among needing to be forgiven, taken care of, and reprimanded, on a cyclical basis. Although the provoker is deeply troubled by the addict's lifestyle, he or she is always there to compensate for any action that might threaten to dissolve the tenuous family unit. The bitterness engendered by the alcoholic's behavior feeds back into the family dynamics and often results in further upset and consequent escalation of drinking by the alcoholic partner.

According to Reverend Kellermann (1970), if recovery from addiction is to occur, it must start with the people who unwittingly maintain the addict's system of denial. The victim and enabler should find a source of information and insight if they are to change their characteristic roles. The provoker should enter some form of ongoing group program, such as Al-Anon, to receive the support that this person will need to make a substantial change in his or her life. Finally, parents are asked to consider that they may be unintentionally playing support roles on the "merry-go-round of denial" for addicted teenagers. "Denial"— disbelief that a member of their family suffers from an addictive disorder—is perhaps the most elemental concept that parents, other family members, and close friends need to understand.

We suggest that the concept of denial is better understood and communicated to those affected by addiction when replaced by the word *defensiveness.* The concept of denial is often perceived as implying poor character (i.e., deliberate lying and deception) and lack of awareness about "what's really going on." Defensiveness, on the other hand, communicates a degree of concern, dissatisfaction with the status quo, and a desire for something different (personal communication with Kenneth Wanberg, January 20, 2009).

Symbols of Change

It is virtually impossible for a friend or family member to accurately gauge the extent to which an addict depends on a neurochemical prop. After tolerance has developed, the addict may appear completely normal during an extended voyage in his or her capsule for transport. By far the most reliable indication of continuing addiction is the person's apparent inability to integrate his or her goals and behaviors. The allegedly recovering person is exposed by an obvious inability to coordinate stated objectives and actual performance. He or she may miss appointments with intimate friends or fail to appear for critical work assignments. These inconsistencies, which might be dismissed among nonaddicts as faux pas, are the telltale signs of a flourishing hedonic dependency.

Figure 17.3 shows the deterioration of a person's values as the journey to oblivion progresses over time. The values closest to the center represent guiding principles in the addict's life. In the pre-addiction (symptomatic) phase, a person's behavior may reflect the entire spectrum of moral precepts that he or she has internalized from well-minded people in society. However, as addiction progresses through prodromal, crucial, and chronic phases, the person's ability to function in accord with his or her own values dwindles to near zero.

With the onset of recovery, the principles that guide one's behavior may become reorganized. The ones that formerly occupied positions of highest priority, such as the experience of excitement, may become peripheral and of minimal importance during the recovery phase of an addict's career. When a person assumes the commitment to get well, the preliminary and possibly the most superficial aspect of the task is to stop the self-defeating behavior, whatever that may be. The greater challenge, which may take years of self-discipline and support from treatment personnel, is to regain the full capacity to operate in accord with the values that the individual has chosen as guiding principles for his or her life.

Figure 17.3 Deterioration of Values As addiction progresses through prodromal, crucial, and chronic phases, the addict's ability to function in accord with his or her own values dwindles to near zero.

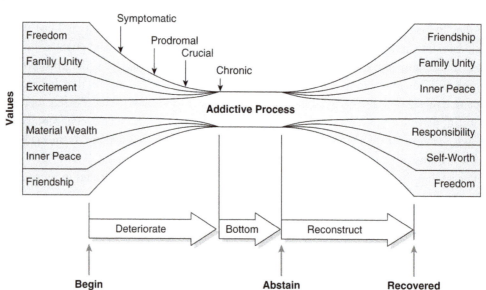

The Robot Pilot

If you have never been enslaved by an irresistible impulse, it is difficult for you to appreciate a person's apparent inability to captain his or her own ship. Whatever the seductive agent—substances, smartphones, or sweets—addicts repeat time and time again, "Whenever it's right there in front of me, I have no choice. I've never been able to turn down a ..." This subordination of rational thought and value-based decision making to the lure of momentary pleasure is at once the most mystifying and destructive aspect of the addictive process. In the case of recovering alcoholics, higher cue sensitivity (increased cravings elicited by alcohol stimuli) was found to be highly predictive of later relapse (Drummond, 2000).

To understand the compulsion to be at craving's beck and call, we must again consider the multifaceted basis of addiction. From the standpoint of biology, our formulation rests on the position that we can become physically dependent on the experiences of arousal, satiation, or fantasy, independent of whether the capsule for transport is a substance or an activity. Behavior in each sphere may be related to a particular kind of neurotransmission, possibly involving specific neural pathways and neurotransmitter combinations. Arousal dependence may be compared to biochemical alterations related to excessive amphetamine use, while satiation effects may be compared to those related to opioid use. Fantasy behaviors can be related to such neurotransmitters as dopamine, norepinephrine, or serotonin, all of which have chemical similarities to certain psychedelic drugs, e.g., MDMA and mescaline. Repetition of each type of activity sets up a compensatory biochemical reaction that restores neurochemical balance in the central nervous system. The individual must increase the level of addictive behavior—for example, risk taking—to continue to achieve a subjective experience of pleasure. Addicts are also motivated by increasing discomfort from withdrawal, when they stop or reduce the need-satisfying activity. The tendency toward reinstatement (doing it again) is encouraged by a substratum of neurochemical instability.

Witkiewitz and Marlatt (2007) have studied the compulsion to repeat destructive behaviors from a combined psychological and social perspective. The irresistible urge to reenter the drab spiral of progressive impairment is based on pressure from the following sources:

- The addict's expectation that some positive effects might be experienced through a brief interlude with the seductive agent
- The initial rush of pleasure produced by the object of craving
- Social pressures to be one of the group

The seasoned addict engages in a fierce battle for control over the object of his or her craving. Episodes of abstinence typically alternate with nearly complete submission and loss of control. The likelihood that an addict will repeat the characteristic pattern of excess and moral depravity is increased by an identified series of psychological reactions. The combined influence from a predictable set of internal messages convinces the addict to abandon control.

This process begins just after the first tastes of forbidden fruit. When a person who tries to be straight, sober, controlled, or clean experiences a slip, he or she becomes confused in self-concept: "I thought I had control over ... but now it appears that I don't." Most often, the individual attributes his or her failure or slip to personal weakness. These two psychological factors—identity conflict and self-blame—are cumulative in effect. The internal discord produced by the discrepant self-concept of "I am in control" versus "I have failed" results in a regressive shift in self-image from responsible person to out of control addict. By attributing the slip to personal weakness, the addict unwittingly creates the expectation for continued failure in the future. The cumulative effect of role confusion and loss of confidence makes submission to the robot pilot an easier choice than abstinence or self-regulation. The intensity of this reaction depends on several factors:

- The degree of personal commitment to maintain abstinence
- The period of sustained abstinence—the longer the duration, the greater the effect
- The importance of the behavior to the individual involved (Witkiewitz & Marlatt, 2007)

The Mutiny

The course of addiction is remarkably resistant to change. Hunt, Barnett, and Branch (1971) found that approximately 75% of all addicts who attempted abstinence from heroin, alcohol, or cigarettes resumed their habits between 3 and 6 months after beginning a program for recovery. The statistics for attempted weight control are equally grim (Kolata, 2007). In other outcome studies, approximately 65% to 70% of patients treated for alcoholism were found to relapse within 1 year of treatment, with the majority relapsing within less than 3 months (Emrick, 1974; W. R. Miller & Hester, 1986). In studies of drug- or polysubstance-dependent patients, relapse rates following treatment are similar to, if not higher than, those found for patients solely dependent on alcohol (McKay, Alterman, Rutherford, Cacciola, & McLellan, 1999). Recidivism rates for juvenile and adult crime range from 70% to 80%, depending on how recidivism is defined (Wanberg & Milkman, 2006).

In consideration of the powerful influences from biological, psychological, and social sources, a continuing pattern of struggle and failure seems inevitable. To be sure, the traveler who survives must organize a powerful mutiny to overthrow the tyrannical "commander." The rebellious survival force must battle a slew of weapons, massively deployed by a malevolent robot whose sophisticated armament includes habitual psychological responses, biochemically-based emotional and physical disturbances, intense social pressure, and the random stress of unavoidable negative circumstance. A successful rebellion must effectively counteract these forces. Each mutiny must be tailor-made to fit the specific requirements of each journey.

In the realm of substance abuse, for example, the initial tactics for recovery are determined by the specific needs of the user and the unique qualities of his or her drug. Withdrawal from a single drug, drugs from the same group, or a combination of drugs from different groups requires diverse detoxification procedures. Withdrawal from opioid dependence, for example, produces a well-defined abstinence syndrome, characterized by gastrointestinal distress, muscle aches, anxiety, insomnia, and narcotics hunger—none of which is life threatening. In contrast, withdrawal from barbiturates, or a barbiturate–alcohol combination, may produce potentially fatal seizures, requiring vigorous medical intervention, often hospital-based care.

Withdrawal from cocaine, amphetamine, or meth usually involves depression and lethargy. For these drugs, the symptoms of high-dose intoxication may become life threatening. Cocaine toxicity may result in brain seizures, heart failure, delusions, hallucinations, and potentially violent behavior. In addition, mixed addiction may result from the alternating use of antagonistic substances as observed in the upper-downer cycle. Some addicts use high doses of stimulants such as amphetamines or cocaine and then use a secondary drug such as alcohol, a short-acting barbiturate, or an opioid to calm the side effects of excessive stimulation. Dependence and tolerance may develop to the secondary depressant drug as well. Dependence on drugs such as opioids, cocaine, phencyclidine (PCP), and cannabinoids has been shown to co-occur with alcohol dependence in 64% of individuals (Compton, Cottler, Phelps, Abdallah, & Spitznagel, 2000). During detoxification, those dependent on more than one drug may experience a complex of symptoms associated with the withdrawal from drugs of different classes.

Sadly, according to SAMHSA's National Survey on Drug Use and Health, 21.0 million people (nearly 8% of the U.S. population) aged 12 or older needed treatment for an illicit drug or alcohol use problem in 2016. Only 3.8 million received any form of substance use treatment that year, with about 2.2 million of these individuals receiving services from specialty treatment programs (SAMHSA, 2017). Some populations may suffer from a lack of availability of quality, specialty treatment programs. For instance, incarcerated individuals have drug dependence rates 4 times greater than that of the general population, but less than 25% of these people will have access to services. Moreover, the services may not be adequate for the needs of the clients, focusing on education and awareness rather than actual treatment (Taxman, Perdoni, and Harrison, 2007).

For non-substance addictions, the primary strategy for recovery usually involves either completely stopping the compulsive activity (as in gambling) or dramatically reducing the pattern of abuse (as in eating disorders). Although addicts take the first steps to recovery for a variety of reasons, including family pressure, the threat of being fired, health concerns, or legal problems, the ensuing battle for control is always decided according to one fundamental principle: the addict must discover alternative means to satisfy the needs that were previously resolved through the addictive activity. Addictions to love, sex, and the Internet pose a more unique challenge, in that the addict's goal is not to completely cease engagement in those activities, but rather to be able to engage in them in an appropriate (i.e., non-excessive, non-compulsive) manner.

An innovative client, whom we shall refer to as Max, developed a set of nonchemical alternatives that he successfully used to overcome his dependence on alcohol. With assistance from his therapist, Max realized that he used alcohol to cope with an identifiable set of psychological and physical needs. He and his therapist devised a program of behavioral alternatives, specifically designed to cope with the emotions and conflicts previously managed through drinking. The program involved the use of sensory isolation, videos, massage, and weekly psychotherapy sessions. After one year, Max could successfully terminate psychotherapy and continue to enjoy a comfortable and responsible life without using drugs or alcohol. Table 17.2 outlines the cognitive (insights gained from psychotherapy) and behavioral (alternative behavior) techniques that Max used to regain control over his own life.

Table 17.2 Max's Innovative Mutiny Against his Dependence on Alcohol

	Isolation Tank	Massage	Fantasy	Psychotherapy
Device	Float in water to alleviate the effects of gravity. As much as possible, eliminate all temperature difference while shutting out light and sound.	Soothing sensations to the skin and musculature are delivered by a qualified practitioner.	Video movies are selected from the complete range of fantasy productions available in the contemporary retail video market.	Individual psychotherapy is delivered by a qualified professional with a cognitive-behavioral orientation.
Rationale	Reduce external stimulation to trigger fantasies of power and immortality. Results in altered state of consciousness.	Reduce tension through internal chemicals released by touch. Diminish unresolved dependency needs.	Movies allow for passive means to achieve relaxation without the unwanted effects of intoxication and hangovers.	Therapist helps client understand the emotional, sensory, and intellectual needs that were previously met through alcohol.
Goals	Fantasies of power help to compensate for feelings of helplessness and lack of self-worth. These are examined during psychotherapy and replaced by self-actualizing behaviors.	Vigorous massage is used to dampen anxiety and aggressive drive. The client gradually learns to subdue emotional discomfort through positive interpersonal relationships.	Provide gratification for aesthetic, intellectual, and emotional needs that have been mismanaged at home or at the bar. Gain insight into origins of anxiety and fear.	The client learns to separate himself from infantile needs previously resolved in a self-destructive fashion. Through a safe, caring, insight-oriented relationship, client enlarges the scope of his coping skills.

Source: From "An innovative approach to methadone detoxification (Milkman, et. al. 1980).

A Guard Must Be Posted

Co-occurring disorder is an almost ubiquitous problem in treatment for addiction. Among drug-dependent clients (not including alcoholics), the co-occurrence of some other form of mental disorder is as high as 84% (Compton et al., 2000). These include a range of mood, anxiety, and personality disorders. In alcohol-dependent subjects, co-occurring depression, bipolar I and II disorders, and personality disorders have also been found at elevated rates. In 2014, among the 20.2 million adults with a past year substance use disorder, 7.9 million (39.1%) had AMI [any mental illness] in the past year. Furthermore, the percentage of adolescents aged 12 to 17 who used illicit drugs in the past year was higher among those with a past year major depressive episode (MDE) than it was among those without a past year MDE (33.0 vs. 15.2%). Youths with a past year MDE in 2014 also were more likely than those without an MDE to be users of marijuana, nonmedical users of psychotherapeutics, users of inhalants, and users of hallucinogens in the past year (Center for Behavioral Health Statistics and Quality, 2015, pp. 32–34).

As reviewed by Sher (2012), individuals with substance abuse disorders are at an elevated risk for suicide. This is compounded with the presence of a co-occurring psychological disorder or with poly-substance abuse. This risk is thought to be linked to dysregulation of neurotransmitter systems (such as serotonin and dopamine) as well as cognitive impairments linked to chronic or excessive drug use. Appropriate precautions should be taken, as it will be some time (on the scale of months) after discontinuance of the drug before regular neurochemical levels will be restored.

From these findings, the case is clear that abstaining from one's drug(s) or activity of choice is likely the first step toward wellness. To that end, not treating an underlying mental disorder can be as detrimental as not treating the substance-dependent individual at all!

The recovering addict must gain the upper hand over negative social or peer influences, internal and external states of conflict, and sometimes excruciating physical discomfort. Often the challenge is too great, and the mindless robot returns. Those who avoid subjugation to the addictive process need to develop a mature set of emotional, intellectual, and behavioral skills that promote attainment of pleasure through internal rewards and life-enhancing activities. This may be accomplished through group therapy or an individually tailored treatment program combined with strong environmental support. We will more fully explore evidence-based treatment for hedonic disorders in the following chapter, "Elements of Effective Treatment."

Chapter Summary

Addiction is regarded by some research scientists as a chronic and relapsing brain disease. On the basis of a questionnaire study of more than 2,000 male alcoholics, Jellinek formulated his four-phase concept of alcohol addiction: the pre-alcoholic symptomatic phase, the prodromal phase, the crucial phase, and the chronic phase. This final stage of alcoholism is characterized by prolonged periods of intoxication, known as binges. Withdrawal symptoms appear as soon as alcohol is no longer present in the body. Finally, the need for alcohol is so great that the addict can no longer pretend that he has control over his drinking.

Since the formulation of Jellinek's phases of alcoholism, the disease model has been embraced by Alcoholics Anonymous, the American Medical Association, and many others. More recently, the disease concept has widened to include many other potentially addictive agents such as gambling, sex, and eating, as well as a host of other addictive substances such as cocaine, amphetamines, and opioids. In fact, any stress-reducing activity—whether ingestion of a psychoactive substance or playing Internet games—may be subject to compulsive overuse and the escalating consequences of loss of control. The disease concept may be applied to the entire spectrum of compulsive problem behaviors. As in viral and bacterial infections, the origin and structure of specific disease carriers may be very different, and yet the consequences of foreign invasion may be the same as far as symptoms, prognosis, and treatment.

A person loses touch with his or her core values as the journey to oblivion progresses over time. In the pre-addiction (symptomatic) phase, where drinking (or the hedonic activity of choice) has not caused any major problems, the individual may maintain functioning with an intact and positive system of morals and values (i.e., progressing toward life goals as a contributing member of society). However, as addiction progresses through prodromal, crucial, and chronic phases, the person's ability to function in accord with his or her own values greatly diminishes. With the onset of recovery, positive values that guide one's behavior may reemerge or become reorganized. This type of prosocial reorientation, however, requires ample support from family and friends, personal commitment, and ample time to become ingrained as a new pattern of thoughts, feelings and actions.

Although addicts take the first steps to recovery for a variety of reasons, the battle for control is always decided according to one fundamental principle: the addict must find alternative means to satisfy the needs that were previously met through the addictive activity.

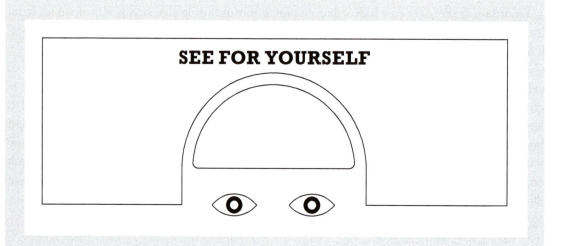

SEE FOR YOURSELF

Secular Organizations for Sobriety.

For those wondering about secular alternatives to traditional 12-step meetings. The number of non-religious people in the nation is rising, and secular support groups for recovery may provide a valuable resource for people who do not make the assumption of a higher power. **http://www.sossobriety.org/**

12 Steps of AA with Father Martin. 1972. Father Martin. 44:59

Father Martin, an iconic speaker on the disease model of alcoholism, explains the 12-Step recovery model associated with Alcoholics Anonymous. **https://www.youtube.com/watch?v=sqKvijuc89k&feature=youtu.be**

Drinking to Oblivion. 2016. Louis Theroux. BBC Two. 3:00

In this short clip, Louis interacts with Mariana, who is trying to support her partner of three years, Pieter, through his alcohol addiction **http://www.bbc.co.uk/programmes/p03rvjd8**

'Unbroken Brain' Offers New Insights on Addiction. 2016. Alva Noë. NPR. Commentary.

This brief article offers commentary on Maia Szalavitz's book, in which she provides an alternative to a disease or moralistic model of addiction. Szalavitz posits that addiction is more akin to a learning disorder than a physiological disease. **http://www.npr.org/sections/13.7/ 2016/04/29/475991514/unbroken-brain-offers-new-insights- on-addiction**

Surgeon General Murthy Wants America to Face Up to Addiction. 2016. Dr. Vivek Murthy interviewed on *Morning Edition*. NPR. 3:50

This brief interview covers Dr. Murthy's perspective on the serious and growing public health problem that is addiction in the U.S. **http://www.npr.org/sections/health-shots/2016/11/17/ 502402409/surgeon-general-murthy-wants-america-to-face-up- to-addiction**

CHAPTER 18

Elements of Effective Treatment

In my early professional years I was asking the question: How can I treat, or cure, or change this person? Now I would phrase the question in this way: How can I provide a relationship which this person may use for his own personal growth?

—Carl R. Rogers

Introduction

Among many addicted individuals, the wisdom of AA (originally formulated in 1935) remains gospel. Overeaters Anonymous, Gamblers Anonymous, Narcotics Anonymous, Cocaine Anonymous, Sexaholics Anonymous (to name just a few) rely on minor tweaking of the original AA doctrine: "Stop drinking [or other compulsive pleasure-seeking activity] ... Go to meetings ... Get a sponsor ... Ask for help." After more than 80 years, the AA model remains a pillar for people, worldwide, to find help with their addiction and support in their recovery. However, the powerful AA philosophy, which is predicated upon calling for help from their "higher power" is not to be equated with the scientific principles of effective treatment.

In this chapter, we discuss the principal evidence-based models for addiction treatment, which apply to the panoply of "hedonic disorders." Excluding "pharmacological criteria" the DSM-5 (2015) definition of Substance Use Disorder easily encompasses the commonalities approach to behavioral and substance abuse problems espoused in this book.

The *Diagnostic and Statistical Manual of Mental Disorders*, Fifth Edition (DSM-5), no longer uses the terms substance abuse and substance dependence, rather it refers to substance use disorders, which are defined as mild, moderate, or severe to indicate the level of severity, which is determined by the number of diagnostic criteria met by an individual. Substance use disorders occur when the recurrent use of alcohol and/or drugs causes clinically and functionally significant impairment, such as health problems, disability, and failure to meet major responsibilities at work, school, or home. According to the DSM-5, a diagnosis of substance use disorder is based on evidence of impaired control, social impairment, risky use, and pharmacological criteria (SAMHSA, 2015).

Most recovery programs—with the usual exception of those designed for eating, sex, love, and the Internet—stress the need for abstinence, although it is recognized that some individuals may benefit from initiating their treatment with the aim of moderating their use, rather than abstaining (Marlatt, 1998). Vaillant (1995, p. 367) summarized the ingredients of effective programs in the mainstream of treatment, all of which are embodied by the tenets of AA:

- Offer the client or patient a non-harmful substitute dependency for the addictive agent.
- Remind him or her ritually that even one encounter with the addictive agent can lead to pain and relapse.
- Support recovery through the formation of new relationships in which addictive behavior is neither encouraged nor tolerated.
- Repair the social and medical damage that has already occurred.
- Promote participation in an inspirational group.
- Restore self-esteem

Depending on the personality and situation of the client, a recovery-oriented self-help group, such as AA or an AA derivative such as Narcotics Anonymous or Sexaholics Anonymous, is often indicated.

The relief effect from participating in a group that offers empathy and belonging while continuously rewarding sobriety may be essential to the recovery process (Litt, Kadden, Kabela-Cormier, & Petry, 2007). A change in social support is often stressed for alcoholics (Litt et al., 2007), rather than trying to white-knuckle the addiction away in isolation (Interlandi, 2008). AA is an existing social network that does all the things listed above. In many cases, group support can be bolstered by individual counseling. In other cases, the only form of treatment that the addict will accept is one-to-one psychotherapy. Most addiction experts agree that addicts attempting to terminate their use will almost always need some sort of psychological support (Interlandi, 2008). Whether individual or group, effective treatment requires a readiness on both sides (client and therapist) for intensive work.

Community residential programs often incorporate the social models of AA, including "frequent on-site presence of alumni and community Alcoholics Anonymous (AA) and Narcotics Anonymous (NA) members, an emphasis on building clean and sober networks, and an ethic of volunteerism which incorporates program upkeep and service" (Witbrodt et al., 2007, p. 948). Most residential rehabilitation centers follow a similar program of a 28-day typical stay, a 12-step program paradigm, and supplemental cognitive-behavioral therapy and motivational interviewing (J. Adler, 2007).

Earlier viewed as generated by lack of willpower, addiction is now more widely understood as a "bio-psycho-social-spiritual disorder" (Interlandi, 2008). Most AA groups are attempting to keep up with the times (Summers, 2007). With the American Medical Association's recognition of addiction as a disease in 1956 and all of the neurological and biochemical evidence that shows malfunctioning of the brain in addicted individuals, society is now accepting addiction as a legitimate illness (Interlandi, 2008).

Is This a Good Idea?
If Congress and President Trump succeed in further dismantling the Affordable Care Act, *aka* Obama Care, what will happen to the legions of drug-dependent patients whose treatment has been paid for by Medicaid? Consider the plight of a former heroin addict who is on Suboxone, a drug that eases withdrawal and cravings for opioids. For many, treatment with this drug has been a godsend. Former addicts report dramatic improvements in their ability to function in mainstream society. Without Medicaid insurance coverage for medication and counseling, there is likelihood that former patients will backslide to using heroin or other illegal narcotics purchased on the street. Return to a life of crime and violence may be the inevitable result.
Source: NYT. Addiction Treatment Grew Under Health Law. Now What? (Seelye, K & Goodnouth, 2017)

Table 18.1 presents a summary, developed by the National Institute on Drug Abuse, of known factors that improve outcomes for people who struggle with substance use disorders. As explained in "Journey to Oblivion," these principles apply to the broad spectrum of addictive behaviors; simply substitute the phrase "hedonic disorder" for references to substances or drugs.

Table 18.1 NIDA Principles of Drug Addiction Treatment

1. Addiction is a complex but treatable disease that affects brain function and behavior. Drugs alter the brain's structure and how it functions, resulting in changes that persist long after drug use has ceased. This may help explain why abusers are at risk for relapse even after long periods of abstinence.

2. No single treatment is appropriate for everyone. Matching treatment settings, interventions, and services to an individual's problems and needs is critical to his or her ultimate success.

3. Treatment needs to be readily available. Because drug-addicted individuals may be uncertain about entering treatment, taking advantage of available services, the moment people are ready for treatment is critical. Potential patients can be lost if treatment is not immediately available or readily accessible.

4. Effective treatment attends to multiple needs of the individual, not just his or her drug abuse. To be effective, treatment must address the individual's drug abuse and any associated medical, psychological, social, vocational, and legal problems.

5. Remaining in treatment for an adequate period of time is critical. The appropriate duration for an individual depends on the type and degree of his or her problems and needs. Research indicates that most addicted individuals need at least 3 months in treatment to significantly reduce or stop their drug use and that the best outcomes occur with longer durations of treatment.

6. Counseling—individual and/or group—and other behavioral therapies are the most commonly used forms of drug abuse treatment. Behavioral therapies vary in their focus and may involve addressing a patient's motivations to change, building skills to resist drug use, replacing drug-using activities with constructive and rewarding activities, improving problem solving skills, and facilitating better interpersonal relationships.

7. Medications are an important element of treatment for many patients, especially when combined with counseling and other behavioral therapies. For example, methadone and buprenorphine are effective in helping individuals addicted to heroin or other opioids stabilize their lives and reduce their illicit drug use. Also, for persons addicted to nicotine, a nicotine replacement product (nicotine patches or gum) or an oral medication (buproprion or varenicline), can be an effective component of treatment when part of a comprehensive behavioral treatment program.

8. An individual's treatment and services plan must be assessed continually and modified as necessary to ensure it meets his or her changing needs. A patient may require varying combinations of services and treatment components during treatment and recovery. In addition to counseling or psychotherapy, a patient may require medication, medical services, family therapy, parenting instruction, vocational rehabilitation and/or social and legal services. For many patients, a continuing care approach provides the best results, with treatment intensity varying according to a person's changing needs.

9. Many drug-addicted individuals also have other mental disorders. Because drug abuse and addiction—both of which are mental disorders—often co-occur with other mental illnesses, patients presenting with one condition should be assessed for the other(s). And when these problems co-occur, treatment should address both (or all), including the use of medications as appropriate

10. Medically assisted detoxification is only the first stage of addiction treatment and by itself does little to change long-term drug abuse. Although medically assisted detoxification can safely manage the acute physical symptoms of withdrawal, detoxification alone is rarely sufficient to help addicted individuals achieve long-term abstinence. Thus, patients should be encouraged to continue drug treatment following detoxification.

11. Treatment does not need to be voluntary to be effective. Sanctions or enticements from family, employment settings, and/or the criminal justice system can significantly increase treatment entry, retention rates, and the ultimate success of drug treatment interventions.

12. Drug use during treatment must be monitored continuously, as lapses during treatment do occur. Knowing their drug use is being monitored can be a powerful incentive for patients and can help them withstand urges to use drugs. Monitoring also provides an early indication of a return to drug use, signaling a possible need to adjust an individual's treatment plan to better meet his or her needs.

13. Treatment programs should assess patients for the presence of HIV/AIDS, hepatitis B and C, tuberculosis, and other infectious diseases, as well as provide targeted risk-reduction counseling to help patients modify or change behaviors that place them at risk of contracting or spreading infectious diseases.

Source: NIDA's Principles of Drug Addiction Treatment: A Research-Based Guide (2012).

Integrated Models

The acronym SCRAM, which colloquially means "leave a place quickly," is a convenient memory device for focusing on integrated models for optimal treatment effects. In the past decade, it has become known that therapeutic outcomes are often synergistically improved by combining treatments, each with a demonstrated track record of effectiveness. (Sederer, 2015).

S-Stages of Change

Prochaska and DiClemente (1992) developed a foundational model for understanding how people move through a series of changes in thoughts and actions as they undergo change. They describe a spiraling process in which people, naturally, and often repetitively, move from a phase of *precontemplation* (marked by lack of motivation to take any steps toward resolving an addiction problem); to *contemplation* (the cornerstone of this period is ambivalence); followed by *determination* (motivation to seek help); to *action* (participating in a program to facilitate change); to *maintenance* (where the person can exit the repetitious cycle of moving forward and then regressing along the spiral pathway of ambivalence and relapse to a period of stable recovery. The implications of the stage of change model are far reaching in that different motivational and treatment strategies may be deployed at distinct phases of the client's progress toward growth and change, e.g., motivational interviewing during the precontemplation and contemplation stages; medication, cognitive-behavioral treatment, and relapse prevention, during the action phase of treatment.

C- Cognitive-Behavioral Therapy

A. Beck (1993) sent shock waves through the recovery field by developing an evidence-based model for treating addictions, outside of the traditional AA approach. Beck's model does not approach addiction as primarily a biological disease (see Jellinek's model Chapter 17, "The Voyage of Hardship and Suffering"), but rather a problem generated by patterns of maladaptive thoughts. By coming to terms with discernable patterns of negative core beliefs and automatic thoughts about the self, ongoing experience, and the outside world, addicts can develop healthy coping strategies regarding how they feel or react to drugs or other seductions (e.g., food, sex, gambling). Chapter 19, "The Cognitive-Behavioral Revolution: How to Manage Thoughts, Feelings, and Behaviors," presents a detailed view of how cognitive-behavior therapy has evolved to being recognized as the core strategy for achieving positive treatment outcomes, not only in the field of addiction, but also in other areas of mental health and criminal conduct.

R- Relapse Prevention

Marlatt's (1985) relapse prevention model, shown in Figure 18.1, is the foundational tool used by cognitive-behavioral therapists to provide substance abuse clients with an understanding of how high-risk situations (e.g., negative feelings, peer influence, stimulus cues, interpersonal conflict, change in self-image) can evoke a progression of thoughts and actions that can lead to full-blown relapse. The usual thinking response to a high-risk situation is loss of confidence in one's ability to cope (decreased self-efficacy) coupled with an expectation that a tension-reducing drug or action will bring relief (positive outcome expectancies). The next stage of relapse is acting out the impulse to use by indulging in the perceived tension-relieving behavior (e.g., ingesting alcohol, taking drugs, eating) in some intended measured and controlled manner (lapse). The cognitive dissonance (tension evoked by having overthrown a primary rule of conduct, e.g., abstinence) leads to the co-occurring process of self-justification (e.g., Who wants to be sober anyway?) and the perception that the drug or behavior is in fact working as intended (perceived effects). Further, the individual is likely to attribute his or her "fall" to personal weakness (self-attribution). Marlatt used the term *rule violation effect* to describe the combined influences of cognitive dissonance, self-attribution, and perceived effects, as they set the stage for return to earlier patterns of abuse and dependence (full relapse). Individuals who are interested in quitting are well-advised to give serious consideration to this model by developing and rehearsing alternative patterns of thoughts and actions at each stage of a potential relapse process.

In relation to in-depth reflection on the progression of relapse and alternative patterns of thoughts and action as indicated above, Table18.2 presents viable strategies for coping with cravings and urges that may threaten our resolve to achieve freedom from any hedonic dependency. By understanding the sequence of thoughts prior to violating a self-defined rule for maintaining personal responsibility regarding substance abuse or other potentially harmful behavior (e.g., binge drinking, promiscuity, overeating), a person can learn to restructure his or her dysfunctional thoughts, feelings, and actions in response to high-risk situations.

Figure 18.1 Marlatt's Model for Relapse Prevention

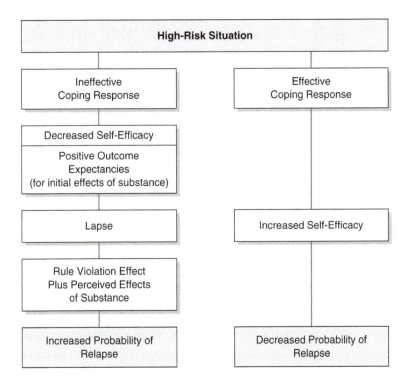

Table 18.2 Strategies for Managing Cravings and Urges

Sharing	Talk to family, friends, or someone you trust and ask for their support.
Toughing It Out	Get control over the craving by accepting the discomfort and implementing the following:
	Notice how you experience the craving. What are your thoughts and feelings about the craving? Where does it occur in your body?
	Is it still a craving, or has it become an urge (when your physical body becomes activated and you take steps to fulfill the craving such as searching out a friend you can get high with)?
Talk Yourself Down	When the craving becomes an urge, focus on your body where you feel the urge. Talk to yourself and take control of your actions, figuring out alternative ways to feel comfortable.
Urge Surfing	Ride out the wave, and visualize relaxing at the shore.
Alternatives	Find another activity that will distract you from the craving or urge.

A–Assessment

With the goal of developing an effective and individualized treatment plan, the therapist engages the client in a collaborative process with shared responsibility for setting goals and agendas, communicating transparently, and putting cognitive-behavioral skills into everyday life (Wright, Fasco, & Thase, 2006). It is general practice of most treatment agencies to use some form of screening to evaluate clients to determine appropriate intervention placement and the need for further assessment. It is also widespread practice to do a comprehensive assessment to determine the more specific needs of the client and to develop an individualized treatment plan (ITP).

Much of the information gathered in these assessment efforts relies on self-report of the client. It is commonly believed by many treatment practitioners and evaluators that these self-reports are often not reliable and are not to be trusted. Given that most would agree that both screening and comprehensive assessment are essential in the process of developing effective treatment placements and plans, how do we approach assessment to resolve the dilemma between this importance and the problem of report validity? Utilization of the convergent validation model (Figure 18,2) provides a basis for resolving this dilemma (Milkman & Wanberg, 2012, p. 281).

Discerning how well self-report represents the client's "true" condition requires the utilization of other-report data. Both sources of data are essential in providing an estimate of the client's "true" condition. We can hypothesize about this condition. Our data then test the hypothesis. If our objective is to measure where the client is and to get the best representation of how willing the client is to report his or her self-perceptions at the time of assessment, then whatever the client tells us is valid. We conclude that this is a valid representation of at least the willingness to report that perception. Even a slapdash response to assessment items is valid—not in terms of content but in terms of the client's response state at the time of assessment.

Within this model, *a self-report is never invalid*. Figure 18.2 provides a graphic representation of this model. The vertical vector (A) represents the "true" or veridical condition of the client in a certain area of assessment (e.g., substance use involvement). Vector B, represents the self-report source of data; and vector C represents the other-report source of data. The magnitude of the angle (B–C) between vectors

Figure 18.2 Convergent Model for Client Assessment

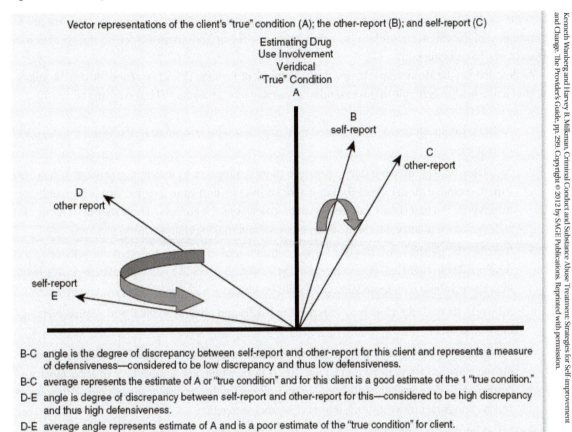

Vector representations of the client's "true" condition (A); the other-report (B); and self-report (C)

Estimating Drug
Use Involvement
Veridical
"True" Condition
A

B
self-report

C
other-report

D
other report

self-report
E

B-C   angle is the degree of discrepancy between self-report and other-report for this client and represents a measure of defensiveness—considered to be low discrepancy and thus low defensiveness.

B-C   average represents the estimate of A or "true condition" and for this client is a good estimate of the 1 "true condition."

D-E   angle is degree of discrepancy between self-report and other-report for this—considered to be high discrepancy and thus high defensiveness.

D-E   average angle represents estimate of A and is a poor estimate of the "true condition" for client.

Kenneth Warnberg and Harvey B. Milkman, Criminal Conduct and Substance Abuse Treatment: Strategies for Self-improvement and Change: The Provider's Guide, pp. 299. Copyright © 2012 by SAGE Publications. Reprinted with permission.

B and C is the theoretical estimate of the level of defensiveness or the willingness of the client to self-disclose. The magnitude of the angle between vector A and vector C represents the validity of the estimate of the client's "true" condition in the area of involvement in drug use, based on the other-report source of data. The B–C set of vectors would indicate a client who is relatively open to self-disclosure and whose self-report is discerned to be congruent with other-report data, and vector A indicates that both sources of data are good estimates of the client's "true" condition. The D–E set of vectors represents a very defensive client whose self-report is quite discrepant from the other-report, but the other-report is also discerned to be not a good estimate of the client's "true" condition.

Motivational Interviewing (MI)

W. Miller and Rollnick's (2013) groundbreaking work on how to motivate clients to participate in treatment has revolutionized the ways in which practitioners facilitate clients' progress through the stages of change. Of principal importance is to create an atmosphere in which clients can discover their own motivations for change. The therapist engages the client in a non-judgmental discussion about reasons for change, exploring ambivalence, and providing feedback about what is being said. Effective counselors are skilled in: (1) asking open ended questions; (2) providing affirmations of clients' willingness to engage in a dialogue about the possibility of change; (3) using the essential skill of reflective listening (reflecting to the client the meaning of their experiences as they discuss aspects of their life); (4) summarizing important components of the client–counselor discussion, to ensure the at both parties agree on the content and meaning of what is being said.

As described in the Motivational Interviewing Network of Trainers (MINT) website (2016), the following characteristics are germane to this essential counseling tool. Motivational Interviewing is:

1. A conversation about change designed to help people who are ambivalent regarding some parts of their life.

2. A collaborative partnership that honors the client's autonomy in the change process. It is not an expert–recipient model where the counselor knows the "best strategies" for the client. Rather, it is inspirational so that clients can look up to themselves as the authors of how they can change. MI is designed to enhance the client's competence about making changes throughout life.

3. It evokes the person's own motivation and commitment to change. A therapeutic relationship is developed with client and counselor coming together as peers in a collaborative exercise. Clients look inward about their motivations and skills for change.

4. MI works through the clinician's interpersonal skills and abilities to elicit and reinforce change talk by the client.

5. MI strengthens personal motivation for and commitment to a specific goal by eliciting and exploring the person's own reasons for change. This is done within and atmosphere of acceptance and compassion. The emphatic, collaborative style allows for the counselor to understand the client's will to change and move through the change process together.

6. MI addresses the widespread problem of ambivalence about change, recognizing that people often become stunted by inside and outside pressures to change. MI removes that pressure; helping people to tap into their own reservoir of abilities to change.

Population Focused Treatments

People who suffer from hedonic disorders come from diverse backgrounds. Effective practitioners pay special attention to the client's life context, e.g., age, cultural background, gender identity, sexual preferences, etc. An exhaustive discussion of the many contexts surrounding client struggles with hedonic disorders is beyond the scope this chapter. For an extensive review of the theory, research, and practice for treating adolescents, one of our most vulnerable populations, readers are referred to *Criminal Conduct and Substance Abuse Treatment for Adolescents: Pathways to Self-Discovery and Change* (Milkman and Wanberg, 2012). Chapter 24, "Meaningful Engagement of Talents", explains two highly successful models for promoting healthy lifestyles and preventing substance abuse among teenagers.

Our discussion now turns to the population of women, who benefit from gender-focused treatment services, and the legions of men and women who suffer from addiction in association with traumatic life experiences. Finally, in the spirit of opportuning synergistic treatment effects, we discuss the integration of medical services with psychological interventions, in the emerging field of medication-assisted treatment (MAT).

Gender-Focused Treatment

Women generally begin substance abuse later than men, and there is some evidence that they respond better to treatment. In an 8-year follow-up, Timko, Moos, Finney, and Connell (2002) found that the outcomes for women were somewhat better than for men using the same services. Jarvis (1992) found that women are likely to do less well in mixed-sex group therapy because of the overrepresentation of men and unfavorable sexual dynamics. Furthermore, women who report sexual or physical abuse tend to prefer a female therapist, while others do equally well with male or female therapists (Connors, Carroll, DiClemente, Longabaugh, & Donovan, 1997).

As summarized by Back, Brady, Jaanimagi, and Jackson (2006), women are less likely to enter substance abuse treatment because of sociocultural factors (e.g., stigma, lack of partner/family support to enter treatment), socioeconomic factors (e.g., child care), pregnancy, fears concerning child custody issues, and complexities associated with increased rates of co-occurring psychiatric disorders. Furthermore, many women seek treatment at other settings (e.g., primary care, mental health). However, once women do enter treatment, they are at least as likely as men to complete therapy and have positive outcomes. Programs that address barriers to treatment that are specific to women (e.g., child care) and provide careful psychiatric assessment and treatment are likely to be the most effective.

The cognitive-behavioral approach (see Chapter 19) is a breakthrough for examining the relapse process and teaching relapse prevention skills for both men and women. However, for women with addictive disorders, *gender-focused* treatment is strongly indicated (Milkman, Wanberg, & Gagliardi, 2008). Table 18.3 presents general principles for treating women in counseling settings (Williams-Quinlan, 2004).

Table 18.3 Guidelines for Treating Women in Counseling Settings

Effective treatment with women should be free of restrictions based on narrowly defined gender stereotypes.

The empowerment process involves recognition that women are able to accomplish what they make a commitment to and that the female substance abuse clients are no different from other women.

Women should not be expected to act in stereotypical ways, and nontraditional role choices should be respected.

Marriage should not be encouraged as a solution to women's problems.

Women should be helped to recognize that the "socially appropriate" ways they have been taught are not ideal for mental health and adjustment (Crawford & Unger, 2000; Gergen & Davis, 1997; Matlin, 1996).

Women should be treated and addressed with respectful language that communicates their equal status to men (Covington, 2000; Matlin, 1996; McMahon, 2000; Pollock, 1998).

Service providers should help women recognize the realities of sexism, racism, and economic discrimination and develop effective means of coping with these issues (Matlin, 1996).

Source: Williams-Quinlan, "Guidelines for Treating Women in Counseling Settings." Copyright © 2004

Women-focused treatment may produce improved outcomes because women perceive the same-sex treatment environment as one in which it is easier to disclose information about themselves, such as issues with children, sexuality, prostitution, sexual abuse, and physical abuse (Milkman et al., 2008; Sun, 2006). In addition, women-only settings eliminate the possibility of negative stereotyping and sexual harassment from their male counterparts (Weisner, 2005).

Perhaps the most important key to empowerment and strengthening women's resiliency lies in provision of a safe and reliable environment for trust, bonding, and intimacy. A typical component of substance abuse is violence in the female's domestic setting (Velez et al., 2006). Treatment that places the source of a woman's problems solely within herself can actually do damage to the recovery process by exacerbating already existing tendencies toward self-blame and feelings of powerlessness (Covington, 2000; Crawford & Unger, 2000; Matlin, 1996; Pollock, 1998). Equally important is helping women to see that assuming a victim stance in response to social realities is not an excuse to avoid personal responsibility for their actions.

The bottom line is that treatment outcomes are enhanced through gender-specific programs. Multiple treatment benefits are realized by empowering women to become self-sufficient and take personal responsibly for their own recovery (Milkman et al., 2008). These include:

- Lower rates of relapse and recidivism;
- Lower rates of inpatient care;
- Greater job constancy; and
- Better parenting relationships resulting in higher rates of child custody.

"Protector (NOT!)," written by a woman with firsthand experience in the treatment system, addresses a woman's journey from abusive relationships and codependence to self-awareness and personal empowerment.

Protector (NOT!)

When I was a child
She taught me to fear the wild ...
You need a protector ...
Need a protector ...
You need a protector
From the BIG BAD WOLF.
And when I was bad (or not)
I was punished by the dad (or what) ...
He's our protector ...
He's our protector ...
But he's also the BIG BAD WOLF.
And when I was grown
I wanted out on my own.

Not without a protector ...
You need a protector ...
Need a protector
From the BIG BAD WOLF.
And so I was married
And tradition carried ...
I had a protector ...
Had a protector ...
I had a protector
Who turned into the BIG BAD WOLF.
LEARN TO PROTECT YOURSELF.

"Protector (NOT!)" Copyright © by LaRee Herod.

Trauma as a Factor in Hedonic Disorders

Victims of traumatic life events tend to cope with heightened levels of anxiety and disturbing memories by escaping into activities that provide instant and powerful relief (e.g., substance use, sexual promiscuity, eating, gambling). Although the diagnosis of PTSD is by no means a prerequisite for addiction, vast numbers of people who struggle with hedonic dependencies have trauma, often recurring and severe, in their background. It has been posited that the problem of addiction arises as the result of being hurt, early in life (e.g., Mate, 2015).

Earnest research concerning PTSD began after the Vietnam War due to the profound psychological problems experienced by its veterans, both men and women. However, it has been reported that PTSD-like symptoms have been observed in all veteran populations, including those of the World Wars, the Korean conflict, and United Nations peacekeeping forces deployed to other war zones. Similar symptoms also occur in veterans from countries outside the United States including Australia and Israel (Beall, 1997). Written accounts of PTSD symptoms are documented from the U.S. Civil War, when it was known as "Da Costa's Syndrome," based on a paper written by Da Costa in 1871 (cited in Beall, 1997), which described it as "sol-dier's heart" or "irritable heart." Holocaust survivors are also discussed in medical literature as having similar symptoms, as are survivors of railway disasters and of the atom bombs dropped on Hiroshima and Nagasaki.

Outside of war, PTSD came to the forefront of public interest when survivors of the September 11, 2001, terrorist attacks in New York City showed symptoms of this disorder; survivors of the 2004 tsunami in southeastern Asia and eastern India, and survivors of the 2005 earthquake in Pakistan and hurricanes in the southeastern United States suffer PTSD as well (e.g., Katrina). It is self-evident that PTSD is a significant burden to those who survived mass assassinations such as (to name just a few): the Orlando nightclub shooting (June 12, 2016); San Bernardino community center shooting (Dec. 2, 2015); Sandy Hook Elementary School shooting (Dec. 14, 2012); Aurora movie theater shooting (July 20, 2012).

Today, PTSD is no longer considered a disorder only of war veterans, as it occurs in both men and women, adults and children, Western and non-Western groups, and at all socioeconomic levels. Only a small minority of people appear to be invulnerable to extreme trauma. These stress-resistant individuals appear to be those with high sociability; a thoughtful coping style; and a strong perception of their ability to control their own destiny, or possessing an "internal locus of control" (Herman, 1997).

At the core of PTSD diagnosis is an etiological agent (i.e., a traumatic event) that is outside the individual, as opposed to a weakness or flaw within the individual. Herman (1997) uses the *Comprehensive Textbook of Psychiatry*'s description of trauma: "intense fear, helplessness, loss of control, and threat of annihilation" (p. 33).

PTSD Population Statistics

The National Center for Posttraumatic Stress Disorder (NCPTSD, 2007) reports that about 8% of the population will have PTSD symptoms at some time in their lives. Approximately 5.2 million adults have PTSD during a given year; however, this is only a small portion of those who have experienced a traumatic event. About 60% of men and 50% of women experience a traumatic event at some time in their lives.

Women are more likely to experience sexual assault and child sexual abuse. Men are more likely to experience accidents, physical assault, combat, or witness death or injury. About 8% of men and 20% of women who experience a traumatic event will develop PTSD (NCPTSD, 2007). Sexual assault is more likely than other events to cause PTSD (Vogt, 2007).

Approximately 30% of men and women who served in war zones experience PTSD symptoms. An additional 20% to 25% have had some symptoms. Specific to the Vietnam War, research shows that of those who served, over 30% of men and 26% of women experienced PTSD symptoms at some time during their lives (Beall, 1997). As many as 10% of Gulf War (Desert Storm) veterans, 6% to 11% of Afghanistan (Enduring Freedom) veterans, and 12% to 20% of Iraq (Iraqi Freedom) veterans are estimated to have experienced, or be likely to experience, PTSD (NCPTSD, 2007).

According to the NCPTSD (2007), those most likely to develop PTSD:

- Were directly exposed to a traumatic event as the victim or as a witness;
- Were seriously injured during the event;
- Experienced a trauma that was long-lasting or very severe;
- Believed their lives were in danger;
- Believed that a family member was in danger;
- Had a severe reaction during the event such as crying, shaking, vomiting, or feeling separated from their surroundings;
- Felt helpless during the trauma, not being able to help themselves or family member(s);
- Had an earlier life-threatening event, such as being abused as a child;
- Had another mental health problem;
- Had family members with mental health problems;
- Had minimal support from family and friends;
- Recently lost a loved one, particularly if it was unexpected;
- Had recent, stressful life changes;
- Drank alcohol in excess; or
- Were women, poorly educated, or relatively young.

While some people may have few problems adjusting and returning to a normal state after a traumatic event, others may be debilitated for years; two people exposed to the same event will have different levels of reaction. Behavioral scientists are unable to predict or measure the potential effect of a traumatic event on different people, but certain variables seem to have the most impact, including:

- The source of the trauma: human-caused is generally more difficult than an event of nature;
- The level of perceived extent of threat or danger, suffering, upset, terror, or fear;
- Sexual victimization, especially when betrayal is involved;
- An actual or perceived responsibility for the event; and
- Prior vulnerability factors including genetics or early onset as in childhood trauma.

Symptoms of PTSD

Chronic PTSD typically involves periods of increase in symptoms, followed by a remission. Some individuals experience symptoms that are unremitting and severe, while others report a lifetime of mild symptoms, with significant increases in symptoms following major life events such as retirement, medical illness, or reminders of military service, such as reunions or media attention to anniversaries of events. Table 18.4 shows common symptoms of PTSD.

Relationship to Substance Abuse

Approximately 74% of men and 29% of women with PTSD had a lifetime diagnosis of alcohol abuse (Ouimette, Wolfe, & Chrestman, 1996) and approximately 30% to 50% of men and 25% to 30% of women with lifetime PTSD also are substance abusers (Kimerling, Prins, Westrup, & Lee, 2004). Co-occurring diagnosis of PTSD and substance use disorder [SUD] is associated with poorer substance use outcomes: those with PTSD relapse more quickly, drink more on days when they do drink, have a greater percentage of heavy drinking days, and suffer greater negative consequences due to their substance abuse than do non-PTSD abusers (P. J. Brown, 2000).

Women are more likely than men to develop substance use disorders after exposure to a traumatic event and symptoms of PTSD, with approximately 65% to 84% of women experiencing PTSD before developing substance use disorders. This points toward the "self-medication" hypothesis for PTSD/SUD co-occurrence among women, where women use alcohol or drugs to cope with trauma-related symptoms. Sharp (2003) calls substance use and abuse "almost inevitable" for women and girls coping with abusive experiences. In contrast, men are more likely to experience trauma due to their behaviors linked to substance use, which then results in PTSD symptoms (Kimerling et al., 2004). Kimerling et al. strongly suggest that clinicians routinely screen clients for SUD when PTSD is suspected.

Table 18.4 shows a list of symptoms commonly associated with PTSD. Note the categories of *Psychological Outcomes* and *Social Manifestations* which include: eating disorders, alcohol and substance use, conduct disorders, and risky sexual behaviors. All qualify as avenues of hedonic dependence with underpinnings in the need to avoid psychological pain.

Table 18.4 **Symptoms of PTSD**

Re-experiencing the trauma

Flashbacks

Nightmares

Intrusive memories and exaggerated emotional and physical reactions to triggers that remind the person of the trauma

Emotional numbing

Feeling detached

Lack of emotions, especially positive ones

Loss of interest in activities

Avoidance

Avoiding activities, people, or places that are reminders of the trauma

Increased arousal

Difficulty sleeping and concentrating

Irritability

Hypervigilance

Exaggerated startle response

PTSD also creates physiological changes in the body including:

Neurobiological changes

Alterations in brainwave activity

Changes in the size of brain structures including decreased size of the hippocampus and abnormal activation of the amygdala

Changes in functioning such as memory and fear responses

Psychophysiological changes

Hyperarousal of the sympathetic nervous system

Increased startle reaction

Sleep disturbances

Increased neurohormonal changes resulting in heightened stress and increased depression

Physical manifestations

Headaches

Stomach or digestive problems

Immune system problems

Asthma or breathing problems

Dizziness

Chest pain

Chronic pain or fibromyalgia

Psychological outcomes can include the following:

Depression, major or pervasive	Employment problems
Anxiety disorders such as phobias, panic, and social anxiety	Homelessness
Conduct disorders	Trouble with the law
Dissociation	Self-destructive behaviors
Eating disorders	Substance abuse
Social manifestations include	Suicidal attempts
Interpersonal problems	Risky sexual behaviors
Low self-esteem	Reckless driving
Alcohol and substance use	Self-injury

Sources: Dryden-Edwards & Stopler, 2007; Kinchin, 2005; M. Smith, Jaffe, & Segal, 2008.

Recovery from Trauma

Recovery from traumatic events is described by Herman (1997) as unfolding in three stages, the first being that of *establishing safety.* The second stage includes the tasks of *remembrance and mourning,* while the third stage encompasses *reconnection with ordinary life.* As with any abstract concept, the stages are not followed exactly nor are they linear. Herman describes traumatic syndromes as "oscillating and dialectical in nature ... defy[ing] any attempt to impose such simpleminded order" (p. 155). These stages are defined here in an attempt to assist clients and clinicians alike in simplifying and gaining control of a seemingly uncontrollable process.

Safety

Survivors of victimization must shift their surroundings from that of unpredictable danger to reliable safety. This includes recognizing and naming the demon. As Herman (1997) discusses, some may feel relieved to learn that there is a name for their problems. Others, however, resist the diagnosis out of fear of the stigma associated with any psychiatric diagnosis; some may deny the condition out of a sense of pride. Many survivors of physical or sexual abuse do not make the connection that their experience of abuse is directly related to their symptoms or behaviors. Herman goes on to emphasize that the process of developing a framework that relates the client's problems to the traumatic history is beneficial, as it assists in developing a therapeutic alliance.

Establishing safety includes allowing the victim to regain control. While those who become dependent on drugs or other tension-reducing behaviors may have attempted to regain control through external stimulation, true control is accomplished when victims feel safe in relation to others, as well as with their own thinking and feeling. As Herman (1997) suggests, gradually developing a safe and trusting therapeutic relationship is key. In addition, family, friends, and lovers who were *not* involved in abuse of the victim should be mobilized to act as a support system.

Further, any attachment to those involved in the victimization must be disconnected, as must use of illicit drugs or alcohol or other addictive agents.

Remembrance and Mourning

After having regained a sense of control, developed a feeling of safety within the self and among others, and discontinued self-destructive behaviors, trauma victims can gradually move on to stage two: *remembrance and mourning*. This is the phase where victims verbally tell the whole in-depth, sordid story. As Herman (1997) notes, the difference between remembering the trauma and retelling the trauma is likened to a series of still snapshots as opposed to full cinematic movies with the inclusion of words and music.

Retelling the story must be repetitive; eventually, the story no longer will arouse such intense feelings (Herman, 1997). Ultimately, it becomes only a part of the survivor's experience rather than the focus of it. The memory fades, and grief loses its strength. The victim's life story begins to take on other aspects rather than only one. This, indeed, is a simple explanation of a complex process, but one that can be accomplished with a knowledgeable and trained clinician who can look past the anger and hatred that may accompany PTSD and its symptoms.

Reconnection

After mourning the loss of the person they were before the trauma, victims must create a new self and a new future. As quoted by Herman (1997), psychiatrist Michael Stone describes this task (specific to his work with incest survivors) thusly:

> All victims ... have, by definition, been taught that the strong can do as they please, without regard for convention. ... *Re-education* is often indicated, pertaining to what is typical, average, wholesome, and "normal" in the intimate life of ordinary people. Victims ... tend to be woefully ignorant of these matters, owing to their skewed and secretive early environments. Although victims in their original homes, they are like strangers in a foreign country, once "safely" outside. (p. 198)

Herman (1997) believes the statement "I know I have myself" is the anchor of the third stage. No longer possessed by past trauma, the survivor now understands the results of the damage done and becomes the person he or she wants to be. Imagination and fantasy, desire and initiative are at the core of this stage, where hopes and dreams are woven into reality.

Herman (1997) emphasizes that resolution of the trauma is never final, and recovery is never complete; the impact of trauma will "reverberate throughout the survivor's lifecycle" (p. 211). While incomplete, recovery will allow the survivor to return to the normal tasks of life. Becoming more interested in the present and future than the past, a survivor of trauma overcomes fear and opposition and gradually engages in new and healthy relationships.

In summary, there are seven criteria for the resolution of trauma (Herman, 1997):

- The physiological symptoms of PTSD have been brought within manageable limits;

- The survivor is able to bear the feelings associated with traumatic memories;

- The person has authority over the memories; for example, he or she can either remember the event or put it aside;

- The memory is coherent and linked with feeling;

- The survivor's self-esteem has been restored;

- Important relationships have been reestablished; and

- A coherent system of meaning and belief concerning the trauma has been constructed (p. 213).

Medication Assisted Therapy (MAT)

Because of the complexity and doggedness of substance use disorders there is no "treatment size" that fits all. Moreover, reliance on one form of intervention (whether it be 12-Step or medication) does not appreciate the multiple points of therapeutic opportunity offered by our current knowledge of brain circuits and cognitive neuroscience (Sederer, 2015).

Comprehensive care should be a standard aspired to by patients, family members, and clinicians. Individual, evidence-based treatments are likely to augment one another, i.e., they operate synergistically (1+1 = >2) evoking a more robust response (Sederer, 2015). Over emphasis on one treatment modality (e.g., medication, cognitive-behavioral therapy, AA) often reflects a practitioner bias and may not be in the best interest of the client. As illustrated in Figure 18.3, a comprehensive treatment plan is generated for a client with a diagnosis of substance use (opioid) disorder (SUD) with co-occurring anxiety and depression.

Figure 18.3 Neuroscience and Addiction Treatment

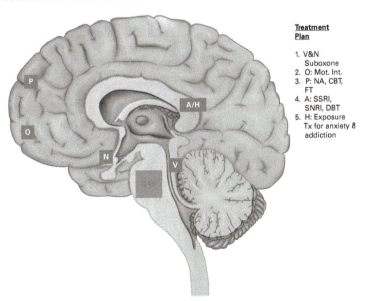

Treatment
Plan

1. V&N
   Suboxone
2. O: Mot. Int.
3. P: NA, CBT,
   FT
4. A: SSRI,
   SNRI, DBT
5. H: Exposure
   Tx for anxiety &
   addiction

Twelve-step programs (AA, NA) for SUDs represent only one of many tools for combatting addiction. Here we describe an integrated plan utilizing community support, cognitive-behavioral and family therapy, along with medication to assist with managing symptoms of withdrawal, craving, depression and anxiety.

The VTA (V) by releasing dopamine ("gas" – G) and the nucleus accumbens (N) send a signal of pleasure by delivering a spike of dopamine to the orbital frontal cortex (O), which is instrumental to human drive and motivation. The dopamine surge motivates the user to seek out the sources of pleasure (opioids). The prefrontal cortex (P) which regulates judgment and reasoning, can inhibit (put the brakes on) the accelerator pedal (N), which is activated by the drug.

The amygdala (A) and hippocampus (H) regulate emotions (A) and store memories (H) of what is so rewarding. In a brain addicted to opioids, this five-region circuit (V, N, O, H/A, P) is pirated because these drugs directly boost dopamine in the V and N. This triggers the circuit to powerfully fire and drives the compulsion to use.

By using MAT, a number of medications can be used that either block the effect of the opioids in the V & N regions (e.g., naltrexone) or control its activity at less intense levels (e.g., Buprenorphine; Suboxone); or methadone.

Motivation to resist the desire to re-experience the spike (the O region) can be enhanced by Motivational Interviewing (MI).

The section of our brain in charge of sound judgment (P), can be enhanced by a variety of interventions, including NA/AA, family psychoeducation and support, and promoting coping skills (being surrounded with people who are not addicts, eating and sleeping well, and stress reduction practices like yoga and slow breathing).

The amygdala/hippocampus (A/H) regions can also be impacted by opioid involvement. Environmental triggers can drive cravings and relapse; these include the sight of a needle or pill, contact with other addicts or dealers, and commercials about pain relief. Cognitive-behavioral Treatment (CBT) can assist a person with a SUD to avoid or have a reduced response to a trigger. Improved regulation of emotions can also be achieved through treatment with Dialectical Behavior Therapy (DBT) a modified form of CBT.

Depression and sadness are based not only maladaptive thoughts, but on chemical imbalances. In cases of unremitting and severe depression, selective serotonin reuptake inhibitors (SSRIs) or serotonin-norepinephrine reuptake inhibitors (SNRIs) can be used to give the amygdala (A) a needed assist. Anxiety-evoking memories of traumatic events, trapped in the hippocampus (H), can be diffused by various forms of exposure therapy.

A comprehensive plan for a person with an opioid addiction with co-occurring anxiety and depression would, therefore, (with the counselor employing Motivational Interviewing) offer the patient, and supportive loved ones, a plan that includes MAT, 12-step recovery, family psychoeducation, CBT, and a number of wellness activities like yoga (and yogic breathing), meditation, exercise, nutritional food, as well as the company of those dedicated to life, not addiction. This formulation is a compressive plan for effective action along a variety of critical brain, cognitive, and behavior pathways (Ross, Travis, & Arbuckle, 2015; Sederer, 2015).

Chapter Summary

The wisdom of AA (originally formulated in 1935) remains a pillar for people, worldwide, to find help with their addiction and support in their recovery. However, the powerful AA philosophy, which is predicated upon calling for help from their "higher power," is not to be equated with the scientific principles of effective treatment. Today, millions of people who suffer from substance use disorders (SUDs) and other hedonic dependencies benefit from a broad array of evidence-based treatment strategies. When integrated into a coherent treatment plan, taking into account contextual factors such as age, gender identity, sexual orientation, and cultural background, individually proven models synergistically improve treatment outcomes.

The principles of treatment that appear to be most useful in an integrated plan for change are: (1) Stages of Change; (2) Cognitive-behavioral therapy; (3) Relapse and Recidivism Prevention; (4) Assessment; and (5) Motivational Interviewing. To serve clients effectively, these approaches are tailored to the specific needs of the individual, taking into account research on treatment efficacy for designated populations, e.g., women, adolescents. Given that a significant portion of hedonic disorders are rooted in traumatic experiences originating either in childhood or later in life, the symptoms and general principles of treatment are addressed.

The final section of this chapter presents the rationale for medication assisted therapy (MAT) in the design of a comprehensive treatment plan for an individual with co-occurring substance use disorder (SUD), anxiety, and depression. The model ties together knowledge from neuroscience, psychiatry, psychology, and community support networks, such as AA or NA.

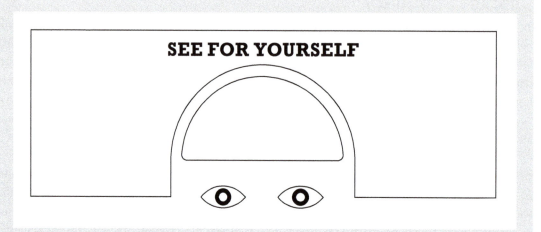

SEE FOR YOURSELF

Trauma, Healing and the Brain: Community Learning Event. (2015). Gabor Mate. 18:38

Dr. Gabor Mate discusses the relationship between trauma in childhood and addiction. **https://youtu.be/I3WzMpjtkrs**

Want to Erase Fear Memories? Choose Weed, Not Booze. 2012. Virginia Hughes. *National Geographic: Only Human.*

Research indicates that alcohol can make recovery from trauma more difficult, while marijuana may improve the brain's ability to unlearn fear memories. **http://phenomena.nationalgeographic.com/2012/09/10/erasing-fear-memories/**

The Irrationality of Alcoholics Anonymous. 2015. Gabrielle Glaser. *The Atlantic.* **Feature article.**

This piece offers a critical perspective on the dominance of AA in American systems of substance abuse treatment. Glaser discusses the conflicting and scant research on the effectiveness of AA's treatment approach, and compares it to other options, such as the Sinclair method. **https://www.theatlantic.com/magazine/archive/2015/04/the-irrationality-of-alcoholics-anonymous/386255/**

SECTION VII

Natural Highs
The Cutting Edge of Mood Alteration

But we should be mindful of the fact that the maps of joy can be falsified by a host of drugs and thus fail to reflect the actual state of the organism.

—Antonio Damasio

Overview: The Era of Self-Regulation and Natural Highs

We have explored hedonic pursuit from multiple perspectives. Culture, social learning, brain chemistry, and genetics all conspire toward the relentless quest for exalted delight. Zest for life is a virtue. Pleasure and relief from suffering, however, easily morph into hardship and despair.

> *Upon the first goblet he read the inscription: monkey wine; upon the second: lion wine; upon the third: sheep wine; upon the fourth: swine wine. These four inscriptions expressed the four descending degrees of drunkenness: the first, that which enlivens; the second, that which irritates; the third, that which stupefies; the fourth, that which brutalizes.*
>
> —Victor Hugo, *Les Misérables*

Hedonic dependencies largely subvert the needs in Maslow's hierarchy (Maslow, 1970). People who are hooked on using drugs or other behaviors may become blind to even their most basic physiological needs (food) or safety (shelter). Needs for love and belonging, as well as esteem, may well fall by the wayside. Self-actualization is out of the picture when one is living day by day or moment by moment. Many of the motivations in Maslow's hierarchy are linked to natural highs. For the person in recovery, it's important to reconnect to these rewards. For everyone, they are healthy (and often less expensive) alternatives that can make artificial ones (drugs, compulsive Internet use, etc.) irrelevant. Certainly, it can be excruciatingly difficult to overcome renegade biological processes that are further encouraged by powerful social and psychological influences. Yet, it can be done, and it is well worth it!

Biologically, the question is, can the human brain gain control over inherited impulses that were appropriate for prehistoric humans but are inappropriate in the 21st century? We know that compulsive pleasure-seeking lifestyles are self-induced and are under both cortical and limbic system control. We also know that the cerebral cortex, the center of thought and memory, is much larger in humans than in other animals. With this great reasoning capacity, we *should* be able to exercise more control over the basic emotions directed by the lower brain centers. In fact, there are rational and healthy means to regulate the universal drive to experience pleasure.

We are in the midst of a revolution in how humans manage stress. The old standbys of being angry, depressed, anxious, drunk, or otherwise misbehaving are no longer acceptable. We have reached an evolutionary junction in self-regulation. Culture now calls upon humans to take charge of their emotions and actions by changing or managing dysfunctional thoughts from which negative feelings and problem behaviors arise. We refer to this perspective as the *cognitive-behavioral revolution*. Cognitive-behavioral therapy, as we have noted previously, has become the predominant treatment modality for the three pillars of maladaptive functioning: addiction, crime, and mental disorder. More than 300 controlled studies of CBT have been completed for a variety of psychiatric and psychological disorders (Butler & Beck, 2000).

However, the value of CBT extends far beyond treating the broad spectrum of social problem behaviors. It has also become the predominant means for better managing the ups and downs of everyday life. By learning the principles and skill sets of cognitive-behavioral restructuring (CBR), readers will take a quantum leap toward improving their overall quality of life. Increased control and flexibility in how we interpret and respond to both crisis and everyday events increase the chances for success and happiness throughout one's life span. As educators, counselors, parents, and friends, we can influence others to take on the mantle of self-discovery and positive change.

A critical step toward positive mood alteration (i.e., natural highs) and enduring happiness is to develop a state of mindfulness or focused awareness on our present thoughts. As William James has said, "The greatest weapon against stress is our ability to choose one thought over another." *Acceptance and commitment therapy* (ACT) (Hayes, Follette, & Linehan, 2004; Hayes & Smith, 2005) and *dialectical behavioral therapy* (DBT) (Linehan, 1993a, 1993b; Robins, Schmidt, & Linehan, 2004) have improved our understanding of mindfulness in prevention, intervention, treatment, and everyday life. The concept of mindfulness generally includes awareness and attention, focusing on the present, sensitivity to surrounding stimuli, awareness of the connections between self and the outside world, and a lack of desire or urge to escape the current situation (Fruzzetti & Iverson, 2004). It is a practice that has to do with being aware of and taking part in everyday living. "It is a way of living awake, with one's eyes wide open" (Robins et al., 2004, p. 37). Rooted in the thoughtful approaches common to Eastern and Western spiritual disciplines, it "allows" experiences rather than suppressing or avoiding them (Robins et al., 2004, p. 37). It is a conscious process of observing, describing, and taking part in the reality of the moment, putting aside judgment, conclusions, and opinions. According to Robins et al., it is looking at thoughts as thoughts, rather than looking *from* thoughts or looking at the world *through* thoughts. We not only have the capacity to diffuse and disengage from risky or harm-directing thoughts; we can also select and focus on those that are in our own and others' best interest.

Linehan (1993a, 1993b) sees mindfulness as involving "what to do" and "how to do" skills. Wanberg and Milkman (2008; 2012) summarize these as follows:

The "what to do" skills in being mindful are

- observing, noticing, awareness of the present.
- verbally describing what has been observed or experienced.
- taking part fully in the behavior and letting go without a lot of conscious activity.

The "how to do" skills involve

- not being judgmental or evaluative or focusing on the "good" or "bad" of the thoughts or experiences.
- focusing on the present, here and now, and on one thing at a time.
- engaging in actions that are congruent with one's life goals, purpose, or values.

Another facet of being in the here and now is accepting the reality of the situation at hand. Robins et al. (2004) describe "radical acceptance" as a process of "focusing on the current moment, seeking reality as it is without 'delusions' and accepting reality without judgment" (p. 39). In DBT, "clients are taught and encouraged to use skills for accepting life completely and radically as well as for changing it" (p. 39). Fruzzetti and Iverson (2004) identify several components or defining features of acceptance:

- The person is fully aware of what is being accepted.

- Regardless of whether the experience is pleasant or unpleasant, wanted or not wanted, the focus is on accepting, rather than mobilizing resources to change the situation or experience.

- The person has some understanding of how the experience is related to stimuli that preceded it.

Acceptance is seen at two levels: pure acceptance with no efforts to change, and acceptance in balance with change. The almost universal appreciation of AA's Serenity Prayer is evidence for the sensibility of this approach:

> God grant me the serenity to accept the things I cannot change
>
> Courage to change the things I can
>
> And the wisdom to know the difference

There are many self-help workbooks, e.g., *Get out of Your Mind and Into Your Life* (Hayes & Smith, 2005) designed to teach mindfulness and acceptance as means to overcome emotional pain and enhancing general well-being. These manuals provide exercises on how to understand and choose, rather than blindly follow, the positive or negative thoughts that constitute ordinary human consciousness. An example of a mindfulness and acceptance exercise is presented below.

EXERCISE: Seashells at the Ocean Shore

This exercise can be done either with your eyes open or closed.

Imagine that you are relaxing on a beautiful ocean sand beach on a perfectly calm summer day. The temperature is ideal, and you are lying in an extremely comfortable position where you can see gentle waves ebbing and flowing on the shoreline. Each oncoming and receding wave causes the movement of a beautiful array of seashells that have temporary residence on the shoreline before being carried back to sea.

Remain at the ocean shore, watching the shells come and go. Don't try to alter the gentle pattern of waves or movement of shells in any way…. Seeing them as they come or go, hearing the sounds of the sea, watching shells coming and going with each new wave.

Now become aware of your thoughts and each time a thought comes to mind, find a seashell to place it on just before being transported back to its ocean home. If your thought is in the form of a picture, place the picture on top of the shell. If your thought is in words, see them written on one of the shells. The idea is to place each new thought on an outgoing shell, watching it gracefully disappear into the hidden ocean floor.

Stay at the shoreline and allow the shells to keep carrying each new thought away. Don't try to rearrange the words or pictures as they appear on the shells in any way. Just let them gently recede into the ocean. If you observe that the shells disappear or you that you are no longer at the beach, or if you are into the wave or on a shell, simply notice what happened and return to your comfortable spot on the beach. Watch a thought come into your mind, place it on a shell and watch it gently recede into the ocean floor.

With a watch at your side, keep doing the exercise for a minimum of 5 minutes. When you are finished please answer the questions below, each designed to assist you as you proceed on this journey to mindfulness.

- How much time went by before you got stuck on one of your thoughts?
- If you left the beach or became unable to visualize thoughts coming and going on the shells, write down what was happening just before the action stopped.
- If you couldn't imagine the scene at the beach and the waves at the shoreline, write down the thoughts which interfered with your being able to imagine the waves and seashells near the shore.

Adapted from: Hayes, S. C., & Smith, S. (2005). Get out of your mind and into your life: The new Acceptance and Commitment Therapy. *Oakland, CA: New Harbinger, pp. 76–77.*

Hayes and Smith (2005) recommend that you do this kind of exercise regularly to see if you can do better in allowing the stream to flow.

According to the World Happiness Report (2015, p. 29), Switzerland, Iceland, and Sweden are, respectively, the happiest countries in the world. It is posited (Brooks, 2008) that the most important determinant of happiness is the extent to which people have free choice in how to manage their lives. The premise of this book is that through self-regulation of thoughts, feelings, and actions, we can orchestrate our natural brain chemistry to evoke positive feeling states and lasting happiness. Hence, the final chapters explore the six basic tenets of the natural highs perspective:

Chapter 19: The Cognitive-Behavioral Revolution: How to Manage Thoughts, Feelings, and Behaviors
Chapter 20: Maintaining Close and Intimate Relationships
Chapter 21: Relaxation, Mindfulness, and Meditation
Chapter 22: Eating Yourself Fit
Chapter 23: Exercise: The Magic Bullet
Chapter 24: Meaningful Engagement of Talents

CHAPTER 19

The Cognitive-Behavioral Revolution
How to Manage Thoughts, Feelings, and Behaviors

The greatest weapon against stress is our ability to choose one thought over another.

—William James

Introduction: Evolution of the Cognitive-Behavioral Model

The goal of this chapter is to capture the essence of cognitive-behavioral restructuring (CBR) and to show how it can be incorporated in everyday life. We begin with a discussion of how the CBR model ascended to its current role as the preeminent tool for self-discovery and change. The basic principles of the cognitive-behavioral model are discussed, with case examples illustrative of how thinking is intimately related to feelings and actions. Readers are encouraged to utilize these principles to improve their overall quality of life.

The perspective that developing a healthy style of thinking can reduce distress or enhance well-being is a common theme across many generations and cultures. The *cognitive-behavioral revolution* is predicated upon fundamental principles from ancient Persian, Buddhist, Roman, and Greek philosophies. According to the Persian prophet and religious poet Zoroaster (estimated to have lived in the 6th century BC), "your good thoughts, good words, and good deeds alone will be your intercessors. Nothing more will be wanted. They alone will serve you as a safe pilot to the harbor of Heaven, as a safe guide to the gates of paradise" (quoted in Barrows, 1893, p. 904). Buddha (563–483 BC) is quoted as saying, "We are what we think.... All that we are arises with our thoughts.... With our thoughts, we make the world" (quoted in Kornfield, 1993, p. 222). Plato (428–347 BC) (De Cuypere, 2008) described "ideal forms" as existing

Figure 19.1 Thinking Makes it So

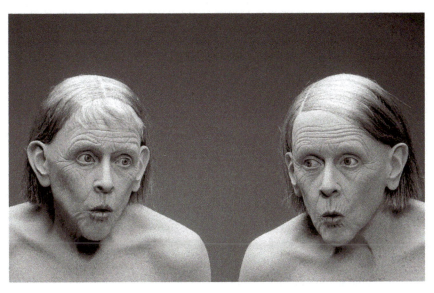

Source: The "Whistlers" Used with permission of Tip Toland from the collection of Doug and Dale Anderson.

within the mind and representing what is real in the world, and Epictetus (55–135 AD), an ancient Greek philosopher, promulgated the idea that "men are not disturbed by things which happen but by their opinions about things" (Templeton, 1998, p. 114). Marcus Aurelius, who presided as emperor of Rome from AD 161 to his death in 180, is reputed to have stated, "Our life is what our thoughts make it" (Goodman & Goodman, 1997, p. 831).

Philosophers of the 17th and 18th centuries also built their view of the world around the idea that the mind determines reality. This is particularly found in René Descartes' concept, "I think, therefore I am," and Immanuel Kant's idea that the mind makes nature (R.G. Collingwood, 1949). According to William James (1842–1910), regarded by many as the father of American psychology, "The greatest discovery of my generation is that a man can alter his life simply by altering his attitude of mind" (quoted in Hamilton, 2008, p. 117). Deepak Chopra stated, "Our minds influence the key activity of the brain, which then influences everything; perception, cognition, thoughts and feelings, personal relationships; they're all a projection of you." (as cited in Martin, 2012).

The National Association of Cognitive-Behavioral Therapists (2008) describes cognitive-behavioral therapy as a general classification of psychotherapy, including several intervention approaches: *rational emotive behavior therapy, cognitive therapy, rational behavior therapy, rational living therapy, schema focused therapy,* and *dialectical behavior therapy.* Each approach has its own developmental history.

Albert Ellis, Grandfather of Cognitive Therapy

Although there are many approaches covered by the rubric of cognitive therapy, Ellis is generally regarded as the grandfather of the cognitive approach. In reaction to his perception of psychoanalysis as "in-efficient and in-directive," Ellis developed *rational emotive therapy* (RET) (Ellis, 1962; Ellis & Harper, 1961). He was influenced by Alfred Adler (1956), a neo-Freudian, who stated, "I am convinced that a person's behavior springs from his ideas" (p. 172).

Having been trained in psychoanalysis, Ellis searched for a more rapid way to facilitate change. He discovered that he was often quicker than his clients at discovering the source of their problems. Furthermore, their difficulties usually stemmed from a common pattern of distorted thinking. He developed *rational therapy* (RT) to enable clients to not only recognize distortions in their thinking but also to "vigorously dispute" them. Ellis soon expanded RT to rational emotive therapy (Ellis, 1962), and more recently to *rational-emotive behavioral therapy* (REBT) (Ellis, 2004). Although his theories have evolved over the past five decades, some common themes emerge from his writings.

1. There is an important distinction between rational and irrational beliefs (Dryden & Ellis, 1986). Whereas rational beliefs are useful in helping individuals get what they want, irrational beliefs are more closed-minded and inflexible and usually interfere with satisfaction of needs and desires. People become disturbed by a self-imposed prison of shoulds (e.g., I should do that) and musts (e.g., I must do this), leading to self-condemnation and negative emotions as they try to satisfy a litany of impossible self-imposed demands.

2. ABC: The **A** (activating event)–**B** (belief)–**C** (consequence) method of cognitive and behavioral analysis and change. It is one's *belief* (B) about the *activating event* (A) that leads to the emotional or behavioral *consequence* (C). From this perspective, clients can change C by changing B, even if the activating events in their lives don't change. REBT typically involves an active and directive therapist who helps the client first identify and then vigorously confront, challenge, and dispute his or her irrational thoughts. Although Ellis uses homework assignments as means for behavioral rehearsal, the primary targets for change are an individual's thoughts and beliefs about certain aspects of life. Like behavioral therapy, REBT is present focused. Inquiry into past events, thoughts, or feelings is deemed unnecessary; rather, it is important to identify and dispute current irrational beliefs (Ellis, 1962).

Contemporary Cognitive Therapy

The preeminent authority on cognitive therapy is Aaron Beck. In the 1960s, Beck (1963, 1964) developed a theory called *thinking and depression*, which set the stage for Beck being recognized as the foremost expert on using cognitive therapy for a spectrum of emotional disorders (Leahy, 1996). The perspectives of several post-Freudian analysts, such as Adler, Honey, and Sullivan, influenced his work, particularly their focus on distorted self-images, which paved the way to more systematized cognitive-behavioral formulations of psychiatric disorders and personality structure. Kelly's (1955) theory of personal constructs (core beliefs or self-schemas) and Ellis's rational emotive therapy (1962) also contributed to the development of Beck's cognitive theories.

Beck's early work considered the role of maladaptive information processing in depression and anxiety disorders. He posited a cognitive conceptualization of depression by relating problems in mood, motivation, and physical malaise to characteristically negative thoughts about the self, world, and future. This became known as the "negative cognitive triad" (A. T. Beck, 1963, 1964). Beck theorized that there are characteristic errors in logic in the automatic thoughts (expectations, appraisals, attributions, and decisions) and other cognitions of persons with emotional disorders. Subsequent research has confirmed the importance of cognitive errors in pathological styles of information processing. As shown in Table 19.1, Beck described six categories of cognitive errors.

In implementing CBT methods for reducing cognitive errors, therapists typically teach clients that the most important aim is to recognize that one is making cognitive errors—not to identify each and every error in logic that is occurring.

Table 19.2 shows Beck's formulation of *schemas,* the core mental structures that guide automatic thinking. Schemas are enduring principles of thinking that start to take shape in early childhood and are influenced by a multitude of life experiences, including parental teaching and modeling, formal and informal educational activities, peer experiences, traumas, and successes (Wright, Fasco, & Thase, 2006). The relationship between schemas and automatic thinking is understood according to the diathesis-stress hypothesis. Beck and others have explained that in depression and other conditions of mental disturbance, maladaptive schemas (diathesis, i.e., mental predisposition) may remain dormant until a condition of stress arises that activates the core beliefs (Beck, Rush, Shaw, & Emery, 1979; Clark, Beck, & Alford, 1999; Miranda, 1992).

In summary, according to the cognitive approach (Wright et al., 2006), the highest level of functioning is consciousness—therapists encourage the development and application of rational thinking and problem solving. In terms of irrational or maladaptive thinking, CBT teaches clients to recognize and change their response to pathological thinking on two levels:

> *Automatic Thoughts*—cognitions that stream rapidly through our minds when we are in the midst of situations (or recalling events): "This talk is boring; get me out; I can't take it anymore."

> *Schemas*—core beliefs that give meaning to information from the environment: "Academics know nothing about the real world."

There is an emphasis on techniques designed to help clients *detect and modify* their inner thoughts, especially those that are associated with emotional symptoms such as depression, anxiety, or anger. One of the most important clues that automatic thoughts might be occurring is the *presence of strong emotions.* In depression and other conditions, maladaptive schemas may remain dormant until a stressful life event occurs that activates the core belief (A. T. Beck et al., 1979). The maladaptive schema is then strengthened to the point that it stimulates and drives the more superficial stream of negative automatic thoughts.

This formulation may be used to explain the breakdown of logic and civility in emotionally charged situations. Consider the example of a celebrity actor/director spewing anti-Semitic remarks upon learning of his DUI arrest.

Table 19.1 Cognitive Errors

Selective Abstraction

Sometimes called the mental filter. A conclusion is drawn after looking only at a small portion of the available information.

A depressed man with low self-esteem doesn't receive a holiday card from an old friend. "I'm losing all my old friends. Nobody cares about me anymore."

Arbitrary Inference

Coming to a conclusion in the face of contradictory evidence or in the absence of evidence.

A woman with a fear of elevators is asked to predict the chance of the elevator falling if she rides in it. She replies, "The chances are 10% or more that the elevator will crash if I ride in it."

Overgeneralization

A conclusion is made about one or more isolated incidents and then extended illogically to cover broad areas of functioning.

A depressed college student gets a B on a test. He considers this unsatisfactory and overgeneralizes when he has these automatic thoughts. "I'm in trouble in this class. . . . I'm falling short everywhere in my life. . . . I can't do anything right."

Magnification and Minimization

The significance of an attribute, event, or sensation is exaggerated or minimized.

A woman with a panic disorder starts to feel light-headed during the onset of a panic attack. She thinks, "I'll faint. . . . I might have a heart attack or a stroke."

Personalization

External events are related to oneself when there is no evidence for doing so. Excessive responsibility or blame is taken for negative events.

In an economic downturn, a previously successful businessman struggles to meet the annual budget. Layoffs are being considered. Although many factors have contributed to the financial crisis, the manager thinks, "It's my fault. . . . I should have seen this coming and done something about it. . . . I've failed everybody in the company."

Dichotomous Thinking

Also called absolutist or all-or-none thinking. Judgments about oneself, personal experiences, or others are placed into one of two categories (e.g., all bad or all good, total failure or total success).

"Ted has everything and I have nothing."

Source: Adapted from Wright, J., Fasco, M., & Thase, M. (2006). Learning cognitive-behavioral therapy: An illustrated guide. Arlington, VA: American Psychiatric Publishing, pp. 11–12.

Table 19.2 Three Main Groups of Schemas

1. Simple schemas

   Rules about the physical nature of the environment, practical management of everyday activities, or laws of nature that may have little or no effect on psychopathology.

   - e.g., "Be a defensive driver;" "A good education pays off;" Take shelter during a storm."

2. Intermediary beliefs and assumptions

   Conditional rules such as if-then statements that influence self-esteem and emotional regulation.

   - e.g., "I must be perfect to be accepted;" "If I don't please others all the time, they will reject me;" "If I work hard, I can succeed."

3. Core beliefs about the self

   Global and absolute rules for interpreting environmental information related to self-esteem.

   - e.g., "I'm unlovable;" "I'm stupid;" "I'm a failure;" "I'm a good friend;" "I can trust others."

Source: From "Learning cognitive-behavioral therapy: An illustrated guide" by J. Wright, M. Fasco, & M. Thase, 2006, Arlington, VA: American Psychiatric Publishing, pp. 11–12.

CASE EXAMPLE: Mel Gibson's Anti-Semitic Tirade

According to a series of widely publicized media reports (see "Gibson's Anti-Semitic Tirade," Marquez, 2006), on July 28, 2006, at 2:36 a.m. PDT, Mel Gibson was arrested on suspicion of driving under the influence (DUI) of alcohol after being stopped for speeding (84 mph in a 45 mph zone). He was apprehended in his 2006 Lexus LS 430 on the Pacific Coast Highway in Malibu, California. Gibson's blood-alcohol level was measured at 0.12 (the legal limit in California is 0.08). A three-quarters-full bottle of Cazadores Tequila was found next to him.

The arresting officer, James Mee, described Gibson as cooperative until the time of his arrest when, while handcuffed in the police car, he became belligerent and made anti-Semitic remarks to Mee, who is of Jewish decent. The entertainment Website TMZ.com reported that Gibson said, "The Jews are responsible for all the wars in the world," and asked the arresting officer, "Are you a Jew?" Citing an unnamed law enforcement source, TMZ further alleged that Gibson asked a female sergeant at the station, "What are you looking at, sugar tits?" Gibson was released on bail at 9 a.m. PDT. The next day, he confessed to driving under the influence and to "despicable" behavior during his arrest. He made several public apologies. A frenzy of media coverage followed (e.g., Chris Suellentrop's article "Mel Gibson's Moment" in the *New York Times,* August 1, 2006).

As shown in Figure 19.2, the cognitive view of the mind shows that under stress, deep-seated beliefs, which under ordinary conditions may remain dormant, become energized and activate automatic thinking (Wanberg & Milkman, 2008 & 2012).

As discussed in the section overview, mindfulness training (Hayes et al., 2004; Hayes & Smith, 2005) can serve as a powerful antidote to the usual knee-jerk stress response of blindly activating maladaptive beliefs, energizing automatic thoughts that fall prey to distortion by errors in logic. Of course, consuming six alcoholic beverages (as is likely in the case of Mr. Gibson, based on the bottle found in his car and his blood-alcohol level) is likely to exacerbate any proclivity toward the above.

Figure 19.2 Model of Cognitive Structures and Processes Stress may activate dysfunctional core beliefs that energize automatic thoughts, which are filtered through characteristic errors in logic.[1]

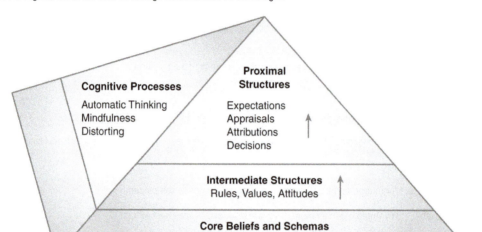

Behaviorist Contributions

The development of behavioral theory in the late 1950s and 1960s provided the foundation for the behavioral component of cognitive-behavioral therapy, but behaviorism itself has a longer history. It dates back to John B. Watson's groundbreaking 1913 publication "Psychology as the Behaviorist Views It" (often referred to as "The Behaviorist Manifesto"):

> Give me a dozen healthy infants, well-formed and my own specified world to bring them up in and I'll guarantee to take any one at random and train him to become any type of specialist I might select—doctor, lawyer, artist, merchant, chief and yes even beggar man and thief, regardless of the talents, penchants, tendencies, abilities, vocations, and race of his ancestors. (J. B. Watson, 1924, p. 104)

Other contributions to the behavioral component are drawn from Ivan Pavlov's (1927) work in "classical conditioning" (involuntary behavior triggered by a stimulus) and the "operant conditioning" models (voluntary behavior encouraged or discouraged by consequences) of B. F. Skinner (1938). Behaviorism, as such, focuses on observable, external behaviors and disregards internal mental processes.

Combining Cognitive and Behavioral Theories

In modern psychology, the cognitive approach was a reaction to the narrower view of behavioral psychology, which did not attend to—and even rejected—the importance of internal thought processes. Bandura's (1969, 1977) pioneering work on *social learning* and Meichenbaum's (1977) focus on an individual's *internal dialogue or self-talk* paved the way for the blending of the cognitive and behavioral approaches to self-discovery and change.

1 Kenneth Wanberg and Harvey B. Milkman, Criminal Conduct and Substance Abuse Treatment: Strategies for Self-improvement and Change. The Provider's Guide, pp. 252. Copyright © 2012 by SAGE Publications. Reprinted with permission.

Albert Bandura's Social Learning Model

Bandura's classic work, *Principles of Behavior Modification* (1969), showed the limitations of a strictly behavioral approach to therapy. Bandura disagreed with traditional behaviorists about there being a direct link between stimulus and response or between behavior and reinforcement. Instead, cognitive processing mediates between stimulus and response. Human functioning is a product of the interaction of environment, behavior, and thinking. Bandura conducted research on the concept of *self-efficacy,* an individual's sense of self-esteem and competence in dealing with life's problems. People with high self-efficacy believe they are capable of dealing effectively with the diverse events in their lives. Conversely, when confronted with a challenge or significant life problem, those with low self-efficacy are likely to give up if their initial problem-solving attempts fail (Schultz & Schultz, 2004).

Bandura (1977) stressed the influence of external reinforcement schedules on such thought processes as beliefs, expectations, and instructions. People are not merely machines that automatically respond to external stimuli. Instead, reactions to stimuli are self-activated, initiated by the person. Bandura's principle of *reciprocal determinism* posits that not only do environmental contingencies influence human behavior, but humans in turn influence themselves and their environment. Bandura showed that a perceived reinforcer was more reinforcing than an actual reinforcer not perceived as such. What happens in the "black box" (the mind) is of crucial importance.

Bandura's work on *modeling* is also of great significance to modern CBT approaches. He discovered that individuals did not have to be reinforced directly for performing a behavior in order for that behavior to increase in probability. In fact, it is sufficient to observe another person (a model) having been reinforced for performing that behavior. Hyper-aggressive adolescents model the aggressive hostile attitudes of their parents (Bandura, 1973; Bandura & Walters, 1959). In his experiments where children were exposed to models demonstrating either violent or nonviolent behaviors toward a "Bobo doll," he contradicted standard learning theory. Simply observing a model without being personally reinforced resulted in aggression. Thus, behavior can be learned without direct reinforcement. In *Social Learning and Personality Development,* Bandura and Walters (1963) demonstrated the principle of vicarious reinforcement: learning occurs through the observation of other people's behavior and seeing the consequences of such behavior. Social learning can affect behavior by teaching new behaviors, increasing the frequency with which already learned behaviors are carried out, encouraging previously forbidden behaviors, and increasing or decreasing similar behaviors (e.g., a child observing his or her parents using alcohol may increase the probability of that child using marijuana or other drugs; Wanberg & Milkman, 2008 & 2012).

Meichenbaum's Stress Inoculation Model

As research in behavioral techniques for managing various forms of behavioral dysfunction (e.g., conduct disorder, phobias, anxiety disorders) expanded in the 1960s and 1970s, a number of prominent researchers such as Meichenbaum (1977) and Lewinsohn, Hoberman, Teri, and Hautzinger (1985) found that the cognitive perspective added *context depth and understanding* to behavioral interventions. Drawing on the work of Soviet psychologists Luria (1973) and Vygotsky (1978), Meichenbaum found that when faced with a task, children talk to themselves about how to perform that task. Private speech serves as an important regulator of behavior. Developmentally, these self-verbalizations are initially overt, but as the child grows older, they become increasingly covert to form the internal dialogue.

Meichenbaum (1977) developed a training program for impulsive children who showed deficits in the ability to regulate their behavior by self-instructions. He set up situations where adult models, while performing a task, would talk out loud about how to perform the task. This training program sequentially facilitated (1) the child performing the task while talking out loud; and (2) the child performing the task while talking covertly. Based on the success of this technique, Meichenbaum formulated a three-stage "stress inoculation" model for improved coping with critical life events. It consisted of (1) an educational phase (mental preparation), (2) modeling and rehearsing the new skills (skills development), and (3) practicing the new skills in the environment (rehearsal). These programs became the blueprint for Meichenbaum's theory of cognitive-behavioral modification.

Clients are first instructed on how to become aware of their behaviors and of the internal dialogues that sustain their behavior. Then they are trained in emitting incompatible behavior and internal dialogue (i.e., talking to themselves differently), and finally they are taught to exhibit this new behavior in the environment and to think differently about this new behavior (Meichenbaum, 1977). The therapist's threefold job is to teach or coach clients to (1) notice the behavior, (2) think about and change the behavior, and (3) reconstruct the internal dialogue about the behavior. Meichenbaum's model assumes that various therapeutic systems simply provide different explanatory constructs to help clients think about their problems differently—in other words, to change the nature and content of their internal dialogue. A refreshing thought is that whether one chooses a 12-step recovery program, RET, Buddhism, or to join a political party, if the new alliance provides a basis for an improved internal dialogue that features optimism and purpose, the participant will experience a process of positive growth and change.

> [A]s a result of therapy a translation process takes place...the translation is from the internal dialogue the client engaged in prior to therapy to a new language system that emerges over the course of treatment. (Meichenbaum, 1977, p. 217)

Examination of the principles outlined by Bandura (social learning), Meichenbaum (internal dialogue), and Beck (cognitive errors) leads to the conclusion that "self-reinforcement" is the combination of cognitive and behavioral approaches (Wanberg & Milkman, 2008 & 2012). Cognitive and behavioral changes reinforce each other. When cognitive change leads to changes in action and behavior, there occurs a sense of well-being that strengthens (reinforces) the change in thought and in turn further strengthens the behavioral changes. This self-reinforcing feedback process is a key element of the cognitive-behavioral approach and is the basis for understanding the cognitive-behavioral process.

The self-reinforcing mechanism of CBR is illustrated in Figure 19.3. This graphic device provides a visual anchor for cognitive-behavioral restructuring. The map is of benefit to people at all stages of addiction or emotional and behavioral unrest, including mild irritability, moderate anxiety, severe depression, and violent anger. Clients, students, and psychologically minded readers can learn to recognize high-risk situations, consider and rehearse lifestyle modifications, and learn a variety of strategies for identifying and changing distorted thinking processes.

The figure shows how stressful life events trigger a cascade of automatic thoughts (shaped by underlying beliefs), which are then translated into emotions that lead to behaviors. If an individual chooses a positive (adaptive) course of action (through rational thought and emotional control) or opts against a negative one (distorted thought and emotional dysregulation), the outcome will likely be good. This in turn strengthens the recurrence of positive behavior and encourages positive thought processes. Conversely, if the individual chooses a negative (maladaptive) course of action, the outcome will likely be bad, strengthening more negative thought processes (Milkman & Wanberg, 2007, Wanberg & Milkman, 2012).

The main idea of this model is to learn skills for self-regulation of emotions and behavior by making conscious choices regarding the thoughts that one selects to explain the events in his or her life. Recall William James's sage remark, "The greatest weapon against stress is our ability to choose one thought over another."

Figure 19.3 The Cognitive-Behavioral Map For Learning and Change Events trigger automatic thoughts (activated by underlying beliefs), which energize emotions that lead to behaviors.

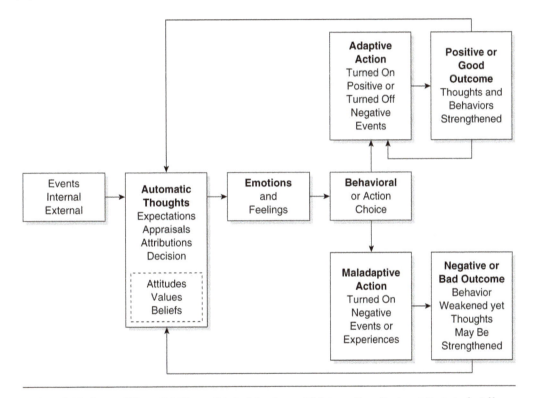

Source: Kenneth Wanberg and Harvey B. Milkman, Criminal Conduct and Substance Abuse Treatment: Strategies for Self-improvement and Change. The Provider's Guide, pp. 251. Copyright © 2012 by SAGE Publications. Reprinted with permission.

Working With Automatic Thoughts and Core Beliefs

Cognitive-behavioral therapy is effective in the treatment of a wide array of conditions including anxiety disorders, eating disorders, schizophrenia, bipolar disorder, chronic pain, personality disorders, and substance abuse (Butler & Beck, 2000; Dobson, 1989; Wright et al., 2006). The case of Rick, below, illustrates how the cognitive model is used as a tool to improve resiliency and decrease vulnerability to stress.

CASE EXAMPLE: Cognitive Restructuring for Relapse Prevention

Rick had a past history of alcohol dependence. During his first years in high school, he felt insecure among his peers, especially with the opposite sex. When he started drinking at the age of 16, Rick found that he could outdrink and outlast his peers, and could overcome his shyness with girls. After about 4 years of abusive drinking, he started to drink every day. During his freshman year, he dropped out of college and his parents signed him into a 30-day, AA-oriented residential treatment center.

Upon discharge, he continued to attend AA meetings where he met his first wife, who was also recovering from alcohol dependence. They soon became engaged and after a year of courtship they decided to marry. After going back to school, Rick graduated from college and was hired as a manager in a large advertising firm. The couple had their first child after Rick's promotion to an executive position during his third year with the company.

Upon receiving the news that he was being dismissed from his "dream job" because the company needed to downsize in an unstable economic climate, Rick began to have recurrent thoughts of returning to drink. He became overwhelmed by self-blame (i.e., getting fired was all his fault) and the belief that his life would be permanently ruined. Soon after his relapse, Rick and his wife agreed to have him admitted to a cognitively oriented outpatient treatment program. Through a trusting relationship with his counselor, Rick became mindful of the dysfunctional mental processes that culminated in relapse.

Beginning with the powerful stressor (loss of employment), Rick's deep-seated distal structures (beliefs)—"I fall apart under pressure;" "I'm damaged;" "Life isn't fair"—become activated. The intermediate structures (attitudes, values, rules) that determine the quality of his automatic thoughts are set into motion: "Who cares, anyway? Life sucks." (attitude) ... "I need peace of mind." (value). . . "I'll do whatever it takes to get over it" (rule). These intermediate thoughts (rules, values, and attitudes) energized an onslaught of automatic thoughts: "It's all my fault." (attribution)..."It will affect everything that I do."..."Getting fired is the worst thing that can happen." (appraisal) . . . "I can't cope; if I have a drink, I'll feel better." (expectation). These proximal cognitive structures triggered what Rick experienced as unbearable emotional states (fear, anxiety, and depression). His decision was to get drunk.

In treatment, Rick was able to successfully challenge the deep-seated belief structures that led to his undoing. In fact, he could recount many times when he did not fall apart under pressure: when his child was born prematurely and Rick had to take care of both his child and wife who became bedridden after a fall; when he got a promotion and turned in some of his best work at a time when he had some of the most difficult clients; when his mother passed away and he made all the proper funeral arrangements and gave a heartwarming eulogy to relatives and friends about her life.

After thoroughly challenging and modifying the underlying beliefs, intermediate structures, and automatic thoughts that characteristically led him back to the bottle, Rick was successfully discharged from the 3-month course of outpatient treatment. He and his counselor were confident of Rick's commitment and capacity to live a comfortable and responsible life without alcohol. To date, Rick and his wife have raised four healthy children and neither one has had a slip or relapse in the past 30 years.

The purpose of cognitive-behavioral counseling is to facilitate the discovery of alternative ways of appraising a given situation, and then identify any barriers to thinking and acting in this more adaptive and satisfying way. Table 16.3 maps Rick's relapse process and the protective cognitive restructuring that led to a healthy and productive lifestyle.

The Trans-Ideological Power of Cognitive-Behavioral Restructuring

In June of 2005, Aaron Beck, who had long been intrigued by the apparent similarities between Buddhist philosophy and cognitive therapy (CT), engaged in a dialogue with the Dalai Lama, the spiritual leader of Tibetan Buddhism. Their meeting took place at the International Congress of Cognitive Psychotherapy in Göteborg, Sweden. In Beck's (2005) "Reflections on My Public Dialogue With the Dalai Lama," he discusses commonalities between Buddhism and CT.

According to Beck (2005), "Buddhism is the philosophy and psychology closest to cognitive therapy and vice versa" (p. 4). Perhaps the most elemental similarity is that both approaches use the mind to understand and cure the mind. The two share common goals of serenity, peace of mind, and relief of suffering. Both adhere to common values that stress the importance of acceptance, compassion, knowledge, and understanding, with a clear focus on altruism (vs. egoism) and universalism (vs. groupism). Personal responsibility for one's actions and science taking precedent over superstition are core principles.

Regarding the causes of distress, there is a common view of the intrinsic goodness of people, which is overlaid by layer after layer of "negative thoughts." In the Buddhist tradition, these can be neutralized by positive thinking (focusing on positive and good things), whereas CT stresses pinpointing thinking errors and facilitating their correction. Both share common methods of focusing on the immediate (here and now), targeting biased thinking through reflectiveness, perspective-taking, use of imagery, identifying toxic beliefs, distancing, and nurturing constructive experiences and positive thoughts.

According to the Dalai Lama in his work *Ethics for the New Millennium* (1999), "If we can reorient our thoughts and emotions, and reorder our behavior, not only can we learn to cope with suffering more easily, but we can prevent a great deal of it from starting in the first place" (p. xii).

At the core of the philosophies embraced by both CBR and the Dalai Lama is *secular ethics*, whereby people of different faiths and cultural backgrounds can accept the importance of positive thought, without necessarily invoking the instrument of religion. These trans-ideological and commonsense aspects of CBR are major factors in its enormous success around the globe. At the time of this writing, a Google search for *cognitive-behavioral therapy* yielded 2,010,000 citations. One of the authors (Milkman), during a Fulbright lectureship at the Psychology Department of the University of Kebangsaang in Malaysia (1985–1986), discovered that CBT was the preferred treatment approach, equally endorsed by ethnic Malay students who were predominantly Muslim, ethnic Chinese students who were Christian and Buddhist, and ethnic Indian students who were raised primarily in the Hindu tradition. As strange as it may seem, a recent approach to combating terrorism in Saudi Arabia is consistent with the cognitive-behavioral psychology described above.

> At a government detention camp an hour outside Riyadh, jihadis are asked to rethink their radicalism.... Welcome to the Care Rehabilitation Center, a three-year-old

experiment to reform malleable minds who have fallen under the sway of Osama bin Laden's radical brand of Islam. To get here, jihadis have to demonstrate during a prison interview a readiness to rethink their extremist views.... The program, developed by a team of Saudi scholars, psychiatrists and sociologists, tries to convince these men of their mistakes and make them productive members of Saudi society which has been rocked by terrorism. (MacLeod, 2007, p. 8)

Table 19.3 Relapse Thoughts and Protective Cognitive Restructuring

Proximal Structures (Automatic Thoughts)	

Decision—GET DRUNK	**Decision**—HANG TOUGH
Expectation	
If I have a drink, I'll feel better; I can't cope.	I don't need a drink; I have a lot to lose.
Appraisal	
Getting fired is the worst thing that can happen.	I can manage tough times; I've done it before.
Attribution	
It's entirely my fault; it will affect everything that I do.	Bad circumstances, but I've still got a lot going for me.
↑ ↓	
Intermediate Structures	
Rules	
Do whatever you can to get over it.	I won't go back to the old crutch
Values	
Peace of mind	Life is often stressful; I can accept challenges.
Attitudes	
Who cares, anyway? Life sucks.	I care about my life and family.
↑ ↓	
Distal Structures Core Beliefs; Schemas	
I'm damaged; life isn't fair. I fall apart under pressure.	A lot of things have gone my way. I can be pretty tough when it comes down to it.
↑ ↓	

Loss of employment

Image sources: Copyright © 2011 Depositphotos/monkeybusiness Source:; Source: https://pixabay.com/en/man-board-drawing-muscles-strong-2037255.

Cognitive-Behavioral Restructuring in Everyday Life

It is our hope and expectation that readers will extrapolate the principles above to improve the quality of their lives. CBR methodologies, which have become preeminent across the spectrum of counseling domains (i.e., mental health, substance abuse, and criminal conduct), are applicable in everyday life. By practicing the techniques of mindfulness, acceptance, and cognitive restructuring, readers can improve their relationships, not only with themselves (dealing more effectively with emotions and behavioral choices), but with others across the board. A parent can better relate to his or her children, employees can increase cooperation and positive feelings among coworkers, project managers can improve relationships with their supervisees, and all of us can achieve improved affective states stemming from our interactions with significant others. It might be of particular benefit to reflect on the cognitive restructuring schema (Table 16.3) and cognitive-behavioral map (Figure 16.3) above as personal checkpoints during an episode of stress or interpersonal conflict. Improved self-regulation and positive outcomes are likely to follow. Anyone struggling with hedonic dependencies is likely to benefit from this approach.

Much of our everyday thinking involves a stream of cognitive processing just below the surface of our conscious awareness. This type of automatic thinking may be regarded as preconscious, because thoughts of this nature can be recognized if attention is brought to them (Clark et al., 1999). Perhaps the most important clue that automatic thoughts are taking place is the presence of *strong feelings* (Wright et al., 2006). People who struggle with depression or anxiety often experience automatic thoughts that, through the errors in logic described above, become maladaptive and distorted. When these thoughts (guided by underlying schemas or core beliefs) are activated by stress, they can generate strong emotional reactions and dysfunctional behavior. Alcohol misuse or maladaptive reliance on any tension-relieving behavior may be the behavioral outcome of maladaptive cognitive processing.

The relationship between events, automatic thinking, and emotions in everyday life is illustrated by the example of Susan, a woman who successfully turned her thoughts around after realizing that they were formative to her depressed feelings.

CASE EXAMPLE: Susan's Automatic Thought

Event	Automatic Thoughts	Emotions
My father calls and asks why I forgot to call him about going to lunch.	There I go again. There's no way that I will ever please him. I can't do anything right; I might as well give up.	Sadness Anger
Thinking about a term paper that is due at school.	I can't handle it. I'll never meet the deadline. I won't be able to face my teacher. I'll get a low grade and screw things up like I do everything else.	Anxiety
My husband complains that I'm cranky every time he sees me.	He's really on my case. I'm not being a good wife. I don't enjoy life. Nobody would like to spend time with me.	Sadness Anxiety

Susan's automatic thoughts are consistent with the common finding of negatively based cognitions in anxiety and depression. Themes of hopelessness, low self-esteem, and failure are common in depressive feeling states. People who find themselves riddled with anxiety usually have automatic thoughts that include prediction of danger, harm, uncontrollability, and inability to manage threats (Wright et al., 2006).

Everyone has automatic thoughts; they do not just occur in people who seek treatment for depression, anxiety, or other emotional disorders. By recognizing our personal automatic thoughts and underlying beliefs and by deploying alternative cognitive-behavioral processes, we can strengthen our empathy for others, enhance our counseling skills, and step up the overall quality of our lives.

Automatic Thoughts Exercise

Write down an example of automatic thoughts. Try this for a situation from your own life. If a personal example does not come to mind, you can use an example from someone you know.

1. Draw three columns on a sheet of paper and label them *Event, Automatic Thoughts,* and *Emotions.*
2. Recall a recent situation or memory of an event that seemed to stir up emotions such as anxiety, anger, sadness, physical tension, or happiness.
3. Try to imagine being back in this situation, just as it happened.
4. What automatic thoughts were occurring in this situation? Write down the event, the automatic thoughts, and the emotions in each column of your record.
5. Try to identify the underlying beliefs that energize these thoughts.
6. What kind of errors in logic might you be using?
7. What alternative cognitive process can you use to alter your emotional states?

Chapter Summary

The perspective that developing a healthy style of thinking can reduce distress or enhance well-being is a common theme across many generations and cultures. The cognitive-behavioral revolution is based on fundamental principles from ancient Persian, Buddhist, Roman, and Greek philosophies.

Albert Ellis is generally regarded as the grandfather of the cognitive approach to therapy. Today, the preeminent authority on cognitive therapy is Aaron Beck. Beck put forth a cognitive conceptualization of depression that relates problems in mood, motivation, and physical malaise to typically negative thoughts about the self, world, and future. This became known as the "negative cognitive triad." Beck theorized that there are characteristic errors in logic in the automatic thoughts (expectations, appraisals, attributions, and decisions) and other cognitions of those with emotional disorders. Subsequent research has confirmed the importance of cognitive errors in pathological styles of information processing.

There is an emphasis on techniques designed to help clients detect and modify their inner thoughts, especially those that are associated with emotional symptoms such as depression, anxiety, or anger. The presence of strong emotions is a prime indicator that automatic thoughts might be occurring. In depression and other conditions, maladaptive schemas may remain dormant until a stressful life event occurs and activates the core belief. The schema is then strengthened to the degree that it stimulates and drives the more superficial negative, automatic thoughts. Emotional discomfort, substance abuse, interpersonal conflict, and other harmful patterns of behavior are seen as sequels to dysfunctional patterns of thought.

The development of behavioral theory in the late 1950s and 1960s provided the foundation for the behavioral component of cognitive-behavioral therapy. Examination of the principles outlined by Bandura (social learning), Meichenbaum (internal dialogue), and Beck (cognitive errors) leads to the conclusion that "self-reinforcement" is the combining element of cognitive and behavioral approaches. Changes in thinking and behavior strengthen one another. When a change in cognition leads to a change in action, which is followed by a positive outcome, the resultant sense of well-being reinforces (strengthens) both the initiating thought and subsequent behavior. This self-reinforcing aspect of the cognitive-behavioral approach facilitates the transition from an effortful form of cognitive-behavioral self-management to a relatively effortless pattern of thinking and acting in a new and more adaptive manner.

People of different faiths and cultural backgrounds can accept the importance of positive thought without necessarily invoking a particular religion or philosophy of life. These trans-ideological and commonsense aspects of CBR are great contributors to its tremendous success around the world. By practicing the techniques of mindfulness, acceptance, and cognitive restructuring, readers can improve how they think and feel about themselves, the world, and their relationships with others.

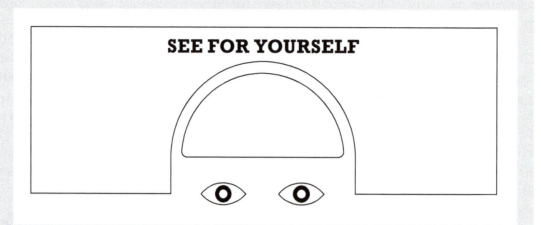

SEE FOR YOURSELF

Unlocking the Healing Power of You. 2016. Erik Vance. Photographs and Videos by Erika Larsen. National Geographic Magazine.

This piece provides a detailed discussion of the power of belief in medicine. The article includes examples of "control" groups experiencing dramatic improvement after receiving no treatment, and the power of religious belief in combatting pain and achieving medical results. **http://www.nationalgeographic.com/magazine/2016/12/healing-science-belief-placebo/**

Rewriting the Story of My Addiction. 2015. Jo Harvey Weatherford. TEDx University of Nevada. 9:41

In this candid talk, Weatherford discusses her own experience reframing her thoughts about her alcohol addiction to find a path to recovery. **https://www.youtube.com/watch?v=OJY4GkpRc7U**

Meeting of the Minds. 2005. Aaron Beck and the Dalai Lama. International Congress of Cognitive Psychotherapy. 1:30:06

Aaron Beck and His Holiness the Dalai Lama discuss the Buddhist and Western approaches to managing thoughts, feelings, and behaviors. **https://www.youtube.com/watch?v=beYldvfwvEw**

CHAPTER **20**

Maintaining Close and Intimate Relationships

Your soul is your relationship with other people. What you say and do does not die.

—Tom Wolfe

Introduction: The Three Faces of Love

"Love represents a cognitive, behavioral and emotional stance toward others that takes three prototypical forms" (Peterson & Seligman, 2004, p. 304). The first and perhaps the foundation for all future attachments is the love that we feel for our first caregivers. We trust them to make our welfare a priority and to be at our side in times of need. They comfort and reassure us when we are disquieted by long periods of separation. The prototype for this form is a child's love for a parent. Another kind of love is for those who depend on us to make them feel safe and looked after. We provide them with comfort and safety, assistance and support when they are in need and put their welfare above our own. We feel uplifted when they are happy and sad when things don't go their way. The prototype of this form is a parent's love for a child. The third form of love is one that involves passionate desire for sexual, physical, and emotional closeness with another person. We consider this person special, and being with him or her makes us feel special. The prototype here is romantic love.

Freud (1905/1962) was among the first to describe the commonalities between love for a child and romantic love. He noted striking similarities between lovers and mother–infant pairs. Both spend a good deal of time in mutual gazing, cuddling, kissing, and having skin-to-skin contact, along with touching body parts that are considered "private." Today, there is biological evidence for a similar neurochemical under-pinning between the two types. Oxytocin, released during suckling/nursing, is thought to induce feelings

413

of bonding and attachment between mother and child. The same chemical is released at sexual climax and is believed to play a role in the cuddling and feelings of closeness that follow intercourse (Carter, 1992; Slater, 2006; Walter, 2008).

This chapter is designed to provide readers with an understanding of the importance of flourishing human relationships to our overall happiness and well-being. In the context of natural highs, the thrust of our discussion is on developing improved ways of satisfying basic needs for love and belonging, for ourselves and those whom we cherish and admire. We begin our discussion of maintaining close and intimate relationships with infant–caretaker attachment. Healthy bonding at this vital stage of development is a critical model for trust and safety in future relationships (Erikson, 1982). The derivative of healthy bonding and security—through infancy, childhood, and adolescence—is secure adult attachment, which is closely linked to healthy relationships. Our discussion of secure attachment sets the stage for examining the qualities of mature love and the importance of consciously engaging in behaviors that sustain interpersonal connections over time and contribute to flourishing relationships (Snyder & Lopez, 2007).

The Universal Need for Love

Maslow (1954/1970) posited that human motives are hierarchically arranged. Ascending in order from a base of *biological* needs, hunger and thirst, next the needs for *safety* (i.e., to become free from threats of danger, both psychological and physical) come into play. Next in the hierarchy is the need for attachment, which leads to our quest for connection to others, to love and to be loved. When these are satisfied, our motives turn toward the need to feel valued or *esteemed* by ourselves and others. The drives toward knowledge, understanding, and novelty are grouped together as *cognitive* needs. We then experience *aesthetic* needs, which become manifest in our desires for order and beauty. At the upper tier of the hierarchy is the need for *self-actualization*—"the full use and exploitation of talents, capacities, and potentialities" (Maslow, 1954/1970, p. 150). The self-actualized individual is characterized by such traits as spontaneity, autonomy, sense of humor, and *deep interpersonal relationships.* At the apex of the hierarchy is the need for *transcendence,* pertaining to spiritual or religious needs.

In their classic work called *Character Strengths and Virtues,* Peterson and Seligman (2004) classify six broad virtues that consistently emerge across history and culture: wisdom, courage, humanity, justice, temperance, and transcendence. From both Peterson and Seligman's and Maslow's perspectives, the capacity to establish and maintain deep interpersonal relationships is germane to the experience of happiness and fulfilling one's potential. This view of the intimate connection between optimal life experience and the capacity to form close interpersonal bonds is also a vital component of our view of natural highs as "self-induced changes in brain chemistry that result in positive feeling states, health, and well-being for the individual and society," as noted in Chapter 1.

The characteristics of Peterson and Seligman's (2004) core virtue of "humanity" are helpful in conceptualizing ideal human connections.

Humanity: Interpersonal strengths that involve tending and befriending others

- *Capacity to Love and Be Loved:* Valuing close relations with others, in particular those in which sharing and caring are reciprocated; being close to other people

- *Kindness [generosity, nurturance, care, compassion, altruistic love, "niceness"]:* Doing favors and good deeds for others; helping them; taking care of them
- *Social Intelligence [emotional intelligence, personal intelligence]:* Being aware of the motives and feelings of other people and oneself; knowing what to do to fit into different social situations; knowing what makes other people tick. (p. 29)

Secure Attachment: A Prototype for Successful Relationships

Studies of human attachment shed light on how people remain "on track" with their needs for love and belonging and how others may become "derailed." As discussed in Section V, "craving for intimacy" can override our sense of right or wrong and judgment concerning harm to the self or others. We may use drugs, join cults, or purchase sexual favors to find relief from loneliness and despair. Thus, positive relationships may help prevent people from "attaching" to unhealthy substances or activities; on the flip side, those looking to recover from hedonic dependencies can bolster their chance of success if they have loving, supportive relationships.

The roots of scholarly work in the area of human connectedness are found in the study of traumatic separation (e.g., Bowlby, 1969) and failed relationships (e.g., Carrere & Gottman, 1999). With the recent turn toward "positive psychology," theorists and researchers have undertaken the study of developmental precursors to successful relationships (e.g., Gable, Reis, & Elliot, 2003; Harvey, Pauwels, & Zickmund, 2001; Peterson & Seligman, 2004; Snyder & Lopez, 2007).

Attachment is a process that may begin *in utero* and continue throughout one's life span. It is the emotional link that forms between an infant and a caregiver, and it physically bonds people together over time (Ainsworth, Bell, & Stayton, 1992). Bowlby (1969), a clinician who worked with delinquent and orphaned children, identified certain styles of caregiving that resulted in secure or insecure patterns of attachment. Maladaptive parental behaviors include chaotic and unplanned attempts to meet the child's needs. Contrastingly, adaptive parenting centers on responsiveness to the child's behavioral cues such as smiling when happy or crying when upset. Inconsistency in responding is associated with anxiety and frustration later in life, whereas consistency is associated with later development of contentment and trust. Lopez (2003) describes the two-way connection between infant and caregiver as "a unique, evolutionary-based motivational system (i.e., independent of gratification of the libidinal needs and drives) whose primary function is the provision of protection and emotional security" (p. 286).

By studying children that became disconnected from their caregivers, Bowlby (1969) realized that insecure attachment sets the stage for a host of developmental struggles. The growing child may have difficulty in mood regulation or in cooperating with others. On the other hand, those children who were raised under conditions of secure attachment became more appealing to their caregivers and those around them. In time, mutually beneficial patterns of interaction allow for positive growth and development in children as well as their caregivers. Ainsworth, Blehar, Waters, and Wall (1978) developed the "Strange Situation" technique, which is regarded as the classic assessment strategy to explore the attachment system in infants and toddlers. A child is exposed to a novel situation (new room) in the company of his or her caregiver. Then the caregiver leaves and is reintroduced into the situation twice. A stranger first enters the room in the presence of the caregiver and tries to engage the child in play. Then the caregiver leaves the child alone with the stranger. Then the caregiver returns for the first reunion and the stranger leaves unobtrusively. The caregiver then leaves and the child is alone. Then the stranger returns and tries to settle the child. The caregiver returns for the second time and the stranger leaves unobtrusively. During this time, the child's responses are coded by trained observers.

Table 20.1 shows the categorization of the quality of the child's attachment in the Strange Situation (Ainsworth, 1979).

Table 20.1 Qualities of Attachment in the Strange Situation

Secure Attachment	Balance between exploration of the environment and contact with the caregiver.
	As the situation unfolds, the child seeks more proximity to and contact with the caregiver.
	He or she explores the environment only to return for comfort as necessary.
Insecure Attachment	Increasing tension between child and parent.
Insecure-Avoidant	Child avoids the caregiver when he or she returns.
Insecure-Resistant/Ambivalent	Child passively or actively demonstrates hostility toward the caregiver while simultaneously wanting to be held or comforted.

Source: Based on "Infant-mother attachment," by M. D. S. Ainsworth, 1979, American Psychologist, 34, 932–937.

As measured by the Strange Situation, quality of attachment is predictive of a child's behavior many years later. Bretherton and Walters (1985) found that among preschoolers, insecurely attached children had difficulty in relating to adults and their caregivers and they were less able to cope with their parents' absence. Belsky and Nezworski (1988) found that long-term consequences of insecure attachment include relationship problems, emotional disorders, and conduct problems.

Conversely, infants and toddlers with secure attachment were more likely to manifest healthy personalities through late childhood and into adolescence (Bowlby, 1988; Shaver, Hazan, & Bradshaw, 1988). These findings may be understood as the result of children being able to form an internal model of themselves and others. Children with secure attachment develop positive perceptions of themselves as competent, appealing, and loveable, and internal constructs for caregivers as accessible, responsive, and consistent. These models remain relatively stable during development because they are self-reinforcing (i.e., when the child responds with affection to the caregiver, he or she receives more consistent attention and love from caregivers).

> If people carry forward a secure mindful state, they see the world as safe and others as reliable. Unfortunately, negative or insecure schema also may be perpetuated. For example, people who see the world as unpredictable and other people as unreliable have difficulty overcoming their desires to keep others at a distance. (Snyder & Lopez, 2007, p. 303)

Of course, having achieved a state of secure attachment as an infant or toddler does not guarantee healthy adjustment later in life. However, of all the predictors of overall adjustment, the quality of social functioning is among the strongest. "Being securely attached to a caregiver in the first year of life provides a solid foundation for affect regulation and exploration as well as the expectation of future responsiveness from and the tendency to turn to and rely on others during times of need" (Peterson & Seligman, 2004, p. 314).

Interestingly, neuroscience research in rats has revealed that parenting affects brain development. As summarized by Cozolino (2014), a mother rat's nurturing contact—licking is a major form of mother-pup interaction for these creatures—influences brain structures related to stress responses, coping (emotion regulation), learning, and brain plasticity (the ability of the brain to regenerate neurons and alter based on experiences). Moreover, the mother's early nurturance is related to how her female pups function as mothers once they mature. As you have probably guessed, higher levels of maternal attention are associated with better functioning in these areas, as are higher levels of oxytocin, GABA receptors, and opioid receptors. Additional research is needed to confirm these findings in humans.

Attachment theory has been extended across the life span in an attempt to understand how adolescents relate to their peers and how adults relate to each other and to the children for whom they are caregivers. Hazan and Shaver (1987) found that Ainsworth's (1979) three categories of attachment—secure, avoidant, and anxious—accurately described adult attachments to a significant other. Secure adult attachment involves comfort and emotional closeness and a general lack of anxiety about being abandoned. The most important benefit of having secure adult attachment is that it provides avenues to healthy development and even enhanced survival. By cultivating support from significant others, children and adults become more adept at managing threats. Furthermore, by being open to exploring individual growth experiences without fear of rejection or abandonment, we can pursue self-actualization, or optimal human functioning. Kobak and Hazan (1991) found that secure attachment in adolescence and adulthood is related to more supportiveness and less rejection toward partners in tasks that require joint problem solving. Brennan and Shaver (1995) showed secure attachment to be related to safer sex practices.

> In sum, secure adolescents and adults cope more effectively with the stresses of life and are more skilled at forming social ties that are enduring, satisfying and characterized by trust and intimacy. Both of these skills predict better psychological adjustment and physical health (Peterson & Seligman, 2004, p. 315).

Attachment theory is one of the most prominent frameworks used to study relationships. Given all of the emphasis on healthy (secure) attachments, one might wonder if someone with an insecure attachment style is "doomed" to a lifetime of unhealthy relationships. According to Kinley and Reyno (2013), Bowlby's model allowed for attachments to shift over time, based upon experience. Kinley and Reyno's data support that attachment style can be altered through interventions. Using a 6-week intensive group therapy intervention, they took relationship measures linked to attachment both before and after the intervention. They noted increases in secure attachments and decreases in fearful attachments (although there was less of an effect on preoccupied and no effect at all on dismissive attachment styles). The changes in the secure and fearful attachments were associated with improved interpersonal functioning. Other researchers have also reported changes in attachment consistent with these findings (e.g., Kilmann et al., 1999; Levy et al., 2006; Travis et al., 2001; cited in Kinley and Reyno, 2013). The benefits of improving attachments can have a positive impact on both the psychotherapy relationship as well as clients' relationships in their personal lives.

Healthy Love

Four constructs, denoted by Greek terms, are highlighted by I. Singer (1984a, 1984b, 1987) in what many refer to as the definitive history of love: (1) eros—search for the beautiful; (2) philia—affection in friendship; (3) nomos—submission and obedience to the divine; and (4) agape—bestowal of love by the divine. S. Hendrick and Hendrick (1992) asserted that although it has only been in the last 300 years that people have been able to develop a sense of self, capable of loving and caring for a romantic partner, "Life without love would be for many people like a black-and-white movie—full of events and activities but without the color that gives vibrancy and provides a sense of celebration" (p. 117).

Aron and Aron's "self-expansion theory of love" (A. Aron & Aron, 1986; E. N. Aron & Aron, 1996), which was influenced by Eastern conceptualizations, posits that humans have a basic drive to expand the self, which strives to include everyone and everything. The emotions, thoughts, and actions of love energize self-development. According to this model, satisfying relationships are the natural by-products of self-expansion. Being in a love relationship brings on positive feeling states, which in turn reinforce or strengthen the commitment to the relationship.

Triangular Theory of Love

Sternberg's (1986) prominent "triangular theory of love" explains various dimensions of the love experience. He posits that love is a mix of three primary factors: (1) passion, or physical attractiveness and romantic drives; (2) intimacy, or feelings of closeness or connectedness; and (3) commitment, involving the decision to initiate and sustain a relationship. Various combinations of these components result in eight forms of love. For example, when intimacy and passion are combined, they form the basis of romantic love. The combination of intimacy and commitment result in companionate love. According to Sternberg, consummate love, the most durable (long-lasting) form, is manifested when all three components are present in high levels and in balance across both partners. Silberman (1995), in a study of 104 couples who were married an average of 13 years, found that marital satisfaction was highest for couples who were high on intimacy, followed by passion.

Romantic Competence

Joanne Davila, Ph.D., is a clinical psychologist who is the Director of Clinical Training as well as the Director of the Relationship Development Center in the Department of Psychology at Stony Brook University and a vocal advocate for something that she refers to as "romantic competence" (or RC for short). What is RC? According to Davila and colleagues (2009, 2017), RC is a set of three skills that are essential to healthy relationships: insight, mutuality, and emotion regulation. *Insight* involves being able to think about one's partner and the relationship, recognize the potential impact of events on the relationship, and be able to learn from experiences. *Mutuality* addresses the fact that there are two people whose needs are to be respected in the relationship. *Emotion regulation* refers to the person's ability to not overreact but rather to remain calm when issues arise in the relationship. Overall, these skills allow a person to have more open communication with their partner.

Davila and her colleagues developed a Romantic Competence Interview (2009) which was originally used in 13–14 year-old adolescents; the interview was later modified for use with young adults (2017). Data from the young adult study demonstrated that RC is linked to greater relationship satisfaction, greater feelings of security with the relationship, healthier decision making concerning the relationship, and fewer problems such as depression and anxiety. Note that these are correlational data, as no efforts were made to manipulate RC.

This brings us to one of Davila's primary points: RC should be taught to people, ideally when they are young (adolescents or emerging adults) so that they have the skills to enable them to make healthy decisions about relationships. Davila recognizes that unhealthy relationships are a source of distress (promoting anxiety and depression); by promoting RC, it may be possible to decrease the number of negative relationships a person experiences—and give them the skills to recognize and get out of those unhealthy relationships when they do occur. (To hear Dr. Davila speak about RC, check out her TEDx Talk in See for Yourself.)

Intimacy and Sexuality

Intimacy helps to satisfy our needs to feel connected, to give and receive affection, and to develop self-esteem. Intimate relationships provide our support system when life gets difficult. Intimacy can best be described as a caring and trusting relationship in which thoughts, needs, and feelings can be openly expressed and unconditionally accepted. Therefore, freedom in communication is an essential aspect of an intimate relationship. Developing true intimacy requires taking risks. It means exposing some of our most guarded emotions and vulnerable areas to another person. It is through this kind of risk taking that genuine trust can develop. If partners are unaccustomed to heartfelt emotional communication, the thought of revealing one's feelings can seem quite threatening. Many relationships must learn to allow intimacy to develop.

When emotional intimacy fails to develop or is purposely avoided, sex often becomes a goal-oriented performance. That is, sex is perceived as a single, instantly gratifying act that blocks emotional awareness to the point of diminished interest in sex or one's partner. Sexual responsiveness declines, and any sense of intimacy may be lost (Masters & Johnson, 1974). Negotiating differences in a sexual relationship requires commitment and practice. Conflict doesn't have to be viewed as a negative situation; it can instead be considered a stimulus for growth, provided both partners are working toward resolution. In *The Pleasure Bond*, Masters and Johnson (1974) explain that couples can achieve resolution of conflict using two principles: *neutrality* and *mutuality*.

Neutrality means that each partner respects the good intentions of the other and trusts that those intentions are genuine and sincere. Each partner takes personal responsibility for his or her actions and sexual responses. If a couple is to enjoy a positive physical relationship, each must strive to be responsive to the other, not responsible for the other. The principle of *mutuality* defines the sexual interaction between two persons. Whether by speech or by actions, all sexual exchanges should occur in the spirit of working toward a mutual cause. The common goal of partners in a healthy sexual relationship is to discover and accept what pleases each other; to be sensitive to individual needs and differences; and to be committed to working together toward mutual satisfaction, knowing that their sexual preferences will not always match perfectly.

The key is a commitment to full communication of our honest feelings in order to remain attuned to our partner's needs as well as our own. We have a responsibility to accept each other as unique individuals and to honor each other's wants or desires in a way that enables us to satisfy our sexual needs. This is the mutually cooperative effort that will sustain a healthy and successful sexual relationship.

Some fundamentally important aspects are involved in developing and maintaining a healthy sexual relationship. First, honesty and direct communication form the cornerstone to building trust and intimacy. When problems arise, it is important to find resolution rather than solution. That is, both partners must be committed to openly expressing their feelings in a caring way and to accepting those ideas with concern and respect for individual likes and differences. Freedom of expression and effective communication are essential elements of an intimate relationship and are the key to conflict resolution (Peterson & Seligman, 2004). We are not automatic interpreters of body language or semi-audible verbal cues. It takes effort and assertiveness for partners to discover what is best for each other. Both partners are responsible for expressing thoughts and feelings as clearly as possible. If clear communication is lacking, neither partner will be able to respond effectively, and satisfaction will slip into frustration.

Second, partners should strive to not bring "old garbage" into a new relationship. If, for instance, one person has been betrayed in a previous relationship, it is crucial to future relationships to work on feelings of hurt and trust so that this sort of unfinished business is not brought into the current relationship. Expecting that a previously negative experience is going to repeat itself is harmful to the relationship. When a partner brings remnants of the past, it invalidates the other individual's uniqueness. It puts a new person in an old scenario, which is destructive.

Third, it is important to the success of the relationship that both parties remain individuals with their own interests. Maintaining independence within a relationship gives us the capacity to set goals, pursue new interests, and function well as an individual and partner. The self-actualization and personal satisfaction that are enjoyed enhance the quality of the relationship and make each partner more interesting to the other. Pursuing outside interests not only encourages self-awareness, but also promotes personal autonomy, preventing partners from becoming overly dependent on each other. When autonomy fails to develop (insecure attachment) before a serious relationship is formed, dependencies are simply transferred from parents to partners (Masters & Johnson, 1974).

Last, sexual commitment involves sexual responsibility. That is, each of us takes responsibility for clearly expressing our sexual wants and needs and for remaining attuned to our partner's wants and needs. The responsibility, however, does not end with the mutual satisfaction of the sexual encounter; rather, it includes the obligation of full commitment of both partners to the responsibility of pregnancy and birth control as well as protecting against sexually transmitted diseases. Every potential outcome of sexual interaction is the mutual responsibility of both partners.

Intimacy Versus Individuality

Whether sexual or platonic, healthy intimacy is predicated upon reconciliation of two fundamental human needs: belonging and individuality. Needs for intimacy and closeness and needs for individuality and separateness are often in conflict. A healthy balance of closeness and separateness is key to developing mature and healthy relationships, predicated on a foundation of secure attachment. Figure 20.1 depicts healthy and unhealthy balances between closeness and individuality (Wanberg & Milkman, 2006, p. 223).

Table 20.2 provides a set of guidelines for keeping a healthy closeness with one's friends or significant other.

Figure 20.1 **Relational Balance Between Closeness and Separateness** Ideal relationships maintain a healthy balance between individuality and closeness.

Circle One: Enmeshed
Relationship dominates
individuals, little separation or
individuality

Circle Two: Detached
Individual needs dominate,
little giving to the relationship

Circle Three: Balanced
Healthy balance between closeness and
separateness, between
individuality and relationship

Source: Kenneth Wanberg and Harvey B. Milkman, Criminal Conduct and Substance Abuse Treatment: Strategies for Self-improvement and Change: Pathways to Responsible Living: The Participant's Workbook, pp. 223. Copyright © 2006 by SAGE Publications. Reprinted with permission.

Table 20.2 Guidelines for Intimacy and Uniqueness

Be proactive and active.	Put energy into the relationship. Make things happen. Do your share of planning activities.
Let your partner be proactive and active.	Respect and support your partner's effort to energize the relationship.
Interact rather than react to what your partner does.	Use active listening and active sharing to interact. When you react, you make your partner responsible rather than taking responsibility.
Keep a balance between closeness and separateness.	Be okay even when your partner is not. When you are not okay, let your partner be okay. Each safeguards the self and the relationship.
Always work for a win–win when settling problems.	Keep the focus on the problem, not on the other conflicts. Restate the other person's side to make sure you understand it. Talk about yourself, not the other person. Use "I" messages, not "you" messages. After a conflict is resolved, be sure that each of you is better off.

Help the other person	Show enthusiasm, appreciation, and respect for the other's achievements. Celebrate that success.
Combine strengths for the good of attracted each other.	Be proud of and profit from the other person's strengths. What attracted you to each other was the strength of your differences.
Don't let things build up between you.	Tell your partner what bothers you. Don't expect your partner to read your mind, to know what you want or feel or think.
Keep your relationship fresh and romantic.	Take trips, go to different places, have fun. Keep up the romance. See physical and sexual intimacy as more than having sex. Take part in healthy play—to move freely in space together.
Give and receive compliments and praise.	Show that you appreciate the other person. Make the positives outweigh the negatives. All parts of the relationship improve when there are positive expressions. Sexual intimacy occurs when there are positive feelings between people.

Source: Kenneth Wanberg and Harvey B. Milkman, "Guidelines for Intimacy and Uniqueness," Criminal Conduct and Substance Abuse Treatment: Strategies for Self-improvement and Change: Pathways to Responsible Living: The Participant's Workbook, pp. 222.

Optimizing Relationships

Positive psychologists have focused on identifying elements of highly successful relationships and what skills partners can learn to optimize their interpersonal connections. Three interrelated constructs have emerged from this area of study: (1) minding relationships, (2) creating a culture of appreciation, and (3) capitalizing on positive events (Snyder & Lopez, 2007).

Minding Relationships

Harvey et al. (2001) developed a five-component model of what they refer to as *minding relationships*. Minding is the "reciprocal knowing process involving the nonstop interrelated thoughts, feelings and behaviors of people in a relationship" (p. 424). Minding is a conscious knowing process that involves a moment-to-moment awareness of the workings of our conscious mind. Couples seeking to optimize their relationship are encouraged to develop skills according to the following guidelines:

- Through an in-depth knowing process, both partners are united by a common purpose of knowing the other and being known by the other.
- Both members of the partnership are invested in using the information gained through "knowing" to enhance their relationship.
- There is mutual acceptance concerning what is learned and respect for the person they learn about.
- Both partners agree to continue this process (minding relationships) indefinitely until a synchrony of thought, feeling, and behavior arises.
- In time, both partners develop a deep sense of being unique and appreciated in the relationship.

Creating a Culture of Appreciation

Using what was learned from observing couples, Gottman, with the assistance of a group of mathematicians (Gottman, Murray, Swanson, Tyson, & Swanson, 2003), developed the "magic ratio" for successful marriages—five positive interactions to one negative (5:1) is formulaic for a flourishing relationship. As the ratio approaches 1:1, divorce is likely. Adhering to a positive ratio does not mean avoiding all arguments. Rather, by infusing warmth, humor, respect, and good listening skills into difficult conversations, couples are able to thrive. A lack of positive interactions during emotionally charged situations can lead to contempt and the ultimate breakdown of the relationship.

Crystallizing decades of research on his "sound marital house" theory, Gottman and his colleagues (Gottman, Driver, & Tabares, 2002) developed a marital counseling strategy designed to move partners from conflict to comfortable interactions. Therapeutic goals include enhancing *communication and social skills* and *mindfulness* of the downsides of negative communication messages (i.e., criticism, contempt, defensiveness, and stonewalling). By creating a culture of appreciation, regardless of marital status or sexual involvement, partners experience more rewarding and fulfilling relationships. Expressing gratitude for the small behaviors that often go unnoticed is the primary vehicle for infusing a relationship with positive energy. Saying thanks to a spouse for tidying up the house, making a fellow student aware that you value his or her comments in class, thanking a friend for taking the time to listen—all of these contribute to the sense of mutual appreciation that then becomes normative for the relationship.

Capitalizing on Positive Events

Gable, Reis, Impett, and Asher (2004) found that the process of *capitalization* (i.e., telling partners about the good things in your life) reaps many benefits. When a partner responds enthusiastically to your good fortune, you experience personal gain by reliving the experience. *Active/constructive* responses are most beneficial for capitalizing (i.e., amplifying the pleasure) on a good event or situation. Those in flourishing relationships were apt to characterize their partner's response to hearing good news in the following ways:

- My friend/relative/partner reacts enthusiastically.
- My friend/relative/partner appears to be even more happy than I am about the event.
- My friend/relative/partner typically asks many questions and shows genuine interest in the positive event.

The strategy for achieving capitalization on positive events simply involves making a point of telling trusted friends about the daily events that bolster your spirit. If there are people in your life who tend to undermine your communication of happiness (e.g., "That promotion at work will probably mean you'll have to bust your butt with long hours ..."), then they probably shouldn't remain privy to news of your good fortune. The skill of offering positive responses (mirroring happiness and asking meaningful questions) about the good fortune of others is relatively easy to attain and well worth pursuing. It will not only enhance the quality of the relationship for your partner; through your example, it will also most likely encourage reciprocal responses to your disclosures as well.

Chapter Summary

This chapter deals with the concept of intimacy from the perspective of natural highs. Caring and close relationships are viewed as instrumental in orchestrating thoughts, feelings, and behaviors toward happiness and fulfillment for the individual, for his or her partner, and for society at large. Three forms of love are articulated: love for our caregivers, love for those who depend on us, and passionate desire.

Maslow (1954/1970) posited that human motives are hierarchically arranged. Near the top of the hierarchy is the need for *self-actualization*. The self-actualized individual is characterized by spontaneity, autonomy, sense of humor, and deep interpersonal relationships. Peterson and Seligman's core virtue of "humanity" is helpful in conceptualizing ideal human connections. Humanity is defined as "interpersonal strengths that involve tending and befriending others." Love is seen as the valuing of close relationships with others, especially those where sharing and caring are reciprocal, and being close to people.

Studies of human attachment show how people stay "on track" with their needs for love and belonging. Attachment is a process that may begin in utero and continue throughout one's life. It is the emotional link between an infant and a caregiver and it physically bonds people together over time. Bowlby identified certain styles of caregiving that resulted in secure or insecure patterns of attachment. Maladaptive parental behaviors include inconsistent attempts to meet the child's needs. Adaptive parenting is focused on responsiveness to the child's behavioral cues. Inconsistency in responding is associated with anxiety and frustration later in life, whereas consistency is associated with later development of contentment and trust.

Attachment theory has been extended to explore how adolescents relate to their peers and how adults relate to each other and to the children for whom they are caregivers. Kobak and Hazan found that secure attachment in adolescence and adulthood is related to more supportiveness and less rejection toward partners in tasks that require joint problem solving. Peterson and Seligman discovered that secure adolescents and adults handle life stresses better and are more able to develop lasting social ties that are characterized by trust and intimacy. These particular skills were found to be the best predictors of good psychological adjustment and physical health. Sternberg's triangular theory of love explains love as a mix of three primary factors: (1) passion, (2) intimacy, and (3) commitment. Consummate love, the most durable type, occurs when all three of the above components are highly present and are balanced across both partners.

Davila's concept of romantic competence (RC) refers to skills that enable healthy relationships. These are insight, mutuality, and emotion regulation. Her research has linked RC to greater relationship satisfaction as well as other positive relationship outcomes. In the future, RC may be taught to adolescents or young adults as a way of empowering them in forming healthy relationships.

Regarding the relationship between intimacy and sexuality, when emotional intimacy fails to develop or is purposely avoided, sex often becomes merely goal-oriented. Masters and Johnson state that couples can achieve intimacy and conflict resolution by using the principles of neutrality and mutuality. Neutrality means that each partner respects the good intentions of the other and trusts that those intentions are genuine and sincere. The principle of mutuality defines the sexual interaction between two persons. All words and actions should occur in the spirit of working toward mutual well-being.

Whether sexual or platonic, healthy intimacy is based on reconciliation of two fundamental human needs: belonging and individuality. Needs for intimacy and closeness and needs for individuality and separateness are often in conflict. A healthy balance of closeness and separateness in relationships is central to forming mature and healthy relationships, predicated on a foundation of secure attachment.

Finally, positive psychologists have focused on identifying elements of highly successful relationships and what skills can be taught to partners to optimize their interpersonal connections. Three interrelated constructs have emerged: (1) minding relationships, (2) creating a culture of appreciation, and (3) capitalizing on positive events. Those who learn and practice these relationship skills have been shown to experience increased intimacy and overall satisfaction from their most cherished relationships.

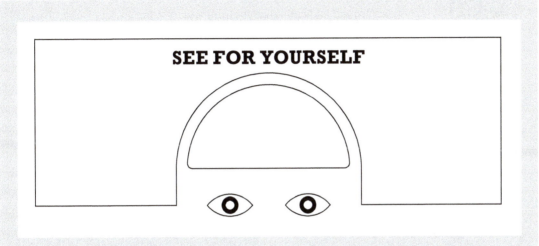

SEE FOR YOURSELF

Joanne Davila, a clinical psychologist, promotes skills for healthy romantic relationships in this TEDx talk:

https://www.youtube.com/watch?v=gh5VhaicC6g

Helen Fisher: Why we love, why we cheat. 2006. Helen Fisher. TED Talks. 23:27

Anthropologist Helen Fisher discusses love in relation to brain systems, evolution, and contemporary social trends. **https://www.ted.com/talks/helen_fisher_tells_us_why_we_love_cheat**

Everything you think you know about addiction is wrong. 2015. Johann Hari. TED Talks. 14:35

 Johann Hari, author of *Chasing the Scream: The First and Last Days of the War on Drugs,* posits that "the opposite of addiction is not sobriety; the opposite of addiction is connection." Hari discusses the mindsets and policies around addiction that contribute to isolating addicts, rather than providing access to the support and meaningful connections that are essential for recovery. **https://www.ted.com/talks/johann_hari_everything_you_think_you_know_about_addiction_is_wrong**

Mary Ainsworth: Attachment and the Growth of Love. 2005. Davidson Films. 37:35

 This film reviews Mary Ainsworth's research on attachment and love. The piece includes narration by Bob Marvin and discussion of Ainsworth's influences, research methodologies, findings, and legacy. **https://youtu.be/yxAwOv7BPFY**

CHAPTER 21

Relaxation, Mindfulness, and Meditation

Now, there are about 20,000 moments of 3 seconds in a 16-hour day, so this is what life consists of; it consists of a sequence of moments. Each of these moments is actually very rich in experience, so if you could stop somebody and ask, "What is happening to you right now?" a great deal is happening to us at any one of these moments. There is a goal, there is a mental content, there is a physical state, there is a mood, there might be some emotional arousal. Many things are happening. And then you might ask, "What happens to these moments?"

—Daniel Kahneman, Nobel Laureate

Wherever you go, there you are.

—Jon Kabat-Zinn

Introduction: The Trouble with You is You Think Too Much!

Consider this passage from an article entitled "The Thinking Mind as Addiction: Mindfulness as Antidote":

> Addiction is a great metaphor for how we suffer. Seeking pleasure and avoiding pain are natural and hard-wired into the primitive part of the brain so that we can survive as a species and procreate. However, as human beings, we have the mental capacity to vastly complicate our physical, instinctual, and emotional experience with our *thinking* mind which cognizes all of the real and perceived

data, devaluates, judges, compares, concludes, and reacts to its own productions as if they were true. Then, because our lives can be so difficult, overwhelming, and despairing, we become attached to food, drugs, alcohol, gambling, sex, shopping, entertainment, and an infinite array of misused behaviors, thoughts, patterns, and means of protection to make our own lives more tolerable or workable.

Peltz and Black, 2014

Figure 21.1 Mindfulness and Stress Management The premise of this chapter is that through learning skills to develop a nonjudgmental attention to stimuli in the internal and external environments, the human stress response is diminished, resulting in improved mental and physical health and a more positive state of mind.

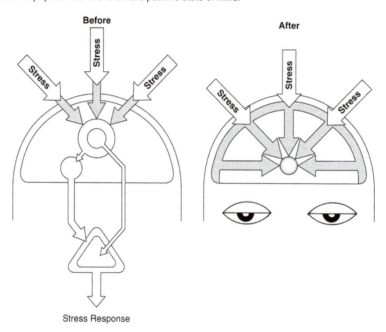

Peltz and Black go on to suggest that thinking itself can be an addiction. The goal with meditative practices is for people to be able to not always believe their own thoughts, and sometimes, to get away from thinking at all for a while. In the words of Jon Kabat-Zinn, we need to "replace thinking with 'awarenessing'" (Google Talk—check this out in See for Yourself).

This chapter begins with an exploration of the basics and a brief history of meditative practices and then moves more specifically into the use of mindfulness-based practices. Meditation appears to be gaining popularity in recent years, with 8% of adults in the U.S. practicing it, according to the National Health Interview Survey (Clarke, Black, Stussman, Barnes, & Nahin, 2015, reported by the National Center for Complementary and Integrative Health). There is a growing body of data that support the benefit of these practices, and not just for people who are suffering from physical disease, psychological disease, or addiction. As you will soon discover, engaging in mindfulness has been shown to boost brain function and enhance quality of life. Towards the end of the chapter, we address how specific forms of mindfulness-based intervention have been developed to help those with substance abuse and addiction issues.

Meditation Comes of Age

By learning techniques for being "in the present," we gain the invaluable opportunity to live life more fully and with increased novelty; diminished stress; greater empathy; fewer value judgments; and a deeper sense of beauty, contentment, and meaning. Today there is an abundance of scientific research on how meditative, self-calming skills can improve physical and mental health (e.g., Oman, Hedberg, & Thoresen, 2006; Parks & Marlatt, 2006; Perez-De-Albeniz & Holmes, 2000; Rausch, Gramling, & Auerbach, 2006; Shigaki, Glass, & Schopp, 2006). In addition, meditation has become a widespread practice throughout Western culture.

Benson's (1975, 1984, 1989, 2000) pioneering work brought meditative practice, formerly regarded by Western health practitioners as "new age" or religiously based, into the domain of respected medical, psychiatric, and psychological interventions.

Increasing Personal Calm (Just Breathe)

- 44% of Americans feel more stressed than they did 5 years ago.

- 1 in 5 Americans experience extreme stress—shaking, heart palpitations, depression.

- Work stress causes 10% of strokes. 60% increase in productivity over the past 20 years plus stagnant wages—working harder for less.

- Stress is the basic cause of 60% of all human illness and disease. 3 out of 4 doctor's visits are for stress-related ailments.

- Stress increases the risk of: heart disease by 40%, heart attack by 25%, and stroke by 50%.

- 40% of stressed people overeat or eat unhealthy foods.

- 44% lose sleep every night.

- Stress shrinks the brain. Extreme stress events (i.e., divorce, job loss) reduce grey matter in regions tied to emotion and physiological functions which can lead to future psychiatric problems.

- Stress-related ailments cost the nation $300 billion every year in medical bills and lost productivity, $100 billion more than what obesity costs Americans. (The American Institute of Stress, n.d.)

After completing medical training in cardiology, Benson, now director emeritus of the Benson-Henry Institute for Mind Body Medicine, became interested in how the mind affects the body, and particularly how high blood pressure might be influenced by emotional states. Benson was trying to gather scientific evidence for what had long been assumed in medical circles: that there is a positive correlation between stress and cardiovascular disease, and, further, that relaxation training could diminish the harmful effects of environmental threat. Colloquial expressions supporting his notion were commonplace: "Keep your cool—your blood pressure will go up;" "Don't get excited—you'll develop hypertension." In the late 1960s, Benson and his colleagues (Benson, 1975; Benson, Greenwood, & Klemchuk, 1975) were able to show that certain environmental influences could, in fact, raise or lower blood pressure in a group of laboratory monkeys. Further, the monkeys could be trained to increase or decrease their blood pressure on cue. One day, a group of young people came in to see Benson with a soft-spoken challenge: "Why are you fooling around with monkeys? Why don't you study us? We practice Transcendental Meditation."

Benson, acting in his role as Harvard scientist, tried to dissuade the group. But they persisted. Finally, he decided that little would be lost by seeing whether or not there might be physiological changes attendant to the practice of Transcendental Meditation (TM). He and his colleagues brought healthy volunteers to the laboratory and had them sit for an entire hour, getting used to the instruments that would measure oxygen consumption (an index of the body's total metabolism) and carbon dioxide elimination (the amount of waste product that parallels oxygen usage). Measurements were taken in three 20-minute intervals corresponding to (1) premeditation; (2) meditation—during which the subjects changed neither their posture nor their activity, only what they were thinking about; and (3) post meditation—wherein participants were instructed to go back to their regular mode of thinking (Benson, 1975, 2000).

Benson (1975, 2000) found a 16% to 17% decrease in oxygen consumption, with a parallel decrease in the amount of carbon dioxide elimination. This meant that by simply changing their thoughts, meditators could induce a significant change in their body's overall metabolism (i.e., they self-induced a hypometabolic state). The fact that the ratio of oxygen to carbon dioxide remained constant between the premeditation and meditation conditions showed that the meditators were neither breathing rapidly nor holding their breath to bring about the observed physiological changes. There was a true decrease in the overall amount of oxygen being used by the body. Correspondingly, during the meditation interval, there was a decrease of about 2 or 3 breaths per minute (dropping from 13 or 14 breaths per minute to about 11 breaths). Subsequently, while studying advanced meditators in India, Benson and his colleagues (1982) were able to document respiratory rates as low as zero to one breath per minute for 3 to 4 minutes on end; the advanced meditators could so quiet their overall metabolism that they could, in effect, stop breathing. Further, there was no change in the arterial concentration of oxygen. The cells were getting enough oxygen; they were simply using less. There was also a precipitous fall in arterial blood lactate, high levels of which are associated with stress, anxiety, or disquietude and low levels with peace and tranquility (Benson, 1975, 2000; Benson, Steinert, Greenwood, Klemchuk, & Peterson, 1975).

To his amazement, Benson (2000; Benson et al., 1982) documented some of the lowest levels of human metabolic activity ever recorded. At the time, there were only two physiological states known to cause these kinds of changes: sleep and hibernation.

A hibernating animal shows a decrease in rectal temperature of 2 to 3 degrees, whereas a sleeping animal shows a change of only 0.2 to 0.3 degrees. According to Benson (1989), after sneaking into the den of some Alaskan grizzly bears and finding the animals sleeping while sitting up, two intrepid physiologists placed several quarts of maraschino cherries in front of one bear, which naturally, because of its love of sweet fruit, leaned forward. The investigators, taking advantage of the postural tilt, proceeded to make their measurements. The bear awoke, was understandably irate, and chased the investigators, who miraculously escaped unharmed, data in hand (so to speak). In fact, bears do not hibernate—they sleep.

Under much less hazardous conditions Benson and his colleagues could show that meditation was not a hibernatory state. But the data could not be explained as a sleep state, either (Benson, Steinert, et al., 1975). The observed increase in alpha and theta wave frequencies of meditating participants was distinctly different from frequency rates measured during ordinary sleep. Benson suspected that the changes brought about through TM were the opposite of what had been described nearly three-quarters of a century earlier by Cannon (1915, 1929) as the *fight-or-flight* response. Cannon showed that stimulation of a region of the hypothalamus leads to a series of physiological changes resulting in a 300% to 400% increase in blood flowing to the muscles. But it made no sense to Benson to say that TM was the *only* way to bring about this reversed, anti-stress response. So he and his colleagues (Benson, 1975, 2000) dissected the TM instructions into two basic components: (1) the repetition of a word, sound, prayer, or muscular activity; and (2) the passive disregard of everyday thoughts when they come to mind.

By examining the religious and secular literatures of the world, Benson found that the same steps existed in virtually every culture (Benson, 1975, 1987). The earliest examples come from the Hindu scriptures—the Upanishads—dating back to the 7th and 8th centuries BC. It was written that to achieve a union with God, one should sit quietly, pay attention to one's breathing, and on each out-breath, repeat a word or phrase from the scriptures, the Vedas, or the Bhagavad Gita. When other thoughts came to mind, one should passively disregard them and come back to the repetition. In a similar manner today, Hindu worshippers can be heard chanting the words "Ohm, shanti, shanty," (God, peace, peace) while sitting in a meditative position.

Other examples from Judaism (dating back to roughly the 2nd century BC to the 1st century AD) and Christianity (early, middle, and late) allow us to trace the evolution of meditative techniques through prayers. To this day, there are hallowed Greek Byzantine monasteries espousing that people twice daily kneel quietly by themselves, pay attention to their breathing, and on each out-breath, say quietly to themselves, "Lord Jesus, have mercy" or "Lord Jesus, have mercy on us sinners." When other thoughts come to mind, the meditator is to passively disregard them and come back to the repetition.

The method of this whole process is called Hesychasm, traced back to Hesychius of Jerusalem, a 5th-century teacher of the uses of the Jesus prayer. Hesychius described prayer as "a spiritual art that releases one completely from passionate thoughts, words and evil deeds, and gives a 'sure knowledge of God the Incomprehensible'" (Goleman, 1988, p. 55). Hesychius described thoughts as "enemies who are bodiless and invisible, malicious and clever at harming us, skillful, nimble and practiced in warfare" (p. 55), who enter through the five senses. The idea is that a mind preoccupied with the senses or thought is distant from Jesus; one can be with him only by overcoming the lure of sensations and by attaining a silent mind. Followers are instructed to find a teacher who carries the spirit within him or her and to devote themselves to the master, obeying all commands.

Virtually the same instructions were given in 14th-century Judaism, where the mystical Kabbalistic tradition was evolving, and remarkably parallel traditions are found in Zen Buddhism, Shintoism, Taoism, and Confucianism—only the words are different. In the so-called primitive or shamanistic religions, people achieve similar states by chanting in time to the stamping of feet or the beating of drums—an echo of their heartbeats.

Benson (1987, 2000) has shown that the *relaxation response* can be viewed as an extraordinary tool for behavior change that can be used in any desired fashion. The method of elicitation, however, is critical. Practitioners select a personally meaningful word, sound, prayer, phrase, or muscular activity for repetition. When given a choice, most people will prefer prayer (e.g., the 23rd Psalm; Lord's Prayer; Hail Mary; or repetition of the Hebrew word for peace, "shalom"). Regular practitioners often report they have made contact with their Higher Power through this process. In effect, the relaxation response is a tailor-made method of complementing each individual's belief system.

> As a matter of fact, many patients say to me, "Thank you, doctor, for telling me to
> pray again. It's something that I've always wanted to do, but felt funny about. But

now that you as a doctor tell me about it, it's something that I'll do." You can then utilize that mind-opening effect brought about by the elicitation of the *Relaxation Response* to change behavior. If you wish the person to be more positive, simply have that individual read affirmations afterwards. It can be anything from Norman Vincent Peale to Robert Schuller, to statements of truth. If the person desires better health, have them think healthy thoughts about themselves. And this isn't just a thought, but these thoughts translate, insofar as mind can affect body, into physiologic change. This is what has been proposed, for example, by the Symingtons as a way of treating cancer. They first elicit the *Relaxation Response* through meditation, and then they visualize white cells in Pac-man fashion sort of chewing up cancer cells. Does that work? We don't know, but it is the same basic mind/body technology that they are utilizing. (Benson, 1989)

Benson (1987, 2000) recommends a series of steps for increasing calm and optimizing life experiences. The steps can be used to promote the development of an array of artistic and recreational skills consistent with one's sense of purpose and meaning. Readers are encouraged to explore how the relaxation response can serve as a physiological bridge to natural highs. By participating in these steps readers may not only develop a sense of inner peace, but also experience enhanced feelings of pleasure, because they are more attuned to dormant proclivities, interests, and abilities that may have been suppressed by inattention, anxiety, or stress. Table 21.1 presents the generic technique taught at the Benson-Henry Institute for eliciting the relaxation response.

Regular elicitation of the relaxation response has been scientifically proven to be an effective treatment for a wide range of stress-related disorders. In fact, to the extent that any disease is caused or made worse by stress, the relaxation response can help.

Table 21.1 Steps to Your Maximum Mind

The following is the generic technique taught at the Benson-Henry Institute:

1. Pick a focus word, short phrase, or prayer that is firmly rooted in your belief system, such as "one," "peace," "The Lord is my shepherd," "Hail Mary, full of grace," or "shalom."

2. Sit quietly in a comfortable position.

3. Close your eyes.

4. Relax your muscles, progressing from your feet to your calves, thighs, abdomen, shoulders, head, and neck.

5. Breathe slowly and naturally, and as you do, say your focus word, sound, phrase, or prayer silently to yourself as you exhale.

6. Assume a passive attitude. Don't worry about how well you're doing. When other thoughts come to mind, simply say to yourself, "Oh well," and gently return to your repetition.

7. Continue for 10 to 20 minutes.

8. Do not stand immediately. Continue sitting quietly for a minute or so, allowing other thoughts to return. Then open your eyes and sit for another minute before rising.

9. Practice the technique once or twice daily. Good times to do so are before breakfast and before dinner.

Source: Based on information from the Benson-Henry Institute for Mind Body Medicine (2006), http://www.mbmi.org/basics/whatis_rresponse_elicitation.asp (retrieved February 7, 2009).

Mindfulness

Benson's work on the relaxation response paved the way for exploration of a range of techniques designed to facilitate the attainment of positive emotional and behavioral experiences. The general practice of learning how to live positively in the moment, with a flexible awareness of what is and what can be, may be subsumed under the construct of *mindfulness.* Langer (2002) defines this construct in general terms:

> It is a flexible state of mind, openness to novelty, a process of actively drawing novel distinctions. When we are mindful we become sensitive to context and perspective; we are situated in the present. When we are mindless, we are trapped in rigid mindsets, oblivious to context or perspective. When we are mindless, our behavior is rule and routine governed. In contrast, when mindful, our behavior may be guided rather than governed by rules and routines. Mindfulness is not vigilance or attention when what is meant by those concepts is a stable focus on an object or an idea. When mindful, we are actively varying the stimulus field. (p. 214)

Snyder and Lopez (2007) offer what they refer to as a "nuts and bolts" definition of mindfulness, one that is used by the practicing community: "attending non-judgmentally to all stimuli in the internal and external environments" (p. 249). In moments of mindfulness, "positive psychological processes" are reported to enter consciousness (Snyder & Lopez, 2007). These include acceptance, patience, generosity, empathy, trust, gratitude, nonattachment, and gentleness (Shapiro, Schwartz, & Santerre, 2002).

From the definitions above, Benson's relaxation response and the cognitive-behavioral restructuring techniques detailed in Chapter 19 may be considered tools for the attainment of mindfulness. By freeing ourselves and taking distance from inflexible patterns of thought, we become open to a non-judgmental awareness of the here and now.

In addition, the principal strategy presented in Chapter 20 is referred to as "minding relationships" (i.e., being attuned to the ongoing stream of thoughts in a close or intimate relationship). In fact, a broad spectrum of meditative and relaxation techniques provides segues to a nonevaluative and present-centered state of consciousness.

We shall now consider *insight meditation* as another tool for the attainment of mindfulness. In *Insight Meditation: The Practice of Freedom,* J. Goldstein (1993) presents a commonsense rationale for the Buddhist approach to meditation and offers specific instructions for its incorporation into everyday life:

> The Buddha's teaching inspires the journey because he articulates so clearly where the path of practice [meditation] leads: to deeper levels of insight and freedom, to that purity and happiness of a mind-heart free from grasping, free from hatred, and free from ignorance. (p. 29)

When we consider the nature of our experience, it is clear that everything we do—whether related to work, family, relationships, or creativity—has some mental representation. Since much, if not all, human endeavor has its origins in our thoughts and feelings, then it would seem exceedingly worthwhile to understand the nature of our mind. The commitment to comprehend more about our own mental processes is at the core of Buddhist meditation.

One of the most obvious facts about the human psyche is that it is not static or fixed. Rather, our ideas, feelings, and fantasies are in a continuous state of evolution and flux. Also, our perceptions—the interpretations we assign to the objects and events in our midst—are colored by emotions. When we feel anger, our consciousness or awareness is tainted by hostility. When we feel love or compassion, there is increased likelihood of benevolence toward others and a positive explanation concerning events in our lives. Meditation aims to clarify the mental conditions that are associated with increased tightness, suffering, or pain, versus the qualities that lead to greater openness, ease, and well-being. But how should one choose from the array of meditative traditions and relaxation practices in the self-help marketplace (e.g., Benson's relaxation response vs. Goldstein's insight meditation)? An ancient Persian story helps to resolve this dilemma.

ANCIENT PARABLE: Finding Truth

The Mullah Nasrudin is a mythical Sufi teaching figure about whom there are hundreds of legends. Nasrudin is half crazy, half saint; half wise man, half fool. One day, a friend came to borrow a donkey and Nasrudin said, "I'm sorry, the donkey isn't here; I don't have it; I can't lend it to you." Just at that moment, when Nasrudin was speaking about not having the donkey, the donkey, which was outside the window, began to bray. The friend became increasingly angry and said, "How can you tell me you don't have the donkey? I hear it outside the window!" And Nasrudin, in turn, became very offended and said, "Well, who are you going to believe—me or the donkey?"

Buddha gave a very definitive answer to this question. "Don't believe anybody," he said. "Don't believe the books or the teachers and don't believe me." He advocated looking into our own mind and investigating the factors that seem conducive to greed, hatred, and delusion. These things are to be abandoned. Buddha taught that we should attend to and develop whatever actions of mind, body, and speech cultivate greater understanding and compassion.

Thus, according to J. Goldstein (1993), the practice of insight meditation is a matter of taking on personal responsibility for understanding the basis or purpose of our actions—for having insight. It has little or nothing to do with dogma, ritual, or religious conviction.

As a prerequisite for gaining insight—deeper understanding and a sense of purpose—one should cultivate "mindfulness," the skill of being able to attend to what is happening in each moment. Although the directive seems quite simple—to pay attention to what is happening in each instant (like now)—it's actually quite difficult to do. A cornerstone of Buddhist teaching is the delineation of succinct practice techniques to develop the quality of awareness. Practitioners are instructed to begin with the most tangible way of cultivating a strong, well-focused attention: "Be mindful of the body." What aspect of ourselves could be more accessible than the sensations that emanate from our own physical processes, particularly the act of breathing?

Concentration on breathing develops the skill to recognize when the mind is wandering or going off—that is, losing the quality of attentiveness. It also promotes a sense of relaxation. As described earlier in the discussion of Benson's relaxation response, Buddhist meditators also report increased calm and feelings of well-being. As a matter of fact, breathing awareness is also used as a means for stress reduction or relaxation, quite apart from any meditative practice. Yet whether the technique is introduced by a mental health counselor, medical adviser, or spiritual leader, the benefits of observing our breathing while detaching ourselves from everyday thoughts are quite similar.

Beginning meditators may, however, quickly lose interest in just attending to routine activities such as breathing. However, when we consider the consequences of not being able to breathe—someone holding our head under water, for example—breathing quickly becomes our number one priority. Practitioners are reminded that in a very literal way, every breath we take is vital to sustaining our life. Not all environmentalists may be Buddhists, but Buddha would have had no objections to their campaign for clean air.

Another aspect of mindfulness of the body is paying attention to every little thing we do: standing up, sitting down, making tea, opening the door, working at our job. A tremendous conservation of energy occurs when we develop the skill to bring our attention back to the simple movements we make throughout the day. How often do we become needlessly lost in thinking, fantasizing, or planning about some event that never takes place? As Mark Twain quipped, "I've had a lot of problems in my life, but most of them never happened." Much of our worrisome rumination is not useful—the mind, by habit, just seems to go on and on. By coming back to the simple movements of the body, we can resume concentration on the moment.

Here is a popular Zen story that illustrates this point:

> It seems this one person had been practicing meditation for a very long time, and he had some great insight. He was sitting in meditation and this cosmic insight unfolded, and he thought he understood the truth of things. Very excited, he went running up to his teacher, who lived in another hut in the forest. It was raining out. Before he went in to visit his teacher, he left his shoes and umbrella outside. He went in and he bowed down to his teacher, all excited about his insight. And his Zen master simply asked him, "On which side of your shoes did you leave your umbrella?" He couldn't remember. And the Master sent him back for 10 more years of practice.

The first half of meditation practice is learning to be aware. Few of us have the opportunity to devote our lives to pure meditation. How can we Westerners daily incorporate meditation into our busy lives? We have to commit to applying the practice to our everyday activities—by noting on which side of our shoes we left our umbrella. One important benefit of increasing mindfulness of our bodies, particularly while sitting, is that we become keenly aware of the tension we carry. We usually remain unaware of this stress and therefore don't release it. By increasing the awareness of our breathing, we take greater notice of the body's condition. When we become aware of the tension, rather than fighting it, we begin to release it. We let go, and stress-related illness begins to reverse its course. There is an abundance of stories from meditation centers in Thailand and Burma about very severe organic diseases actually being cured through the practice of meditation.

Perception of one's mind—thoughts, emotions, feelings—is also increased. While the brain is constantly engaged in thinking—judging, remembering, planning, evaluating, processing sensory input—we spend very little time cognizant of our thoughts; that is, we leave our brain on "automatic pilot." Like a high-flying kite, our mind is often carried astray by random gusts of thought. How often in a day do we get distracted by a thought and get lost in a daydream? Many times these so-called stray thoughts are a learned pattern or reaction to past experiences and cause us to react reflexively, not purposefully. How often do we get carried away by thoughts about our mother, father, lover, or children that have absolutely no basis in reality? *The thought of your mother is not your mother.*

Meditation allows us to explore the nature of thought and how it drives us. By increasing awareness of our thoughts, we can more easily recognize the motivation for the thought, and we can choose to act—rather than react—accordingly. Similarly, we can become more attuned to our emotions. As with thought, it is possible to observe emotions as they arise. We become more accepting and experience them on a more cognitive plane. Because we are able to filter out the "white noise" of our emotions, we can bring about increased personal calm and balance behavior, thoughts, and feelings.

The second half of meditative practice is observing the nature of all these insights, emotions, thoughts, and breaths. The one constant that binds all of these elements together is change. Life is not static or fixed, and neither are we. The greater our understanding of the nature of change, the greater our ability to let go and adapt. One of Buddha's teachings is that we cause suffering in our lives when there's attachment in the mind, because all things change. Buddhists teach their children, before they even enter grade school, that all people at some time must get old, get sick, and die.

A familiar metaphor for teaching the value of detachment describes a monkey trap widely used in Asia.

> A hollowed-out coconut with a small hole in the bottom is attached to a tree. A sweet is placed inside the coconut. A monkey comes along, slips its hand in, and grasps the sweet. The hole is big enough for the monkey to slip its hand in when the monkey's hand is open, but not large enough to allow the monkey to withdraw its hand when the hand is closed. Thus, the monkey is ensnared by its own greed and attachment. It is an extremely rare monkey that will open its hand, release the sweet, and thus extricate itself.

We humans place ourselves in the same predicament. We are trapped by our own attachments. We refuse to acknowledge that we are the cause of our suffering, and we place the blame on external causes. It takes a great deal of sensitivity and openness to accept our responsibility and learn how to release it. When we are successful, our bodies, minds, and lives become more harmonious and free.

> For twenty-five hundred years the practices and teachings of Buddhism have offered a systematic way to see clearly and live wisely. They have offered a way to discover liberation within our own bodies and minds, in the midst of this very world. (Kornfield, 2004, p. x)

As shown in Table 21.2, J. Goldstein (1993) provides the instructions for insight meditation.

Table 21.2 Goldstein's Instructions for Insight Meditation

- Sit fairly still and stable. Frequent changes of position break the concentration. If you become very uncomfortable and painful, shift, but for the most part try to sit as still as possible. Arrange your hands in any comfortable position, either on your knees or in your lap.

- Let your eyes close gently and softly. Take a few deep breaths to connect yourself with the breathing. Begin to feel the rise and fall of the abdomen that happens with each breath. When you breathe in, there's a rising moving of the abdomen, an expansion. When you breathe out there's a natural falling or contraction. Focus your awareness on that movement, feeling the sensations of the rising movement, and the falling movement. Be aware of the movement—from the very beginning, to the middle, and end of the falling movement.

- Don't rush or force the breathing in any way. Let the rising and falling happen in its own time. See how subtle and careful your awareness and attention can be.

- Make a soft mental note of rising at the beginning of the rising movement, and a soft mental note of falling at the beginning of the falling movement. Just a soft whisper in the mind. The words "rising" … "falling" …

- If sounds become distracting and call your attention away from the rising and falling, make a note of hearing, focusing your attention just on the vibration of the sound. Make the note "hearing," "hearing," without thinking of the cause of the sounds, just experiencing the actual phenomenon of hearing, and then return again to the rising and falling.

- Let the sounds simply arise and pass away, noting "hearing" when they are distracting and calling your attention, and returning in a very careful and subtle way to the rising and falling of the abdomen.

- If any sensations in the body become predominant—tightness, pressure, aching, vibration, tingling, itching—make a note of the particular sensation, observing it carefully. Observe what happens to it as you notice. Does it get stronger? Does it get weaker? Does it disappear?

- And again, return to the rising and falling. See how carefully you can feel each breath, making the soft note of "rising" and "falling," and if sounds distract you, calling your attention away, make a note of "hearing." And return to the rising and falling.

- If there are any strong sensations in the body that are more predominant than the breath, make a note of the sensation, feeling it, observing it, and noticing what happens as you note it. Does it get stronger? Does it get weaker? How does it change? And return to the rising and falling.

- Whenever you become aware of a thought in the mind, make a note of "thinking," trying to notice as close to the beginning as possible. Observe what happens to the thought as you note it. Does it continue? Does it disappear?

- Keep the mind alert and wakeful, noting in each moment the rise and fall of the breath, or hearing, or sensations in the body, or thinking—aware in each moment of the predominant object.

- See how carefully you can feel each breath: the entire movement of the rising, the entire movement of the falling.

- As soon as you are aware that the mind is wandering, make a note of "thinking," observe what happens to the thought as you note it, come back to the breathing.

- And if there is any strong mind state or emotion—of boredom, of interest, happiness, sadness, anger, fear, compassion—if any strong emotion should arise, that also should be noted. Feel it, be aware of it, and return again to the breath.

- Feel each rising and falling carefully and accurately, making the soft mental note.

- Make a note of any strong, predominant sensation in the body that may call your attention away from the breathing.

- If there are any images or pictures in the mind, make a note of "seeing;" observe what happens to the picture or image as you note it; then return to the rise and fall.

- Keep your attention on the breath, on any sounds which may become predominant, or any sensations, noting also images as they may come to mind, keeping the mind wakeful and alert in each moment, seeing all phenomena arising and passing away.

Source: Adapted from Goldstein, J. (1993). Insight meditation: The practice of freedom. Boston: Shambhala Publications, p. 34.

Process Meditation

Another, perhaps more active and deliberate, approach to accessing critical aspects of the mind is Progoff's (1975, 1980) *Process Meditation*. His technique of "intensive journal writing" is designed for becoming actively involved in discovering the movement and meaning of your life. Distinctly different from a diary, Progoff's method provides a multilevel feedback system that integrates conscious and unconscious fantasies, gently unfolding the meaning and purpose of one's life. As Progoff (1975) puts it,

> *Process Meditation* enables us to work actively and systematically at this inner level, reaching toward an experience both of personal meaning and of a meaning in life that is more than personal. ... The practice of Process Meditation makes it possible to work tangibly with the dimension of spiritual meaning in the specifics of our individual life history. (p. 9)

Readers are invited to adopt the guidelines, as shown in Table 21.3, for utilizing the amazing gift of fantasy to improve self-understanding and personal intimacy—in Progoff's (1975) words,

> Our workbook becomes a place where a person's private intimations of meaning can be articulated, respected, and explored. More important even than the basic fact of acknowledging our spiritual feelings and treating them as realities, our method gives us a means of working with them in tangible ways so that their intimations of truth can be nurtured, can be considered, altered, or brought to further development. (p. 273)

According to Anaïs Nin (quoted in Kaiser, 2001), a diarist who logged more than 150,000 pages, "The lack of intimacy with one's self and consequently with others is what created the loneliest and most alienated people in the world." In recognition of intimacy as a basic human need, we have dedicated an entire section of this book (Section V) to the topic of "Craving for Intimacy."

Table 21.3 The Way of the Journal

- Where are you right now in your life? Form an image.

- Recapitulations and Remembering—Quick, significant scenes in our lives.

- Stepping Stones—Note important events or people captured in a word or two or an image.

- Intersections—Describe roads taken and not taken.

- Twilight Imagery—Turn your attention inward and wait in stillness, letting yourself observe the various forms of imagery that present themselves.

- Dialogue Dimension—Engage in imaginary conversations with some of the significant people already listed in the Stepping Stones section. Go through a short Stepping Stone exercise for the "other." After the exercise, reread what you have written and write down how you feel.

Source: Adapted from "The way of the journal," by B. Kaiser, 1981, March, Psychology Today.

Meditation as Treatment

In 1974, the late Tibetan teacher Chögyam Trungpa predicted that "Buddhism will come to the West as a psychology." And indeed, it has! There are now several forms of meditation-based therapies, specifically designed to treat psychological conditions. Mindfulness-Based Stress Reduction (MBSR) was developed by Jon Kabat-Zinn (Kabat-Zinn, Lipworth, & Burney, 1985) at Harvard. This is a standardized, 8-week program that involves a 2.5- to 3-hour session once per week and a 6-hour "retreat" session on the Saturday of the 6th week. The program has a manual, and instructors go through training and certification to teach classes. MBSR was originally developed as an alternative treatment for patients who were not benefiting much (if at all) from standard medical treatment. One of the goals is to help ameliorate anxiety and depression associated with chronic illness. It is also intended to help chronic pain patients psychologically deal with their pain. Unlike traditional meditation practices, religious tenets are not included—mindfulness meditation is a secular practice.

Other mindfulness-based interventions soon followed. A specific incarnation of mindfulness meditation, packaged as an 8-week program geared towards preventing depression relapse, emerged with Mindfulness-Based Cognitive Therapy (MBCT) (Segal, Teasdale, & Williams, 2004). Acceptance and Commitment Therapy (ACT, pronounced "act") is a bit more free-form in that it isn't delivered in a manualized program (Hayes, Strosahl, & Wilson, 1999); it is intended to be used with a wide variety of different conditions. Dialectical Behavior Therapy (DBT; Linehan, Armstrong, Suarez, Allmon, & Heard, 1991) also has wide-reaching applications, including borderline personality disorder, eating disorders, and substance use disorders (more on substance use applications forthcoming).

That mindfulness techniques can be effectively married with cognitive therapy should not be surprising. Shigaki et al. (2006) consider mindfulness a form of cognitive therapy in that both techniques focus on directing the client's attention toward improvements in managing harm-generating thoughts and reducing autonomic responses. While traditional cognitive therapy teaches the replacement of maladaptive thoughts with more adaptive ones, mindfulness focuses on one's *approach to thinking*, that is, "emphasizing the awareness of thoughts, appreciation for the transient nature of thoughts, and developing tolerance for observing one's own thoughts and feelings" (Segal et al., 2002, quoted in Shigaki et al., 2006, p. 210). These authors liken "mindfulness" to exposure and desensitization techniques. Through mindfulness, one is given the opportunity to observe thoughts, emotions, and the physical sensations as they occur and without catastrophic consequences. Meditation may allow for exposure and desensitization to "catastrophizing," which may improve adaptive coping styles with issues such as chronic pain and substance abuse.

Oman et al. (2006) evaluated an 8-week, 2-hour per week training for physicians, nurses, chaplains, and other health professionals using nonsectarian, spiritually based self-management tools based on passage meditation. Their Eight-Point Program (EPP) for stress management is outlined below:

- Passage meditation for 30 minutes each morning, which includes the silent repetition in one's mind of memorized inspirational passages (23rd Psalm, Prayer of St. Francis, or Discourse on Goodwill of the Buddha's Sutta Nipata)
- Repetition of a holy word or mantra

- Slowing down, setting priorities, and reducing stress and friction caused by rushing
- Focused attention to the matter at hand
- Training the senses to overcome conditioned habits and learning to enjoy what is beneficial
- Putting others first and gaining freedom from selfishness and separateness; finding joy in helping others
- Spiritual association with others who follow the same program for mutual inspiration and support
- Inspirational reading from scriptures of all religions to draw upon the writings by and about great spiritual figures

Beneficial treatment effects were observed on stress and mental health. When subjects adhered to the study's meditative practices, stress reductions remained large at 19 weeks. The authors concluded that this program reduces stress and may enhance mental health.

Does Meditation Work?

One of the criticisms that has been lodged at mindfulness meditation (see A Word of Caution below) is that we don't know how it works. A more comprehensive question is, "does meditation work, and (if so) why?"

Before tackling these questions, we must first consider what it would mean for meditation to have an effect. Proponents of meditation suggest that possible outcomes could include: (1) improved physical and/or psychological health and well-being; and (2) improved cognitive abilities (attention, memory, executive functions). With those goals in mind, recognize that, although there is an ever-growing mountain of data related to meditation practices, "the findings are often difficult to interpret," according to Davidson and Kaszniak (2015, pg. 582). They discuss a variety of reasons for this quandary, many of which are tied to research design and methodology. For instance, meditation and mindfulness interventions cannot be administered in a blind fashion, and outcome measures are often self-reported. This leaves open the possibility of participant biases influencing the results. It's also difficult to know what the appropriate control (comparison) condition should be. But, with those caveats in mind, let's try to discern if meditation works.

Effects on Physical and Psychological Health and Well-being

Meditation is believed to improve one's sense of physical and psychological well-being. Perez-De-Albeniz and Holmes (2000) report that the physiological effects of meditation include the following:

- Increased cardiac output
- Slower heart rate
- Muscle relaxation
- Decreased renal and hepatic blood flow
- Increased cerebral flow
- Decreased respiratory frequency

- Significantly decreased sensitivity to ambient carbon dioxide

- Less oxygen consumption

- Increased skin galvanic resistance

- Decreased spontaneous electrodermal response

- EEG synchrony with increased intensity of slow alpha in central and frontal regions, and increased theta waves in frontal areas of the brain

- Enhancement of brain stem auditory evoked response, increased alpha and beta coherence

- A shift in hemispheric dominance with greater activation of the centers in the right hemisphere

Goyal and colleagues (2014) published a meta-analysis that ultimately included 47 trials testing either mindfulness meditation or mantra/TM. Their inclusion criteria for their review article required that the studies in their meta-analysis have a control condition that was "matched for time and attention to the intervention group" in order to have a proper comparison (pg. 358). Consequently, an original sample of over 1,600 journal articles got whittled down to a mere 47 that met inclusion criteria, limiting the number of studies that were summarized in their analysis. *Overall, their analysis demonstrated moderate evidence for improving anxiety, depression, and pain.* Their analysis more often associates positive effects with *mindfulness meditation* rather than mantra/TM.

The authors also state that the current evidence *does not show meditation programs to be better than drug, exercise, or behavioral therapies.* This meta-analysis strongly highlights the need for higher-quality research design in this area so that medical doctors who might be asked by their patients if meditation is recommended for them can discern whether effects are real (e.g., not a placebo effect or due to time or other factors). Nonetheless, given that there are demonstrated effects for mindfulness meditation, patients may prefer trying this approach over medication and exercise, or in combination with those other approaches.

Effects on Cognitive Functions

A meta-analysis by Lao, Kissane, and Meadows (2016) found mixed results in terms of cognitive effects. One might be expecting such a review to include dozens of studies. However, because meditation can be delivered in so many ways—an obvious source of variance in results across studies—they specifically selected MBSR and MBCT studies that used 8-week mindfulness training and had neuropsychological measures as dependent variables in the study. Inclusion criteria also required that there was some form of a control (comparison) in the study. Only 18 studies met the criteria. On the one hand, Lao and colleagues concluded that there is preliminary evidence to show that mindfulness improved working memory, autobiographical memory, cognitive flexibility, and meta-awareness. (The qualification of "preliminary" is based on the small number of studies that tested these constructs). On the other hand, they found little support for effects on attention and executive function. Many caveats accompany their conclusions. Some of these include the lack of consistency in measures used across the studies and wide variability in the populations that were sampled—young, old, ill, healthy, etc. Perhaps it is possible—even to be expect-ed—that an 8-week course in and of itself may not be sufficient to yield statistically significant results; ongoing practice may be key in terms of reaping the full cognitive benefits that mindfulness meditation can bring. We will have to await further data (preferably with randomized, controlled designs) to allow firmer conclusions.

Neuroimaging data support brain changes related to meditation and mindfulness practices. For instance, a study by Kang et al. (2013) compared long-term meditators to a control group and found that the meditators had significantly thicker cortex in frontal and temporal lobe regions; these regions are associated with cognitive functions, including executive control and sustained attention. Such findings might leave us thinking that we have to practice meditation for long periods of time to see results. However, a recent meta-analysis (Gotink, Meijboom, Vernooj, Smits, & Hunink, 2016) suggests that even relatively short mindfulness interventions are sufficient: "After 8 weeks of MBSR training, participants demonstrated similar changes in the PFC [prefrontal cortex], the hippocampus, the insula and the cingulate cortex, associated with attention regulation, self-referential processing, and perspective taking, all stimulated in both long-term meditation and MBSR exercises" (pg. 39). Another meta-analysis on neuroimaging data (Tang, Tolzel, & Posner, 2015) reports that both structural and functional imaging data point to a link between mindfulness mediation and brain changes in regions associated with self-awareness, emotional regulation, and attentional processes. However, this review also highlights the need for better (more methodologically rigorous) studies before the neural mechanisms underlying these brain changes can be understood.

A final qualification about neuroimaging data as it relates to meditation: Fox and colleagues (2016) report that there are actually different patterns of activation (and deactivation) of brain regions across different varieties of meditation. While their meta-analysis shows that there is activation of frontal cortex regions, the insula, and portions of the cingulate cortex (i.e., regions related to self-awareness, attention, executive functions, etc.) across different imaging studies, "convergence is the exception rather than the rule" (pg. 1). In short: all types of meditation may not yield the same brain results.

The studies above address the issue of whether meditation can have positive effects—it can. But what about the "why" question: why are mindfulness and other meditation practices helpful for physical and psychological maladies? Here is our guess: decreasing stress levels should lower stress hormone levels, which in turn could boost immune function and growth factors in the brain. A recent study suggests this may be the case. Researchers studied participants at a 3-month retreat that included both yoga and mindfulness-based meditation. In addition to collecting self-report measures (an anxiety inventory) they also measured several biochemicals: cortisol, BDNF (brain-derived neurotrophic factor, a substance that promotes brain cell regeneration), and several blood markers associated with immune responses (pro- and anti-inflammatory chemicals). They found that higher BDNF levels were associated with lower anxiety scores. They also found changes in some of the immune markers. The cortisol data pointed to an enhanced awakening cortisol response; everyone should have a cortisol peak shortly after waking in the morning, but an enhanced cortisol awakening response may be more adaptive to homeostasis, according to the authors.

The bottom line: Clearly some people derive significant benefits from meditation. It is probably not a tool for everyone. Although some studies show that exercise and drug therapies may be as useful in alleviating emotional discomfort, it comes down to a matter of personal choice. What works for one individual may not be helpful to another. If exercise is your thing, do it. If you perceive benefits from mediation, do it! Or why not both?

Meditation and Hedonic Dependencies

Marlatt (2002), an iconic figure in psychological research and treatment for substance abuse, found meditation an invaluable tool for improving treatment outcomes. Marlatt saw how Buddhist philosophy provides a useful framework for addiction treatment. From the Buddhist perspective, "addiction represents 'a false refuge' from the pain and suffering of life" (p. 49). According to Marlatt, the Four Noble Truths of Buddha can be used to gain insight into the addict's experience and potential course of recovery.

First Noble Truth: "Suffering is ubiquitous" and is experienced in multiple ways including anxiety, pain, and misery in association with life changes or existence in general (Kumar, 2002). Engaging in drug use (or other forms of hedonic escape) constitutes a "false refuge," motivated by a desire or "craving" to avoid suffering. The pleasure addict is ignorant of the fact that, in the long run, continuation of addictive behavior prolongs and intensifies suffering rather than reducing pain.

Second Noble Truth: Suffering and pain, essential to all life experience, are caused by craving and attachment. Rather than viewing addiction as a physical disease, the affliction may be conceived as a "disease of the mind," characterized by an intense form of the attachment process, perpetuated by ignorance of the fact that addictive behavior is only a temporary or "false" refuge (Marlatt, 2002).

Third Noble Truth: Cessation of suffering is based on "the complete fading and extinction of this craving, its forsaking and abandonment, liberation from it, detachment from it" (Groves & Farmer, 1994, p. 186).

Fourth Noble Truth: This describes the Noble Eightfold Path leading toward enlightenment: right vision, conception, speech, conduct, livelihood, effort, mindfulness, and concentration (Kumar, 2002).

Meditation is viewed as

> a pathway from the heavy burden of addiction to the freedom of enlightenment. Ignorance can be replaced by a combination of "right conception or understanding" as to the true nature of addiction and the development of new coping skills (right conduct, or "skillful means"). As such the practice of meditation and following the *Eightfold Path* offers a clearer and distinctive alternative to the 12-steps approach and the disease model of addiction. (Marlatt, 2002, p. 46)

Parks and Marlatt (2006) recognized the use of Vipassana meditation (VM), a widely practiced Buddhist form of mindful meditation, as an alternative for individuals who had not succeeded with traditional addiction treatment. They assert that VM allows for an environment that is tolerant of a variety of religious beliefs, has flexible treatment goals, and involves less stigma than traditional treatment programs.

VM courses teach "mindfulness through objective, detached self-observation without reaction" (Parks & Marlatt, 2006, p. 343). Parks and Marlatt first studied the effectiveness of VM courses with adult male and female inmates at a minimum-security jail. Participants showed decreased alcohol-related problems and psychiatric problems and an increase in positive psychosocial outcomes. Three months after release, there was significantly less use of alcohol, marijuana, and crack cocaine, as well as fewer alcohol-related negative consequences. In addition, the former inmates reported lower levels of psychiatric symptoms, more internal alcohol-related locus of control, and higher levels of optimism.

Since Marlatt's initial study using meditation practices to treat individuals with substance use disorders, several other meditation-based approaches have been developed, some of them directly following along Kabat-Zinn's mindfulness meditation approach. These interventions are summarized in Table 21.4.

Table 21.4 Mindfulness-Based Interventions for Hedonic Dependencies

Treatment Approach	Features	Example
Acceptance & Commitment Therapy (ACT)	Accept reactions & be present; Choose a valued direction; Take action	Gifford et al. (2004): At one year follow-up ACT participants had better abstinence rates compared to clients on nicotine replacement
Mindfulness-Based Relapse Prevention (MBRP)	Combines CBT-based relapse prevention with mindfulness; Structured aftercare (to follow inpatient or intensive outpatient program)	Bowen et al. (2014): At one year follow-up MBRP participants had fewer days of use, less heavy drinking compared to relapse prevention and treatment as usual
Mindfulness-Oriented Recovery Enhancement (MORE)	Combines CBT with positive psychology principles and mindfulness; emphasizes savoring healthy experiences and reconnecting to natural rewards	Garland et al. (2017): Improved positive affect and decreased perception of pain compared to support group; decreased risk of misusing opioids post-treatment

At a very basic level, the application of mindfulness meditation to the issue of addiction seems to be a good fit because the process is intended to help the person deal with stress, a factor long known to trigger relapse. Teaching mindfulness to clients essentially provides them with skills for stress management that will hopefully benefit them well into the future. One of the skills is "urge surfing:" riding the wave of a craving without succumbing to the temptation to take the substance. As described by Houlihan and Brewer (2016), the participants learn to dissect the craving into its sensory parts, which might include "hot" or "tingly" or some other aspect. Focusing on the sensory components helps take the emphasis away from thinking about using. Participants learn that cravings pass if they wait them out. By learning to not act on them, the person works on breaking the urge-behavior (craving-using) connection in their brains.

Obviously, there are many similarities between mindfulness and cognitive-behavioral treatment. In evidence-based practice, CBT is the most widely utilized treatment modality for the sometimes independent, but usually intersecting, problems of substance abuse, mental disorder, and criminal conduct. Teasdale et al. (2002) draw some interesting distinctions between traditional CBT and CBT combined with a mindfulness training approach. Unlike CBT, where there is great emphasis on changing the contents of thoughts, mindfulness-based cognitive therapy (MBCT) teaches individuals to be more aware of thoughts and feelings and to relate to them with a more detached, broader perspective, as "mental events" that can be observed and not necessarily associated with accurate reflections of reality. The CBT model for growth and change, as discussed in Chapter 19, integrated with the mindfulness perspective, as presented here, are the mental underpinnings of our natural highs approach.

A Word of Caution

A 2015 article in *The Washington Post* provided a skeptical view of mindfulness meditation (Farias & Wikholm, 2015). Apart from mentioning the unknowns of mindfulness interventions—such as why it works, who is most likely to respond, and how long the effects will last—the authors criticize mindfulness meditation as something that has been sold to the public as an intervention with *only* positive results and no negative effects. The first two issues may be less concerning, given that interventions have been used in the past (e.g., lithium for bipolar disorder) without knowing how they work or who will best respond; the medication works for some and has made their lives much more manageable. Meanwhile, data have emerged that have addressed the "how" and "who" questions of lithium. Therefore, with further research on mindfulness, we may expect answers forthcoming regarding the "how", "who", and even "how long" questions.

Of greater concern, however, are the negative effects resulting from meditation practices. Some researchers addressed the phenomenon of meditation-related problems, even before the mindfulness craze hit full force in the 21st century (Craven, 1989; Kutz, Borysenko, and Benson, 1985; Lukoff, Lu, & Turner, 1998; Perez-De-Albeniz & Holmes, 2000; D.H. Shapiro, 1992), although these reports seem to have slipped under many people's radar. A review article by Lustyk, Chawla, Nolan, and Marlatt (2009), which Farias and Wikholm, 2015, link to their *Washington Post* article) compiles adverse reactions from 12 published reports on meditation (not all of which are mindfulness-based). The most commonly reported side effects are psychological in nature: depersonalization, derealization, disorientation, mania, psychotic symptoms (including hallucinations and delusions), cognitive problems (such as impaired judgement and insight), and emotional responses (e.g., depression, dysphoria, anxiety). Other negative reactions include insomnia, loss of appetite, increased risk of seizures, and perceptual distortions (double vision, sense of seeing things from outside of one's body). Some participants reported physical pain. One very rare individual attempted suicide. Lustyk et al. (2009) point out that the reports of psychotic behavior may be linked to extended meditation experiences, such as retreats that last multiple days. Some practices will put the participants into essentially sensory deprivation (where these is limited outside stimulation), sleep deprivation, or food deprivation states; this could potentially pose a trigger for aberrant reactions, including psychotic symptoms. Moreover, certain types of practices may not be appropriate for individuals with muscle or joint issues; people with arthritis might rightfully expect that sitting for long periods of time will aggravate symptoms. Although mindfulness programs do typically use mindful walking as one of the skills they teach, it is only a portion of the program. So, care must be taken in either selecting participants for research studies or for making recommendations about adoption of mindfulness as a treatment intervention. Lustyk and colleagues ultimately recommend that the risk of negative outcomes could be decreased through appropriate screening of participants and informed consent.

In some cases, adverse emotional reactions are linked to triggered memories that emerge during meditation. The following quotation by Perez-De-Albeniz and Holmes (2000) highlights the need for caution and guidance in managing some of the mental contents that may arise in relation to the meditative experience:

> Sobbing and hidden memories and themes from the past, such as incest, rejection, and abandonment appeared in intense, vivid forms. ... [However,] it is not uncommon to encounter a meditator who claims to have found "the answers" when in fact he has been actively engaged in a subtle [maneuver] of avoiding his basic questions. (p. 52)

Meditation has the potential to bring about serious side effects, even among long-term practitioners. The tendency of meditation to release unconscious material (e.g., Perez-De-Albeniz & Holmes, 2000) implies that the beginning meditator should approach the practice with moderation. Meditation, as with other need-gratifying activities discussed throughout this book, can slip over the line into hedonic dependency (see Chapter 1). However, by approaching time-proven and research-validated meditative techniques with respect and professional guidance, the odds are certainly in favor of positive mental and physical health outcomes.

Science-Based Relaxation Techniques

While the specific meditative techniques described above (i.e., relaxation response and insight meditation) have been of enormous value, a related and overlapping set of relaxation skills also have the potential to diminish stress and elicit some qualities of mindfulness. *Progressive muscle relaxation* (PMR), the most widely studied relaxation method, has been shown to reduce anxiety, decrease cortisol levels, reduce pain, and re-regulate physiological processes, thereby increasing the general quality of life (Rausch et al., 2006). Table 21.5 provides a summary of prominent science-based techniques for relaxation. In each case, there is an instruction to repetitiously focus on something outside the realm of ordinary thought, with passive disregard for intruding ideas or stimuli.

Managing Stress in the Here and Now

We have developed the acronym BRAIN to highlight five essential skills to diffuse stress in a myriad of provocative situations (e.g., problems at work, at home, in the community). The BRAIN formula integrates many of the techniques germane to the relaxation and meditative strategies discussed throughout this chapter.

B—*Breathing:* Concentrate on focusing your attention on the area of your body near your heart. Inhale deeply for about 5 seconds, imagining the breath flowing in through your heart. Then exhale for about 5 seconds, visualizing the breath flowing out from your solar plexus (the area in the center of your body just below the middle of your rib cage).

R—*Recognize and disengage:* Notice your mood and the physical signs of distress (e.g., knot in the stomach, raising the level of your voice, tenseness of muscles, flushing of face). Make a decision to "freeze the frame" of this discomfort, almost like pressing the pause button on your VCR, and then move on to a different experience—a bit like skipping over an e-mail that holds no interest for you.

A—*Ask yourself, "Is there a better alternative?"* Is there a different way of managing the situation without feeling angry, depressed, or guilty? What other thoughts might we use to replace those that are leading to uncomfortable emotions? Use self-talk skills: "Why am I angry? What can I do about it positively?" Discover what thoughts are causing the feelings, and then replace them with some of your positive thoughts.

I—*Invoke a positive feeling:* Focus on images that make you feel good. An example might be a walk in the woods, or laughing with some childhood friends on the playground, or being on top of your game in some sport that you have enjoyed.

N—*Note the change in perspective:* In a very quiet manner, notice any change in your mood, physical sensations, or negative thoughts. Maintain these positive changes as long as you can.

Source: Adapted from Cryer, B., McCraty, R., & Childre, D. (2003). Managing yourself: Pull the plug on stress. Harvard Business Review, 81(7), 102–107.

Table 21.5 Prominent Relaxation Techniques

Technique	Instruction
Progressive Muscle Relaxation (PMR)	The most extensive relaxation technique used today, this method involves the systematic focus of attention on the gross muscle groups throughout the body: "Actively tense each muscle group for a few seconds and then release the muscles and relax; for example, I want you to stop tensing, and simply concentrate on what these muscles feel like as you learn to relax." The sequence of tension release and attention is sequentially applied to the dominant hand and forearm; dominant upper arm; nondominant hand and forearm, forehead; eyes, nose, cheeks, and mouth; neck and throat; chest; back and respiratory muscles; abdomen; dominant upper leg, calf, and foot; nondominant upper leg, calf, and foot. Progression to each muscle group is predicated upon successful and complete relaxation of the prior group.
Calm Scene and Breathing	Imagine a personally calming scene: for example, peacefully walking on a beach with a toddler; watching a sunset; relaxing near a cool stream on a summer day. Breathe from your diaphragm, slow and steady, in and out for several minutes, focusing on the rising of the abdomen on the in-breath and the falling of the abdomen on the out-breath.
Deep Breathing	Beginning with normal breathing, slowly start to make each breath deeper until you have inhaled deeply five times. Inhale through the nose and exhale through the mouth, making a small opening through the lips and breathing out slowly. Return to normal breathing after five deep breaths.
Active Relaxation	Walk or jog 15 minutes each day. Vary your body posture; for example, swing your arms, and then put them behind your back, while reflecting on your positive state of mind. Work out a few times a week by playing a sport, swimming, or going to the gym.

Grounding	Turn attention to the outside world and focus on the here and now, not the past or future. Describe what is around you at this moment in time: for example, the chair is wood, the sky is blue, the breeze is cool.
Massage	Via the manipulation of soft tissues and muscles with massage, relaxation is produced, thereby relieving muscle aches and pain. Various massage techniques have developed based on cultural idioms. Examples include Swedish, reflexology, Rolfing, Hellerwork, Alexander technique, and Feldenkrais. Evidence shows that massage reduces anxiety scores in short-term care settings.
Freeze-Frame Technique	Conscious perception is like watching a movie, and we perceive each moment as an individual frame. When the so-called scene becomes stressful, the freeze-frame technique allows one to "freeze," or isolate, the perceptual frame so that one can observe it from a detached and objective view.

- Recognize and disengage, taking time out to temporarily retreat from thoughts and feelings, particularly stressful ones.
- Breathe through your heart, focusing breaths through the area of your solar plexus.
- Invoke positive feelings by making a sincere effort to be positive.
- Ask yourself if there is a better alternative and what would be an efficient, effective attitude or action in order to reduce stress.
- Note how your perspective has changed; sense your change in perception or feelings and sustain it as long as possible.

Source: Derived from Cryer, McCraty, & Childre (2003); Davidson & Schwartz (1976); Mamtani & Cimino (2002); Najavits (2006); Wanberg & Milkman (2006).

Mindfulness in Everyday Life

Advocates of mindfulness see it as a practice that should be engaged in regularly to promote everyday well-being rather than something only to be turned to when a person is dealing with illness, severe stress, or addiction. Our daily activities—from cooking to walking—provide opportunities to metaphorically close all of our browser windows and deal with "now." Although there's an absence of published literature on these topics, there are many activities that seem to fit with mindfulness: staring at the flames in a campfire, watching the ocean waves ebb and recede, minding your fishing line while you float on a lake, gazing at jellyfish undulating in an aquarium, or coloring in your adult coloring book. All of these promote focusing on the sensory aspects of the present moment and require nothing more of you than just being and experiencing. Carve out a portion of your day—maybe 20 minutes—to engage in a mindful activity, whether it is formal meditation or something else. See if you value being "off line" for a few minutes to clear your cache.

Chapter Summary

Meditation and other calming techniques are evidence-based means for stress reduction and improved quality of life. Using principles derived from ancient meditative practice, Benson's relaxation response is discussed as a Western prototype for the use of meditation as a technique to reduce stress and achieve a positive state of mind. By examining the religious and secular literatures of the world, Benson found that the same steps exist in virtually every culture.

1. The repetition of a word, sound, prayer, or muscular activity
2. The passive disregard of everyday thoughts when they come to mind

Those who practice Benson's relaxation response are instructed to select a personally meaningful focus word or phrase (aka mantra), followed by muscle relaxation and attention to their breathing. The focus word or phrase is repeated upon exhaling. The steps are used to promote the development of an array of artistic and recreational skills consistent with one's sense of purpose and meaning.

Based on Buddhist tradition, insight meditation presents an alternative pathway to peace of mind. By increasing awareness of our thoughts, we can more easily recognize the motivation for the thought, and we can *choose to act*—rather than react—accordingly. Similarly, we can become more attuned to our emotions. As with thought, it is possible to observe emotions as they arise. We become more accepting and experience them on a more cognitive plane, gaining freedom from actions based on transient feelings. The chapter further explains how Buddhist philosophy provides a useful framework for addiction treatment. From the Buddhist perspective, addiction represents a "false refuge" from the pain and suffering of life.

Another approach to accessing critical aspects of the mind is Progoff's process meditation technique of intensive journal writing. This technique provides a multilevel feedback system that integrates conscious and unconscious fantasies, gently stimulating insight into the meaning and purpose of one's life. Instructions are given for utilizing fantasy to improve self-understanding and personal intimacy.

Related forms of instruction are germane to other techniques for achieving relaxation or peace of mind. Progressive muscle relaxation (PMR), the most widely studied relaxation method, has been shown to reduce anxiety, decrease cortisol levels, reduce pain, and re-regulate physiological processes, thereby increasing the overall quality of life. A summary of prominent science-based techniques for relaxation shows that in each case there is an instruction to repetitiously focus on something outside the realm of ordinary thought, with passive disregard for intruding ideas or stimuli.

Research data from psychology and medicine support the use of meditation and relaxation exercises as important tools for improving health and one's overall sense of well-being. Meditation has been shown to improve memory; provide acceptance and tolerance of affect; increase happiness, joy, and positive thinking; increase confidence and productivity; improve problem-solving skills; enhance the acceptance of, compassion for, and tolerance of self and others; and improve relaxation, resilience, and the ability to control feelings. A growing body of data support the notion that meditation (especially mindfulness meditation) is linked to structural and functional brain changes in areas related to attention, self-awareness, executive functions, and emotional regulation.

Specific adaptations of mindfulness-based interventions have been applied to promoting recovery and preventing relapse in those struggling with substance abuse or addiction. Data support the notion that there is lower risk of relapse and less extreme relapse in those who have utilized mindfulness meditation as part of their treatment or post-treatment programming.

Meditation, like other need-gratifying activities, can cross the line into hedonic dependency. However, by approaching the discipline with preparation, respect, and professional guidance when needed, there is great likelihood that these time-honored strategies will result in improved states of physical and mental well-being, not only for the individual, but for society at large. We conclude this section with advice from the Dalai Lama:

We are visitors on this planet. We are here for ninety, a hundred years at the very most. During that period, we must try to do something good, something useful with our lives. Try to be at peace with yourself and help others share that peace. If you contribute to other people's happiness, you will find the true goal, the true meaning of life. (quoted in J. Goldstein, 1993, p. 160)

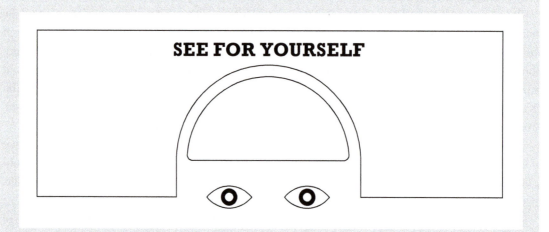

SEE FOR YOURSELF

Jon Kabat-Zinn: Guided Mindfulness.

Undergo a half hour of mindfulness meditation with Jon Kabat-Zinn in this Google talk. Note: the first 23 minutes serve as an introduction to mindfulness mediation, which is then followed by almost 30 minutes of guided mindfulness. During the last portion of the video, Kabat-Zinn addresses audience questions, including what he calls "the occupational hazard of mediation:" falling asleep. **https://www.youtube.com/watch?v=3nwwKbM_vJc**

All It Takes Is 10 Mindful Minutes. 2012. Andy Puddicombe. TED Talks. 9:24

Meditation expert Andy Puddicombe shares his experience with meditation and describes a simple, practical approach to familiarizing oneself with the present moment. **https://www.ted.com/talks/andy_puddicombe_all_it_takes_is_10_mindful_minutes?language=en**

Addiction in the Age of Brain Science. **2016. Markus Heilig. TEDxNorrköping. 17:13**

Psychiatrist and addiction specialist Markus Heilig discusses the important intersection between social science and neuroscience that may unlock new options for addiction treatment. Heilig highlights this with experimental research linking stress associated with social exclusion to specific brain activity and drug cravings. **https://youtu.be/4un3XxMqN3I**

Transcendental Meditation Technique—A Complete Introduction. 2014. Bob Roth. Transcendental Meditation. 20:14

Renowned meditation educator Bob Roth offers an introductory explanation of Transcendental Meditation, including how it can be learned, and the affect it has on the body and mind. **https://youtu.be/fO3AnD2QbIg**

Neuroscientists and the Dalai Lama Swap Insights on Meditation. 2013. Christof Koch. *Scientific American.*

This article discusses the interchange of ideas between Western scientists and the Dalai Lama's monastic community. **https://www.scientificamerican.com/article/neuroscientists-dalai-lama-swap-insights-meditation/**

Brains of Buddhist monks scanned in meditation study. 2011. Matt Danzico. BBC News. 2:32

This piece includes a short video explaining research that includes brain scans of accomplished Tibetan monks. **http://www.bbc.com/news/world-us-canada-12661646**

16: Moments. 2009. William Hoffman. Radiolab WNYC. 4:16

This artistic representation is described as a "visual experiment." The brief film offers the artists' attempt to distill and define individual moments. **https://youtu.be/jNVPalNZD_I**

22

Eating Yourself Fit

We are what we absorb.
—Julia Rucklidge

Introduction: A Healthy Relationship between You and Food

In this chapter, we explore healthy eating as a means of positively impacting physical and mental health. Before getting started, let's say a few words about "diet." As a noun, "diet" can simply refer to the foods a person eats. Your doctor might inquire about the sources of protein in your diet, or an individual might be on a gluten-free diet. Then, there is the verb meaning, where "diet" denotes altered food intake with the intention of losing weight. This distinction might seem moot to some readers, but we want to highlight that there are plenty of normal weight individuals (i.e., people who don't need to diet) who could benefit from changes to their diet (i.e., altering the specific foods that they eat). A major point of this chapter is that people can reap health benefits by altering their food choices. Proper nutrition promotes natural highs by providing your nervous system with the raw materials to synthesize neurotransmitters such a serotonin and dopamine.

We begin this chapter by discussing the issue of dieting, integrating concepts from cognitive-behavioral therapy (CBT) that have been successful for many people. We then move into discussions of food intake recommendations, based on the food pyramid, which alone no longer represents health dogma. New data address the importance of micronutrients (vitamins, minerals, amino acids), which some people may not be able to obtain in sufficient levels from their diet alone. Additionally, we briefly explore the issue of the microbiota (your gut's flora or "good bacteria") and its role in health. This chapter promotes a healthy relationship with food in which proper nutrients are consumed in appropriate amounts to serve as the foundation of sound physical and mental health.

Does Dieting Work?

In *Rethinking Thin*, Kolata (2007), a science writer for the *New York Times*, argues that scientists have a far better understanding of factors that lead to obesity than of how to lose weight permanently. Paradis and Cabanac (2008) find that people have "set points," and their bodies will slow down or speed up metabolic activity in order to keep their weight constant. Given that biological influences are important determinants of a person's weight, is there any recourse for the huge proportion of American adults who qualify as being obese?

> C. D. Gardner et al. (2007) published the results of one of the longest and most persuasive comparisons of weight-loss programs ever conducted. Three of the four diets in the study are heavily promoted regimens that have made their originators famous: the Atkins diet and the Zone diet, which both emphasized high-protein foods and the Ornish diet, a plan that prohibits most fatty foods. The fourth was the no-frills, low-fat diet that most nutrition experts recommend. (Raeburn, 2007, quoted in Nestle, 2007, p. 66)

A year after starting their diets, people on the Atkins plan had dropped an average of 10 pounds. Subjects on the other diets lost between 3 and 6 pounds, and members of the Atkins group showed no jump in cholesterol levels, despite the high levels of cholesterol in their diet. All groups showed modest weight loss and improvement in individuals' levels of cholesterol, blood pressure, and insulin (see Figure 22.1). "Contrary to expectations, the high-fat Atkins diet produced greater weight losses than three other popular weight-reduction plans" (Raeburn, 2007, quoted in Nestle, 2007, p. 67).

However, Mann et al. (2007) analyzed 31 long-term studies and found that although most participants lost about 5% to 10% of their total body mass, using all kinds of diets, most also regained all that weight over the long term and some put on even more than they had lost. Gorman (2004) reported on long-term weight loss among people who'd dropped at least 30 pounds and kept them off for a year, with an average 70-pound weight loss maintained for 6 years. Although there appears to be no commonality regarding how people in the study lost the weight, there is a striking similarity in how they succeeded in keeping it off—*exercise*, with an average of about an hour of physical activity a day! (Stay tuned for benefits of physical activity: it's covered next in Chapter 23, "Exercise: The Magic Bullet.")

Figure 22.1 Battle of the Diet Plans

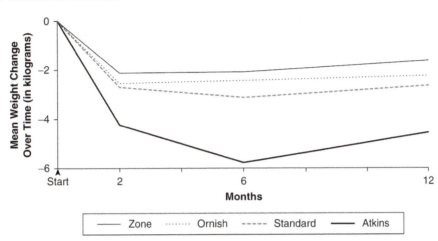

The Natural Highs Alternative: Think Thin, Moderate, Work Out!

Success in weight loss—especially if one is looking to lose large amounts of weight—is not solely dependent on just changing what one eats. We need to think about long-lasting lifestyle changes that not only promote weight loss but sustain it.

Although there are a plethora of regimens designed to encourage exercise and restrained caloric intake, *state of mind* is a critical ingredient regarding one's ability to follow through. People who desire to lose weight permanently while remaining healthy and productive must take a serious inventory of their behavioral budget. They must become converts to "thin thinking" and be prepared for a degree of persistent discomfort from relentless dieting. They must first recognize that they eat too much and exercise too little.

A few commonsense recommendations set the stage for a healthy approach to weight control. Crash dieting is not helpful, as the diet is almost always broken, resulting in rapid weight gain (and the consequent erosion of the individual's confidence that he or she can succeed). Eating when emotionally aroused is another hazard, as food serves as a means to reduce stress, with calorie consumption far outpacing nutritional need. Weight loss should be planned as a gradual process taking place over a period of several months (as opposed to a few weeks as in crash dieting) with a usual goal of about a pound per week. Moderation and portion control are the rules of thumb, with the inclusion of regular (planned and incidental) exercise as a part of the overall weight management scheme. A small excess of calories, even as little as a handful of peanuts or one alcoholic beverage, consumed on a regular basis, can add one pound per month, and in as little as one year can advance the dieter from petite to plump without the person ever appearing to lose control.

Developing the Right State of Mind

In *The Beck Diet Solution,* Dr. Judith Beck (2007) applies the principles of cognitive-behavioral therapy to include goals, values, and rational thinking in any program for weight loss. The basic ideas of her approach are summarized in Table 22.1.

Table 22.1 Thinking Like a Thin Person

Create Your Advantages Response Card: Write down all the reasons you want to lose weight and rate how important these are to you. Then read the card 2x daily plus whenever you are threatened by cravings.

Pick Two Reasonable Diets: Pick any reasonable and healthy one that seems appealing to you and a second one in case the first doesn't work out.
Eat Sitting Down: Unplanned eating is much more likely if you eat while standing up.

Give Yourself Credit: Recognize all the positive things you are doing each day so when you make a mistake you don't magnify it out of proportion.

Eat Slowly and Mindfully: Concentrate on what you are eating in order to derive satisfaction from smaller portions; i.e., savor each bite.

Get a Diet Support Coach: The coach helps with motivation, accountability, keeping perspective, and giving yourself credit.

Arrange Your Environment: Eliminate foods at home and work that trigger your cravings.
Make Time and Energy for Dieting: Devote time to shopping, preparing meals, exercising, etc.

Select an Exercise Plan: Exercise should be both incidental and planned.
Pick a Reasonable Goal: An attainable short-term goal might be to lose 5 pounds.

Differentiate Between Hunger, and Desire and Cravings: If the time elapsed after a reasonable sized meal is less than 3 hrs., the probability is that you are dealing with the urge to eat, not hunger.

Practice Hunger Tolerance: Hunger comes and goes; as you attend to other things, hunger diminishes.
Overcome Cravings: The more you wait out your cravings, the less frequently and intensely they will occur.
Plan for Tomorrow: Prepare a food plan that each day describes what you will eat tomorrow.

Prevent Unplanned Eating: Establish the rule that there is "no choice" about giving in to unplanned eating.
End Overeating: Remember that excess food will go to waste in your body; it is better to go to waste in the garbage.

Change Your Definition of Full: Think about how easily you could take a moderately brisk walk before eating. If you can't imagine keeping the same pace after a meal, you have overeaten.

Stop Fooling Yourself: Beck lists examples of fake excuses, such as "I'll eat less later," or "It's not that fattening," or "I'm so upset and I just don't care."

Get Back on Track: Acknowledge the mistake and recommit to the diet instead of giving in to relapse.

Get Ready to Weigh In: The advantages of weekly weigh-ins are that they celebrate success, build confidence, keep us honest if we've gained weight, and help us stay committed.

Deal With Discouragement: When faced with thoughts of giving up, it's important to challenge those by focusing on the here and now, reminding ourselves that we can do what we need to do.

Identify Sabotaging Thoughts: It is important to learn how to spot thoughts that undermine your resolve, e.g., "Dieting is too hard" or "I'm treating myself."

Recognize Thinking Mistakes: Thoughts are transient; just because you're thinking something doesn't mean it's true or that you have to act on the thought.

Master the Seven Questions Technique:
1. What kind of thinking error could I be making? 2. What's the evidence that this thought might not be true? 3. Is there an alternative explanation or another way of viewing this? 4. What is the most realistic outcome of this situation? 5. What is the effect of my believing this thought, and what could be the effect of changing my thinking? 6. What should I tell a close friend/family member if he or she were in this situation and had this thought? 7. What should I do now?

Monitor Your Eating: By keeping a written record of what you are eating and following your daily food plan, you increase the chances of losing weight and keeping it off.

Say, "Oh Well" to Disappointment: Accept your cravings and hardships around not eating what you want, acknowledging that although you might not like dieting, it is necessary to achieve your goals.

Countering the Unfairness Syndrome: "Everyone has some unfairness in life; having to regulate my food intake is mine and I can handle it."

Resist Food Pushers: Be direct; do not communicate any wiggle room or ambiguity in your refusal to indulge.

Decide About Drinking: Know how many calories are in an alcoholic beverage and plan accordingly, making sure that any loss of judgment does not provoke unplanned eating.

Source: Reprinted with permission from The Beck Diet Solution: Train Your Brain to Think Like a Thin Person. Published by Oxmoor House, © Judith S. Beck, PhD, 2007.

The immediate benefits of maintaining a healthy lifestyle are looking good, feeling good, and being a positive role model. In the long term, a balanced program of exercise and nutrition can help prevent chronic diseases such as heart disease, diabetes, and some cancers.

Eating Schedules: Partial Fasting vs. Grazing

The Bible says that Moses and Jesus fasted for 40 days for spiritual renewal. Hippocrates, Socrates, and Plato recommended fasting for health reasons. According to Neufeld (quoted in Neighmond, 2007), an endocrinologist at UCLA, by studying newborns we can gain a clearer picture of how the body reacts to a lack of food. Babies may need to feed every few hours because their bodies cannot produce enough glycogen, the body's form of stored sugar required to make energy. Glycogen is needed for basic functions of the brain and body: thinking, muscle action, and cell survival. According to Neufeld, adults require about 2,000 calories a day to make energy or glycogen and it might help the body to fast, that is, to stop eating for short periods of time (24 hours once a week) while still consuming water. "You re-tune the body, suppress insulin secretion, reduce the taste for sugar, so sugar becomes something you're less fond of taking" (n.p.).

Mattson (2007), of the National Institute on Aging, says that when we convert food into energy, our bodies create a lot of unnecessary by-products including free radicals, which attack proteins, DNA, the nuclei of cells, and cell membranes. Mattson cites studies where rats and mice were fed every other day. The finding of reduced disease in comparison to regularly fed rats suggests that humans could also benefit from partial (also known as intermittent) fasting. From Mattson's perspective, partial-fasting benefits range from improving glucose regulation, which can protect against diabetes, to lowering blood pressure. Some animal studies have also shown that partial fasting has very beneficial effects on the brain, protecting against Alzheimer's, Parkinson's, and stroke. Partial fasting may even extend the life span because eating less sends a message to the cells of the body that they should conserve and use energy more efficiently. "When they're exposed to a mild stress, [the body's cells] sort of expect that maybe this is going to happen again. … So maybe next time I may have to go longer without food, so I'd better be able to deal with that when it comes on" (Mattson, 2007, p. 337).

There seems to be a lot of hype but relatively little data on partial fasting—at least in humans. A review by Patterson and Sears (2017) includes both animal and human data in an effort to reach a consensus view. Human studies are often plagued by small sample sizes; worse, there are a variety of different types of fasting that fits the notion of "intermittent," although few are as extreme as the alternate day fasting advocated by Mattson. Several studies investigated this approach to intermittent fasting (with complete or near-complete fasting except fluid on fasting days and normal eating on intervening days). Although there are some human data to support that such a feeding schedule can promote weight loss, it might not be viable: participants commonly complained about hunger on fasting days. These complaints were often accompanied by reports of mental distraction, low mood, and low energy. Perhaps more disappointing (at least for believers in fasting) is that, overall, the data do not suggest that alternate day fasting is better at promoting weight loss than calorie restriction associated with traditional dieting.

But what about the other extreme? Perhaps you have heard people advocate for more frequent (>3 meals per day) that are smaller—a practice humorously referred to as "grazing." The rationale is that by eating more frequently one can stave off hunger and food cravings but without overindulging. On the surface it seems to make sense, especially to those of us who find ourselves distracted by hunger and cravings. The data, however, are mixed as to whether this is an effective approach for weight loss. A review by Raynor et al. (2015) summarizes both animal and human studies and points out that there is a lack of data in general as well as wide variability in terms of how the existing studies were conducted. Nonetheless, Raynor and colleagues report that over half of the studies (61.5%) showed no effect on calorie consumption due to increased frequency of meals. Most of the human studies do not report significant changes in "anthropometric data" (decreases in body weight, waist measurements, etc.). There is not even consistency in the results with regard participants' self-reports of hunger: 3 out of 6 studies reported significantly lower hunger ratings when participants were eating more frequent meals, while 2 other studies reported no effect (and one study didn't report any data on this).

So what's the "skinny" on grazing vs. partial fasting? To our knowledge, there is not a study that directly compares these. The data on both of these approaches show mixed results, and more studies seem warranted before we can draw any solid conclusions. In the meantime, if you are considering switching up your meal schedule in an effort to help lose weight, perhaps consider the issue of hunger ratings. Some people may find hunger sensations and food cravings distracting enough to interfere with their ability to focus on daily tasks, making adherence to decreased eating frequency difficult. The data addressing intermittent fasting and grazing also do not show consistent results with regard to effects on metabolism rate, so we probably shouldn't expect feeding schedules to be the "magic bullet" that solves our caloric issues. Moderation of intake still matters.

What Is a Healthy Diet?

Willett and Stampfer (2006), at the Harvard School of Public Health, strongly emphasize weight control through exercising daily and avoiding excessive caloric intake. The majority of our diet should contain healthy fats (liquid vegetable oils, e.g., olive, canola, soy, corn, sunflower, and peanut) and healthy carbohydrates (whole grain foods such as whole wheat bread, oatmeal, and brown rice). Fruits (2–3 servings) and vegetables (eaten liberally) should be included with moderate amounts of healthy proteins (nuts, legumes, fish, poultry, and eggs) limited to two servings per day. Willett and Stampfer recommend minimizing the consumption of red meat, butter, refined grains (e.g., white bread, white rice, and white pasta), potatoes, and sugar. Trans fats should be avoided entirely, and a multivitamin is suggested for most people. If not contraindicated by medical conditions (including but not limited to prior alcohol abuse/alcoholism issues) or medication, moderate consumption of alcohol of any kind (wine, beer, or spirits) can be a healthy option.

The U.S. Department of Agriculture food pyramid (*The Washington Post*, 2005) breaks food categories into a spectrum to emphasize variety. Exercise was introduced as a component of the food pyramid, and 12 individualized intake profiles were added. Their recommendations for a healthy diet are shown in Figure 22.2.

Figure 22.2 The Food Pyramid

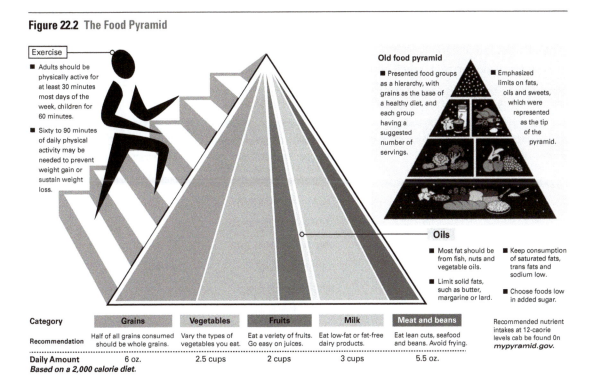

It's wise to mind both your macronutrients (proteins, fats, and carbohydrates) as well as your micronutrients (vitamins, minerals, and amino acids). With regard to macronutrients, a balanced diet needs to include a mix of these three constituents. A review by Duranti, Ferrario, van Sinderen, Ventura, and Turroni (2017) discusses that a balanced diet consists of 55–60% carbohydrates and 15–30% proteins in terms of energy intake (with the rest made up from fats). While the Western diet commonly consumed in the U.S. fits within the range of these macronutrients, issues exist with many of the highly-processed foods in our environment; refined sugars and vegetable oils are common, foods may have lots of saturated fats and trans fats, and many people don't get sufficient fiber in their diet. These details regarding macronutrients can matter in terms of promoting weight gain and negative health markers (increased cholesterol, insulin resistance, etc.).

People should pay attention to specific choices regarding macronutrients to bolster their micronutrients. In other words, pick foods that are rich sources of proteins, amino acids, vitamins, and minerals. Micronutrients play important roles in basic body functions. For instance, the nervous system uses amino acids (often found in protein-rich foods) to produce neurotransmitters. Table 22.2 lists some of our key neurotransmitters, the amino acids they are produced from, and dietary sources. For people specifically looking to increase serotonin by pumping up dietary tryptophan, a few words of caution are in order. First, amino acids require active transport via carrier proteins to cross the blood-brain barrier and reach the brain. Protein sources rich in tryptophan are generally rich in other amino acids, too. As a result, tryptophan competes with other amino acids to get transported across the blood-brain barrier. Eating some carbs will favor tryptophan's passage into the brain. Second, data suggest that it would be better to go for balance of neurotransmitters rather than specifically trying to elevate one (such as serotonin) in particular. Because serotonin and dopamine share synthesizing and degrading enzymes, specifically trying to pump up serotonin through tryptophan or 5-HTP supplements—5-HTP is the intermediary between tryptophan and serotonin—can ultimately lead to depletion of dopamine (Hinz, Stein, and Uncini, 2012). So we advise people to eat for their entire system and go for balance.

Table 22.2 Neurotransmitters, Amino Acids, and Common Dietary Sources

Neurotransmitter	Amino Acid Precursor	Dietary Sources	Important Functions
Acetylcholine	Choline	eggs, poultry, meat, fish, dairy products, peanuts, broccoli, Brussel sprouts, cauliflower, kidney beans	Movement, cognition; brain development
Dopamine	Tyrosine	eggs, poultry, meat, fish, dairy products, soy, some seeds and nuts, peanuts, lima beans bananas, avocados	Movement, cognition, reward
Serotonin	Tryptophan	eggs, poultry, meat, fish, dairy products, soy, peanuts, some seeds, lima beans, bananas, white rice, white flour, oats, russet potatoes	Mood, sleep, appetite
Glutamate	Glutamine	eggs, poultry, meat, fish, dairy products, beans, beets, cabbage, spinach, carrots, parsley, wheat, papaya, Brussel sprouts, kale, celery, fermented food	Primary excitatory NT; important for memory

Notes: The neurotransmitter/hormone norepinephrine (noradrenaline) is made from dopamine, and the neurotransmitter/hormone epinephrine (adrenaline) is made from norepinephrine. The neurotransmitter GABA, our primary inhibitory neurotransmitter, is synthesized from glutamate. Melatonin, which promotes sleep, is made from serotonin. So numerous neurotransmitters depend on a handful of amino acids for synthesis.

Some researchers argue that micronutrient supplementation may be helpful for treating a variety of different psychological conditions because vitamins and minerals are involved in basic cellular functions and some are involved in neurotransmitter synthesis. Rucklidge and Kaplan (2013) reviewed studies looking at broad-spectrum micronutrient formulas (which contain many vitamins and minerals and sometimes amino acids or omega-3 fatty acids) on a variety of different psychological conditions. At this point, readers should not be surprised to hear that results are mixed and that some of the studies are not as well-conducted as one would hope. Adding to the complexity of the situation is the variability of what ingredients are included in the supplements. It's also possible that efficacy depends on whether those taking the supplements were nutrient-deficient in the first place.

One of the more rigorous studies is by Rucklidge and colleagues (2014) who conducted a double-blind randomized control study investigating micronutrient supplementation as a treatment for ADHD. Participants were not on psychiatric medications, and the study lasted 8 weeks. Improvement was based on clinicians' ratings of the clients' symptoms, obtained through clinical interviews; the treatment group showed greater improvements over the course of the study compared to the control group, suggesting that micronutrient supplements may be a viable alternative to medication for this condition. Notably, there were not differences between the two groups with regard to adverse events, indicating that supplementation may be well tolerated. This research supports the notion that nutrients affect psychological functioning, even if how they accomplish their roles are not fully understood, although Stevens, Rucklidge, and Kennedy (2017) suggest they may impact gene expression in addition to affecting basic cellular and neurotransmitter function. Dr. Rucklidge is a leader in this area of research; to hear her speak on micronutrients as a treatment, check out her TEDx talk (See for Yourself).

But a word of caution is in order: people should not try to "self-medicate" by taking large doses of vitamins daily. Although some vitamins are water soluble, not everything in nutritional supplements is—for instance, iron can build up in tissues and have harmful effects. There are upper limits to how much of any vitamin or mineral is considered tolerable. So follow the recommended daily intake instructions.

Micronutrients as Treatment for Substance Addiction

A major premise of this chapter is that if the body and brain have the nutrients they need for optimal functioning, then the individual should feel better both physically and mentally. In essence, the person is experiencing feel-good neurochemistry (a natural high) through proper food intake. We recommend that for anyone, regardless of whether they have ever suffered from a hedonic dependency.

But what about those who have suffered from substance abuse? Are there data to show that nutritional interventions can be helpful in recovery? Although research is limited, there are data to suggest that this may be the case. For instance, a study in China (Chen et al., 2012) used dietary supplements containing amino acids to boost the levels of dopamine, serotonin, glutamate, and acetylcholine. In a 6-day study using detoxified heroin addicts in a hospital setting, participants were randomly assigned to supplement treatment or placebo and were blind to their conditions. The treatment group showed improved withdrawal symptoms and sleep, and at the end of the study, reported more energy and better moods compared to the control condition. The efficacy of this sort of intervention makes sense, given that chronic drug abuse throws neurotransmitter levels out of balance. Previous work has tested amino acid supplements in cocaine abusers (Blum et al., 1988) and alcohol, opioid, and cocaine DUI offenders (Brown, Blum, & Trachtenberg, 1990) with some success. Overall, these results are promising, suggesting that nutritional supplements may enhance functioning in substance abusers.

A Look to the Future: Microbiota

Actually, microbiota (microbes living in our body) are already here—and apparently have been throughout the evolution of our species. What lies in the future is a better understanding of them. If you're a germaphobe, it may disturb you that bacteria and other types of flora live in your gut, but think of these as "good bugs." They are the ones we take for granted. Only recently have scientists begun to realize the vast diversity of our microbiota. Knight and Buhler's (2015) book *Follow Your Gut: The Enormous Impact of Tiny Microbes* gives an excellent overview of research in the field and is the basis for our description below.

Although obesity is influenced by a number of factors (genetics, activity levels, food choices, quantity of intake, etc.), gut bacteria also play a critical but underappreciated role. Not all of our food digestion is dependent on our own enzymes. Gut bacteria help digest complex carbohydrates and absorb fat. Some microbes are better than others at extracting energy from foods. Research shows that there is less diversity (fewer strains) of gut microbes in obese people. These bacteria help regulate energy metabolism and storage, so it makes sense that they play a role in obesity.

It may sound sinister—like something from a bad sci-fi movie in which alien entities take control of human bodies from within—but our gut microbiota communicate with our brains! This is known as the gut-brain axis. Currently, researchers are linking gut bacteria to neurological conditions. Gut bacteria also play a role in immune functioning. Our understanding of the human condition seems to be unfolding on a whole new (microscopic) level. Study of microbiota may very well help explain individual differences in health, given that everyone has a somewhat different microbiota profile (sort of like bacterial fingerprints).

But back to obesity: suppose imbalances in a person's microbes could lead to weight gain. These bacteria influence the gut's release of a variety of chemicals involved in hunger and satiety (signals that are detected in the brain). Our microbiota are sensitive to a variety of influences, such as what we eat, whether we feast or fast, and consumption of antibiotics for infections. What if an overweight person has the "wrong" microbiota because some of their gut bacteria have died off? Researchers have done experiments in rodents in which microbiota from non-obese animals are transplanted into experimental animals fed high-fat diets, and the transplants bestowed resiliency to becoming overweight. Other researchers are looking to probiotics ("good bacteria" that you can buy in the form of supplements at your local grocery or health food store) as a means of improving digestion, metabolism, energy, and weight control. Knight and Buhler (2015) warn that this is one of those "Buyer beware!" situations—yet another example where there's more hype than data to support claims of "fixing" our health. Check the latest scientific literature first because specific species and strains of bacteria have different effects (assuming that the microbes are alive after sitting on a store shelf for who knows how long). But keep microbiota on your radar because in the future they may be viable treatments for a whole host of conditions, including obesity.

For more information on the weird and wonderful world of microbiota, check out Dr. Knight's TED Talk (See for Yourself). Perhaps you will come to appreciate these symbiotic (not parasitic) life forms that may be so important to how we function that we should probably consider them to be a part of ourselves (like an extra endocrine organ). Research in this area may revolutionize how a variety of conditions—including obesity, anorexia, neurodegenerative diseases, psychological disorders, and others—are treated.

The Bottom Line

Excluding not smoking, the World Cancer Research Fund (cited in "To Avoid the Big C, Stay Small," *The Economist*, 2007) makes the recommendations shown in Table 22.3 concerning nutrition and reducing the risk of cancer and other health problems:

Finally, "the simplest message may be the best: do not overeat, exercise more, consume mostly fruits, vegetables and whole grains, and avoid junk foods" (Nestle, 2007). People gain weight when intake exceeds expenditure and lose weight when expenditure exceeds intake. Energy intake (right side of scale in Figure 22.3) is determined by the sum of the calories contained in the carbohydrate (hexagons, 4 kcal/g), fat (circles, 9 kcal/g), and protein (ovals, 4 kcal/g) components of the diet. Total daily energy expenditure (left side of scale) is the sum of the energy needed to sustain vital functions at rest (RMR, the resting metabolic rate), the energy expended during exercise (TEE, the thermic effect of exercise), and the energy used to digest and absorb food (TEF, the thermic effect of feeding).

Table 22.3 Nutrition Recommendations to Reduce Risk of Cancer

Body fatness	Be as lean as possible within the normal range of body weight, BMI 21–23.
Physical activity	Be physically active; for example, walk briskly at least 30 minutes a day.
Foods and drinks weight gain	Limit consumption of energy foods. Average energy intake should be that promote 125kcal/100g of food. Avoid sugary drinks.
Plant foods	Eat mostly foods of plant origin; fruits and nonstarchy vegetables at least 600g a day.
Animal foods	Limit intake of red meat, no more than 300g a week. Avoid processed meat including bacon and ham.
Alcoholic drinks	Limit alcoholic drinks, two a day for men and one a day for women.
Preservation, processing, and preparation	Limit consumption of salt to less than 5g per day.
Dietary supplements	Aim to meet nutritional needs through diet alone.
Breastfeeding	Mothers should breastfeed; children should be breastfed.
Cancer survivors	Follow the recommendations for cancer prevention.

Source: World Cancer Research Fund, cited in Nestle, 2004.

Figure 22.3 Energy Balance Body mass depends on the balance between energy intake and energy expenditure.

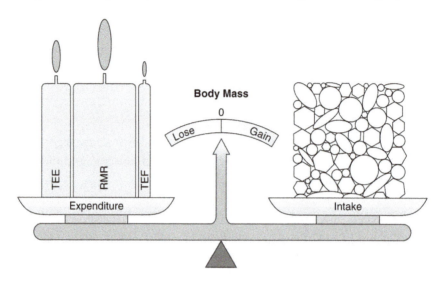

RMR = Resting Metabolic Rate; TEE = Thermic Effect of Exercise; TEF = Thermic Effect of Feeding.

Chapter Summary

Given that biological influences are important determinants of a person's weight, is dieting a viable option for the huge proportion of American adults who qualify as overweight or obese? It appears that many diets will facilitate short-term weight loss; however, those who manage to sustain control over their weight include a healthy quantum of exercise in their daily and weekly schedules. Successful dieters realize that they eat too much and exercise too little. Crash dieting is ill-advised as it results in nothing more than a setup for failure and lowered self-esteem. The diet is almost always broken, and whatever weight has been lost is rapidly regained. Dr. Judith Beck's work is described, as she applies the principles of cognitive-behavioral therapy to weight loss programs.

Some weight-loss gurus are extolling the advantages of partial (intermittent) fasting. Other gurus advocate for multiple, small meals per day. Data are mixed on both of these approaches in terms of health effects and weight loss. People attempting to lose weight need to think about whether these approaches are sustainable or whether they should stick with the traditional wisdom of not taking in more calories than one can expend.

With respect to healthy dieting, Willet and Stampfer strongly emphasize weight control through exercising daily and avoiding excessive caloric intake. They recommend minimizing the consumption of red meat, butter, refined grains, potatoes, and sugar. Trans fats should be eliminated, and multivitamins are suggested for most people. Moderate consumption of alcohol is okay if not contraindicated by medical conditions or medication. Perhaps the most succinct and coherent statement about food and fitness is: consume moderate portions; make exercise a priority; avoid junk foods; and eat plenty of fruits, vegetables, and whole grains.

Make certain you are getting adequate micronutrients to allow your body to synthesize neurotransmitters. Be kind to your stomach and intestinal flora, given your intimate relationship with them. They appear to influence physical and mental health and may have an impact on body weight and obesity.

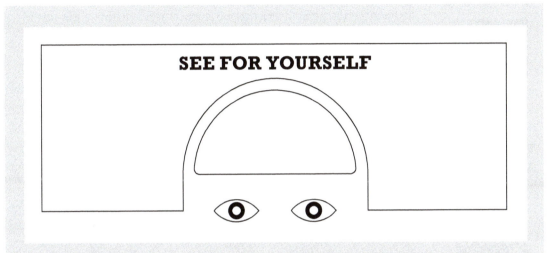

SEE FOR YOURSELF

Julia Rucklidge, a clinical psychologist at University of Canterbury in Christ Church, New Zealand, discusses micronutrients in this TEDx Talk. Her research specifically focuses on how micronutrients (or, rather, lack thereof) may play a role in a number of psychological conditions, such as depression and ADHD.

https://www.youtube.com/watch?v=3dqXHHCc5lA (17:42)

Rob Knight, biology professor of University of California at San Diego, discusses the importance of our microbes to our physical and mental health in this TED Talk.

https://www.youtube.com/watch?v=i-icXZ2tMRM

Minifasting: How Occasionally Skipping Meals May Boost Health. 2015. Allison Aubrey and Eliza Barclay. NPR: *All Things Considered*. 5:02.

This interview discusses the science and practical use of intermittent fasting to promote a variety of health benefits. **http://www.npr.org/sections/thesalt/2015/01/12/376712920/minifasting-how-occasionally-skipping-meals-may-boost-health**

The Evolution of Diet. 2013. Ann Gibbons. Photographs by Matthieu Paley. *National Geographic Magazine*. Feature Article.

This piece examines the evolution of the human diet and discusses the contemporary diet in terms of individual health and environmental impact. Researchers are looking at groups of indigenous people whose current food habits are more similar to ancient ways of eating. **http://www.nationalgeographic.com/foodfeatures/evolution-of-diet/**

About the Diet Trap Solution. 2016. Dr. Judith Beck and Deborah Beck Busis. Beck Institute of Cognitive Behavior Therapy. 3:47

Dr. Judith Beck and Deborah Beck Busis introduce their book, which provides a resource for application of their cognitive behavioral approach to dieting and weight loss. **https://youtu.be/MQZjTgj79ec**

Why Dieting Doesn't Usually Work. 2013. Sandra Aamodt. TED Talks. 12:42

Neuroscientist Sandra Aamodt presents the research indicating that the culture dieting can do more harm than good, and suggests mindful eating as alternative. **https://www.ted.com/talks/sandra_aamodt_why_dieting_doesn_t_usually_work**

23

Exercise
The Magic Bullet

Introduction: It's Not Just About Burning Calories

*No drug in current or prospective use holds as much promise for
sustained health as a lifetime program of physical exercise.*
—Walter Bortz, Stanford University Medical School

Take care of your body. There's not a spare in the trunk.

—Bumper sticker

The purpose of this chapter is to develop a better understanding of the whole-life benefits of a sensible exercise program. Physical fitness is not just for those who wish to lose weight. It is also a prescription for participating in the fullness of life. Exercise can enhance self-esteem, social interaction, motivation, and self-image as well as decreasing stress levels, anxiety, and depression (Perham & Accordino, 2007). Another benefit of regular exercise is enhanced energy and decreased fatigue (Puetz, O'Connor, & Dishman, 2006). It is clearly associated with improved physical and mental health. For those with a bent toward sensation seeking and excitement, exercise (and competitive sports) can supply a natural high alternative to such risk-taking behaviors as gambling, promiscuity, and the abuse of stimulant drugs. Health and psychological benefits have been shown to accrue when exercise is used as an adjunct to treatment in complex mental health problems such as alcohol and drug rehabilitation (Donaghy, 2007). To put icing on the cake, regular exercisers have been found to be 10 years younger physiologically than their sedentary counterparts (Cherkas et al., 2008)!

There is an abundance of research that shows exercise as conducive to improved intellectual functioning (Hillman, Erickson, & Kramer, 2008), mood adjustment (Donaghy, 2007), and physical health (Cherkas et al., 2008). According to Hillman et al., "research strongly supports the positive effects of exercise on cognition: aerobic activity improves learning and task acquisition, increases the secretion of key neurochemicals associated with synaptic plasticity and promotes the development of new neuronal architecture" (p. 63). These findings are supported by neuroimaging studies that show positive changes in brain structure from exercise.

In terms of mental health, exercise increases blood flow to the brain, stimulating the release of "those wonderful endorphins" (Donaghy, 2007). Animal studies have shown increases in serotonin, dopamine, and norepinephrine during exercise (Chaouloff, 1997). As graduates of Neurochemistry 101, we know that these neurotransmitters allow for elevated moods and good feelings. So not only can exercise help your intellectual capacity and your mental and physical health, it also slows aging. If you don't want to be spending all your money on beauty creams and potentially carcinogenic tanning salons, go outside for a jog and keep your body moving.

Exercise of Choice

So, what is "sensible" exercise? Doesn't this word *sensible* sound a little wimpy? Isn't the old marathoner adage, "No pain, no gain," the real way to exercise for good health as well as muscular fitness? Absolutely not! Health benefits are not directly proportional to the total amount of energy expended. If your exercise of choice is running and you run more than 20 miles a week, you are most likely running for more than reasons of health. Although this level of commitment is not necessarily harmful, don't expect to achieve greater health benefits than those who run 12 to 15 miles a week. The operative concept here is health, not "Olympian Superstar." Cherkas et al. (2008) found that people who participate in moderate exercise for 30 minutes at least 5 days a week are effectively reducing their vulnerably to a host of illnesses. Regular workouts have been linked to lower rates of cardiovascular disease, type 2 diabetes, cancer, high blood pressure, obesity, and osteoporosis (Stein, 2008b).

To be effective, exercise must suit your lifestyle, including your personal and professional life. Finding an exercise that you enjoy should not be difficult, since hundreds of different options are available. All of these alternatives can be broken down into five categories: isometric, isotonic, isokinetic, anaerobic, and aerobic. Figure 23.1 represents the four dimensions of an exercise plan set to meet a given individual's needs and preferences.

Isometric Exercise

Bodybuilder Charles Atlas popularized this form of exercise (97-pound weakling punches out beach bully), which he termed *dynamic tension*. In isometric exercise, muscles push hard against each other. While this does produce a gain in strength, isometrics do not lead to overall body conditioning. The advantage is that these exercises can be performed anywhere, anytime. This is beneficial for those who must sit for long periods or who are immobilized; however, such exercise may be insufficient for improving cardiovascular health.

Figure 23.1 Exercise Prescription The four components of an exercise prescription are intensity (how hard), duration (how long), frequency (how many times per week), and mode (type of exercise, e.g., swimming or running). For example, an exercise prescription to increase cardiopulmonary endurance could be to run (mode) at a heart rate of 150 beats/min (intensity) for 20 minutes per day (duration) three times per week (frequency) (K. Axen & K.V. Axen, 2001, p. 232).

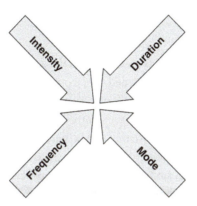

Isotonic Exercise (Pumping Iron)

The difference between isometric and isotonic exercise is that in isotonic exercise (e.g., weightlifting and push-ups), muscles contract with the accompanying movement of the joints. Generally speaking, weight-training programs oriented toward bodybuilding are based on isotonic exercises. A number of popular magazines are devoted entirely to isotonic workouts (e.g., *Muscle and Fitness*). While pumping iron might lead to a cover-page physique, it is woefully insufficient as the sole source of exercise for individuals seeking improved overall conditioning or who have a history of heart disease.

For those not wishing to join an exercise gym, a weight bench with an attached knee exerciser and accompanying weight set can be purchased for less than $100 at discount stores. Obviously, the bench must be sturdy; this is much more important than having a number of costly attachments that may never be used. Individuals attempting weight training should either do it under the guidance of a trained instructor or very carefully follow the instructions given with the exercise equipment. It is possible to do both muscle and structural damage to the body by attempting to move too quickly from a sedentary lifestyle to an Arnold Schwarzenegger–type workout.

Isokinetic Exercise (Work Those Pecs!)

Isokinetic exercises are very much like isotonic ones, except that exertion is required both going from the starting position and then returning to it. This form of exercise usually requires special equipment, such as a Nautilus machine, in which the individual can adjust the tension according to his or her level of training. Isokinetic exercise is not only expensive, but also inconvenient, in that it requires the individual to belong to a health club in order to use its equipment. This may be a plus for those who enjoy the social atmosphere of a gym. Unfortunately, taken by itself, it does not provide a complete exercise program.

Anaerobic Exercise (No Sweat)

As the name implies, anaerobic exercise does not require an overall increase in the consumption of oxygen. Many everyday activities fall into this category. Exercises such as calisthenics, playing Frisbee, bounding up stairs two at a time, running to the copy machine, hailing a cab in New York City, playing softball, and other activities requiring short but rather intensive bursts of energy are considered anaerobic. Clearly, this is not a complete exercise program, in that it does nothing to increase overall cardiovascular and respiratory fitness. The benefit of such exercises is that they are often fun, which is a major reason to engage in them.

Aerobic Exercise (Gasp)

As the name implies, aerobic exercise requires an increase in the amount of oxygen used by the body. For aerobic exercise to be effective, it must be performed over a prolonged length of time, preferably 20 to 30 minutes at submaximal effort. The most common forms of this exercise are running, jogging, and formal aerobic workouts. Other forms of aerobic exercise can, however, be equally beneficial. Rapid walking and bicycling are other examples of aerobic exercise that can be performed by nearly everyone. For walking, all that's needed is a good pair of comfortable walking shoes, which cost around $80 and are good for up to 2,000 miles. For people living in congested areas such as cities, walking, as well as running during rush hour, can be quite harmful due to the pollution from traffic. It is recommended that any exercise in which oxygen consumption is significantly increased be performed away from polluted areas.

Whereas people often argue that aerobic exercise is best, many fitness gurus argue for a mix of aerobic and anaerobic for overall fitness. A mix of strength training, body toning, and stretching, combined with walking, jogging, biking, or swimming will help firm and trim the body as well as increase overall endurance and cardiovascular health. Brain research indicates that both of these produce brain benefits, even if the cardio-vascular benefits are favored by aerobic workouts.

The Chemistry of Burning Calories

Many undertake exercise programs to lose weight (or to maintain their weight loss after dieting) rather than to enhance their overall health or to achieve euphoria. Happily, unless the desire to lose weight is pathological, these benefits are closely related. A loss of excess body fat will nearly always lead to better health and an improved sense of well-being. Obviously, the body's repository of excess fat (rather than muscle) is the appropriate target of weight-loss programs. To discover how different kinds of exercise can lead to the maximum loss of body fat, we need to learn some basic truths about the physiology of exercise.

Exercise requires energy in order to propel the muscles of the body. This comes from a molecule known as adenosine triphosphate (ATP), which releases energy as it breaks down during exercise. After breaking down, ATP must then be regenerated in order for the muscles to continue working. The fuel that the body uses to regenerate ATP is either fats or carbohydrates. This fuel is burned in the body by using oxygen, just as a stove uses oxygen to burn coal or wood. Fats and carbohydrates are completely consumed under aerobic (oxygen-rich) conditions to produce carbon dioxide and water. Fat, however, has more than twice the fuel capacity (9 calories per gram) of carbohydrates (4 calories per gram). Although fat has more calories, it burns more slowly than carbohydrates during exercise, just as coal burns more slowly than wood, but releases more total energy. When you are simply puttering around the house or garden, you do not have a high-energy demand. During these activities, fat is the primary source of energy consumed to regenerate ATP. But if you start jogging or running, you suddenly need more energy and more oxygen to supply your muscles with ATP. Because you need more energy immediately, the body quickly shifts from burning fat to burning carbohydrates, such as glucose or glucose from glycogen (a starch-like substance stored in the liver). Carbohydrates produce ATP faster but less efficiently than fat in terms of the calories contained per gram (Axen & Axen, 2001).

Figure 23.2 shows how glucose (fuel) is broken down to provide energy needed to perform exercise. After this glycogen is gone, or even before it is completely gone, the exerciser will begin to falter and be unable to continue the pace. Marathoners and long-distance cyclists call this experience of glycogen deficiency "hitting the wall." The individual has pushed him- or herself until all of the stored glycogen in the muscles and the liver is nearly exhausted. At this time, the primary fuel available to continue is fat. As indicated, fat burns very slowly, and an individual is unable to continue vigorous running or cycling by burning fat alone.

Figure 23.2 **ATP Production** A 6-carbon molecule of glucose is broken down to two 3-carbon molecules of pyruvic acid (pyruvate) in the anaerobic pathway of glycolysis (no oxygen is required). The energy released during this process is sufficient to synthesize two molecules of ATP, a stored form of energy. The 3-carbon molecules of pyruvate can then enter aerobic pathways (which require a continuous supply of oxygen) where they get broken down to carbon dioxide and water with a net yield of 34 ATP molecules per molecule of glucose (Axen & Axen, 2001).

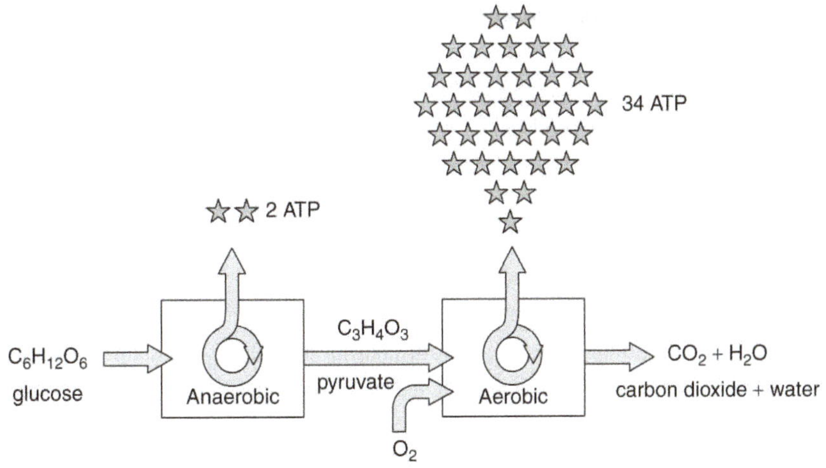

Individuals who hit the wall will stagger about and sometimes collapse. Running to this level of carbohydrate depletion is extremely dangerous, since the brain itself needs glucose (a carbohydrate) in order to function. To avert depletion of glycogen during the race, marathoners may load up with pasta and other forms of carbohydrates for several days before running. The goal is to build up a supply of glycogen in the muscles and in the liver in order to minimize the chances of hitting the wall.

CASE EXAMPLE: Hitting the Wall

Sandy had not run a marathon for some time when she first began to train for an upcoming race. The night before the marathon, she was at a dinner party where considerable amounts of protein, in the form of fish, and carbohydrates, in the form of rice, were served. Her friend, thinking of the upcoming marathon, urged Sandy to eat more rice and less fish. Yet, as the fish was exceedingly good, Sandy proceeded to ignore the rice, which is rich in carbohydrates, and ate primarily fish. Her friend later described the race:

The next day, during the race, I went back to a point about 4 or 5 miles from the finish line to cheer Sandy on as she ran past. I saw her about 300 yards away and I knew immediately that something was wrong. She was not running with her usual confident and strong stride. I quickly hurried back to the finish and arrived just as she crossed the line and collapsed. Fortunately, because she was in superb physical condition, she was soon revived.

Can we use present knowledge of physiology to achieve our optimum physical state? Let's imagine that you went for a vigorous run after some hours of light exercise in the garden or around the house. As you began to run, fat consumption dropped dramatically, because it is slow to furnish energy. Carbohydrate consumption increased dramatically, as it burns faster than fats and can immediately furnish the energy needed for the larger demand from the muscles. At this point in the aerobic process, the body, by necessity, is consuming carbohydrates much more rapidly than fat. In fact, the consumption of carbohydrates will increase to about 85% of total energy consumed almost immediately after one begins to run, and use of fat will fall dramatically. After a short period of time (20 to 30 minutes), however, if the initial pace is not too fast (slow jogging or fast walking), the consumption of fat now begins to rise slowly. As you continue exercising, the body will attempt to conserve carbohydrates (glycogen) and begin to burn fat more efficiently. Provided the intensity of the exercise is below maximal, consumption of fat exceeds carbohydrate consumption after about 30 to 40 minutes. At the end of an hour, fat consumption will be much more prevalent than carbohydrate consumption. This is the typical pattern of energy supplied during an aerobics class or a 5- to 10-mile jog. Another added benefit, and a *bona fide* motivator for strenuous exercise, is that you will continue burning both fat and carbohydrates even after you have stopped exercising. The longer you exercise, the longer you will continue to burn calories after you have quit the exercise.

It should be very clear that longer periods of submaximal aerobic exercise are more productive for weight loss than shorter bursts of intense anaerobic exercise. During the more intense, short-term maximal exercise, the body's demand for energy is so great that it cannot be furnished by fat and the body will utilize primarily carbohydrates. On the other hand, with exercise less intense than fast running, such as rapid (but not power) walking, the body soon converts from carbohydrate consumption to fat consumption. In other words, if your exercise intensity is somewhat below maximum, the efficiency of oxygen use is high, and this permits the body to utilize fat for fuel as opposed to using carbohydrates. Conversely, if your workout is extremely intense, as you approach your maximum oxygen uptake, your consumption of fats will decrease and the consumption of glycogen will increase. Therefore, three workouts of an hour or so at lower intensity will burn more fat than six workouts of 30 minutes or so at a higher intensity. In addition, high-intensity exercises are more likely to result in muscular or skeletal injury.

The bottom line is that not everyone needs to be a marathon runner in order to be physically fit. The myth that one must "go for the burn" and that with "no pain, no gain" is just not true and keeps what may otherwise be motivated people on the couch. Now that we know how we need carbohydrates as well as fats to fuel our aerobic body, how can we use this information to devise a suitable exercise program and help us achieve a better physique as well as a healthier mind and body?

Exercise for Body Trimming

> *O, that this too, too solid flesh would melt, thaw and resolve itself into a dew!*
> —William Shakespeare, *Hamlet*

It is certainly true that not everyone is, nor should everyone be, satisfied with his or her present body weight or condition. For these individuals, exercise offers a mechanism but certainly not a guarantee of success; tenacity and dedication do. It is sad but true that the body gives up its pound (or even ounce) of fat very grudgingly. The body's conservation of fat is an evolutionary survival mechanism, resulting from its experience with periods of food deprivation. For early humans, it was equally important for survival that the stored body fat not be depleted too rapidly, even when normal activity was maintained. The fact that you are here today is due in great measure to the large amount of energy (9 calories per gram) stored in fat. The bad news is that to reduce your weight by 1 gram (454 grams are equal to 1 pound), you need to burn at least this amount (1 gram) of fat.

Table 23.1 shows the estimated amount of calories expended during various activities for a 160-pound person (people with more body weight will burn more calories per hour; e.g., a 160-pound person will burn an estimated 183 calories after walking at the rate of 2 mph for an hour, whereas a 200-pound person will burn an estimated 228 calories and a 240-pound person will burn around 273 calories). Calorie expenditure varies widely depending on the type of exercise, the level of intensity, and the individual's unique physical characteristics.

Table 23.1 Calories Expended per Hour of Activity

Activity	Calories
Walking, 2 mph	183
Dancing, ballroom	219
Walking, 3.5 mph	277
Bicycling, 10 mph	292
Golf, carrying clubs	329
Skiing, downhill	365
Swimming laps	511
Tennis, singles	584
Stair treadmill	657
Rope jumping	730
Rollerblading	913
Running, 8 mph	986

Source: "Calories Expended per Hour of Activity," Mayo Foundation for Medical Education and Research (MFMER). Copyright © 2007.

The information presented in Table 23.1 is discouraging for anyone trying to lose weight by exercise alone. Exercise, even hard exercise, does not burn that many calories. If your sole purpose is to lose body fat, the facts are even worse than the table indicates. Unfortunately, as we have seen, the aerobically active body needs to burn carbohydrates as well as fat. Remember that, for about 30 minutes into your exercise workout, you are burning more calories in the form of carbohydrates than fat. It is only after this time that fat calories are being consumed in greater amounts. Even more discouraging is the fact that even if you are burning equal calories from fat and carbohydrates, you must expend more than twice as many calories to consume 1 pound of fat as those needed to consume 1 pound of carbohydrates.

Assuming that your exercise program consumes 50% of total calories as fat and 50% as carbohydrates, walking for 1 hour at 3.75 miles per hour would burn off 150 calories of fat at 9 calories per gram, or less than 0.04 pounds. (For reference, there are 100–120 calories in a slice of many kinds of bread.) Put in practical terms, you would need to walk 25 miles at this speed to burn off 1 pound of fat. Very depressing, isn't it? And they say exercise helps depression!

Clearly, the most effective way to shape up our bodies, including enhancing muscle tone and reducing fat, is to combine a sensible exercise program with an equally sensible diet (see Chapter 22, "Eating Yourself Fit"). In fact, dieting programs to lose weight nearly always fail unless they are combined with a regular exercise program. It is critical for each person to choose an exercise program and diet that fits into his or her lifestyle and is consistent with his or her personal preferences. If the exercise is not enjoyable and the diet barely palatable, this is a recipe for failure. The Personal Pleasure Inventory (see Appendix A) should be useful in helping you to select an exercise program that is both enjoyable and beneficial. If spending time outdoors and enjoying nature is a natural high for you, why not consider running, walking, hiking, cycling, cross-country skiing, or playing tennis, rather than an aerobics class or swimming in an indoor pool?

Training for Physical Health

It has been said that the human body is the only machine that wears out when not used. Probably no single factor is as important to your health as a sensible program of exercise. People with active lifestyles are far less likely to die from cancer and heart disease than their physically out-of-shape contemporaries.

Over the course of almost five decades, Paffenbarger and Lee (1996) of Stanford University conducted large epidemiologic studies proving that increased exercise lowers the chance of death from heart disease. Paffenbarger used periodic questionnaires to chronicle the personal characteristics, physical activity levels, illnesses, and deaths of over 50,000 college alumni. He examined the role of multiple factors in coronary heart disease: blood pressure, body mass, physical activity, cigarette smoking, history of hypertension, and family history of hypertension and heart attacks. Of all these factors, physical inactivity ranked ahead of all except hypertension as a predictor of coronary heart disease (CHD). The health benefits of physical activity were found to be independent of all the other variables tested. For example, inactive men who had a history of hypertension and smoked ("suicide in the fast lane") had a rate of CHD more than twice that of physically active smokers.

According to the American College of Sports Medicine (Pescatello et al., 2004),

Exercise remains a cornerstone therapy for the primary prevention, treatment, and control of hypertension. The optimal training frequency, intensity, time, and type (FITT) need to be better defined to optimize the BP [blood pressure] lowering capacities of exercise, particularly in children, women, older adults, and for certain ethnic groups. Based upon the current evidence, the following exercise prescription is recommended for those with high blood pressure:

- Frequency: on most, preferably all, days of the week
- Intensity: moderate intensity
- Time: 30 min of continuous or accumulated physical activity per day
- Type: primarily endurance physical activity supplemented by resistance exercise (p. 533)

Besides the well-established relationship between exercise and reduced cardiovascular disease, working out has been shown to have benefits in preventing a host of other life-threatening ailments including obesity, type 2 diabetes, osteoporosis, and cancer (Stein, 2008b). By examining blood samples of some 2,400 twins, Cherkas and her colleagues (2008) at Kings College London determined that telomeres (repeated DNA sequences) on the ends of chromosomes in white blood cells (leukocytes) were longer in subjects who exercised the most (an average of 199 minutes weekly) compared with more sedentary subjects who exercised an average of 16 minutes or less per week. Telomeres are believed to be markers of aging because they shrink over time. Individuals who exercised regularly were found to have telomeres equal in length to sedentary types who were on average 10 years younger. The researchers speculate that stress, inflammation, and oxidative stress (damage to cells caused by exposure to oxygen) may have caused the shortening of telomeres in sedentary types.

Another spectacular finding has been reported by Dean Ornish (2008), founder and president of the Preventive Medicine Research Institute at the University of California, San Francisco. Ornish and his colleagues found that the activity of more than 500 genes in the normal tissue of 30 men with low-risk prostate cancer changed after the patients began to exercise regularly, practice yoga stretching, and eat diets that were low in red meats and fat, and heavy in fruit, vegetables, and whole grain (supplemented by soy, fish oil, selenium, and vitamins C and E). According to the research team, the study shows that lifestyle changes of stress management, regular exercise, and sound nutrition may prompt swift and profound differences in the behavior of tumor-suppressing genes (turning them on) whereas certain disease-promoting ones (including oncogenes implicated in both prostate and breast cancer) were down-regulated or switched off. The study challenges the widely held belief that "it's all in my genes and there is nothing I can do." Ornish refers to this type of reasoning as "genetic nihilism," arguing that "genes may be our disposition but not our fate" (quoted in Stein, 2008a).

Healthy Body, Healthy Mind

The natural healing force within us is the greatest force in getting well.

—Hippocrates

*Opposite to Exercise is Idleness or want of exercise, the bane
of body and mind … and a sole cause of Melancholy.*

—Robert Burton, 1632

We know that a healthy mind free from stress promotes good bodily health, but can a healthy body produce a healthy mind? Can there actually be a connection between bodily fitness and mental health? Clearly, this concept is not new. Holistic medicine, which regards the mind and body as a single entity, has been a tenet of Hindu philosophy for centuries. As we have seen, modern research clearly indicates a correlation between mind and body. But how does it work? In order to understand this relationship, we shall review and look more closely at the mind-body connection, discussed earlier in Chapter 3 (Figure 3.4) and Chapter 10 (Figure 10.4) as the hypothalamus-pituitary-adrenal (HPA) axis.

Figure 23.3 shows the HPA axis, including beta-endorphins, which traditionally are thought to play a role in the runner's high and general feelings of well-being after vigorous exercise. The release of endorphins during exercise may step down the body's response to stress.

In reaction to outside stimuli, including stress, higher centers in the brain, such as the hippocampus, relay messages to the hypothalamus, the portion of the brain that regulates emotion as well as many other basic processes of life, such as eating and body temperature. The hypothalamus then relays the stress signals by sending certain chemicals (corticotropin-releasing hormone) to the pituitary gland, which lies at the base of the brain. This gland then releases other molecules, including endorphins (in the brain and in the blood) and ACTH, which in turn alert the outer layer (cortex) of the adrenal glands, which are situated on top of the kidneys. The adrenal cortex secretes other molecules, known as corticosteroids such as cortisol, which control a number of body functions. These include preparing the body for an emergency by releasing adrenaline and norepinephrine. As seen in Figure 23.3, in our HPA system, one of the regulating mechanisms is a negative feedback loop to the hypothalamus that is activated by corticosteroids from the adrenal glands. This in turn inhibits sending the molecular message from the hypothalamus to the pituitary gland. There are other molecular organizations that regulate the HPA system, including the now familiar neurotransmitters dopamine, norepinephrine, and serotonin (Donaghy, 2007), as well as the equally familiar endorphins (Mutrie & Faulkner, 2003).

Once again, it seems that molecules of the mind literally have the power to control our lives both physically and mentally. It is well-known that stress can upset the HPA system and that continued, unrelenting stress can lead to depression. Nemeroff (1998) argues that in depressed people, the homeostasis of the HPA axis is upset. Since stress can upset HPA homeostasis and possibly lead to depression, it would seem logical that exercise, which we have shown to relieve stress, would at least reduce depression by reestablishing homeostasis in the HPA system.

Figure 23.3 Regulation of the HPA Axis The activity of the HPA axis is inhibited by beta-endorphins, which act on the hypothalamus and pituitary gland, as well as by negative feedback from the adrenal cortex. These effects reduce the amount of cortisol released during stress (see Fig. 3.4).

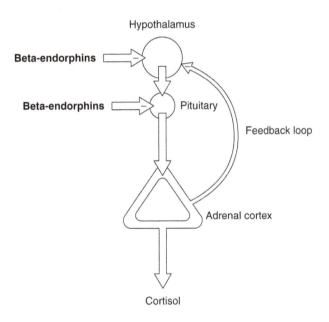

Running Away from Depression

In a pioneering study of the relationship between exercise and mental health, Griest and colleagues (1978) found that a program of regular jogging reduced symptoms in a group of depressed outpatients more than a regimen of psychotherapy. Even more encouraging was the one-year follow-up, which found that most of the members of the running group had become regular runners and remained symptom free. Since that time, dozens of studies (Donaghy, 2007) have been conducted on the effect of both acute (usually single aerobic events) and chronic (long-term physical fitness) exercise. In nearly all cases, exercise—even anaerobic exercise—was found to be beneficial in reducing symptoms of depression, although moderate aerobic training seems to be most beneficial (Netz, Wu, Becker, & Tenenbaum, 2005).

As encouraging as these results may be, they do not necessarily relate to most of us, who are not clinically depressed but do have occasional episodes of mild depression that rob us of some of life's joys. Most research indicates that exercise can help rid us of the often too frequent "blahs." I. L. McCann and Holmes (1984) at the University of Kansas randomly assigned a group of mildly depressed females into three groups: (1) an aerobic exercise group, (2) a group that practiced muscle relaxation, and (3) a no-treatment group. At the end of 10 weeks, only those in the aerobic group showed dramatic decreases in depression. Nearly every study since has confirmed that exercise provides excellent protection against depression. According to Donaghy (2007), "Fifteen randomized controlled trials (RCTs) and three meta-analyses provide evidence that exercise can reduce depression and that it can be as effective as cognitive therapy" (p. 76). A more recent meta-analysis suggested that the actual effect size of exercise on alleviating depression is small to moderate, but it may be as effective as psychological or medication treatments (Cooney et al., 2013).

Why does exercise help with depression? The effects of elevating serotonin and regulating the HPA-axis are thought to be key. Increasing serotonin (and norepinephrine) allows for better cortisol regulation; additionally, when serotonin increases and cortisol decreases, the levels of BDNF (brain-derived neurotropic factor) increases. BDNF is a growth factor that promotes neurogenesis. Research shows that treatment with SSRI antidepressants promotes neurogenesis, and this may actually be what's responsible for the antidepressant effects—which explains why it generally takes a couple of weeks or more for depression to lift after medication has begun (Mahar, Rodriguez Bambico, Mechawar, & Nobrega, 2014). Exercise also has epigenetic effects on the gene that encodes for BDNF, causing an increase in transcription that upregulates BDNF production (Fernandes, Arida, & Gomez-Pinilla, 2017). By the way, this neurogenesis has been specifically linked to the hippocampus, a brain region important for memory. The increase in neurogenesis helps explain exercise's boosts on both mood and cognitive function.

For those starting an exercise program with the hope of feeling better, don't expect to feel better *immediately*. Stick with the program because it may take some time before alleviation of depression or anxiety is felt. But the same is true of antidepressant medication, and antidepressants don't have the cardiovascular and other health benefits that exercise does!

Exercise as Ancillary Treatment for Substance Abuse

As reviewed by Weinstock et al. (2017), several studies have investigated exercise programs as augments to traditional substance abuse treatment. The rationale makes sense: data already support the use of exercise to help alleviate symptoms of depression and anxiety. Not only are these commonly co-occurring conditions for addictions, but they are also commonly experienced by individuals going through drug withdrawal. Given that stress can be a trigger for relapse, and exercise helps decrease people's reactivity to stress, exercise could provide a cost-effective, non-pharmaceutical means of coping with stress.

Lynch and colleagues (2013) did a comprehensive review of exercise as a treatment for drug addiction, integrating both human and animal data. The authors assessed the literature based upon when the exercise was implemented—during initiation of drug use, progression from use to addiction, or withdrawal—and provide a rationale based on neurobiology as to why this would be helpful. Their conclusion: *"While exercise generally produces an efficacious response, certain exercise conditions may be ineffective or lead to detrimental effects depending on the level/type/timing of exercise exposure, the stage of addiction, the drug involved, and the subject population"* (p. 1622; italics in original). One reason why exercise may be helpful during initiation of drug use and withdrawal is it boosts dopamine levels, providing feelings of pleasure. Moderate levels of exercise may also help prevent the progression from occasional use to addiction. However, there are data that show that excessively *high levels* of exercise during initiation of drug use may increase the risk of abuse by inducing changes in the reward pathway similar to those produced by chronic drug abuse. Moreover, humans have social factors that are tied to their exercise—for instance, playing team sports—and sometimes those social factors work against exercise as a protective effect for drug abuse. For instance, imagine a sports team whose members shun smoking but think binge drinking at parties is "cool."

Weinstock et al. (2017) note some degree of success using exercise as an additional form of treatment for substance abuse, although there is a limited number of studies available. Generally, results point to increased quality of life for those who engage in exercise as part of treatment. For example, three studies by Brown and colleagues (2009, 2010, 2014; cited by Weinstock et al., 2017) implemented exercise as part of 12-week outpatient alcohol treatment programs and found decreased drinking over the course of the program, compared to individuals in treatment who didn't engage in exercise. A major limitation of most studies published in this area, however, is a lack of follow-up, so there's no indication if the gains achieved through exercise are sustained.

Weinstock and colleagues (2017) further critique use of exercise as part of substance abuse treatment. Unfortunately, there are relatively few programs that use it, and those that do generally do not incorporate a high enough "dose" (frequency, intensity, and duration) of exercise to produce benefits. Another problem is lack of participation, compounded by high drop-out rates. It seems that many people struggling in addiction recovery have low motivation for exercising. To counter this, Weinstock and colleagues developed an exercise intervention that is being tested in treatment programs. They call for incorporating incentives to increase participation and for monitoring clients to ensure they are really participating. They also recommend having someone skilled in exercise training work directly with the clients on exercises the clients choose. In accordance with American College of Sports Medicine (2013, cited in Weinstock et al., 2017) recommendations, they suggest establishing session frequency at the outset but adjusting intensity and duration based upon the individual client's fitness level.

Runner's High: Fact or Fiction?

CASE EXAMPLES

Runner A

Thirty minutes out and something lifts. Legs and arms become light and rhythmic. My snake brain is making the best of it. The fatigue goes away, and feelings of power begin. I think I'll run 25 miles today. I'll double the size of the research grant request. I'll have that talk with the dean. ...

Then, sometime into the next hour comes the spooky time. Colors are bright and beautiful, water sparkles, clouds breathe, and my body, swimming, detaches from the earth. A loving contentment invades the basement of my mind, and thoughts bubble up without trails. I find the place I need to live.

Runner B

All of a sudden, my throat opens up, [and] the air flows back into my lungs. All the tension in my body is released, and at that moment, a rush of power surges through my body. I can feel the tautness of every muscle in my being. I hear and feel my breath billowing out through my mouth, and I feel a moment of exhilaration. It's as if I'm looking through the eyes of a new and baptized person. And at that moment, I feel like I could run forever.

The above descriptions capture the experience of runner's high—a euphoric, drug-like state accompanied by decreased anxiety and pain sensations. A pleasant mental state and sense of relaxation may continue for a while after the exercise session ends. Anecdotal accounts of runner's high abound, although there do not appear to be data indicating how common this experience really is. Gupta and Mittal (2015, p. 207) wrote: "There are many sceptics who dismiss the very notion of runner's high because they consider it to be nothing but a mere confabulatory act, which stems from the sense of achievement felt upon successful completion of a physical activity." In other words, some people think it's a myth.

There are actually a number of biochemicals that increase during exercise: norepinephrine, serotonin, and dopamine, in addition to cortisol. At this point, we might think that dopamine alone could be responsible for the euphoria. For decades, however, endogenous opioids have been thought to provide runner's high because they could account not just for the mood changes but also for differences in pain sensitivity. There are some data to support the role of endorphins in runner's high. For instance, a PET imaging study by Boecker et al. (2008) examined levels of endogenous opioid binding in 10 athletes' brains under two different conditions: at rest and after 2 hours of running. Ratings of euphoria were higher after the running condition and were associated with higher levels of endogenous opioids, compared to the resting condition.

More recently, however, some researchers have questioned the role of endogenous opioids in runner's high. The reason is that, although blood levels of endogenous opioids increase during exercise, these chemical molecules do not readily cross the blood-brain barrier. Therefore, researchers looked to other chemical messengers that also increase during exercise—endocannabinoids, which do readily cross into the brain. In a series of studies with mice, Fuss and colleagues (2015) demonstrated the role of endocannabinoids in this phenomenon. Mice were allowed free access to an exercise wheel for three days, then denied access for 2 days. On day 6 of the study, some mice were given access to their running wheels for 5 hours while others were still denied access. Data showed that mice with exercise wheel access prior to behavioral testing had decreased anxiety and increased pain thresholds; these are two measures consistent with runner's high. Moreover, treatment with drugs that block endocannabinoid receptors eliminated the anxiety- and pain-reducing effects of the wheel running. On the contrary, blocking endogenous opioid receptors did not decrease these effects. The authors argue that these data support the role of endocannabinoids over endogenous opioids in runner's high.

So which is it—are endocannabinoids or endogenous opioids responsible for positive mood states produced during exercise? Perhaps it is both! The mouse model of runner's high has no way of accessing euphoria (the actual "high" part of the runner's high). Yes, the runner mice showed decreased pain responses and anxiety reactions, but were they "buzzed"? We just don't know. Endogenous opioids can be released within the brain itself and would not have to cross the blood-brain barrier to produce euphoria. We suggest that perhaps runner's high could be a combination of several neurochemicals: endogenous opioids, endocannabinoids, and maybe even dopamine.

Make Life a Moving Experience

Table 23.2 presents a few simple ways to increase our everyday physical movement. These "incidental" activities may not burn many calories, but they are likely to increase your odds of having a longer, healthier, and happier life.

Table 23.2 Incidental Exercise

- Use the stairs (up and down) instead of the elevator. Start with one flight and gradually build up to more.
- Park a few blocks from your destination and walk the rest of the way. If you ride on public transportation, get off a few stops early.
- Take an exercise break—get up from your computer, stretch, walk around, and give your muscles and mind a chance to relax.
- Instead of snacking, take a walk.
- When traveling, choose a hotel with a good exercise facility or near a walking trail and make use of it.
- Instead of using the cell phone while driving, try phoning while walking.
- Some physical activity can save you money: mow the lawn or do your own housework.
- When you walk the dog, try walking a little faster and a little longer. If you don't have a pet, adopt one.
- Try "aerobic shopping": wear track shoes and take a few extra laps around the mall. Stretch to reach items in high places and squat or bend to look at items at floor level. Trying this in the supermarket will extricate you from the "impulse buying" zone at eye level that's easy to reach.
- Add any moving activity that you find to be enjoyable and stress free.

Obligatory Words of Caution!

Despite its many benefits, exercise needs to be done sensibly to avoid potential risks. One piece of advice is the same given for determining medication dosing to treat various conditions: "start low and go slow." This pertains to people who have not exercised for a long time and are out of shape. They will not have the endurance to be able to jog or work-out for long periods of time, and attempting to do so can make exercise feel aversive. Exercise novices should start at lower levels of intensity for shorter periods of time and build from there. The person should have a positive relationship with their exercise program!

A less obvious piece of advice is that there can be physical risks associated with overdoing exercise that extend beyond the typical musculoskeletal injuries. Occasionally, people work out so intensely that they end up with a condition called rhabdomyolysis in which muscle tissue breaks down, releasing proteins into the blood stream that damage the kidneys. The person won't experience the worst of it until a day or more after their workout: fatigue, pain, muscle swelling, nausea, and brown-colored urine. This is a serious condition requiring a trip to the emergency room because the kidneys can fail. Several articles over the past few years have highlighted cases associated with spin classes (Brogan, Ledesma, Coffino, & Chandler, 2017) and cross-training (Meyer, Sundaram, & Schafhalter, 2017; Paidoussis & Dactis, 2013). Brogan et al.'s article regarding spin class-induced cases notes that out of 46 cases that had been reported, 42 were first-timers. Their article calls for greater public awareness of the risks and establishment of guidelines for safe spinning for beginners. But regardless of the kind of exercise—don't "overdose" by overdoing!

A final word of caution pertains to a subset of individuals who seem to get hooked on exercise. The prevalence of exercise addiction is difficult to determine, although Szabo et al. (2015) suggest it may be as high as 3% of regular exercisers in the general population, with the risk being substantially higher among athletes. Landolfi (2013) reviews theories about why people get hooked on exercise. One theory—and perhaps most people's initial assumption—is that it's due to the biochemistry of runner's high. Over time, the person may develop tolerance and need to increase exercise in order to get their buzz; when deprived of exercise, they feel anxiety, depression, and agitation (withdrawal symptoms). But other theories point to personality factors and motivations for exercising. Landolfi concludes that those who are exercising due to body image and weight concerns, rather than for psychological effects, are most at risk (there can be an overlap with those who are susceptible to eating disorders).

If you need to try to decide how much is too much, Adkins and Keel (2005, cited in Landolfi, 2013) point to the amount of exercise: when the duration, intensity and/or frequency of exercise exceeds what is needed for physical health benefits and the person is injuring him/herself from this activity, it's time to consider this is an addiction. Ultimately, the goal is not to make the person stop exercising completely but rather to bring them back to a moderate, non-injurious, level of exercise so that they can reap health benefits as others do.

Chapter Summary

The focus of this chapter is on developing a better understanding of the whole-life benefits of regular exercise. Exercise can build self-esteem, provide social interaction, increase motivation, and improve self-image as well as decrease stress levels, anxiety, and depression.

For those who like sensation-seeking and excitement, exercise can offer a natural high alternative to riskier activities such as gambling, promiscuity, and the abuse of stimulant drugs. It can also be useful as an adjunct treatment for complex mental health problems such as alcohol and drug addiction.

People who exercise moderately for 30 minutes at least 5 days a week are effectively reducing their vulnerably to a range of illnesses from cardiovascular disease to cancer. It is important to develop an exercise regimen that is consistent with one's lifestyle and personal preferences. All of the different exercise modalities can be grouped into five categories: isometric, isotonic, isokinetic, anaerobic, and aerobic. For aerobic exercise to be effective, it must be performed over a prolonged length of time, preferably 20 to 30 minutes at submaximal effort.

Exercise may be used for body trimming, but most successful weight reduction programs involve significant attention to diet as well. During less vigorous activities (e.g., gardening), fat is the primary source of energy consumed. But if you start jogging or running, you suddenly need more energy and more oxygen to supply your muscles with ATP. Because you need more energy immediately, the body quickly shifts from burning fat to burning carbohydrates, such as glucose or glycogen (a starch-like substance stored in the liver). Carbohydrates produce ATP faster but less efficiently than fat in terms of the calories contained per gram. Provided the intensity of the exercise is below maximal, consumption of fat exceeds carbohydrate consumption after about 30 or 40 minutes. At the end of an hour, fat consumption will be much more prevalent than carbohydrate consumption. Longer periods of submaximal aerobic exercise are more productive for weight loss than shorter bursts of intense anaerobic exercise.

In addition to the well-established relationship between exercise and protection against a host of life-threatening ailments, exercise preserves youth. Individuals who exercised regularly were found to have cells marked by the aging process to a degree consistent with those found in sedentary types who were on average 10 years younger. Another spectacular finding is that regular exercise and sound nutrition may prompt tumor-suppressing genes to "turn on," and certain disease-promoting genes are down-regulated or switched off. In short, genes may be our predisposition but not our destiny. Exercise also stimulates neurogenesis—generation of nerve cells. This can be a basis for both positive cognitive and mood effects of exercise.

Studies examining the relationship between exercise and mental health confirm that exercise offers excellent protection against depression. Such studies show that exercise can reduce depression and that it can be as effective as cognitive therapy. Stress can upset HPA homeostasis and possibly lead to depression; therefore, exercise, which is known to relieve stress, is likely to reduce depression by reestablishing homeostasis in the HPA system.

Does exercise produce a runner's high? Research findings on exercise and mood show that prolonged, submaximal exercise produces endorphins, whereas short bouts of acute exercise produce norepinephrine. Prolonged vigorous exercise causes peripheral increases in the level of endorphins. Interviews with runners suggest that running has two phases: the norepinephrine phase, followed by the endorphin phase. Exercise also promotes increased dopamine levels. More recently, endocannabinoids have been implicated in runner's high, so the entire "cocktail" of brain chemicals involved in this phenomenon may not be fully understood yet.

Finally, the health benefits of exercise are more attainable when integrated into one's daily routine. Such minor lifestyle modifications as using the stairs, walking the dog longer, vigorous mall shopping, and getting away from your computer can result in longer life and improved happiness.

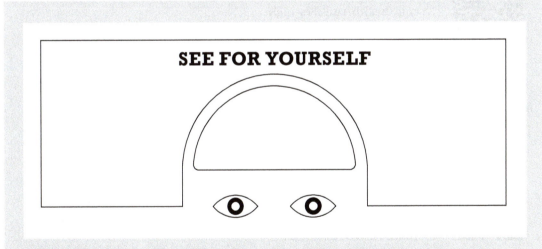

SEE FOR YOURSELF

Social psychologist Emily Balcetis talks about the importance of perception about exercise in this TED Talk.

https://www.youtube.com/watch?v=QeIrdqU0o9s

Neuroscientist Wendy Suzuki talks about exercise and brain function in this TEDx Talk. Dr. Suzuki was inspired to incorporate exercise into one of her neuroscience classes based on her own personal experience. The video shows a demonstration of the exercise used (19:25). **https://www.youtube.com/watch?v=BzCxpNUxg2U**

To learn more about her and her research on exercise and cognition in humans, visit her website: **http://www.wendysuzuki.com/intensati/**

This brief video and accompanying article explains the basic chemistry behind the experience of the Runner's High. **http://www.menshealth.com/health/runners-high**

How Running Makes You High. 2014. K. Aleisha Fetters. *Men's Health Magazine.* 1:11

The Disruptive Power of Exercise. 2016. Dr. Wendy Suzuki. TEDx Talks. 19:25

Neuroscientist and fitness instructor Dr. Wendy Suzuki discusses her research and experience studying the impact of exercise on the brain. The talk includes a demonstration of the exercise program Suzuki implemented, which includes movement paired with spoken affirmation. **https://youtu.be/BzCxpNUxg2U**

Why Some People Find Exercise Harder Than Others. 2014. Emily Balcetis. TEDxNewYork. 14:08

Social psychologist Emily Balcetis presents her research on how visual perception affects our choices and how to shift our perspective. **https://www.ted.com/talks/emily_balcetis_why_some_people_find_exercise_harder_than_others**

Run When You're 25 for a Sharper Brain When You're 45. 2014. Maanvi Singh. *NPR: Shots*. Brief Article.

Research shows that exercise has long term cognitive benefits. **http://www.npr.org/sections/health-shots/2014/04/02/297910425/run-when-youre-25-for-a-sharper-brain-when-youre-45**

What's Good for the Heart is Good for the Brain. 2016. Patti Neighmond. *NPR: Morning Edition*. 3:27

Research suggests that heart health is correlated with brain health in older Americans. **http://www.npr.org/sections/health-shots/2016/05/02/476209760/whats-good-for-the-heart-is-good-for-the-brain**

Mayo Clinic: Exercise for weight loss: calories burned in 1 hour

Source: Selected activities derived from Mayo Foundation for Medical Education and Research (MFMER).(2007). *Weight loss*. Retrieved February 11, 2009, from http://www.mayoclinic.com/health/exercise/SM00109.

24

Meaningful Engagement of Talents

The artist, at the moment of creating, does not experience gratification or satisfaction.... Rather it is a joy, joy defined as the emotion that goes with heightened consciousness, the mood that comes with the experience of actualizing one's own potentialities.

—Rollo May, *The Courage to Create*

Introduction: Where Do We Go from Here?

So, you've made it this far. You've learned that healthy relationships, proper diet, exercise, and mindfulness all promote positive physical and psychological states, enhance quality of life, and provide natural highs. At this point, you may be thinking that there's no way to go up from here. We beg to differ! Tapping into your talents is a way of finding rewards and helping to fulfill that elusive top rung of Maslow's hierarchy: self-actualization. In this last chapter, we explore how to identify your talents and passions (even if you believe you don't have any), and how utilizing them can give you a dopamine buzz. We also examine programs for at-risk youth that enable teens to grow their talents—not only to provide reward and build self-esteem, but also to provide positive social interactions. Moreover, the fruits of their labors may provide joy to others, allowing transcendence into the realm of self-actualization.

Capitalizing on Abilities and Strengths

Howard Gardner (1983, 1993; Hatch & Gardner, 1993) points our attention to children who, at a very early age, evidence great talent in such domains as music, art, mathematics, language, and athletics. Since prodigies appear only in certain areas of endeavor, these proclivities seem to tap biological abilities inherent in the human species. Gardner views intelligence as a plural characteristic, that is, a set of distinct and specific abilities.

Gardner (1983) initially formulated a provisional list of seven intelligences. As described below, linguistic and logical-mathematical abilities are traditionally valued in schools; musical, bodily-kinesthetic, and spatial abilities are usually associated with the arts; intrapersonal and interpersonal capacities are referred to as "personal intelligences" (Gardner, 1999). M. K. Smith (2008) outlined the components of Gardner's pluralistic model of intelligence as follows:

Linguistic intelligence involves sensitivity to spoken and written language, the ability to learn languages, and the capacity to use language to accomplish certain goals. This intelligence includes the ability to effectively use language to express oneself rhetorically or poetically, and as a means to remember information. Writers, poets, lawyers, and speakers are among those that Gardner (1983, 1993) sees as having high linguistic intelligence.

Logical-mathematical intelligence consists of the capacity to analyze problems logically, carry out mathematical operations, and investigate issues scientifically. It encompasses the ability to detect patterns, reason deductively, and think logically. This intelligence is most often associated with scientific and mathematical thinking.

Musical intelligence involves skill in the performance, composition, and appreciation of musical patterns. It encompasses the capacity to recognize and compose musical pitches, tones, and rhythms. According to Gardner (1983, 1993), musical intelligence runs in an almost structural parallel to linguistic intelligence.

Bodily-kinesthetic intelligence entails the potential of using one's whole body or parts of one's body to solve problems. It is the ability to use mental abilities to coordinate bodily movements. Gardner (1983, 1993) sees mental and physical activity as related.

Spatial intelligence involves the potential to recognize and use the patterns of wide space and confined areas.

Interpersonal intelligence is concerned with the capacity to understand the intentions, motivations, and desires of other people. It allows people to work effectively with others. Educators, salespeople, religious and political leaders, and counselors all need a well-developed interpersonal intelligence.

Intrapersonal intelligence entails the capacity to understand oneself and to appreciate one's feelings, fears, and motivations. In Gardner's (1983, 1993) view, it involves having an effective working model of ourselves, and being able to use such information to regulate our lives.

Since Gardner's (1983) original formulation of multiple intelligences, he and his colleagues have examined the possibility of additional constructs for intelligence: naturalistic, spiritual, existential, and moral (Gardner, 1999). After much research and scholarly discussion of the four proposed constructs, *naturalist intelligence*—one that permits humans to recognize, categorize, and draw upon certain features of the environment—has been added to the list. Gardner (1983) believes that the challenge of effectively utilizing human capital is "how to best take advantage of the uniqueness conferred on us as a species exhibiting several intelligences" (p. 45).

Go with Your Flow!

The manifestation of any intellectual trait is most likely the result of the combination of innate propensity and environmental support. While intelligence is traditionally considered as the "ability to solve problems," psychologists posit a "group of 'hot' intelligences, so called because they process 'hot' information: signals concerning motives, feelings, and other domains of direct relevance to an individual's well-being and survival" (Peterson & Seligman, 2004, p. 338). When intelligence is considered in the context of evolution, the brain would be expected to provide reward (neurochemically mediated pleasure) upon realization of one's intellectual capacity. There is an abundance of corroborative evidence to support this view.

Csikszentmihalyi was intrigued by the stories of artists who lost themselves in the passion for their work. Over the past 30 years, he has interviewed and observed thousands of people who described the experience as being in a state of "flow." Nakamura and Csikszentmihalyi (2002) characterize flow as follows:

- Intense and focused concentration on what one is doing in that present moment
- Merging of action and awareness
- Loss of reflective self-consciousness (i.e., loss of awareness of oneself as a social actor)
- A sense that one can control one's actions—that is, a sense that one can, in principle, deal with the situation because one knows how to respond to whatever happens next
- Distorting of temporal experience, typically a sense that time has passed faster than normal
- Experience of the activity as intrinsically rewarding such that often the end goal is just an excuse for the process.
- Most of us have experienced flow even if we didn't know the word "flow." Perhaps you think of this a "being in the zone." But see if Csikszentmihalyi's description rings a bell:

Flow denotes the holistic sensation present when we act with total involvement. It is the kind of feeling after which one nostalgically says: "that was fun," or "that was enjoyable." It is the state in which action follows upon action according to an internal logic which seems to need no conscious intervention on our part. We experience it as a unified flowing from one moment to the next, in which we feel in control of our actions, and in which there is little distinction between self and environment; between stimulus and response; or between past, present, and future. (Csikszentmihalyi, 2014, p. 136–137).

Csikszentmihalyi (1975, 2000) graphically depicted the necessary elements and trajectory of flow experiences by comparing relationships between perceived challenges and skills. As shown in Figure 24.1, three domains of momentary experience were identified: (1) *flow*—when an individual is profoundly engaged in a task, feeling competent and fulfilled; (2) *boredom*—a lack of interest and a sense of discomfort when opportunities to perform are too easy relative to one's skills; and (3) *anxiety*—a sense of discomfort when demands of the task at hand exceed one's ability to perform.

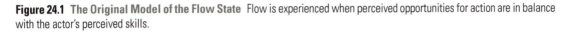

Figure 24.1 The Original Model of the Flow State Flow is experienced when perceived opportunities for action are in balance with the actor's perceived skills.

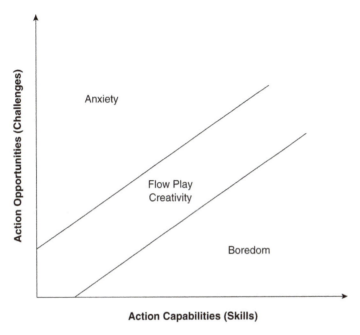

The likelihood of achieving a state of flow increases as challenges and skills move beyond an individual's average level. Whatever the type of intelligence (e.g., music, art, mathematics, sports), the desired state of "flow" requires pushing the envelope beyond one's comfort zone (e.g., in sports, your opponent may have a bit more skill; in mathematics, the answers are not so easy to come by; in art, the task requires heightened attention and deep concentration).

Longitudinal studies provide evidence of the positive relationship between flow and long-term success. Csikszentmihalyi, Rathunde, and Whalen (1993) followed the development of teenagers throughout high school. Students who, at the age of 17, were committed to a talent (academics, work, or sports) reported having experienced their talent as a source of flow 4 years earlier during the initial data gathering when they were 13 years old. Similarly, Heine (1996) showed that students who excelled in the second half of a math class (controlling for initial abilities and grade point average) were the ones who experienced flow in the first half. Extrapolating from these findings, attributes such as commitment and perseverance—factors necessary for lasting satisfaction and success—are related and are possible offshoots from the experience of flow. "The experience of absorption provides intrinsic rewards that encourage persistence and return to the activity" (Snyder & Lopez, 2007, p. 258).

By this point in time, the mention of any kind of rewards, including "intrinsic rewards" in the previous paragraph, may lead you to wonder if dopamine plays a role in flow. Although there are not definitive answers, Di Domenico and Ryan (2017) suggest that dopamine is an important player. However, dopamine does not appear to be the sole answer: brain imaging data reveal activation in regions related to "salience detection, attentional control, and self-referential cognition" (pg. 1). Dopamine circuits are clearly involved in salience detection and attentional control. Although not directly discussed by Di Domenico and Ryan, it is notable that activation of attentional control and self-referential circuits are also linked to meditation.

Integrating Models for Self-Discovery and Change

The implication of flow research is that pleasure, achievement, satisfaction, and productivity are enhanced by access to states of flow. Csikszentmihalyi (1990, 1996, 2014) and his colleagues (Csikszentmihalyi & Robinson, 1990; Jackson & Csikszentmihalyi, 1999) and Perry (1999) describe two paths to becoming meaningfully engaged in one's talents or abilities: (1) identifying and shaping environments that are conducive to flow experiences, and (2) identifying personal characteristics and attentional skills that can be honed to make the experience of flow more likely.

With the goal of facilitating natural highs for at-risk youth as healthy alternatives to drugs, crime, and emotional distress, Milkman and colleagues (Milkman, 2001; Milkman, Wanberg, & Robinson, 1996) integrated Gardner's theory of multiple intelligences and Csikszentmihalyi's conceptualization of flow. Youth were recruited from three at-risk populations: (1) criminal justice referrals from probation and parole, (2) mental health referrals from the department of social services, and (3) students at risk for suspension or expulsion from high school. They were encouraged to join Project Self-Discovery (PSD) to discover and expand their abilities and talents.

The results of offering art in students' preferred area of interest (music, dance, or visual art), adventure-based counseling (beyond the comfort zone), and cognitive-behavioral psychology (interpersonal and intrapersonal intelligences) to transform the lives of this "covert" treatment population are striking. Milkman et al. (1996, 2001) were able to show that PSD had a positive impact on participants by increasing their ability to use artistic involvement to replace drugs and crime.

The spirit of this unique program is captured through the case example, "Better Than Dope," presented below.

CASE EXAMPLE: Better Than Dope[1]

"Living" is a word David never understood. To him, living meant running for his life from gangs and guns. It meant trying to avoid drugs and drinking. It meant being afraid. When he was growing up, he lived in a bad neighborhood. Down the street from him was a group of the worst people you would ever wish to avoid. He had to walk past them every day. In his neighborhood, death was an everyday occurrence; he fell asleep to the sound of gunshots.

At home, his mother had men visiting at all hours. She would ignore David and his sisters. She loved to drink with her men friends. When she let one of them move in, he thought he was king of the world. He would beat David and his sisters. David missed his dad because his dad didn't beat him. His dad didn't treat him like dirt. Still, he wasn't a stable father figure, either. In fact, David didn't have an adult male figure he could talk with.

At school, he didn't think he would fit in. At lunch hour, he would sit by himself. Later, he figured the only way to fit in was by using drugs and drinking. When he joined the Junior Reserves Officers Training

Corps, he found the common link was doing drugs. The more he hung out with this crowd, the more he used drugs. Because of his habits, he was failing most of his classes. During his sophomore year, he went to class only 9 days. Soon, he didn't go at all. His life fueled his self-loathing. He hated himself so much, he even attempted suicide. He tried a number of methods—hanging himself, overdosing on aspirin, and drinking way beyond any safe amount.

At about that time, he started to eat a lot. In less than a year, he had gained over 100 pounds. He was so alienated from his family that he barely spoke to his mom. Whenever she asked to talk, he would tell her to go to hell. Sadly, she also began abusing drugs, which made their relationship even worse. She had her drug addiction and David had his. Then, at age 16, David had a mild heart attack. The drugs were the reason behind his heart problems. Right then, he decided to quit.

After that summer, he enrolled in school. His guidance counselor told David about Project Self-Discovery. PSD is a community-based, after-school program that provides artistic alternatives to teenagers who have problems with school, their family, or the community. Participants use music, art, and dance to reach their goals. Students also receive school credit for attending. David signed up for the music program.

Although David's story is unique, his needs are similar to the majority of youth who participate in the project. Artistic activities have proven to be powerful antidotes to emotional distress, drug abuse, crime, and violence. In fact, PSD evolved into a model for treating a broad spectrum of teenage problems. At PSD, one could find youths with varied backgrounds and behaviors.

Betty Jo, a 15-year-old African American, lives at Daybreak, a community corrections residential placement. She describes her mother as "a bitch" and "evil," and she (Betty Jo) has attempted suicide twice by overdosing on Tylenol. Betty Jo's art teacher says she is interacting nicely with other students and "demonstrates an orderly, precise, and methodical way of working on projects."

Peter, age 16, is diagnosed as schizoaffective. Since the age of 8, he bounced around foster homes, some of which were sexually abusive. Now in custody of the Department of Social Services, he is excited about learning to act at PSD so he will be "noticed" and begin his career in theater arts. His dance teacher reports that he is interacting well with his peers while benefiting from her coaching and her advice.

Rosa, a 15-year-old Latina, has decided to never again "bang" with her sect of the gang, Gangster Disciples. Five of her close friends have died or have been murdered during the past year. She is considered highly motivated by her music teacher and is getting along well with her fellow students and staff.

The usual outcome for kids like Rosa, Peter, and Betty Jo is enormous frustration and failure. These teenagers have a variety of mental disorders and behavioral problems and come from radically diverse backgrounds. "Mental health is a key component of a child's overall wellbeing. There are approximately 30 million youth in the U.S. between the ages of 10 and 17— enough to populate an entire country! In 2015, an estimated 3 million adolescents aged 12 to 17 had at least one major depressive episode in the past year. This number represented 12.5% of the U.S. population aged 12 to 17." (National Institute of Mental Health, 2015, n.p.). "A total of 13%–20% of children living in the United States experience a mental disorder in a given year, and the prevalence of these conditions appears to be increasing." (Perou, et al., 2013, n.p.).

The inspiration for PSD came from viewing substance abuse as just one of many forms of dangerous pleasure-seeking behaviors (Jessor, 1998; Milkman & Sunderwirth, 1983, 1987, 1993, 1998; Shaffer, LaPlante, et al., 2004). Any action that deposits a hearty dose of dopamine in the brain's reward center—be it drink, money, sex, calories, crime, or cocaine—can trigger addiction. Yet rather than using drugs, people can bring about self-induced changes in brain chemistry through natural highs. Drugs and alcohol are seen as "chemical prostitutes," or counterfeit molecules that compromise the clockwork of nature's most complex and delicate entity: the brain.

PSD began serving teenagers in January 1993 as the result of a 4-year national grant through the Center for Substance Abuse Prevention. The project was designed to show that natural highs could serve as viable alternatives to drug abuse and associated high-risk lifestyles. Teenagers were targeted because of their extreme vulnerability to substance abuse, crime, and violence. The most common causes of death among young adults between ages 15 and 24 are accidents (unintentional injuries) at 41.1%, suicide at 17.6%, and assault (homicide) at 17.6%. (Centers for Disease Control and Prevention, 2016, n.p.). Juan talks about his brush with death in the description that follows.

The Hood

They came up the dirt hill. There were eight or nine of them and there was just six of us. My homeboy gave me a .25 [.25 caliber pistol]. It was already loaded, cocked, and ready to bust some caps. So I went up to them and said, "I know you, the punk motherfucker who just tagged up my locker. You disrespected my hood. Just kill me motherfucker. Get it over with." So he pulls out this crowbar. And I pulled out the .25. I put it to his head and said, "What hood you from?' He said "CMG Blood." And I said "WHAT FUCKIN' HOOD YOU FROM?" And he said, "CMG Blood." Then he said, "Crip." I made that fool cry and shit. When you gotta strap [gun], you feel like you got the power to do anything in the world. You can make anybody scared of you with a strap.

—Juan

While dance connects one to sensuality, music provides a safe vehicle for the expression of emotional unrest. Painting and drawing provide an opportunity to visualize topics that may be too difficult for words. In this excerpt from Paula's script, it is evident that through writing and drama, she is discovering important means to transcend the wounds of her childhood.

The Family

He's my father. I don't even know what that means. I don't even know what a father is. I don't even know what a father is supposed to be. I used to think it was someone who took me fishing, or maybe camping. Someone who I could talk to, who protected me, took care of me. But if you ask me, I'd say a father is someone who beats up his family. A father is someone who screams, yells, and cusses out his family. A father is someone who breaks things, smashes things, ruins things. I HATE HIM! I HATE THIS HOUSE WHEN HE'S IN IT! It's like a war zone and he is the enemy. Every second, I'm looking over my shoulder to see if he's coming after me. He didn't tear up my drawings. He tore up my dreams. I HATE HIM! I hate it when he beats on my mom. I hate seeing my mother on the floor; I hate feeling like I have to protect her from the enemy and I HATE THAT THE ENEMY IS HIM. WHY AM I PROTECTING THE ENEMY? He's my father. I love him.

—Paula

At-risk teens experience traditional talking therapies as invasive and persecutory. We have discovered that adventure-based counseling, using hands-on games and physical challenges—like providing stilts to "feel 10 feet tall"—are far more engaging than standard lecture presentations. A kid who has a strong drive for thrill seeking and novelty can avoid gang violence by satisfying their needs through the performance of poetry, hip hop, or rap. Almost magically, the conga, paintbrush, or guitar can become formidable substitutes for pistols or joints.

It is no secret that people who are hopelessly dependent on drugs can still participate in the creative process. The necessary complement to artistic skill development is learning to restructure habitual patterns of thought (e.g., "I can't cope") and feelings (e.g., fear, anger, sadness) that trigger destructive actions (e.g., drugs, crime, violence). We raise the question, "What else is possible?" To this end, PSD youth participated in a 32-session life-skills curriculum entitled Pathways to Self-Discovery and Change (PSD-C): A Guide for Responsible Living (Milkman & Wanberg, 2005; 2012). The Pathways curriculum, now widely used in youth correctional and substance abuse treatment settings in the United States and abroad, is predicated upon the use of modeling, role-plays, skits, comic strips, and interactive exercises to groove in neuropsychological pathways for prosocial thought and behavior.

The client's workbook (PSD-C) is geared toward a range of reading and conceptual abilities and uses comic strip illustrations (e.g., Figure 24.2) and interesting stories that are presented through the narrative voice of adolescents who experience a broad spectrum of problems with substance abuse, criminal conduct, and mental health issues. This allows the clients to engage in active discussion about the situations, thoughts, emotions, and behaviors that have become embroidered in life problems. An excerpt from Jeb's Story is shown below.

I started smoking weed when I was 12. I didn't really listen to my mom when she gave me her anti-drug lecture. After all, what did she know? She was always at work anyway. So I started hanging out with the people around my block, and realized that there was a potential job scene. People wanted drugs, but they couldn't get them on a regular basis. That is when I became a drug pusher. I could make money, they could get their drugs, and I wasn't hurting anyone by doing it. After all, these people already chose their path in life.

Things were going good until some other dealers moved into the neighborhood. They were selling cheaper drugs, and I had to struggle to keep up with my old customers. I started pushing on the streets instead of just quitting the game. Ended up trying to sell to an undercover, and now I'm here in jail, waiting to be tried as an adult.

Figure 24.2 Jeb's Story Comic strip illustrations are used to engage client interest in cognitive-behavioral restructuring.

CHAPTER 1

Building Trust and Motivation to Change

JEB'S STORY

GOAL OF THIS CHAPTER

To discuss the progam

Getting to know each other

To learn how thoughts affect feeling and actions

To recognize the importance of change

Figure 24.3 shows the visual model used throughout the curriculum for restructuring thoughts, emotions, and actions. Events experienced by an individual trigger automatic thoughts (shaped by underlying beliefs), which are then translated into emotions that lead to behaviors. As presented in Chapter 19, if an individual chooses a positive (adaptive) course of action (through rational thought and emotional control), or opts against a negative one (distorted thought and emotional dysregulation), the outcome will likely be good, which strengthens the recurrence of positive behavior and encourages positive thought processes. Conversely, if the individual chooses a negative (maladaptive) course of action, the outcome will likely be bad, strengthening more negative thought processes (Milkman & Wanberg, 2012).

David Describes his Experience in the Pathways Course

We gathered in a theater and talked about our past experiences with gangs, drugs, and all the other things that teens face. We also talked about ways we could avoid these situations. I tried to be quiet, but my mouth would just shoot open. When it came to bad situations, I thought that I had a lot to offer the group.

David was making great progress. He had successfully embarked on the first stage of our three-tiered program, each phase providing the foundation for the next level of growth and change. Level I, called the Intervention Program, lasted 12 weeks and the youth met after school for 3 hours, 2 days a week. Level II, the Graduate Program, was on an ongoing, scheduled meeting one afternoon a week. Level III, the Mentorship Program, allowed graduate students who had demonstrated leadership skills to serve as facilitators and mentors to youth in the initial, 12-week Intervention Program.

Figure 24.3 Pathways to Learning and Change The cognitive-behavioral map for change is artistically enhanced to appeal to the teenage mind-set.

Kenneth Wanberg and Harvey B. Milkman, Pathways to Self-discovery and Change: Criminal Conduct and Substance Abuse Treatment for Adolescents. The Participant's Workbook, pp. 15. Copyright © 2005 by SAGE Publications. Reprinted with permission.

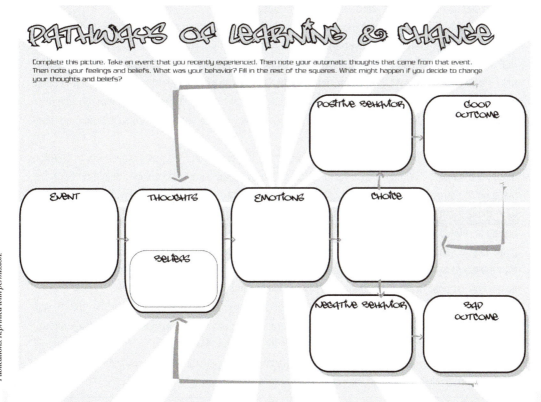

The Rites of Passage is another component designed to transform the participants. Here is David's description:

We went up to the mountains and froze our butts off for the sake of getting to know each other and ourselves. There was a ropes course that scared me beyond belief. I had always thought that I was afraid of nothing. But we were hooked up to a rope that was connected to a wire between two large poles. I kept thinking, I am going to die.

When David hooked up his harness, everyone in the group started to cheer for him. Suddenly, his face took on a funny expression, like the Grinch learning the meaning of Christmas. "I got the strength to hurry through the course and when I got down, it felt as though a huge weight had been lifted off my shoulders." Later that night, the kids and staff sat in the cabin and talked about the course, and all the students wrote in their journals about their day. The thing that David remembers most was "the acceptance between everyone."

Around the campfire, all participants shared their thoughts. David, for example, spoke about his drug abuse and his plans for the future: "When we returned from the mountains, I felt a change in me."

David stayed with the program for 2 additional years. He learned the guitar and the drums, performed on stage, acted in a video film, and became a mentor for others who were new to the program. He felt wanted and he helped others realize they were wanted, too.

The results of PSD have been impressive. During 10 years of program operation (1992–2002), PSD received 1,700 referrals from Denver-area youth advocates. Short- and long-term outcome data show that artistic endeavor and adventure-based counseling are effective antidotes to drugs and other high-risk behaviors (Milkman, 2001; Milkman et al., 1996). Not only do participants show test scores reflecting improved mental health and family functioning, but they also reveal decreased reliance on negative peer influences and decreased drug and alcohol use. These positive outcomes are sustained long after graduation.

As David puts it, because of PSD he has "become a better person." He has learned how to care for others and himself. "Without this experience, I don't know what I would be doing. I would probably be living on the streets using drugs, and not having any direction," he says. Today, David shares a house with an old friend from school, has a full-time job, and visits his mother once a week. He has also started boxing to relieve stress and lose weight. And for the last 4 years, he has been completely drug free. He plans to go to college and major in business and computer science. In David's words: "PSD showed me that the world is full of possibilities. The program also showed me that when a door is closed a window is open. What does living mean to me now? Living is knowing that you are not alone."

Project Self-Discovery demonstrated that so-called at-risk youth are amenable to positive growth and development, providing that the means for engagement are perceived as nonjudgmental, adventurous, and creatively rewarding. Those who completed the program showed significant improvements on scores that measure mental health, resistance to negative peers, sustained drug or alcohol use, criminal conduct, and family functioning.

Promoting Healthy Lifestyles Before Serious Problems Emerge

The most important lesson from PSD is that when at-risk teenagers are provided with positive role models and healthy alternatives to drugs and crime (in sync with their passions, abilities, and natural proclivities) then "dope" (including crime and other destructive forms of pleasure-seeking) become undesirable choices. The obvious sequel to the PSD success story is to create environments with some of the attributes of Project Self-Discovery as a form of primary prevention, i.e., before youth even begin to have problems with unhealthy means of coping with life-stress. This is exactly what happened. Of all places, the country of Iceland has developed a model, whereby youth, nationwide, are guided by the provision of healthy lifestyle opportunities, from middle childhood through adolescence. As shown in the case study below, the Iceland model has had enormous success and is being replicated in multiple cities throughout Europe.

CASE STUDY: Iceland Succeeds at Reversing Teenage
Substance Abuse: The U.S. Should Follow Suit[1]

The tide began to turn in 1997 when substance abuse among Icelandic youth was approaching epidemic proportions; e.g., 17% of 15-year olds had already tried hashish and wanton binge drinking was becoming the norm. Despite a concerted approach to provide school-based education about the negative effects of drugs, alcohol and drug abuse appeared to be spiraling out of control.

As explained by Professor Inga Dóra Sigfúsdóttir (Director of Research at the Icelandic Centre for Social Research and Analysis – ICSRA) at the April 19, 2016, United Nations General Assembly Special Session (UNGLASS) on the World Drug Problem: "A visionary group of policy makers, researchers and practitioners – decided to gather their strengths, try out a new approach, and see whether it might be possible to reverse this negative, upward trend in substance use among young people."

"We wanted to change what looked like this: research, policy and practice {as} three separate aspects with scientists publishing their findings, not knowing, and often not caring much whether they would come to any use in society."

We wanted to change from this: To this:

Figure 24.4[2]

The seminal group of activists for the health and safety of Icelandic youth initiated an inter-sectoral collaboration (i.e., uniting multiple sectors of society) among a broad network of stakeholders in adolescent well-being, i.e., parent groups, schools, research scientists, politicians, media, sports organizations, and corporations. A highly-publicized annual "Prevention Day" was launched in 2007 by the President of Iceland, the goals of which were:

- Increase time spent together by adolescents and their families
- Postpone the onset of alcohol use until 18 years of age and over
- Increase adolescent participation in structured and organized youth activities supervised by adults

---

1 Source: http://www.huffingtonpost.com/harvey-b-milkman-phd/iceland-succeeds-at-rever_b_9892758.html.
2 24.4a: Icelandic Centre for Social Research and Analysis, Youth in Europe Evidence-based Drug Prevention. Copyright © by The Icelandic Centre for Social Research and Analysis (ICSRA).

24.4b: Icelandic Centre for Social Research and Analysis, Youth in Europe Evidence-based Drug Prevention. Copyright © by The Icelandic Centre for Social Research and Analysis (ICSRA).

The high value placed on political support for evidence-based drug prevention is epitomized by the policies of Dagur Eggertsson, Mayor of Reykjavik. "My vision is that politics should be in a much closer dialogue and discussion with academia and researchers, and that good monitoring of policies are instrumental to having good results."

Understanding the Icelandic Model

The Icelandic model is predicated upon three pillars of success: (1) evidence-based practice; (2) using a community-based approach; and (3) creating a dialogue among research, policy, and practice.

Core elements of the model:

- A holistic model, not a program
- Views adolescents as social attributes
- A primary prevention approach
- Requires long-term commitment, not a fixed time-period
- Emphasizes environmental change and not within-person change

Every year, nationwide, Icelandic children and teenagers 10–16 years of age take part in a comprehensive survey of "Life and Living Conditions of Youth" (85–87% response rate). Youth are promised anonymity and instructed to mark answers to multiple choice questions about risk and protective factors including: self-esteem; patterns of alcohol or other drug use; family living conditions; neighborhood characteristics; attitudes about school; leisure time activities; religious affiliations; quality of parental supervision; love and guidance; support from peers; neighborhood support; anxiety, depression, and suicide; etc.

Analysis of these surveys shows that affiliations with family, peer group effects, and types of recreational activities available are the strongest predictors of the paths taken by adolescents.

Jón Sigfússon (ICSRA Director of Youth in Iceland and Youth in Europe) explains the essence of the Icelandic model:

> "Well it's not magic. It's simply organized, structured work. We collect data in Iceland in February among the 10–16-year olds and within a period of about two months we have processed this data and made the report. They know from this data the situation in their municipalities approximately two months after the actual data collection.
>
> Today we have contact persons within all these municipalities and we regularly communicate with them. We tell them what's up next in the research field and in the data collection. When they get their reports, or even before that, they have set up meetings and someone from our research institution comes and we go through the data...with them.
>
> They gather people working in the field... teachers, politicians, people from the health care center, the church, the sports club. They also gather parents. We go through the situation and just talk about how the situation is. This is how

your children are feeling, this is what they want and here there is a rise, here is a decline. We follow this up so that the information gets into action as soon as possible."

Positive Outcomes

Iceland's progress is evident from the information presented in Figure 24.5 below. From 1998 to 2017, the percentage of 15–16-year-old Icelandic youth drunk in the past 30 days declined from 42% to 5%; daily cigarette smoking dropped from 23% to 3%; and having used cannabis one or more times, fell from 17% to 5%.

Figure 24.5 Substance Abuse Decrease Among 15–16 Year Adolescents in Iceland

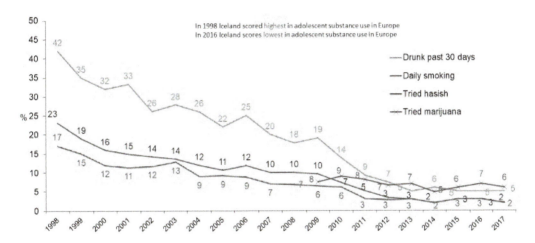

Future Directions: Benefitting from the Icelandic Experience

In her closing remarks at the UN Special Session, Professor Sigfúsdóttir presented her view on how to move forward:

> In a world where there are practically no cultural or national boundaries any-more—AND cyberspace is without limits— teenagers are mobile in more than one sense of the word.
>
> In this kind of world, we know that it is only through joining forces, by learning from each other and basing our work on trustworthy research, by which we will succeed in fighting substance use. It is not an easy task. But—based on research—we know it can be done—with guardianship, community attachment and informal social control. We will not change anything by single project solutions. Prevention needs to be consistent and comprehensive—not one campaign, but a quiet revolution!

If you want to replicate what happened in Iceland, here is what I recommend you to do:

- Minimize unsupervised adolescent time periods
- Create more activity, frequently and in structured ways
- Delay "first drink" onset
- Base your efforts at a community level—where things can get done, practically and quickly
- Get your elected leadership to campaign for this venture "first drink" onset

Source: Adapted from: Milkman, H. (2017). Iceland Succeeds at Reversing Teenage Substance Abuse: The U.S. Should Follow Suit. Huffington Post

Self-Discovery in Everyday Life

The positive outcomes derived from participation in PSD show that many types of dysfunctional patterns of thinking, feeling, and acting are improved though artistic engagement, adventure-based counseling, and cognitive-behavioral restructuring. These results seem almost too good to be true. How could a single program be restorative for so many different types of problems?

Certainly the common malaise of depression underlies many faces of emotional and behavioral disorder. In *Listening to Prozac,* Kramer (1997) convincingly argues that there are many manifestations of mood disorders with a common biological underpinning—low levels of the neurotransmitter serotonin. Prozac seems to have beneficial effects on a range of personality problems, including shyness; sensitivity to rejection; obsessive traits; and of course, depression. From our discussion of the reward cascade in Chapter 3, we learned that by increasing the availability of serotonin (common to Prozac and other SSRIs), the flow of dopamine is increased in the nucleus accumbens. But the jury is still out on the wisdom of relying so heavily on antidepressant medications. Recent discoveries in brain science point to the conclusion that a broad array of mood disturbances and problem behaviors can be effectively reduced through behavioral means (Lambert, 2008). The data suggest that the flow of dopamine can be enhanced through anticipating and engaging in complex and challenging tasks, that is, meaningful engagement of talents.

Lambert (2008) was intrigued by research reports of dramatically increased rates of depression among those born in the middle third of the 20th century compared with those who were born in the first third. In fact, one study showed that the rate of depression was 10 times greater for people born in the latter part of the 20th century than it was for those born earlier. Lambert reasoned that since the anatomy of the human brain probably has not changed much in the last few decades, the answer to the question of increased rates of depression probably resides in lifestyle changes. We have dramatically decreased our reliance on physical effort to enhance survival. Microwave ovens eliminate the complex tasks of food preparation, computers save us from retyping our manuscripts, and online games save us from scuffing our knees playing schoolyard sports.

Our brains are programmed to receive rewards when we carry out tasks that enhance our survival. When our physical effort produces something tangible, that is, visible and meaningful toward survival, we are hardwired to derive a deep sense of satisfaction and pleasure. Lambert (2008) refers to this emotional payoff as "effort-driven rewards" (p. 33). These rewards are rooted in the chemical messages and neural infrastructure of our brain.

As shown in Figure 24.6, the nucleus accumbens, which we have discussed throughout this book as the brain's primary pleasure center, is positioned in close proximity to the motor system, or striatum, and the limbic system, a series of structures that control emotions and learning. The closely linked motor and emotional systems also extend to our frontal cortex, which is a vast assembly of neurons responsible for problem solving, planning, and judgment. "Essentially the accumbens is a critical interface between our emotions and our actions....It is the proposed neuroanatomical network underlying the symptoms of depression" (Lambert, 2008, p. 35). In fact, according to Lambert, all of the major symptoms of depression can be correlated to a brain part on the accumbens-striatal-cortical network. "Loss of pleasure? The nucleus accumbens. Sluggishness and slow motor responses? The striatum. Negative feelings? The limbic system. Poor concentration? The prefrontal cortex" (p. 35).

Figure 24.6 Accumbens-Striatal-Cortical Network The nucleus accumbens forms a critical interface between the motor system (striatum) and the prefrontal cortex that controls thought.

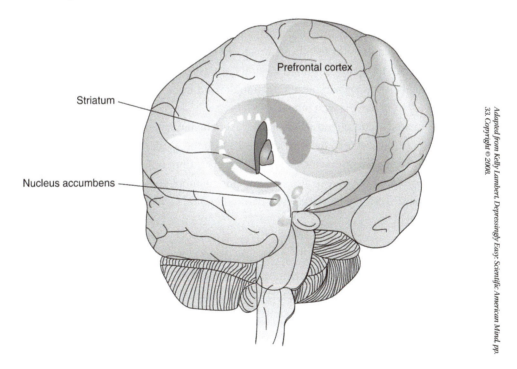

Adapted from Kelly Lambert, Depressingly Easy: Scientific American Mind, pp. 33. Copyright © 2008.

The upshot of this analysis is that "effort-driven rewards" derived from the accumbens-striatal-cortical network are seen as behavioral antidotes to depression. By engaging in complex tasks that engage our innate capacities for multiple intelligences (e.g., kinesthetic, spatial, musical), we can achieve a state of neurochemical balance conducive to happiness and well-being. Engaging one's talents such as playing a favorite sport, sketching a waterfall, hip hop dancing, or campaigning for political office—especially if the activities are perceived as meaningful—is likely to charge up the reward cascade. Through meaningful engagement of talents, we can orchestrate the natural release of serotonin, endorphins, and dopamine, thereby reducing our reliance on alcohol, drugs, or other false props to improve mental and physical well-being.

The Personal Pleasure Inventory

A secret to deriving happiness and meaning in life is to integrate an array of enjoyable activities with the values that guide our existence. Too often we remain largely unaware of not only our value priorities, but also the very activities we find enjoyable. By bringing our pleasure orientations to the forefront of our awareness, we increase the likelihood of achieving a balance between what we deem important and the things we actually do. Wanberg and Milkman (2008) have classified the kinds of activities from which human beings derive pleasure. After having administered the *Personal Pleasure Inventory* (PPI) to a diverse population of adults, four broad-pleasure dimensions have been identified: (1) Physical Expression, (2) Self-Focus, (3) Aesthetic Discovery, and (4) Collective Harmony.

Each dimension is defined by a specific group of related activities. The dimension of *Physical Expression* includes sports, challenging nature, and physical fitness. Within the dimension of *Self-Focus* are the factors for romance, calming sensations, and material comforts. The dimension of *Aesthetic Discovery* includes seeking adventure, enjoying nature, home involvement, mental relaxation, and artistic stimulation. *Collective Harmony* combines the factors of mental exercise, people closeness, spiritual involvement, and helping others. Pleasure orientations are not mutually exclusive; that is, aesthetic appreciation of music and art may coincide with pleasurable stimulation derived from learning to play a musical instrument, combined with joy from playing with others.

Readers are invited to complete the Personal Pleasure Inventory as presented in Appendix A. The scoring system allows respondents to measure themselves on the 15 aforementioned pleasure orientations. By focusing on the activities from which you derive pleasure, not only will you become more mindful of your needs and desires, but you will also begin to pursue more goal-directed pathways to pleasure. By challenging yourself to engage more deeply in your identified pleasure preferences, you will most likely orchestrate natural highs.

Chapter Summary

At a very early age, some children show tremendous talent in such areas as music, art, mathematics, language, and athletics. These talents appear to tap biological abilities inherent in the human species. Howard Gardner views intelligence as a plural characteristic, that is, a set of distinct and specific abilities. Gardner initially formulated a provisional list of seven intelligences: linguistic and logical–mathematical abilities; musical, bodily–kinesthetic, and spatial abilities; and intrapersonal and interpersonal capacities ("personal intelligences"). After much research and scholarly discussion, naturalist intelligence has been added to the list. Gardner believes that the challenge of the future is to effectively capitalize on our species' unique capacity for multiple intelligences.

Csikszentmihalyi was intrigued by the stories of artists who lost themselves in the passion for their work. Over 30 years, he and his colleagues developed the concept of "flow:" intense and focused concentration on what one is doing, merging of action and awareness, loss of reflective self-consciousness, a sense that one can control one's actions, distorting of temporal experience, and experience of the activity as intrinsically rewarding.

The likelihood of achieving a state of flow increases as challenges and skills move beyond an individual's average level. Whatever the type of intelligence (e.g., music, art, writing, mathematics, sports), the desired state of flow requires pushing the envelope beyond one's comfort zone. Longitudinal studies provide evidence of the positive relationship between flow and long-term success. Extrapolating from these research studies, such attributes as commitment and perseverance—factors necessary for lasting satisfaction and success—are related and possible offshoots from the experience of flow. The experience of absorption provides intrinsic rewards that encourage persistence and return to the activity.

The implication of flow research is that pleasure, achievement, satisfaction, and productivity are enhanced by access to states of flow. Csikszentmihalyi and his colleagues describe two paths to becoming fully absorbed in one's talents or abilities: (1) identifying and shaping environments conducive to flow experiences, and (2) identifying personal characteristics and attentional skills that can be honed to make the experience of flow more likely.

With the goal of facilitating natural highs as healthy alternatives to drugs, crime, and emotional distress, Milkman and colleagues integrated Gardner's theory of multiple intelligences and Csikszentmihalyi's conceptualization of flow, resulting in a program for at-risk high school students called Project Self-Discovery (PSD). Program participants showed evidence of improved mental health and family functioning, and they also experienced decreased reliance on negative peer influences and decreased drug and alcohol use. These positive outcomes were sustained long after graduation.

PSD results show that many types of dysfunctional patterns of thinking, feeling, and acting are improved though artistic engagement, adventure-based counseling, and cognitive-behavioral restructuring. The logical sequel to Project Self-Discovery is to promote and provide healthy alternatives for all youth, before they fall by the wayside and begin to experiment with unhealthy means to manage stress. The Iceland Prevention Model, has succeeded in developing a national strategy which has dramatically reduced teenage substance abuse and associated problem behaviors.

Recent discoveries in brain science point to the conclusion that a broad array of mood disturbances and problem behaviors can be effectively reduced through behavioral means. The data suggest that the flow of dopamine, which leads to absorption, commitment, and success in personally meaningful tasks, can be enhanced through anticipating and engaging in complex and challenging multisensory activities. Readers are invited to complete the Personal Pleasure Inventory in the Appendix to become more mindful of the activities and experiences that are likely to promote natural highs.

Note

1. Project Self-Discovery: Artistic Alternatives to Teenage Drug Abuse, Crime, and Violence received the 2000 Coming Up Taller Award from the National Endowments for the Arts and Humanities and the President's Committee on the Arts and the Humanities—one of 10 programs nationwide to receive this honor.

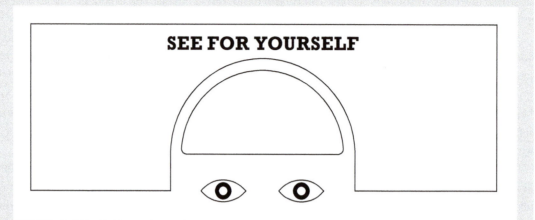

SEE FOR YOURSELF

Flow, the Secret to Happiness. 2004. Mihaly Csikszentimihalyi. TED Talks. 18:55

Positive psychologist Mihaly Csikszentimihalyi describes his work on flow, and includes various examples of individuals in flow, and how this state is measured and identified. **https://www.ted.com/talks/ mihaly_csikszentmihalyi_on_flow**

Beyond Wit and Grit: Rethinking the Keys to Success. 2015. Howard Gardner. TEDxBeaconStreet. 17:03

Psychologist Howard Gardner presents his theory of multiple intelligences, or MI. Dr. Gardner introduces each of the 8 intelligences he has identified, and discusses the practical application of this approach to intelligence. Gardner goes on to discuss the concept of grit and what it means to be successful in terms of creating "good work"—that which is excellent, engaged, and ethical. **https://www.youtube.com/watch?v=IfzrN2yMBaQ**

Better Than Dope. 2001. Harvey Milkman. *Psychology Today*.

Dr. Milkman describes Project Self Discovery through experiences of some of the young people who have engaged in the program. **https://www. psychologytoday.com/articles/200103/better-dope**

Do Schools Kill Creativity? 2006. Ken Robinson. TED Talks. 19:24

Creativity expert and educator Sir Ken Robinson posits that teaching creativity is as important as teaching literacy. **https://www.ted.com/talks/ken_robinson_says_schools_kill_creativity**

APPENDIX A

The Personal Pleasure Inventory

Personal Pleasure Inventory: Using one of the five choices below, rate the degree of pleasure you get from each activity. Place the number (0 through 4) of your choice on the blank line by the activity.

0 = Never engaged in activity or no pleasure derived from activity

1 = Low degree of pleasure derived

2 = Moderate degree of pleasure derived

3 = High degree of pleasure derived

4 = Very high degree of pleasure derived

Work Sheet

1. SPORTS
    - ____ Playing basketball
    - ____ Tennis
    - ____ Watching sports
    - ____ Softball
    - ____ Going to sporting events
    - ____ Playing golf
    - ____ Playing team sports
    - ____ Playing volleyball
    - Total Score___

2. CHALLENGING NATURE
    - ____ Climbing
    - ____ Canoeing
    - ____ White water rafting
    - ____ Camping out
    - ____ Hiking
    - ____ Skiing/snowboarding
    - Total Score___

3. PHYSICAL FITNESS

____ Eating healthy foods

____ Exercising/stretching

____ Biking/rollerblading

____ Swimming

____ Walking/running

Total Score___

4. ROMANCE

____ Making love

____ Kissing and cuddling

____ Giving gifts to your lover

____ Sharing intimate moments

____ Being together in nature

Total Score___

5. CALMING SENSATIONS

____ Listening to soft music

____ Warming self by fire

____ Soaking in hot tub

____ Having back rubbed

____ Massage

____ Eating in nice restaurant

Total Score___

6. MATERIAL COMFORTS

____ Making money

____ Shopping/spending money

____ Taking a luxury vacation

____ Having a nice car

____ Improving outward appearance

Total Score___

7. SEEKING ADVENTURE

____ Driving to new places

____ Visiting different cities

____ Experiencing new places

____ Experiencing new things

_____ Traveling to foreign cities

_____ Visiting different cultures

Total Score___

8. ENJOYING NATURE

_____ Being in nature

_____ Being in the woods/mountains/seashore

_____ Watching wildlife

_____ Watching the stars/moon

_____ Watching the sunrise/sunset

Total Score___

9. HOME INVOLVEMENT

_____ Redecorating your home

_____ Remodeling your home

_____ Working on home projects

_____ Painting your house

_____ Working in the yard and gardening

Total Score___

10. MENTAL RELAXATION

_____ Meditation

_____ Relaxation exercises

_____ Yoga

_____ Self-reflection

_____ Journal writing

Total Score___

11. ARTISTIC STIMULATION

_____ Going to movies/theater/concerts

_____ Going to museums/art galleries

_____ Creating art work

_____ Reading books/poetry/fiction

_____ Writing poetry/fiction

_____ Playing musical instrument

Total Score___

12. MENTAL EXERCISE

   ____ Word games

   ____ Playing cards/board games

   ____ Crossword or other puzzles

   ____ Solving mystery games

   ____ Playing computer games

   Total Score____

13. PEOPLE CLOSENESS

   ____ Helping family members

   ____ Playing with children

   ____ Being with family

   ____ Time with friends

   ____ Hugging

   ____ Being with your partner

   Total Score____

14. RELIGIOUS INVOLVEMENT

   ____ Spiritual thinking

   ____ Worship

   ____ Religious study

   ____ Church work

   ____ Going to services

   ____ Praying/meditation

   Total Score____

15. HELPING OTHERS

   ____ Counseling others

   ____ Helping others

   ____ Teaching others

   ____ Volunteering services

   ____ Supporting friends or family

   Total Score____

End of Inventory

When you have finished, put the total score for each group of activities on the Total Score line. Then, put that score on the PPI Profile. Find your score on the row for each activity and mark it with an X. Find your percentile rank for that activity. The percentile score shows how you compare with a sample of adult men and women. For example, if your raw score for SPORTS is 15, you enjoy this pleasure activity more than 65% of the people in that sample.

WORKSHEET   Personal Pleasure Inventory Profile

NAME: _____ DATE: _____ GENDER: ☐ MALE ☐ FEMALE AGE: _____

| | SCALE NAME | RAW SCORE | DECILE RANK | | LOW-MEDIUM | | | HIGH-MEDIUM | | | HIGH | |
			LOW 1	2	3	4	5	6	7	8	9	10
PHYSICAL	1. SPORTS		0 2 3 4	5 6 7	8 9 10	11 12	13	14 15	16 17	18 19 20	21 22 23	24 26 32
	2. CHALLENGING NATURE		0 2 3 5	6 7	8	9 10	11 12	13	14 15	16 17	18 19	20 21 24
	3. PHYSICAL FITNESS		2 5 6 7	8	10	11		12	13	14	15	16 18 20
	4. ROMANCE		1 6 8 9	10 11 12	13	14	15	16	17	18		19 20
SELF FOCUS	5. CALMING SENSATIONS		4 10 11	12 13 14	15	16	17	18	19	20	21 22	23 24
	6. MATERIAL COMFORTS		4 7 8 9	10 11	12	13	14	15	16	17	18	19 20
	7. SEEKING ADVENTURE		4 7 8 9	10 11 12	13	14 15	16	17 18	19	20 21	22	23 24
AESTHETIC DISCOVERY	8. ENJOYING NATURE		1 6 7 8	9 10	11	12	13	14	15	16 17	18	19 20
	9. HOME INVOLVEMENT		0 1 2	3	4	5 6	7	8	9	10	11 12 13	14 15 20
	10. MENTAL RELAXATION		0 1 2	3	4	5	6	7	8	9 10	11 12	13 15 20
	11. ARTISTIC STIMULATION		0 2 3	4 5 6	7	8	9	10 11	12	13 14	15 16 17	18 20 24
	12. MENTAL EXERCISE		0 1 2	3 4	5	6	7		8	9	10 11	12 14 20
HARMONY	13. PEOPLECLOSENESS		4 11 12	13 14	15 16	17	18	19	20	21	22	23 24
	14. RELIGIOUS INVOLVEMENT		0	1 2	3	4 5	6	7 8	9 10	11 12	13 14 15	16 19 24
	15. HELPING OTHERS		1 6 7	8	9	10	11	12	13	14	15	16 17 20

PERCENTILE: 0   10   20   30   40   50   60   70   80   90   99

Source: The personal pleasure inventory, Wanberg, Milkman and Harrison.
Copyright 2009 © K.W. Wanberg and H.B. Milkman

APPENDIX B

Contemporary Drugs and Their Effects

Drug	Street Names	Possible Effects	Withdrawal Symptoms	Adverse/Overdose Reactions
Narcotics				
Heroin	Brown sugar, China White, Dope, H, Horse, Junk, Skag, Skunk, Smack, White Horse With OTC cold medicine and antihistamine: Cheese	Euphoria, alternating wakeful and drowsy states, dry mouth, heavy extremities, itching, clouded mental functioning	Drug craving, restlessness, muscle and bone pain, insomnia, diarrhea and vomiting, cold flashes with goose bumps ("cold turkey"), kicking movements ("kicking the habit")	Low blood pressure, rapid heart rate, shallow breathing, convulsions, coma, possible death, collapsed veins, infection of the heart lining and valves, abscesses, cellulitis, and liver disease
Prescription Opioids Codeine	Captain Cody, Cody, Lean, Schoolboy, Sizzurp, Purple Drank With glutethimide: Doors & Fours Loads, Pancakes and Syrup	Lowered inhibition, enhanced sensory perception, pain relief, drowsiness, nausea, consti-pation, euphoria, confusion, slowed breathing, death	Restlessness, muscle and bone pain, insomnia, diarrhea, vomiting, cold flashes with goose bumps ("cold turkey"), leg movements	Confusion; depression; sleep problems; anxiety; increased heart rate and blood pressure; muscle tension; teeth clenching; nausea; blurred vision; faintness; chills or sweating; sharp rise in body temperature leading to liver, kidney, or heart failure and death
Oxymorphine	Biscuits, Blue Heaven, Blues, Mrs. O, O Bomb, Octagons, Stop Signs			Long-term: Long-lasting confusion, depression, problems with attention, memory, and sleep; increased anxiety, impulsiveness, aggression; loss of appetite; less interest in sex

Drug	Street Names	Possible Effects	Withdrawal Symptoms	Adverse/Overdose Reactions
Fentanyl	Apache, China Girl, China White, Dance Fever, Friend, Goodfella, Jackpot, Murder 8, Tango and Cash, TNT			
Vicodin	Hydrocodone or dihydrocodeinone (Vicodin®, Lortab®, Lorcet®, and others)			
Dilaudid	D, Dillies, Footballs, Juice, Smack Hydromorphone			
Demerol	Demmies, Pain Killer			
Methadone	Amidone, Fizzies With MDMA: Chocolate Chip Cookies			
Morphine	M, Miss Emma, Monkey, White Stuff			
Oxycodone	O.C., Oxycet, Oxycotton, Oxy, Hillbilly Heroin, Percs			
Depressants				
Xanax Valium Nembutal	Xanies, vals, Vs, downers, nerve pills, tranks	Calming effect, slows normal brain functioning, psychomotor slowing, drowsiness, poor concentration, ataxia, dysarthria, motor incoordination, diplopia (double vision), muscle weakness, vertigo, and mental confusion	Seizures, increased heart rate and blood pressure level, tremulousness, insomnia and sensory hypersensitivity, delirium, depression	Slow breathing, slowing of the heart, death vomiting, dizziness, blackouts, death

Drug	Street Names	Possible Effects	Withdrawal Symptoms	Adverse/Overdose Reactions
Alcohol	Booze, liquor, juice, sauce, brew, brewski, vino, forty, hooch	Difficulty walking, blurred vision, slurred speech, slowed reaction times, impaired memory, disturbed sleep, nausea	Feeling jumpy and nervous, shakiness, anxiety, irritability, emotional volatility, depression, fatigue, headache, sweating, nausea, vomiting, loss of appetite, insomnia, paleness, rapid heart rate, dilated pupils, clammy skin, tremor of the hands, delirium tremens, agitation, fever, convulsions	**Heart:** Drinking a lot over a long time or too much on a single occasion can damage the heart, causing problems including: • Cardiomyopathy—Stretching and drooping of heart muscle • Arrhythmias—Irregular heart beat • Stroke • High blood pressure • Research also shows that drinking moderate amounts of alcohol may protect healthy adults from developing coronary heart disease. **Liver:** Heavy drinking takes a toll on the liver, and can lead to a variety of problems and liver inflammations including: • Steatosis, or fatty liver • Alcoholic hepatitis • Fibrosis • Cirrhosis **Pancreas:** Alcohol causes the pancreas to produce toxic substances that can eventually lead to pancreatitis, a dangerous inflammation and swelling of the blood vessels in the pancreas that prevents proper digestion. **Cancer:** Drinking too much alcohol can increase the risk of developing certain cancers, including cancers of the: • Mouth • Esophagus • Throat • Liver • Breast **Immune System:** Chronic drinkers are more liable to contract diseases like pneumonia and tuberculosis. Drinking a lot on a single occasion slows the body's ability to ward off infections—even up to 24 hours after getting drunk.

Drug	Street Names	Possible Effects	Withdrawal Symptoms	Adverse/Overdose Reactions
Stimulants				
Metham-phetamine	Meth, speed, crank, ice, glass, chalk, crystal	Euphoria, wakefulness, increased energy, decrease in appetite, increased respiration, rapid heart rate, irregular heartbeat, increased blood pressure, hyperthermia	Fatigue, disturbed sleep, irritability, intense hunger, moderate to severe depression, hallucinations and delusions (psychotic reactions), anxiety	Tremors, muscle twitches, rapid breathing, confusion, hallucinations, panic, aggressiveness, fever or flu symptoms, nausea, vomiting, diarrhea, stomach pain, uneven heartbeats, feeling light-headed, fainting, convulsions, coma, or death
Cocaine	Coke, blow, snow, flake, yay-yo	Euphoria increased energy and alertness; reduced fatigue and appetite; constricted blood vessels; dilated pupils; increased temperature, heart rate, and blood pressure	Fatigue, lack of pleasure, anxiety, irritability, sleepiness, agitation or extreme suspicion, cravings, depression	Paranoid psychosis, auditory hallucinations, heart attacks, chest pain and respiratory failure, strokes, seizures, headaches, gastrointestinal complications such as abdominal pain and nausea
Dexedrine Ritalin Adderall	Bennies, speed, uppers, beans, dexies, black beauties, go pills, LA turnarounds	Increased alertness, attention, and energy; euphoria; increased blood pressure and heart rate; constricted blood vessels; increased breathing	Fatigue, depression, insomnia, hostility, paranoia	Irregular heartbeat, dangerously high body temperatures, potential for cardiovascular failure or seizures, paranoia, hallucinations
khat	Abyssinian Tea, African Salad, Catha, Chat, Kat, Oat	Euphoria, increased alertness and arousal, increased blood pressure and heart rate, depression, inability to concentrate, irritability, loss of appetite, insomnia.	Depression, nightmares, trembling, and lack of energy	Tooth decay and gum disease; gastrointestinal disorders such as constipation, ulcers, stomach inflammation, and increased risk of upper gastrointestinal tumors; cardiovascular disorders such as irregular heartbeat, decreased blood flow, and heart attack

Drug	Street Names	Possible Effects	Withdrawal Symptoms	Adverse/Overdose Reactions
Synthetic Cathinones (Bath Salts)	Bloom, Cloud Nine, Cosmic Blast, Flakka, Ivory Wave, Lunar Wave, Scarface, Vanilla Sky, White Lightning	Increased heart rate and blood pressure; euphoria; increased sociability and sex drive; paranoia, agitation, and hallucinations; psychotic and violent behavior; nosebleeds; sweating; nausea, vomiting; insomnia; irritability; dizziness; depression; suicidal thoughts; panic attacks; reduced motor control; cloudy thinking	Depression, anxiety, problems sleeping, tremors, paranoia	Breakdown of skeletal muscle tissue; kidney failure; death. Risk of HIV, hepatitis, and other infectious diseases from shared needles.
Tobacco				
	Butts, stogies, squares, coffin nails, fags, snuff, chew, cig, chaw, skag, gasper	Increased heart rate and respiration, relaxation, calmness, alertness	Anger, hostility, aggression, headache, anxiety, nausea, cravings, tingling in hands and feet, nausea, cramps	Nausea, vomiting, cancer, stroke, coronary heart disease, emphysema, aneurysm
Hallucinogens				
Salvia	Magic mint, Maria Pastora, Sally-D, Shepherdess's Herb, Diviner's Sage	Short-lived but intense hallucinations; altered visual perception, mood, body sensations; mood swings, feelings of detachment from one's body; sweating	Unknown	Unknown
Ayahuasca	Aya, Yagé, Hoasca	Strong hallucinations including perceptions of otherworldly imagery, altered visual and auditory perceptions; increased blood pressure; vomiting	Unknown	Unknown

Drug	Street Names	Possible Effects	Withdrawal Symptoms	Adverse/Overdose Reactions
LSD	Acid, blotter, microdot	Dilated pupils; increased heart rate, body temperature, and blood pressure; sweating; loss of appetite; sleeplessness; dry mouth; magnified emotions; fascination with ordinary objects; heightened aesthetic responses to color and texture	No withdrawal symptoms reported	Delusions, visual hallucinations, panic, severe and terrifying thoughts and feelings, fear of losing control, fear of insanity, despair, sometimes death
Psilocybin	Mushrooms, shrooms, boomers, God's flesh, little smoke, Mexican mushrooms, musk, sacred mushroom, silly putty, simple simon	Euphoria, disorientation, lethargy, enhancement of colors and sensations, confusion, hilarity, general feeling of connection to nature and the universe	No reported withdrawal symptoms	Nausea, vomiting, muscle weakness, drowsiness, lack of coordination, hallucinations, inability to discern fantasy from reality, panic, psychosis
PCP	Angel dust, wack, rocket fuel, ozone, hog, shermans, embalming fluid	Distorts perceptions of sight and sound; produces feelings of detachment from the environment and self; increased breathing, blood pressure, and pulse; flushing; profuse sweating; numbness of extremities; loss of muscular coordination	No withdrawal symptoms reported	Blood pressure, pulse rate, and respiration drop; nausea; vomiting; blurred vision; flicking up and down of the eyes; drooling; loss of balance; dizziness; seizures; coma; death; delusions; hallucinations; paranoia; disordered thinking; sparse and garbled speech
Marijuana				
	Pot, herb, weed, grass, Mary Jane, reefer, Aunt Mary, skunk, boom, gangster, kif, ganja	Euphoria, relaxed inhibitions, distorted perceptions, impaired coordination, difficulty in thinking and problem solving, problems with learning and memory	Irritability; sleeplessness; decreased appetite, anxiety, and drug craving	Rare but include paranoia, fatigue, panic, psychosis

Drug	Street Names	Possible Effects	Withdrawal Symptoms	Adverse/Overdose Reactions
Inhalants				
	Whippets, poppers, snappers	Slurred speech, lack of coordination, euphoria, dizziness, light-headedness, hallucinations, delusions	Not common but can include anxiety, depression, loss of appetite, irritation, aggressive behavior, dizziness, tremors, nausea	Heart failure and death, hearing loss, peripheral neuropathies or limb spasms, central nervous system or brain damage, bone marrow damage
Club Drugs				
MDMA (Ecstasy/Molly)	Adam, Clarity, Eve, Lover's Speed, Peace, Uppers	Lowered inhibition; enhanced sensory perception, mental stimulation, emotional warmth, increased physical energy, increased blood pressure and body temperature, dry mouth, euphoria	Fatigue, loss of appetite, depression, trouble concentrating	Confusion; depression; sleep problems; anxiety; increased heart rate and blood pressure; muscle tension; teeth clenching; nausea; blurred vision; faintness; chills or sweating; sharp rise in body temperature leading to liver, kidney, or heart failure and death.
Ketamine	Cat Valium, K, Special K, Vitamin K	Problems with attention, learning, and memory; dreamlike states, hallucinations; sedation; confusion and problems speaking; loss of memory; problems moving, to the point of being immobile	Unknown	Raised blood pressure; unconsciousness; slowed breathing that can lead to death. Long-term: Ulcers and pain in the bladder; kidney problems; stomach pain; depression; poor memory; sometimes used as a date rape drug; risk of HIV, hepatitis, and other infectious diseases from shared needles.
GHB	G, Georgia Home Boy, Goop, Grievous Bodily Harm, Liquid Ecstasy, Liquid X, Soap, Scoop, easy lay	Euphoria, drowsiness, decreased anxiety, confusion, memory loss	Insomnia, anxiety, tremors, sweating, increased heart rate and blood pressure, psychotic thoughts	Hallucinations, excited and aggressive behavior, nausea, vomiting, unconsciousness, seizures, slowed heart rate and breathing, lower body temperature, coma, date rapes, death.

Drug	Street Names	Possible Effects	Withdrawal Symptoms	Adverse/Overdose Reactions
Rohypnol	Circles, Date Rape Drug, Forget Pill, For-get-Me Pill, La Rocha, Lunch Money, Mexican Valium, Mind Eraser, Pingus, R2, Reynolds, Rib, Roach, Roach 2, Roaches, Roachies, Roapies, Rochas Dos, Roofies, Rope, Rophies, Row-Shay, Ruffies, Trip-and-Fall, Wolfies	Drowsiness, sedation, sleep; amnesia, blackout; slurred speech; decreased anxiety; muscle relaxation, impaired reaction time and motor coordination; impaired mental functioning and judgment	Headache; muscle pain; extreme anxiety, tension, restlessness, confusion, irritability; numbness and tingling of hands or feet; hallucinations, delirium, convulsions, seizures, or shock	Blackouts, loss of memory, dizziness, disorientation, nausea, difficulty with motor movements and speaking, vomiting, headache, rapid mood changes and violent outbursts. In combination with alcohol: severe sedation, unconsciousness, and slowed heart rate and breathing, which can lead to death.
Steroids	Juice, roids, gym candy, pumpers, stackers, balls, bulls, weight trainers, Arnies, As, anabolics	Rapid weight gain, rapid muscle devel-opment, increased endurance	Mood swings, fatigue, restlessness, loss of appetite, insomnia, reduced sex drive, steroid cravings	Acne flare-up, fluid retention, jaundice, mood swings, depression, aggressive behavior, premature balding, high blood pressure, paranoid jealousy, manic episodes, extreme irritability, delusions, stunted growth, shrinking testicles, growth of body and facial hair

Sources: NIDA (2017); Longo & Johnson (2000); U.S. Department of Health and Human Services (2004); Web sites for the following: American Council for Drug Education; MedIndia.com; National Institutes of Health; National Drug Intelligence Center; National Institute on Drug Abuse; Partnership for a Drug-Free America; Smack Foundation.

REFERENCES

Acevedo, B. P., & Aron, A. P. (2014). Romantic love, pair-bonding, and the dopaminergic reward system. In M. Mikulincer, & P. R. Shaver (Eds.), *Mechanisms of social connection: From brain to group* (55–69). Washington, D.C.: American Psychological Association.

Acohido, B., & Swartz, J. (2005). Meth addicts' other habit: Online theft. In H. T. Wilson (Ed.), *Annual editions: Drugs, society, and behavior 2007/2008* (pp. 117–121). Dubuque, IA: McGraw-Hill. (Originally published in *USA Today*, December 15, 2005).

Adamson, S. J., Kay-Lambkin, F. J., Baker, A. L., Lewin, T. J., Thornton, L., Kelly, B. J., & Sellman, J. D. (2010). An improved brief measure of cannabis misuse: The Cannabis Use Disorder Identification Test-Revised (CUDIT-R). *Drug & Alcohol Dependence, 110,* 137–143.

Adler, A. (1956). *The individual psychology of Alfred Adler.* H. Rowena & R. Ansbacher (Eds.). New York: Basic Books.

Adler, J. (2007, November 5). Rehab reality check. *Newsweek.* Retrieved July 9, 2008, from http://www.newsweek.com/id/68441

Ahmed, S. H., Guillem, K., & Vandaele, Y. (2013). Sugar addiction: Pushing the drug-sugar analogy to the limit. *Current Opinions in Clinical Nutrition & Metabolic Care, 16,* 434–439.

Ainsworth, M. D. S. (1979). Infant-mother attachment. *American Psychologist, 34*(10), 932–937.

Ainsworth, M. D. S., Bell, S. M., & Stayton, D. J. (1992). Infant-mother attachment and social development: "Socialization" as a product of reciprocal responsiveness to signals. In M. Woodhead, R. Carr, & P. Light (Eds.), *Becoming a person* (pp. 30–55). London: Routledge.

Ainsworth, M. D. S., Blehar, M. C., Waters, E., & Wall, S. (1978). *Patterns of attachment: Assessed in the strange situation and at home.* Hillsdale, NJ: Lawrence Erlbaum.

Ainsworth, M. D. S., & Bowlby, J. (1991). An ethological approach to personality development. *American Psychologist, 46,* 333–341.

Alanez, T. (2016, March 4). Flakka's rise and fall: From crisis to clampdown. *SunSentinel.* Retrieved from http://www.sun-sentinel.com/local/broward/fl-flakka-decline-20160304-story.html

Allen J.G., Flanigan S.S., LeBlanc M., Vallarino J., MacNaughton P., Stewart J.H., Christiani D.C. (2016). Flavoring chemicals in e-cigarettes: diacetyl, 2,3-pentanedione, and acetoin in a sample of 51 products, including fruit-, candy-, and cocktail-flavored e-cigarettes. Environmental Health Perspectives;124(6):733–9.

Allison, S. E., von Wahlde, L., Shockley, T., & Gabbard, O. (2006). The development of the self in the era of the Internet and role-playing fantasy games. *American Journal of Psychiatry, 163,* 381–385.

American College of Neuropsychopharmacology (2007). Nicotine Addiction Might Be Controlled By Influencing Brain Mechanisms. Retrieved on February 5, 2018.

American Heart Association. (2008). Cigarette smoking and cardiovascular disease. Retrieved June 5, 2008, from http://www.americanheart.org/presenter.jhtml? identifier=4545

American Heart Association (2015, October 23). Illegal drugs and heart disease. Retrieved on March 26, 2017 from http://www.heart.org/HEARTORG/Conditions/More/MyHeartandStrokeNews/Illegal-Drugs-and-Heart-Disease_UCM_428537_Article.jsp#.WNfDUYWcFPY

American Psychiatric Association. (1994). *Diagnostic and statistical manual of mental disorders* (4th ed.). Washington, DC: American Psychiatric Association.

American Psychiatric Association. (2000). *Diagnostic and statistical manual of mental disorders* (4th ed., text revision). Washington, DC: American Psychiatric Association.

American Psychiatric Association. (2013). Diagnostic and statistical manual of mental disorders (5th ed.). Arlington, VA: American Psychiatric Publishing.

Amoroso, T (2015) The psychopharmacology of ±3,4 methylenedioxymethamphetamine and its role in the treatment of posttraumatic stress disorder. *J Psychoactive Drugs* 47: 337–344.

Anderson, K. (1999, August). *Internet use among college students: Should we be concerned?* Paper presented at the American Psychological Association, Boston.

Anderson, R. N. (2002). *Deaths attributable to obesity: Making sense of the numbers.* Washington, DC: National Center for Health Statistics. Retrieved January 6, 2009, from http://www.cdc.gov/nchs/ppt/bsc/anderson.ppt

Andreassen, C. S. (2014). Shopping addiction: An overview. *J. Nor. Psychol. Ass. 51,* 194–209.

Aron, A., & Aron, E. N. (1986). *Love and the expansion of self: Understanding attraction and satisfaction.* New York: Hemisphere.

Aron, E. N., & Aron, A. (1996). Love and expansion of the self: The state of the model. *Personal Relationships, 3,* 45–58.

Arria, A.M., & Compton, W.M. (2017). Complexities in understanding and addressing the serious public health issues related to the nonmedical use of prescription drugs. *Addictive Behaviors, 65,* 215–217.

Arria, A. M., Wilcox, H. C., Caldeira, K. M., Vincent, K. B., Garnier-Dykstra, L. M., & O'Grady, K. E. (2013). Dispelling the myth of "smart drugs": Cannabis and alcohol use problems predict nonmedical use of prescription stimulants for studying. *Addictive Behaviors, 38,* 1643–1650.

Arterburn, S., & Felton, J. (1991). *Toxic faith: Experiencing healing from painful spiritual abuse.* Nashville, TN: Oliver-Nelson.

Atran, S. (2002). *In gods we trust: The evolutionary landscape of religion.* New York: Oxford University Press.

Auslander, J. (2016, January 11). Wave of fake driver's licenses, IDs hits Aspen. *The Aspen Times.* Retrieved from http://www.aspentimes.com/news/wave-of-fake-drivers-licenses-ids-hits-aspen/

Axen, K., & Axen, K. V. (2001). *Illustrated principles of exercise physiology.* Englewood Cliffs, NJ: Prentice Hall.

Baan, R., Straif, K., Grosse, Y., Secretan, B., El Ghissassi, F., Bouvard, V., … Cogliano, V. (2007). Carcinogenicity of alcoholic beverages. *Lancet Oncology, 8*(4), 292–293.

Back, S. E., Brady, K. T., Jaanimagi, U., & Jackson, J. L. (2006). Cocaine dependence and PTSD: A pilot study of symptom interplay and treatment preferences. *Addictive Behavior, 31,* 351–354.

Bainbridge, S. W. (2007). The scientific research potential of virtual worlds. *Science, 317,* 472–476.

Baker, H. S., & Baker, M. N. (1987). Heinz Kohut's self psychology: An overview. *American Journal of Psychiatry,* 144(1), 1–9.

Bandura, A. (1969). *Principles of behavior modification.* Oxford, UK: Holt, Reinhart & Winston.

Bandura, A. (1973). *Aggression: A social learning analysis.* Englewood Cliffs, NJ: Prentice Hall.

Bandura, A. (1977). *Social learning theory.* Oxford, UK: Prentice Hall.

Bandura, A., & Walters, R. H. (1959). *Adolescent aggression.* New York: Ronald Press.

Bandura, A., & Walters, R. H. (1963). *Social learning and personality development.* New York: Holt, Rinehart & Winston.

Barnes, G. M., Welte, J. W., Tidwell, M. O., & Hoffman, J. H. (2015). Gambling and substance use: Co-occurrence among adults in a recent general population study in the United States. *International Gambling Studies, 15*(1), 55–71.

Barrett, P. M. (2012, June 21). The new republic of porn. *Bloomberg Businessweek.* Retrieved from http://www.businessweek.com/printer/ articles/58466-the-new-republic-of-porn

Barrows, J. (1893). *The world's parliament of religions.* Chicago: The Parliament Publishing Company.

Barton, B. (2002). Dancing on the Mobius strip: Challenging the sex war paradigm. *Gender & Society, 16*(5), 585–602.

Battleday, R. M., & Brem, A. (2015). Modafinil for cognitive neuroenhancement in healthy non-sleep-deprived subjects: A systematic review. *European Neuropsychopharmacology: The Journal of the European College of Neuropsychopharmacology, 25*(11), 1865–1881.

BBC News. (2008, April 22). *Professor, 49, died from anorexia.* Retrieved on February 19, 2017, from http://news.bbc.co.uk/2/hi/uk_news/england/dorset/7360470.stm

Beall, L. S. (1997). Post-traumatic stress disorder: A bibliographic essay. *Choice, 34*(6), 917–930. Retrieved February 20, 2007, from http://www.lib.auburn.edu/socsci/docs/ptsd.html

Bearak, B. (1997, April 28). Eyes on glory: Pied pipers of Heaven's Gate. *The New York Times.* Retrieved from http://0go.galegroup.com.skyline.ucdenver.edu/ps/i.do?p=GRGM&u=auraria_main&id=GALE%7CA150340640&v=2.1&it=r&sid=summon

Beck, A. T. (1963). Thinking and depression: I. Idiosyncratic content and cognitive distortions. *Archives of General Psychiatry, 9*(4), 324–333.

Beck, A. T. (1964). Thinking and depression: II. Theory and therapy. *Archives of General Psychiatry, 10*(6), 561–571.

Beck, A. T. (1993). Cognitive approaches to stress. In P. M. Lehrer & R. L. Woolfolk (Eds.), *Principles and practice of stress management* (2nd ed.). New York: Guilford.

Beck, A. T. (2005). Reflections on my public dialogue with the Dalai Lama. *Cognitive Therapy Today, 10*(2), 4.

Beck, A. T., Rush, A. J., Shaw, B. F., & Emery, G. (1979). *Cognitive therapy of depression.* New York: Guilford.

Beck, J. S. (2007). *The Beck diet solution: Train your brain to think like a thin person.* Des Moines, IA: Oxmoor House.

Begley, D. J. (2007). Structure and function of the blood-brain barrier. In E. Touitou & B. Barry (Eds.), *Enhancement in drug delivery* (pp. 571–590). Boca Raton, FL: CRC Press.

Bell, J. (2012). Pharmacological maintenance treatments of opiate addiction. *British Journal of Clinical Pharmacology, 77*, 253–263.

Belsky, J., & Nezworski, T. (Eds.). (1988). *Clinical implications of attachment.* Hillsdale, NJ: Lawrence Erlbaum.

Benson, H. (1975). *The relaxation response.* New York: Morrow.

Benson, H. (1984). *Beyond the relaxation response.* New York: Berkley Press.

Benson, H. (1987). *Your maximum mind.* New York: Random House.

Benson, H. (1989, August). *Meditation: A physiological bridge to natural highs.* Keynote address, Natural Highs Conference, Boulder, CO.

Benson, H. (2000). *The relaxation response—updated and expanded (25th anniversary edition).* New York: Avon.

Benson, H., Greenwood, M., & Klemchuk, H. (1975). The relaxation response: Psychophysiologic aspects and clinical applications. *International Journal of Psychiatric Medicine, 6*(1–2), 87–98.

Benson, H., Lehmann, J., Malhotra, M., Goldman, R., Hopkins, J., & Epstein, M. (1982, January 21). Body temperature changes during the practice of g Tum-mo yoga. *Nature, 295*, 234–236.

Benson, H., Steinert, R. F., Greenwood, M. M., Klemchuk, H. M., & Peterson, N. H. (1975). Continuous measurement of O_2 consumption and CO_2 elimination during a wakeful hypometabolic state. *Journal of Human Stress, 1*, 37–44.

Beral, V., Hamajima, N., Hirose, K., Rohan, T., Calle, E. E., Heath, C. W., ... Kosmelj, K. (2002). Alcohol, tobacco and breast cancer—collaborative reanalysis of individual data from 53 epidemiological studies, including 58,515 women with breast cancer and 95,067 women without the disease. *British Journal of Cancer, 87*(11), 1234–1245.

Bessiere, K., Seay, A. F., & Kiesler, S. (2007). The ideal elf: Identity exploration in World of Warcraft. *CyberPsychology & Behavior, 10*(4), 530–535.

Bettelheim, B. (1976). *The uses of enchantment: The meaning and importance of fairy tales.* New York: Knopf.

Betz, C., Milhalic, D., Pinto, M. E., & Raffa, R. B. (2000). Could a common biochemical mechanism underlie addictions? *Journal of Clinical Pharmacy and Therapeutics, 25*, 11–20.

Bimbi, D.S. (2007). Male prostitution: Pathology, paradigms, and progress in research. *Journal of Homosexuality, 53*(1–2), 7–35.

Bjornsen, C. A. & Archer, K. J. (2015). Relationship between college students' cell phone use during class and grades. *Scholarship of Teaching & Learning in Psychology, 1*(4), 326–336.

Black, S. (1819). *Clinical and pathological reports.* Newry, UK: Alex Wilkinson.

Blanchard, A., & Lyons, M. (2016). Sex differences between primary and secondary psychopathy, parental bonding, and attachment style. *Evolutionary Behavioral Sciences, 10*(1), 56–63.

Blanchard, G. T. (1995). Sexually addicted lust murders. *Sexual Addiction & Compulsivity, 2*(1), 62–71. doi 10.1080/10720169508400067

Blonigen, D. M., Hicks, B. M., Patrick, C. J., Krueger, R. F., Iacono, W. G., & McGue, M. (2005). Psychopathic personality traits: Heritability and genetic overlap with internalizing and externalizing pathology. *Psychological Medicine, 35,* 637–648.

Blum, K. (1991). *Alcohol and the addictive brain: New hope for alcoholics from biogenetic research.* New York: Free Press.

Blum, K., Allison, D., Trachtenberg, M. C., Williams, R. W., & Loeblick, L. A. (1988). Reduction of both drug hunger and withdrawal against advice rate of cocaine abusers in a 30-day inpatient treatment program by the neuronutrient Tropamine. *Current Therapeutic Research, 43*(6), 12041214.

Blum, K., Gardner, E., Oscar-Berman, M., & Gold, M. (2012). "Liking" and "Wanting" linked to Reward Deficiency Syndrome (RDS): Hypothesizing differential responsivity in brain reward circuitry. *Current Pharmaceutical Design, 18*(1), 113–118.

Blum, K., Han, D., Hauser, M., Downs, B. W., Giordano, J., Borsten, J., Barh, D. (2013). Neurogenetic impairments of brain reward circuitry links to reward deficiency syndrome (RDS) as evidenced by genetic addiction risk score (GARS): A case study. *IIOAB Journal, 4*(1), 4–9.

Blumberg, A. (2017, April 27). How North Korea's politcal ideology became a de-facto religion. *The World Post.* Retrieved on July 5, 2017, from http://www.huffingtonpost.com/entry/how-north-koreas-political-ideology-be-came-a-de-facto-religion_us_58ffaf4ee4b091e8c711108e?utm_hp_ref=kim-jong-un

Bobzean, S. A. M., DeNobrega, A. K., & Perrotti, L. I. (2014). Sex differences in the neurobiology of drug addiction. *Experimental Neurology, 259,* 64–74.

Boecker, H., Sprenger, T., Spilker, M. E., Henriksen, G., Koppenhoefer, M., Wagner, K. J., ... & Tolle, T. R. (2008). The runner's high: Opioidergic mechanisms in the human brain. *Cerebral Cortex, 18,* 2523–2531.

Boellstorff, T. (2008). *Coming of age in Second Life: An anthropologist explores the virtually human.* Princeton, NJ: Princeton University Press.

Booth, L. (1991). *When God becomes a drug: Breaking the chains of religious addiction & abuse.* Los Angeles: J.P. Tarcher; New York: St. Martin's Press.

Booth, L. (1998). *When God becomes a drug: Understanding religious addiction & religious abuse.* SCP Limited.

Borio, G. (1993). *The tobacco timeline.* Retrieved from http://grace4life.com/History_of_Tobacco-by_Gene_Borio.pdf

Bowden, M. (2017, July/August). How to deal with North Korea. *The Atlantic.* Retrieved on July 5, 2017, from https://www.theatlantic.com/magazine/archive/2017/07/the-worst-problem-on-earth/528717/

Bowen, S., Witkiewitz, K., Clifasefi, S. L., Grow, J., Chawla, N., Hsu, S. H., ... Larimer, M. E. (2014). Relative efficacy of mindfulness-based relapse prevention, standard relapse prevention, and treatment as usual for substance use disorders: A randomized clinical trial. *JAMA Psychiatry, 71*(5), 547–556. doi:10.1001/jamapsychiatry.2013.4546

Bowlby, J. (1969). *Attachment and loss: Vol. 1. Attachment.* London: Tavistock.

Bowlby, J. (1988). *A secure base: Parent-child attachment and healthy human development.* New York: Basic Books.

Brady, K. T., Grice, D. E., Dustan, L., & Randall, C. (1993). Gender differences in substance use disorders. *American Journal of Psychiatry, 150,* 1707–1711.

Brand, M., Laier, C., & Young, K.S. (2014). Internet Addiction: Coping styles, expectancies, and treatment implications. *Frontiers in Psychology 5.* doi: 10.3389/fpsyg.2014.01256

Brand, M., Young, K.S., & Laier, C. (2014). Prefrontal control and Internet addiction: A theoretical model and review of neuropsychological and neuroimaging findings. *Frontiers in Human Neuroscience 8.* doi: 10.3389/fnhum.2014.00375

Bratskeir, K. (2015). 21 Percent of Americans are online basically all the time. *Huffpost Healthy Living.* Retrieved from http://www.huffingtonpost.com/entry/american-time-spent-online-is-outrageous_us_566863cfe4b080eddf567867

Bren, L. (2006). Some cold medicines move behind counter. *FDA Consumer.* In H. T. Wilson (Ed.), *Annual editions: Drugs, society, and behavior 2007/2008* (pp. 109–110). Boston: McGraw-Hill.

Brenhouse, H. C., & Anderson, S. L. (2008). Delayed extinction and stronger reinstatement of cocaine conditioned place preference in adolescent rats, compared to adults. *Behavioral Neuroscience, 122*(2), 460–465.

Brennan, K. A., & Shaver, P. R. (1995). Dimensions of adult attachment, affect regulation, and romantic relationship functioning. *Personality and Social Psychology Bulletin, 23,* 23–31.

Breslau, N., Fenn, N., & Peterson, E. L. (1993). Early smoking initiation and nicotine dependence in a cohort of young adults. *Drug & Alcohol Dependence, 33,* 129–137.

Bretherton, I., & Waters, E. (Eds.). (1985). Growing points of attachment theory and research. *Monograph of the Society for Research in Child Development, 50*(209).

Brewster, Z. W. (2003). Behavioral and interactional patterns of strip club patrons: Tipping techniques and club attendance. *Deviant Behavior, 24*(3), 221–243.

Briere, J., & Rickards, S. (2007). Self-awareness, affect regulation, and relatedness: Differential sequels of childhood versus adult victimization experiences. *Journal of Nervous and Mental Disease, 195,* 497–503.

Brogan, M., Ledesma, R., Coffino, A., & Chandler, P. (2017). Freebie rhabdomyolysis: A public health concern. Spin class-induced rhabdomyolysis. *American Journal of Medicine, 130*(4), 484–487.

Brooks, A. C. (2008). *Gross national happiness: Why happiness matters for America—and how we can get more of it.* New York: Basic Books.

Brooks-Gunn, J., & Donahue, E. H. (2008). Introducing the issue: Children and electronic media. *Future of Children, 18*(1), 3–10.

Brown, D. J. (2007, December 28). Psychedelic healing? Hallucinogenic drugs which blew minds in the 1960s soon may be used to treat mental ailments. *Scientific American,* 66–71. Retrieved from http://www.sciam.com/article.cfm?id=psychedelic-healing

Brown, P. J. (2000). Outcome in female patients with both substance use and posttraumatic stress disorder. *Alcoholism Treatment Quarterly, 18*(3), 127.

Brown, R. J., Blum, K., & Trachtenberg, M. C. (1990). Neurodynamics of relapse prevention: A neuronutrient approach to outpatient DUI offenders. *Journal of Psychoactive Drugs, 22*(2), 173–187.

Brown University Health Education. (2008, December 15). *Caffeine and energy boosting drugs: Energy drinks.* Retrieved December 20, 2008, from http://www.brown.edu/Student_Services/Health_Services/Health_Education/atod/energydrinks.htm

Browning, R. (1888). *The poetical works of Robert Browning.* London: Smith, Elder & Co.

Bruch, H. (1961). Transformation of oral impulses in eating disorders: A conceptual approach. *Psychiatric Quarterly, 35,* 458–481.

Buddie, A. M., & Parks, K. A. (2003). The role of the bar context and social behaviors on women's risk for aggression. *Journal of Interpersonal Violence, 18*(12), 1378–1393.

Budney, A. J., Hughes, J. R., Moore, B. A., & Novy, P. L. (2001). Marijuana abstinence effects in marijuana smokers maintained in their home environment. *Archives of General Psychiatry, 58*(10), 917–924.

Budney, A. J., Hughes, J. R., Moore, B. A., & Vandrey, R. (2004). Review of the validity and significance of cannabis withdrawal syndrome. *American Journal of Psychiatry, 161*, 1967–1977.

Budney, A. J., Roffman, R., Stephens, R. S., & Walker, D. (2007). Marijuana dependence and its treatment. *Addiction Science and Clinical Practice, 4*, 4–16.

Bulik, C. M., Reba, L., Siega-Riz, A. M., & Reichborn-Kjennerud, T. (2005). Anorexia nervosa: Definition, epidemiology, and cycle of risk. *International Journal of Eating Disorders, 37*, S2–S9.

Burt, S. A., McGue, M., Krueger, R. F., & Iacono, W. G. (2005). Sources of covariation among the child-externalizing disorders: Informant effects and the shared environment. *Psychological Medicine, 35*(8), 1133–1144.

Burton, R. (1632). *The anatomy of melancholy.* Oxford, UK: Henry Cripps.

Butler, A. C., & Beck, J. S. (2000). Cognitive therapy outcomes: A review of meta-analyses. *Journal of the Norwegian Psychological Association, 37*, 1–9.

Cadet, J., Ordonez, S., & Ordonez, J. (1997). Methamphetamine induces apoptosis in immortalized neural cells: Protection by the proto-oncogene, bcl-2. *Synapse, 25*(2), 176–184.

California Department of Health, Office of AIDS. (2015). Retrieved on September 12, 2016, from https://www.cdph.ca.gov/programs/aids/Documents/List%20-%20SEPs%20November%202015.pdf

Calleja, G. (2007, July). Digital game involvement. *Games and Culture, 2*(3), 236–260.

Campbell, S. W. (2006). Perceptions of mobile phones in college classrooms: Ringing, cheating, and classroom policies. *Communication Education, 55*, 280–294.

Campbell, U. C., Thompson, S. S., & Carroll, M. E. (1998). Acquisition of oral phencyclidine (PCP) self-administration in rhesus monkeys: Effects of dose and an alternative non-drug reinforce. *Psychopharmacology, 137*(2), 132–138.

Campo-Flores, A., & Smalley, S. (2008, March 15). On top of the world? *Newsweek.* Retrieved January 20, 2009, from http://www.newsweek.com/id/123566

Canadian Broadcasting Corporation (CBC) News. (2007, September 27). Red Bull promotion near Halifax schools halted: energy drink maker tells province promotion was a mistake. Retrieved on September 3, 2010 from http://www.cbc.ca/news/canada/nova-scotia/red-bull-promotion-near-halifax-schools-halted-1.679980

Canadian Broadcasting Corporation (CBC) News. (2013, November 5). Mayor Rob Ford won't step down despite crack use: Toronto mayor says he has 'nothing left to hide' and still has work to do at city hall. Retrieved from http://www.cbc.ca/news/canada/toronto/mayor-rob-ford-won-t-step-down-despite-crack-use-1.2415533

Cannon, W. B. (1915). *Bodily changes in pain, hunger, fear, and rage: An account of recent researches into the function of emotional excitement.* New York: Appleton.

Cannon, W. B. (1929). *Bodily changes in pain, hunger, fear, and rage.* New York: Appleton.

Carelli, R. M. (2002). The nucleus accumbens and reward: Neurophysiological investigations in behaving animals. *Behavioral and Cognitive Neuroscience Reviews, 1*(4), 281–296.

Carhart-Harris, R. O., Leech, R., Hellyer, P. J., Shanahan, M., Feilding, A., Magliazucchi, E., . . . Nutt, D. (2014). The entropic brain: A theory of conscious states informed by neuroimagaing research with psychedelic drugs. *Fontiers in Human Neuroscience, 8*, Article 20. doi: 10.3389/fnhum.2014.00020

Carlisle, A. (2014). *The development of the violent mind: The case of Ted Bundy: I'm not guilty.* (2nd ed.). Encino, CA: Genius Books.

Carpenter, J. (2014). Finding truth in the fictional TV bar. *Punch.* Retrieved on March 19, 2017, from http://punchdrink.com/articles/finding-truth-in-the-fictional-tv-bar/

Carrere, S., & Gottman, J. (1999). Predicting divorce among newlyweds from the first three minutes of a marital conflict discussion. *Family Process, 38*, 293–301.

Carroll, J. S., Padilla-Walker, L. M., Nelson, L. J., Olson, C. D., Barry, C. M., & Madsen, S. (2008). Generation XXX: Pornography acceptance and use among emerging adults. *Journal of Adolescent Research, 23*(1), 6–30.

Carter, C. S. (1992). Oxytocin and sexual behavior. *Neuroscience and Biobehavioral Review, 16,* 131–144.

Carter, R. (1998). *Mapping the mind.* Berkeley: University of California Press.

Carter, C., Reissig, M., Johnson, M., & Klinedinsth, R. (2013). Acute cognitive effects of high doses of dextromethorphan relative to triazolam in humans. *Drug and Alcohol Dependence,* Volume 128, Issue 3, 1 March 2013, Pages 206-213.

Center for Behavioral Health Statistics and Quality. (2015). *Behavioral health trends in the United States: Results from the 2014 National Survey on Drug Use and Health* (HHS Publication No. SMA 15-4927, NSDUH Series H-50). Retrieved from http://www.samhsa.gov/data/sites/default/files/NSDUH-FRR1-2014/NSDUH-FRR1-2014.pdf

Centers for Disease Control and Prevention. (2015a). *Prevalence of self-reported obesity among U.S. adults by state and territory, BRFSS, 2016.* Retrieved on February 19, 2017, from https://www.cdc.gov/obesity/data/prevalence-maps.html

Centers for Disease Control and Prevention. (2015b, May 29). Global tobacco control. Retrieved May 31, 2016, from http://www.cdc.gov/tobacco/global/

Centers for Disease Control and Prevention. (2015c, August 18). *Smoking and tobacco use.* Retrieved May 31, 2016, from http://www.cdc.gov/tobacco/data_statistics/fact_sheets/health_effects/tobacco_related_mortality/index.htm

Centers for Disease Control and Prevention. (2016). *Prescription opioid overdose data.* Retrieved from www.cdc.gov/drugoverdose/data/overdose.html

Centers for Disease Control and Prevention. (2017). *Smoking & tobacco use: Health effects of cigarette smoking.* Retrieved from www.cdc.gov/tobacco/data_statistics/fact_sheets/health_effects/effects_cig_smoking/index.htm

Cerda, M., Bordelois, P., Keyes, K. M., Roberts, A. L., Martins, S. S., Reisner, S. L., . . . Koenen, K. C. (2014). Family ties: Maternal-offspring attachment and young adult nonmedical prescription opioid use. *Drug & Alcohol Dependence, 142,* 231–238.

Chan, A. (2016, January 20). Diet foods are tanking. So the diet industry is now selling 'Health'. *NPR: Eating and Health.* Retrieved on February 8, 2017, from http://www.npr.org/sections/thesalt/2016/01/20/462691546/as-diet-foods-tank-confusing-health-labels-replace-them

Chandler, R. K, Fletcher, B. W., & Volkow, N. D. (2009). Treating drug abuse and addiction in the criminal justice system: Improving public health and safety. *JAMA, 301*(2), 183–190.

Chang, L., Ernst, T., Speck, O., Patel, H., DeSilva, M., Leonido-Yee, M., & Miller, E. N., (2002). Perfusion MRI and computerized cognitive test abnormalities in abstinent methamphetamine users. *Psychiatry Research, 114*(2), 65–79.

Chaouloff, F. (1997). Effects of acute physical exercise on central serotonergic systems. *Medicine and Science in Sports Exercise, 29,* 58–62.

Chapkis, W. (2000). Power and control in the commercial sex trade. In R. Weitzer (Ed.), *Sex for Sale: Prostitution, pornography, and the sex industry* (pp. 181–201). New York: Routledge.

Chein, I., Gerard, D. L., Lee, R. S., & Rosenfeld, E. (1981). The road to H: Narcotics, delinquency, and social policy. In H. Shaffer & M. Burglass (Eds.), *Classic contributions in the addictions* (pp. 95–116). New York: Brunner/Mazel.

Chen, A. (2016, January 20). Diet foods are tanking. So the diet industry is now selling 'health'. *NPR: Eating and Health.* Retrieved on February 8, 2017, from http://www.npr.org/sections/thesalt/2016/01/20/462691546/as-diet-foods-tank-confusing-health-labels-replace-them

Chen, C. H., Lee, M. H., Chen, Y. C., & Lin, M. F. (2011). Ketamine-snorting associated cystitis. *Journal of Formosan Medical Association, 11,* 787–791.

Chen, J. F. (2014). Adenosine receptor control of cognition in normal and disease. *International Review of Neurobiology, 199,* 257–307.

Cheng, C. & Li, A. Y. -I. (2014). Internet addiction prevalence and quality of (real) life: A meta-analysis of 31 nations across seven world regions. *Cyberpsychology, Behaviors, and Social Networking, 17*(2). doi: 10.1089/cyber.2014.0317

Cherkas, L. F., Hunkin, J. L., Kato, B. S., Richards, J. B., Gardner, J. P., Surdulescu, G. L., . . . Aviv, A. (2008). The association between physical activity in leisure time and leukocyte telomere length. *Archives of Internal Medicine, 168*(2), 154-158. doi:10.1001/archinternmed.2007.39

Childs, E., & de Wit, H. (2008). Enhanced mood and psychomotor performance by a caffeine-containing energy capsule in fatigued individuals. *Experimental and Clinical Psychopharmacology, 16*(1), 13–21.

Chögyam Trungpa, R. (1975). Transpersonal cooperation at Naropa. *The Journal of Transpersonal Psychology, 7*(1), 81.

Christie, M. J. (2008). Cellular neuroadaptations for chronic opioids: Tolerance, withdrawal, and addiction. *British Journal of Pharmacology, 154*, 384–396.

Christy, M. M., (1994). *Your own perfect medicine.* Scottsdale, AZ: Future Medicine.

Ciccocioppo, R., Economidou, D., Fedeli, A., Angeletti, S., Weiss, F., Heilig, M., & Massi, M. (2004). Attenuation of ethanol self-administration and of conditioned reinstatement of alcohol-seeking behaviour by the antiopioid peptide nociceptin/orphanin FQ in alcohol-preferring rats. *Psychopharmacology, 172*(2), 170–178.

Cicero, T. J., Ellis, M. S., Surratt, H. L., & Kurtz, S. P. (2014). The changing face of heroin use in the United States: A retrospective analysis of the past 50 years. *JAMA Psychiatry, 71*(7), 821–826.

Clapp, J. D. (2008, January 6). College drinking games lead to higher blood alcohol levels. *HealthDay News.* Retrieved June 30, 2008, from http://www.washington post.com/wp-dyn/content/article/2008/01/06/AR2008010600771.html

Clark, D. A., Beck, A., & Alford, B. A. (1999). *Scientific foundations of cognitive theory and therapy of depression.* New York: Wiley.

Clarke, T. C., Black, L. I., Stussman, B. J., Barnes, P. M., & Nahin, R. L. (2015). *Trends in the use of complementary health approaches among adults: United States, 2002–2012. National health statistics reports; no 79.* Hyattsville, MD: National Center for Health Statistics. Retrieved from https://nccih.nih.gov/research/statistics/NHIS/2012/mind-body/meditation

Cleckley, H. M. (1941). *The mask of sanity: An attempt to reinterpret the so-called psychopathic.* Oxford, UK: Mosby.

Cloninger, C. R. (2004). *Feeling good: The science of well-being.* New York: Oxford University Press.

Cloninger, C. R., Svrakic, D., & Przybeck, R. (1993). A psychobiological model of temperament and character. *Archives of General Psychiatry, 50*, 975–990.

Cloyd, J. W. (1976). The market-place bar: The interrelation between sex, situation, and strategies in the pairing ritual of Homo Ludens. *Journal of Contemporary Ethnography, 5*, 293–312.

Cobb C., Ward, K. D., Maziak, W., Shihadeh, A. L., & Eissenberg, T. (2010). Waterpipe tobacco smoking: An emerging health crisis in the United States. *American Journal of Health Behavior, 34*(3), 275–285.

Cohen, L. (2006). *Book of longing.* New York: HarperCollins.

Cole, J. M. (29 August 2013). *Memorandum for all states attorneys: Guidance regarding marijuana enforcement.* Retrieved from https://www.justice.gov/iso/opa/resources/3052013829132756857467.pdf

Cole, H., & Griffiths, M. D. (2007). Social interactions in massively multiplayer online role-playing gamers. *CyberPsychology and Behavior, 10*(4), 575–583.

Collingwood, J. (2016). Preferred music style is tied to personality. *Psych Central.* Retrieved from http://psychcentral.com/lib/preferred-music-style-is-tied-to-personality/0001438

Collingwood, R. G. (1949). *The idea of nature.* London: Oxford University Press.

Comings, D. E., Gonzales, N., Saucier, G., Johnson, J. P., & MacMurray, J. P. (2000). The DRD4 gene and the spiritual transcendence scale of the character temperament index. *Psychiatric Genetics, 10*(4), 185–189

Commins, D. L., Vosmer, G., Virus, R. M., Woolverton, W. L., Schuster, C. R., & Seiden, L. S. (1987). Biochemical and histological evidence that methylenedioxymethylamphetamine (MDMA) is toxic to neurons in the rat brain. *Journal of Pharmacology and Experimental Therapeutics, 241*, 338–345.

Compton, W. M., Cottler, L. B., Phelps, D. L., Abdallah, A. B., & Spitznagel, E. L. (2000). Psychiatric disorders among drug-dependent subjects: Are they primary or secondary. *American Journal of Addiction, 9*(2), 126–134.

Connery, H.S. (2015). Medication-assisted treatment of opioid use disorder: Review of the evidence and future directions. *Harvard Review of Psychiatry, 23*, 63–75.

Connors, G. J., Carroll, K. M., DiClemente, C. C., Longabaugh, R., & Donovan, D. M. (1997). The therapeutic alliance and its relationship to alcoholism treatment participation and outcome. *Journal of Consulting and Clinical Psychology, 41*, 588–598.

Conway, K. P., Compton, W., Stinson, F. S., & Grant, B. F. (2006). Lifetime comorbidity of DSM-IV mood and anxiety disorders and specific drug use disorders: Results from the National Epidemiologic Survey on Alcohol and Related Conditions. *Journal of Clinical Psychiatry, 67*, 247–257.

Cooney, G. M., Dwan, K., Greig, C. A., Lawlor, D. A., Rimer, J., Waugh, F. R. . . . Mead, G. E. (2013). Exercise for depression. *The Cochrane Database of Systematic Reviews*, (9), CD004366.

Cooper, A., Delmonico, D. L., & Burg, R. (2000). Cybersex users, abusers, and compulsives: New findings and implications. *Sexual Addiction & Compulsivity, 7*, 5–29.

Cooper, M. J. (2005). Cognitive theory in anorexia nervosa and bulimia nervosa: Progress, development, and future directions. *Clinical Psychology Review, 25*(4), 511–531.

Courtwright, D.T. (2001). *Dark paradise: A history of opiate addiction in America.* Cambridge, MA: Harvard University Press.

Covington, S. S. (2000). Helping women to recover: Creating gender-specific treatment for substance-abusing women and girls in community corrections. In M. McMahon (Ed.), *Assessment to assistance: Programs for women in community corrections* (pp. 171–234). Lanham, MD: American Correctional Association.

Cozolino, L. J. (2014). *The neuroscience of human relationships: Attachment and the developing social brain* (2nd ed.). New York: W.W. Norton & Company.

Crabbe, J. C. (2002). Alcohol and genetics: New models. *American Journal of Medical Genetics (Neuropsychiatric Genetics), 114*, 969–974.

Craig, A. H. (1897). A temperance address—The nickel behind the bar. In *Pros and cons: Complete debates.* New York: Hinds & Noble.

Craven, J. L. (1989). Meditation and psychotherapy. *Canadian Journal of Psychiatry, 34*(7), 648–653.

Crawford, M., & Unger, R. (2000). *Women and gender: A feminist psychology* (3rd ed.). Boston: McGraw-Hill.

Crick, F. H. C. (1995). *The astonishing hypothesis: The scientific search for the soul.* New York: Scribner.

Cryer, B., McCraty, R., & Childre, D. (2003). Pull the plug on stress. *Harvard Business Review, 81*(7), 102–107.

Csikszentmihalyi, M. (1975). *Beyond boredom and anxiety.* San Francisco: Jossey-Bass.

Csikszentmihalyi, M. (1990). *Flow: The psychology of optimal experience.* New York: Harper & Row.

Csikszentmihalyi, M. (1996). *Creativity: Flow and the psychology of discovery and invention.* New York: HarperCollins.

Csikszentmihalyi, M. (2000). *Beyond boredom and anxiety* (25th anniversary ed.). San Francisco: Jossey-Bass.

Csikszentmihalyi, M., Rathunde, K., & Whalen, S. (1993). *Talented teenagers.* Cambridge, UK: Cambridge University Press.

Csikszentmihalyi, M., & Robinson, R. (1990). *The art of seeing.* Malibu, CA: J. Paul Getty Museum/Getty Center for Education in the Arts.

Csikszentmihalyi, M., & SpringerLink (Online service). (2014). *Flow and the foundations of positive psychology: The collected works of Mihaly Csikszentmihalyi* (2014, ed.). Dordrecht: Springer Netherlands. doi:10.1007/978-94-017-9088-8

Cullen, D. (2005). The depressive and the psychopath: At last we know why the Columbine killers did it. www.slate.com/articles/news_and_politics/assessment/2004/04/the_depressive_and_the_psychopath.html

Cullen, D. (2009). *Columbine.* New York: Twelve.

Cunningham, J. A., Hodgins, D. C., & Toneatto, T. (2014). Relating severity of gambling to cognitive distortions in a representative sample of problem gamblers. *Journal of Gambling Issues, 29.* http://dx.doi.org/10.4309/jgi.2014.29.2

Curran, H. V., Freeman, T. P., Mokrysz, C., Lewis, D. A., Morgan, C. J. A., & Parsons, L. H. (2016). Keep off the grass? Cannabis, cognition and addiction. *Nature Reviews Neuroscience, 17,* 293–306.

Dalai Lama. (1999). *Ethics for the new millennium.* New York: Riverhead.

Danaei, G., Ding, E. L., Mozaffarian, D., Taylor, B., Rehm, J., Murray, C. J. L., & Ezzati, M. (2009). The preventable causes of death in the United States: Comparative risk assessment of dietary, lifestyle, and metabolic risk factors. *PLoS Medicine, 6*(4), 1–23.

Das S., Barnwal, P., Ramasamy, A., Sen, S., & Mondal, S. (2016). Lysergic acid diethylamide: A drug of "use"? *Therapeutic Advances in Psychopharmacology, 6,* 214–228.

Davidson, R. J., & Kaszniak, A. W. (2015). Conceptual and methodological issues in research on mindfulness and meditation. *American Psychologist, 70*(7), 581–592.

Davidson, R. J., & Schwartz, G. E. (1976). The psychobiology of relaxation and related states: A multiprocess theory. In D. I. Mostofsky (Ed.), *Behavior control and the modification of physiological activity* (pp. 399–442). Englewood Cliffs, NJ: Prentice Hall.

Davidson, T., & Odle, T. G. (2015). Energy Drinks. In J. L. Longe (Ed.), *The Gale Encyclopedia of Medicine* (5th ed., Vol. 3, pp. 1776–1779). Farmington Hills, MI: Gale.

Davila, J., Mattanah, J., Bhatia, V., Latack, J. A., Feinstein, B. A., Eaton, N. R., ... & Zhau, J. (2017). Romantic competence, healthy relationship functioning, and well-being in emerging adults. *Personal Relationships, 24,* 162–184.

Davila, J., Sternberg, S. J., Ramsay, M., Stroud, C. B., Starr, L., & Yoneda, A. (2009). Assessing romantic competence in adolescence: The romantic competence interview. *Journal of Adolescence, 32,* 55–75.

Davis, C. (2014). Evolutionary and neuropsychological perspectives on addictive behaviors and addictive substances. *Substance Abuse and Rehabilitation, 5,* 129–137.

De Boer, A., Van Buel, E. M., & Ter Horst, G. J. (2012). Love is more than just a kiss: A neurobiological perspective of love and affection. *Neuroscience, 201,* 114–124.

De Cuypere, L. (2008). *Limiting the iconic: From the metatheoretical foundations to the creative possibilities of iconicity in language.* Amsterdam: John Benjamins.

de Kemp, R. A. T., Scholte, R. H. J., Overbeek, G., & Engels, R. C. (2006, August). Early adolescent delinquency: The role of parents and best friends. *Criminal Justice and Behavior, 33*(4), 488–510.

Delgado, M. R. (2007). Reward-related responses in the human striatum. *Annals of the New York Academy of Sciences, 1104,* 70–88.

De Luca, M. T., & Badiani, A. (2011). Ketamine self-administration in the rat: Evidence for a critical role of setting. *Psychopharmacology, 214*(2), 549–556.

Demasio, A. (2003). *Looking for Spinoza: Joy, sorrow, and the feeling brain.* New York: Harcourt.

De Rossi, P. (2010). *Unbearable lightness: A story of loss and gain.* New York: Atria Books.

Deshotels, T., & Forsyth, C. (2006). Strategic flirting and the emotional tab of exotic dancing. *Deviant Behavior, 27,* 223–241.

De-Sola Gutierrez, J., Rodriguez de Fonseca, F., & Rubio, G. (2016). Cell-phone addiction: A review. *Frontiers in Psychiatry,* doi:10.3389/fpsyt.2016.00175

Diamond, S., Bermudez, R., & Schensul, J. (2006, May). What's the rap about ecstasy? Popular music lyrics and drug trends among American youth. *Journal of Adolescent Research, 21*(3), 269–298.

Di Chiara, G., & Imperto, A. (1988). Drugs abused by humans preferentially increase synaptic dopamine concentrations in the mesolimbic system of freely moving rats. *Proceedings of the National Academy of Sciences, 85*, 5274–5278.

Di Domenico, S. I., & Ryan, R. M. (2017). The emerging neuroscience of intrinsic motivation: A new frontier in self-determination research. *Frontiers in Human Neuroscience.* Doi: 10.3389/fnhum.2017.0014

Dietary Guidelines Advisory Committee. (2015). *Scientific report of the 2015 dietary guidelines advisory committee.* Washington (DC): USDA and U. S. Department of Health and Human Services.

Dietz, P. E. (1983). Recurrent discovery of autoerotic asphyxia. In R. R. Hazelwood, P. E. Dietz, & A. W. Burgess (Eds.), *Autoerotic fatalities* (pp. 13–44). Lexington, MA: Lexington.

DiFranza, J. R. (2008, May 3). Hooked from the first cigarette. *Scientific American,* 84–87.

DiFranza, J. R., Savageau, J. A., Fletcher, K., Ockene, J. K., Rigotti, N. A., McNeill, A. D., … Wood, C. (2002). Measuring the loss of autonomy over nicotine use in adolescents: The Development and Assessment of Nicotine Dependence in Youths (DANDY) study. *Archives of Pediatric Adolescent Medicine, 156,* 397–403.

DiFranza, J., Savagean, J. A., Fletcher, K., Pbert, L., O'Loughlin, J., McNeill, A. D., … Wellman, R. J. (2007). Susceptibility to nicotine dependence: The Development and Assessment of Nicotine Dependence in Youth-2 Study. *Pediatrics, 120*(4), e974-e983.

Dinis-Oliveira, R. J. (2016). Metabolomics of 9-tetrahydrocannabinol: Implications in toxicity. *Drug Metabolism Reviews, 48,* 80–87.

Dobson, K. A. (1989). A meta-analysis of the efficacy of cognitive therapy for depression. *Journal of Consulting and Clinical Psychology, 57*(3), 414–419.

Donaghy, M. (2007). Exercise can seriously improve your mental health: Fact or fiction? *Advances in Physiotherapy, 9*(2), 76–89.

Donovan, D. M. (2005). Assessment of addictive behaviors for relapse prevention. In D. M. Donovan & G. A. Marlatt (Eds.), *Assessment of addictive behaviors* (2nd ed., pp. 1–48). New York: Guilford.

Dowd, M. (2014, June 3). Don't harsh our mellow, dude. *The New York Times.* Retrieved from https://www.nytimes.com/2014/06/04/opinion/dowd-dont-harsh-our-mellow-dude.html?_r=0

Downing, Jr, M. J., Schrimshaw, E., Antebi, N., & Siegel, K. (2014). Sexually explicit media on the internet: A content analysis of sexual behaviors, risk, and media characteristics in gay male adult videos. *Archives of Sexual Behavior, 43,* 811–821.

Dozier, M., Stovall, K. C., & Albus, K. E. (2008). Attachment and psychopathology in adulthood. In J. Cassidy, & P. R. Shaver (Eds.), *Handbook of attachment: Theory, research, and clinical applications* (2nd ed.). (pp. 718–744). New York, NY: Guildford Press.

Drexler, P. (2015, January 30). The Blog: Millennial women are taking a laissez-faire approach to romance. *The Huffington Post.* Retrieved on February 25, 2017, from http://www.huffingtonpost.com/peggy-drexler/-millennial-women-are-tak_b_6578116.html

Drummond, D. C. (2000). What does cue-reactivity have to offer clinical research? *Addiction, 95,* S129–S144.

DrugAbuse.com (2015). Instagram, drugs, rock and roll: The growth of concerts and music festivals. Retrieved from http://drugabuse.com/featured/instagram-drugs-and-rock-n-roll/

Dryden-Edwards, R., & Stopler, M. C. (2007). Post-traumatic stress disorder (PTSD). *MedicineNet.com.* Retrieved March 4, 2008, from http://www.Medicinenet.com/posttraumatic_stress_disorder/article.htm

Dryden, W., & Ellis, A (1986). Rational-emotive therapy. In W. Dryden & W. Golden (Eds), *Cognitive-behavioral approaches to psychotherapy* (pp. 129–168). London: Harper & Row.

Dufour, M. C. (1999). What is moderate drinking? Defining "drinks" and drinking levels. *Alcohol Research & Health, 23*(1), 5–14.

Duggan, P., Shear, M. D., & Fisher, M. (1999, April 22). Shooter pair mixed fantasy, reality. *Washington Post*, p. A1.

Dukes, R. L., Basel, T. M., Borega, K. N., Lobato, E., & Owens, M.D. (2003). Expression of love, sex, and hurt in popular songs: A content analysis of all-time greatest hits. *The Social Science Journal, 40*, 643–650.

Dunham, W. (2014, May 28). Weight of the world: 2.1 billion people obese or overweight. *Reuters. Health News*. Retrieved on February 20, 2017, from http://www.reuters.com/article/us-health-obesity-idUSKBN0E82HX20140528

DuPont, R. L., & Ford, B. (2000). *The selfish brain: Learning from addiction*. New York: Hazelden.

Duranti, S., Ferrario, C., van Sinderen, D., Ventura, M., & Turroni, F. (2017). Obesity and microbiota: An example of an intricate relationship. *Genes & Nutrition, 12*, 18. Doi: 10.1186/sl2263-017-0566-2

Dusfresnes, C., Jan, C., Bienert, F., Goudet, J., & Fumagalli, L. (2017). Broad-scale genetic diversity of Cannabis for forensic applications. *PLoS ONE, 12*, e0170522. doi: 10.1371/journal.pone.0170522

Earleywine, M. (2002). *Understanding marijuana: A new look at the scientific evidence*. Oxford, New York: Oxford University Press.

Earp, B. D., Wudarczyk, O. A., Foddy, B., & Savulescu, J. (2017). Addicted to love: What is love addiction and when should it be treated? *Philosophy, Psychiatry, & Psychology, 24*(1), 77–92.

Edenberg, H. J., & Foroud, T. (2006). The genetics of alcoholism: Identifying specific genes through family studies. *Addiction Biology, 11*(3/4), 386–396.

Egan, R. D. (2003). I'll be your fantasy girl if you'll be my money man: Mapping desire, fantasy, and power in an exotic dance club. *Journal of Psychoanalysis, Culture and Society, 8*(1), 109–120.

Einstein, A. (1956). Moral decay. In A. Einstein, *The Einstein Reader*. New York: Kensington. (Original work published 1937).

Elkind, D. (1970). Origins of religion in the child. *Review of Religions Research, 12*, 35–42.

Ellis, A. (1962). *Reason and emotion in psychotherapy*. Oxford, UK: Lyle Stuart.

Ellis, A. (2004). *The road to tolerance: The philosophy of rational emotive behavior therapy*. Amherst, NY: Prometheus Books.

Ellis, A., & Harper, R. A. (1961). *A guide to rational living*. Oxford, UK: Prentice Hall.

ElSohly, M. A., Mehmedic, Z., Foster, S., Gon, C., Chandra, S., & Church, J. C. (2016). Changes in cannabis potency over the last two decades (1995–2014): Analysis of current data in the United States. *Biological Psychiatry, 79*, 613–619

Emrick, C. (1974). A review of psychologically oriented treatment of alcoholism. *Journal of Studies on Alcohol, 35*, 523–549.

Enck, G. E., & Preston, J. D. (1988). Counterfeit intimacy: A dramaturgical analysis of an erotic performance. *Deviant Behavior, 9*, 369–381.

Englert, H. (2003). Sussing out stress. *Scientific American Mind, 14*(1), 56–61.

Erickson, D., & Tewksbury, R. (2000). The 'gentlemen' in the club: A typology of strip club patrons. *Deviant Behavior, 21*(4), 271–293.

Erikson, E. H. (1964). *Insight and responsibility*. New York: Norton.

Erikson, E. H. (1982). *The life cycle completed*. New York: Norton.

Eriksson, C. J. P. (2015). Genetic-epidemiological evidence for the role of acetaldehyde in cancers related to alcohol drinking. In V. Vasiliou, S. Zakhari, H. K. Seitz, & J. B. Hoek (Eds.), *Biological basis of alcohol-induced cancer: Advances in experimental medicine and biology 815* (pp. 41–58). DE: Springer Verlag.

European Association for the Study of Obesity (EASO). (2013). *Obesity facts and figures*. Retrieved on June 6, 2016, from http://easo.org/education-portal/obesity-facts-figures/

Fadiman, J. (2011). *The psychedelic explorer's guide: Safe, therapeutic, and sacred journeys*. Park Street Press.

Fagg, E. (1989, January 24). Utahns knew and liked university law student. *Deseret News*. Retrieved from http://www.deseretnews.com/article/31872/UTAHNS-KNEW-AND-LIKED-U-LAW-STUDENT.html

Falkowski, C. L. (2003). Methamphetamine across America: Misconceptions, realities, and solutions. *State Government News*. In H. T. Wilson (Ed.), *Annual editions: Drugs, society, and behavior 2007/2008* (pp. 9–12). Dubuque, IA: McGraw-Hill.

Fantegrossi, W. E., Murnane, K. S., & Reissig, C. J. (2008). The behavioral pharmacology of hallucinogens. *Biochemical Pharmacology, 75*(1), 17–33.

Farias, M., & Wikholm, C. (2015, June 5). Meditation and mindfulness aren't as good for you as you think. *The Washington Post*. Retrieved from https://www.washingtonpost.com/posteverything/wp/2015/06/05/meditation-and-mindfulness-arent-as-good-for-you-as-you-think/?utm_term=.518e1386233b

Farley, F. (1986, May). The big T in personality. *Psychology Today*, 45–52.

Fass, M. (2004, March 21). A sort of love story. *New York Times*, sec. 14, p. 4.

Fattore, L., Melis, M., Fadda, P., & Fratta, W. (2014). Sex differences in addictive disorders. *Frontiers in Neuroendocrinology, 35*(3), 272–284.

FDA (2017). Pulling Pain Medication Opana ER from Market, Is This the Beginning of the End for Chronic Pain Sufferers? Retrieved from http://nationalpainreport.com/fda-pulling-pain-medication-opana-er-from-market-is-this-the-beginning-of-the-end-for-chronic-pain-sufferers-8833817.html

Feeney, J. A., & Noller, P. (1990). Attachment style as a predictor of adult romantic relationships. *Journal of Personality & Social Psychology, 58*(2), 281–291.

Ferguson, M. A., Nielsen, J. A., King, J. B., Dai, L., Giangrasso, D. M., Holman, R.,… Anderson, J. S. (2016). Reward, salience, and attentional networks are activated by religious experience in devout Mormons. *Social Neuroscience*. Retrieved from http://www.tandfonline.com/doi/full/10.1080/17470919.2016.1257437?scroll=top&needAccess=true

Ferguson, R. A., & Goldberg, D. M. (1997). Genetic markers of alcohol abuse. *Clinica Chimica Acta, 257*(2), 199–250.

Fernandes, J., Arida, R. M., & Gomez-Pinilla, F. (2017). Physical exercise as an epigenetic modulator of brain plasticity and cognition. *Neuroscience & Biobehavioral Reviews, 80*, 443–456.

Ferracuti, F. (1982). A sociopsychiatric interpretation of terrorism. *Annals of the American Academy of Political and Social Science, 463*(1), 129–140.

Fields, R. D. (2011, March 11). The deadliest disorder. *Psychology Today*. Retrieved on February 9, 2017, from https://www.psychologytoday.com/blog/the-new-brain/201103/the-deadliest-disorder-0

Fine, D. (2017, June 14). Science calls out Jeff Sessions on medical marijuana and the "historic drug epidemic." *Scientific American*. Retrieved from https://www.scientificamerican.com/article/science-calls-out-jeff-sessions-on-medical-marijuana-and-the-historic-drug-epidemic/

Finn, K., & Salmore, R. (2016). The hidden costs of marijuana use in Colorado: One emergency department's experience. *The Journal of Global Drug Policy & Practice, 10*, 1–24.

Fishel, F. M. (2009). Pesticide toxicity profile Neonictinoid pesticides IFAS Ext. *Publication PI-80*. Retrieved from http://edis.ifas.ufl.edu/pi117

Fisher, H., Aron, A., & Brown, L. L. (2005). Romantic love: An fMRI study of a neural mechanism for mate choice. *Journal of Comparative Neurology, 493*(1), 58–62.

Fisher, H. E., Xu, W., Aron, A., & Brown, L. L. (2016). Intense, passionate, romantic love: A natural addiction? How the fields that investigate romance and substance abuse can inform each other. *Frontiers in Psychology, 7*, 687. Doi: 10.3389/fpsyg.2016.00687

Fisher, M. L., Worth, K., Garcia, J. R., & Meredith, T. (2012). Feelings of regret following uncommitted sexual encounters in Canadian university students. *Culture, Health & Sexuality, 14*(1), 45–57. doi:10.1080/13691058.2011.619579

Fitzgerald, K. T., Bronstein, A. C., & Newquist, K. L. (2013). Marijuana poisoning. *Topics in Companion Animal Medicine, 28*(1), 8–12.

Flack, W. F., Daubman, K. A., Caron, M. L., Asadorian, J. A., D'Aurelli, N. R., Gigliotti, S. N., . . . Stine, E. R. (2007). Risk factors and consequences of unwanted sex among university students: Hooking up, alcohol, and stress response. *Journal of Interpersonal Violence, 22*(2), 139–157.

Flanagan, L. (2014, September 3). Putting the brakes on adolescent impulse. *The Huffington Post.* Retrieved from http://www.huffingtonpost.com/linda-flanagan/putting-the-brakes-on-ado_b_5758032.html

Floresco, S. B. (2007). Dopaminergic regulation of limbic-striatal interplay. *Journal of Psychiatry & Neuroscience, 32*(6), 400–411.

Ford, B. M., Tai, S., Fantegrossi, W. E., & Prather, P. L. (2017). Synthetic pot: Not your grandfather's marijuana. *Trends in Pharmacological Sciences, 38,* 257–276.

Ford, M. (2011, January 26). Old habits die hard for ageing addicts. *The Guardian.* Retrieved from https://www.theguardian.com/society/2011/jan/26/older-drug-users-habits-die-hard

Forsyth, C. J., & Deshotels, T. H. (1997). The occupational milieu of the nude dancer. *Deviant Behavior: An interdisciplinary journal, 18*(2), 125–142.

Forsyth, C. J., & Deshotels, T. H. (1998). A deviant process: The sojourn of the stripper. *Sociological Spectrum, 18,* 77–82.

Fort, J. (1969). *The pleasure seekers: The drug crisis, youth, and society.* New York: Grove Press.

Fox, K. C. R., Dixon, M. L., Nijeboer, S., Girn, M., Floman, J. L., Lifshitz, M., . . . Christoff, K. (2016). Functional neuroanatomy of meditation: A review and meta-analysis of 78 functional neuroimaging investigations. *Neuroscience & Biobehavioral Review, 65,* 208–228.

Fox, M. (2013, January 23). Linda Riss Pugach, whose life was ripped from headlines, dies at 75. *The New York Times.* Retrieved from http://www.nytimes.com/2013/01/24/nyregion/linda-riss-pugach-whose-life-was-ripped-from-headlines-dies-at-75.html

Foye, L. (2016). Virtual reality: Market dynamics & future prospects 2015–2020. *Juniper Research Group.*

Freud, S. (1962). *Three essays on the theory of sexuality* (J. Strachey, Trans.). New York: Basic Books. (Original work published 1905).

Freud, S. (2005). *Civilization and its discontents* (J. Strachey, Ed., Trans.). New York: Norton. (Original work published 1929).

Frishman, W. H., Del Vecchio, A., Sanal, S., & Ismail, A. (2003). Cardiovascular manifestations of substance abuse: Part 2: Alcohol, amphetamines, heroin, cannabis, and caffeine. *Heart Dis., 5*(4), 253–271.

Fruzzetti, A. E., & Iverson, K. M. (2004). Mindfulness, acceptance, validation, and "individual" psychopathology in couples. In S. C. Hayes, V. M. Follette, & M. M. Linehan (Eds.), *Mindfulness and acceptance: Expanding the cognitive-behavioral tradition* (pp. 168–191). New York: Guilford.

Furlow, B. (2017). Recreational cannabis legislation in the USA outpaces research into health effects. *The Lancet Respiratory Medicine, 5,* 385–386.

Fuss, J., Steinle, J., Bindila, L., Auer, M. K., Kirchherr, H., Lutz, B., & Gass, P. (2015). A runner's high depends on cannabinoid receptors in mice. *Proceedings of the National Academy of Sciences, 112*(42), 13105–13108.

Gable, S. L., Reis, H. T., & Elliot, A. J. (2003). Evidence for bivariate systems: An empirical test of appetition and aversion across domains. *Journal of Research in Personality, 37*(5), 349–372.

Gable, S. L., Reis, H. T., Impett, E. A., & Asher, E. R. (2004). What do you do when things go right? The intrapersonal and interpersonal benefits of sharing positive events. *Journal of Personality and Social Psychology, 87,* 228–245.

Gaher, R. M., & Simons, J. S. (2007). Evaluations and expectancies of alcohol and marijuana problems among college students. *Psychology of Addictive Behaviors, 21*(4), 545–554. doi:10.1037/0893-164X.21.4.545

Galician, M.-L. (2009). *Sex, love, and romance in the mass media: Analysis and criticism of unrealistic portrayals and their influence.* New York: Routlege.

Gaoni, Y. & Mechoulam, R. (1964). Isolation, structure and partial synthesis of an active constituent of hashish. *Journal of the American Chemical Society, 86,* 1646–1647.

Garcia, J., Reiber, C., Massey, A., & Merriwether, A. (2012). Sexual hook-up culture: A review. *American Psychological Association, 16*(2), 161–176. Retrieved on February 25, 2017, from http://www.apa.org/monitor/2013/02/sexual-hookup-culture.pdf

Gardner, C. D., Kiazand, A., Alhassan, S., Kim, S., Stafford, R. S., Balise, R. R., et al. (2007). Comparison of the Atkins, Zone, Ornish, and LEARN diets for change in weight and related risk factors among overweight premenopausal women: The A to Z weight loss study: A randomized trial. *Journal of the American Medical Association, 297,* 969–977.

Gardner, H. (1983). *Frames of mind: The theory of multiple intelligences.* New York: Basic Books.

Gardner, H. (1993). *Frames of mind: The theory of multiple intelligences* (10th ed.). New York: Basic Books.

Gardner, H. (1999). *Intelligence reframed: Multiple intelligences for the 21st century.* New York: Basic Books.

Garland, E. L., Bryan, C. J., Finan, P. H., Thomas, E. A., Priddy, S. E., Riquino, M. R., & Howard, M. O. (2017). Pain, hedonic regulation, and opioid misuse: Modulation of momentary experience by Mindfulness-Oriented Recovery Enhancement in opioid-treated chronic pain patients. *Drug & Alcohol Dependence, 173,* S65–S72.

Garland, T. S., Hughes, M. F., & Marquart, J. W. (2004). Alcohol, sexual innuendos, and bad behavior: An analysis of a small town bar. *Southwest Journal of Criminal Justice, 1*(2), 11–29.

Garvey, A. J., Bliss, R. E., Hitchcock, J. L., Heinold, J. W., & Rosner, B. (1992). Predictors of smoking relapse among self-quitters: A report from the normative aging study. *Addictive Behaviors, 17,* 367–377.

Gately, I. (2001). *Tobacco: A cultural history of how an exotic plant seduced civilization.* New York: Grove Press.

Gaudiosi, J. (2016). Fortune Tech: Virtual reality video game industry to generate $5.1 billion in 2016. Retrieved on April 29, 2017, from http://fortune.com/2016/01/05/virtual-reality-game-industry-to-generate-billions/

Gergen, M. M., & Davis, S. N. (Eds.). (1997). *Toward a new psychology of gender: A reader.* New York: Routledge.

Giedd, J. (2015). The amazing teen brain. *Scientific American, 312*(6), 32–37.

Gifford, E. V., Kohlenberg, B. S., Hayes, S. C., Antonuccio, D. O., Piasecki, M. M., Rasmussen-Hall, M. L., & Palm, K.M. (2004). Acceptance-based treatment for smoking cessation. *Behavior Therapy, 35,* 689–705.

Gilman, S. E., & Abraham, H. D. (2001). A longitudinal study of the order of onset of alcohol dependence and major depression. *Drug and Alcohol Dependence, 63,* 277–286.

Glassman, A. H., Jackson, W. K., Walsh, B. T., Roose, S. P., & Rosenfeld, B. (1984). Cigarette craving, smoking withdrawal, and clonidine. *Science, 226*(4676), 864–866.

Glaze, L.E., & Herberman, E.J. (2013).Correctional Populations in the United States, 2012. *Office of Justice Programs: Bureau of Justice Statistics.*

Goertzel, T. (2002). Terrorist beliefs and terrorist lives. In C. Stout (Ed.), *The psychology of terrorism* (Vol. 1, pp. 97–111). Westport, CT: Praeger.

Goffman, E. (1959). *The presentation of self in everyday life.* Garden City, NY: Doubleday.

Goffman, E. (1963). *Stigma: Notes on the management of spoiled identity.* Englewood Cliffs, NJ: Prentice Hall.

Goffman, E. (1967). *Interaction ritual.* Garden City, NY: Doubleday.

Goldstein, J. (1993). *Insight meditation: The practice of freedom.* Boston: Shambhala.

Goleman, D. (1988). *The meditative mind.* Los Angeles: Tarcher.

Goodman, C., & Goodman, T. (1997). *The Forbes book of business quotations: 14,266 thoughts on the business of life.* New York: Black Dog & Leventhal.

Gorman, C. (2004, June 28). Dieting: The secrets of their success. *Time.*

Gorwood, P., Blanchet-Collet, C. Chartrel, N., Duclos, J., Dechelotte, P., Hanachi, M., ... Epelbaum, J. (2016). New insights into anorexia nervosa. *Frontiers in Neuroscience, 10,* 256.

Gosline, A. (2007, December). Bored? *Scientific American*. Retrieved February 1, 2009, from http://www.sciam.com/article.cfm?id=bored—find-something-to-live-for

Gotink, R. A., Meijboom, R., Vernooj, M. W., Smits, M., & Hunink, M. G. M. (2016). 8-week mindfulness-based stress reduction induces brain changes similar to traditional long-term meditation practice: A systematic review. *Brain & Cognition, 108*, 32–41.

Gottman, J. M., Driver, J., & Tabares, A. (2002). Building the sound marital house: An empirically derived couple therapy. In A. S. Gurman & N. S. Jacobson (Eds.), *Clinical handbook of couple therapy* (pp. 373–399). New York: Guilford.

Gottman, J. M., Murray, J. D., Swanson, C., Tyson, R., & Swanson, K. R. (2003). *The mathematics of marriage: Dynamic nonlinear models*. Cambridge: MIT Press.

Gould, S. J. (1997). The adaptive excellence of spandrels as a term and prototype. *Proceedings of the National Academy of Sciences USA (94)*, 10750–10755.

Gould, S. J. (2002). *The structure of evolutionary theory*. Cambridge, MA: Belknap.

Goyal, M., Singh, S., Sibinga, E. M. S., Gould, N. F., Rowland-Seymour, A., Sharma, R., … Haythornthwaite, J. A. (2014). Meditation programs for psychological stress and well-being: A systematic review and meta-analysis. *JAMA Internal Medicine, 174*(3), 357–368. doi:10.1001/jamainternmed.2013.13018

Graham, A., & Glickauf-Hughes, C. (1992). Object relations and addiction: The role of "transmuting externalizations." *Journal of Contemporary Psychotherapy, 22*, 1.

Grant, B. F., Dawson, D. A., Stinson, F. S., Chou, S. P., Dufour, M. C., & Pickering, R. P. (2004). The 12-month prevalence and trends in DSM-IV alcohol abuse and dependence: United States, 1991–1992 and 2001–2002. *Drug and Alcohol Dependence, 74*, 223–234.

Greaney, T. M. (2015, September 16). It's an intimacy disorder! Please don't call it sex and love addiction. *Addiction Professional*. Retrieved from https://www.addictionpro.com/article/its-intimacy-disorder-please-dont-call-it-sex-and-love-addiction

Greenberg, H. R. (1975). *The movies on your mind*. New York: Dutton.

Greenberg, J. T., Pyszczynski, T., & Solomon, S. (1986). The causes and consequences of a need for self-esteem: A terror management theory. In R. F. Baumeister (Ed.), *Public self and private self*. New York: Springer-Verlag.

Greenemeier, L. (2007, December 28). For the holidays: Good things come in virtual packages. *Scientific American*. Retrieved October 15, 2008, from http://www.sciam.com/article.cfm?id=2007-year-in-robots

Greenfield, P. (2009). Women and Alcohol: Why excessive drinking among women is on the rise—and what that means. *Women's Health*.

Greenfield, S. F., Back, S. E., Lawson, K., & Brady, K. T. (2010). Substance abuse in women. *Psychiatric Clinics of North America, 33*(2), 339–355.

Greenspan, S. I. (1985). Research strategies to identify developmental vulnerabilities for drug abuse. Etiology of Drug Abuse: Implications for Prevention. *NIDA Research Monograph Series, 56*, 136–154.

Grey, A. (2015). Jesus on LSD. *Boom, (5)*4. Retrieved on July 11, 2016, from http://www.boomcalifornia.com/2015/12/jesus-on-lsd/

Griest, H., Klein, M. H., Eischens, R. R., Paris, J., Gurman, A. S., & Morgan, W. P. (1978). Running through your mind. *Journal of Psychosomatic Research, 22*, 259–264.

Griffiin D., Black, N., & DiCarlo, P. (2015, November 2). 9 things everyone should know about the drug Molly. *CNN Investigations*. Retrieved on April 12, 2017, from http://edition.cnn.com/2013/11/22/health/9-things-molly-drug/index.html

Griffin, S. (2012, March). *When booze comes off the battlefield*. The New York Times Company.

Griffiths, M. D., Davies, M. N. O., & Chappell, D. (2003). Online computer gaming: A comparison of adolescent and adult gamers. *Journal of Adolescence, 27*(1), 87–96.

Grimm, O. (2007, April/May). Addicted to food. *Scientific American Mind, 36*–39.

Grinspoon, L., & Sagan, C. (1971). *Marihuana reconsidered.* New York: Bantam.

Grof, S. (1975). *Realms of the Human Unconscious: Observations from LSD Psychotherapy.* New York: Viking.

Grof, S. (1996). *Realms of the human unconscious: Observations from LSD research.* Condor Books. London: Souvenir Press.

Grof, S., & Grof, C. (1980). *Beyond death.* Thames and Hudson.

Groves, I., & Farmer, R. (1994). Buddhism and addictions. *Addiction Research, 2,* 183–194.

Gunter, M. J. (2017). Coffee Drinking and Mortality in 10 European Countries, Annals of Internal Medicine, published online. Retrieved February 5, 2018, from https://www.coffeeandhealth.org/2017/07/m-j-gunter-et-al-2017.

Gupta, R., Derevensky, J. L., & Ellenbogen, S. (2006). Personality characteristics and risk-taking tendencies among adolescent gamblers. *Canadian Journal of Behavioural Science, 38*(3), 201–213.

Gupta, S. (2013, August 8). Why I changed my mind on weed. *CNN.* Retrieved from http://www.cnn.com/2013/08/08/health/gupta-changed-mind-marijuana/

Gupta, S., & Mittal, S. (2015). Runner's high: A review of the plausible mechanisms underlying exercise-induced ecstasy. *Saudi Journal of Sports Medicine, 15*(3), 207.

Gurpegui, M., Jurado, D., Luna, J. D., Fernandez-Molina, C., Moreno-Abril, O., & Galvez, R. (2007). Personality traits associated with caffeine intake and smoking. *Progress in Neuro-Psychopharmacology & Biological Psychiatry, 31,* 997–1005.

Gutiérrez-Cebollada, J., de la Torre, R., Ortuno, J., Garcés, J. M., & Cami, J. (1994). Psychotropic drug consumption and other factors associated with heroin overdose. *Drug & Alcohol Dependence, 35,* 169–174.

Hakim, D., & Rashbaum, W. K. (2008, March 11). Spitzer is linked to prostitution ring. *New York Times,* p. 1.

Halliburton, R. (2005). HIV/1: Crystal clear danger. *New Statesman, 10*(1).

Halperin, S., & Bloom, S. (2007). *Pot culture.* New York: Abrams Image.

Hamblin, J. (2016, Oct 25). Millennial women have closed the drinking gap: Decoupling alcohol and masculinity. *The Atlantic.*

Hamilton, A. (2008). *The cure within: A history of mind-body medicine.* New York: Norton.

Haney, M., Ward, A. S., Comer, S. D., Foltin, R. W., & Fischman, M. W. (1999). Abstinence symptoms following smoked marijuana in humans. *Psychopharmacology, 14,* 395–404.

Harris, L. (2002, August/September). Al Qaeda's fantasy ideology: War without Clausewitz. *Policy Review.* Retrieved January 27, 2008, from http://www.hoover.org/publications/policyreview/3459646.html

Hartley, N. (1997). In the flesh. In J. Nagle (Ed.), *Whores and other feminists* (pp. 57–65). New York: Routledge.

Hartogsohn, I. (2016). Set and setting, psychedelics and the placebo response: An extra-pharmacological perspective on psychopharmacology. *Journal of Psychopharmacology, 30,* 1259–1267. doi: 10.1177/0269881116677852

Harvard School of Public Health. (2008). The nutrition source: Alcohol and heart disease. Retrieved October 21, 2008, from http://www.hsph.harvard.edu/nutritionsource/what-should-you-eat/alcohol-and-heart-disease/index.html

Harvey, J. H., Pauwels, B. G., & Zickmund, S. (2001). Relationship connection: The role of minding in the enhancement of closeness. In C. R. Snyder & S. J. Lopez (Eds.). *The handbook of positive psychology* (pp. 423–433). New York: Oxford University Press.

Hasin, D. S., Saha, T. D., Kerridge, B. T., Goldstein, R. B., Chou, S. P., Zhang, H., … Grant, B. F. (2015). Prevalence of marijuana use disorders in the United States between 2001–2002 and 2012–2013. *JAMA Psychiatry, 72*(12), 1235–1242. doi:10.1001/jamapsychiatry.2015.1858

Hasin, D. S., Stinson, F. S., Ogburn, E., & Grant, B. F. (2007). Prevalence, correlates, disability, and comorbidity of DSM-IV alcohol abuse and dependence in the United States: Results from the National Epidemiologic Survey on Alcohol and Related Conditions. *Archives of General Psychiatry, 64*(7), 830–842.

Hatch, T., & Gardner, H. (1993). Finding cognition in the classroom: An expanded view of human intelligence. In G. Salomon (Ed.), *Distributed cognitions. Psychological and educational considerations* (pp. 164–187). New York: Cambridge University Press.

Hawkley, L. C., Masi, C. M., Berry, J. D., & Cacioppo, J. T. (2006). Loneliness is a unique predictor of age-related differences in systolic blood pressure. *Psychology and Aging, 21*(1), 140–151.

Hayes, S. C., Follette, V. M., & Linehan, M. M. (Eds.). (2004). *Mindfulness and acceptance: Expanding the cognitive-behavioral tradition.* New York: Guilford.

Hayes, S. C., & Smith, S. (2005). *Get out of your mind and into your life: The new acceptance and commitment therapy.* Oakland, CA: New Harbinger.

Hayes, S. L., Strosahl, K. D., & Wilson, K. G. (1999). *Acceptance and commitment therapy: An experiential approach to behavior change.* New York: Guildford Press.

Hazan, C., & Shaver, P. (1987). Romantic love conceptualized as an attachment process. *Journal of Personality and Social Psychology, 52,* 511–524.

Heath, A. C., Bucholz, K. K., Madden, P. A. F., Dinwiddie, S. H., Slutske, W. S., Bierut, L. J., ... Martin, N. G. (1997). Genetic and environmental contributions to alcohol dependence risk in a national twin sample: Consistency of findings in women and men. *Psychological Medicine, 27*(6), 1381–1396.

Heath, A. C., & Martin, N. G. (1994). Genetic influences on alcohol consumption patterns and problem drinking: Results from the Australian NH&MRC twin panel follow-up survey. *Annals of the New York Academy of Sciences, 708,* 72–85.

Heine, C. (1996). Flow and achievement in mathematics. Unpublished doctoral dissertation. University of Chicago.

Heinz, A. (2006, April/May). Staying sober. *Scientific American Mind,* 57–61.

Helliwell, J. F., Layard R., & Sachs, J. (Eds.). (2015). *World Happiness Report 2015.* New York: Sustainable Development Solutions Network.

Hendrick, S. S., & Hendrick, C. (1992). *Romantic love.* Newbury Park, CA: Sage Publications.

Henig, R. M. (2007, March 4). Darwin's God. *New York Times.* Retrieved July 29, 2008, from http://www.nytimes.com/2007/03/04/magazine/04evolution.t.html?n= Top/Reference/Times%20Topics/People/D/Dawkins,%20Richard

Herman, J. (1997). *Trauma and recovery: The aftermath of violence—from domestic abuse to political terror.* New York: Basic Books.

Hewlett, P., & Smith, A. (2006). Correlates of daily caffeine consumption. *Appetite, 46,* 97–99.

Hiatt, E. (2017, Spring). Cannabinoids without cannabis: Exploring alternate sources of THC. *THC Mag,* 96–76.

Hicks, B. M., Bernat, E., Malone, S. M., Iacono, W. G., Patrick, C. J., Krueger, R. F., & McGue, M. (2007). Genes mediate the association between P3 amplitude and externalizing disorders. *Psychophysiology, 44*(1), 98–105.

Higgins, J. P., Tuttle, T. D., & Higgins, C. L. (2010). Energy beverages: Content and safety. *Mayo Clinic Proceedings, 85*(11), 1033–1041.

Hillman, C. H., Erickson, K. I., & Kramer, A. F. (2008). Be smart, exercise your heart: Exercise effects on brain and cognition. *Nature Reviews Neuroscience, 9,* 58–65.

Hinz, M., Stein, A., & Uncini, T. (2012). 5-HTP efficacy and contraindications. *Neuropsychiatric Disease and Treatment, 2*(8), 323–328.

Hoek, H. W. (2006). Incidence, prevalence, and mortality of anorexia nervosa and other eating disorders. *Current Opinions in Psychiatry, 19,* 389–394.

Hoffman, J., & Froemke, S. (2007). *Addiction.* New York: Rodale.

Hofmann, A. (1980). *LSD, my problem child: Reflections on sacred drugs, mysticism, and science* (J. Ott, Trans.). Mt. View, CA: Wiretap.

Hogg, R. C. (2016). Contribution of monoamine oxidase inhibition to tobacco dependence: A review of the evidence. *Nicotine & Tobacco Research, 18*, 509–523.

Holden, S. (2008, January 2). John Lennon's death revisited through the words of his killer. *New York Times.*

Holliday, E., & Gould, T. J. (2016). Nicotine, adolescence, and stress: A review of how stress can modulate the negative consequences of adolescent nicotine abuse. *Neuroscience & Biobehavioral Reviews, 65*, 173–84.

Hopwood, C. J., Baker, K. L., & Morey, L. C. (2008). Personality and drugs of choice. *Personality and Individual Differences, 44*, 1413–1421.

Hosenball, M., & Conant, E. (2007, July 23). An elite escort service. *Newsweek.* Retrieved January 20, 2009, from http://www.newsweek.com/id/35004/output/print

Houlihan, S. D., & Brewer, J. A. (2016). The emerging science of mindfulness as a treatment for addiction. In E. Shonin, W. Van Gordon, & M. Griffiths (Eds.), *Mindfulness- and Buddhist-derived approaches to mental health and addiction.* Switzerland: Springer International.

Hu, J., & Quick, M. W. (2008). Substrate-mediated regulation of aminobutyric acid transporter 1 in rat brain. *Neuropharmacology, 54*, 309–318.

Hu, M. C., Davies, M., & Kandel, D. B. (2006). Epidemiology and correlates of daily smoking and nicotine dependence among young adults in the United States. *American Journal of Public Health, 96*, 299–308

Huddle, T. S., Kertesz, S. G., & Nash, R. R. (2014). Health care institutions should not exclude smokers from employment. *Academic Medicine, 89*, 843–847.

Hudson, J. I., Hiripi, E., Pope, H. G., & Kessler, R. C. (2007). The prevalence and correlates of eating disorders in the National Comorbidity Survey Replication. *Biological Psychiatry, 61*, 348–358.

Hughes, J. (1975). Isolation of an endogenous compound from the brain with pharmacological properties similar to morphine. *Brain Research, 88*, 295–308.

Hunt, W., Barnett, L., & Branch, L. (1971). Relapse rates in addiction programs. *Journal of Clinical Psychology, 27*, 455–456.

Iacono, W. G., Malone, S. M., & McGue, M. (2003). Substance use disorders, externalizing psychopathology, and P300 event-related potential amplitude. *International Journal of Psychophysiology, 48*, 147–178.

Ikegami, A., Olsen, C. M., D'Souza, M. S., & Duvauchelle, C. L. (2007). Experience-dependent effects of cocaine self-administration/conditioning on prefrontal and accumbens dopamine responses. *Behavioral Neuroscience, 121*(2), 389–400.

Ingraham, C. (2017, April 19a). Marijuana has truly gone mainstream. *The Denver Post.* Retrieved from http://www.denverpost.com/2017/04/19/marijuana-mainstream-study-finds/

Ingraham, C. (2017, February 17b). Just how mainstream is marijuana? There's now a "Congressional Cannabis Caucus." *The Washington Post.* Retrieved from https://www.washingtonpost.com/news/wonk/wp/2017/02/17/just-how-mainstream-is-marijuana-theres-now-a-congressional-cannabis-caucus/?utm_term=.615bdd99dd89

Institute of Medicine. (2013). Substance use disorders in the U. S. Armed Forces. C. P. O'Brien, M. Oster., & E. Morden (Eds.). Washington, DC: The National Academies Press.

Interlandi, J. (2008, February 23). What addicts need. *Newsweek.* Retrieved July 9, 2008, from http://www.newsweek.com/id/114716

International Agency for Research on Cancer. (2007). Working group on ultraviolet (UV) light and skin cancer: The association of use of sunbeds with cutaneous malignant melanoma and other skin cancers: A systematic review. *International Journal of Cancer, 120*(5), 1116–1122.

Ivilieva, N. Y. (2012). Neurobiological mechanisms of addictive behavior. *Neuroscience and Behavioral Physiology, 42*(7), 678–691.

Jabar, F. (2013). Gambling on the brain. *Scientific American, 309*(5), 28–30.

Jackson, S., & Csikszentmihalyi, M. (1999). *Flow in sports.* Champaign, IL: Human Kinetics.

James, W. (1890). *Principles of psychology.* New York: Henry Holt.

James, W. (1902). *The varieties of religious experience: A study in human nature.* Cambridge, MA: Riverside Press.

Jarvis, T. J. (1992). Implications of gender for alcohol treatment research: A quantitative and qualitative review. *British Journal of Addiction, 87,* 1249–1261.

Jefferson, D. J. (2005). America's most dangerous drug. *Newsweek.* In H. T. Wilson (Ed.), *Annual editions: Drugs, society, and behavior 2007/2008* (pp. 16–19). Dubuque, IA: McGraw-Hill.

Jellinek, E. M. (1952). The phases of alcohol addiction. *Quarterly Journal of Studies on Alcohol, 13,* 672–684.

Jenkins, C. S. I. (2017). 'Addicted'? To 'love'? *Philosophy, Psychiatry, & Psychology, 24*(1), 93–96.

Jerome, L., Schuster, S., & Yazar-Klosinski, B. B. (2013). Can MDMA play a role in the treatment of substance abuse? *Current Drug Abuse Review, 6*(1), 54–62.

Jessor, R. (1998). *New perspectives on adolescent risk behavior.* New York: Cambridge University Press.

John, O. P., & Srivastava, S. (1999). The big-five trait taxonomy: History, measurement, and theoretical perspectives. In L. A. Pervin & O. P. John (Eds.), *Handbook of personality: Theory and research* (Vol. 2, pp. 102–138). New York: Guilford Press.

Johnson, E. O., Chen, L. S., Breslau, N., Hatsukami, D., Robbins, T., Saccone, N. L., . . . & Bierut, L. J. (2010). Peer smoking and the nicotinic receptor genes: An examination of genetic and environmental risks for nicotine dependence. *Addiction, 105,* 2014–2022.

Jones, .I., Pastor, P. N., Simon, A. E., & Reuben, C. A. (2014). Use of selected nonmedication mental health services by adolescent boys and girls with serious emotional or behavioral difficulties: United States, 2010–2012. *Centers for Disease Control and Prevention, NCHS Data Brief No. 163, August 2014.*

Joseph, M. H., Young, A. M. J., & Gray, J. A. (1998, December 4). Are neurochemistry and reinforcement enough? Can the abuse potential of drugs be explained by common actions on a dopamine reward system in the brain? *Human Psychopharmacology: Clinical and Experimental, 11*(Suppl. 1), S55–S63.

Juliano, L. M., Huntley, E. D., Harrell, P. T., & Westerman, A. T. (2012). Development of the caffeine withdrawal symptom questionnaire: Caffeine withdrawal symptoms cluster into 7 factors. *Drug and Alcohol Dependence, 124,* 229–234.

Julien, R. M., Advokat, C. D., & Comaty, J. E. (2008). *A primer of drug action: A comprehensive guide to the actions, uses, and side effects of psychoactive drugs* (11th ed.). New York: Worth Publishers.

Jung, J., & Yi, S. (2014). Assessment of heterogeneity of compulsive buyers based on affective antecedents of buying lapses. *Addiction Research & Theory, 22*(1), 37–48.

Kabat-Zinn, J., Lipworth, L., & Burney, R. (1985). The clinical use of mindfulness meditation for the self-regulation of chronic pain. *Journal of Behavioral Medicine, 8*(2), 163–190

Kahneman, D. (2003, August 17). Toward a science of wellbeing. Transcript of interview with Nobel Laureate Daniel Kahneman, interviewed by Natasha Mitchell on ABC Radio National program *All in the Mind.* Retrieved on October 11, 2008, from http://www.abc.net.au/rn/allinthemind/stories/2003/923773.htm.

Kahr, B. (2008). *Who's been sleeping in your head.* Cambridge, MA: Perseus.

Kaisar, M. A., Prasad, S., Liles, T., & Cucullo, L. (2016). A decade of e-cigarettes: Limited research and unresolved safety concerns. *Toxicology, 365,* 67–75.

Kaiser, R. B. (2001, March). The way of the journal. *Psychology Today.*

Kandel, D. B., & Maloff, D. R. (1983). Commonalities in drug use: A sociological perspective. In P. K. Levison, D. R. Gerstein, & D. R. Maloff (Eds.), *Commonalities in substance abuse and habitual behavior* (pp. 3–28). Lexington, MA: Lexington Books.

Kang, D. H., Jo, H. J., Jung, W. H., Kim, S. H., Jung, Y. H., Choi, C. H., … Kwon, J. S. (2013). The effect of meditation on brain structure: Cortical thickness mapping and diffusion tensor imaging. *Social Cognitive & Affective Neuroscience, 8*(1), 27–33.

Karim, S. (2014). Erotic desires and practices in cyberspace: 'Virtual reality' of the non-heterosexual middle class in Bangladesh. *Gender, Technology and Development, 18*(1), 53–76.

Katz, N. (2011). Life-size Barbie's shocking dimensions): Would she be anorexic? CBS News April 21, 2011, 11:45 AMKeller, H. (1957). *The open door.* Garden City, N.Y.: Doubleday.

Kellermann, J. L. (1970). *Alcoholism: A merry-go-round named denial* [Pamphlet]. New York: Hazelden.

Kelley, D., & Wilson, T. (1997, April 2). Suicide cultist left area for 'kingdom' in '75. *Los Angeles Times*, http://articles.latimes.com/1997-04-02/local/me-44424_1_bob-rowland

Kelly, G. A. (1955). *The psychology of personal constructs: Vol. 1. A theory of personality; Vol. 2. Clinical diagnosis and psychotherapy.* Oxford, UK: Norton.

Kendler, K. S., Bulik, C. M., Silberg, J., Hettema, J. M., Myers, J., & Prescott, C. A. (2000). Childhood sexual abuse and adult psychiatric and substance use disorders in women: An epidemiological and cotwin control analysis. *Archives of General Psychiatry, 57,* 953–959.

Kendler, K. S., Myers, J., Damaj, M. I., & Chen, X. (2013). Early smoking onset and risk for subsequent nicotine dependence: A monozygotic co-twin control study. *American Journal of Psychiatry, 170,* 408–413.

Kendler, K. S., Neal, M. C., Heath, A. C., Kessler, R. C., & Eaves, L. J. (1994). A twin-family study of alcoholism in women. *American Journal of Psychiatry, 151,* 707–715.

Kendler, K. S., Prescott, C. A., Myers, J., & Neale, M. C. (2003). The structure of genetic and environmental risk factors for common psychiatric and substance use disorders in men and women. *Archives of General Psychiatry, 60,* 929–937.

Kessler, D. (2001). *A question of intent: A great American battle with a deadly industry.* New York: Public Affairs.

Kessler, R. C. (2004). The epidemiology of dual diagnosis. *Biological Psychiatry, 56,* 730–737.

Kessler, R. C., Berglund, P., Demler, O., Jin, R., & Walters, E. E. (2005). Lifetime prevalence and age-of-onset distributions of DSM-IV disorders in the National Comorbidity Survey Replication. *Archives of General Psychiatry, 62*(6), 593–602.

Khajehdaluee, M., Zavar, A., Alidoust, M., & Pourandi, R. (2013). The relation of self-esteem and illegal drug usage in high school students. *Iranian Red Crescent Medical Journal, 15*(11), 1–7.

Khantzian, E. J. (1997). The self-medication hypothesis of substance use disorders: A reconsideration and recent applications. *Harvard Review of Psychiatry, 4*(5), 231–244.

Khantzian, E. J. (2001). Understanding addiction as self medication: Finding hope behind the pain. Keynote Address, 2000 American Academy of Addiction Psychiatry Annual Meeting Proceedings.

Khantzian, E.J. (2012). Reflections on Treating Addictive Disorders: A psychodynamic perspective. *The American Journal on Addictions, 21,* 274–279.

Khokhar, J. Y., Ferguson, C. S., Zhu, A. Z. X., & Tyndale, R. F. (2010). Pharmacogenetics of drug dependence: Role of gene variations in susceptibility and treatment. *Annual Review of Pharmacology & Toxicology, 50,* 39-61.

Kilpatrick, D. G., Resnick, H. S., Saunder, B. E., & Best, C. L. (1998). Victimization, posttraumatic stress disorder, and substance use and abuse among women. In C. L. Wetherington & A. B. Roman (Eds.), *Drug addiction research and the health of women* (pp. 285–307) (NIH Publication No. 98-4290). Rockville, MD: U.S. Department of Health and Human Services.

Kim, K. H., Kabir, E., & Jahan, S. A. (2016). Waterpipe tobacco smoking and its human health impacts. *Journal of Hazardous Materials, 317,* 229–236.

Kimerling, R., Prins, A., Westrup, D., & Lee, T. (2004). Gender issues in the assessment of PTSD. In J. P. Wilson & T. M. Keane (Eds.), *Assessing psychological trauma and PTSD* (2nd ed., pp. 565–602). New York: Guilford.

Kinchin, D. (2005). *Post-traumatic stress disorder: The invisible injury.* Oxfordshire, UK: Success Unlimited.

King, S. M., Iacono, W. G., & McGue, M. (2004). Childhood externalizing and internalizing psychopathology in prediction of early substance use. *Addiction, 99,* 1548–1559.

King County Bar Association Drug Policy Project. (2005). *Drugs and the drug laws: Historical and cultural contexts.* Seattle, WA: Author, 3.

Kinley, J. L. & Reyno, S. M. (2013). Attachment style changes following intensive short-term group psychotherapy. *International Journal of Psychotherapy, 63*(1), 53–75.

Klaassen, M. J. E., Peter, J. (2015). Gender (in)equality in Internet pornography: A content analysis of popular pornographic internet videos. *The Journal of Sex Research 52*(7), 721–735.

Klam, M. (2001) Experiencing Ecstasy. *New York Times Magazine.* Retrieved February 6, 2018, from http://www.nytimes.com/2001/01/21/magazine/experiencing-ecstasy.html

Klatsky, A. L. (2006, December 23–29). Drink to your health? *Scientific American Reports, 288,* 74–81.

Klebold, S. (2009 November). I will never know why. *O Magazine.* Retrieved February 14, 2018, from http://www.oprah.com/world/Susan-Klebolds-O-Magazine-Essay-I-Will-Never-Know-Why#ixzz3fFMokMc6

Klein, D., & Liebowitz, M. (1979). Hysteroid disphoria. *Psychiatric Clinics of North America, 2,* 555–575.

Klump, K. L., Kaye, W. H., & Strober, M. (2001). The evolving genetic foundations of eating disorders. *Psychiatric Clinics of North America, 24*(2), 215–225.

Knight, R., & Buhler, B. (2015). *Follow your gut: The enormous impact of tiny microbes* (First T Books hardcover ed.). New York: Ted Books, Simon & Schuster.

Knishkowy B., & Amitai, Y. (2005). Water-pipe (Narghile) smoking: An emerging health risk behavior. *Pediatrics, 116*(1), e113–e119.

Kobak, R. R., & Hazan, C. (1991). Attachment in marriage: Effect of security and accuracy of working models. *Journal of Personality and Social Psychology, 60,* 861–869.

Kohut, H. (1977). *The restoration of the self.* New York: International Universities Press.

Kolata, G. (2007). *Rethinking thin: The new science of weight loss—and the myths and realities of dieting.* New York: Farrar, Straus & Giroux.

Koob, G.F. (2013). Theoretical frameworks and mechanistic aspects of alcohol addiction: Alcohol addiction as a reward deficit disorder. In W. H. Sommer & R. Spanagel (Eds.), *Behavioral Neurobiology of Alcohol Addiction.* (pp. 3–30). New York; Heidelberg: Springer.

Kormendi, A., Brutoczki, Z., Vegh, B. P, & Szekely, R. (2016). Smartphone use can be addictive? A case report. *Journal of Behavior Addictions, 5,* 548–552.

Kornfield, J. (1993). *A path with Heart: A guide through the perils and promises of spiritual life.* New York: Bantam Books.

Kornfield, J. (Ed.). (2004). *Teachings of the Buddha.* Boston: Shambhala Publications.

Kosterlitz, H. W., & Hughes, J. (1975). Some thoughts on the significance of enkephalin, the endogenous ligand. *Life Science, 17*(1), 91–96.

Kouri, E. M., Pope, H. G., Jr., & Lukas, S. E. (1999). Changes in aggressive behavior during withdrawal from long-term marijuana use. *Psychopharmacology, 143*(3), 302–308.

Kovacs Harbolic, B. (n.d.) Caffeine. *MedicineNet.com.* Retrieved on February 28, 2017, from http://www.medicinenet.com/caffeine/article.htm

Krakowski, M. (2003). Violence and serotonin: Influence of impulse control, affect regulation, and social functioning. *Journal of Neuropsychiatry and Clinical Neuroscience, 15,* 294–305.

Kramer, P. D. (1997). *Listening to Prozac: The landmark book about antidepressants and the remaking of the self* (Rev. ed.). New York: Penguin.

Krall, E. A., Garvey, A. J., & Garcia, R. I. (2002). Smoking relapse after 2 years of abstinence: Findings from the VA Normative Aging Study. *Nicotine & Tobacco Research, 4*, 95–100.

Krueger, R. F., Hicks, B. M., Patrick, C. J., Carlson, S. R., Iacono, W. G., & McGue, M. (2002). Etiologic connections among substance dependence, antisocial behavior, and personality: Modeling the externalizing spectrum. *Journal of Abnormal Psychology, 111,* 411–424.

Kumar, S. M. S. (2002). An introduction to Buddhism for the cognitive behavioral therapist. *Cognitive and Behavioral Practice, 9*(1), 40–43.

Kuss, D. J. (2013). Internet gaming addiction: Current perspectives. *Psychology Research and Behavior Management, 6,* 125+. Retrieved from http://0-go.galegroup.com.skyline.ucdenver.edu/ps/i.do?id=GALE%7CA375581093&sid=summon&v=2.1&u=auraria_main&it=r&p=AONE&sw=w&asid=09a5740d06b401d7e64f8249317dd9f1

Kuss, D. J. & Griffiths, M. D. (2012). Online gaming addiction: A systematic Review. *International Journal of Mental Health and Addiction, 10,* 278–296.

Kutz, I., Borysenko, J. Z., & Benson, H. (1985). Meditation and psychotherapy: A rationale for the integration of dynamic psychotherapy, the relaxation response, and mindfulness meditation. *American Journal of Psychiatry, 142*(1), 1–8.

LaBrie, J. W, Ehret, P. J., & Hummer, J. (2013). Are they all the same? An exploratory, categorical analysis of drinking game types. *Addictive Behaviors, (38)*5, 2133–2139.

Ladika, S. (2005). Meth madness. In H. T. Wilson (Ed.), *Annual editions: Drugs, society, and behavior* (pp. 166–169). Dubuque, IA: McGraw-Hill.

Lamb, C., Burns, J. E., Scaffidi, J., & Murdock, J. (October, 1994). Paper presented at the Association for Education in Journalism and Mass Communication Annual Convention: *Karaoke: Research with a two drink minimum.* Washington, DC.

Lambert, K. (2008, August/September). Depressingly easy. *Scientific American Mind,* 31–37.

Landolfi, E. (2013). Exercise addiction. *Sports Medicine,* 43, 111–119.

Langer, E. J. (2002). Well-being: Mindfulness versus positive evaluation. In C. R. Snyder & S. J. Lopez (Eds.), *Handbook of positive psychology* (pp. 214–230). New York: Oxford University Press.

Lao, S.-A., Kissane, D., & Meadows, G. (2016). Cognitive effects of MBSR/MBCT: A systematic review of neuropsychological outcomes. *Consciousness & Cognition, 45,* 109–123.

LaPlante, D. A., & Shaffer, H. J. (2007). Understanding the influence of gambling opportunities: Expanding exposure models to include adaptation. *American Journal of Orthopsychiatry, 77,* 616–623.

Lask, B., & Bryant-Waugh, R. (Eds.). (2000). *Anorexia nervosa and related eating disorders in childhood and adolescence.* Hove, UK: Psychology Press.

Leahy, R. L. (1996). *Cognitive therapy: Basic principles and applications.* Northvale, NJ: Jason Aronson.

Leger, D. L. (2012, April 12). 'Bath salt' poisonings rise as legislative ban tied up. *USA Today.*

Legrand, L. N., Iacono, W. G., & McGue, M. (2005). Predicting addiction. *American Scientist, 93,* 140–147.

Lehner, K. R., & Bauman, M. H. (2013). Psychoactive 'bath salts': Compounds, mechanisms, and toxicities. *Neuropsychopharmacology Reviews, 38*(1), 243–244.

Lejuez, C. W., Bornovalova, M. A., Reynolds, E. K., Daughters, S. B., & Curtin, J. J. (2007). Risk factors in the relationship between gender and crack/cocaine. *Experimental and Clinical Psychopharmacology, 15*(2), 165–175.

Leonard, K. E., Quigley, B. M., & Collins, R. L. (2002). Physical aggression in the lives of young adults: Prevalence, location, and severity among college and community samples. *Journal of Interpersonal Violence, 17,* 533–550.

Leshner, A. (2007). Addiction is a brain disease. *Issues in Science and Technology.* University of Texas at Dallas. Retrieved February 11, 2009, from http://www.issues.org/17.3/leshner.htm

Lesieur, H. R., & Blume, S. B. (1993). Pathological gambling, eating disorders, and the psychoactive substance use disorders. *Journal of Addictive Diseases, 12*(3), 89–102.

Leutwyler, K. (2006, December). Dying to be thin. *Scientific American Reports.*

Levin, F. R., & Kleber, H. D. (2008). Use of dronabinol for cannabis dependence: Two case reports and review. *American Journal on Addictions, 17*(2), 161–164. doi:10.1080/10550490701861177

Lewinsohn, P. M., Hoberman, H. M., Teri, L., & Hautzinger, M. (1985). An integrated theory of depression. In S. Reiss & R. Bootzin (Eds.), *Theoretical issues in behavior therapy* (pp. 331–359). New York: Academic Press.

Lewis, J.R. (Ed.). (2006). *The order of the solar temple: The temple of death.* Burlington, VT: Ashgate Publishing.

Lieber, C. S. (2001). Alcohol and hepatitis C. *Alcohol Research and Health, 25*(4), 245–254.

Liebowitz, M. R. (1983). *The chemistry of love.* Boston: Little, Brown.

Liepe-Levinson, K. (2002). *Strip show: Performances of gender and Desire.* London: Routledge.

Lindsey, H. (1970). *Late great planet earth.* Grand Rapids, MI: Zondervan.

Linehan, M. M. (1993a). *Cognitive-behavioral treatment of borderline personality disorder.* New York: Guilford.

Linehan, M. M. (1993b). *Skills training manual for treating borderline personality disorder.* New York: Guilford.

Linehan, M. M., Armstrong, H. E., Suarez, A., Allmon, D., & Heard, H. L. (1991). Cognitive-behavioral treatment of chronically parasuicidal borderline patients. *Archives of General Psychiatry, 48,* 1060–1064.

Litt, M. D., Kadden, R. M., Kabela-Cormier, E., & Petry, N. (2007). Changing network support for drinking: Initial findings from the Network Support Project. *Journal of Consulting and Clinical Psychology, 75*(4), 542–555.

Lopez, F. G. (2003). The assessment of adult attachment security. In S. J. Lopez & C. R. Snyder (Eds.), *Positive psychological assessment: A handbook of models and measures* (pp. 285–299). Washington, DC: American Psychological Association.

Lopez-Quintero, C., Pérez de los Cobos, J., Hasin, D. S., Okuda, M., Wang, S., Grant, B. F., & Blanco, C. (2011). Probability and predictors of transition from first use to dependence on nicotine, alcohol, cannabis, and cocaine: Results of the national epidemiologic survey on alcohol and related conditions (NESARC). *Drug and Alcohol Dependence, 115*(1), 120–130. doi:10.1016/j.drugalcdep.2010.11.004

Love, T. (2014, April). Oxytocin, motivation and the role of dopamine. *Pharmacology Biochemistry and Behavior, 119,* 49–60.

Lukoff, D., Lu, F. G., & Turner, R. P. (1998). From spiritual emergency to spiritual problem: The transpersonal roots of the new DSM-IV category. *Journal of Humanistic Psychology, 38*(2), 21–50.

Luria, A. R. (1973). *The working brain.* New York: Basic Books.

Lustig, R. (2009). The Skinny on Obesity. *UCTV Prime: University of California.* Retrieved from http://www.uctv.tv/skinny-on-obesity

Lustig, R. (2012). Fat chance: Beating the odds against sugar, processed food, obesity, and disease. *UCTV Prime: University of California.* Retrieved from http://www.uctv.tv/skinny-on-obesity

Lustyk, M. K. B, Chawla, N., Nolan, R. S., & Marlatt, G. A. (2009). Mindfulness meditation research: Issues of participant screening, safety procedures, and researcher training. *Advances, 24*(1), 20–30.

Lutfullah. (1985). *Autobiography of Lutfullah.* New Delhi, India: International Writers Emporium. (Original work published 1857).

Lynch, W. J., Peterson, A. B., Sanchez, V., Abel, J., & Smither, M. A. (2013). Exercise as a novel treatment for drug addiction. A neurobio and stage-dependent hypothesis. *Neuroscience & Biobehavioral Reviews, 37,* 1622–1644.

Maass, P. (2001, October). Emroz Khan is having a bad day. *New York Times,* pp. 48–51.

Macht, M.; Mueller, J. (2007). Immediate effects of chocolate on experimentally induced mood states. *Appetite, 49,* 667–674.

MacKay, T. L., & Hodgins, D. C. (2012). Cognitive distortions as a problem gambling risk factor in Internet gambling. *International Gambling Studies, 12*(2), 163–175. doi: 10.1080/14459795.2011.648652

MacLeod, S. (2007, October 29). Postcard: Saudi Arabia. *Time,* p. 8.

Maguire, M.H. & Schnurbush, K. (Eds.). (2016). *Annual editions: Drugs, society, and behavior,* (30th ed.). New York, NY: McGraw-Hill.

Mahar, I., Rodriguez Bambico, F., Mechawar, N., & Nobrega, J. N. (2014). Stress, serotonin, and hippocampal neurogenesis in relation to depression and antidepressant effects. *Neuroscience and Biobehavioral Reviews, 38,* 173–192.

Mahler, M. (1967). On human symbiosis and the vicissitudes of individuation. *Journal of the American Psychoanalytic Association, 15,* 740–763.

Mamtani, R., & Cimino, A. (2002). A primer of complementary and alternative medicine and its relevance in the treatment of mental health problems. *Psychiatric Quarterly, 73*(4), 367–381.

Mander, J. (1978). *Four arguments for the elimination of television.* New York: Harper Perennial.

Manhart, K. (2005, September 22). Lust for danger. *Scientific American Mind.* Retrieved June 18, 2008, from http://www.sciam.com/article.cfm?id=lust-for-danger&print=true

Mann, T., Tomijama, A. J., Westling, E., Lew, A. M., Samuels, B., & Chatman, J. (2007). Medicare's search for effective obesity treatments: Diets are not the answer. *American Psychologist, 62*(3), 220–233.

Mansvelder, H. D., & McGehee, D. S. (2002). Synaptic mechanisms underlie nicotine-induced excitability of brain reward systems. *Neuron, 33*(6), 905–919.

Marazziti, D., & Dell'osso, M. C. (2008). The role of oxytocin in neuropsychiatric disorders. *Current Medical Chemicals, 15*(7), 698–704.

Markham, F., Young, M., & Doran, B. (2012). The relationship between alcohol consumption, gambling behavior and problem gambling during a single visit to a gambling venue. *Drug and Alcohol Review, 31,* 770–777.

Marlatt, G. A. (1998). Highlights of harm reduction: A personal report from the first national harm reduction conference in the United States. In G. A. Marlatt (Ed.), *Harm Reduction: Pragmatic strategies for managing high-risk behaviors* (pp. 3-29). New York, NY: The Guilford Press

Marlatt, G. A. (2002). Buddhist philosophy and the treatment of addictive behavior. *Cognitive and Behavioral Practice, 9,* 44–49.

Marlatt, G. A., & Gordon, J. R. (Eds.). (1985). *Relapse prevention: Maintenance strategies in the treatment of addictive behaviors.* New York: Guilford.

Marlatt, G. A., Miller, W. R., Duckert, F., Goetestam, G., Heather, N., Peele, S., Sanchez-Craig, M., Sobell, L. C., Sobell, M. B. (1985). Abstinence and controlled drinking: Alternative treatment goals for alcoholism and problem drinking. *Bulletin of the Society of Psychologists in Addictive Behaviors, 4*(3), 123–150.

Marlatt, G. A., & Witkiewitz, K. (2005). Relapse prevention for alcohol and drug problems. In G. A. Marlatt & D. M. Donovan (Eds.), *Relapse prevention: Maintenance strategies in the treatment of addictive behavior* (pp. 1–44). New York: Guilford.

Marquez, J. (2006, July 31). Mel Gibson's anti-Semitic remarks cited in official police report. *San Francisco Chronicle.* Retrieved January 26, 2009, from http://www.sfgate.com/cgi-bin/article.cgi?f=/n/a/2006/07/31/entertainment/e143903D69.DTL&type=politics

Marsanic, V. B., Margetic, B. A., Jukic, V., Matko, V., & Grgic, V. (2014). Self-reported emotional and behavioral symptoms, parent-adolescent bonding and family functioning in clinically referred adolescent offspring of Croatian PTSD war veterans. *European Child & Adolescent Psychiatry, 23*(5), 295–306.

Marshall, K., Gowing, L., Ali, R., & Le Foll, B. (2014). Pharmacotherapies for cannabis dependence. *Cochrane Database of Systematic Reviews, 12.* doi: 10.1002/14651858.CD008940.pub2

Martin, J. (2012, December 20). Deepak Chopra on your "Super Brain," work stress and creativity. *Forbes.* Retrieved on October 3, 2016, from http://www.forbes.com/sites/work-in-progress/2012/12/20/deepak-chopra-on-your-super-brain-work-stress-and-creativity/#5a7c290a297d

Maslow, A. (1970). *Motivation and personality.* New York: Harper. (Original work published 1954).

Mason (2007). Nicotine has significant effects on brain GABA. *News: Medical: Sciences.* Retrieved on October 4, 2016, from http://www.news-medical.net/news/2007/12/10/33328.aspx

Masters, W. H., & Johnson, V. E. (1974). *The pleasure bond*. New York: Bantam.

Masterson, P. (2017). *Ted Bundy's last interview*. Posted on YouTube. Retrieved from https://www.youtube.com/watch?v=6pv-O8VnIwA

Mate, G. (2015, November 27). Trauma, healing and the brain: Community learning event. Retrieved on July 22, 2017, from https://youtu.be/I3WzMpjtkrs

Matlin, N. W. (1996). *The psychology of women*. Fort Worth, TX: Harcourt Brace.

Mattson, M. (2007). Calcium and neurodegeneration. *Aging Cell, 6*, 337–350.

Mayo Clinic Staff (2014). Caffeine content for coffee, tea, soda and more. Healthy Lifestyle: Nutrition and healthy eating. Retrieved on March 22, 2017, from http://www.mayoclinic.org/healthy-lifestyle/nutrition-and-healthy-eating/in-depth/caffeine/art-20049372

McCann, I. L., & Holmes, D. S. (1984). Influence of aerobic exercise on depression. *Journal of Personality and Social Psychology, 46*(5), 1142–1147.

McCaughan, J. A., Carlson, R. G., Falck, R. S., & Siegal, H. A. (2005). From "Candy-kids" to "Chemikids": A typology of young adults who attend raves in the Midwestern United States. *Substance Use and Misuse, 40*(9–10), 1503–1523.

McClelland, G. M., Elkington, K. S., Teplin, L. A., & Abram, K. M. (2004). Multiple substance use disorders in juvenile detainees. *Journal of the American Academy of Child & Adolescent Psychiatry 43*(10), 1215–1224.

McCoy, T. (2015, August 9). How this chemist unwittingly helped spawn the synthetic drug industry. *The Washington Post*. Retrieved from https://www.washingtonpost.com/local/social-issues/how-a-chemist-unwittingly-helped-spawn-the-synthetic-drug-epidemic/2015/08/09/94454824-3633-11e5-9739-170df8af8eb9_story.html?utm_term=.a6497097650f

McCutcheon, J. C., Mustaine, E. E., & Tewksbury, R. (2016). Working the stroll: Prostitutes, pimps, and johns, *Deviant Behavior, 37*(12), 1449–1458.

McDonald, S.E. (2013). The effects and predictor value of in-class texting behavior on final course grades. *College Student Journal, 47.1*, 34–40.

McGonigal, K. (2013). *How to make stress your friend*. You tube TED talk. Retrieved on July 8, 2017, from https://www.youtube.com/watch?v=RcGyVTAoXEU

McKay, J. R., Alterman, A. I., Rutherford, M. J., Cacciola, J. S., & McLellan, A. T. (1999). The relationship of alcohol use to cocaine relapse in cocaine dependent patients in an aftercare study. *Journal of Studies on Alcohol, 60*, 176–180.

McKee, S. A., Sinha, R., Weinberger, A. H., Sofuoglu, M., Harrison, E. L., Lavery, M., & Wanzer, J. (2011). Stress decreases the ability to resist smoking and potentiates smoking intensity and reward. *Journal of Psychopharmacology, 25*, 490–502.

McMahon, M. (Ed.). (2000). *Assessment to assistance: Programs for women in community corrections*. Lanham, MD: American Correctional Association.

McMurray, M. S., Oguz, I., Rumple, A. M., Paniagua, B., Styner, M. A., & Johns, J. M. (2015). Effects of prenatal cocaine exposure on early postnatal rodent brain structure and diffusion properties. *Neurotoxicology and Teratology, 47*, 80–88.

Mears, B. (2005). Supreme Court allows prosecution of medical marijuana. Retrieved February 25, 2018, from http://www.cnn.com/2005/LAW/06/06/scotus.medical.marijuana/

Mears, C. (2007). Computer gaming: When virtual violence becomes real. *Psychiatric Times, 24*(13), 1–3.

Mechoulam, R., Peters, M., Murillo-Rodriguez, E., & Hanus, L. O. (2007). Cannabidiol: Recent advances. *Chemistry & Biodiversity, 4*, 1678–1692.

Meichenbaum, D. (1977). Dr. Ellis, please stand up. *Counseling Psychologist, 7*(1), 43–44.

Melby, T. (2008). How Second Life seeps into real life. *Contemporary Sexuality, 41*(12), 3–5.

Meredith, S. E., Juliano, L. M., Hughes, J. R., & Griffiths, R. R. (2013). Caffeine use disorder: A comprehensive review and research agenda. *Journal of Caffeine Research, 3*(3), 114–130.

Meule A., & Gearhardt, A. N. (2014). Food addiction in the light of DSM-5. *Nutrients, 6*(9), 3653–3671.

Meule, A., Hermann, T., & Kubler, A. (2014). A short-version of the Food Cravings Questionnaire-Trait: The FCQ-T-reduced. *Frontiers in Psychology, 5*, 1–10.

Meyer, A. C., Rahman, S., Charnigo, R. J., Dwoskin, L. P., Crabbe, J. C., & Bardo, M. T. (2010). Genetics of novelty seeking, amphetamine self-administration and reinstatement using inbred rats. *Genes, Brain and Behavior, 9*, 790–798. doi:10.1111/j.1601-183X.2010.00616.x

Meyer, M., Sundaram, S., & Schafhalter, I. (2017). Exertional and cross-fit-induced rhabdomyolysis. *Clinical Journal of Sport Medicine.* Doi: 10.1097/JSM0000000000000480

Meyers, J. (1992). *Edgar Allan Poe: His life and legacy.* New York: Cooper Square.

Michaud, S. G. & Aynesworth, H. (1999). *The only living witness: The true story of serial sex killer Ted Bundy.* Irving, TX: Authorlink Press.

Milkman, H. (1981). Trip to China. Unpublished notes.

Milkman, H. (1987). Interview with Detective Daril Cinquanta. In H. Milkman & S. Sunderwirth, *Craving for ecstasy: The consciousness and chemistry of escape* (p. 115). Lexington, MA: Lexington Books.

Milkman, H. (2001, April/May). Better than dope. *Psychology Today.*

Milkman, H. (2016). Iceland succeeds at reversing teenage substance abuse: The U.S. should follow suit. *The Huffington Post.* Retrieved on July 30, 2017, from http://www.huffingtonpost.com/harvey-b-milkman-phd/iceland-succeeds-at-rever_b_9892758.html

Milkman, H., & Frosch, W. (1973). On the preferential abuse of heroin and amphetamines. *Journal of Nervous and Mental Disease, 156*(4), 242–248.

Milkman, H., & Hunter, A. (1987, October 3–5). *Say Yes to Natural Highs: A Conference on New Directions* [conference brochure]. Sponsored by the Colorado Alcohol and Drug Abuse Division, Clarion Hotel, Boulder.

Milkman, H., & Hunter, A. (1988, September 16–18). Natural Highs: New Directions for Individual, Family, and Community Well-*Being* [conference brochure]. Sponsored by the Colorado Alcohol and Drug Abuse Division, in association with the Colorado Department of Education, Clarion Hotel, Boulder.

Milkman, H., Metcalf, D., & Reed, P. D. (1980). An innovative approach to methadone detoxification. *International Journal of the Addictions, 15*(9), 1199–1211.

Milkman, H., & Sunderwirth, S. (1982). Addictive processes. *Journal of Psychoactive Drugs, 14*, 177–192.

Milkman, H., & Sunderwirth, S. (1983, October). The chemistry of craving. *Psychology Today*, 36–44.

Milkman, H., & Sunderwirth, S. (1987). *Craving for ecstasy: How our passions become addictions and what we can do about them.* San Francisco: Jossey-Bass.

Milkman, H., & Sunderwirth, S. (1993). *Pathways to pleasure: The consciousness and chemistry of optimal living.* Lexington, MA: Lexington Books.

Milkman, H., & Sunderwirth, S. (1998). *Craving for ecstasy: How our passions become addictions and what we can do about them* (paperback reissue of 1987 ed.). San Francisco: Jossey-Bass.

Milkman, H., & Wanberg, K. (2005). *Criminal conduct and substance abuse treatment for adolescents: Pathways to self-discovery and change.* Thousand Oaks, CA: Sage Publications.

Milkman, H., & Wanberg, K. (2007). *Cognitive-behavioral treatment: A review and discussion for corrections professionals.* Washington, DC: National Institute of Corrections. (NIC Accession No. 021657)

Milkman, H. & Wanberg, K. (2012). *Criminal conduct and substance abuse treatment for adolescents: Pathways to self-discovery and change.* Thousand Oaks, CA: Sage Publications.

Milkman, H., Wanberg, K., & Gagliardi, B. (2008). *Criminal conduct and substance abuse treatment for women in correctional settings: Adjunct provider's guide.* Thousand Oaks, CA: Sage Publications.

Milkman, H., Wanberg, K., & Robinson, C. (1996). *Project Self-Discovery: Artistic alternatives for high-risk youth.* Hoboken, NJ: Wiley.

Miller, C. H., & Hedges, D. W. (2008). Scrupulosity disorder: An overview and introductory analysis. *Journal of Anxiety Disorders, 22*(6), 1042–1058. doi:10.1016/j.janxdis.2007.11.004

Miller, M. E., Badger, G. J., Heil, S. H., Higgins, S. T., & Sigmon, S. C. (2015). Associations between sensation seeking and d-amphetamine reinforcement. *The American Journal on Addictions, 24,* 435–442.

Miller, P., Wells, S., Hobbs, R., Zinkiewicz, L., Curtis, A., & Graham, K. (2014). Alcohol, masculinity, honour and male barroom aggression in an Australian sample. *Drug and Alcohol Review, 33*(2), 136–143. doi:10.1111/dar.12114

Miller, R. J. (2013, December 27). Religion as a product of psychotropic drug use. *The Atlantic.* Retrieved from http://www.theatlantic.com/health/archive/2013/12/religion-as-a-product-of-psychotropic-drug-use/282484

Miller, W. R., & Hester, R. K. (1986). The effectiveness of treatment for substance abuse treatment: What research reveals. In W. R. Miller & N. Heather (Eds.), *Treating addictive behaviors: Processes of change* (pp. 121–174). New York: Plenum.

Miller, W. & Rollnick, S. (2013). Motivational interviewing: Helping people change. (3rd ed.). New York: The Guilford Press.

Milrod, C., Monto, M. (2012). The hobbyist and the girlfriend experience: Behaviors and preferences of male customers of internet sexual service providers. *Deviant Behavior 33*(10), 792–810.

Miranda, J. (1992). Dysfunctional thinking is activated by stressful life events. *Cognitive Therapy and Research, 16,* 473–483.

Mitchel, A. (2015). *It was me all along: A memoir.* Clarkson Potter.

Mokdad, A. H., Marks, J. S., Stroup, D. F., & Gerberding, J. L. (2004). Actual causes of death in the United States. *Journal of the American Medical Association, 291,* 1238–1245.

Montemurro, B. (2001). Strippers and screamers: The emergence of social control in a noninstitutionalized setting, *Journal of Contemporary Ethnography, 30*(3), 275–304.

Moore, K., & Miller, S. (2005, August). Living the high life: The role of drug taking in young people's lives. In H. T. Wilson (Ed.), *Annual editions: Drugs, society, and behavior 2007/2008* (pp. 5–8). Dubuque, IA: McGraw-Hill. (Originally published in *Drugs and Alcohol Today*).

Morahan-Martin, J. (2001). Impact of Internet abuse for college students. In C. Wolfe (Ed.), *Learning and teaching on the World Wide Web* (pp. 191–219). San Diego: Academic Press.

Morain, S. R., Winickoff, J. P., & Mello, M. M. (2016). Have tobacco 21 laws come of age? *The New England Journal of Medicine, 374*(17), 1601.

Morasco, B. J., Pietrzak, R. H., Blanco, C., Grant, B. F., Hasin, D., & Petry, N. M. (2006). Health problems and medical utilization associated with gambling disorders: Results from the National Epidemiologic Survey on Alcohol and Related Conditions. *Psychosomatic Medicine, 68,* 976–984.

Motivational Interviewing Network of Trainers (MINT). (2016). Retrieved on July 21, 2017, from http://motivationalinterviewing.org/

Mueller, A., Mueller, U., Albert, P., Mertens, C., Silbermann, A., Mitchell, J. E., & de Zwaan, M. (2007). Hoarding in a compulsive buying sample. *Behaviour Research & Therapy, 45,* 2754–2763.

Mukamal, K. J., Conigrave, K. M., Mittleman, M. A., Camargo, C., Stampfer, M., Willett, W. C., & Rimm, E. B. (2003). Roles of drinking pattern and type of alcohol consumed in coronary heart disease in men. *New England Journal of Medicine, 348,* 109–118.

Mumola, C.J., & Karberg, J. C. (2006). Drug use and dependence, State and Federal prisoners, 2004. Washington, DC: Bureau of Justice Statistics.

Mutrie, N., & Faulkner, G. (2003). Physiotherapy and occupational therapy in mental health: An evidence-based approach. In T. Everett, M. Donaghy, & S. Fever (Eds.), *Physical activity and mental health* (pp. 211–215). Oxford, UK: Butterworth Heinemann.

Najavits, L. M. (2006). Present- versus past-focused therapy for PTSD/substance abuse: A study of clinician preferences. *Brief Treatment and Crisis Intervention, 6*(3), 248–254.

Nakamura, J., & Csikszentmihalyi, M. (2002). The concept of flow. In C. R. Snyder & S. J. Lopez (Eds.), *The handbook of positive psychology* (pp. 89–105). New York: Oxford University Press.

National Academies of Sciences, Engineering, and Medicine (2017). *The health effects of cannabis and cannabinoids: The current state of evidence and recommendations for research.* Washington, D.C.: The National Academies Press. doi: 10.17226/24625

National Association of Cognitive-Behavioral Therapists. (2008). *What is cognitive-behavioral therapy (CBT)?* Retrieved from http://www.nacbt.org/whatiscbt-htm/

National Center for Posttraumatic Stress Disorder. (2007). *How common is PTSD?* [fact sheet]. Washington, DC: U.S. Department of Veterans Affairs. Retrieved August 29, 2007, from http://www.ncptsd.va.gov/ncmain/ncdocs/fact_shts/fs_how_common_is_ptsd.html

National Council on Alcoholism and Drug Dependence. (2015). *Alcohol, drug dependence & seniors.* Retrieved from https://www.ncadd.org/about-addiction/seniors/alcohol-drug-dependence-and-seniors

National Eating Disorder Association. (2016). *Overview and statistics.* Retrieved from https://www.nationaleatingdisorders.org/binge-eating-disorder

National Geographic. (n.d.). *Drugs Inc.* Retrieved from http://channel.nationalgeographic.com/drugs-inc/

National Geographic. (2013, August 19). *The Science of Stress.* Retrieved from https://www.bing.com/videos/search?q=you+tube+stress&view=detail&mid=0149D2EFCD4B919D33A40149D2EFCD4B919D33A4&FORM=VIRE

National Institute of Mental Health. (2015). *Major depression among adolescents.* National Institutes of Health (NIH). Retrieved on November 18, 2016, from https://www.nimh.nih.gov/health/statistics/prevalence/major-depression-among-adolescents.shtml

National Institute on Alcohol Abuse and Alcoholism (NIAAA). (2004, Winter). *NIAAA Council approves definition of binge drinking.* NIAAA Newsletter. Retrieved on September 19, 2016, from http://pubs.niaaa.nih.gov/publications/Newsletter/winter2004/Newsletter_Number3.pdf

National Institute on Alcohol Abuse and Alcoholism of the National Institutes of Health. (2005). *Helping patients who drink too much: A clinician's guide.* Bethesda, MD: Author.

National Institute on Alcohol Abuse and Alcoholism of the National Institutes of Health. (2016). *Rethinking drinking: Alcohol and your health.* Bethesda, MD: Author. Retrieved from pubs.niaaa.nih.gov/publications/RethingDrinking/Rethinking_Drinking.pdf

National Institute on Drug Abuse. (2001). *Hallucinogens and dissociative drugs.* Washington, DC: U.S. Department of Health and Human Services: Author.

National Institute on Drug Abuse. (2005a). *Inhalant abuse.* Research report series (Publication No. 05-3818). Washington, DC: Author.

National Institute on Drug Abuse. (2005b). *Marijuana abuse.* Research report series (Publication No. 05-3859). Washington, DC: Author.

National Institute on Drug Abuse. (2007a, June). *NIDA Info Facts: Club drugs (GHB, ketamine, and Rohypnol).* Retrieved July 14, 2008, from http://www.nida.nih.gov/infofacts/Clubdrugs.html

National Institute on Drug Abuse. (2008). *Drugs, brains, and behavior: The science of addiction.* Retrieved from https://www.drugabuse.gov/sites/default/files/soa_2014.pdf

National Institute on Drug Abuse. (2008, August). *NIDA InfoFacts: Crack and cocaine.* Retrieved February 1, 2009, from http://www.nida.nih.gov/Infofacts/cocaine.html

National Institute on Drug Abuse. (2009, May 15). *The impact of third hand smoke on risk for genetic mutations wins first place Addiction Science Award at 2009 Intel ISEF Competition.* Retrieved from https://archives.drugabuse.gov/newsroom/09/NR5-15a.html

National Institute on Drug Abuse. (2011). *Drug facts—Comorbidity: Addiction and other mental disorders.* Retrieved from https://www.drugabuse.gov/publications/drugfacts/comorbidity-addiction-other-mental-disorders

National Institute on Drug Abuse. (2012a). *Principles of drug addiction treatment: A research-based guide.* Retrieved from https://d14rmgtrwzf5a.cloudfront.net/sites/default/files/podat_1.pdf

National Institute on Drug Abuse. (2012b). *Principles of drug addiction treatment: A research-based guide.* Retrieved on July 21, 2017, from https://www.drugabuse.gov/publications/principles-drug-addiction-treatment-research-based-guide-third-edition/principles-effective-treatment

National Institute on Drug Abuse. (2014a). *Principles of drug abuse treatment for criminal justice populations - A research-based guide.* Retrieved from https://www.drugabuse.gov/publications/principles-drug-abuse-treatment-criminal-justice-populations/introduction

National Institute on Drug Abuse. (2014b). *Drug facts: Heroin.* Bethesda, MD: National Institute on Drug Abuse. Retrieved from www.drugabuse.gov/publications/drugfacts/heroin

National Institute on Drug Abuse. (2015a). Research reports: Substance use in women. Retrieved from https://d14rmgtrwzf5a.cloudfront.net/sites/default/files/substanceuseinwomenrr_final_09162016.pdf

National Institute on Drug Abuse. (2015b). *Monitoring the future figures 2015.* Retrieved from https://www.drugabuse.gov/related-topics/trends-statistics/monitoring-future/overview-findings-2015/monitoring-future-figures-2015

National Institute on Drug Abuse. (2016a). *Research reports: Substance use in women.* Retrieved from https://www.drugabuse.gov/publications/research-reports/substance-use-in-women/sex-gender-differences-in-substance-use-disorder-treatment

National Institute on Drug Abuse (2016b). *Treatment approaches for drug abuse.* Retrieved from https://www.drugabuse.gov/publications/drugfacts/treatment-approaches-drug-addiction

National Institute on Drug Abuse. (2016c). *Commonly abused drugs charts: Methamphetamine.* Retrieved on April 6, 2017, from https://www.drugabuse.gov/drugs-abuse/commonly-abused-drugs-charts#methamphetamine

National Institute on Drug Abuse. (2016d). *Synthetic cathinones. ("bath salts").* Retrieved on April 11, 2017, from https://www.drugabuse.gov/publications/drugfacts/synthetic-cathinones-bath-salts

National Institute on Drug Abuse. (2016e). *Drug facts: Cocaine.* Retrieved on June 21, 2016, from https://www.drugabuse.gov/publications/drugfacts/cocaine

National Institute on Drug Abuse. (2016f). *Commonly abused drugs charts: Cocaine.* Retrieved on April 6, 2017, from https://www.drugabuse.gov/drugs-abuse/commonly-abused-drugs-charts#cocaine

National Institute on Drug Abuse. (2016g). *Club Drugs.* Retrieved on April 11, 2017, from https://www.drugabuse.gov/drugs-abuse/club-drugs

National Institute on Drug Abuse. (2016h). *Hallucinogens.* Retrieved from https://www.drugabuse.gov/publications/drugfacts/hallucinogens

National Institute on Drug Abuse. (2016i). *DrugFacts: High school and youth trends.* Retrieved on September 5, 2016, from https://www.drugabuse.gov/publications/drugfacts/high-school-youth-trends

National Institutes of Health (2018). Methamphetamine Summary Chart. Retrieved on February 6, 2018, from https://www.drugabuse.gov/drugs-abuse/commonly-abused-drugs-charts

National Institutes of Mental Health (2011). *The Teen Brain: Still Under Construction.* Retrieved March 26, 2017, from https://infocenter.nimh.nih.gov/pubstatic/NIH%2011-4929/NIH%2011-4929.pdf

National Survey on Drug Use and Health. (2005). *Alcohol: A women's health issue.* Washington, DC: U.S. Department of Health and Human Services. (NIH Publication No. 04-4956, revised)

National Survey on Drug Use and Health. (2006). *SAMHSA's latest National Survey on Drug Use and Health.* Washington, DC: U.S. Department of Health and Human Services. Retrieved April 6, 2009, from http://www.oas.samhsa.gov/NSDUHlatest.htm

NBC News Channel (2010). Countries ban popular energy drink ingredient. Retrieved February 5, 2018, from http://www.nbcnews.com/video/nbc-news-channel/26608339

Neighmond, P. (2007, November 21). Retune the body with a partial fast [transcript of radio broadcast]. *All Things Considered.* National Public Radio. Retrieved July 1, 2008, from http://www.npr.org/templates/story/story.php?storyId=16513299

Nelson E. E. & Panksepp, J. (1998). Brain substrates of infant-mother attachment: Contributions of opioids, oxytocin, and norepinephrine. *Neuroscience & Biobehavioral Reviews, 22,* 437–452.

Nelson, K. G., & Oehlert, M. E. (2008). Evaluation of a shortened South Oaks Gambling Screen in veterans with addictions. *Psychology of Addictive Behaviors, 22*(2), 309–312.

Nemeroff, C. B. (1998, June). The neurobiology of depression. *Scientific American,* 42–49.

Nestle, M. (2007, August). Eating made simple: How do you cope with a mountain of conflicting advice? *Scientific American,* 60–69. Retrieved July 1, 2008, from http://www.sciam.com/article.cfm?id=eating-made-simple

Netz, Y., Wu, M., Becker, B. J., & Tenenbaum, G. (2005). Physical activity and psychological well-being in advanced age: A meta-analysis of intervention studies. *Psychology and Aging, 20*(2), 272–284.

Nichols, D. E. (1997). Role of serotonergic neurons and 5-HT receptors in the action of hallucinogens. In H. G. Baumgarten & M. Gothert (Eds.), *Handbook of experimental pharmacology: Serotoninergic neurons and 5-HT receptors in the CNS* (pp. 563–585). Heidelberg, Germany: Springer-Verlag.

Nichols, C. & Sanders-Bush, E. (2001). Serotonin receptor signaling and hallucinogenic drug action. *The Heffter Review of Psychedelic Research, 2.* Retrieved from https://heffter.org/docs/hrireview/02/chap5.pdf

Nicoll, R. A., & Alger, B. E. (2004). The brain's own marijuana. *Scientific American, 291*(3), 67–75.

Nikoshkov, A., Drakenberg, K., Wang, X., Horvath, M., Keller, E., & Hurd, Y. L. (2008). Opioid neuropeptide genotypes in relation to heroin abuse: Dopamine tone contributes to reversed mesolimbic proenkephalin expression. *Proceedings of the National Academy of Sciences of the United States of America, 105*(2), 786–791.

Nimitvilai, S., You, C., Arora, D. S., McElvain, M. A., Vandegrift, B. J., Brodie, M. S., & Woodward, J. J. (2016). Differential effects of toluene and ethanol on dopaminergic neurons of the ventral tegmental area. *Frontiers in Neuroscience, 10*(434), 1–12.

Nizza, M. (2007, November 7). A deadly school shooting, this time in Finland. *New York Times.*

North, A. C. and Hargreaves, D. J. (2008). The social and applied psychology of music. Oxford: Oxford University Press.

Nutt, D.J., Lingford-Hughes, A., Erritzoe, D., & Stokes, P.R.A. (2015). The dopamine theory of addiction: 40 years of highs and lows. *Nature Reviews Neuroscience, 16,* 305–312.

Oates, W. E. (1971). *Confessions of a workaholic: The facts about work addiction.* New York: World Publication Company.

Obituary: Albert Hofmann. (2008, May 8). *Economist,* p. 90.

O'Connor, A., & Sanger-Katz, M. (2016, November 26). As soda taxes gain wider acceptance, your bottle may be next. *The New York Times.* Retrieved on February 9, 2017, from https://mobile.nytimes.com/2016/11/26/well/eat/as-soda-taxes-gain-wider-acceptance-your-bottle-may-be-next.html

Ofcom. (2015). Adults' media use and attitudes: Report 2015. Retrieved on August 4, 2016, from https://www.ofcom.org.uk/__data/assets/pdf_file/0014/82112/2015_adults_media_use_and_attitudes_report.pdf

Office of Disease Prevention and Health Promotion. (2015). *Dietary guidelines 2015–2020. Appendix 9. Alcohol.* Retrieved from https://health.gov/dietaryguidelines/2015/guidelines/appendix-9/

Office of National Drug Control Policy. (2008). *Club drugs facts & figures.* Retrieved January 13, 2009, from http://www.ondcp.gov/drugfact/club/club_drug_ff.html

Ogden, C.L., Carroll, M.D., Fryar, C.D., & Flegal, K.M. (2015). *Prevalence of obesity among adults and youth: United States, 2011–2014,* NCHS data brief, no 219. Hyattsville, MD: National Center for Health Statistics.

Ohia-Nwoko, O., Kosten, T.A., & Haile, C.N. (2016). Animal models and the development of vaccines to treat substance use disorders. *International Review of Neurobiology, 126,* 263–291.

Olds, J., & Milner, P. (1954). Positive reinforcement produced by electrical stimulation of septal area and other regions of the rat brain. *Journal of Comparative Physiology & Psychology, 47,* 419.

Oman, D., Hedberg, J., & Thoresen, C. E. (2006). Passage meditation reduces perceived stress in health professionals: A randomized, controlled trial. *Journal of Consulting and Clinical Psychology, 74,* 714–719.

Oncken, C., Cooney, J., Feinn, R., Lando, H., & Kranzler, H. (2007). Transdermal nicotine for smoking cessation in postmenopausal women. *Addict Behaviors, 32,* 296–309.

Ornish, D. (2008). *Dean Ornish shows how to reverse prostate cancer with nutrigenomics.* Retrieved on July 27, 2008, from http://articles.directorym.net/Dean_ Ornish_Shows_How_to_Reverse_Prostate_Cancer_with_Nutrigenomics_Sacramento_CA-r861391-Sacramento_CA.html

Ornstein, R., & Sobel, D. (1987). *The healing brain: Breakthrough discoveries about how the brain keeps us healthy.* New York: Simon & Schuster.

Orwell, G. (1977). *1984: A novel.* New York, N.Y: Published by Signet Classic.

Osborne, G., & Fogel, G. (2008). Understanding the motivations for recreational marijuana use among adult Canadians. *Substance Use and Misuse, 43*(3–4), 539–572.

Ott, A., Andersen, K., Dewey, M. E., Letenneur, L., Brayne, C., Copeland, J. R. M., ... & Stijnen, T. (2004). Effect of smoking on global cognitive function in nondemented elderly. *Neurology, 62*(6), 920–924.

Ouimette, P. C., Wolfe, J., & Chrestman, K. R. (1996). Characteristics of posttraumatic stress disorder—alcohol abuse comorbidity in women. *Journal of Substance Abuse, 8*(3), 335–346.

Owen, F. (2007). *No speed limit: Meth across America.* New York: St. Martin's Press.

Ozelli, K. L. (2007). This is your brain on food. *Scientific American, 297*(3), 84.

Paffenbarger, R. S., & Lee, I. M. (1996). Physical activity and fitness for health and longevity. *Research Quarterly for Exercise and Sport, 67*(3), S11–S28.

Paidoussis, D., & Dachs, R. J. (2013). Severe rhabdomylosis associated with a popular high-intensity at-home exercise program. *Journal of Medical Cases, 4*(1), 12–14.

Palamar, J. J., Griffin-Tomas, M., & Ompad, D.C. (2015). Illicit drug use among rave attendees in a nationally representative sample of U.S. high school seniors. *Drug and Alcohol Dependence, 152,* 24–31.

Palmer, I. (2007). Terrorism, suicide bombing, fear, and mental health. *International Review of Psychiatry, 19*(3), 289–296.

Paradis, S., & Cabanac, M. (2008). Dieting and food choice in grocery shopping. *Physiological Behavior, 93*(4–5), 1030–1032.

Park, S.Y, Freedman, N.D,, Haiman, C., Marchand,L, Wilkens, L,. Setiawan, V. (2017). Association of Coffee Consumption With Total and Cause-Specific Mortality Among Nonwhite Populations. Annals of Internal Medicine.

Parker, G., Parker, J., & Brotchie, H. (2006). Mood state effects of chocolate. *Journal of Affective Disorders, 92,* 149–159.

Parks, G. A. (2005). Use relapse prevention techniques. In S. Sacks & R. K. Ries (Eds.), *Substance abuse treatment for persons with co-occurring disorders: Treatment Improvement Protocol (TIP) 42* (pp. 127–133). Rockville, MD: U.S. Department of Health and Human Services, Substance Abuse and Mental Health Services Administration, Center for Substance Abuse Treatment.

Parks, G. A., & Marlatt, G. A. (2006). Mindfulness meditation and substance use in an incarcerated population. *Psychology of Addictive Behaviors, 20*(3), 343–347.

Parks, K. A., Miller, B. A., Collins, R. I., & Zetes-Zanatta, L. (1998). Women's descriptions of drinking in bars: Reasons and risks. *Sex Roles, 38,* 701–717.

Partnership for Drug-Free Kids. (2015, September 24). CVS will sell Naloxone without prescription in 14 states. Retrieved on September 9, 2016, from http://www.drugfree.org/news-service/cvs-will-sell-naloxone-without-prescription-14-states/

Parrot, A.C. (2007). The psychotherapeutic potential of MDMA (3,4-methylenedioxymethamphetamine): an evidence-based review. *Psychopharmacology*, 191:181–193

Pasko, L. (2002). Naked power: The practice of stripping as a confidence game. *Sexualities*, 5(1), 49–66.

Passsie, T., Halpern, J., Stichtenoth, D., Hinderk, E. & Annelie, H (2008). The Pharmacology of Lysergic Acid Diethylamide: A Review. *CNS Neuroscience & Therapeutics*. Volume 14, Issue 4, Winter 2008, pp. 295–314.

Patrick, C. J., Bernat, E., Malonel, S. M., Iacono, W. G., Krueger R. F., & McGue, M. K. (2006). P300 amplitude as an indicator of externalizing in adolescent males. *Psychophysiology*, 43, 84–92.

Patterson, R. E., & Sears, D. D. (2017). Metabolic effects of intermittent fasting. *Annual Review of Nutrition*. Doi: 10.1146/annurev-nutr-071816-064634

Pavlov, I. (1927). *Conditioned reflexes.* New York: Oxford University Press.

Peele, S., & Brodsky, A. (1975). *Love and addiction.* New York: Taplinger. Retrieved from www.peele.net/lib/laa4.html

Peltz, L., & Black, D. S. (2014). The thinking mind as addiction: Mindfulness as antidote. *Substance Use and Misuse*, 49(5), 605–607.

Perez-De-Albeniz, A., & Holmes, J. (2000). Meditation: Concepts, effects, and uses in therapy. *International Journal of Psychotherapy*, 5(1), 49–59.

Perham, A. S., & Accordino, M. P. (2007). Exercise and functioning level of individuals with severe mental illness: A comparison of two groups. *Journal of Mental Health Counseling*, 29(4), 350–362.

Perou, R., Bitsko, R. H., Blumberg, S. J., Pastor, P., Ghandour, R. M., Gfoerer, J. C. . . . Huang, L.N. (2013). Mental health surveillance among children–United States, 2005-2011. *Centers for Disease Control and Prevention, Morbidity and Mortality Weekly Report (MMWR)*, 62(02), 1–35

Perry, S. K. (1999). *Writing in flow.* Cincinnati, OH: Writer's Digest Books.

Pescatello, L. S., Franklin, B. A., Fagard, R., Farquhar, W. B., Kelley, G. A., & Ray, C. A. (2004, March). American College of Sports Medicine position stand: Exercise and hypertension. *Medicine & Science in Sports & Exercise*, 36(3), 533–553.

Peschek-Böhmer, F., & Schreiber, G. (1999). Urine Therapy: Nature's Elixir for Good Health. *Healing Arts Press*.

Peterson, C., & Seligman, M. E. P. (2004). *Character strengths and virtues: A handbook and classification.* New York: Oxford University Press.

Peterson, D., & Dressel, P. (1982). Equal time for women: Social notes on the male strip show, *Urban Life, 11*, 185–208.

Phillips, P., Stuber, G., Heien, M., Wightman, R., & Carelli, R. (2003). Subsecond dopamine release promotes cocaine seeking. *Nature, 422*, 614–618.

Pilcher, K. (2009). Empowering, degrading or a 'mutually exploitative' exchange for women?: Characterising the power relations of the strip club. *Journal of International Women's Studies, 10*(3), 73.

Pilcher, K. (2012). Dancing for women: Subverting heteronormativity in a lesbian erotic dance space? *Sexualities, 15*(5), 521–537.

Pink, D. H. (2005). *A whole new mind.* New York: Riverhead Books.

Ploj, K., Roman, E., & Nylander, I. (2003). Long term effects of short and long periods of maternal serparation on brain opioid peptide levels in male Wistar rats. *Neuropeptides, 37*, 149–156.

Plumridge, E. W., Chetwynd, J. W., Reed, A., & Gifford, S. J. (1997). Discourses of emotionality in commercial sex: The missing client voice. *Feminism and Psychology, 7*, 165–181.

Poe, E. A. (1849). Annabel Lee. *Sartain's Union Magazine.*

Pollan, M. (2015, February 2). The Trip Treatment. *New Yorker*. Retrieved on May 3, 2017, from http://www.newyorker.com/magazine/2015/02/09/trip-treatment

Pollock, M. J. (1998). *Counseling women in prison*. Thousand Oaks, CA: Sage Publications.

Popkin, B. M. (2007). Understanding global nutrition dynamics as a step towards controlling cancer incidence. *Nature Reviews Cancer, 7*(1), 61–67.

Popkin, B. M. (2011). Does global obesity represent a global public health challenge? *The American Journal of Clinical Nutrition, 93*(2), 232–233.

Potenza, M. N. (2001). The neurobiology of pathological gambling. *Seminars in Clinical Neuropsychiatry, 6,* 217–226.

Potter, B. (1991). *The tale of Peter Rabbit*. New York: Penguin. (Original work published 1902).

Prescott, C. A., & Kendler, K. S. (1999). Genetic and environmental contributions to alcohol abuse and dependence in a population-based sample of male twins. *American Journal of Psychiatry, 156,* 34–40.

Price, K. (2000). Stripping women: Workers control in strip clubs. *Current Research on Occupations and Professions, 11,* 3–33.

Proctor, R.N. (2012). The history of the discovery of the cigarette-lung cancer link: Evidentiary traditions, corporate denial, global toll. *Tobacco Control, 21,* 87–91.

Prochaska, J.O. & DiClemente, C.C. (1992). Stages of change in the modification of problem behaviors. Progress in Behavior Modification, 28, 183–218.

Prochaska, J. O., DiClemente, C. C., & Norcross, J. C. (1992). In search of how people change: Applications to addictive behaviors. *American Psychologist, 47*(9), 1102–1114. doi:10.1037/0003-066X.47.9.1102

Progoff, I. (1975). *At a journal workshop: The basic text and guide for using the intensive journal process*. New York: Dialogue House.

Progoff, I. (1980). *The practice of process meditation: The intensive journal way to spiritual experience*. New York: Dialogue House.

Prus, A.J. (2017). *Drugs and the neuroscience of behavior: An introduction to psychopharmacology*. (2nd ed.). Los Angeles, CA: Sage.

Puetz, T. W., O'Connor, P. J., & Dishman, R. K. (2006). The effect of chronic exercise on feelings of energy and fatigue: A quantitative synthesis. *Psychological Bulletin, 132,* 866–876.

Pynchon, T. (2012). *The crying of lot 49*. New York: The Penguin Press.

Pyszczynski, T. (2004). What are we so afraid of? A terror management theory perspective on the politics of fear. *Social Research, 71*(4), 827–848.

Radó, S. (1984). The psychoanalysis of pharmacothymia (drug addiction). *Journal of Substance Abuse Treatment, 1*(1), 60–68. doi:10.1016/0740-5472(84)90055-2

Ramirez, J. (2008, June 16). Feeling the pinch: Nevada's brothels hit hard times. *Newsweek*. Retrieved January 20, 2009, from http://www.newsweek.com/id/141848

Rasch, W. (1979). Psychological dimensions of political terrorism in the Federal Republic of Germany. *International Journal of Law and Psychiatry, 2,* 79–85.

Rausch, S. M., Gramling, S. E., & Auerbach, S. M. (2006). Effects of a single session of large-group meditation and progressive muscle relaxation training on stress reduction, creativity, and recovery. *International Journal of Stress Management, 13*(3), 273–290.

Ray, R., Tyndale, R. F., & Lerman, C. (2009). Nicotine dependence pharmacogenetics: Role of genetic variation in nicotine-metabolizing enzymes. *Journal of Neurogenetics, 23,* 252–261.

Raylu, N., & Oei, T. P. (2004). The Gambling-Related Cognitions Scale (GRCS): Development, confirmatory factor validation, and psychometric properties. *Addiction, 99,* 757–769. doi: 10.1111/j.1360-0443.2004.00753.x

Raynor, H. A., Goff, M. R., Poole, S. A., & Chen, G. (2015). Eating frequency, food intake, and weight: A systematic review of human and animal experimental studies. *Frontier in Nutrition, 2,* 38. Doi: 10.3389/fnut.2015.00038

Read, K. W. (2013). Queering the brothel: Identity construction and performance in Carson City, Nevada. *Sexualities, 16*(3), 467–486.

Rehm, J., Patra, J., & Popova, S. (2007). Alcohol drinking cessation and its effect on esophageal and head and neck cancers: A pooled analysis. *International Journal of Cancer, 121*(5), 1132–1137.

Reich, A. (1960). Pathologic forms of self-esteem regulation. *Psychoanalytic Study of the Child, 15,* 215–232.

Reissig, C., Strain, E., & Griffiths, R. (2008). Caffeinated energy drinks—a growing problem. *Drug Alcohol Dependency, 165*(10), 1256–1260.

Reissig, C. J., Strain, E. C., & Griffiths, R. R. (2009). Caffeinated energy drinks—a growing problem. *Drug and Alcohol Dependence, 99*(1), 1–10.

Reith, G. (2007). Gambling and the contradictions of consumption: A genealogy of the "pathological" subject. *American Behavioral Scientist, 51*(1), 33–56.

Renoux, M. (2016, September 30). Fake IDs for pot a problem in Breckenridge. *9 News KUSA.* Retrieved from http://www.9news.com/news/local/fake-ids-for-pot-a-problem-in-breckenridge/328115226

Reuter, J., Raedler, T., Rose, M., Hand, I., Glascher, J., & Buchel, C. (2005). Pathological gambling is linked to reduced activation of the mesolimbic reward system. *Nature Neuroscience, 8,* 147–148.

Reynaud, M., Karila, L., Blecha, L., & Benyamina, A. (2010). Is love passion an addictive disorder? *The American Journal of Drug and Alcohol Abuse, 36,* 261–267.

Rice, R.A. (2006). *MMO evolution.* Raleigh, NC: Lulu Press.

Rideout, V. J., Foehr, U. G., & Roberts, D. F. (2010). Generation M2: Media in the lives of 8- to 18-year-olds. *Henry J. Kaiser Family Foundation.*

Rigamonti, A.E., Piscitelli, F., Aveta, T., Agosti, F., De Col, A., Bru, S., … Sartono, A. (2015). Anticipatory and consummatory effects of (hedonic) chocolate intake are associated with increased circulating levels of the orexigenic peptide ghrelin and endocannabinoids in obese adults. *Food and Nutition Research, 59.*

Rilke, R. M. (1954). *Letters to a young poet.* New York: Norton.

Rimm, E. B., Klatsky, A., Grobbee, D., & Stampfer, M. J. (1996). Review of moderate alcohol consumption and reduced risk of coronary heart disease: Is the effect due to beer, wine, or spirits. *British Medical Journal, 312,* 731–736.

Rivas-Vasquez, R. A., & Delgado, L. (2002). Clinical and toxic effects of MDMA ("Ecstasy"). *Professional Psychology: Research and Practice, 33*(4), 422–425.

Robins, C. J., Schmidt, H., III, & Linehan, M. M. (2004). Dialectical behavior therapy: Synthesizing radical acceptance with skillful means. In S. C. Hayes, V. M. Follette, & M. M. Linehan (Eds.), *Mindfulness and acceptance: Expanding the cognitive-behavioral tradition* (pp. 30–44). New York: Guilford.

Robinson, T. E. & Berridge, K. C. (1993). The neural basis of drug craving: An incentive-sensitization theory of addiction. *Brain Research Review, 18*(3), 247–291.

Robinson, T. E., & Berridge, K. C. (2008). The incentive-sensitization theory of addiction: Some current issues. *Philosophical Transactions of the Royal Society B Biological Sciences, 363,* 3117–3146.

Ronai, C. R., & Ellis, C. (1989). Turn-ons for money: Interactional strategies of the table dancer. *Journal of Contemporary Ethnography, 18*(3), 271–298.

Rosell, D. R. & Siever, L. J. (2015). The neurobiology of aggression and violence. *CNS Spectrums, 20*(3), 254–279

Rosenberg, N. L., Grigsby, J., Dreisbach, J., Busenbark, D., & Grigsby, P. (2002). Neuropsychologic impairment and MRI abnormalities associated with chronic solvent abuse. *Journal of Clinical Toxicology, 40,* 21–34.

Ross, D. A., Travis, M. J., & Arbuckle, M. R. (2015). The future of psychiatry as clinical neuroscience: Why not now? *JAMA Psychiatry, 72*(5), 413–414. doi:10.1001/jamapsychiatry.2014.3199

Rossel Waugh, E.-J. (2006, August 25). A short history of electronic arts. *Business News.* Retrieved January 29, 2009, from http://www.businessweek.com/print/innovate/content/aug2006/id20060828_268977.htm

Routtenberg, A. (1978). The reward system of the brain. *Scientific American, 239*(5), 154–164.

Rucklidge, J. J., Frampton, C. M., Gorman, B., & Boggis, A. (2014). Vitamin-mineral treatment of attention-deficit hyperactivity disorder in adults: Double-blind randomized placebo-controlled trial. *British Journal of Psychiatry, 204*(4), 306–315.

Rucklidge, J. J., & Kaplan, B. J. (2013). Broad-spectrum micronutrient formulas for the treatment of psychiatry symptoms: A systematic review. *Expert Review of Neurotherapeutics, 13*(1), 49–73.

Rupp, J. C. (1973). The love bug. *Journal of Forensic Sciences, 18,* 259–262.

Ryan, T., Chester, A., Reece, J., & Xenos, S. (2014). The uses and abuses of Facebook: A review of Facebook addiction. *Journal of Behavioral Addictions, 3*(3), 133–148.

Sabelli, H. (2002). Phenylethylamine deficit and replacement in depressive illness. In *Natural medications for psychiatric disorders: Considering the alternatives.* Philadelphia, PA: Lippincott, Williams, & Wilkins. Pp. 83–100

Sabelli, H.C., Mosnaim, A.D., Vazquez, A.J., Giardina, W.J., Borison, R.L., & Pedemonte, W.A. (1976). Biochemical plasticity of synaptic transmission: A critical review of Dale's Principle. *Biological Psychiatry, 11*(4), 481–524

Sabol, W. J., West, H.C., & Cooper, M. (2009). Prisoners in 2008. *Office of Justice Programs: Bureau of Justice.* Retrieved from http://bjs.ojp.usdoj.gov/index.cfm?ty=pbdetail&iid=1763

Safko, L., & Brake, D. K. (2009). *The social media bible: Tactics, tools, and strategies for business success.* Hoboken, N.J: John Wiley & Sons.

Samuel, D. B., & Widiger, T. A. (2007). Describing Ted Bundy's personality and working towards DSM-V. *Independent Practitioner, 27*(1), 20–22.

Sanders, T. (2005) *Sex work: A risky business.* Cullompton, Devon, UK: Willan.

Santora, M. (2016, December 14). Drug 85 times as potent as marijuana caused a "zombielike" state in Brooklyn. *The New York Times.* Retrieved from https://www.nytimes.com/2016/12/14/nyregion/zombielike-state-was-caused-by-synthetic-marijuana.html?_r=0

Santucci, A. C. (2008). Adolescent cocaine residually impairs working memory and enhances fear memory in rats. *Experimental and Clinical Psychopharmacology, 16*(1), 77–85.

Sang-Hun, C. (2010). South Korea expands aid for Internet addiction. *New York Times,* May 28, 2010. p.4,

Sapolsky, R. M. (1994). *Why zebras don't get ulcers.* New York: Henry Holt.

Satir, V. (1972). *People making.* Palo Alto, CA: Science and Behavior Books.

Satir, V., & Baldwin, M. (1983). *Satir step by step: A guide to creating change in families.* Palo Alto, CA: Science and Behavior Books.

Satran, A., Bart, B. A., Henry, C. R., Murad, B., Talukdar, S., Satran, D., & Henry, T. D. (2005). Increased prevalence of coronary artery aneurysms among cocaine users. *Circulation, 111,* 2424–2429.

Sauvageau, A. (2014). Current reports on autoerotic deaths: Five persistent myths. *Current Psychiatry Reports, 16*(1), 1–4.

Schaefer-Jones, J. (2007). *Preparing for the worst: A comprehensive guide to protecting your family from terrorist attacks, natural disasters, and other catastrophes.* Westport, CT: Greenwood.

Schindler, A., Thomasius R., Peterson, K., & Sack, P. M. (2009). Heroin as an attachment substitute? Differences in attachment representations between opioid, ecstasy, and cannabis abusers. *Attachment & Human Development, 11,* 307–330.

Schlosser, E. (2003). *Reefer madness: Sex, drugs, and cheap labor in the American black market.* Boston: Houghton Mifflin Company.

Schmich, M.T. (1986). A stopwatch on shopping. *Chicago Tribune,* Dec 24, 1986.

Schmidt, R. L. (2011). Little girl blue: The life of Karen Carpenter. *Chicago Review Press*. Retrieved from http://www. autopsyfiles.org/reports/Celebs/carpenter,%20karen_report.pdf

Schneider, J. P., & Irons, R. R. (2001). Assessment and treatment of addictive sexual disorders: Relevance for chemical dependency relapse. *Substance Use and Misuse, 36*(13), 1795–1820.

Scholey, A., & Kennedy, D. (2004, November). Cognitive and physiological effects of an "energy drink": An evaluation of the whole drink and of glucose, caffeine and herbal flavouring fractions. *Psychopharmacology, 176*(3–4).

Schultz, D. P., & Schultz, S. E. (2004). *A history of modern psychology* (8th ed.). Belmont, CA: Wadsworth/Thompson.

Schuppe, J. (2016, June 19). *30 Years after Basketball Star Len Bias' Death, Its Drug War Impact Endures.* NBC News.

Schwartz, J. P., Thigpen, S. E., & Montgomery, J. K. (2006). Examination of parenting styles of processing emotions and differentiation of self. *Family Journal: Counseling and Therapy for Couples and Families, 14*(1), 41–48.

Sederer, L. (2015). How doctors think: Addiction, neuroscience and your treatment plan. Retrieved on June 29, 2015, from http://www.huffingtonpost.com/lloyd-i-sederer-md/how-doctors-think-addicti_b_7687986.html

Seelye, K. Q., & Goodnough, A. (2017, February 11). Without health law, addicts could have the most to lose. (national desk). *New York Times.*

Segal, Z. V., Teasdale, J. D., & Williams, J. M. G. (2004). Mindfulness-based cognitive therapy: Theoretical rationale and empirical status. In S. C. Hayes, V. M. Follette, & M. M. Linehan (Eds.), *Mindfulness and acceptance: Expanding the cognitive behavioral tradition.* (45–65). New York: Guildford Press.

Seligman, M. E. P. (2002). *Authentic happiness: Using the new positive psychology to realize your potential for lasting fulfillment.* New York: Free Press.

Selye, H. (1956). *The stress of life.* Boston: McGraw-Hill.

Selye, H. (1971). *Hormones and resistance.* New York: Springer-Verlag.

Selye, H. (1974). *Stress without distress.* Philadelphia: Lippincott.

Shaffer, H. J., Hall, M. N., & Vander Bilt, J. (1999). Estimating the prevalence of disordered gambling behavior in the United States and Canada: A research synthesis. *American Journal of Public Health, 89,* 1369–1376.

Shaffer, H. J., & Korn, D. A. (2002). Gambling and related mental disorders: A public health analysis. *Annual Review of Public Health, 23,* 171–212.

Shaffer, H. J., LaBrie, R., LaPlante, D., Nelson, S., & Stanton, B. (2004, August). The road less traveled: Moving from distribution to determinants in the study of gambling epidemiology. *Canadian Journal of Psychiatry, 49*(8), 504–516.

Shaffer, H. J., LaPlante, D. A., LaBrie, R. A., Kidman, R. C., Donato, A., & Stanton, M. V. (2004). Toward a syndrome model of addiction: Multiple manifestations, common etiology. *Harvard Review of Psychiatry, 12*(6), 367–374.

Shaheen, P. E., Walsh, D., Lasheen, W., Davis, M. P., & Lagman, R. L. (2009). Opioid equianalgesic tables: Are they all equally dangerous? *Journal of Pain and Symptom Management, 38,* 409–417.

Shapiro, D. H. (1992). Adverse effects of meditation: A preliminary investigation of long-term meditators. *International Journal of Psychosomatics, 39*(1–4), 62–67.

Shapiro, S. L., Schwartz, G. E. R., & Santerre, C. (2002). Meditation and positive psychology. In C. R. Snyder & S. J. Lopez (Eds.), *The handbook of positive psychology* (pp. 632–645). New York: Oxford University Press.

Sharp, S. (2003). *The incarcerated woman: Rehabilitative programming in women's prisons.* Englewood Cliffs, NJ: Prentice Hall.

Shaver, P., Hazan, C., & Bradshaw, D. (1988). Love as attachment. In R. J. Sternberg & M. L. Barnes (Eds.), *The psychology of love* (pp. 68–99). New Haven, CT: Yale University Press.

Sheehan, W., & Garfinkel, B. D. (1987). Adolescent autoerotic deaths. *Journal of the American Academy of Child and Adolescent Psychiatry, 27,* 367–370.

Sher, L. (2012). Suicidal behavior in alcohol and drug abuse. In J.C. Vester, K. Brady, M. Galanter, & P. Conrad (Eds). *Drug abuse and addiction in medical illness: Causes, consequences, and treatment* (pp. 479-488). New York: Springer Science and Business Media.

Siegel, D. J. (1999). *The developing mind: Toward a neurobiology of interpersonal experience.* New York, NY: Guilford Press.

Shigaki, C. L., Glass, B., & Schopp, L. H. (2006). Mindfulness-based stress reduction in medical settings. *Journal of Clinical Psychology in Medical Settings, 13*(3), 209–216.

Shin, D.H. (2012). The dynamic user activities in Massive Multiplayer Online Role Playing Games. *International Journal of Human Computer Interaction, 26,* 317–344.

Shropshire, T. (2017) Top 10 cannabis festivals in the US. *Rolling Out.* Retrieved on July 7, 2017, from http://rollingout.com/2017/04/20/top-10-cannabis-festivals-us/

Siegel, R.K. (1986). MDMA: Nonmedical Use and Intoxication. J. Psychoactive Drugs 18 34.

Siegel, S., Hinson, R.E., & Krank, M.D. (1982). Heroin "overdose" death: Contribution of drug-associated environmental cues. *Science, 216,* 436–437.

Sigfúsdóttir, D. (2016, April 19). *United Nations General Assembly Special Session (UNGLASS) on the World Drug Problem.*

Silberman, S. W. (1995). The relationship among love, marital satisfaction, and duration of marriage. *Dissertation Abstracts, 56,* 2341.

Silke, A. (1998). Cheshire-cat logic: The recurring theme of terrorist abnormality in psychological research. *Psychology, Crime, and Law, 4,* 51–69.

Singer, I. (1984a). *The nature of love: Vol. 1. Plato to Luther* (2nd ed.). Chicago: University of Chicago Press.

Singer, I. (1984b). *The nature of love: Vol. 2. Courtly and romantic.* Chicago: University of Chicago Press.

Singer, I. (1987). *The nature of love: Vol. 3. The modern world.* Chicago: University of Chicago Press.

Singer, J. L. (1976). Towards the scientific study of imagination. *Imaginations, Cognition, and Personality, 1*(1), 5–28.

Singer, J. L., & Kolligian, J. (1987, January). Personality: Developments in the study of private experience. *Annual Review of Psychology, 38,* 533–574.

Sinha, R., & Rounsaville, B. J. (2002). Sex differences in depressed substance abusers. *Journal of Clinical Psychiatry, 63,* 616–627.

Skinner, B. F. (1938). *The behavior of organisms: An experimental analysis.* Oxford, UK: Appleton-Century.

Skipp, C., & Campo-Flores, A. (2008, June 30). Rough ride above the South Beach "brothel bus." *Newsweek.* Retrieved January 20, 2009, from http://www.newsweek.com/id/144102/output/comments

Slater, L. (2006, February). Love. *National Geographic Magazine,* 32–49.

Smedley, R. L. (2015). Coping mechanisms as behavioral addictions. *Addiction Professional, 13*(1), 42.

Smith, C. (2002). Shiny chests and heaving g-strings: A night out with the Chippendales, *Sexualities, 5*(1), 67–89.

Smith, D., Smith, R., & Misquitta, D. (2016). Neuroimaging and violence. *Psychiatric Clinics of North America, 39,* 579–597.

Smith, M., Jaffe, J., & Segal, J. (2008). *Post-traumatic stress disorder: Symptoms, types, and treatment. Helpguide.org.* Retrieved March 3, 2008, from http://www.Helpguide.org/mental/post-traumatic-stress-disorder-symptoms-treatment.htm

Smith, M. K. (2008). *Howard Gardner, multiple intelligences and education.* Retrieved July 10, 2008, from http://www.infed.org/thinkers/gardner.htm.

Snyder, C. R., & Lopez, S. J. (2007). *Positive psychology: The scientific and practical explorations of human strengths.* Thousand Oaks, CA: Sage Publications.

Society for Neuroscience. (2003, October). Sugar addiction. *Brain Briefings*. Washington, DC: Author. Retrieved January 5, 2009, from http://www.sfn.org/skins/main/pdf/BrainBriefings/BrainBriefings_Oct2003.pdf

Soderpalm, B., & Ericson, M. (2013). Neurocircuitry involved in development of alcohol addiction: The dopamine system and its access points. In W. H. Sommer & R. Spanagel (Eds.), *Behavioral Neurobiology of Alcohol Addiction*. (pp. 127–162). New York; Heidelberg: Springer.

Solomon, R. L. (1980). The opponent-process theory of acquired motivation: The costs of pleasure and the benefits of pain. *American Psychologist, 35*(8), 691–712.

Solomon, S., Greenberg, J., & Pyszczynski, T. (1991). Terror management theory of self-esteem. In C. R. Snyder & D. Forsyth (Eds.), *Handbook of social and clinical psychology: The health perspective* (pp. 21–40). New York: Pergamon.

Spear, L.P. (2016). Consequences of adolescent use of alcohol and other drugs: Studies using rodent models. *Neuroscience and Biobehavioral Reviews, 70*, 228–243.

Stanciu, C. N., Penders, T. M., & Rouse, E. M. (2016). Recreational use of dextromethorphan, "Robotripping"—a brief review. *American Journal on Addictions, 25*, 374–377.

Star Wars Episode II: The Bar Scene. (2015). Retrieved from https://www.bing.com/videos/search?q=u+tube+bar+scene+from+star+wars&&view=detail&mid=9730068391A158D-168B79730068391A158D168B7&FORM=VRDGAR

Steenbergh, T.A., Meyers, A.W., May, R.K., and Whelan, J.P. (2002). Development and validation of the Gamblers' Beliefs Questionnaire. *Psychology of Addictive Behaviors, 16*(2), 143–149. doi: 10.1037///0893-164x.16.2.143

Stein, L. (2008a). Work it out: More activity equals slower aging. *Scientific American*. Retrieved June 18, 2008, from http://www.sciam.com/article.cfm?id=new-study-links-exercise-to-longevity

Stein, L. (2008b). Can lifestyle changes bring out the best in genes? *Scientific American*. Retrieved July 27, 2008, from http://www.sciam.com/article.cfm?id=can-lifestyle-changes-bring-out-the-best-in-genes

Steinke, L., Lanfear, D. E., Dhanapal, V., & Kalus, J. S. (2009). Effect of "energy drink" consumption on hemodynamic and electrocardiographic parameters in healthy young adults. *The Annals of Pharmacotherapy, 43*(4), 596–602.

Stern, J. (2004). *Terror in the name of God: Why religious militants kill*. New York: HarperCollins.

Sternberg, R. J. (1986). A triangular theory of love. *Psychological Review, 93*, 119–135.

Stetka, B. S., & Volkow, N. D. (2013, July 16). Can obesity be an addiction? *Medscape*. Retrieved from http://www.medscape.com/viewarticle/807684

Stevens, A. J., Rucklidge, J. J., & Kennedy, M. A. (2017). Epigenetics, nutrition and mental health. Is there a relationship? *Nutritional Neuroscience*. Doi: 10.1080/1028415X.2017.1331524

St. Leger, A. S., Cochrane, A. L., & Moore, F. (1979). Factors associated with cardiac mortality in developed countries with particular reference to the consumption of wine. *Lancet, 1,* 1017–1020.

Stockwell, T., Zhao, J., Panwar, S., Roemer, A., Naimi, T., & Chikritzhs, T. (2016). Do "moderate" drinkers have reduced mortality risk? A systematic review and meta-analysis of alcohol consumption and all-cause mortality. *Journal of Studies on Alcohol and Drugs, (77)*2, 185–198. Retrieved from http://www.jsad.com/doi/full/10.15288/jsad.2016.77.185

Strassman, R. (2001). *The spirit molecule: A doctor's revolutionary research into the biology of near-death and mystical experiences*. Rochester, VT: Park Street Press.

Subrahmanyam, K., & Greenfield, P. (2008). Online communications and adolescent relationships. *Future of Children, 18*(1), 119–146.

Substance Abuse and Mental Health Services Administration. (2008). *Results from the 2007 National Survey on Drug Use and Health: National Findings* (Office of Applied Studies, NSDUH Series H-34, DHHS Publication No. SMA 08-4343). Rockville, MD.

Substance Abuse and Mental Health Services Administration, Center for Behavioral Health Statistics and Quality. (2014). *Treatment Episode Data Set (TEDS): 2002-2012. National Admissions to Substance Abuse Treatment*

Services. BHSIS Series S-71, HHS Publication No. (SMA) 14-4850. Rockville, MD: Substance Abuse and Mental Health Services Administration. Retrieved from http://archive.samhsa.gov/data/2k14/TEDS2012NA/TEDS2012NTbl1.3a.htm

Substance Abuse and Mental Health Services Administration (2016). *Key Substance Use and Mental Health Indicators in the United States: Results from the National Survey on Drug Use and Health.* Retrieved on February 25, 2018 from https://www.samhsa.gov/data/sites/default/files/NSDUH-FFR1-2015/NSDUH-FFR1-2015/NSDUH-FFR1-2015.htm#illicit02.

Substance Abuse and Mental Health Services Administration. (2016a). *2015 National Survey on Drug Use and Health (NSDUH).* Table 2.46B—Alcohol Use, Binge Alcohol Use, and Heavy Alcohol Use in Past Month among Persons Aged 12 or Older, by Demographic Characteristics: Percentages, 2014 and 2015. Retrieved on January 18, 2017, from https://www.samhsa.gov/data/sites/default/files/NSDUH-DetTabs-2015/NSDUH-DetTabs-2015/NSDUH-DetTabs-2015.htm#tab2-46b

Substance Abuse and Mental Health Services Administration. (2016b). *Binge drinking: Terminology and patterns of use.* Retrieved on January 18, 2017, from https://www.samhsa.gov/capt/tools-learning-resources/binge-drinking-terminology-patterns

Substance Abuse and Mental Health Services Administration (2017). *Key Substance Use and Mental Health Indicators in the United States: Results from the National Survey on Drug Use and Health.* Substance Abuse and Mental Health Services Administration. (2017). *Key substance use and mental health indicators in the United States: Results from the 2016 National Survey on Drug Use and Health* (HHS Publication No. SMA 17-5044, NSDUH Series H-52). Rockville, MD: Center for Behavioral Health Statistics and Quality, Substance Abuse and Mental Health Services Administration Retrieved on February 26, 2018, from https://www.samhsa.gov/data/sites/default/files/NSDUH-FFR1-2016/NSDUH-FFR1-2016.htm#summary.

Suellentrop, C. (2006, August 1). Mel Gibson's moment. *New York Times.*

Summers, N. (2007, August 21). A struggle inside AA. *Newsweek.* Retrieved July 9, 2008, from http://www.newsweek.com/id/35018

Sumnall, H. R., Woolfall, K., Edwards, S., Cole, J. C., & Beynon, C. M. (2008). Use, function, and subjective experiences of gamma-hydroxybutyrate (GHB). *Drug and Alcohol Dependence, 92,* 286–290.

Sun, A. P. (2006). Program factors related to women's substance abuse treatment retention and other outcomes: A review and critique. *Journal of Substance Abuse Treatment, 30,* 1–20.

Sussman, S. (2010). Love addiction: Definition, etiology, treatment. *Sexual Addiction & Compulsivity, 17*(1), 31–45.

Svetkey, B. (1997, July 18). Making contact. *Entertainment Weekly.* Retrieved February 6, 2007, from http://www.ew.com/ew/article/0,,288672,00.html.

Swift, A. (2016). Support for legal marijuana use up to 60% in U.S. *Gallup.* Retrieved from http://www.gallup.com/poll/196550/support-legal-marijuana.aspx

Szabo, A., Griffths, M. D., de La Vega Marcos, R., Mervo, B., & Demetrovics, Z. (2015). Methodological and conceptual limitations in exercise addiction research. *Yale Journal of Biology & Medicine, 88,* 303–308.

Tanda, G., Pontieri, F. E., & Di Chiara, G. (1997). Cannabinoid and heroin activation of mesolimbic dopamine transmission by a common opioid receptor mechanism. *Science, 276,* 2048–2050.

Taneja, C. (2014). The psychology of excessive cell phone use. *Delhi Psychiatry Journal, 17,* 448–451.

Tang, Y. Y., Holzel, B. K., & Posner M. I. (2015). The neuroscience of mindfulness meditation. *Neuroscience, 16*(4), 213–225.

Tarm, M., & Forliti, A. (2016, June 2). Autopsy report: Prince died of fentanyl overdose. *Associated Press.* Retrieved from bigstory.ap.org/article/3c5f1efbd3a4ae1zdd3a3d787864475/apnewsbreak-official-says-prince-died-opioid-overdose

Taubes, G. (2011, April 13). Is Sugar Toxic? *New York Times Magazine.* Retrieved on February 9, 2017, from http://www.nytimes.com/2011/04/17/magazine/mag-17Sugar-t.html

Taxman, F. S., Perdoni, M. L., & Harrison, L. D. (2007). Drug treatment services for adult offenders: The state of the state. *Journal of Substance Abuse Treatment, 32*(3), 239–254. doi:10.1016/j.jsat.2006.12.019

Taylor, C.Z. (2002). Religious addiction: Obsession with spirituality. *Pastoral Psychology, 50*, 291–315

Teasdale, J. D., Moore, R. G., Hayhurst, H., Pope, M., Williams, S., & Segal, Z. V. (2002). Metacognitive awareness and prevention of relapse in depression: Empirical evidence. *Journal of Consulting and Clinical Psychology, 70*, 275–287.

Templeton, J. (1998). W*orldwide laws of life: 200 eternal spiritual principles.* West Conshohocken, PA: Templeton Foundation Press.

Tennov, D. (1979). *Love and limerence: The experience of being in love.* New York: Stein and Day.

Ter Bogt, T. F. M., & Engels, R. C. M. E. (2005). "Partying" hard: Party style, motives for, and effects of MDMA use at rave parties. *Substance Use and Misuse, 40*(9–10), 1479–1502.

Tewksbury, R. (1993). Male strippers: Men objectifying men. In C. Williams (Ed.), *Doing women's work: Men in non-traditional occupations* (168–181). London: Sage.

Tewksbury, R., & Lapsey, D. (2016). It's more than just a big dick: Desires, experiences, and how male escorts satisfy their customers. *Deviant Behavior.* doi: 10.1080/01639625.2016.1263076

The American Institute of Stress. (n.d.) *Stress is killing you.* Retrieved on October 24, 2016, from http://www.stress.org/stress-is-killing-you/

The Economist. (2016, November 2). *The global crisis of obesity.* Retrieved on February 19, 2017, from http://www.economist.com/events-conferences/emea/global-crisis-obesity-2

The Economist. (2007, November 21). To avoid the big c, stay small. Retrived on February 23, 2018, from http://www.economist.com/node/10062421

The Josiah Macy Foundation. (n.d.). *Seven case studies of people with substance abuse problems.* J. DiDominico (Ed.). Retrieved on October 24, 2016, from http://www.cnsproductions.com/pdf/casestudies.pdf

The Manhattan Project: An enduring legacy. (1999, December 6). *PhysicsWorld.com.* Retrieved January 30, 2009, from http://physicsworld.com/cws/article/print/855

The National Academies of Sciences, Engineering, and Medicine (2017). *The health effects of cannabis and cannabinoids: The current state of evidence and recommendations for research.* Washington, D.C.: The National Academies Press.

The New York Times. (2016, June 22). *'My first gay bar': Rachel Maddow, Andy Cohen and others share their coming-out stories.* Retrieved from https://www.nytimes.com/2016/06/23/fashion/my-first-gay-bar-rosie-odonnell-rachel-maddow-alexander-wang-andy-cohen-share.html?_r=0

The Washington Post. (2005). *The new food pyramid.* Retrieved on July 29, 2017, from http://www.washingtonpost.com/wp-srv/nation/daily/graphics/diet_042005.html

The Washington Post. (2015, January 11). *Southwest border drug seizures.* Retrieved on April 7, 2017, from http://apps.washingtonpost.com/g/page/world/southwest-border-drug-seizures/1543/

Thombs, D. L. (2006). *Introduction to Addictive Behaviors* (3rd ed.). New York: Guilford Press.

Timko, C., Moos, R. H., Finney, J. W., & Connell, E. G. (2002). Gender differences in help-utilization and the 8-year course of alcohol abuse. *Addiction, 97,* 877–889.

Titova, O.E., Hjorth, O.C., Schloth, H.B., & Brooks, S.J. (2013). Anorexia nervosa is linked to reduced brain structure in reward and somatosensory regions in a meta-analysis of VBM studies. BMC Psychiatry, 13:110. Doi: 10.1186/1471-224X-13-110

Trevisan, L. A., Boutros, N., Petrakis, I. L. & Krystal, J. H. (1998). Complications of alcohol withdrawal: Pathophysiological insights. *Alcohol Health & Research World, 22,* 61–66.

Trigo, J. M. & Le Foll, B. (2017). The role of the endocannabinoid system in addiction. In E. Murillo-Rodriguez (Ed.), *The endocannabinoid system: Genetics, biochemistry, brain disorders, and therapy.* London: Academic Press.

Tupper, K. W., Wood, E., Yensen, R., & Johnson, M. W. (2015). Psychedelic medicine: A re-emerging therapeutic paradigm. *CMAJ, 187*(14), 1054–1059.

Tyler, K., Schmitz, R., & Adams, S. A. (2015, June 30). Alcohol expectancy, drinking behavior, and sexual victimization among female and male college students. *Journal of Interpersonal Violence*, 19.

Tyre, P. (2005). Fighting anorexia: No one to blame. *Newsweek.* Retrieved July 1, 2008, from http://www.msnbc.msn.com/id/10219756/site/newsweek/print/1/displaymode/1098

Uhl, G. R., Liu, Q. R., & Naiman, D. (2002, August). Substance abuse vulnerability loci: Converging genome scanning data. *Trends in Genetics, 18,* 420–425.

U.S. Department of Agriculture. (2015). Scientific Report of the 2015 Dietary Guidelines Advisory Committee, Part D. Chapter 2, Table D2.3, p. 43. Available at: https://health.gov/dietaryguidelines/2015-scientific-report/pdfs/scientific-report-of-the-2015-dietary-guidelines-advisory-committee.pdf. Accessed January 18, 2017.

U.S. Department of Health and Human Services. (n.d.). The real cost: Taking control. Retrieved from https://therealcost.betobaccofree.hhs.gov/taking-control.html

U.S. Department of Health and Human Services. (2004, October). *Alcohol alert: Alcohol's damaging effects on the brain.* Retrieved July 14, 2008, from http://pubs.niaaa.nih.gov/publications/aa63/aa63.htm

U.S. Department of Health and Human Services. (2014). *The health consequences of smoking: 50 years of progress.* A report of the Surgeon General. Atlanta, GA: U.S. Department of Health and Human Services, Centers for Disease Control and Prevention, National Center for Chronic Disease Prevention and Health Promotion, Office on Smoking and Health.

U.S. Department of Health, and Human Services, Centers for Disease Control and Prevention, National Center for Chronic Disease, Prevention and Health Promotion, Office on Smoking and Health (2016). E-Cigarette Use Among Youth And Young Adults: A Report of the Surgeon General — Executive Summary; 2016. https://e-cigarettes.surgeongeneral.gov/documents/2016_SGR_Exec_Summ_508.pdf. Accessed February 21, 2017.

U.S. Department of Transportation. (2016, April). Traffic safety facts: Distracted driving 2014. Retrieved from https://crashstats.nhtsa.dot.gov/Api/Public/ViewPublication/812260

U.S. Food & Drug Administration. (2014, April 3). FDA approves new hand-held auto-injector to reverse opioid overdose. Retrieved on September 1, 2016 from https://www.fda.gov/NewsEvents/Newsroom/PressAnnouncements/ucm391465.htm

U.S. Food & Drug Administration. (2015). FDA consumer advice on pure powdered caffeine. Retrieved from http://www.fda.gov/food/recallsoutbreaksemergencies/safetyalertsadvisories/ucm405787.htm

U.S. Food & Drug Administration. (2016a). FDA drug safety communication: FDA warns about serious heart problems with high doses of the antidiarrheal medicine loperamide (Imodium), including from abuse and misuse. Retrieved from www.fda.gov/Drugs/DrugSafety/ucm504617.htm

U.S. Food & Drug Administration. (2016b). Tobacco products: Rules, regulations & guidance. Retrieved from https://www.fda.gov/TobaccoProducts/Labeling/RulesRegulationsGuidance/

Uva, J. L. (1995). Review: Autoerotic asphyxiation in the United States. *Journal of Forensic Sciences, 40,* 574–581.

Vadivelu, N., Kaye, A. D., & Urman, R. D. (2014). Perioperative analgesia and challenges in the drug-addicted and drug-dependent patient. *Best Practices in Research & Clinical Anesthesiology, 28,* 91–101.

Vaillant, G. (1983). *The natural history of alcoholism.* Cambridge, MA: Harvard University Press.

Vaillant, G. E. (1995). *The natural history of alcoholism revisited.* Cambridge, MA: Harvard University Press.

Vanderheyden, P. A. (1999). Religious addiction: The subtle destruction of the soul. *Pastoral Psychology, 47*(4), 293-302. doi:10.1023/A:1021351428976

van Holst, R. J., van den Brink, W., Veltman, D. J. & Goudriaan, A. E. (2010). Brain imaging studies in pathological gambling. *Current Psychiatry Reports, 12*(5), 418–425.

Vare, E. A. (2011). *Love addict: Sex, roman, and other dangerous drugs.* Deersfield Beach, FL: Health Communications, Inc.

Vazquez, V., Giros, B., & Dauge, V. (2006). Maternal deprivation specifically enhances vulnerability to opiate dependence. *Behavioural Pharmacology, 17*, 715–24

Vegting, Y., Reneman, L, & Booij, J. (2016). The effects of ecstasy on neurotransmitter systems: A review on the findings of molecular imaging studies. *Psychopharmacology, 233*(19–20), 3473–3501.

Velez, M. L., Montoya, I. D., Schwietzer, W., Golden, A., Jansson, L. M., Walters, V., et al. (2006). Exposure to violence among substance-dependent pregnant women and their children. *Journal of Substance Abuse Treatment, 30,* 31–38.

Venniro, M., Mutti, A., & Chiamulera, C. (2015). Pharmacological and non-pharmacological factors that regulate the acquisition of ketamine self-administration in rats. *Psychopharmacology, 232*(24), 4505–4514.

Vergara, D., Bidwell, L. C., Gaudino, R., Torres, A., Du, G., Rutherburg, T. C., … Kane, N. C. (2017). Compromised external validity: Federally produced *Cannabis* does not reflect legal markets. *Scientific Reports, 1,* 46528. Doi: 10.1038/srep46528

Vergara, D., Kane, N., & Pauli, C. (2017, April 29). *Diversity in Cannabis sativa.* Presentation at the 1st Annual Institute of Cannabis Research Conference, Pueblo, CO.

Vestal, C. (2016). Stateline: As more women drink, some states take action. *The Pew Charitable Trusts.* Retrieved on February 23, 2017, from http://www.pewtrusts.org/en/research-and-analysis/blogs/stateline/2016/12/19/as-more-women-drink-some-states-take-action

Virtual online worlds. (2006, September 28). Living a Second Life. *The Economist.*

Viveros, M. P., Llorente, R., Suarez, J., Llorente-Berzal, A., Lopez-Gallardo, M., & Rodriguez de Fonseca, F. (2012). The endocannabinoid system in critical neurodevelopmental periods: Sex differences and neuropsychiatric implications. *Journal of Psychopharmacology, 26,* 164–176

Vogt, D. (2007). *Women, trauma, and PTSD. National Center for Posttraumatic Stress Disorder Fact Sheet.* Washington, DC: U.S. Department of Veterans Affairs.

Volkow N.D.(2013). Foreword. Journal of Food and Drug Analysis. Dec; 21(4):S2.

Volkow, N. D., Fowler, J. S., Wang, G. J., Swanson, J. M., Telang, F. (2007). Dopamine in drug abuse and addiction: Results of imaging studies and treatment implications. *Archives of Neurology, 64*(11), 1575–1579.

Volkow, N.D., & McClellan, A.T. (2016). Opioid abuse in chronic pain—misconceptions & mitigation strategies. *The New England Journal of Medicine, 374,* 1253–1263.

Volkow, N. D., & Morales, M. (2015). The brain on drugs: From reward to addiction. *Cell, 162,* 713–725.

Volkow, N. D., Wang, G. J., Fowler, J. S., Tomasi, D., & Baler, R. (2011). Food and drug reward: Overlapping circuits in human obesity and addiction. In *Brain imaging in behavioral neuroscience* (pp. 1–24). Springer: Berlin Heidelberg.

Volkow, N. D., Wang, G., Logan, J., Alexoff, D., Fowler, J. S., Thanos, P. K., … Tomasi, D. (2015). Caffeine increases striatal dopamine D2/D3 receptor availability in the human brain. *Translational Psychiatry, 5,* e549. doi:10.1038/tp.2015.46

Vygotsky, L. S. (1978). *Mind in society: The development of higher psychological processes.* Cambridge, MA: Harvard University Press.

Wacker, D., Wang, S., McCorvy, J. D., Betz, R. M., Venkatakrishnan, A. J., Levit, A., … Roth, B.L. (2017). Crystal structure of an LSD-bound human serotonin receptor. *Cell, 168*(3), 377–389.

Wade, T. D., Bulik, C. M., Neale, M., & Kendler, K. S. (2000). Anorexia nervosa and major depression: Shared genetic and environmental risk factors. *American Journal of Psychiatry, 157*(3), 469–471.

Waldman, A. (2017). A really good day: How microdosing made a mega difference in my mood, my marriage, and my life. NY: Alfred A. Knopf (a division of Penguin Random House).

Wall, T. L., Luczak, S. E., & Hiller-Sturmhöfel, S. (2016). Biology, genetics, and environment: Underlying factors influencing alcohol metabolism. *Alcohol Research: Current Reviews, 38,* 59–68.

Wallace, A. (2016, August 11). DEA declines to reschedule marijuana, saying drug has no accepted medical use. *The Denver Post*. Retrieved from http://www.denverpost.com/2016/08/11/dea-not-rescheduling-marijuana/

Wallace, K. (2016, July 29). Half of teens think they're addicted to their smartphones. *CNN*. Retrieved from http://www.cnn.com/2016/05/03/health/teens-cell-phone-addiction-parents/

Walter, C. (2008, January 31). Affairs of the lips: Why we kiss. *Scientific American*. Retrieved October 21, 2008, from http://www.freerepublic.com/focus/f-chat/1967046/posts

Wanberg, K. W., & Milkman, H. B. (2006). *Criminal conduct and substance abuse treatment: Strategies for self-improvement and change: The participant's workbook* (2nd ed.). Thousand Oaks, CA: Sage Publications.

Wanberg, K. W., & Milkman, H. B. (2008). *Criminal conduct and substance abuse treatment: Strategies for self-improvement and change: The provider's guide* (2nd ed). Thousand Oaks, CA: Sage Publications.

Wanberg, K. W., & Milkman, H. B. (2012). *Criminal conduct & substance abuse treatment for adolescents: Pathways to self-discovery and change* (2nd ed.). Los Angeles, CA: Sage Publications.

Watson, J. B. (1924). *Behaviorism*. New York: Norton.

Webmd.com. (2016). *Teen abuse of cough and cold medicine*. Retrieved on July 11, 2016, from http://www.webmd.com/parenting/teen-abuse-cough-medicine-9/teens-and-dxm-drug-abuse?page=3

Weil, A. (2004). The Marriage of the Sun and Moon: Dispatches from the Frontiers of Consciousness. New Youk: Houghton Mifflin Company

Weinstock, J. W., Farney, M. R., Elrod, N. M., Henderson, C. E., & Weiss, E. P. (2017). Exercise as an adjunctive treatment for substance use disorders: Rational and intervention description. *Journal of Substance Abuse Treatment, 72*, 40–47.

Weisner, C. (2005). Substance misuse: What place for women-only treatment programs? *Addiction, 100*, 7–8.

Wexler, A., & Wexler, S. (1992). *Facts on compulsive gambling and addiction*. Trenton: Council on Compulsive Gambling of New Jersey. (ERIC Document Reproduction Service No. ED372337)

Werner, E. (1989, April). Children of the Garden Island. *Scientific American*, p. 106.

White, A., Castle, I. J., Chen, C. M., Shirley, M., Roach, D., & Hingson, R. (2015). Converging patterns of alcohol use and related outcomes among females and males in the United States, 2002 to 2012. *Alcohol Clin Exp Res. 39*(9), 1712–1726.

White, T. L., Lejuez, C. W., & de Wit, H. (2007). Personality and gender differences in effects of d-amphetamine on risk taking. *Experimental and Clinical Psychopharmacology, 15*(6), 599–609.

Wiesenfeld-Hallin, Z. (2005). Sex differences in pain perception. *Gender Medicine, 2*, 137–145.

Wikler, A. (1973). Dynamics of drug dependence: Implications of a conditioning theory for research and treatment. *Archives of General Psychiatry, 28*, 611–616.

Will, G. F. (2002). Electronic morphine. *Newsweek, 140*(22), 92.

Willett, W. C., & Stampfer, M. J. (2006). Eating to live: Rebuilding the food pyramid. *Scientific American, 16*, 18.

Williams-Quinlan, S. L. (2004). Guidelines for treatment of women in psychotherapy. In G. Koocher, J. Norcross, & S. Hill (Eds.), *Psychologists' Desk Reference* (2nd ed.). New York: Oxford University Press.

Wise, R. A. (1996). Addictive drugs and brain stimulation reward. *Annual Review of Neuroscience, 19*, 319–340.

Wise, R. A., & Koob, G. F. (2014). Circumspectives: The development and maintenance of drug addiction. *Neuropsychopharmacology, 39*, 254–262.

Witbrodt, J., Bond, J., Kaskutas, L. A., Weisner, C., Pating, D., & Moore, C. (2007). Day hospital and residential addiction treatment: Randomized and nonrandomized managed care clients. *Journal of Consulting and Clinical Psychology, 75*(6), 947–959.

Witkiewitz, K. A., & Marlatt, G. A. (2007). High-risk situations: Relapse as a dynamic process. In K. A. Witkiewitz & G. A. Marlatt (Eds.), *Therapist's guide to evidence-based relapse prevention* (pp. 19–33). London: Academic Press.

Witt, E. (2015, November 23). The trip planners. *The New Yorker.* Retrieved on May 3, 2017 from http://www.newyorker.com/magazine/2015/11/23/the-trip-planners

Wolfe, T. (1980). *The right stuff.* New York: Bantam.

Wood, G. (2015, March). What ISIS really wants. *The Atlantic* March 2015. Retrieved on July 6, 2017, from https://www.theatlantic.com/magazine/archive/2015/03/what-isis-really-wants/384980/

World Health Organization. (1948). *Preamble to the Constitution of the World Health Organization as adopted by the International Health Conference,* New York, 19 June–22 July 1946 (Official Records of the World Health Organization, no. 2, p. 100) and entered into force on April 7, 1948.

World Health Organization. (2007, December). *Third meeting on influenza vaccines that induce broad spectrum and long-lasting immune responses.* Geneva, Switzerland. Retrieved October 21, 2008, from http://www.who.int/vaccine_research/diseases/influenza/meeting_071203/en/print.html

World Health Organization (2015, July). *Tobacco: Fact sheet.* Retrieved on May 31, 2016, from http://www.who.int/mediacentre/factsheets/fs339/en/

World Health Organization. (2016a). *10 Facts on obesity.* Retrieved on June 6, 2016, from http://www.who.int/features/factfiles/obesity/en/

Wosick-Correa, K. R., & Joseph, L. J. (2008). Sexy ladies sexing ladies: Women as consumers in strip clubs, *The Journal of Sex Research, 45*(3), 201–216.

Wright, J., Fasco, M., & Thase, M. (2006). *Learning cognitive-behavioral therapy: An illustrated guide.* Arlington, VA: American Psychiatric Publishing.

Wright, W. (2000), CNN - Will Wright on creating 'The Sims' and 'SimCity. Retrieved on February 6, 2018, from www.cnn.com/chat/transcripts/2000/12/1/wright.chatWu, X.-S., Zhang, Z.-H., Zhao, F., Wang, W.J., Li, Y.-F., Bi, L., … Sun, Y-H. (2016). Prevalence of internet addiction and its association with social support and other related factors among adolescents in China. *Journal of Adolescence, 52,* 103–111.

Wurtman, J. J., & Marquis, N. F. (2006). *The serotonin power diet: Use your brain's natural chemistry to cut cravings, curb emotional overeating, and lose weight.* Emmaus, PA: Rodale Books.

Wurtman, R. J., & Wurtman, J. J. (1989). Carbohydrates and depression. *Scientific American,* January, 68–75.

Wurtman, R. J., & Wurtman, J. J. (1995). Brain serotonin, carbohydrate craving, obesity, and depression. *Obesity Research, 4,* 477S–480S.

Wurtzel, E. (2002). *More, now, again.* New York: Simon & Schuster.

Wyatt, K. (2017, March 9). Marijuana clubs approved in Colorado Senate. *Associated Press.* Retrieved from https://www.usnews.com/news/best-states/colorado/articles/2017-03-09/marijuana-clubs-approved-in-colorado-senate

Yildirim, B. O., & Derksen, J. J. L. (2015). Mesocorticolimbic dopamine function in primary psychopathy: A source of within-group heterogeneity. *Psychiatry Research, 229,* 633–677.

Yoo, H. J., Cho, S. C., Ha, J., Yune, S. K., Kim, S. J., Hwang, J., … Lyoo, I.K. (2004). Attention deficit hyperactivity symptoms and Internet addiction. *Psychiatry & Clinical Neurosciences, 58,* 487–494.

Young, K.S. (1996). Addictive use of the Internet: A case that breaks the stereotype. *Psychological Reports, 79,* 899–902.

Young, K. S. (2004). Internet addiction: A new clinical phenomenon and its consequences. *American Behavioral Scientist, 48*(4), 402–415.

Zalewska-Kaszubska, J. (2015). Is immunotherapy an opportunity for effective treatment of drug addiction? *Vaccine, 33,* 6545–6551.

Zaraki, K. (2013). Nazi Underworld Series, Hitler's Drug Use Revealed. Retrieved from https://www.youtube.com/watch?v=IaWTDzR1mRI

Zeller, B. E. (2014). *Heaven's Gate: America's UFO religion.* New York: University Press.

Zernike, K. (2006). A more addictive meth emerges as states curb homemade type. In H. T. Wilson (Ed.), *Annual editions: Drugs, society and behavior 2007/2008* (pp. 71–72). Dubuque, IA: McGraw-Hill.

Zhai, H., Yang, Y., Sui, H., Wang, W., Chen, L., Qiu, X., ... Zhu, X. (2015). Self-Esteem and problematic drinking in China: A mediated model. *PLoS ONE 10*(10): e0140183. doi: 10.1371/journal.pone.0140183

Zhu, W., Ding, Z., Zhang, Y., Hashimoto, K., & Lu, L. (2016). Risks associated with misuse of ketamine, as a rapid-acting antidepressant. *Neuroscience Bulletin, 32*(6), 557–564.

Zimmer, C. (2008, September 1). Spore: When games and science collide. *Discover.* Retrieved January 15, 2009, from http://blogs.discovermagazine.com/loom/2008/09/01/spore-when-games-and-science-collide

Zinberg, N. E. (1984). *Drug, set, and setting: The basis for controlled intoxicant use.* New Haven, CT: Yale University Press.

Zindel, L.R., & Kranzler, H.R. (2014). Pharmacotherapy of alcohol use disorders: Seventy-five years of progress. *Journal of Studies on Alcohol & Drugs, Suppl 17,* 79–88

Zucconi, S., Volpato, C., Adinolfi, F., Gandini, E., Gentile, E., Loi, A., & Fioriti, L. (2013). Gathering consumption data on specific consumer groups of energy drinks. *EFSA Supporting Publications, 10*(3), n/a. doi:10.2903/sp.efsa.2013. EN-394

Zuckerman, M. (1994). *Behavioral expressions and biosocial bases of sensation seeking.* New York: Cambridge University Press.

Zuckerman, M. (2007). *Sensation seeking and risky behavior.* Washington, DC: American Psychological Association.

Zukov, I., Ptacek, R., Kozelek, P., Fischer, S., Domluvilova, D., Raboch, J., ... Susta, M. (2009). Brain wave P300: A comparative study of various forms of criminal activity. *Medical Science Monitor, 15*(7), CR349–354.

Zunes, S. (2017, October 18). *U.S. Middle East policy and strategic nonviolent action: Where faith and violence coincide. (Colloquium Abstract).* Auraria Campus, Denver, CO.

INDEX

Eight-Point Program (EPP) for stress management, 439

Einstein, A., 227

Electronic media, 230. *See also* Internet; Virtual reality
  addiction issues, 4
  adolescent exposure, 10
  parent substitutes, 5

Elkind, D., 237

Ellis, Albert, 397

Enabler, 359

Endocannabinoids, 179

Endorphins, 8, 14, 76
  alcohol dependence and, 34
  eating and satiation, 111
  exercise and, 443
  overeating/obesity relationship, 146
  pain perception and, 80
  regulatory mechanisms, 81
  running and, 468

Energy balance, 464

Energy drinks, 170

Energy metabolism, 462

Engels, R. C., 219

Enkephalin, 57, 60–61

Enzymes, 26

Epictetus, 397

Epinephrine (adrenaline), 169, 460

Erickson, D., 336

Erikson, Erik, 11, 281

Eros, 305

Erotic dance venues, 336

Ethanol, chemical structure, 92

Ethnic differences, 282

Excitatory neurotransmission, 187

Exercise, 394–395
  aerobic, 468
  anaerobic, 468
  body trimming, 473–474
  bulimia and, 149
  chemistry of, 161
  endorphins and, 79–80
  energy balance, 464
  energy expenditure and weight, 161
  energy metabolism, 462
  health and psychological benefits, 467
  hitting the wall, 471
  incidental activities, 480
  isokinetic, 482

  isometric, 468
  isotonic, 468
  mental health and, 496
  neurochemistry, 51–52
  "no pain, no gain" mentality, 472
  physical health and, 428
  prescription drug abuse, 39
  runner's high, 476
  sensible, 467
  training for health, 474–475
  weight loss and, 454

Experience and addiction, 228

Externalizing disorders, 5

External reinforcement, 403

Extreme sports, 126

F

Fairy tales, 229

Family relationships, 14

Fantasy, 22, 24, 26, 28. *See also* Hallucinogenic
    drugs; Religion and myth
  active, 115
  child's use of, 229
  coping styles and drugs/behaviors of choice, 439
  dreams, xviii
  personal heroes, 189
  receptive, 228
  schizophrenic, 23
  sexual, 24
  shared delusions, 274–275
  slippery slope, 272
  television viewing, 286
  terrorist mind-set, 281–282

Farley, F., 186

Fasting, 457–458

Fat cells, 161

Fat metabolism, 169

Female substance use, 377

Fentanyl, xviii, 355

Ferracuti, F., 282

Fight-or-flight response, 430

Fischman, M. W., 324

Flack, W. F., 115

Flow, 488–489

Fogel, G., 315

Foltin, R. W., 324

"Four Noble Truths" of Buddhism, 443

dopaminergic reward system, 62
morphine replacement, 65
overdose, 75
tolerance, 81
withdrawal, 83
Hesychasm, 431
Hibernation, 430
Hinduism, 233
Hinkley, John, 238
Hippocampus, 320
Hofmann, Albert, 11–12
Holistic medicine, 476
Holmes, D. S., 477
Holmes, J., 440
Holocaust survivors, 379
Hooked on Nicotine Checklist (HONC), 131
Howard, Greg, 73
Hudson, J. L., 149
Hughes, J. R., 324
Human immunodeficiency virus (HIV), 128
Humanity, 287, 357
Human needs hierarchy, 421
Hypertension, 174, 216
Hypothalamic-pituitary-adrenal (HPA) axis, 55, 56, 182
Hypothalamus, 55, 57
    overeating/obesity and, 147
    reward cascade, 500
Hysteroid dysphoria, 298

I

Identity conflict, 361
Identity theft, 197
Imagination. See Fantasy
Immune function, 442, 462
Imperto, A., 62
Impett, E. A., 423
Incidental exercise, 481
Individuality, intimacy versus, 246
Individuation process, 10
Infant satiation, 38
Infatuation, 294
    hysteroid dysphoria, 298
    neurochemistry, 303
Inhalants, 320, 357
Inhibitory neurotransmission, 97
Inoculation, 403

Insight meditation, 433
Intelligences, 487
Internet
    associated compulsive behaviors, 16
    online role-playing games, 229, 242, 245–246
    pornography, 6, 230
    positive and negative aspects, 9
    terrorism and, 283
Interpersonal intelligence, 487
Interpersonal relationships. See also Intimacy; Romantic love
    attachment and, 299, 499
    capitalization, 423
    communication and, 423
    cyber affairs, 249
    Ecstasy effects, 261
    family and child development, 77
    healthy love, 298
    magic ratio, 423
    minding relationships, 425
    need for love, 414–415
    optimizing, 422–423
    sensation seeking compatibility, 467
Intimacy, 9, 215. See also Interpersonal relationships; Romantic love
    communication and, 423
    Ecstasy effects, 28
    forms of love, 418
    Gentlemen's clubs, 166
    individuality versus, 246
    prostitutes and, 343
    sexuality and, 345
    universal need for love, 414–415
Intrapersonal intelligence, 487
IQ, 323
ISIS, 288
Isokinetic exercise, 469
Isometric exercise, 468
Isotonic exercise, 469
Iverson, K. M., 393

J

James, William, 169, 263, 272
Jellinek, E. M., 351–352
Jewish meditative practices, 428
Jocks, 114
Johnson, V. E., 420

Johnston, L. D., 50
Joseph, M. H., 62
Journal writing, 438
Jung, Carl, 31, 258

K

Kabbalistic meditation, 431
Kahneman, Daniel, 427
Kahr, B., 238
Kandel, D. B., 26
Kauai, 10
Kellerman, Joseph L., 359
Kennedy, D., 175
Ketamine, 196, 214–215, 218–219
Khantzian, R. C., 22, 30, 45
Kimerling, R., 381
Kissing, 300
Klatsky, A. L, 91
Klein, D., 298
Kobak, R. R, 417, 424
Kolata, G., 454
Kolligian, J., 231
Kouri, E. M., 324
Kramer, P. D., 468

L

Lambert, K., 500
Langer, E. J., 433
Lap dances, 335
Leary, Timothy, 260
Lee, R. S., 381
Lee, T., 306
Left-hemisphere activity, 24
Legba, 216
Lennon, John, 238
Leutwyler, K., 151
Librium, 355
Liebowitz, M., 298, 304
Life cycle of natural highs, 11
Limbic system, 23, 24
Limerence, 296
Linehan, M. M., 393
Linguistic intelligence, 487
Liver damage, 76
Locus coeruleus, 180
Logical-mathematical intelligence, 487
Loneliness, 160, 292

Lopez, S. J., 323, 414
Love, 414–415. *See also* Romantic love
  self-expansion theory, 418
  triangular theory of, 418
  universal need for, 414–415
LSD, 7, 11, 13, 20–21, 516
  compulsive use, 23
  coping styles and drugs of choice, 21
  user-observer discord, 25
Lukas, S. E, 324
Lung cancer, 34, 128
Lung health, marijuana use and, 331

M

Madonnas, 114
Magical thinking, 236
Magic ratio, 423
Magnetic resonance imaging (MRI), 303
Mahler, M., 188
Maintenance phase of addiction, 16–17
Major depressive disorder (MDD), 34.
    See also Depression
Maladaptive parenting, 392
Maloff, D. R., 15
Mander, J., 243
Marazziti, D., 307
Marijuana, 313
  beneficial uses, 330
  brain and, 319
  cognitive impairment, 364
  compulsive use, 20
  dopaminergic reward system, 62
  endocrine system and, 463
  extent of use, 8
  health effects, 133
  immune system and, 319
  medical use, 327
  mental health issues, 493
  pain and, 265
  prevalence, 6
  Reefer Madness, 294
  withdrawal effects, 131, 209
Marital counseling, 423
Mark of the beast, 285
Marlatt, G. A., 361, 369
Marquis, N. F., 160
Martyrdom, 282

Maslow, A., 292, 392

Massage, 343

Massively multiplayer online role-playing games (MMORPGs), 242, 255

Masters, W. H., 419

Mattson, M., 457

May, Rollo, 486

McCann, I. L., 477

MDA, 215

MDMA. *See* Ecstasy

Medication, 34, 38

Meditation, 386, 395
 dependency, 9
 efficacy of, 65
 hedonic dependencies and, 131
 insight meditation, 433
 mental and physical health effects, 446
 mindfulness and self-awareness, 394
 passage, 439
 process, 431
 side effects, 445

Meichenbaum, D., 402–404

Mental-behavioral impaired control cycle, 19

Mental health. *See also* specific disorders
 co-occurring disorders, 32
 dopamine imbalances and, 35
 exercise and, 443
 gender differences, 123
 marijuana use and, 331
 meditation and stress management, 439
 neuronal disturbances, 468
 obsessive love and, 500
 parental controls and, 293
 post-traumatic stress disorder and, 380
 psychedelic drug effects, 262
 risk factors for addictive behaviors, 370
 smoking and, 106
 social connectedness and, 254
 substance abuse comorbidity, 268

Mermaids, 236

Mescaline, 229, 259

Metabolic rate, 463, 464

Methadone, 46, 65

Methamphetamine, 56, 62, 65
 brain and, 67
 case example, user experiences, 243
 chemical structure, 261
 health effects, 133

manufacture of, 197
 personality and drugs of choice, 21
 physical dependence, 13
 risky sex and, 197
 withdrawal, 218

Mexico, 197

Meyers, R. D., 306

Microbiota, 454, 462

Milk, 78, 117

Milkman, H., 187, 233, 236

Milner, P., 57

Mind expansion, 24

Mindfulness, 393, 409, 423, 433–434.
  See also Meditation

Mindfulness-based cognitive therapy (MBCT), 439

Mindfulness-based stress reduction (MBSR), 439

Minding relationships, 433

Monkey trap, 436

Monoamine oxidase (MAO) inhibitors, 129

Moore, B. A., 197

Morphine, 204

Mortality rate
 alcohol-related, 34
 autoerotic fatalities, 185–186
 gender differences, 111
 smoking-related, 126
 substance use, 152

Mother's milk, 78

Multiple intelligences, 487

Multiple sclerosis, 326

Murray, J. D., 423

Mushrooms, 22

Musical intelligence, 487

Mutuality, 418

Mythology. *See* Religion and myth

N

Nakamura, J., 488

Naloxone, 78

Naltrexone, 79

Narasinha, 234

Narcotics. *See* specific drugs

Narcotics Anonymous (NA), 369

Nasrudin, Mullah, 434

Natural highs, 455–456. *See also* Abilities and talents; Eating; Exercise; Meditation; Positive psychology

Oxycontin, 355
Oxytocin, 414, 417

P

Pain, 39, 41
Palfrey, Deborah, 342
Parenting, 371, 378
Parkinson's disease, 65, 172
Parks, G. A., 218
Partial fasting, 457–458
Passage meditation, 439
Patients in the street, 45–46
Patra, J., 106
Pavlov, I., 402
PCP, 218, 261, 265–266
Perez-De-Albeniz, A., 429
Performance
    arousal and, 53
    energy drinks and, 175
Personal intelligences, 487
Personality and addictive behaviors, 5
    drugs or behaviors of choice, 21
    thrill-seeking, 166
Personal Pleasure Inventory, 474
Peter Rabbit, 232
Peterson, C., 335
Peyote, 22
Pharmaceutical supports, 39
Pharmacotherapy. *See* Medication
Phenethylamine, 261
Phenylalanine, 64
Philia, 418
Phillips, P., 61
Phone sex, 278
Physical activity. *See* Exercise
Physical dependence. *See* Dependence
Pituitary gland, 476
Plato, 396
Play, 462
Pleasure and addiction, 474
Plumridge, E. W., 343
Poe, Edgar Allen, 306
Pontieri, F. E., 62
Pope, H. G., Jr., 149
Popova, S., 106
Pornography, 230
"Porphyria's Lover,", 306

Positive psychology, 415. *See also* Cognitive-
    behavioral therapy; Natural highs
    BRAIN, 446
    definition, 9
    mindfulness, 393–394
    self-regulation, 395
Post-traumatic stress disorder (PTSD), 33
    brain function and, 150
    diagnosis, 37
    population statistics, 380
    recovery, 383
    substance abuse, 368
    symptoms, 379
Potter, Beatrix, 232
Poverty, obesity and, 10
Prayer, 237
Prefrontal cortex, 251
Preventing substance abuse, 376.
        See also Cognitive-behavioral therapy
Prins, A., 381
Process meditation, 438–439
Progesterone, 35
Progoff, I., 438
Progressive muscle relaxation (PMR), 446
Project Self-Discovery (PSD), 490
Prostitution, 19, 24
Protective factors, 15
"Protector (NOT!)", 378
Provoker, 359
Prozac, 57, 59, 500
Pryor, Richard, 205
Pseudoephedrine, 197
Psilocybin, 214, 229
Psychedelic drugs. *See* Hallucinogenic drugs
Psychopathology. *See also* Depression; Mental
        health; specific disorders
Pugach, Burton, 307
Pulque, 91

R

Rathunde, K., 489
Rational and irrational thinking, 399
Rational-emotive behavioral therapy (REBT), 398
Rational therapy (RT), 398
Raves, 196
Receptive fantasy, 228
Receptor sites, 55

Virtual reality, 229. *See also* Electronic media
   addiction issues, 302
   online role-playing games, 229, 242, 245–246
   sex, 205
   video games, 229
   virtual mental hospital, 248
Vivitrol, 86
Volkow, Nora, 155

W

Walter, C., 304
Wanberg, K., 359, 362, 374
Ward, R. W., 324
Watson, John B., 402
Waugh, Rosel, 243
Weight loss, 454, 456. *See also* Obesity and
       overweight
   appetite-suppressing drugs, 144
   dieting, 148
   eating disorders, 152–153
   energy balance, 464
   exercise and, 443, 455, 457
   healthy diet, 458–461
   natural highs alternative, 455–456
   partial fasting, 457–458
   pathological, 180–183
   right state of mind, 456–457
   set points, 454
Weil, A., 215
Werner, E., 10
Westrup, D., 381
Whalen, S., 489
White wine syndrome, 123
Wightman, R., 61
Wikler, A., 16
Willett, W. C., 458
Wine cooler, 123
Withdrawal, 13, 20, 41, 73
   alcohol, 72, 75, 83
   cocaine, 75, 87
   conditioned, 82, 99
   marijuana, 103, 122
   MDMA, 196
   methamphetamine, 196
   nicotine, 371
   opiate, 66, 76
   treatment, 86

Witkiewitz, K. A., 361
Wolfe, Tom, 381, 413
"Wolves", 115
Women-focused treatment, 378
Woods, S. C., 12
World Health Organization (WHO), 6, 143
World of Warcraft, 190, 229, 245
Wright, Will, 252
Wurtman, J., 160
Wurtman, R. J., 160

X

Xanax, 22

Y

Yeager, Chuck, 189
Yellowlees, Peter, 248
Yerkes-Dodson law, 168
Young, A. M., 248
Young, K. S., 249

Z

Zinberg, N. E., 315
Zoroaster, 396
Zuckerman, M., 187

CPSIA information can be obtained
at www.ICGtesting.com
Printed in the USA
LVHW010003011221
704760LV00004B/14